MW00860762

It's Coming to America:

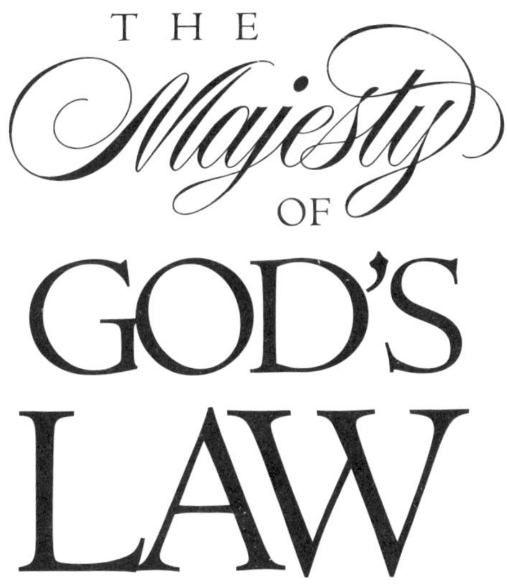

W. CLEON SKOUSEN

Ensign Publishing

ISBN 978-1630720-00-1

Ensign Publishing
PO Box 298
Riverton, UT 84065
www.skousen2000.com

Printed in the United States of America
Second edition, First printing
SEP 2010 5M

Third edition, First printing
MAY 2017 2.5M
Second printing
DEC 2020 2M

DEDICATION

This book is affectionately dedicated to our fifty grandchildren and their parents.

Grandchild	Birthdate	Parents
1. Richard N. Skousen	1966	Eric and Cheryl Skousen
2. W. Daniel Skousen	1968	Eric and Cheryl Skousen
3. Candace Kimber	1968	Glenn and Julianne Kimber
4. Jered Skousen	1970	Eric and Cheryl Skousen
5. Jay Kimber	1971	Glenn and Julianne Kimber
6. Eldon Skousen	1972	Eric and Cheryl Skousen
7. Kathryn Skousen	1972	David and Judith Skousen
8. Jewel Kimber	1972	Glenn and Julianne Kimber
9. Laurel Skousen	1973	Harold and Anne Skousen
10. David A. Skousen	1973	David and Judith Skousen
11. Angelyn Krey	1974	Russell and Sharon Krey
12. Sheresa Skousen	1974	Eric and Cheryl Skousen
13. Melissa Skousen	1975	Harold and Anne Skousen
14. Clifton Kimber	1975	Glenn and Julianne Kimber
15. Dayne Krey	1975	Russell and Sharon Krey
16. Deborah Skousen	1976	David and Judith Skousen
17. John Eric Skousen	1976	Eric and Cheryl Skousen
18. Krystal Kimber	1976	Glenn and Julianne Kimber
19. Karen Skousen	1976	Harold and Anne Skousen
20. Jacob Skousen	1977	Paul and Kathy Skousen
21. Daniel W. Skousen	1977	David and Judith Skousen
22. Kenneth Kimber	1978	Glenn and Julianne Kimber
23. Heather Skousen	1978	Harold and Anne Skousen
24. Michelle Skousen	1978	Paul and Kathy Skousen
25. Tiffany Skousen	1978	Eric and Cheryl Skousen
26. Melanie Skousen	1979	Brent and Myralynne Skousen
27. Douglas Kimber	1979	Glenn and Julianne Kimber
28. J. Richard Skousen	1979	David and Judith Skousen
29. Misty Krey	1980	Russell and Sharon Krey
30. Joseph M. Skousen	1980	Paul and Kathy Skousen
31. Ashley Skousen	1981	Brent and Myralynne Skousen
32. Jennifer Skousen	1981	Harold and Anne Skousen

33. Geoffrey Skousen	1981	Eric and Cheryl Skousen
34. Benjamin Skousen	1981	Paul and Kathy Skousen
35. John R. Skousen	1981	David and Judith Skousen
36. Joy Kimber	1981	Glenn and Julianne Kimber
37. Heidi Skousen	1982	Harold and Anne Skousen
38. Adam Skousen	1983	Brent and Myralynne Skousen
39. Laureen Skousen	1983	David and Judith Skousen
40. Patricia Skousen	1983	Paul and Kathy Skousen
41. Matthew Skousen	1984	Harold and Anne Skousen
42. Natalie Skousen	1985	Brent and Myralynne Skousen
43. Amy Skousen	1986	Harold and Anne Skousen
44. Wendy Skousen	1986	Paul and Kathy Skousen
45. Krystalee Krey	1986	Russell and Sharon Krey
46. Julie Skousen	1987	Paul and Kathy Skousen
47. Marilee Skousen	1988	Brent and Myralynne Skousen
48. Maryann Skousen	1990	Paul and Kathy Skousen
49. Joshua Skousen	1992	Paul and Kathy Skousen
50. Elisabeth Skousen	1994	Paul and Kathy Skousen

Author's Preface

In 1967 a great leader whom I admired and loved said that a crisis was coming to America and the legal minds of the nation were not getting ready to deal with it.

He indicated that the Founding Fathers knew this would happen and they knew what to do about it. He suggested, as he had to many other lawyers of his acquaintance, that I take time to get acquainted with the things the Founders knew.

This dear friend died in 1970 and by that time I had just begun to realize some profound and inspiring things about the Founders I had never known before. Much of it was in their letters and private communications with each other. I found they knew much more about the manifest destiny of America than any text I had ever read.

For over a quarter of a century I have been struggling to put it all together. This book is the result of that labor but the author is entirely responsible for the concepts presented and conclusions I have drawn from them.

Early in this study, I discovered that the Founders were in-depth students of the Bible, and equally familiar with secular history, both ancient and modern. Their beliefs and convictions grew out of these carefully analyzed sources.

I was surprised that they knew we Americans would one day fulfill a prophecy of the ancient prophet, Moses; that in America we would one day practice the revealed code of righteous law given to the Israelites by God. Some of the Founders even experimented with parts of that law or rewrote the code of their own states to reflect the fundamental elements of God's law.

In this sense *It's Coming to America: The Majesty of God's Law* is a book for Americans about America.

In the dark hours through which this nation seems to be passing, there is a tangible shaft of light and hope. The Founders knew about it and only regretted that it would not happen in their day. But they knew it would happen some day—after the cleansing.

Not only lawyers and political scientists but all Americans should find it heartening to know that the Holy Bible contains a promise of a magnificent, brighter day for this choice land.

The challenge in writing this book was my own sincere attempt to try and put it all together so that anyone could see what the Founders saw, and generate through study and prayerful meditation the same great vision for the future.

It will be observed that nearly all of the references in this book are from the Bible or from well-established and authoritative secular sources. Occasionally, however, I have quoted from some of my other books where additional scriptures are discussed.

Acknowledgements

My entire family and a host of friends have provided vast quantities of assistance and encouragement during the quarter of a century I have been working on this book.

This is my thirty-sixth book and my wife, Jewel, has been the editor and proof-reader for all of them. What a joy and a blessing to have a wife and companion who is "precious beyond rubies!"

Then my children combined to give me a birthday present of the latest computer equipment and a lovely desk and chair to go with it. My son, Eric, has been my computer "Guru" with my sons, Harold, Brent and Paul providing the emergency backup service. Harold also videotaped the course when it was presented for the first time to an invited audience of relatives and friends. My son, David, specializes in health products, and has kept me well supplied with vitamins.

My grandson, Richard, and his wife Jill, volunteered to finance and publish the first edition of this book and patiently went through the pagination and corrections that are always innumerable right down to press time.

Several dozen names of friends also run through my mind who deserve my affectionate appreciation for all they did to help bring this rather monumental undertaking to a final conclusion. To all of them I extend my heartfelt thanks.

W. Cleon Skousen
Salt Lake City, Utah
August 13, 1996

Contents

CHAPTER ONE

In the Beginning Politicians Studied the Bible

Very often we hear people say, "Where did the Founding Fathers get so many of their great ideas?"

Recently, Dr. Donald S. Lutz and Dr. Charles S. Hyneman made an extensive study to determine which books the Founders relied upon for the basic ideas that went into the formulation of the United States Constitution.

They reviewed an estimated 15,000 items, and closely perused the political content of 2,200 books, pamphlets, newspaper articles, and monographs which were published between 1760 and 1805. The most significant items were selected which amounted to 916 articles. These were carefully analyzed and numerically coded as to content as well as the references cited by the leaders of that era.

It very quickly became apparent where the focus of interest was concentrated in the minds of the Founding Fathers. Of the thousands of citations quoted to support their ideas, 34% came from one source—the Bible. Most of these were from the book of Deuteronomy which is the *Book of God's Law*.

Other citations were scattered over a broad spectrum of writings from historians, philosophers and political thinkers including Montesquieu, Blackstone, Locke, Coke, Cicero, and other intellectual luminaries from the so-called "Enlightenment." [1] But the linchpin that united their thinking on every important principle was the Bible.

Where the Founders Received Most of Their Education

The Founders' exceptional insight into the Bible was the direct result of their college training. In America at that time every major institution of higher learning was designed to train ministers. Consequently, the sponsoring church of each college or university required a comprehensive study of

1. Donald S. Lutz, The Relative Influence of European Writers on Late Eighteenth Century American Political Thought, 78 American Political Science Review, p. 189; cited by John Eidsmoe in Restoration of the Constitution, H. Wayne House, ed. Dallas: Probe Books, 1987, p. 78.

the Bible for all students even though they were studying law or intending to follow some profession other than the ministry.

Here is a list of the colleges and universities which were founded during the colonial period. We have indicated the names of the churches which provided most of the funding to maintain each one of them.

1. *Harvard University* was founded in 1636 at Cambridge, Massachusetts. It was sponsored and primarily funded by the Congregational churches.

2. *Yale University* was founded in 1701 at New Haven, Connecticut. It was sponsored and primarily funded by the Congregational churches.

3. *Princeton University* was founded in 1746 at Princeton, New Jersey. It was sponsored and primarily funded by the Presbyterian churches.

4. *Columbia University* was founded in 1754 at New York City. It was sponsored and primarily funded by the Episcopalian churches.

5. *Brown University* was founded in 1764 at Providence, Rhode Island. It was sponsored and primarily funded by the Baptist churches.

6. *Rutgers University* was founded in 1766 at New Brunswick, New Jersey. It was sponsored and primarily funded by the Dutch Reformed churches.

7. *Dartmouth University* was founded in 1769 at Hanover, New Hampshire. It was sponsored and primarily funded by the Congregational churches.

John Jay—An Example of a Bible-reading Founding Father

Among all the Founding Fathers, none had a deeper appreciation of the debt which the American people owed to the Holy Bible than John Jay.

He became the president of the American Bible Society and raised money to distribute thousands of Bibles throughout colonial America. He wanted the people to know what it meant to be a "covenant" society and someday enjoy the blessing of living under God's law.

Born in New York in 1745, John Jay was one of the youngest members of the Constitutional Convention. It was he who joined with James Madison and Alexander Hamilton to write the famous *Federalist Papers*. These papers were the first commentaries on the purpose and meaning of the United States Constitution, and have remained among the great classics in American political science studies ever since.

Although John Jay was a careful student of the Greek and Roman classics as well as other books on world history, here is what he had to say about the Bible:

> "I believe the fact to be, that except [for] the Bible there is not a true history in the world." [2]

As for God's law set forth in the Bible, Jay stated:

> "Uninspired commentators have dishonored the law, by ascribing to it, in certain cases, a sense and meaning which it did not authorize, and which our Saviour rejected and reproved.
>
> "The inspired prophets, on the contrary, expressed the most exalted ideas of the law. They declared that the law of the Lord is perfect; that the statutes of the Lord are *right*; and that the commandment of the Lord is *pure*; that God would magnify the law and make it honorable." [3]

John Jay did not get to sign the Declaration of Independence because he had been called back to New York to help draft the new constitution for that state. He ended up as chairman of the committee and much of the New York constitution which received such great praise by the other Founders reflects the thinking of John Jay.

Jay's Life of Service

In September, 1777, Jay was made chief justice of the New York Supreme Court. However, two years later he was appointed plenipotentiary to work out a treaty with Spain. Then, in 1781 he joined Franklin, John Adams and Henry Laurens to work out the details of the peace treaty with England following the Revolutionary War.

In 1784 Congress made him "Secretary of Foreign Affairs," and he served in that capacity until Thomas Jefferson returned from France and this position was called "Secretary of State" after 1790.

John Jay was made the first Chief Justice of the United States Supreme Court and served from 1790 to 1795. As Chief Justice, he went to England in 1794 and negotiated the Jay Treaty with England. In 1795 he resigned as Chief Justice and was elected governor by the State of New York. He served two terms.

---

2. John Jay's letter to Jedediah Morse, February 28, 1797, quoted by Norman Cousins, In God We Trust, New York: Harper Brothers, 1958, p. 362.
3. Ibid., p. 367. Emphasis by author in this and all other quotations. .

Jay ended his public career in 1801 and retired to his estate near Bedford, New York, in Westchester County. He was then 57 years of age.

John Jay died on the 17th of May, 1829. One of his last acts was to express his profound admiration and devotion to the principles of the Bible. These views were set forth in a lengthy article published by the American Bible Society. In his writings, Jay's major themes were as follows:

1. The need for the practice of righteous Biblical principles in the daily lives of the people.

2. The desire of the Almighty to have peace between nations.

3. The importance of promoting temperance in every community of America.

4. And finally, his strong belief in the anti-slavery movement.

Among the Founders, John Jay was a much admired example of Christian virtue and dedicated public service.

John Adams Searches for the Divine Science of Good Government

Another Founder who wanted to set up America according to the Bible was John Adams. He had carefully studied the Old Testament in Latin and the New Testament in Greek. As we shall see later, Adams was inspired with the hope that someday there would be a society where their only law book would be the Bible.[4]

He felt that once the divine formula for God's law was understood, the American leaders could proceed to structure their entire political system upon it. In chapter 23 Rev. Samuel Langdon traces the close parallel between the Bible and the original design of the American system of government.

During this period there were many great scholars in both Europe and America who felt the solutions to the problems plaguing mankind could be found in the Bible.

William Blackstone, the famous English legal authority, had agreed with the English philosopher, John Locke, and the French scholar, Baron Charles de Montesquieu, that just as scientists seek to learn the divine principles by which God rules the universe, so students of political science should seek to

4. John Adams' Diary, February 21, 1756; quoted by Adrienne Koch, The American Enlightenment, New York: George Braziller, 1965, p. 167.

discover the divine principles for the most ideal human government which would propel mankind toward a blessed age of peace on earth, good will toward men.

John Adams looked upon his own generation as a corps of modern political scientists who had a mission to identify and revive the divine principles of sound politics revealed by God in ancient times.

He felt that if they were successful, America would become the mighty vanguard that would usher in a great new epoch of human progress that would begin to satisfy the physical and social needs of human beings all over the world.

On June 17, 1782, John Adams wrote from Holland to James Warren and said, "Politics are the divine science, after all." [5]

His wife, Abigail Adams, was accustomed to hearing her husband speak of the "divine science" of good government. In 1780 he had written a letter from Paris in which he said:

> "The science of government is my duty to study, more than all other sciences; the arts of legislation and administration and negotiation ought to take place, indeed to exclude, in a manner, all other arts. I must study politics and war, that my sons may have liberty to study mathematics and philosophy. My sons ought to study mathematics and philosophy, geography, natural history and naval architecture, navigation, commerce, and agriculture, in order to give their children a right to study painting, poetry, music, architecture, statuary, tapestry, and porcelain." [6]

John Adams was very critical of the corrupt systems of government he found in Europe. He vented an outburst of disgust in one of his letters to James Warren. He wrote:

> "How is it possible that any man should ever think of making it [politics] subservient to his own little passions and mean private interest? ... Is the end of politics a fortune, a family, a gilded coach, a train of horses, and a troop of livery servants, ball at Court, splendid dinners and suppers? Yet the divine science of politics is at length in Europe reduced to a mechanical system composed of these materials." [7]

---

5. John Adams' letter to Abigail Adams, no date except 1780; quoted by Adrienne Koch, in The American Enlightenment, op cit., p. 189.
6. Ibid., p. 188.
7. A letter to James Warren, June 17, 1782; quoted in Ibid., p. 189.

As we mentioned earlier, John Adams, like the rest of the Founders, agreed with Sir William Blackstone, John Locke, and Baron Charles de Montesquieu, that the most reliable textbook for the study of the divine science of good government is the Bible.

Remarkable Insights of Benjamin Franklin

Benjamin Franklin was largely self-taught which means he became his own tutor. The thoroughness of his studies persuaded him that the key to good government and happy living was centered in the Bible. He wrote his own creed and a devotional for private worship at the age of 22. At the age of 41 he wrote:

> "As the scriptures are given for our reproof, instruction and warning, may we make a due use of this example, before it is too late." [8]

To unite the American people, the Founders undertook to find those basic beliefs set forth in the Bible on which people of all religious faiths could agree. It turned out that Benjamin Franklin struck the most harmonious chord for everyone in his own personal creed. In a letter to Ezra Stiles, president of Yale University, the 81-year-old Franklin wrote:

> "Here is my creed: I believe in one God, the Creator of the universe. That he governs it by his providence. That he ought to be worshipped. That the most acceptable service we render to him is in doing good to his other children. That the soul of man is immortal, and will be treated with justice in another life respecting its conduct in this. These I take to be the fundamental points in all sound religion." [9]

A careful analysis of Franklin's creed reflects five points of fundamental religious belief which are either expressed or implied and these have been guideposts for Americans for over two centuries. Perhaps these could be summarized as follows:

1. There exists a Creator who made all things, and mankind should recognize and worship him.

2. The Creator has revealed a moral code of behavior for happy living which distinguishes right from wrong.

3. The Creator holds mankind responsible for the way they treat one another.

---

8. Ibid.
9. Ibid., 10:84.

4. All mankind live beyond this life.

5. In the next life mankind are judged for their conduct in this one.

All five of these tenets are abundantly evident throughout the writings of the Founding Fathers.

How These Basic Beliefs Could Unite All Mankind

Samuel Adams said that this group of basic beliefs which constitute "the religion of America is the religion of all mankind." [10]

In other words, these fundamental beliefs are the very foundation of all world faiths and therefore they could be taught without being offensive to any "sect or denomination."

In the "Northwest Ordinance" of 1787 the Congress stated that three things should be taught in the schools.[11] These were:

1. Religion.

2. Morality.

3. Knowledge.

Of course, teaching religion in school raised a monumental question. Everyone wanted to know, "Whose religion would be taught?" Franklin answered that question by setting forth in his own creed that which expressed or implied the fundamental precepts of all "sound religion." Samuel Adams had supported Franklin's position by saying that these basic truths constitute the "religion of all mankind." [12] This being true, it seemed obvious that it should be possible to teach these great truths in the schools without offending any sect or denomination.

Basic Religious Beliefs Constitute The Glue That Binds a Nation Together

John Adams called these tenets the "general principles" on which the American civilization had been founded.[13]

---

10. Adam's letter to Jefferson cited by Albert Ellery Bergh, The Writings of Thomas Jefferson, Washington, D.C.: The Thomas Jefferson Memorial Association, 1907, 13:293.
11. George B. de Huszar, ed., Basic American Documents, Ames, Iowa: Littlefield, Adams and Company, 1953, pp. 62-68.
12. William V. Wells, The Life and Public Services of Samuel Adams, Boston: Little, Brown and Company, 1965, 3:23.
13. Letter to Thomas Jefferson; cited by Bergh in The Writings of Thomas Jefferson, op. cit., 13:293.

Thomas Jefferson called these basic beliefs the principles "in which God has united us all." [14]

From these statements it is obvious how significantly the Founders looked upon the fundamental precepts of religion and morality as the cornerstones of a free government.

This gives additional importance to the warning of Washington:

> "Of all the dispositions and habits which lead to political prosperity, religion and morality are indispensable supports. ... Who that is a sincere friend to it can look with indifference upon attempts to shake the foundation of the fabric?" [15]

Washington issued this solemn warning because in France, shortly before he wrote his Farewell Address (1796), the promoters of atheism and amorality had seized control of that nation and turned the French Revolution into a shocking blood bath of wild excesses and violence. Washington obviously never wanted anything like that to happen in the United States. Therefore he had said:

> "In vain would that man claim the tribute of patriotism, who should labor to subvert these great pillars of human happiness [religion and morality]." [16]

Jefferson Made a Life-long Study of the Bible

Thomas Jefferson also studied the Bible as his principal source for the discovery of the ancient principles of divine law revealed by God. Few of the Founders knew the Bible better than he.

Jefferson was particularly skillful in his knowledge of the law and constitutional principles set forth in the five books of Moses.

When the American Bible Association was organized to expand the distribution of Bibles, Jefferson sent along a monetary contribution and said:

> "I had not supposed there was a family in this state [of Virginia] not possessing a Bible ... When, in earlier life, I was intimate with every class, I think I never was in a house where that was not the case. However, circumstances may have changed, and the [Bible] Society, I presume, have evidence of the fact. I therefore enclose

14. Ibid., 14:198.
15. Huszar, Basic American Documents, op. cit., pp. 108-109.
16. Ibid.

> you cheerfully an order ... for fifty dollars, for the purposes of the society." [17]

James Madison Promotes Complete Freedom of Religion

Another outstanding Bible scholar among the Founders was James Madison. He studied religion and law simultaneously.

When George Mason wrote a Bill of Rights for the state of Virginia it included a statement on religion. James Madison was on the committee which reviewed this provision and he changed it to fit his own views on religion. Here is what he wrote:

> "The Religion or the duty we owe to our Creator, and the manner of discharging it, being under the direction of reason and conviction only, not of violence or compulsion, all men are equally entitled to the full and free exercise of it according to the dictates of conscience; and therefore that no man or class of men ought, on account of religion, to be invested with peculiar emoluments or privileges; nor subject to any penalties or disabilities unless under color of religion, any man disturb the peace, the happiness, or safety of Society. And that it is the mutual duty of all to practice Christian forbearance, love, and charity, toward each other." [18]

At the age of 36, it fell Madison's lot to provide the leadership for the Virginia delegation at the Constitutional Convention. From the Virginia delegates came the agenda for the convention and James Madison became known as "the father of the Constitution." It was his goal, as it was with Thomas Jefferson, to weave together in the American Constitution those principles of government portrayed in the Bible.

The Bible Provides the Key to Understanding the Genius of the American System of Government

Once it is recognized that the Founders were using the divine science of government revealed to the Israelites (and the remarkably similar system used by the Anglo-Saxons who seemed to have copied the Israelites), it then becomes important to identify the specific ideas which the Founders used to create the political framework for the first free people in modern times.

Nevertheless, until Donald S. Lutz and Dr. Charles S. Hyneman completed their analysis of the principal writings of the Founders, it might have seemed

17. Bergh, The Writings of Thomas Jefferson, op. cit., 14:81.
18. Irving Brant, James Madison, Indianapolis: The Bobbs-Merrill Company, 1941, 1:245.

incredible that they would have gleaned so many of their great ideas from this single source—the Bible.

Topics for Reflection and Discussion

1. According to the Lutz-Hyneman study approximately what percentage of the Founders' "great ideas" came from the Bible? In the days of the Founders what kind of organizations sponsored every major college and university in America? Was a study of the Bible required?

2. Which of the Founders became president of the American Bible Association? What book did he consider the most reliable world history? What prevented him from signing the Declaration of Independence?

3. Who was the Founder who described what a nation would be like if it adopted the Bible as its only law book? Why did he think the Founders were a body of divinely appointed political scientists for the modern age? Did he believe there was an ideal system of government based on the "divine science" of God's law?

4. Name three great European scholars of political science who believed that the most reliable text for the study of good government was the Bible.

5. In the Northwest Ordinance adopted in 1787—the same year the Constitution was written—what were the three things the schools were to teach? What was the biggest problem connected with the first item? Can you identify the five basic beliefs on which all "sound religions" agree?

6. Who said these five basic beliefs that constitute the "religion of America" actually constitute the "religion of all mankind?" Do these basic beliefs fit all major denominations/religions with which you are acquainted?

7. What did George Washington say were "indispensable supports" to "political prosperity"? What did Washington consider a person to be who would undermine these important elements in our society?

8. When Thomas Jefferson was asked to contribute money for a wider distribution of the Bible, why was he surprised? As he travelled around the country what had he observed? Did he contribute anyway?

9. Which of the Founders is best remembered for his campaign to insure freedom of religion in all of the states? Why is he called the "Father of the Constitution?"

10. Can you think of at least two advantages a Bible-reading Founding Father would have over the vast majority of the politicians in our own day?

CHAPTER TWO

The American Founders Make an Exciting Discovery

It was through a careful reading of the Bible that the Founders discovered a whole new perspective concerning God's plans for America. They found that what God had promised ancient Israel he had also promised to restore in "the latter days."

To appreciate what the Founders had discovered, we have to remind ourselves that God gave ancient Israel the formula for an ideal society that could have made the Israelites the wealthiest and most powerful nation on earth. Here is the way the Lord said it the first time:

> "Now therefore, if ye will obey my voice indeed, and keep my covenant, then ye shall be a peculiar treasure unto me above all people: for all the earth is mine."[1]

A little later on the Lord repeated it. He said:

> "For thou art an holy people unto the Lord thy God: the Lord thy God hath chosen thee to be a special people unto himself, above all people that are upon the face of the earth."[2]

As the Lord was in the midst of teaching the people about the advanced civilization they were expected to build, he once more reminded them with these words:

> "Thou art an holy people unto the Lord thy God, and the Lord hath chosen thee to be a peculiar people unto himself, *above all the nations that are upon the earth.*"[3]

By this time one would assume that the Israelites should have realized how fortunate they were to be chosen by God to receive such a marvelous blessing.

---

1. Exodus 19:5.
2. Deuteronomy 7:6.
3. Deuteronomy 14:2.

The Blessings and the Cursings

But the Lord knew something the Israelites would never have guessed. In spite of all these marvelous promises, the Lord knew these liberated Egyptian slaves were going to run off braying into the wilderness and lose everything he had promised them.

And just to accentuate the intensity of the consequences in case they rebelled and apostatized, the Lord made a list of blessings and a list of cursings. As we proceed with this study we will examine both the blessings and the cursings in detail. It is almost incomprehensible that these descendants of Abraham would make the worst of all possible choices.

Moses Is Commanded to Give Israel the Bad News

It is probably impossible to imagine the anguish of Moses as the Lord revealed to him what the people would do to themselves after Moses was gone. The Lord told the prophet:

> "Behold, thou shalt sleep with thy fathers; and this people will rise up, and go a whoring after the gods of the strangers of the land, whither they go to be among them, and will forsake me, and break my covenant which I have made with them. Then my anger shall be kindled against them in that day, and I will forsake them, and I will hide my face from them, and they shall be devoured, and many evils and troubles shall befall them." [4]

Probably the saddest day of his entire life was when Moses finished writing the statutes of God's law and then told the Levites to put "this book … in the side of the ark … that it may be there for a witness against them." [5]

Then he said to the people:

> "I know that after my death ye will utterly corrupt yourselves, and turn aside from the way which I have commanded you; and evil will befall you in the latter days; because ye will do evil in the sight of the Lord, to provoke him to anger through the work of your hands." [6]

---

4. Deuteronomy 31:16-17.
5. Deuteronomy 31:26.
6. Deuteronomy 31:29.

How the Collapse of the Israelites Changed the History of the World

If the Israelites had set up the most powerful nation on earth the way God had commanded them, it would have stabilized the political and economic affairs of all other nations. The Israelites could have repeated everything the City of Enoch had accomplished centuries before. For 365 years it had stabilized the political and economic structure of the civilized world during the Enochian age. One account says:

> "The fear of the Lord was upon *all nations* so great was the glory of the Lord, which was upon his people. And the Lord blessed the land, and they were blessed upon the mountains, and upon the high places, and did flourish." [7]

But a thousand years later, Israel failed the Lord miserably. It had the same assignment as the City (actually the nation) of Enoch, but this benighted people degenerated into such a cesspool of debauchery that God's cursings descended on the Israelites like a plague of leprosy.

Four Blood-thirsty Empires Arise

Israel's collapse left a huge vacuum in the political and economic structure of the civilized world. Beginning about 600 B.C.—when Israel should have been at the height of her power—Babylon began spilling blood all over Asia to set up her mighty empire. (612-539 B.C.)

Then the Persians conquered Babylon and repeated the slaughter and conquest from nation to nation in order to establish the Persian empire. (539-331 B.C.)

Next came Alexander the Great who tried to satisfy his passion for power by overthrowing the Persians and setting up an empire that extended from the tip of Europe to India. (331-161 B.C.)

Finally Rome imposed her iron-clad law over the largest territory the world had ever known and ruled until she split in two in 395 A.D. and then finally disintegrated into numerous independent nations on three continents.

This disastrous sequence of imperial conquests cost the human family more than a thousand years of bloodshed, rapine, massacres, burning and ruthless ravaging of cities and farms. It decimated thirty-five consecutive generations of the Father's children. Much if not all of this could have been

7. See W. Cleon Skousen, The First 2,000 Years, Salt Lake City: Bookcraft, 1953, p. 167.

prevented if Israel had just simply fulfilled her destined role and had become the most powerful nation on earth. Instead, like a wild ass, she went off braying into the wilderness and drank to the very dregs the bitter brew of terrifying curses which God knew Israel would have to endure if she rejected the blessings God had planned for her. Moses declared:

> "And the Lord shall scatter thee among all people, from the one end of the earth even unto the other; and there thou shalt serve other gods, which neither thou nor thy fathers have known, even wood and stone. And among these nations shalt thou find no ease, neither shall the sole of thy foot have rest: but the Lord shall give thee there a trembling heart, and failing of eyes, and sorrow of mind: And thy life shall hang in doubt before thee; and thou shalt fear day and night, and shalt have none assurance of thy life: In the morning thou shalt say, Would God it were even! and at even thou shalt say, Would God it were morning! for the fear of thine heart wherewith thou shalt fear, and for the sight of thine eyes which thou shalt see." [8]

The Founders Discovered Some Good News For Themselves Amidst the Bad News for the Israelites

Among the black, thundering clouds of prophetic disaster which Moses predicted for the apostate Israelites, there was a silver lining that Moses flashed briefly across the future horizon dealing with modern times.

Moses said that after the Israelites had been scattered across the world and endured the lashes of a thousand years of curses and suffering, they would begin to recall God's generous promises to them if they would obey his divine law. Moses said:

> "And it shall come to pass, when all these things are come upon thee, the blessing and the curse, which I have set before thee, and thou shalt *call them to mind* among all the nations whither the Lord thy God hath driven thee.
>
> "And [thou] shalt return unto the Lord thy God, and shalt obey his voice according to *all that I command thee this day,* thou and thy children with all thine heart, and with all thy soul." [9]

Here are three divine promises:

8. Deuteronomy 28:64-67.
9. Deuteronomy 30:1-2; see also verse 8.

1. The remnants of God's people throughout the world will begin to remember the promises made to them.

2. They will then begin to "return unto the Lord," which implies that they will start to gather to some choice land.

3. There they will begin to establish God's law and obey it with all their hearts and souls.

Why this Was Such Good News to the Founders

As careful students of the Bible, the Founders saw the possibility of this beginning to come to pass in their day. They began to look upon America as the place where the remnants would begin to gather and they saw themselves as divinely appointed servants of the Almighty in restoring the sacred law given to Moses.

And they didn't miss the magnificent legacy that went with this law. If people lived it in righteousness they were promised the same blessings that ancient Israel was promised. But they knew it would require a virtuous people to merit such blessings.

Several times the Lord had told Israel what treasures of freedom, peace and prosperity this people could inherit if they would sincerely embrace this law and valiantly magnify its principles in righteousness.

Of course, these promises were made to *ancient* Israel right after they came out of slavery around 1,500 B.C., but God's promise to Moses in Deuteronomy 30:1-9 transferred those same promises to the remnants of Israel who would gather in the latter days and live under the principles of God's law. All through the writings of the Founders there is the expressed anticipation that it will be in *their* day that this will take place.

President Ezra Stiles of Yale University Rejoices in this Divine Promise

The discovery of this remarkable passage of scripture by the Founders generated the most elevated aspirations for themselves and their posterity. They exhibited a determined resolution that they would grasp this opportunity to make the prophecy of Moses a visible reality.

On May 8, 1783, Ezra Stiles, the President of Yale University, addressed the Governor and members of the state legislature on the subject: "The United

States Elevated to Glory and Honor."[10] In this talk he made special reference to the prophecy which Moses made at the close of his earthly ministry. President Stiles declared:

> "Here Moses, the man of God … recapitulated and gave them a second publication of the sacred jural institute [legal declaration] delivered thirty-eight years before, with the most awful solemnity at Mount Sinai. A law dictated with sovereign authority by the Most High … .
>
> "God determined that a remnant should be saved … recovered and gathered … from the nations whither the Lord had scattered them in his fierce anger … and multiply them over their fathers—and rejoice over them for good, as he rejoiced over their fathers (Deuteronomy 30:3-9.)
>
> "Then the words of Moses … will be literally fulfilled; when this branch of the posterity of Abraham shall be nationally collected, and become a very distinguished and glorious people under the Great Messiah, the Prince of Peace.
>
> "He will then make them 'high above all nations which he hath made in praise, and in name, and in honor,' and they shall become 'a holy people unto the Lord' their God."[11]

The Great Gathering

Moses was very specific about the scattered remnants of Israel being gathered together in the latter days. He said:

> "Then the Lord thy God will turn thy captivity, and have compassion upon thee, and will return and gather thee from all the nations, whither the Lord thy God hath scattered thee."[12]

Later prophets indicate that the great gathering of the latter days will bring the Jews back to Old Jerusalem, but the rest of the Israelites will gather to a new land which Isaiah and others call "Zion." Even Old Jerusalem was called Zion in its earlier history but when the prophets began talking about the Zion of the latter days they clearly distinguished it from Old Jerusalem. For example, Isaiah says:

---

10. This entire address appears in God's New Israel by Conrad Cherry, Englewood, N.J.: Prentice-Hall, Inc., 1971, pp. 82-92.
11. Ibid., pp. 82-83.
12. Deuteronomy 30:3.

> "And it shall come to pass *in the last days* ... out of Zion shall go forth the law, and the word of the Lord from Jerusalem." [13]

In thirty-three different verses the prophets distinguish between Old Jerusalem and the new "Zion" of the latter days.[14]

Micah speaks of the new Zion of the latter days as follows:

> "But in the last days it shall come to pass, that the mountain of the house of the Lord shall be established in the top of the mountains, and it shall be exalted above the hills; and people shall flow unto it. And many nations shall come, and say, Come, and let us go up to the mountain of the Lord, and to the house of the God of Jacob; and he will teach us of his ways, and we will walk in his paths: for the law shall go forth out of Zion, and the word of the Lord from Jerusalem." [15]

What Made Bible Scholars Think the "New Zion" of the Latter Days Would Be in America?

When students of the Bible in both Europe and America began looking around for the new prophetic Zion that was separate from Old Jerusalem, the characteristics of America seemed to fit the requirements of the Bible better than any other place.

In their studies they depended heavily on the writings of the prophet Isaiah both as to the location of the New Zion and the description of its native inhabitants.

When Isaiah saw a vision of God's great land of destiny in the latter days he said it was located among the "islands of the sea" and "beyond the rivers of Ethiopia" or Africa.[16] Of course America is a vast continent in its own right, but it is completely surrounded by water which is undoubtedly the reason Isaiah referred to it as one of the "isles." Isaiah also saw the native inhabitants of America and described them as:

> "A nation scattered and peeled ... a people terrible from their beginning hitherto; a nation meted out and trodden down, whose land the rivers have spoiled." [17]

---

13. Isaiah 2:3.

14. Psalms 51:18; 102:21; 128:5; 147:12; Isaiah 2:3; 4:3; 4:4; 10:12; 24:23; 31:9; 37:22; 37:32; 40:9; 41:27; 52:1; 64:10; Lamentations 1:17; 2:10; 2:13; Joel 2:32; 3:16; 3:17; Amos 1:2; Micah 3:10; 3:12; 4:2; 4:8; Zephaniah 3:14; 3:16; Zechariah 1:14; 1:17; 8:3; 9:9.

15. Micah 4:1-2.

16. Isaiah 18:1.

17. Isaiah 18:2.

Furthermore, the prophet Zephaniah refers to the latter days when God will "gather the nations" [18] and he speaks of the inhabitants of a land "beyond the rivers of Ethiopia" or Africa which would seem to be the same land seen by Isaiah. He says:

> "From beyond the rivers of Ethiopia my suppliants [supplicants] even the daughters of *my dispersed*, shall bring mine offering ... In that day shalt thou not be ashamed for all thy doings?... I will ... leave in the midst of thee an afflicted and poor people, and they shall trust in the name of the Lord, the *remnants of Israel* shall not do iniquity, nor speak lies." [19]

Notice that Zephaniah is saying that these native inhabitants of America are "remnants of Israel."

For obvious reasons, Bible scholars attached great significance to this verse. It indicates that those primitive people on the "isle" of the sea are actually remnants of ancient Israel, and in spite of their being scattered and trodden down as Isaiah mentioned, they will bring an offering to the Lord, thereby signifying that they would turn from their wicked ways and seek the favor of the Lord.

America Seen as a Choice Land of God with a Divine Destiny

When an English clergyman, Andrew Burnaby, visited the American colonies in 1759-60 he was rather amazed to discover the way in which many people looked upon the future role of America. He wrote:

> "An idea—strange as it is visionary—has entered into the minds of the generality of mankind that empire is travelling westward; and every one is looking forward with eager and impatient expectation to the destined moment, when America is to give the law to the rest of the world." [20]

It was expected that America, as the new Zion of the latter days, would fulfill the prophecy of Isaiah when he said "out of Zion shall go forth the law, and the word of the Lord from Jerusalem." [21]

18. Zephaniah 3:8.
19. Zephaniah 3:10-13.
20. Andrew Burnaby, Travels in the Middle Settlements in North America in the Year 1759 and 1760, 2nd ed. in John Pinkerton, ed., A General Collection of the Best and Most Interesting Voyages and Travels, London, 1812, 13:750; and quoted by Ernest Lee Tuveson, Redeemer Nation, Chicago: University of Chicago Press, 1968, p. 101.
21. Isaiah 2:3.

The well-known historian, Clinton Rossiter, wrote an essay entitled "The True American Mission." In this treatise he provided the best possible definition of precisely how the early Americans felt about their mission. He wrote:

> "It assumes that God, at the proper stage in the march of history, called forth certain hardy souls from the old and privilege-ridden nations; that He carried these precious few to the new world and presented them and their descendants with an environment ideally suited to the development of a free society; and that in bestowing His grace He also bestowed a peculiar responsibility for the success of popular institutions. Were the Americans to fail in their experiment in self-government, they would fail not only themselves, but all men wanting or deserving to be free." [22]

John Adams caught the spirit of the age when he said:

> "I always consider the establishment of America with reverence and wonder, as the opening of a grand scene and design in Providence for the illumination of the ignorant, and the emancipation of the slavish part of mankind *all over the earth*." [23]

It was commonplace for early Americans to speak of America as the "New Israel" or the new Zion. Conrad Cherry wrote a whole book about it called *God's New Israel*.[24]

As Reverend Abiel Abbot said in his Thanksgiving Sermon of 1799:

> "Our American Israel is a term frequently used; and common consent allows it apt and proper." [25]

Would the Restoration of Biblical Christianity Begin in New England?

Furthermore, it was believed that the pure religion of Biblical Christianity would be restored in New England. Jonathan Edwards, one of America's best known ministers of the Gospel, made this preliminary statement:

> "God presently goes about doing some great thing in order to make way for the introduction of the church's latter-day glory—which is to have its first seat in, and is to rise from [this] new world." [26]

Then he declared:

22. Tuveson, Redeemer Nation, op. cit., p. 22.
23. Quoted by Cherry in God's New Israel, op. cit., p. 65.
24. New York: Prentice-Hall, 1971.
25. Quoted by Cherry in God's New Israel, op. cit., the preface page.
26. Ibid., p. 57.

> "I think—if we consider the circumstances of the settlement of New England—it must needs appear the most likely of all American colonies to be the place whence this work shall principally take its rise."[27]

Thomas Jefferson also believed the restoration of the true Gospel would take place in America although he was fearful it would be after his time. He wrote in 1820:

> "If the freedom of religion . . . can . . . prevail, the genuine doctrines of Jesus . . . will again be restored to their original purity. This reformation will advance with the other improvements of the human mind, but too late for me to witness it."[28]

On another occasion Jefferson wrote that he was "Happy in the prospect of a restoration of primitive Christianity."[29]

Would America Be the Site of God's Latter-day Kingdom Seen by Daniel?

We have already mentioned the four blood-thirsty empires that arose as a result of Israel apostatizing and leaving a massive political vacuum in the world. These were the four empires described by the prophet Daniel when he was interpreting a dream for king Nebuchadnezzar in Babylon around 600 B.C. He concluded by saying:

> "And in the days of these kings shall the God of heaven set up a kingdom which shall never be destroyed: and the kingdom shall not be left to other people, but it shall break in pieces and consume all these [other] kingdoms, and it shall stand forever."[30]

Bible scholars began suggesting that this great kingdom of God that would last forever might very well be set up in the New Zion which they had already decided was America. Other distinguished scholars agreed with this interpretation.

---

27. Ibid., p. 59.
28. A letter to Jaret Sparks, Bergh, The Writings of Thomas Jefferson, op. cit., 15:288; quoted in The Real Thomas Jefferson, by Andrew Allison, Washington, D.C.: The National Center for Constitutional Studies, 1983, p. 366.
29. Letter to Dr. Benjamin Waterhouse, Bergh, The Writings of Thomas Jefferson, op. cit., 15:391.
30. Daniel 2:44.

Bishop George Berkeley of Ireland Felt Daniel's Great Prophecy Would Be Fulfilled in America

Throughout Europe the name of George Berkeley represented one of the most famous philosophers of the day. He was an ordained bishop of the Episcopal Church. The passage in the book of Daniel which we have just quoted was of paramount importance to this good churchman. He knew Daniel had predicted that four great empires would destroy one another in historic sequence and then God's kingdom would arise and endure forever.[31]

As Bishop Berkeley looked back through history he felt all of Daniel's prophecy had been fulfilled except the rise of God's kingdom. And he felt that this final epoch in Daniel's magnificent prophecy would be fulfilled in the new Zion of America.

So Bishop Berkeley wrote a poem pointing toward the manifest or divine destiny of America. In it he said:

> "Westward the course of empire takes it way;
>
> The four first acts, already past,
>
> A fifth shall close the drama with the day;
>
> Time's noblest offspring is the last." [32]

And what were the "first four acts, already past?"

Bishop Berkeley pointed to the four bloodthirsty empires of Babylon, Persia, Greece, and Rome. Rome, the last kingdom, had split in two and then divided into a multitude of independent nations like the toes of iron and clay.[33] One by one the four bloodthirsty kingdoms had been destroyed just as Daniel had predicted. Now it was time for the final glorious kingdom to be set up by God. Daniel said it would never be given to another people but would last forever.

Furthermore, Bishop Berkeley concluded from the Bible that it would not be just the hosts of the scattered Israelites who would come to America to set up this kingdom, but the natives—who had been trodden down as seen by Isaiah—would also arise and bring an offering to the Lord just as Zephaniah predicted.

---

31. Daniel chapter 2.
32. Tuveson, Redeemer Nation, op. cit., p. 94.
33. Daniel 2:33.

To Bishop Berkeley this called for action to prepare the American natives for their future destiny. He petitioned the British government for a special grant to set up an Indian cultural center in the Bahamas where the natives could be trained and educated. Having been assured there would be a grant of twenty thousand pounds, he set out for America.[34]

Since Bishop Berkeley had married at the age of 43 he took his new wife with him. They settled at Newport, Rhode Island, and patiently waited for three years hoping the money would arrive. But it did not. Finally, he became entirely discouraged with the unfulfilled promises of the British government and returned to England.

But he never lost interest in the need to educate the American natives about their manifest destiny. He sent books to both Harvard and Yale which could be made available to the natives if circumstances ever permitted the setting up of an all-American college for the Indians.

America's Strength to Be in the West

Lyman Beecher (1775-1863) was not only a notable minister but the father of a family of famous writers and speakers. Reverend Beecher said in 1835 that he believed, along with Jonathan Edwards, that the Millennium would begin in America. But even though it was popular to refer to New England as the land of the New Jerusalem, Lyman Beecher wrote:

> "It is equally plain that the religious and political destiny of our nation is to be decided in the West. There is the territory, and there soon will be the population, the wealth, and the political power. The Atlantic commerce and manufactures may confer always some peculiar advantages on the East, but the West is destined to be the great central power of the nation, and under heaven, must effect powerfully the cause of free institutions and the liberty of the world."[35]

Few orators could express themselves more eloquently about Western America than Lyman Beecher. He described the heartland of the west as follows:

> "The territory is eight thousand miles in circumference, extending from the Allegheny to the Rocky mountains, and from the Gulf of Mexico to the Lakes of the North; and it is the largest territory,

34. Encyclopedia Britannica, Cambridge: Cambridge University Press, scholars ed. (11th), 1910, 3:780.

35. Quoted by Cherry in God's New Israel, op. cit., p. 123.

and most beneficent in climate, and soil, and mineral wealth, and commercial facilities, ever prepared for the habitation of man, and qualified to sustain in prosperity and happiness the densest population on the globe. By twenty-four thousand miles of steam navigation, and canals and rail roads, a market is brought near to every man, and the whole is brought into near neighborhood....

"This vast territory is occupied now by ten states and will soon be twelve. Forty years since it contained only about one hundred and fifty thousand souls; while it now contains little short of five million. At the close of this [nineteenth] century, if no calamity intervenes, it will contain probably one hundred million—a day which some of our children may live to see; and when fully peopled, may accommodate three hundred million. It is half as large as all Europe, four times as large as the Atlantic states, and twenty times as large as New England." [36]

Americans Become Ardent Students of the Bible And Consider Making Hebrew the National Language

Since Americans felt that they were expected by God to pick up where Moses left off, there was a tremendous gravitational pull to identify themselves with ancient Israel. The foundation of this trend was reflected in the widespread popularity of university courses in the Hebrew language. People wanted to read the Old Testament in the original tongue. Many colleges made Hebrew a required course. There was even a suggestion that Hebrew be adopted as the national language in place of English. As one writer states:

"During the American Revolution, a movement was launched to replace English with Hebrew as the official language of the new nation.

"In 1776, anything associated with the British monarchy had a bad taste to the American rebels. Hebrew, on the other hand, was held in high regard by the former British colonists, who viewed it as the mother of all languages, the key to the scriptures and the cornerstone of liberal education.

"They named their towns after those cited in the Bible such as Salem and Bethlehem, and their children were named after Biblical figures.

36. Ibid., pp. 125-126.

"Until 1817, annual commencement addresses at Harvard were delivered in Hebrew, and at Yale the language [of Hebrew] was required for freshmen. Many lower schools also stressed Hebrew.

"Several members of the new Congress reportedly urged that English be banned altogether and replaced by Hebrew. Though the idea never caught on, Hebrew remained a required course at many major American universities well into the 19th century." [37]

A Phase of American History Modern Americans Have Virtually Forgotten

Stephen Birmingham describes the early American sense of affinity with the people of the Bible, both ancient and modern:

"From the beginning … the spirit that guided the American Revolution had strong Judaic overtones. The Old Testament had become, in many ways, a Revolutionary textbook. For one thing, the Puritans of Colonial New England considered themselves the spiritual offspring of Old Testament characters. Like the Jews, they gave their children Old Testament names. It was to the Old Testament that the Puritans turned to find God ….

"In England, the Puritans had been called 'Jewish fellow travelers,' and they had compared their flight to America with the Jews' escape from Egypt. They called the Massachusetts Bay Colony 'the New Jerusalem.' There was a proposal that Hebrew be made the official language of the Colonies (it was on the regular curriculum, along with Latin and Greek, when Harvard was founded, a knowledge of the language being considered part of the equipment of a cultivated man).

"John Cotton had suggested that the Mosaic Code be used as the basis for Massachusetts laws. There is a manifestation of the code, meanwhile, in the wording of the American Constitution." [38]

The Founders Attempt to Popularize Biblical Law

In 1639, the first written Constitution in America was prepared for Connecticut by Rev. Thomas Hooker and his friends. It was based on the first

37. Irving Wallace, et al., "Hebrew: National Language of the U.S.," Parade Magazine, New York: Parade Publications, May 30, 1982, p. 16.

38. Stephen Birmingham, The Grandees, New York: Harper and Roe, 1971, p. 146.

chapter of Deuteronomy. Later, the settlers of Rhode Island copied it for their own constitution.

Around 143 years later, following the Declaration of Independence, these two states were the only ones that had the political structure required for a self-governing commonwealth, and they were the only states that did not have to write new constitutions after the national Constitution was adopted.

For these two states, the principles of God's Law in the first chapter of Deuteronomy proved superior to any precepts used by the other states.

Eventually, most of New England took a leaf from the first chapter of Deuteronomy and organized their communities on the basis of approximately 100 families per unit just as Moses had organized ancient Israel. These units in New England consisting of approximately 100 families were called "wards"—which in the Bible meant a "watched over" or "guarded" place.[39] Later on, we will discuss the New England wards in greater detail.

Meanwhile, Jefferson spent two years in the legislature of Virginia trying to get his own state—which was the largest state in the Union—to adopt many elements of the "perfect law" that had been revealed to Moses.

In fact, to facilitate the adoption of statutes from the pattern of the Bible, he personally rewrote the entire criminal code as well as the civil code of Virginia. Each of these codes was restructured in terms of the principle of "reparation to the victim" as described in the Bible. He wanted the members of the legislature to see what a tremendous advantage God's law would be over English common law.[40]

When Jefferson was sent to France as the American diplomatic agent, he left this reform of the law in the hands of James Madison whom Jefferson had tutored in constitutional principles. However, for many years even Madison had little success in getting the state legislature to catch the vision of a Biblical system of law and justice. They were too deeply immersed in English law, and too comfortable in their professional traditions to see the advantages of a change back to the Biblical system.

However, after ten years, the legislature did finally pass Jefferson's proposal to disestablish the Virginia state church and allow freedom of religion.[41]

---

39. Hastings' Dictionary of the Bible, Edinburgh: T. and T. Clark, 1942 ed., vol. 4, under "ward."
40. Saul K. Padover, ed., The Complete Jefferson, New York: Tudor Publishing Company, 1943, pp. 88-102.
41. Allison, The Real Thomas Jefferson, op. cit., p. 88.

Virginia also permitted passage of Jefferson's bills outlawing primogeniture and the "entail estates." [42] Both of these English statutes had been imposed by the British crown to insure the perpetuation of the aristocratic class.

But other than these three bills, Jefferson's reformed codes on which he had labored so diligently, were tabled and, for the most part, forgotten until after the Revolutionary War. Jefferson commented on the difficulty of getting these reforms adopted. He said:

> "The main body of the work was not entered on by the legislature until after the general peace in 1785, when, by the unwearied exertions of Mr. Madison, in opposition to the endless quibbles, chicaneries, perversions, vexations, and delays of lawyers and demi-lawyers, most of the bills were passed by the legislature, with little alterations." [43]

Warm Friendships Develop Between the Founders and Wealthy American Jews

The American affinity for the Israelites of the past made it easy for Jews in America to develop a warm affinity with the leaders of the Revolution. The Jewish financial support for the Revolution was a critical factor throughout the war.

Take, for example, the friendship which the nation's Revolutionary leaders had with Haym Salomon. Here is his background:

He was born in Poland—around 1740—and migrated to New York. At the age of 37 he married into one of the most illustrious American Jewish families—the Franks of Philadelphia where the newlyweds eventually made their home. His bride, Rachel Frank, was then fifteen. Haym Salomon not only had the advantage of a fortunate marriage, but much earlier he had the exceptional distinction (for a young Jew in Poland) of being allowed to receive a university education. By the time he came to America he spoke French, Polish, Russian, Italian, Hebrew and Yiddish.

When the Revolution was floundering for lack of funds, Haym Salomon was recruited by Robert Morris to sell government bonds. He was so good at this assignment that Robert Morris called him "the most successful of the war brokers." Other brokers were helping to sell bonds, but Robert Morris was so impressed with the valiant services of Haym that he allowed him to advertise

42. Ibid., pp. 78-79.
43. Ibid., p. 80.

as "Broker to the Office of Finance." Salomon charged only a quarter of one percent for his services to the government, but he was so energetic in his work that his deposits at the Bank of North America came close to matching the account of Robert Morris.

This was fortunate for many American leaders, including George Washington, who leaned upon this generous Israelite for funds when they were not to be had from any other source.

Under the Law of Moses, funds extended to the needy were to be provided without interest. This was the policy of Haym Salomon in his effort to support the cause of the Revolution and loan money without interest to the men who were sacrificing their own fortunes to stay in the fight.

James Madison, who later became the "father of the Constitution," described to his friend, Edmund Randolph, the kindness extended to him by Haym Salomon. He wrote:

> "I am almost ashamed to reiterate my wants so incessantly to you, but they begin to be so urgent that it is impossible to suppress them. The kindness of our little friend in Front Street, near the coffee house, is a fund which will preserve me from extremities, but I never resort to it without great mortification, as he so obstinately rejects all recompense. The price of money is so usurious that he thinks it ought to be extorted from none but those who aim at profitable speculations. To a necessitous delegate [like Madison] he gratuitously spares a supply out of his private stock."[44]

During one of the great crises of the Revolution, Washington found his soldiers on the verge of mutiny because they had not been paid for months and their families were in dire straits. Washington sent a night rider posthaste to Haym Salomon in Philadelphia pleading for a loan of $400,000. Of course, this far exceeded the resources of Haym, but the messenger found him at the local synagogue. After whispering to the Jewish patriot the urgent message from Washington, Haym gathered together his friends so that among them they sent the money to Washington that same night. Legend has it that Haym put up $240,000 himself. At that time there would have been few fortunes in America that could have survived such a drain.[45]

Many Jews responded to the friendly spirit of Americans toward their ancient Israelite culture and many with substantial wealth became the nation's first major philanthropists.

44. Birmingham, The Grandees, op. cit., p. 154.
45. Ibid., p. 153.

The Story of Judah Touro

In this connection we should briefly mention a curious man named Judah Touro whose people were from the West Indies and were among the earliest settlers in Rhode Island. However, Judah Touro moved from his native Newport to New Orleans as a young man. Some said he was a miser. He bought land but never sold any. He lived in the poor section of the city and by reputation was said to be extremely frugal. His business operations were always relatively small and involved a wide variety of moderate enterprises. Nevertheless, he slowly accumulated a huge fortune, one of the ten largest fortunes in America.

When he died his executor distributed sixty-five separate bequests totalling $483,000. Some of these went to Christian organizations. Many went to community projects from Boston to New Orleans. A number of Jewish synagogues were also beneficiaries. It was the biggest philanthropic largesse in the early history of the western hemisphere.

Jewish philanthropy became a tradition among wealthy Jewish families and subsequent generations were never allowed to forget that the Jews were among the first philanthropists in the United States. Jewish children were taught that under God's law and according to Jewish tradition, charitable needs must never be forgotten or neglected.[46]

The Vision of the Founders

Before closing this chapter, we should comment briefly on the long-range vision of the Founders concerning America. Their writings clearly demonstrate that these highly motivated leaders believed they were raised up by God to establish the United States as the first free people in modern times.

They believed that their new commonwealth of freedom would eventually encompass the entire North American continent, and they held to this view in spite of the claims of England, Russia, France, and Spain to substantial parts of it.[47]

In fact, the American leaders were deeply disappointed when the four French colonies in Canada declined to accept the invitation extended to them in the Articles of Confederation to become an important part of the United States.[48]

---

46. Ibid., pp. 142-143.
47. Albert Weinberg, Manifest Destiny, Gloucester, Mass.: Peter Smith Publishers, 1958, pp. 1-2, 43; Cherry, God's New Israel, op. cit., p. 1.
48. Ibid.

Nevertheless, the Founders continued to express their complete confidence that their commonwealth would continue to expand, and many new states would be added to the Union until it extended from the Atlantic seaboard to the shores of the Pacific.[49]

As for population, the Founders predicted that within a century the population of the United States (which was then 3.5 million) would be at least 50 million. The 1890 census showed a total of 62.9 million.

John Adams said they were preparing the Constitution and the structure of the United States for a population of 200 to 300 million freemen. By 1990, the estimated population had already reached nearly 250 million.[50]

It was clearly the intention of the Founders to structure the new nation so it could fulfill the promise made to ancient Israel. They wanted God's "new Israel" to become a flourishing example of a righteous community and be "above all the nations that are upon the earth."[51]

---

49. Ibid.
50. 1996 World Almanac, Mahwah, New Jersey: Funk and Wagnalls Corp., p.385.
51. Deuteronomy 14:2.

Topics for Reflection and Discussion

1. How great did the Lord say the people of Israel would become if they obeyed God's commandments? What were the "blessings?" What were the "cursings?" Which did Moses predict the Israelites would inherit?

2. In what way was the assignment of the Israelites identical with that of Enoch? How long did Enoch maintain peace and order among the nations of the earth? In what way did the Israelites fail the Lord?

3. When the Israelites collapsed what was the first blood-thirsty empire to rise up and fill the void? What was the second? What was the third? What was the fourth?

4. What did Moses say would happen to the Israelites if they failed in their mission? But what would they remember in the latter days? Did Moses prophesy that eventually they would be gathered again? Would they eventually be ruled by God's law?

5. How did the Founders know that the Zion of the latter days is different than Jerusalem? Where would the Jews gather in the latter days? Is this now being fulfilled? Why did Micah say the remnants of Israel from the other tribes would gather to the top of the mountains in the latter-day Zion?

6. When Isaiah saw the latter-day Zion in vision where did he say it was located? What kind of inhabitants would be there? Were they a remnant of Israel? What made Bible scholars think Isaiah was talking about America?

7. Why did the early settlers on the Atlantic seaboard speak of America as the "new Israel?" Did the Early Americans believe that eventually God's law would be established in America and then go forth to the rest of the world? Where does Isaiah predict this?

8. Where did Thomas Jefferson and many of the early Americans predict the original purity of Biblical Christianity would be restored? Where did some of them say the Millennium would begin?

9. Although the American people were first established on the Atlantic seaboard, where did Lyman Beecher say the great center of power and population would eventually be? Between what two ranges of mountains did he say America's greatest strength would lie? How many people did he say this one area could accommodate?

10. Why were early Americans so fascinated with Biblical culture and the Hebrew language? Why did some think Hebrew should become America's official language? What did Jefferson do to popularize Biblical Law? Which two states based their Constitutions on the Bible?

CHAPTER THREE

The Marvelous Manner in Which God's Law Was Revealed to Ancient Israel

Moses had the honor of receiving and recording the most famous code of laws in human history, and he received these laws under some amazing circumstances. To appreciate what happened we have to know a little about Moses himself.

A Child Born under a Death Sentence

According to the latest Bible chronology, Moses was born around 1597 B.C. He was the grandson of the patriarch, Levi, who was the great grandson of Abraham.[1] This tells us that contrary to the belief of some, Moses was not of the tribe of Judah. He was a Levite.

Moses was born in Egypt, the child of two slaves who were Israelites. It will be recalled that the Pharaoh had ordered all male babies killed in order to reduce the rapidly expanding slave population; therefore Moses was born under a death sentence and had to be hidden during the daytime in the reeds along the Nile so the soldiers of the Pharaoh would not slay him.[2] However, as every student of the Bible knows, he was discovered by the daughter of Pharaoh,[3] and she adopted him as her son because she had no children of her own.[4]

The Bible says Moses was trained in all of the skills of the Egyptians,[5] and Josephus, the best-known Jewish historian, says he was made the leader of the Egyptian armies, and became a military hero in the war with Ethiopia.[6]

However, Moses was taught nothing about political science other than ruler's law which was the code of tyranny imposed on all nations in ancient times. Moses knew the Egyptian Pharaoh had power over life and death, and when he offended the Pharaoh he fled for his life. At this time he was forty years of age.[7]

1. W. Cleon Skousen, The Third Thousand Years, Salt Lake City: Bookcraft Inc., 1964, p. 193.
2. Exodus 1:22; 2:1-4.
3. Exodus 2:5.
4. Exodus 2:10, The Third Thousand Years, op. cit., p. 198.
5. Acts 7:22.
6. Skousen, The Third Thousand Years, op. cit., pp. 199-203.
7. Acts 7:23, 29.

Moses Flees to Midia

The Bible says Moses fled across the desert of Egypt, passed over the Sinai peninsula and finally reached the land of Midia on the Aqaba gulf of the Red Sea. There he was befriended by the leader of the Midianites, a priest named Jethro, who was also a descendant of Abraham.[8] Moses gained favor with Jethro, married his daughter[9] and was made the manager of Jethro's flocks.[10] Thus, he shifted from the career of a proud prince of Egypt to the role of a humble desert shepherd where he served for another period of forty years.[11]

But he was about to be called to the most important mission of his life—the calling of a prophet. This would be his last assignment and it would also last for forty years.[12]

The Bible says Moses was eighty when he had his first encounter with God.[13] This was a frightening experience, and when it was over Moses found that he had not only witnessed several miraculous demonstrations of God's power, but he had received a command from the Almighty to go to Egypt and lead the enslaved Israelites to freedom.

Moses used every plausible excuse to get out of this assignment. Finally he agreed to go, after Aaron—his older brother—came to meet him at Mount Sinai and they agreed to undertake the mission together.

Upon arriving in Egypt, Moses learned that the old Pharaoh was dead, but the new Pharaoh virtually laughed Moses and Aaron out of the palace when they requested that the Pharaoh allow the Israelites to depart out of Egypt and return to the land of their inheritance in Canaan or Palestine.

Then things began to happen. The power of the Almighty began to take over.

How the Israelites Escaped from Egypt

In all Bible history there has never been such a series of spectacular miracles as those which occurred in quick succession and finally compelled the Egyptians to allow the slave population of around three million Israelites to march triumphantly out of Egypt.[14]

8. Genesis 25:1-2; The Third Thousand Years, op. cit., pp. 207-208.
9. Exodus 2:21.
10. Exodus 3:1.
11. Acts 7:30.
12. Deuteronomy 34:7; Acts 7:36, 42.
13. Acts 7:30.
14. Exodus, chapters 4 to 10.

But the Israelites had not quite escaped from the borders of Egypt when the Egyptians changed their minds and the Pharaoh himself led his hosts out to recapture them. By this time the Israelites had reached the Red Sea and suddenly realized they were about to be trapped. The greatest miracle of all occurred when Moses lifted his rod and the sea suddenly divided. According to Exodus 14:22, the hosts of Israel marched forth on dry ground between the walls of water which stood up on either side. The Israelites had barely crossed when the Egyptians came charging in behind them, but the walls of water instantly collapsed and the Egyptians were all drowned, including the Pharaoh.[15]

Moses hurriedly led this huge host of former slaves southward to the foot of Mount Sinai where they made their encampment. He then ascended the mountain to receive further instructions.

The Lord disclosed to Moses that he desired to enter into a sacred covenant with these people.[16] He ordered Moses to prepare the people for three days and then the power of God would be made manifest and the people would be allowed to hear the voice of the Lord as he dictated to Moses the commandments and statutes for a divine pattern of righteous government.[17]

The Israelites See a Glorious Manifestation of God's Power

When the great event took place, it exceeded their wildest expectations. First of all, a luminous cloud descended on the Mount. Thunders roared out across the wilderness and crashing bolts of lightning caused the earth to quake. Then the people heard the sounding of a trumpet which blew louder and louder until the people were actually trembling with fear.[18]

At this point, Moses brought the hosts of Israel out of their camps and had them converge around the boundaries which had been set up at the base of the mountain. A fearful display of sight and sound then took place:

> "And Mount Sinai was altogether on a smoke, because the Lord descended upon it in fire: and the smoke thereof ascended as the smoke of a furnace, and the whole mount quaked greatly." [19]

Then a near tragedy occurred as some of the more impetuous Israelites determined to ascend the mountain and behold the glory of God the

15. Exodus, chapter 14.
16. Exodus 19:5.
17. Exodus 19:10-11.
18. Exodus 19:16.
19. Exodus 19:18-19.

way Moses had seen it. Everything was held in abeyance until Moses had positively determined that every Israelite had returned to the confines of the sacred boundaries at the foot of the mountain.[20]

Not until later would any of the Israelites—besides Moses—actually see God. They had to be better prepared before they could endure the glory of his presence.[21]

Nevertheless, there was something the Lord could share with the people immediately. He would allow them to hear his voice as he spoke to Moses. This would fulfill an earlier promise when he had told Moses:

> "Lo, I come unto thee in a thick cloud, that the people may hear when I speak with thee, and believe thee forever."[22]

The People Hear God Talking to Moses

The people then heard God begin to declare his law to Moses in the presence of all the people. The first thing Moses received was the Ten Commandments. Later, God would write these commandments on tablets of stone with his own finger, but first he wanted the people to hear them as he proclaimed these sacred edicts to Moses by his own voice.

One would have thought that these sign-seeking Israelites would have rejoiced to be allowed to hear God talking to Moses. Hadn't some of them risked their lives that very day to see the glory of God? Wouldn't hearing God's voice make them "scientific witnesses" of this historic event? But it was not to be. Their reaction to the voice of God was not one of joy, but one of abject terror. The Bible says they panicked and fled "afar off."[23]

Moses could not stop them, but he tried. They said, "Speak thou with us, and we will hear: but let not God speak with us, lest we die."[24]

Moses replied, "Fear not: for God is come to prove you, and that his fear may be before your faces, that ye sin not."[25]

But they were too frightened to prove anything. They not only refused to stand before the Lord, but they pleaded with Moses to go back and get the word of the Lord for them. Meanwhile, they would remain at a safe distance.

---

20. Exodus 19:21-25.
21. Exodus 19:24; 24:9-10.
22. Exodus 19:9.
23. Exodus 20:18.
24. Exodus 20:19.
25. Exodus 20:20.

So Moses went back to receive the rest of the law from the Lord. The scripture says Moses confidently moved up "near unto the thick darkness, where God was." [26]

> "And the Lord said unto Moses, Thus thou shalt say unto the children of Israel, *ye have seen that I have talked with you from heaven.*" [27]

So the purposes of God were fulfilled. As we shall see later, only a few of them were allowed to see God, but all of them would have to testify that they had heard his voice.

The Structure of God's Law

Throughout his writings Moses continually refers to the Law of the Covenant or God's law as having three separate parts. Both the Lord and his prophet refer to these as follows:

1. *The Commandments*. This is the famous decalogue of ten commandments given to Moses in the presence of all of Israel at the foot of Mount Sinai[28] and later inscribed on two stone tablets by the finger of God.[29]

2. *The Statutes*. These are God's laws that John Adams called the "divine science" of good government for happy living and the complete formula for an ideal society which we quoted in chapter two. The Psalmist referred to these statutes as being "perfect ... right ... and pure." [30] These statutes will be treated separately in a section at the end of the book.

3. *The Judgments*. These are the two kinds of judgments which God has held in reserve for the righteous who deserve "blessings" [31] and the punishment for the wicked who deserve "cursings." [32]

Why God Added the Carnal Commandments Which He Hated

As we mentioned earlier, God first revealed his perfect code of law to Moses while he was standing at the foot of Mount Sinai and the Israelites were fearfully waiting at a distance.[33]

26. Exodus 20:21.
27. Exodus 20:22.
28. Exodus 20:1-17
29. Exodus 32:15-16.
30. Psalms 19:7-9.
31. Deuteronomy 28:1-13.
32. Deuteronomy 28:16-68.
33. Exodus 20:18-21.

Later, it will be recalled, Moses went up to the top of the Mount to meet the Lord and received the two tablets on which these laws had been inscribed by the finger of God. It will also be recalled that while he was gone, the people betrayed both Moses and their Lord. Three thousand of them stripped naked, became drunken and began indulging themselves in the vile debauchery of sex worship around a golden calf the way they had seen it done in Egypt.[34] Apparently the rest of the Israelites stood all around gawking at the sight.

As a result of this tragic event, God felt compelled to impose on the Israelites a "schoolmaster law" to teach these rebellious renegades the rhythm of obedience.[35] This burden of tedious rituals, diets, sacrifices, special sabbaths, and boring litany was repulsive to God. He hated it. This is reflected in the first chapter of Isaiah which is sometimes called God's lamentation. To Israel of that day he said:

> "To what purpose is the multitude of your sacrifices unto me? saith the Lord: I am full of the burnt offerings of rams, and the fat of fed beasts; and I delight not in the blood of bullocks, or of lambs, or of he goats ….
>
> "Bring no more vain oblations; incense is an abomination unto me; the new moons and sabbaths, the calling of assemblies, I cannot away with [it]; it is iniquity, even the solemn meeting.
>
> "Your new moons and your appointed feasts my soul hateth: they are a trouble unto me; I am weary to bear them.
>
> "And when ye spread forth your hands, I will hide mine eyes from you: yea, when ye make many prayers, I will not hear: your hands are full of blood."[36]

Then we read how this loving and long suffering Heavenly Parent pleaded with these obstreperous and rebellious people with the following words:

> "Wash you, make you clean; put away the evil of your doings from before mine eyes; cease to do evil;
>
> "Learn to do well; seek judgment, relieve the oppressed, judge the fatherless, plead for the widow.

34. Exodus 32:19, 25.
35. Galatians 3:24.
36. Isaiah 1:11-15.

> "Come now, and let us reason together, saith the Lord: though your sins be as scarlet, they shall be as white as snow; though they be red like crimson, they shall be as wool.
>
> "If ye be willing and obedient, ye shall eat the good of the land." [37]

The Carnal Commandments Are Not Part of God's Law

It will be obvious as we go through God's law why we have not included any of the hated, tedious, boring ritual, diets, and litany of the Carnal Commandments in this study.

As Paul explains, the law of Carnal Commandments was designed to teach the people the rhythm of obedience and hold the remnant of Israel together until Christ was born. Once this had transpired, the purpose of the Schoolmaster Law was fulfilled and its requirements repealed.[38] Jesus verified that his life and ministry fulfilled the need for the Law of Carnal Commandments when he said:

> "Think not that I am come to destroy the law … but to *fulfill*." [39]

Why the Ten Commandments Were Separated from the Rest of the Statutes

All of God's laws are commandments but he wanted to summarize those special commandments which clearly reflected two things:

1. The divine relationship between God and man.
2. The divine relationship that we have with one another as God's children.

The Lord refers to these laws as his "*Ten* Commandments," [40] but he does not number them individually. As a result, some religious denominations number them in a slightly different manner than others. To assist in memorizing these commandments, we have simplified them slightly and summarized them in the numerical order used by most denominations.

1. Thou shalt have no other God before me.
2. Thou shalt not worship false gods or graven images.
3. Thou shalt not take the name of the Lord thy God in vain.

---

37. Isaiah 1:16-19.
38. Hebrews 9:10.
39. Matthew 5:17.
40. Exodus 34:28; Deuteronomy 4:13; 10:4.

4. Remember the sabbath day to keep it holy.
5. Honor thy father and thy mother.
6. Thou shalt not kill.
7. Thou shalt not commit adultery.
8. Thou shalt not steal.
9. Thou shalt not bear false witness.
10. Thou shalt not covet.

It is interesting that during his ministry Jesus was "tempted" by a lawyer to name the most important single commandment among the 613 laws the Jewish scribes and scholars had identified in the scriptures.

The lawyer who asked him the question was trying to trick Jesus because he thought that no matter which law the Savior selected as his favorite, there would be loud protests by those who preferred others. But what Jesus came up with astonished the lawyer. Without any hesitation Jesus said:

> "Thou shalt love the Lord thy God with all thy heart, and with all thy soul, and with all thy mind, and with all thy strength, this is the first and great commandment." [41]

Then Jesus quickly added:

> "And the second is like unto it, Thou shalt love thy neighbor as thyself.[42] On these two commandments hang all the law and the prophets." [43]

According to St. Mark, the lawyer was so amazed that a humble carpenter from Galilee could give such an astute answer, that he said in admiration:

> "Well, Master, thou hast said the truth: for there is one God; *and there is none other but he*: And to love him with all the heart, and with all the understanding, and with all the soul, and with all the strength, and to love his neighbour as himself, is more than all whole burnt offerings and sacrifices.
>
> "And when Jesus saw that he answered discreetly, he said unto him, Thou art not far from the kingdom of God. And no man after that durst ask him any question." [44]

---

41. Mark 12:30; Deuteronomy 6:5.
42. Leviticus 19:18.
43. Matthew 22:40.
44. Mark 12:32-34.

When God's Judgments Bring Blessings

Having considered God's "Commandments" which comprise one of the three parts of God's divine science of good government, let us now consider his "Judgments" which were carefully delineated as "blessings" and "cursings." We mentioned these briefly in the previous chapter, but now let us examine them more closely.

Since God's government was only designed to work for a righteous people, these blessings and cursings were specifically set up like red and green traffic signals so Israel would know what to expect as the people maneuvered their way along life's hazardous highway.

To keep these traffic signals clearly visible to every generation of Israelites, the Lord commanded Joshua to erect huge stones on Mount Ebal in the center of the promised land. He was commanded to do this as soon as this area was conquered.

As it turned out, he ascended Mount Ebal with the hosts of Israel shortly after his second military victory. God had instructed him to set up these huge stones and then smooth them over with plaster so that the law of God could be carefully inscribed on these stones together with the blessings and the cursings.[45]

There was to be a sacred ceremony held near the altar after appropriate prayers and sacrifices. Half of the tribes were to face toward Mount Gerizim (just south of Mount Ebal) and pronounce each of the promised blessings. The other half of the tribes were to face Mount Ebal and pronounce each of the cursings, following which "all the people were to answer and say Amen."[46]

In 1985, several Hebrew University archaeologists found a huge Israelite altar on Mount Ebal dating back to the time of Joshua. This author and a group of friends touring Israel obtained permission through Dr. Joseph Ginat of the Prime Minister's office, to see it. Dr. Ginat said we were the first foreign group allowed to visit this site, since it was located in a dangerous off-limits military zone.[47]

---

45. Deuteronomy 27:1-8.
46. Deuteronomy 27:11-15.
47. Our visit to this altar is shown in the Living Scriptures videotape entitled, "Prophecy -- A Visit to the Holy Land with Dr. W. Cleon Skousen."

The Blessings[48]

1. They would become the greatest nation on earth.

2. They would be blessed with an abundance of food, raiment, and comfortable homes.

3. They would be blessed with good health and strong children.

4. They would be blessed with great military strength so that no nation would dare attack them, and in case of war they would be blessed with victory.

5. They would be blessed with abundant rains and flourishing crops.

6. They would be blessed with so much wealth that other nations would come to borrow, but Israel would never have to borrow from others.

The Cursings[49]

In direct contrast to all these marvelous blessings, here are the afflictions which would be heaped upon the heads of the Israelites if they defied God and desecrated his commandments:

1. They would become a wandering, scattered, homeless, poverty-stricken people.

2. They would be cursed, despised and abused wherever they went.

3. They would suffer terrible diseases, plagues, pestilences, famine, thirst, and, in time of siege, they would eat their own dead.

4. They would be weak, vulnerable, and continually conquered by their enemies. Their land would be confiscated, their crops devoured, their wives ravished, and their daughters carried away into slavery.

5. Among the nations of the world, they would never be the head but always the tail.

6. In the end, there would be pitifully few of them left compared to the vast multitude they might have been.

In summary, the Lord was simply saying to the Israelites: for blessings there is nothing you could possibly desire that will not come to you if you are righteous. And, on the other hand, there is nothing you can imagine as terrible as that which will come to you, if you are wicked.

48. Deuteronomy 28:1-13.
49. Deuteronomy 28:16-68.

The Israelites Enter into a Covenant with God

So, with this elaborate smorgasbord of blessings and cursings lying on the table before them, the Israelites entered into their covenant to obey God and hopefully qualify for the rich blessings he had promised.

To achieve this, here is what the Lord said:

> "Ye have seen what I did unto the Egyptians, and how I bare you on eagles' wings, and brought you unto myself. Now therefore, if ye will obey my voice indeed, and keep my covenant, then ye shall be a peculiar treasure unto me above all people … and an holy nation." [50]

It is always easy to make promises but sometimes extremely difficult to keep them. Later on the Israelites would discover just how difficult it was, but at this moment they were eager to make their promises and so the scripture says:

> "And all the people answered together, and said, All that the Lord hath spoken we will do." [51]

Next, the People Had to Be Organized in God's Own Way

In order to make the Law of the Covenant work efficiently, the Israelites had to be organized in a very special way.

It will be recalled that Moses had been originally trained in government as a prince of Pharaoh. All he knew was "ruler's law" where the ruler commands and the people obey.

Under that system the ruler makes the law, interprets the law, and enforces the law. When Moses brought approximately three million Israelites out of Egypt he ruled them in this manner until they reached Mount Sinai. There he was met by Jethro, his father-in-law, who immediately realized that Moses needed to be trained in the efficient self-governing system of law which had been revealed by God to his servants clear back in the days of Adam.

No doubt Jethro was amused and perhaps amazed as he watched Moses trying to govern the people and settle all their problems by himself. Jethro watched Moses a whole day and then he said:

---

50. Exodus 19:4-6.
51. Exodus 19:8.

"What is this thing that thou doest to the people? why sittest thou thyself alone, and all the people stand by thee from morning unto even?

"And Moses said unto his father in law, Because the people come unto me to inquire of God: When they have a matter, they come unto me; and I judge between one and another, and I do make them know the statutes of God, and his laws.

"And Moses' father in law said unto him, The thing that thou doest is not good.

"Thou wilt surely wear away, both thou, and this people that is with thee: for this thing is too heavy for thee; thou art not able to perform it thyself alone." [52]

Jethro Understood God's Law and Shared the Wisdom of the Patriarchs with Moses

In his state of exhaustion, no doubt Moses listened intently as his wise old father-in-law said to him:

"Hearken now unto my voice, I will give thee counsel, and God shall be with thee ....

"Thou shalt teach them [the people] ordinances and laws, and shalt shew them the way wherein they must walk, and the work that they must do.

"Moreover, thou shalt provide out of all the people able men, such as fear God, men of truth, hating covetousness; and place such over them, to be rulers of thousands, and rulers of hundreds, rulers of fifties, and rulers of tens:

"And let them judge [govern] the people at all seasons: and it shall be, that every great matter they shall bring unto thee, but every small matter *they* shall judge: so shall it be easier for thyself, and they shall bear the burden with thee.

"If thou shalt do this thing, and God command thee so, then thou shalt be able to endure, and all this people shall also go to their place in peace." [53]

---

52. Exodus 18:15-18.
53. Exodus 18:19-23.

Forty Years Later Moses Describes What He Did

Forty years later, just as the Israelites were preparing to cross the Jordan into the promised land, Moses reflected on the genius of the system of government which Jethro, that venerable priest of God, had shared with him. He said to the Israelites:

> "And I spake unto you at that time, saying, I am not able to bear you myself alone ....
>
> "How can I myself alone bear your cumbrance, and your burden, and your strife?
>
> "Take [elect] you wise men, and understanding, and known among your tribes, and I will make them rulers over you.
>
> "And you answered me, and said, The thing which thou hast spoken is good for us to do.
>
> "So I took the chief of your tribes, wise men, and known, and made them heads over you, captains over thousands, and captains over hundreds, and captains over fifties, and captains over tens, and officers among your tribes."[54]

Judges must Be Righteous Men Acting in the Name of God

Although the people were allowed to "take" or elect their own judges, they had to be brought to Moses for approval. These men had to be capable of wise and compassionate decisions. They had to govern the people of their particular group. In time of war, they had to be "captains." This selection process called for a very high caliber of men.

Moses brought these leaders together to give them their instructions. He said:

> "And I charged your judges at that time, saying, Hear the causes between your brethren, and judge righteously between every man and his brother, and the stranger that is with him.
>
> "Ye shall not respect persons in judgment; but ye shall hear the small as well as the great; ye shall not be afraid of the face of man; for the judgment is God's: and the cause that is too hard for you, bring it unto me, and I will hear it."[55]

---

54. Deuteronomy 1:9-15.
55. Deuteronomy 1:16-17.

Moses was well aware that when he initiated this new program at Mount Horeb some forty years earlier, he was unloading a mountain of responsibility onto these newly elected officials. He also knew many of them had no experience in administration or handling judicial problems. Even now they still needed constant supervision and advice. Nevertheless, the Lord had told him that his leadership was about to be terminated and they will be compelled to carry on without him. Moses therefore decided to share this last morsel of advice:

> "If there arise a matter too hard for thee in judgment … then shalt thou arise, and get thee up into the place which the Lord thy God shall choose;
>
> "And thou shalt come unto the priests the Levites, and unto the judge that shall be in those days, and inquire; and they shall shew thee the sentence of judgment:
>
> "And thou shalt do according to the sentence, which they of that place which the Lord shall choose shall shew thee; and thou shalt observe to do according to all that they inform thee:
>
> "According to the sentence of the law which they shall teach thee, and according to the judgment which they shall tell thee, thou shalt do: thou shalt not decline from the sentence which they shall shew thee, to the right hand, nor to the left.
>
> "And the man that will do presumptuously, and will not hearken unto the priest that standeth to minister there before the Lord thy God, or unto the judge, even that man shall die: and thou shalt put away the evil from Israel." [56]

Under the Law of the Covenant, justice was administered with dispatch. The matter was to be thoroughly investigated, and a decision rendered which gave the victim prompt relief and the offender speedy punishment.

To the judges, Ezra later emphasized:

> "And whosoever will not do the law of thy God … let judgment be executed speedily upon him, whether it be unto death, or to banishment, or to confiscation of goods, or to imprisonment." [57]

---

56. Deuteronomy 17:8-12.
57. Ezra 7:26.

The People must Be Taught the Law

The genius of a peaceful, prosperous society is having the people thoroughly aware of what is expected of them and highly motivated to conform to their commitments. This is what Moses had in mind when he told his judges and other leaders:

> "And thou shalt teach them ordinances and laws, and shalt shew them the way wherein they must walk, and the work that they must do." [58]

One of the principal reasons for recording the Law of the Covenant on the Mount was so that Moses would have a permanent study guide which covered all the ramifications of the law which the people were to be taught:

> "And the Lord said unto Moses, Come up to me into the mount, and be there: and I will give thee tables of stone, and a law, and commandments which I have written; that thou mayest teach them." [59]

Many have thought the tablets only had the Ten Commandments inscribed on them, but we now know the entire Law of the Covenant was recorded by the Lord. We therefore read:

> "And the Lord spake unto Aaron, saying … teach the children of Israel all the statutes which the Lord hath spoken unto them by the hand of Moses." [60]

The Lord wanted the people to rehearse the principles of the Law of the Covenant until they were deeply impressed on their hearts:

> "Ye shall teach them [to] your children, speaking of them when thou sitteth in thine house, and when thou walkest by the way, when thou liest down, and when thou risest up." [61]

The Statutes of God's Law

Up to this point we have examined the Commandments, the Judgments [blessings and curses], and the responsibilities which God placed on the people to ingrain these principles into their hearts.

---

58. Exodus 18:20.
59. Exodus 24:12.
60. Leviticus 10:8-11.
61. Deuteronomy 11:19.

Now we come to the biggest undertaking of all: learning the genius of the "Statutes" of God's law, and how the judges were supposed to interpret and enforce them.

Beginning with the next few chapters and then jumping to an appendix in the back we commence the most challenging assignment in this entire study.

Topics for Reflection and Discussion

1. How old was Moses when he was forced to flee from Egypt to Midia? How long did he serve as a shepherd managing the flocks of Jethro? How long was he a prophet? Why was it such a great privilege for the Israelites to hear God speaking to Moses? What was their reaction?

2. Did God's law begin with Moses or did it go back to the ancient patriarchs? What was written on the two tablets given to Moses? Who wrote it? By what means?

3. When Moses came down from the Mount, what did he see that brought a great curse upon the Israelites? Did God hate the "carnal commandments" which were added to the Law? Then why did he add them? How would you define the term, "rhythm of obedience?"

4. The Lord divides his laws of the covenant into three parts. What are they? See if you can repeat the shortened version of each of the Ten Commandments.

5. What did Jesus say when he was asked to select the greatest of all the commandments? Which did he say was the second greatest?

6. List five of the blessings Israel would receive if they obeyed the laws of God.

7. List five of the cursings Israel would receive if they apostatized and disobeyed the law of God.

8. How did the father-in-law of Moses (Jethro) tell Moses to organize the twelve tribes of Israel? Did he do it? Was it a genuine improvement?

9. What kind of men did Moses choose as leaders or judges over the people? List three of the qualifications for a good judge. What were the judges to do with a case which was too hard for them?

10. After the people were taught the law, what did the Lord require the people to do? Why was this so important?

CHAPTER FOUR

THE FAMOUS STATUTES OF GOD'S LAW

We are now going to study the only system of law which was given by direct revelation from God. It is sometimes called the Law of the Covenant, but usually we refer to it as "God's Law." The Christian historian Eusebius says the gospel law which is centered in Christ was first revealed in the days of Adam.[1]

Apparently each of the ancient patriarchs had this law,[2] but it was recordėd for the first time in our scriptures when it was put in the Torah (the books of the law) by Moses.

The scripture it is referred to as the "perfect law." As the Psalmist says:

> "The law of the Lord is perfect, converting the soul: the testimony of the Lord is sure, making wise the simple. The statutes of the Lord are *right*, rejoicing the heart: the commandment of the Lord is pure, enlightening the eyes."[3]

Here we are told that the justice and goodness of God is reflected in his righteous commandments or God's law. They convert the soul. Furthermore, these commandments are so direct, so understandable, and so pure that anyone who proclaims and practices them is immediately perceived as being exceedingly wise even though by nature, he or she may be "simple" in both temperament and personal inclination.

We are assured that experience will teach us that the statutes of the Lord are truly inspired. They are right. They give us a sense of belonging to an orderly world which rejoices the soul. These commandments are also clear and pure so that they give us a sense of direction. They enlighten the eyes.

In summary, these passages suggest that one need not be schooled in the sophistry of legal lore to understand God's law. But one does need to know the law. As the Lord told Moses:

---

1. The Nicene and Post-Nicene Fathers of the Christian Church, Grand Rapids, Michigan: William B. Eerdmans Publishing Company, 1952, 1:87.
2. Ibid.
3. Psalms 19:7-8.

> "Teach them ordinances and laws … shew them the way wherein they must walk, and the work that they must do." [4]

Today, probably not even one person in many thousands has gone through God's law carefully and methodically as you are doing in this present course of study. It is reassuring to know that a study of this law is in accordance with a commandment of God.

The Importance of Voluntary Obedience

God's law is to be obeyed voluntarily rather than by compulsion. Therefore Moses read the entire law to his people and then we read:

> "Moses came and called for the elders of the people, and laid before their faces all these words which the Lord commanded him. And all the people answered together, and said, All that the Lord hath spoken we will do. And Moses returned the words of the people unto the Lord." [5]

When it says "Moses returned the words of the people unto the Lord," it simply means that they had heard the law, they understood the law, and they were willing to abide by it.

The People Were to Be Very Careful in Selecting Their Leaders

It will be recalled that the judges or "captains" were to be elected by each division of families. These families were divided by tens, fifties, hundreds, thousands, tens of thousands, etc., and Moses made it clear that he wanted the people to elect men of superb qualities.

Earlier, Moses was told by the Lord the type of men who should be elected judges. The Lord said:

> "Thou shalt provide out of all the people able men, such as fear God, men of truth, hating covetousness; and place such over them, to be rulers of thousands, and rulers of hundreds, rulers of fifties, and rulers of tens: And let them judge the people at all seasons: and it shall be, that every great matter they shall bring unto thee, but every small matter they shall judge: so shall it be easier for thyself, and they shall bear the burden with thee." [6]

---

4. Exodus 18:20.
5. Exodus 19:7-8.
6. Exodus 18:21-22.

The judges were to be "wise men, and understanding, and known among your tribes." [7]

They were to accept no gifts for "a gift doth blind the eyes of the wise, and pervert the words of the righteous." [8]

Judges were not to make decisions until after they had conducted a thorough investigation. They were to "inquire diligently" concerning the facts in each case.[9]

Judges were not to find a person guilty of a capital crime unless there were at least "two or three witnesses" who could prove his guilt. One witness was never sufficient. The prisoner would have to be released and left to the judgment of God if he were guilty.[10]

When a matter had been appealed to the chief judge or High Priest, and the matter had been settled, it was a capital offense to stir up an insurrection against the decision.[11] Honoring a judicial decree applied to the judges of original jurisdiction who might object to the ruling of the higher court. And of course it applied to the complainants or the accused who might be inclined to object if the final appeal went against either of them.

Before leaving this topic we should remind ourselves that each judge was more than merely a judicial officer. He was a "ruler" over those who had elected him.[12] This gave him a wide variety of administrative—and sometimes military—responsibilities. However, deciding disputes between contending parties comprised an important part of an elected leader's work and therefore they were often referred to as "judges." But in the New Testament, the presiding official over each congregation or ward was called a "bishop" which is the Greek word for leader or "overseer." [13]

Instructions to the Judges

It will also be recalled that Moses gave the following instructions to the first contingent of judges:

> "Hear the causes between your brethren, and judge righteously between every man and his brother, and the stranger that is with

7. Deuteronomy 1:13.
8. Deuteronomy 16:19.
9. Deuteronomy 19:18.
10. Numbers 35:30; Deuteronomy 17:6.
11. Deuteronomy 17:12.
12. Deuteronomy 1:13.
13. Hastings' Dictionary of the Bible, under "bishop."

> him. Ye shall not respect persons in judgment; but ye shall hear the small as well as the great; ye shall not be afraid of the face of man; for the judgment is God's: and the cause that is too hard for you, bring it unto me, and I will hear it." [14]

On another occasion, Moses said:

> "Ye shall do no unrighteousness in judgment: thou shalt not respect [discriminate against] the person of the poor, nor honor the person of the mighty: but in righteousness shalt thou judge thy neighbour." [15]

The Judges had the responsibility of selecting the appropriate penalty in each case. Many of the statutes of God's Law list the maximum penalty but this was not mandatory. The maximum penalty only applied in extreme cases. That is why the judges were expected to apply whatever punishment was applicable to the circumstances of each case.

The Philosophy of Penology under God's Law

1. The object of each judgment was not to avenge the wrong, but to restore the victim or offended party to his original position as far as humanly possible. This was done by compensation for injuries he had suffered, loss of time at his employment, the fear or other trauma to which the victim was subjected, or further damages appropriate to the circumstances. None of these fines or payments went to the court or the government. Everything went to the victim.

2. In addition to these damages, there could be punitive damages to discourage the offender from committing this offense in the future. Punitive damages also went to the victim.

3. In trespass cases, the offender had to pay for whatever damages occurred plus one-fifth to discourage any trespass in the future.

4. The death penalty was mandatory for any premeditated or deliberate and intentional slaying of another. This is indicated in the following verse:

> "Moreover ye shall take no satisfaction for the life of a murderer, which is guilty of death: but he shall be surely put to death." [16]

This meant that no "satisfaction"—i.e. compensatory damages, labor, or goods—could be worked out for a murderer. But in this same passage it

14. Deuteronomy 1:16-17.
15. Leviticus 19:15.
16. Numbers 35:31.

clearly implies that "satisfaction" could be worked out for lesser offenses. This gives special meaning to the concept so frequently quoted:

> "Eye for eye, tooth for tooth, hand for hand, foot for foot, Burning for burning, wound for wound, stripe for stripe." [17]

In all of these offenses which did not involve the deliberate taking of human life, the offender is allowed to negotiate with the offended person to provide "satisfaction" so that he does not have to lose his eye or be burned or wounded, etc.

5. Ezra describes four devices by which the judges could compel an offender to provide "satisfaction" to his victim.

> "And whosoever will not do the law of thy God, and the law of the king, let judgment be executed speedily upon him, whether it be unto death, or to banishment, or to confiscation of goods, or to imprisonment." [18]

However, in the case of murder, a person could not be convicted unless there were at least two witnesses. The Lord said:

> "Whoso killeth any person, the murderer shall be put to death by the mouth of witnesses: but one witness shall not testify against any person to cause him to die." [19]

If there were only one witness and the accused did not confess, the judges would be required to release the prisoner unless someone came forth as a "corroborating" witness. Today, the second witness is often a crime laboratory technician testifying concerning hairs, fibers, blood or fingerprints at the scene of the crime which testifies against the offender. Of course, sometimes the testimony and items of evidence will not convince the jury and the offender is turned loose. But as we mentioned earlier this does not mean that the offender is "getting away with his or her crime." It simply means that the offender's guilt and punishment is being left up to the judgment of God either in this life or the life to come.

6. When a fine was imposed on an individual and he refused to pay, the judge could have him delivered "to the tormentors [whip masters] till he should pay all that was due." [20]

---

17. Exodus 21:24-25.
18. Ezra 7:26.
19. Numbers 25:30.
20. Matthew 18:34.

However, the stripes could not be excessive, and the judge had to witness the punishment to make certain there was no abuse. The scripture states:

> "And it shall be, if the wicked man be worthy to be beaten, that the judge shall cause him to lie down, and to be beaten before his face, according to his fault, by a certain number. Forty stripes he may give him, and not exceed: lest, if he should exceed, and beat him above these with many stripes, then thy brother should seem vile unto thee."[21]

7. Under number 5 it will be noticed that Ezra refers to banishment. This was the penalty when a person tried to destroy the culture of God's law and behaved like a heathen. When the offender refused to respond to love and persuasion, the judge could sentence him to live with the heathens and make the threat of death the penalty if he ever tried to return and continue corrupting God's people. A number of offenses list "death" as the penalty, but except for murder this is referring to banishment and the threat of death if the offender ever tries to return.

The Major Offenses under God's Law

We have endeavored to make it easy to find any provision of the law by listing each item alphabetically according to the type of offense. We have also tried to make each provision more readily understood in a modern context by adding a brief commentary where needed. A listing of these statutes begins on page 561, and include:

Abortion
Adultery
Animals: Responsibility of owner
Animals: Purebred Strains to be maintained
Appeals
Arrest: Authority for
Arson or Fire-setting
Assassination
Assault
Asylum
Banishment
Battery
Bestiality
Blasphemy
Bond Servant
Borrowing
Breach of Trust
Bribery
Burglary
Business Ethics
Castraton
Children: Their Rights and Responsibilities
Child Abuse
Children: Their Age of Accountability
Contracts

21. Deuteronomy 25:2-3.

Cults: Religious and Fraternal
Debts
Divorce
Drunkenness
Emasculation
Embezzlement by a Trustee
Elderly People Entitled to Respect
Employer-Employee Relations
Enforcement of the Law
Exile
Eye for an Eye
Familiar Spirits
Father
Fire Hazard
First Fruits
Fornication
Fraud
Gossiping
Hate
Handicapped Should Be Treated with Compassion and Kindness
Homosexuality
Human Sacrifices
Idolatry
Incest
Jubilee
Judges
Juvenile Delinquency
Kidnaping
Kings—Their Calling and Responsibility
Land
Law of the Covenant
Lending
Levites
Lying
Mayhem
Military Service
Military Attack—Three Modes
Mobocracy
Mother
Murders and Accidental Homicides
Neighbors—Duty Towards
Oaths
Parents
Penalties
Phylacteries
Poll Tax
The Poor
Private Property
Prophets—True or False?
Prostitution
Public Nuisances
Punishments
Ransom—An Offender May Ransom His Life
Rape
Sabbath Day
Servitude
Seventy Elders—A Permanent Senate
Sodomy
Spiritualism
Stealing
Strangers, Treatment of
Tattooing
Theft
Tithes
Transvestites
Trees—In Wartime Spare the Trees
Trespassing
Usury
Weights and Measures
Whipping
Widows and Orphans
Witchcraft
The Law of Witnesses

Conclusion

As we can see after our review of what John Adams called God's "divine science" of law and good government, we cannot help but consider once again the writings of the Psalmist when he said:

"The law of the Lord is *perfect*, converting the soul: the testimony of the Lord is *sure*, making wise the simple. The statutes of the Lord are *right*, rejoicing the heart: the commandment of the Lord is *pure*, enlightening the eyes.

"The fear of the Lord is clean, enduring for ever: the judgments of the Lord are true and righteous altogether. More to be desired are they than gold, yea, than much fine gold: sweeter also than honey and the honeycomb. Moreover by them is thy servant warned: and in keeping of them there is great reward." [22]

---

22. Psalms 19:7-11.

CHAPTER FIVE

What the Founders Learned from a Study of God's Law

The political science of ancient Israel is scattered through four sacred books written by Moses—Exodus, Leviticus, Numbers, and Deuteronomy.

The Founders had carefully scrutinized the foremost scholars of their day such as John Locke, William Blackstone and Baron Charles de Montesquieu—but not Alexis de Tocqueville, who would come later.

They had also studied the political theories of the Persians, Babylonians, Greeks and Romans. They had studied the history of England and the major countries in Europe.

In other words, their minds were ripe for the nuggets of God's political science as they carefully read the writings of Moses. As we shall see later, this penetrating insight led them to reject the most elementary aspects of British political science on which they had been tutored from early youth. Instead, they gave top priority to the teachings of Moses. It all began with the national structure of Israel.

When New Hampshire was contemplating the ratification of the Constitution—and thereby becoming the ninth state that would put the Constitution into operation—Samuel Langdon addressed the legislators June 5, 1788, and carefully traced the close comparison between the U.S. Constitution and the inspired government of ancient Israel.[1]

In the final analysis he said it was God's will that the people do their public business through freely elected representatives, the very essence of republican principles. Then he turned to the Bible to make his case.

The National Assembly

The great national assembly of Israel was convened for major decisions, such as the acceptance of the original Mosaic Code:

> "And Moses came and called for the elders [representatives] of the people, and laid before their faces all these words which the Lord commanded him.

1. Quoted in its entirety by Cherry in God's New Israel, op. cit., pp. 103-107.

> "And all the people [through their representatives] answered together, and said, All that the Lord hath spoken we will do. And Moses returned the words of the people unto the Lord."[2]

Later, when Israel wanted a king, the constitution of Israel still required that Saul be accepted by the National Assembly.[3]

After the death of Saul, it says:

> "Then all Israel [meaning all the elders or representatives of all the tribes] gathered themselves to David.... Therefore came all the elders of Israel to the king to Hebron; and David made a covenant with them in Hebron before the Lord; and they anointed David king over Israel, according to the word of the Lord by Samuel."[4]

The same thing happened when Solomon was made king.[5]

However, when Solomon died, and his son, Rehoboam, was offered to the people, ten of the tribes absolutely rejected him and set up a king of their own.[6]

It is interesting that the General Assembly of Israel did not have to hold legislative sessions. This was because they had received a complete code of laws adequate for all their needs. In fact, just a few weeks before the end of his earthly life, Moses told the people:

> "Ye shall not add unto the word which I command you, neither shall ye diminish ought from it, that ye may keep the commandments of the Lord your God which I command you."[7]

Why the Founders Felt Compelled to Adopt the Separation of Powers

The Mosaic code was made for a unitary republic of one nationality and one faith.

When the American Founders discussed how it might be possible to apply these concepts to a pluralistic society of many nationalities and many faiths, they finally accepted the suggestion of John Adams. This doctrine was called "the separation of powers."

2. Exodus 19:7-8.
3. 1 Samuel 10:24.
4. 1 Chronicles 11:1, 3.
5. 1 Chronicles 29:22.
6. 1 Kings 12:16-19.
7. Deuteronomy 4:2.

They would protect the rights of the people by separating the powers of government and thereby playing each of the three branches of government against the other so there would never be a complete concentration of power or a dictatorship. One branch would pass all the laws, another branch would administer all the laws, and the judiciary, or third branch would make sure the Constitution was accurately interpreted and applied by both of the other departments.

At first, the proposal of John Adams that they separate the government into three branches was very unpopular, but after extensive discussion, it was adopted. He suggested a careful structuring of the Constitution so that the legislature would have authority to make laws but only in specific, enumerated areas. He further suggested that contravening powers be delegated to the executive and the judiciary to check the legislature if it went beyond its parameters.[8]

The Senate

The Senate—as set up under God's law—was a body of seventy "wise men," whom God instructed Moses to choose from among the "Elders of Israel."[9] (see *Seventy Elders* in *The Statutes–A List of God's Laws*, page 619-620)

About a year earlier the Lord had given a special spiritual testimony to "seventy elders" who had been chosen from among the various tribes. The Lord allowed them to come up part way into Mount Sinai and there they were allowed to see the Lord "from a distance."[10]

So, a year later the Lord told Moses to select seventy of the elders of Israel and bring them to the Tabernacle. We are not sure these were the same seventy but they might have been. In any event, when Moses brought them to the Tabernacle they received a powerful blessing. The scripture says:

> "And the Lord came down in a cloud, and spake unto him, and took of the spirit that was upon him [Moses] and gave it unto the seventy elders: and it came to pass, that, when the spirit rested upon them, they prophesied."[11]

The great council of seventy set up by Moses is believed by authorities to be the origin of the body which became known in later centuries

8. Koch, The American Enlightenment, op. cit., pp. 163-164.
9. Numbers 11:16.
10. Exodus 24:9-11.
11. Numbers 11:25.

as the Sanhedrin. However, there is no distinct historical paper trail to prove it. However, it seems clear that as Israel apostatized and lost the privilege of having direct revelation through a prophet, the Sanhedrin took over the three branches of Israel's domestic government—executive, legislative and judicial.

Until the destruction of Jerusalem in 70 A.D., the Sanhedrin met in a hall called Gazith, or the Chamber of Hewn Stone situated on the southern edge of the inner court of the temple. After the destruction of Jerusalem it was moved to Tiberias on the south-western shore of the Sea of Galilee. It met there until it became extinct in 425 A.D. It has never met since.[12]

The Founders Copy Many Aspects of the Mosaic Senate

The powers of the United States Senate set forth in the Constitution are very interesting.

1. It must approve all legislation passed by the House or it cannot become law.[13]

2. It must approve all presidential nominations to important positions in both the Executive and Judicial branches of the government.[14]

3. No treaty shall become law until it has been approved by two-thirds of the Senate.[15]

4. In all cases of impeachment, the Senate sits as the supreme tribunal to make the final decision. If the President is being impeached, the Chief Justice of the Supreme Court presides.[16]

The Executive

Under the Law of the Covenant (see *Law of the Covenant* in *The Statutes–A List of God's Laws*, pages 597-598), the executive had the responsibility to administer the law, collect the taxes, control expenditures, set up the financial and monetary system, provide for the national defense, and insure domestic tranquility.

12. Peloubet's Bible Dictionary, under "Sanhedrin."
13. Article I, Section 1.
14. Article II, Section 2, clause 2.
15. Ibid.
16. Article I, Section 3, clause 6.

This office fell upon Moses and Joshua while they were in charge, but Moses prophesied that eventually Israel would demand a king to preside over them. He said when this happened the king should realize that he would not be like the kings of other nations. Under the Law of the Covenant the executive, whether called a chief judge or a king, he was to be no more than "first among equals," and he was to abhor the behavior of pagan kings. The Lord said that if they were determined to have a king, here were the basic requirements:

First of all, he must be chosen "from among thy brethren ... thou mayest not set a stranger over thee, which is not thy brother." [17]

Second, he was not to "multiply horses" which pagan kings accumulated for their private cavalry and royal chariots.[18]

Third, the king was not to "multiply wives" which pagan kings did to cement their relations with surrounding tribes and territories. This was a warning which Solomon did not heed, and the whole nation of Israel suffered from the idolatrous corruption which some of his wives from idolatrous tribes brought into the nation.[19]

Fourth, he was to have his own private copy of the law:

> "And it shall be with him, and he shall read therein all the days of his life: that he may learn to fear the Lord his God, to keep all the words of this law and these statutes, to do them." [20]

Fifth, he must guard against pride and any sense of superiority:

> "That his heart be not lifted above his brethren, and that he turn not aside from the commandment, to the right hand, or to the left: to the end that he may prolong his days in his kingdom, he, and his children, in the midst of Israel." [21]

Having considered the efficient administration of the House, the Senate and the Executive, we must next turn to the organizing of the people themselves, and then we can talk about the administration of justice.

---

17. Deuteronomy 17:15.
18. Deuteronomy 17:16.
19. Deuteronomy 17:17.
20. Deuteronomy 17:18-19.
21. Deuteronomy 17:20.

Organizing the People into Small, Manageable Groups

If the foundation of good government is its law—a simple, carefully structured system of well-understood rules of conduct—then the efficiency of government will depend upon a very solid system of political structure.

We recall that it was Jethro, the priest of Midian, who first instructed Moses on the fundamentals of a godly political structure. He said to begin by setting up a hierarchy of small, manageable groups where everyone had a voice and vote. Moses later describes how he followed Jethro's instructions and said to the people:

> "Take you wise men, and understanding, and known among your tribes, and I will make them rulers over you. And you answered me, and said, The thing which thou hast spoken is good for us to do. So I took the chief of your tribes, wise men, and known, and made them heads over you, captains over thousands, and captains over hundreds, and captains over fifties and captains over tens, and officers among your tribes." [22]

Notice that when Moses took a census of the people he had approximately 600,000 men over age 20 who would be, in most instances, heads of families.[23]

It will be readily apparent that if there were over 600,000—with practically all of them heads of families—the total population would undoubtedly number at least 3,000,000—counting wives, children, and elderly people not included in the military rolls.

We also note that Moses said the people would "take" their captains from their various groups and bring them to him for approval. In other words, each group of ten families would elect a leader whose name would be given to Moses for approval. Then five of these groups of ten would unite to make fifty families.

A captain of fifty would be elected and his name submitted to Moses. In the same manner, two groups of fifty would unite to make a hundred families and they would elect a leader to represent them as a captain of a hundred.

Finally, ten groups of a hundred would unite together and elect a captain of a thousand.

---

22. Deuteronomy 1:13-15.
23. Numbers 1:2, 24, 46.

In this way the armies could be organized and the civil government set up so as to accommodate a huge population. There would not only be captains of ten, fifty, a hundred, or a thousand families, but it would extend upwards to captains of ten thousand families, fifty thousand families, or a hundred thousand families.

So what we have presented here is a hierarchy of manageable units where every family head had a voice and a vote. He not only had a direct vote in selecting the leader of his own unit of ten families, but he had a vote in selecting each of the leaders on the higher levels.

An Abundance of Competent Leaders

To gain some idea of the tremendous number of leaders which this system produces, consider the following:

Six-hundred thousand families divided into groups of ten would produce 60,000 local leaders, each presiding over ten families.

These, in turn, would be combined into groups of fifty families and they would elect 12,000 leaders on their level.

Then these would be combined into groups of a hundred families and they would elect 6,000 leaders on that level.

Finally, these would be combined into groups of a thousand families and they would elect 600 leaders on the top level.

Altogether, this provided Moses with 78,600 leaders to help bear the burden of governing approximately 3,000,000 people.

Americans Seek to Organize Themselves on the Same Basis

The American Founders recognized the merit of this vertical hierarchy of power. On each level the people were governed by their own elected representatives and it allowed most problems to be solved on the level where they originated. It also allowed the government to be structured from the bottom up in direct contrast to a monarchy or centralized government which is always structured from the top down.

In a very real sense this gave the Israelites a government of the people, for the people, and by the people.

The Genius of Strong Local Self-Government

New England was the most successful area in adopting this pattern of strong local self-government. Thomas Jefferson commented:

> "These wards [of around 100 families], called townships in New England, are the vital principle of their governments, and have proved themselves the wisest invention ever devised by the wit of man for the perfect exercise of self government, and for its preservation."[24]

Jefferson also pointed out that the early Anglo-Saxons brought this Israelite system of government into England:

> "In ancient England, local self-government is found in connection with the political territorial division of tythings, hundreds, burghs, counties, and shires, in which the body of inhabitants had a voice in managing their own affairs. Hence it was the germinal idea of the Anglo-Saxon polity."[25]

Dividing the Undeveloped Land into Plots Six Miles Square

To encourage strong local self-government along these same lines, men like Thomas Jefferson and John Adams induced the Congress—in 1785—to have a federal survey of all the undeveloped land and plot the land into townships six miles square. The Anglo-Saxons in England had determined that it required about six miles square to accommodate 100 families with their needs for farms, pastures and a place of settlement.

Today, anyone flying over the prairie states of the midwest or west can see the checkerboard pattern of this survey which anticipated the land being settled by small manageable units. They had taken a page from the writings of Moses which demonstrated that strong local self-government is the cornerstone of freedom.

Now we can talk about the administration of justice under God's law.

---

24. Thomas Jefferson, Letters, New York: The Library of America, 1984, 1399:2.
25. Richard Frothingham, The Rise of the Republic of the United States, Boston: Little, Brown and Company, 1873, p. 14.

The Judiciary under the Law of the Covenant

The captains of tens, fifties, hundreds and thousands were not only military leaders and administrators of the law, but they were required to settle disputes and keep peace among the people. For these assignments the people were commanded to select the most mature and honest people they could find in each of their groups. Here is the way Jethro described the judicial responsibilities of the elected leaders.

> "Moreover thou shalt provide out of all the people able men, such as fear God, men of truth, hating covetousness; and place such over them, to be rulers of thousands, and rulers of hundreds, rulers of fifties, and rulers of tens:
>
> "And let them judge the people at all seasons: and it shall be, that every great matter they shall bring unto thee [Moses], but every small matter they shall judge: so shall it be easier to thyself, and they shall bear the burden with thee."[26]

Moses followed Jethro's instructions implicitly. He then addressed the elected captains who would have to judge conflicts within their various groups, and said:

> "Hear the causes between your brethren, and judge righteously between every man and his brother, and the stranger that is with him.
>
> "Ye shall not respect [favor] persons in judgment, but ye shall hear the small as well as the great; ye shall not be afraid of the face of man; for the judgment is God's: and the cause that is too hard for you, bring it unto me, and I will hear it."[27]

As the years went by, Moses felt compelled to give additional instructions to the elected leaders when they were serving as judges. He said:

> "Thou shalt not wrest [force] judgment; thou shalt not respect [favor] persons, neither accept a gift: for a gift doth blind the eyes of the wise, and pervert the words of righteousness."[28]

These leaders were also instructed to make a thorough investigation of the facts before reaching a decision and pronouncing judgment. They were

26. Exodus 18:21-22.
27. Deuteronomy 1:16-17.
28. Deuteronomy 16:19.

to be particularly alert to any who might give perjured testimony as false witnesses. He said:

> "And the judges shall make diligent inquisition: and, behold, if the witness be a false witness, and hath testified falsely against his brother, then shall ye do unto him, as he had thought to have done unto his brother; so shalt thou put evil away from you." [29]

Penalties for Various Offenses

God gave Israel a unique system of penalties for those who violated the law. First of all, it required the offender to repair the damage he had done, which is true justice. Then a rather severe penalty was added to discourage the culprit from doing it again.

How Did This System Work?

Let us take, for example, the law which said "An eye for an eye, and tooth for tooth." [30] (see *Eye for an Eye* in *The Statutes—A List of God's Laws,* page 583-584) Modern students visualize a wretched prisoner having his eye destroyed with a hot iron or his tooth extracted by a pair of pincers. But this is not what happened.

The purpose of God's law was not revenge, but reparation. Therefore, if an assailant poked out the eye of his victim, the judges required the offender to provide full "satisfaction" to his victim or have his own eye put out. In other words, the threat of losing his own eye was the reason why the offender would desperately extend himself to make it right with his victim.

In nearly all cases the "satisfaction" was in the form of money payments.[31]

If the offender did not have the money, he could sell his personal services[32] for any period of time up to six years.[33]

Today, for a similar offense, a man may be sentenced to many years in prison where his time is virtually wasted and where he is completely separated from his family and the community. Under the Law of the Covenant, the offender could continue his normal life while working out the necessary "satisfaction" for the person he had injured. Of course, if he were a dangerous

29. Deuteronomy 19:18-19.
30. Leviticus 24:20.
31. See, for example, Exodus 21:22, 30.
32. Exodus 22:3.
33. Exodus 21:2.

criminal and could not be trusted by the community, God's law provided a variety of remedies which we will consider in a moment.

But for nearly all offenses against an individual or his property, the offender was allowed to provide "satisfaction" to the victim. The exception was first degree murder. The Lord said:

> "Ye shall take no satisfaction for the life of a murderer ... he shall surely be put to death." [34]

As we mention in our discussion on penalties (see *Penalties* in THE STATUTES—*A* LIST OF GOD'S LAWS, page 609-612), in addition to making a reparation equal to the extent of the damages or losses suffered by the victim, Moses was instructed to compel the wrongdoer to give the victim an additional value in money or property to compensate for the inconvenience, pain or mental suffering which the victim had suffered. Requiring this "additional" penalty of punitive damages was also designed to deter the offender from similar acts in the future.

For example, if a person stole a sheep or a goat, he had to return two for each one stolen.[35] However, if he stole the sheep to sell on the commercial market, then he had to return four sheep for every one stolen.[36] Notice that fines or damages always went to the victim, not the court, the community, or the nation. Notice also that the punitive damages were sufficiently severe to send forth the message, "Among God's people, crime does not pay!"

Thomas Jefferson was so impressed by this method of achieving true justice, that he rewrote the entire criminal code of Virginia, and hoped the other states would then have the wisdom to follow Virginia's example. For all offenses against an individual or his property, Jefferson provided a stipulation that the offender had to compensate the victim and pay heavy punitive damages besides.

Take, for example, Jefferson's recommended penalty for arson. The offender had to pay for the damages threefold.[37] If a person should steal a "sea vessel or goods laden on board thereof, or plunder or pilfer any wreck, he shall be condemned to hard labor five years in the public works, and shall make good the loss of the sufferers threefold." [38] In the case of robbery the

34. Numbers 35:31.
35. Exodus 22:4.
36. Exodus 22:1.
37. Julian P. Boyd, ed., The Papers of Thomas Jefferson, Princeton, N.J.: Princeton University Press, 1950, 1:499.
38. Ibid.

offender "shall be condemned to hard labor four years in the public works, and shall make double reparation to the victim.[39] The same penalty was applied to burglaries committed at night, but if it occurred in the daytime, the penalty was three years of hard labor in the public works and equal reparation to the victim.[40]

It is noteworthy that Jefferson, who was trained in English Common Law, wanted to completely restructure the penalty formula of the Common Law system and adopt the procedures prescribed by God's law which gave the fines and damages to the victim, instead of the court or the crown.

Unfortunately, Jefferson's revised code for Virginia was not accepted by that state or any other state at that time. It was not until recent years that some of the states have allowed their judges to sentence a convicted criminal to imprisonment "without parole" unless the criminal promises to secure employment and compensate the victim of his crime. Of course, this is only done where the offender is not otherwise considered a danger to society.

What about the Offenses Carrying the Death Penalty?

The Mosaic code has seemed particularly harsh to modern minds because it imposes the death sentence for what appear to be minor offenses. Take, for example, violating the sabbath day:

> "Ye shall keep the sabbath, therefore; for it is holy unto you; and every one that defileth it shall surely be put to death … that soul shall be cut off from among his people."[41]

Here we have a problem, for we find only one instance where a person was executed for violating the sabbath.[42] In certain other cases where the penalty could be "death" we find no instances of it ever being carried out. The only exception was the case of first degree murder. This always required the death penalty as we have already noted.

Why would the penalty for a number of offenses be "death," yet in actual practice it was scarcely ever carried out?

As we have mentioned earlier, it turns out that the death penalty was attached primarily to those offenses that would be destructive to the Zion

39. Ibid.
40. Ibid., 1:500.
41. Exodus 31:14.
42. Numbers 15:32-36.

society or higher order of culture that had been promised the Israelites. Anyone who was subverting this culture was jeopardizing God's promise to make Israel the greatest nation on earth. For example, the Lord had said:

> "Now therefore, if ye will obey my voice indeed, and keep my covenant, then ye shall be a peculiar treasure *unto me above all people*: for all the earth is mine: and ye shall be unto me a kingdom of priests, and an holy nation." [43]

However, even with this marvelous promise in mind, why should a little sabbath-breaking merit the death penalty? Or conversely, precisely just what did it mean to keep the sabbath day holy?

As we point out in our discussion about the Sabbath (see *The Sabbath* in THE STATUTES—A LIST OF GOD'S LAWS, page 618), this was the day set aside for the people to meet together, renew their covenants, study the law, attend worship services, and minister to the needs of those who needed spiritual or temporal support.

Now supposing some renegade decides that the sabbath is not so much a holy day for worship, study, and social services, but a holiday for revelry and carousing around. Others might begin to follow his example until it became popular and thereby constitute a threat to their whole culture and the loss of God's great promise to them.

Rabbinical writings indicate that the threat of death was sufficient to induce the renegade to either change his ways or leave the society of the Israelites forever. In other words, if he wished to live like the pagans, he was free to do so, but not among the Israelites who were trying to live a higher law. When a person did not respond to counseling and urging, the judges would simply set a date, and, if the offender had not changed his ways he remained in the community at the risk of his life.

Notice that the scripture says he "shall be cut off from among his people." [44] However, it will be observed that he is to be cut off from his people, not all people. In other words, we are talking about banishment, not execution.

So the penalty of death which is associated with many of the more serious cultural violations, can be better understood when we realize that this was simply the means of forcing into exile those who were defiant and would not mend their ways. It was an automatic cleansing device for their society.

43. Exodus 19:5-6.
44. Exodus 31:14.

God had used this same device during an earlier age—the era of the patriarchs. Abraham was told that any of his people who refused to enter into God's higher law and be circumcised as a token of their commitment to obey its statutes, "shall be cut off from his people."[45] Once again, it is his people, not all people.

Of course, this method of compulsory exile under threat of death would only work in a unitary society similar to the Israelites or the Anglo-Saxons. It would not work in a pluralistic society like the United States. Therefore, the Founders did not adopt this remedial procedure of compulsory exile even though it was being used by some of the European countries. Instead, the Founders used traditional punishments appropriate to the severity of the crime.

At the end of this study we will discuss a future time when Jefferson's dream will come true and the whole nation will be organized into "wards" or townships of around a hundred families. At that time the remedy of threatened banishment will be very practical, and therefore of great remedial value when circumstances warrant it.

What about the Penalty of Whipping?

There was one category of offenses for which no "satisfaction" could be given since the misconduct would be against the whole community rather than any particular individual. Examples would include such offenses as public drunkenness, prostitution, breach of the peace, instigating a riot, and so forth. Since there was no "satisfaction" due any particular individual, the remedy was whipping (see *Penalties* in The Statutes–A List of God's Laws, page 609-612). The Mosaic code stated:

> "And it shall be, if the wicked man be worthy to be beaten that the judge shall cause him to lie down, and to be beaten before his [the judges] face, according to his fault, by a certain number. Forty stripes he may give him, and not exceed: lest, if he should exceed and beat him above these [the specified number] with many stripes, then thy brother should seem vile unto thee."[46]

Notice that in order to safeguard a prisoner against possible abuse by his guards, and, at the same time, to prevent the assigned number of stripes being either exceeded or diminished, the judge who gave the sentence was required to personally witness the whipping. The number of stripes depended upon the seriousness of the offense, but the absolute maximum was forty. To

45. Genesis 17:14.
46. Deuteronomy 25:2.

make certain this limit was not exceeded, it became customary to make the maximum number of stripes thirty-nine.

After the prisoner was whipped he was released. Under the Mosaic code the authorities could not throw an offender down into some dark dungeon to starve or die, nor could they mutilate him, torture him, or subject him to any of the brutal and inhuman cruelties which were customary until 1789 when the United States became the first country to outlaw "cruel and unusual punishment."

Today, "whipping" has also been eliminated because too many officials turned the whipping into a brutal flogging. When Jesus used a whip to cleanse the temple in Jerusalem, the whip was made "with small cords."[47] These cords or thongs were usually of rope or leather and were attached to a wooden handle. The thongs were designed to sting and welt the skin, but not to lacerate it.

When herdsmen and caravan drivers found this type of whip to be ineffective in dealing with tough-skinned animals such as oxen, donkeys, and camels, they tied pieces of bone or metal on the thongs which would cut deeply into the flesh. This type of whip became known as the infamous "cat o' nine tails." When this type of whip was used on human beings it literally cut them to pieces, and gave the whole idea of whipping a repulsive and uncivilized reputation.

However, in Canada, until recent years, any person who was found guilty of a misdemeanor, was allowed the option of receiving a certain number of stripes with a flat strap rather than lose his job and spend six months in jail.[48]

It is interesting that a careful study shows that those who elected to feel the sting of a flat strap rather than go to jail, gained greater therapeutic value from their experience than those who chose to be incarcerated. Practically none of those who elected to take the whipping ever again became involved in criminal activity.[49]

Of course, whipping is almost universally outlawed today, even in Canada. Delaware was the last state to eliminate this practice in the United States. In all of the states whipping has been replaced by fines or mandatory jail sentences. Nevertheless, the Canadian experience with offenders who elected to take the flat strap, demonstrates the wisdom of God in recommending rea-

47. John 2:15.
48. Skousen, The Third Thousand Years, op. cit., p. 360.
49. Ibid.

sonable and humane whipping for persons who had committed an offense for which no satisfaction could be given. The whipping was not nearly as cruel as spending long years in the depressing depravity which characterizes so many of our prisons today.

The Administration of Good Government Requires That the People Know the Law

At this point it can be readily seen why it is important for the smooth operation of the whole system to have the people thoroughly familiar with the requirements of the law.

It is the primary responsibility of parents and leaders to teach the people the laws under which they are to be governed and by which they will be judged if they commit any offense.

It is equally important for the precepts of law to be kept simple, easy to understand, and easy to memorize.

The Founding Fathers wanted this to be the case with American law. They knew the Anglo-Saxons had kept their law so basic and simple that everyone was able to recite the law without referring to any written manuscript.[50] James Madison—often called the father of the Constitution—said:

> "It will be of little avail to the people that the laws are made by men of their own choice if the laws be so voluminous that they cannot be read, or so incoherent that they cannot be understood; if they be repealed or revised before they are promulgated, or undergo such incessant changes that no man, who knows what the law is today, can guess what it will be tomorrow. Law is defined to be a rule of action; but how can that be a rule, which is little known and less fixed?"[51]

Notice that Madison defines law as a "rule of action." What about laws that are so stringent and oppressive that action is inhibited? Obviously, if the action is destructive of the rights of others, it should be prohibited, but if the law is simply designed to control the voluntary activities of the people, it has defeated the entire purpose of the law. John Locke emphasized this point when he said:

> "The end of law is *not* to abolish or restrain, but to preserve and enlarge freedom. For in all the states of created beings, capable of

50. Sharon Turner, The History of the Anglo Saxons, London: Longman Reese, et al., 1936, 2:19.

51. James Madison, Federalist Papers, New York: New American Library, Mentor's Book edition, Number 62, p. 381.

laws, where there is no law there is no freedom. For liberty is to be free from restraint and violence from others, which cannot be where there is no law."[52]

What the Founders Hoped to Adopt from Israel's Law

So the Founders studied the Law of the Covenant with the belief that it contained the ingredients for a free, prosperous, peaceful and happy society. Even though it required certain restructuring to accommodate the needs of a pluralistic society, they nevertheless recognized in it the promise of an abundant life (see *Law of the Covenant* in *The Statutes–A List of God's Laws*, page 597-598).

Based on the writings of the Founders, here is a summary of the political, economic, and social structure they hoped the United States could become:

1. A covenant society following somewhat the pattern of the Mayflower Compact signed by 41 men on November 11, 1620.

2. "A Constitution"—as John Adams said—"made only for a moral and religious people." Then he added, "It is wholly inadequate to the government of any other."[53]

3. A nation of virtuous citizens who are prudent, responsible, and public spirited.

4. A cadre of virtuous leaders with a vibrant sense of public service and a high resolve to fulfill the aspirations of the Founders.

5. A population divided into small, manageable units where every adult has a voice and a vote.

6. A system of strong, local self-government, with only limited and necessary powers assigned to the state and national governments.

7. A structure of society built on close-knit family unity.

8. A strong moral and religious people who recognize the divine destiny of the United States and the clear evidence of divine intervention in the affairs of this nation from its beginning.

9. A universal moral and religious ethic in business, government and society, but a clear separation of church and state.

---

52. John Locke, Second Essay on Civil Government, Great Books of the Western World, Chicago: Britannica Encyclopedia, 35:37, par. 57.

53. John R. Howe, The Changing Political Thought of John Adams, Princeton, N.J.: Princeton University Press, 1966, p. 189.

10. A system of justice based on reparation to the victim where possible, and appropriate punishment where necessary.

11. A corps of honest, firm and fair-minded judges who will faithfully guard the Constitution against subversion or unlawful usurpation of power by the various departments of government.

12. The protection of life and property with a law enforcement policy which makes certain that crime does not pay.

13. A well-informed citizenry with comprehensive education in basic knowledge and practical skills.

14. A dynamic competitive economy based on a strong and efficient work ethic and high production goals.

15. A sound monetary system based on gold and silver and no credit or currency except that which is backed 100% by tangible assets and precious metal.

16. A low tax structure designed to encourage home ownership and the launching of new business enterprises.

17. No national debt except that which can be readily paid off by each generation.

18. A strong emphasis on private social security with a home free and clear and a community life that can insure its inhabitants against disability, unemployment, retirement, and provide comprehensive health service.

19. Compassionate concern for the poor, the weak, and the handicapped.

20. Encouragement of private loans to the poor without interest to help them become independent and self-sufficient.

How Samuel Langdon Closed His Sermon on June 5, 1788

Here is a condensation of the final plea of Samuel Langdon to the governor and state legislature of New Hampshire just before they voted on the ratification of the Constitution. This was a very critical vote since New Hampshire was the ninth state to vote and if she ratified, it would put the Constitution into full force and effect. The following is taken from *God's New Israel* by Conrad Cherry, pp. 100-105.

> "I will now lift my voice and cry aloud to the people.... From year to year be careful in the choice of your representatives and all the higher powers of government.

"Fix your eyes upon men of good understanding and known honesty; men of knowledge improved by experience; men who fear God and hate covetousness; who love truth and righteousness and sincerely wish the public welfare.

"Beware of such as are cunning rather than wise; who prefer their own interest to every thing; whose judgment is partial or fickle; and whom you would not willingly trust with your own private interests.

"When meetings are called for the choice of your rulers, do not carelessly neglect them or give your vote with indifference ... but act with serious deliberation and judgment.

"Let no men openly irreligious and immoral become your legislators. If the legislative body are corrupt, you will soon have bad men for Counsellors, corrupt judges, unqualified justices, and officers in every department who will dishonor their stations.

"Let a superior character point out the man who is to be your head. In this choice ... be always on your guard against parties and unworthy men. Let distinguished merit always determine your vote.

"Never give countenance to turbulent men who wish to distinguish themselves and rise to power by forming combinations and exciting insurrections against government. For this can never be the right way to redress real grievances.

"I call upon you to support schools in all your towns. It is a debt you owe to your children.

"I call upon you to preserve the knowledge of God in the land and attend to the revelation written to us from heaven. If you neglect or renounce that religion taught and commanded in the holy scriptures, think no more of freedom, peace, and happiness.

"Avoid all the vices and corruption of the world; the judgments of heaven will pursue you. There will be a resurrection of the dead, both of the just and the unjust, and a day of solemn judgment when all mankind must give an account of their conduct in this world.

> "Will you permit me now to pray in behalf of the people, that all the departments of government may be constantly filled with the wisest and best [people]."

Topics for Reflection and Discussion

1. List the specific ways in which the Constitution of the United States reflects the structure of ancient Israel.

2. Under the system of government set up by Moses, it was said that everyone "had a voice and a vote." How was that possible?

3. How did the organization set up by Moses produce such an abundance of leaders?

4. What is a "republican" form of government? Was ancient Israel a republic?

5. What does it mean to have the top government officials consider themselves merely "first among equals?"

6. List three ways in which the Lord says the kings of Israel should be different than the kings of the pagan nations.

7. How did the Lord's "law of reparation" work?

8. Under what circumstances was whipping considered more effective than the mode of punishment used today? What did Canada discover concerning the criminals who had been whipped?

9. What was the purpose of having some culture-destroying offenses carry the death penalty? What was the real intent?

10. Describe five of the qualities of life the Founders hoped to achieve for America under the law of the Covenant.

CHAPTER SIX

Lessons Learned by the Founders from the Old Testament

It now becomes our task to go back and trace the highlights of Old Testament history to which the Founders so often referred.

In these pages are recorded many of the bitter lessons the Founders hoped the American people would not have to learn the hard way. It is said that those who do not learn the lessons of history are bound to repeat them.

The reason the Bible is the most popular resource for the study of ancient history, is the fact that the information contained therein is based on the knowledge of those who were living at the time. All other resources covering the ancient origins of the human family are based on tradition or myths.

As we indicated earlier, even the revelatory information provided in the Bible is based on the experience of individuals who were allowed the scientific or historic experience of enjoying a direct communication from the Creator or his emissaries. It is interesting that the same revelatory information was repeated by God's selected spokesmen from dispensation to dispensation, even down to and including the ministry of Jesus Christ.

We begin with some of the lessons learned clear back in the days of Moses.

It will be recalled that in the beginning Moses had hoped to make a great people out of the Israelites after he had rescued them from slavery in Egypt. He knew that God wanted them to become a great people. The Lord had even given them the formula which would make them the richest, most populous, and most powerful nation on earth. Moses said:

> "The Lord thy God hath chosen thee to be a special people unto himself, above all people that are upon the face of the earth."[1]

In all human history, no generation of human beings ever experienced such an outpouring of God's miraculous power as that which the Israelites received during a period of forty years. They even heard God speaking to

---

1. Deuteronomy 7:6.

Moses as the Lord commenced to give his prophet the commandments which all of the Israelites accepted and promised to obey.[2]

Seventy-three of them actually had the sublime experience of beholding the glorious personage of God just as Moses had done.[3]

What more could Moses have done as their leader, or what more could God have done as their Divine Benefactor? How could these three million people be so immersed in God's overflowing beneficence and still fail in their mission? But they did.

They had the formula, they had the leadership, but in nearly every crisis during a period of forty years, they faltered or completely collapsed. All of this demonstrates the shocking and tragic fact the neither mountains of miracles nor a flood of blessings can save a people who will not obey God's commandments.

This lesson was not lost on the American Founders. Franklin exclaimed:

> "As the scriptures are given for our reproof, instruction and warning, may we make a due use of this example before it is too late!"[4]

Jefferson added,

> "Whatever is to be our destiny, wisdom as well as duty dictates that we should acquiesce in the will of Him whose [power] it is to give and take away ...."[5]

In his Thanksgiving Proclamation of 1789, just a few months after he became our first President, George Washington said:

> "It is the duty of all nations to acknowledge the providence of Almighty God, to obey his will, to be grateful for his benefits, and humbly to implore his protection and favor."[6]

He had also said:

> "Purity of morals [is] the only sure foundation of public happiness in any country."[7]

2. Exodus 24:9-10.
3. Exodus 24:10-11.
4. Smyth, The Writings of Benjamin Franklin, op. cit., 2:340.
5. Bergh, The Writings of Thomas Jefferson, op. cit., 1:32.
6. John C. Fitzpatrick, The Writings of George Washington, 39 vols., Washington, D.C.: U.S. Government Printing Office, 30:427.
7. Ibid., 13:118.

These men belonged to a generation of Americans who continually studied the scriptures to glean from the lessons of the past the inspired principles that would guide the building of a great new nation in modern times. They believed the scriptures. As John Jay, the first Chief Justice of the Supreme Court said:

> "I believe that fact to be that except for the Bible, there is not a true history in the world."[8]

Moses Approaches the Beginning of the End

As we have mentioned earlier, it was in great sorrow that Moses came toward the end of his earthly life with a full realization that Israel would miss their great opportunity to become a nation of righteous supremacy "above all people." He said:

> "For I know thy rebellion, and thy stiff neck: behold, while I am yet alive with you this day, ye have been rebellious against the Lord; and how much more after my death?"[9]

The apostasy and rebellion of God's chosen people would not only turn out to be a terrible disaster for Israel, but it would be equally tragic for the whole human race. It would leave a great political vacuum for blood-thirsty tyrants to build massive empires one after the other. First there would be the Babylonian empire, then the Medes and Persians. After that there would be the conquest of the civilized world by Alexander the Great and the Greeks. Finally, the iron-shod wheels of the Roman legions would roll out across the western world.

Millions would be slaughtered during these cruel and brutal conquests. No doubt Moses was aware that all of this terrible destruction of human life could have been prevented if the Israelites had only remained faithful and fulfilled their role which God had assigned to them.

The only comfort Moses received during these dark hours was God's promise that in the latter days, after Israel had suffered both a dispersion and a gathering, God's perfect law would be reinstated and practiced in righteousness.[10]

Meanwhile, Moses was instructed to bring the people together and repeat to them God's magnificent Law of the Covenant. This "second giving of the

---

8. Jay's letter to Jedeiah Morse, February 28, 1797; see Cousins, In God We Trust, op. cit., pp. 2-3.
9. Deuteronomy 31:27.
10. Deuteronomy 30:1-8.

law," called Deuteronomy, was ever afterwards called "the Book of the Law." During the ministry of Jesus, he quoted more frequently from Deuteronomy than any other text.

It will be recalled that Moses was forbidden to lead the Israelites into the promised land,[11] but just before his passing he was allowed to see it from the heights of Mount Pisgah. This is part of the Nebo range on the east side of the Dead Sea.

Josephus describes his ascent into the mount. Moses had told the people he was now leaving them and would never return. Josephus says:

> "He withdrew among the tears of the people; the women beating their breasts, and the children giving way to uncontrollable wailing. At a certain point in his ascent he made a sign to the weeping multitude to advance no farther, taking with him only the elders, the high priest Eleazar, and the general Joshua." [12]

When this group of leaders later returned, Moses was not with them.

Joshua Assumes Command

God had chosen as the successor to Moses, the great military leader named Joshua, whose Greek name was Jesus. He was from the tribe of Ephraim, the largest tribe of Israel. He and Caleb were the only two survivors of the original Egyptian slaves who were allowed to enter the promised land. All the rest had died during the 40 years of wandering in the wilderness.[13]

This was a terrifying assignment for Joshua. In fact, even the Lord declared that it was "a terrible thing" he was going to ask Israel to do.[14] What was this "terrible thing?"

For centuries God had listened to the agonizing screams of the children being sacrificed to the pagan gods of the Hittites, the Amorites, the Canaanites, the Perizzites, the Hivites, and the Jebusites. Now these nations would be declared anathema. He wanted their cultures completely obliterated in this sacred land. The Lord said:

> "But of the cities of these people … thou shalt save alive nothing that breatheth: thou shalt *utterly* destroy them." [15]

---

11. Deuteronomy 31:2.
12. Josephus, Antiquities of the Jews, Grand Rapids, Michigan: Kregel Publications, 1966, book VI, chapter 8:48.
13. Numbers 14:28-31.
14. Exodus 34:10.
15. Deuteronomy 20:16-17.

Of course there were two things these people could do to save themselves. The Lord said the Israelites must first "proclaim peace unto them." [16] If they decided to repent and come under the Law of the Covenant, they would be spared. Or, secondly, they had the option of escaping by fleeing out of the land and settling in some other territory. However, if they defied the Lord's invitation, and refused to forsake their human sacrifices, their depraved sex worship, and other forms of debauchery, then Joshua was told to utterly destroy them.

When Joshua and the hosts of three million Israelites were finally camped on the eastern bank of the Jordan River, the Lord's new prophet received his marching orders. The Lord said:

"... arise, go over this Jordan, thou, and all this people, unto the land which I do give to them, even to the children of Israel.... There shall not any man be able to stand before thee all the days of thy life: as I was with Moses, so I will be with thee: I will not fail thee, nor forsake thee." [17]

The Lord also wanted the people to know that the power of God was with Joshua just as it had been with Moses. The Lord therefore said to him:

"This day will I begin to magnify thee in the sight of all Israel, that they may know that, as I was with Moses, so I will be with thee." [18]

Joshua then called all the people together and told them to get all their baggage loaded up so that their possessions could be carried with them across the river. He even promised them in advance that they were about to see a miracle similar to the dividing of the Red Sea when their fathers came out of Egypt.

As the hosts moved forward, Joshua ordered the priests to proceed ahead of the multitude and march directly into the river!

The scripture says that as the feet of the priests touched the swirling tide along the river banks the great miracle occurred. Before the eyes of all Israel a clean break appeared in the midst of the torrent of water even though it was at flood tide. It seemed as though a huge invisible dam had been thrown across the river in an instant.

The amazed Israelites watched as "the waters which came down from above stood and rose up upon an heap ...." [19]

16. Deuteronomy 20:10-11.
17. Joshua 1:2, 5.
18. Joshua 3:7.
19. Joshua 3:16.

The waters below drained off and disappeared into the Dead Sea. Furthermore, the muddy bottom of the river and the marshlands along its banks became dry land so that the priests bearing the Ark of the Covenant were able to march down into the river bed and stand on "dry ground" while the great wall of water piled up miraculously just above them.[20]

When the three million Israelites had crossed to the western side of the Jordan river, Joshua said to the priests,

"Come ye up out of the Jordan."[21]

Barely had the priests reached the high ground when suddenly the huge invisible dam seemed to crumble away, and "the waters of Jordan returned into their place, and flowed over all his banks, as they did before."[22]

Joshua later learned that this great miracle had not only been experienced by the Israelites, but the pagan spies of the surrounding nations had witnessed it as well.[23]

The Cleansing of the Land

Joshua was forced to annihilate Jericho, the wealthy walled city just a few miles up from the west bank of the Jordan river. The Israelite spies learned that the king of Jericho and his people knew all about the miracles God had performed for Israel.[24] The king knew about the crossing of the Red Sea. He even knew that they had orders to bring the people of this land under the Law of the Covenant or eliminate their culture from the entire region. Amazingly, the king decided to rely on the god of his city to demonstrate his superiority over the Lord God Jehovah. He locked the gates and dared the Israelites to attack.

Six consecutive days Joshua led a sortie around the city to give the king of Jericho a chance to change his mind. When Joshua came forth the seventh day he still marched around the city walls seven times before the priests were ordered to blow their trumpets. When they did the mighty walls of Jericho began to tremble and quake until finally they came tumbling down with soldiers, stones, mortar and bricks all grinding and crashing together in one mammoth avalanche of devastating destruction.[25]

20. Joshua 3:17.
21. Joshua 4:17.
22. Joshua 4:18.
23. Joshua 5:1.
24. Joshua 2:10-11.
25. Joshua, chapter 6.

Only one woman and her family escaped the scorched earth assault on Jericho. Her name was Rahab, the woman who had protected the spies that were sent over by Joshua to determine the attitude of the king and his people. Because of her kindness, the spies had promised her that she and her family would be spared when the attack occurred.[26]

From then on the armies of Israel went about their grizzly task of cleansing the land. Of all the nations which were offered the opportunity to come in under the Law of the Covenant, only one small tribal group consented to the Lord's terms. They were the Gibeonites of the Hivite nation. All the rest conspired together to fight the Israelites with one accord. From then on, it was one mighty battle after another. In one of the crucial conflicts with these tribes, Joshua found that the battle was going well for the Israelites, but the light of day was essential for several more hours. Joshua therefore climbed to some high place "in the sight of Israel" and shouted, "Sun, stand thou still upon Gibeon; and thou Moon, in the valley of Ajalon." [27]

At first it would have been impossible for the people to discern whether the commands of Joshua were real or not, but as the hours passed, it became definitely apparent that neither the sun nor the moon was moving. As the scripture says,

> "So the sun stood still in the midst of heaven, and hastened not to go down about a whole day. And there was no day like that before it or after it, that the Lord hearkened unto the voice of a man …." [28]

The Blessings and the Cursings

In the central part of this new land were two famous mountain peaks with a narrow valley dividing them. One mountain was called Mount Gerazim and the other was called Mount Ebal.

It was in the midst of all these great battles that Joshua took time out to assemble his armies at the foot of these two mountains along with all the hosts of Israel. They had a very sacred ceremony to perform which Moses had commanded them to carry out as soon as it was feasible.[29]

First of all they were to erect two huge stone monuments.

26. Joshua 6:25. Note that she is called a "harlot" but Dr. Adam Clarke says this word should have been translated "innkeeper." See Skousen, The Third Thousand Years, op. cit., p. 475.
27. Joshua 10:12.
28. Joshua 10:13-14.
29. Joshua 8:30-35.

Then they were to plaster them so they could be written upon.

Next they were to write all of the commandments of God on these monuments. Finally, they were to build a great altar for burnt offerings, and hold a great feast at this place.

As mentioned in chapter 3, the University of Jerusalem finally located a huge altar on Mount Ebal. This writer was taken by Dr. Joseph Ginat to see it soon after the altar was found. Its antiquity has been established by scientific methods, and it belongs to Joshua's era. It was a moving experience to stand there and contemplate what must have taken place on that mountain over three thousand years ago.

Following the feast, Moses had told Joshua to assemble six of the tribes of Israel on Mount Gerizim to pronounce blessings, and six of the tribes on Mount Ebal to pronounce cursings. After a blessing was pronounced the great host of people were to shout, "Amen!" which means "so be it." After a cursing was pronounced, the people were also to shout, "Amen."

Although we have already summarized the blessings and the cursings in chapter 3, let us repeat them here in more detail.[30] The blessings promised by the Lord were as follows:

1. They would become the greatest nation on earth.
2. They would be blessed with an abundance of food, raiment, and comfortable homes.
3. They would be blessed with good health and strong children.
4. They would be blessed with great military strength so that surrounding nations would fear to attack them. Nevertheless, if there was a war, Israel would be blessed with victory.
5. They would be blessed with abundant rains and flourishing crops.
6. They would be blessed with so much wealth that other nations would come to borrow from them, but Israel would never have to borrow.

Now, in contrast to these superlative promises we have the inventory of cursings[31] which would come upon the Israelites if they became wicked and debauched:

1. Instead of prosperity, there would be poverty.
2. Instead of health, there would be pestilence.

30. Deuteronomy 28:1-13.
31. Deuteronomy 28:15-68.

3. Instead of fertility, the land would become a desert.

4. Instead of military victory, there would be humiliating defeat.

5. Instead of happy marriages, wives would be kidnapped and ravished.

6. Instead of happy families, children would be sold into slavery.

7. Instead of flourishing flocks and herds, they would be left destitute.

8. Instead of being the highest, Israel would be the lowest.

9. Instead of enjoying religious freedom, they would be compelled to worship man-made idols.

10. Instead of comfort and abundance, there would be hunger, thirst and nakedness.

If these people rejected God and betrayed the trust God had placed in them, Moses saw their cities ravaged, their walls of protection demolished and the people scattered to the four winds.

Fearful that this might happen, Moses declared with a voice of thundering doom:

> "And the Lord shall scatter thee among all people, from the one end of the earth even unto the other; and there thou shalt serve other gods, which neither thou nor thy fathers have known, even wood and stone.
>
> "And among these nations shalt thou find no ease, neither shall the sole of thy foot have rest: but the Lord shall give thee there a trembling heart, and failing of eyes, and sorrow of mind. And thy life shall hang in doubt before thee; and thou shalt fear day and night."[32]

The Death of Joshua

Having built the great altar on Mount Nebo and having performed the ceremony of the blessings and the cursings, Joshua sent the civilian hosts of Israel back to Gilgal near the ruins of Jericho and braced himself for the final cleansing of the land.

There were seven heroic years of ferocious wars and sometimes near defeat, but in the end the Israelites always won. Joshua had hoped to completely cleanse the land before he was too old to fight, but he didn't quite

---

32. Deuteronomy 28:64-66.

make it. The Lord therefore allowed him to retire from the cleansing process and divide the land among the tribes.

Unfortunately, several of the rich Canaanite cities along the coast remained unscathed. Therefore the inheritances of some of the tribes included highly dangerous enemy territory not yet conquered. The tribe of Dan became so unhappy with exposure to frequent attacks that it eventually moved most of its population northward to a completely new region.

As Joshua saw his life ebbing away he called a conference of all the people. He reminded them that the Lord's work in cleansing the land of the idolatrous heathens was far from finished. Under no circumstances were they to become indifferent to this assignment nor be negligent in driving the Canaanites out. He prophesied they would corrupt the Israelites if they were allowed to remain in the land. Said he:

> "If ye do in any wise go back, and cleave unto the remnant of these nations … and shall make marriages with them, and go in unto them, and they to you: know for a certainty that the Lord God will no more drive out any of these nations from before you: but they shall be snares and traps unto you, and scourges in your side, and thorns in your eyes, until ye perish from off this good land which the Lord your God hath given you."[33]

Joshua pleaded with the elders of Israel to use their hard-won freedom to choose the right. Like Moses, he felt the ominous presence of horribly evil forces that would eventually erode away their legacy of righteousness and bring curses instead of blessings. He concluded with a final plea which is one of the most frequently quoted passages from the Bible. Said he:

> "Choose you this day whom ye will serve … but as for me and my house, we will serve the Lord."[34]

So Joshua had preached his last sermon, fought his last battle and made his final plea to the people of Israel. It was now up to them.

> "And it came to pass after these things, that Joshua the son of Nun, the servant of the Lord, died, being an hundred and ten years old. And they buried him in the border of his inheritance in Timnath-serah, which is in Mount Ephraim …."[35]

---

33. Joshua 23:12-13.
34. Joshua 24:15.
35. Joshua 24:29-30.

Israel Plunges into the Dark Ages

When Joshua died the national spirit of Israel died also. No longer was there a massive gravitating force of unity which had been so apparent during the crusade in Canaan. With the death of Joshua the great federation of military and political solidarity melted away.

Every man departed to his own inheritance and each tribe began to look to its own resources without giving help or asking aid from their fellow Israelites. The scripture tells the story:

> "... and there arose another generation after them [meaning Joshua and his generation] which knew not the Lord, nor yet the works which he had done for Israel. And the children of Israel did evil in the sight of the Lord and served Baalim [heathen fertility sun god]:
>
> "And they forsook the Lord God of their fathers, which brought them out of the land of Egypt, and followed other gods, of the gods of the people that were round about them, and bowed themselves unto them, and provoked the Lord to anger." [36]

The great appeal of idolatry was the ritual which went with it. The fertility rites gave religious justification for the most bizarre sexual orgies, drunkenness, and riotous revelry. Furthermore, the theology of heathen idolatry called for human sacrifices, especially of children, and often involved burning them to death or violently spilling their blood.[37]

God hates these two features of pagan worship. And he had told Abraham that when his cup of wrath was filled to overflowing he would feel justified in erasing this ghastly pagan culture from the face of the earth. Of course, he could have done it by fire or flood, but he chose to test the Israelites as his instrument of justice. But they failed. In fact, they joined the enemy.

During the next thousand years, the Israelites went through a long, ambivalent, but steady descent into oblivion. It was a whole series of dark ages interrupted occasionally by the splendor of some brilliant personality like a Deborah or a Gideon, but always smothered in the following generation with a return of the darkness.

For example, three hundred years after Joshua, Israel had become a tributary of the Canaanites. The Lord raised up a Samuel, who liberated them,

---

36. Judges 2:10-12.
37. W. Cleon Skousen, The Fourth Thousand Years, Salt Lake City: Bookcraft, 1966, pp. 319-326.

but in his old age even his own sons became corrupt and Samuel could not reform them.[38]

The People Wanted a King

The people wanted a king, so the Lord told Samuel to give them one. It turned out to be Saul. But Saul had barely won his first major war before he decided to be a priest as well as a general, and God rejected him for his presumptuous arrogance.[39]

By about 1,000 B.C., Saul was killed and David replaced him.[40] The Lord loved David and blessed him for his valiant spirit. As the king of Israel, David expanded the kingdom from the Euphrates river to the river of Egypt. But he lusted after the beautiful wife of Uriah, and arranged for Uriah's death in battle so he could have the woman he coveted. For this, David lost his fabulous blessings. He had even received the plans for a beautiful temple, but he was never allowed to build it. That privilege was reserved for his son, Solomon.[41]

The name "Solomon" is taken from a Hebrew word which means peace, and the years during which king Solomon ruled Israel was the longest period of peace in the history of that people. Solomon not only administered the affairs of Israel with wisdom and justice, but the whole nation became so rich that silver was plentiful beyond need, and became valued at little more than common stones. The Israelites were as powerful and wealthy as any nation known to have existed on the earth at that time, and Solomon was famous from Mesopotamia to the kingdom of Sheba for his wisdom.

But during the last three years of his life, Solomon felt his kingdom was beginning to fracture, therefore he married upwards of a thousand wives from every tribe and prominent family from the numerous nations that had become tributaries of Israel.

This political tactic was popular among rulers in all ages. Such marriages were looked upon as treaties or alliances between families, tribes, and countries. But "multiplying wives" in this manner was contrary to the commandment of God. The scripture indicates that Solomon had no children from these many political wives, but he made the monumental mistake of capitulat-

38. Ibid., pp. 356-358.
39. Ibid., p. 7.
40. Ibid., pp. 197-198, 205-206.
41. Ibid., pp. 146-280.

ing to the teasing of the wives from heathen nations. He allowed them to build their pagan temples on the Mount of Olives.

Israel never recovered from the effect of that error.

Israel Splits in Two

When Solomon died around 922 B.C., the whole kingdom split asunder. Ten of the tribes voted against Rehoboam, the son of Solomon, and set up their headquarters with their own king near Mount Ebal (the mountain of cursings!).

Furthermore, the northern ten tribes drove out all the Levites, so the priests and teachers of the people ended up in the south with Judah.

As might have been expected, the northern ten tribes dropped back into the dark ages almost immediately. Within two generations, a heathen princess from Phoenicia named Jezebel had married the king of the northern tribes. His name was Ahab.[42] Almost over night an inferno of depraved venality exploded among the northern tribes.

God raised up a whole consortium of prophets to stem the tide of carnal iniquity, but the current was running too fast and too strong. Most of the prophets were slaughtered, and even when the magnificent Elijah was allowed to call down fire from heaven,[43] it scarcely made a dent in the calloused conscience of the defiled Israelites.

During the next century, (800 B.C.), Elisha,[44] the successor to Elijah, performed every miracle Jesus later performed, including the raising of the dead, but it was a blessing primarily to those who were close to Elisha or belonged to the school of the prophets. Nevertheless, the king had respect for Elisha and when he heard the good man was dying, the scripture says:

> "And Joash the king of Israel … wept over his face, and said, O my father, my father, the chariot of Israel, and the horsemen thereof."[45]

This was like saying "O my father, thou servant of God, thou art the only defense of Israel!" And this astonishing statement came from a king that tolerated Egyptian golden calf worship all during his reign. It illustrates that

42. Ibid., p. 316.
43. Ibid., pp. 343-351.
44. Ibid., pp. 392, 443.
45. 2 Kings 13:14.

even in their wickedness, the Israelites were conscious that God's servants were their real source of hope, especially in case of some unexpected crisis.

The Captivity of the Northern Ten Tribes

Around 750 B.C., the highly educated Isaiah from Jerusalem began to warn the dissident tribes to the north that their fate of doom was about to descend upon them unless they repented.

The threat was not from the Canaanites on the Mediterranean coast, but from the Assyrians who ruled with venomous cruelty from their famous walled capital of Nineveh on the Tigris River.

Isaiah knew what the Assyrians had in store for the northern tribes of Israel. Eventually, Isaiah wrote the longest book in the Bible. He was apparently shown nearly 2,700 years of future history, and much of his writings dealt with modern times and the glories of the Millennium when the lamb would lie down with the lion, and there would be peace on earth for a thousand years.

However, Isaiah's most immediate prophecies were directed against the northern Ten Tribes.[46] Isaiah even identified the nation that would conquer them and carry them away.

It all came to pass when the Assyrians launched a three-year assault against the Ten Tribes about 722 B.C. This was just 200 years after these rebellious Israelites had defiantly declared their independence from Judah and Levi. Now they not only lost their independence, but also their freedom. The Assyrians butchered most of the Israelites and then carried the remnant off to Halah and Habor by the river of Gozan.

The Assyrians Attack Judah

Twenty years later, the fierce assault troops of Assyria marched down the Mediterranean coast on the way to conquering Egypt. But they never got to Egypt. The king of Assyria, named Sennacherib, became worried about the hostile territory of Judah on their left flank. He therefore decided to put Judah out of action before proceeding south.[47] In 601 B.C., the Assyrians destroyed 46 walled cities of Judah and then prepared to attack Jerusalem.

Although the inhabitants of Jerusalem were virtually petrified with fear, Isaiah assured the good king Hezekiah that he had a message from the Lord. Here was the message:

---

46. Skousen, The Fourth Thousand Years, op. cit., chapter 18.
47. Ibid., pp. 635-636.

> "Thus saith the Lord, be not afraid … the servants of the king of Assyria have blasphemed me, behold, I will send a blast upon him, and he shall hear a rumour, and shall return to his own land; and I will cause him to fall by the sword in his own land." [48]

The king of Judah wanted to believe Isaiah but common sense told him that there was just no way to stop the 185,000 Assyrian troops from invading the city.

Isaiah therefore comforted the king with another message which said:

> "Thus saith the Lord concerning the king of Assyria, He shall not come into this city, nor shoot an arrow there, nor come before it with shield, nor cast a bank against it." [49]

Just about the time Sennacherib was planning to leave the coastal plain and march his massive army up to destroy Jerusalem, a terrible thing happened. Whether God's blast was by plague or by storm we are not told. The Bible simply says:

> "And it came to pass that night, that the angel of the Lord went out, and smote the camp of the Assyrians an hundred fourscore and five thousand: and when they [the survivors] arose early in the morning, behold they were all dead corpses." [50]

Notice that the "blast" had wiped out 185,000 Assyrians!

Sennacherib survived, but he forgot all about attacking Jerusalem. He took the remnants of his shattered army and raced back to his capital city of Nineveh on the Tigris. The rest of Isaiah's prophecy was fulfilled some time later when two of Sennacherib's sons conspired together and murdered their father.

The Fall of Assyria and the Rise of Babylon

A century after the murder of Sennacherib, the Assyrian kingdom was no more. A new power had risen in the earth—Babylon.

The capital of Babylon was located on the Euphrates river close to the point where it converges with the Tigris.

In 612 B.C. a mighty army besieged Nineveh.[51] These were the hosts of the Babylonians and their allies. Shortly after the siege began, the Tigris river

48. 2 Kings 19:6-7.
49. 2 Kings 19:32.
50. 2 Kings 19:35.
51. Skousen, The Fourth Thousand Years, op. cit., pp. 570-571.

flooded and washed away a large segment of the walls of Nineveh which were a hundred feet high.

This left the city indefensible. The Babylonians rushed in and completely devastated Nineveh so that when the Greek historian Herodotus visited the site in his day, it was nothing but mounds of mud.

The fall of Assyria allowed their captive Israelites to escape. They traveled over the Caucasus Mountains which extend between the Black Sea and Caspian Sea, and briefly settled in that area. Before long they had completely disappeared from history and became known as "The Lost Tribes."

Next, the Babylonians turned their attention toward Jerusalem. The king of Babylon was Nebuchadnezzar.

By this time another great prophet had been raised up among the Jews to succeed Isaiah. His name was Jeremiah. Jeremiah had a strange message for the Jews: "Be ye subject to Nebuchadnezzar and live!" In other words, pay a little tribute to the Babylonians and they will leave you alone. The Jewish leaders flatly rejected the words of Jeremiah. His advice was treated as virtually treasonous, and he was thrown in prison.

Meanwhile, the first visit of Nebuchadnezzar to Jerusalem was not a major attack. He simply asked the king of the Jews to pay an annual tribute and departed. However, Nebuchadnezzar took along young Daniel and a few of his bright friends to be trained as administrators in Babylon.

Even though Nebuchadnezzar induced the king of Judah to start paying tribute on his first visit, it did not last long. Therefore when Nebuchadnezzar came back again around 600 B.C., he attacked briefly to let Judah know he meant business. He invaded Jerusalem, took vessels from the temple, and carried off ten thousand of their best artisans. This included a young twenty-five year old Jew named Ezekiel who later became a prophet to the Jews in captivity after the fall of Jerusalem.

The fall of Jerusalem occurred around 587 B.C.[52] It was totally catastrophic. The attack began with a long siege that reduced the starving people to cannibalizing their own dead. Then, when practically all resistance had ceased, Nebuchadnezzar had his generals rescue Jeremiah from the city, and then they began destroying everything. The beautiful temple of Solomon was demolished, the walls of the city were torn down. The homes of the people were reduced to ashes. Thousands of the people were slain, and the remainder were rounded up to be taken captive to Babylon.

52. Ibid., pp. 708-709.

Perhaps they would never have been allowed to return to Jerusalem if it had not been for Cyrus of Persia.

The Fall of Babylon

The Babylonians reigned supreme until 539 B.C. During that year a fatal banquet was held by king Belshazzar. He was feeding a great crowd of guests on the golden plateware taken from the temple in Jerusalem. Suddenly the ghostly specter of a human hand was seen writing on the wall. The words were plain for all to read: "Mene, Mene, Tekel, Upharsin."

Belshazzar was of a different dynasty than Nebuchadnezzar and therefore he had never met the prophet Daniel. Nevertheless, the people urged the king to summon him and interpret the strange message on the wall. Daniel arrived and interpreted the words as follows:[53]

Mene: God hath numbered thy kingdom and finished it.

Tekel: Thou art weighed in the balance and found wanting.

Peres or Upharsin: Thy kingdom is divided, and given to the Medes and Persians.

It all came to pass that very night. Belshazzar was murdered by two of his lords, and Cyrus, the Persian conqueror, was within the gates with his army of Medes and Persians before sunup.

The Rise of Persia and the Return of the Jews

Over 150 years before he came to power, Cyrus was described by name in the writings of Isaiah.[54]

Although a pagan, Isaiah spoke of Cyrus as a great friend of God, who was "anointed" to do a great work.

The very next year after coming to power, Cyrus called the Jewish leaders to him and issued the rather amazing proclamation:

> "Thus saith Cyrus king of Persia, The Lord God of heaven hath given me all the kingdoms of the earth; and he hath charged me to build him an house at Jerusalem, which is in Judah. Who is there among you of all this people? his God be with him, and let him

53. Daniel 5:25-28.
54. Isaiah 44:28; 45:1.

> go up to Jerusalem, which is in Judah, and build the house of the Lord God of Israel … which is in Jerusalem."[55]

At first glance it would seem as though Cyrus had become a convert to Jehovah, the God of Abraham, Isaac and Jacob. But such was not the case. We know Cyrus was honoring heathen deities with equal fervor about this same time. But at least he was honest about it—honest enough to include the true God Jehovah, along with whatever others he had been taught to accept. It was a typical pagan approach to pan-theism.

The king invited Jews from all regions to contribute to the temple fund, and also to the support of the temple builders. Cyrus, himself, brought forth 5,400 vessels of gold and silver which had been captured during the earlier conquests of Judah, and turned them over to the Jewish leaders in charge of the expedition to Jerusalem. He also ordered that the expenses for the restoration of the temple should be paid out of the king's personal account.

The temporal leader of the Jewish people at this time was a man named Zerubbabel (meaning "born in Babylon") therefore the temple they built is usually called the Zerubbabel temple so as to distinguish it from the temple of Solomon.[56]

A great throng of approximately 50,000 Jews made the long trek back to Jerusalem, and, after extremely strenuous efforts, they completed the new temple and dedicated it in the year 516 B.C.

The Coming of Ezra and Nehemiah

In these ancient times, the scriptures were copied by hand and were therefore very expensive. Furthermore, in time of war the books or writings of a people were among the first things to be destroyed. This had happened to the Jews. In their conquest and their captivity, it would seem that their scriptures had practically disappeared from among them.

Even though the Jews had built a new temple in Jerusalem, they were not following the Law of the Covenant. They were not organized with judges over them, and in any event, the local Persian authorities did not allow them to exercise capital punishment even for the most heinous crimes. The situation was becoming further complicated by the fact that some of the Jewish men were taking wives from among the surrounding pagan communities. Consequently, the temple service had been neglected and had seriously deteriorated.

55. Ezra 1:2-3.
56. Skousen, The Fourth Thousand Years, op. cit., p. 768.

There was a desperate need for vigorous spiritual leadership.

About 458 B.C. a very learned scribe and priest named Ezra[57] who had been born in Babylon under Persian rule, gained permission to go to Jerusalem and teach the people.

Fortunately, he brought with him all of the rolls of scripture in his possession, and these became the entire source for our modern Old Testament. Many of the historical books were written by rabbinical scholars and Ezra had these instead of the books of early prophets on which the historical books were based. The modern student of the Bible will therefore observe that while the scripture makes reference to these earlier writings of the prophets, they are not yet part of our canon of holy writ today.

Ezra collected considerable funds and received authority from the king to restore the system of judges to enforce the law of Moses. He even authorized Ezra to impose the death penalty in prescribed cases.

Ezra brought 1,500 leading members of the Babylonian-Jewish community with him. However, he was shocked when he reached Jerusalem to find that it was still a ghost town. The people had settled in the surrounding fields and valleys. Practically no effort had been made to clean up the rubble of the destroyed city or rebuild the walls. Ezra wrote an urgent report to the Jewish leaders back in Babylon.

Undoubtedly Ezra's report had something to do with the determination of the king's cupbearer, named Nehemiah, to restore the Jewish capital. He did not arrive until fourteen years after Ezra first came, but he brought a commission from the king to build up the land, restore the walls, and clean up the city. Even more important, Nehemiah was appointed governor of Jerusalem.[58]

Nehemiah and Ezra became working partners in the great undertaking of making Jerusalem a beautiful city again. Surrounding pagan communities launched an attack against the Jews and they had to rebuild the walls with a weapon in one hand and a trowel in the other. Nevertheless, the walls were finished in 52 days.

A great conference was held and Ezra read the law to the people three hours at a time. To reach the vast throng, Ezra set up a network of "speakers." He would read a line and the speakers nearest him would repeat it. The sentence was then picked up by the next contingent of speakers and then the next until the entire population had heard the law. Thereafter, Ezra set up the

57. Ibid., pp. 787-796.
58. Ibid., pp. 790-796.

synagogues so the law could be carefully studied on a regular basis. Every adult was expected to know the law in detail, but since only a few of the top leaders had a copy of the law, the people relied on their synagogue session to learn the will of the Lord as they restructured their society.

The End of the Old Testament

By 400 B.C. the last of the Old Testament prophets had arrived on the scene. His name was Malachi.[59] He left a treasure of admonition, and a promise that there would be prophets revealed to them in the future, then he closed his record and the Old Testament epoch came to an end.

But it was not the end of Jewish history. The next four centuries before the birth of their Messiah were turbulent years. During the campaign of Alexander the Great they were conquered by the Greeks. They won their independence from the Greeks about 165 B.C. but in 63 B.C. they were conquered by the Romans.

Jesus was therefore born into a conquered country. However, this had some advantages. The Romans had a policy of religious toleration which allowed Pagan, Christian and Jew to worship without interference. The motto of Pax Romana was simply, "Pay your taxes and keep the peace!"

This created a protected climate in which the next great dispensation of God's eternal law for human happiness could be revealed 400 years after Malachi.

59. Ibid., pp. 800-803.

Topics for Reflection and Discussion

1. In what way did the Founders recognize the history of Israel as a "warning" to Americans in modern times?

2. Did Moses know Israel would miss its opportunity to be the greatest nation on earth? Could he have prevented them from apostatizing?

3. What were the four oppressive empires which succeeded one after another as a result of the political vacuum left by the Israelites in consequence of their apostasy and rebellion?

4. Why was the genocidal destruction of the pagan nations in the Holy Land required by the Lord? What could these nations do to escape destruction? Did any of them take advantage of it?

5. In what way were the "cursings" on Israel literally fulfilled?

6. When Israel demanded a king, the Lord granted it even though he knew it would bring them sorrow and oppression. What does this tell you about the Lord?

7. David was greatly loved of the Lord. When David fell did the Lord treat him any differently than anyone else? What does this indicate about the Lord's sense of justice?

8. Have any of the tribes of Israel begun to gather in our day? What does this indicate?

9. Why was the Roman occupation of the Holy Land an advantage to Jesus during his ministry?

10. What kind of an impact did the study of the Old Testament have on the Founders?

CHAPTER SEVEN

The Founders Study God's Law under Biblical Christianity

The Founders knew that Christianity, when properly understood, contained the ingredients for America's highest achievements, both politically and socially. As Thomas Jefferson said:

> "There never was a more pure and sublime system of morality delivered to man than is to be found in the four Evangelists." [1]

The Founders pondered the words of the apostles and noticed that all who came to a unity of the faith and entered into the new Christian covenant, attained the most sublime level of human relationships recorded anywhere in history.[2] It was eventually broken up but only because of bitter persecution emanating from Rome and Jerusalem.

It is interesting that most of the Founders knew Greek, and they therefore studied the New Testament in its original text. They knew that originally the New Testament was called the book of the New Covenant. In fact, the Greek word for "testament" means "covenant." This title emphasized that within the pages of this sacred book could be found the key elements of God's new covenant which came through the ministry of Jesus Christ.

Three Fundamentals of the New Covenant

The New Covenant emphasized three fundamental principles:

1. That once the Savior had fulfilled his mission, all of the ceremonies, ordinances, feast days, and sacrifices pointing to his coming were fulfilled. Therefore, they were to be discontinued.[3]

2. Nevertheless, all of the original laws of the covenant relating to personal conduct, duties to God, and responsibilities toward other human beings, were a permanent part of the gospel. They would therefore remain in full force and effect.[4]

---

1. Bergh, The Writings of Thomas Jefferson, op. cit., 14:81.
2. Acts 4:32.
3. Matthew 5:17.
4. Matthew 5:19.

3. Under the new covenant the level of values enunciated in the original covenant of the Old Testament would not only be retained, but greatly elevated and refined so that under the New Covenant Christians were expected to achieve the same sublimated order of life that Enoch and his people were able to attain in his day.[5]

Changes in the Jewish Religion under the First Principle

Let us briefly consider the many traumatic changes which occurred in the ritual and lifestyle of the Jews who became Christians under the New Covenant.

It will be recalled that when the law of the covenant was first given to Moses, it was fairly simple. It consisted of the commandments, the statutes and the judgments which we have previously discussed.

However, when the Israelites rebelled after all the miracles and fantastic blessings God had given them, it was necessary to impose upon the recalcitrant Israelites a whole new pattern of discipline that would teach them the rhythm of obedience. For this reason, God determined to put them under a "schoolmaster" system of carnal commandments by requiring them to live under a strict dietary law, and perform numerous rituals and ceremonies as a teaching device to assure their survival as a nation until the coming of Christ. As Paul said:

> "The [carnal] law … was added because of transgressions, till the seed [Christ] should come to whom the promise was made.… Wherefore the law was our schoolmaster to bring us unto Christ…."[6]

After Jesus had completed his assignment and had become the Great Mediator following his resurrection, all of the carnal commandments became obsolete. They were no longer required because they had fulfilled their purpose.

Of course, the Jews had become so immersed in the carnal law culture that it seemed almost irreligious to discontinue this elaborate network of "schoolmaster" ceremonies and all their tedious rituals. Therefore, a most challenging task resting upon the Apostles was to get the newly converted Jewish

5. Genesis 5:22-24; Hebrews 11:5.
6. Galatians 3:19, 24.

disciples to accept the fact that the carnal commandments were fulfilled and therefore obsolete.

Most of Paul's epistles to the Hebrews as well as the Jews in Rome, Galatia, Corinth and several other missionary centers, were designed to explain why the carnal laws were no longer relevant. It was necessary to persuade them that when they accepted the New Covenant, they were released from the supplementary carnal commandments given to Moses, and they must now structure their lives and their thinking under the new, higher order.

The Shock of Learning That Circumcision Would No Longer Be Required for Either Jews or Gentiles

The most difficult task of all was to change the mind-set of the Jews concerning the practice of circumcision. The Israelites had been practicing circumcision since the days of Abraham. Now the Apostles were saying that circumcisions could be eliminated or done voluntarily if it were desired. In any event, it was no longer a ceremonial requirement of God. It turned out that this change in perspective was virtually mind shattering to many devout Jews.

Most of the Jews had forgotten the history of circumcision. They had forgotten that there was no requirement of ceremonial circumcision in the days of Adam, Enoch or Noah. However, by 2,000 B.C. the pagans had made it popular to initiate tribal members with a "cutting in the flesh" or some other tribal identification. Some nations, including the Egyptians and Canaanites, were already using circumcision as their "mark in the flesh," and no doubt the practice was becoming increasingly popular. However, it was for a different reason that God initiated circumcision among the descendants of Abraham.

The Bible tells us that when it came time to put Abraham and his people under covenant, the Lord took advantage of the cultural popularity of a "cutting of the flesh," by initiating circumcision as a sign or token of the contract between God and Abraham's people.

The Lord explained the special significance of this new ordinance by saying:

> "My people have gone astray from my precepts, and have not kept mine ordinances, which I gave unto their fathers; and they have not observed mine anointing, and the *burial, or baptism, wherewith I commanded them* … And I will establish a covenant of circumcision with thee … that thou mayest know forever that

> the children are not accountable before me until they are eight years old."[7]

The Lord then went on to say that just as male children were to be circumcised when they were eight days old,[8] it was to remind parents that all children were to be baptized when they were eight years old.

This command not only applied to Abraham but to all the people who wanted to come under the covenant and blessings promised to Abraham. At this time Abraham was 99 years old and his only son was Ishmael who was 13 years of age.[9]

In connection with God's new covenant with Abraham, the Lord said:

> "And ye shall circumcise the flesh of your foreskin; and it shall be a token of the covenant betwixt me and you."[10]

Circumcision was ceremonially mandated for all of those related or associated with Abraham when the Lord said:

> "And the uncircumcised manchild whose flesh of his foreskin is not circumcised, that soul shall be cut off from his people; he hath broken my covenant."[11]

In other words, an uncircumcised male could not remain in the congregation with those whom God had called his chosen people.

With this background it will be appreciated why the Jews, after conversion to Christianity, found it extremely difficult to accept the teaching of the Apostles that circumcision would no longer be required. For many this remained a problem even when the Apostles explained that since circumcision was a carnal commandment, Jesus had said its purpose had been fulfilled.

The problem became increasingly difficult as more and more non-Jewish converts became Christians. The Jewish Christians insisted that the male Gentiles be circumcised before they could be baptized and become Christians.

This became such a hotly debated issue throughout Christendom, that finally around 51 A.D. the Apostles called a special council at Jerusalem. At this conference the Apostles sought the special guidance of the Holy Spirit in reaching a decision. When the conference was concluded it was announced to

7. JST Genesis 17:4-11, emphasis added; see Skousen, The Third Thousand Years, op. cit., p. 12.
8. Genesis 17:12.
9. Genesis 16:16 plus 17:1.
10. Genesis 17:11.
11. Genesis 17:14.

all the churches that the Gospel no longer required mandatory circumcision for anyone, whether Jew or Gentile.[12]

The Overthrow of Nearly All Traditional Jewish Rituals

In addition to eliminating circumcision as a ceremonial requirement, it was made clear that all the "schoolmaster laws" and rituals related to the carnal commandments were also to be eliminated under the New Covenant. Consider how revolutionary this would be to a faithful Pharisee who had turned Christian. Practically all of the sacred rituals were being declared obsolete. This new teaching eliminated:

1. The Burnt Offering.[13]
2. The Sin Offering.[14]
3. The Trespass Offering.[15]
4. The Meal Offering.[16]
5. The Peace Offering.[17]
6. The Wave Offering.[18]
7. The Drink Offering.[19]
8. The Dietary Laws.[20]
9. Laws of Purification.[21]
10. The Annual Day of Atonement.[22]
11. The Feast of the Unleavened Bread.[23]
12. The Feast of the Tabernacles.[24]

---

12. Acts, chapter 15.
13. Leviticus, chapter 1; Skousen, The Third Thousand Years, op. cit., p. 339.
14. Leviticus, chapter 4; Skousen, Ibid.
15. Leviticus, chapter 5; Skousen, Ibid., p. 340.
16. Leviticus 5:11; Skousen, Ibid., p. 341.
17. Leviticus 7:11; Skousen, Ibid., p. 340.
18. Leviticus, chapter 8; Skousen, Ibid., p. 340.
19. Leviticus 23:13; Skousen, Ibid., p. 341.
20. Leviticus, chapter 11; Skousen, Ibid., pp. 346-347.
21. Leviticus chapter 16; Skousen, Ibid., p. 349.
22. Leviticus, chapter 16; Skousen, Ibid., p. 349.
23. Exodus 23:15; Skousen, Ibid., p. 258.
24. Leviticus 23:34-36.

13. The Feast of Pentecost.[25]

14. The Feast of the Ingathering.[26]

15. The Feast of Weeks.[27]

16. The Feast of Dedication or Feast of Lights.[28]

17. Sacrifices at the new moon.[29]

The Christians Were Given a Whole New View of Traditional Jewish Rituals

The apostles taught that all of these rituals and sacrifices were merely teaching devices which were "added" as a schoolmaster to bring the Jews to their prophetic rendezvous with destiny in the meridian of time when their Messiah would be born.

Meanwhile, to the Lord these tedious rituals were a burden. In fact, when they failed to be effective as a teaching device to produce better people, God considered them totally abhorrent. It will be recalled that the Lord made this very clear in the first chapter of Isaiah when he compared the wickedness of the Israelites with the ancient abominations of Sodom and Gomorrah. With sorrow and anguish he cried out:

> "To what purpose is the multitude of your sacrifices unto me [when they fail to improve the lives of the people]? I am full of the burnt offerings of rams, and the fat of fed beasts: and I delight not in the blood of bullocks, or of lambs, or of he goats … Bring no more vain oblations: incense is an abomination unto me; the new moons and sabbaths, the calling of assemblies … It is iniquity, even the solemn meeting. Your new moons and your appointed feasts my soul hateth: they are a trouble to me; I am weary to bear them. And when ye spread forth your hands, I will hide mine eyes from you: yea, when ye make many prayers, I will not hear: your hands are full of blood."[30]

Following this sorrowful lamentation, we hear this loving and forgiving Heavenly Parent pleading with these rebellious descendants of Abraham as

25. Leviticus 23:16.
26. Exodus 23:16.
27. Deuteronomy 16:10.
28. John 10:22.
29. Numbers 10:10; Leviticus 23:24-25.
30. Isaiah 1:11-15.

though he were already anticipating the Beatitudes and the Sermon on the Mount. Said he:

> "Wash you, make you clean; put away the evil of your doings from before mine eyes; cease to do evil; learn to do well; seek judgment, relieve the oppressed, judge the fatherless, plead for the widow. Come now and let us reason together, saith the Lord: though your sins be as scarlet, they shall be as white as snow: though they be red like crimson, they shall be as wool. *If ye are willing and obedient ye shall eat the good of the land.*" [31]

The lesson from all of this is obvious. The Lord is simply saying that there is no particular redeeming virtue in sacrifices, feasts, and convocations. They are merely teaching devices. They are null and void unless the lives of the people are improved. If the people continue in their wickedness, then the feasts, sacrifices and convocations are a mockery before God.

As we mentioned earlier, once these schoolmaster rituals were eliminated under the New Covenant, the task of the apostles was to have the new Christian converts recognize a whole new system of values, a new pattern of worship, and the great new dispensation of freedom that could now be enjoyed under the New Covenant.

Paul expressed his own feelings when he told the Colossians:

> "Let no man therefore judge you in meat, or in drink, or in respect of a [feast] day, or of the new moon, or of the sabbath days, which … [were anciently designed as] a shadow of things to come." [32]

Even a New Sabbath!

Note that even the ancient sabbath was being changed. It was a gradual process. For a time Christians memorialized the traditional Jewish sabbath on the seventh day of the week, but commemorated the day of Christ's resurrection on the first day as the true sabbath. Eventually however, the Christians ceased to memorialize the seventh day but simply made it a day of rest.[33]

Paul realized what a shock it was to the orthodox Jews to have all these new changes suddenly threaten the most sacred traditions of the people. As a missionary, Paul decided to continue showing respect for those traditions lest

31. Isaiah 1:16-19.
32. Colossians 2:16-17.
33. Hastings' Bible Dictionary under "sabbath."

he offend those he wanted to gradually convert to the new order of things. He said:

> "Wherefore, if meat make my brother to offend, I will eat no flesh … lest I make my brother to offend."[34]

In the same spirit, he said to the Romans:

> "It is good neither to eat flesh, nor to drink wine, nor any thing whereby thy brother stumbleth, or is offended, or is made weak."[35]

Christianity under the Second Principle Maintained All of the Original Gospel Elements

It will be recalled that the second aspect of Christianity was the fact that even though the carnal laws, ceremonies and ordinances were fulfilled with the coming of Christ, the rest of God's law as it existed in the original Gospel Covenant was still in full force and effect.

In the Sermon on the Mount Jesus emphasized this very point. He referred to all of the elements of the original covenant as it existed from Adam to Moses, and said:

> "Whosoever therefore shall break one of these least commandments, and shall teach men so, he shall be called the least in the kingdom of heaven: but whosoever shall do and teach them, the same shall be called great in the kingdom of heaven."[36]

But it turned out that some missed this part of the Gospel message. In fact, they thought Christianity did away with all restraints in all of the laws because Jesus had done it all, and paid for all sins, past, present and future. To them this meant that by accepting Christ as one's Savior, a person would be saved no matter what he did.

Certainly, this seemed to be a great new religion!

The Apostles Wrestle with the False Doctrine of "Antinomianism"

Historians tell us that some of the new converts to Christianity gained the idea that since Christ took on the burden of all the sins of "believers" it thereafter allowed Christ's followers to "eat, drink and be merry" because

34. 1 Corinthians 8:13.
35. Romans 14:21.
36. Matthew 5:19.

Christ had liberated them from all restraints under the law. This new Christian heresy was called "Antinomianism," which means "against the law." Philosophically, it might be called a kind of Christian hedonism that says "anything goes and you will still be saved."

The Apostle Paul was horrified when he discovered that these people were quoting him as the church leader who taught them this exciting new doctrine. Here is how this came about.

Early in his ministry, Paul's missionary work had been exclusively among the Jews. However, it was extremely difficult to get the Jews to overcome their deep-rooted tradition that salvation was "earned by good works." To the Jews, this meant fulfilling all the rituals and ceremonial requirements of the law. In his effort to convert the Jewish people to Christianity, Paul tried to teach them just three simple things:

1. Salvation is a free gift given by God through the mediation of the Savior's sacrifice. It is not dependent on "earned salvation" through good works.
2. Nevertheless, a person must repent and covenant through baptism to obey God's commandments in order to become eligible for this great gift.
3. The church, the ritual and ceremonies, are all supplementary support systems to help each individual obey the commandments and thereby qualify for the Savior's great gift.

In preaching to the Jews, Paul was trying to shift the focus from "earned" salvation—which is a false concept—to the atoning sacrifice of Jesus Christ which was being offered as a free and gracious gift by Christ to all who would believe, repent, and make a commitment through the waters of baptism to obey God's commandments so they could receive the enlightenment of the Holy Ghost.

But in Paul's anxiety to teach this doctrine he sometimes left the impression that belief alone was sufficient. To Paul "belief" meant obeying Christ's command to repent and be baptized, but to his listeners it sounded as though he was simply asking them to shout out "I believe," and then they could go out and sin to their heart's content. It was a question of hearing but not understanding. Some of Paul's teachings which were being misinterpreted included the following:

> "Believe on the Lord Jesus Christ, and thou shalt be saved, and thy house."[37]

37. Acts 16:31.

Another time he said:

> "If thou shalt confess with thy mouth the Lord Jesus and shalt believe in thine heart that God hath raised him from the dead, thou shalt be saved."[38]

And again:

> "Whosoever shall call on the name of the Lord shall be saved."[39]

Paul assumed that to "believe" or "confess" Christ automatically meant that a person was willing to follow the Savior and obey his commandments. But, as we have already mentioned, that is not the way many of his disciples translated it. They reasoned that by sinning they were demonstrating how completely they trusted in Christ to take away their sins. Since they had confessed Christ and bore witness of their belief in him they could now be disdainful of all restraints under the law. This disdain was called "Antinomianism" or indifference to the requirements of the law.

No wonder Paul was horrified when he saw what was happening. Frantically, he wrote to the Jewish converts in Rome:

> "Let not sin therefore reign in your mortal body, that ye should obey it in the lusts thereof. Neither yield ye your members as instruments of unrighteousness unto sin: but yield yourselves unto God, as those that are alive from the dead, and your members as instruments of righteousness unto God. For sin shall not have dominion over you: for ye are not under the law, but under grace.
>
> "What then? shall we sin, because we are not under the law, but under grace? God forbid. Know ye not, that to whom ye yield yourselves servants to obey, his servants ye are to whom ye obey; whether of sin unto death, or of obedience unto righteousness?"[40]

Obviously, in his anxiety to emphasize the true origin of salvation through Christ rather than the law, Paul was suffering some fallout he had not expected. So he wanted the Jewish converts in Rome to know that good works are an essential ingredient of true "belief in Christ," and that unless they eschew evil and obey the law of the New Covenant, they will be servants of Satan rather than Christ.

---

38. Romans 10:9.
39. Acts 2:21..
40. Romans 6:12-16.

Paul was actually saying in a rather complicated way what the Lord himself had said much more simply. He closed his Sermon on the Mount on this theme:

> "Not every one that saith unto me, Lord, Lord, shall enter into the kingdom of heaven; but he that doeth the will of my Father which is in heaven."[41]

So "works" turn out to be important after all—not to "earn" salvation as the rabbis had taught, but to qualify as an heir with Christ and enjoy the marvelous free gift of eternal life in the presence of the Father following the judgment.

James Seeks to Eliminate the Confusion

James, who is believed to have been the brother of the Lord, wrote an epistle to the twelve tribes scattered abroad to emphasize the true doctrine that faith or "belief alone" would not save them. He wrote:

> "What doth it profit, my brethren, though a man say he hath faith, and have not works? can faith save him? If a brother or sister be naked, and destitute of daily food, and one of you say unto them, Depart in peace, be ye warmed and filled; notwithstanding ye give them not those things which are needful to the body; what doth it profit?
>
> "Even so faith, if it hath not works, is dead, being alone. Yea, a man may say, Thou hast faith, and I have works: shew me thy faith without thy works, and I will shew thee my faith by my works.
>
> "Thou believest that there is one God; thou doest well: the devils also believe, and tremble. But wilt thou know, O vain man, that faith without works is dead?"[42]

It is rather amazing that in spite of everything the apostles did, Antinomianism continued down through the centuries. As late as 1527 A.D., Johann Agricola was preaching Antinomianism in Germany with great success even though it was strongly opposed by Martin Luther. In other words, why buy "indulgences" when you can get free indulgences by simply confessing Jesus and casting your sins on him.

---

41. Matthew 7:21.
42. James 2:14-20.

During the Middle Ages, Antinomianism had been kept alive by certain mystical sects, and after that by the Libertines, then the Familists, the Ranters, and the followers of Ann Hutchinson who was expelled from Boston and settled in Rhode Island, but was afterwards killed by Indians when she moved to Long Island.

Changes under the New Law of the Christian Covenant

While Paul was wrestling with the Antinomianists, Peter and the other apostles were making significant changes in the structure and ritual of the Church.

For forty days following his resurrection, Jesus had instructed the Apostles in the changes that were to be made. These instructions are not available for us to study, but it is clear from the decisive manner in which the Apostles immediately went about their labors, that they knew exactly what to do. For example:

1. As we have already pointed out, circumcision was no longer by "cutting in the flesh." It had been replaced by the precept of a purification or "circumcision of the heart."[43]

2. The first day of the week, as we have already noted, was celebrated as the sabbath in honor of the Savior's resurrection.[44]

3. Instead of blood sacrifices to memorialize the coming of the Savior, they partook of bread and wine to memorialize what had already taken place—that is, the suffering of Christ's body represented by the broken bread, and the spilling of his blood represented by the wine.[45]

4. The people no longer depended upon the synagogues for their worship service, but met in the homes of the people or in other accommodations when they were available.[46]

5. They no longer depended upon the rabbis or priests to preside over their services. An elder or bishop was installed over each of the congregations.[47]

---

43. Romans 2:28-29; Colossians 2:11; Philippians 3:3.

44. Acts 20:7; 1 Corinthians 16:2; Revelation 1:10.

45. Matthew 26:26; Luke 22:19; Mark 14:22-24; Acts 2:46; 1 Corinthians 11:23-29.

46. Acts 2:46; James L. Barker, Apostasy from the Divine Church, published by Kate Montgomery Barker, Salt Lake City, 1960, p. 72.

47. Hastings' Bible Dictionary, under "bishop."

6. They set up deacons in each congregation to minister to the needs of the poor.[48]

7. They conducted their affairs in each congregation and made all their appointments by common consent of the people.[49]

8. They functioned under a corps of officers who were different than the officers of the synagogues. These included apostles, prophets, seventies, bishops, evangelists, pastors, teachers, elders, and deacons.[50]

9. Spiritually speaking, they were not under the high priest or the Sanhedrin. The entire Church was governed by the central authority of the apostles.[51]

10. The worship services were very simple, without robes, ostentatious ceremonies, or pageantry.[52]

11. There was no paid ministry. Each of the disciples had his own occupation or craft. Peter, James and John were fishermen and practiced their craft after being called to be apostles.[53] Paul followed his occupation of tent maker after he became an apostle.[54] Paul said he had never taken up collections or sought money for himself.[55] Everyone assigned a duty in the church fulfilled it voluntarily as a godly service.

12. No person could perform ordinances, or function in leadership positions in the Church without first being called, approved by the congregation, and ordained by those holding the proper authority to do so.[56]

13. The women were organized for their mutual improvement and assisted the deacons in taking care of those in need.[57]

14. The elders administered to the sick, and many miracles constantly attended the ministry of the Apostles and other leaders who functioned under them.[58]

---

48. Hastings' Bible Dictionary, under "deacon."
49. Hastings' Bible Dictionary, "bishop"; Apostasy from the Divine Church, op. cit., pp. 100-101.
50. Ephesians 4:11-13; 1 Timothy 3:8; Philippians 1:1; Luke 9:10, Titus 1:5.
51. Acts 1:15-26; Ephesians 2:19; Barker, Apostasy from the Divine Church, op. cit., p. 97.
52. Barker, Apostasy from the Divine Church, op. cit., pp. 72-73.
53. John 21:1-3.
54. Acts 18:1-3.
55. Acts 20:33-34.
56. Hebrews 5:4; James 5:14.
57. John Laurence von Mosheim, Institutes of Ecclesiastical History, London: Longman, Brown, Green and Longman, 1850, 1:90.
58. James 5:14; Matthew 4:24; 10:8; Luke 9:2.

15. The people met together often to be instructed in the principles and doctrines of the New Covenant.[59]

Thus a whole new pattern of godly government of the people began to take shape.

Did the Early Christians Practice Communism?

As students of later generations tried to visualize the good life under Christianity, some of them gained the impression that the apostles practiced communism. This means giving up all private property and putting one's possessions in a common pool to be administered by the community leaders.

There are two passages in the New Testament which led some, including the Anabaptists, to conclude that this was what the apostles did. Here is the first passage:

> "And all that believed were together, and had all things common; and sold their possessions and goods, and parted them to all men, as every man had need." [60]

Taken by itself, this passage does indeed sound like the pooling of property and dividing it up among the people according to their various needs. However, what they actually did is more clearly stated in another passage:

> "And the multitude of them that believed were of one heart and of one soul: neither said any of them that ought of the things which he possessed was his own; but they had all things common." [61]

Here we have a declaration indicating the common effort was not a legal pooling of resources in a communal fund, but rather a feeling of unity in dealing with common *problems* so that no man *said* his possessions were his own but treated them as a stewardship from God which should be developed and used to help others as well as support himself and his family.

Our authority for this interpretation of these passages is the apostle Peter in the fifth chapter of Acts. Here is what happened.

The Case of Ananias and Sapphira

It appears that the apostles had asked the saints to exert a special effort to help take care of the poor. Ananias and his wife, Sapphira, decided to sell a

59. Barker, Apostasy from the Divine Church, op. cit., p. 272.
60. Acts 2:44-45.
61. Acts 4:32.

piece of their property and make a contribution. However, after they sold the property they decided to hold out some of the proceeds but tell Peter that the smaller amount was all they got from the sale.

Apparently the Spirit whispered to Peter that the contribution was being made under the pretense that this was all they were able to raise from the sale of the land. Now notice what Peter said:

> "While it [the property] remained, was it not thine own? and after it was sold, was it [the money] not in thine own power? why hast thou conceived this thing in thine heart? thou hast not lied unto men, but unto God." [62]

In other words, when Ananias and Sapphira became Christians they had never surrendered their legal rights to this property by placing it in a commune or turning it over to the apostles. Even though they became Christians the title to their property remained in their own names. If they wished to sell it and help the poor, so be it. But if they wanted to keep it, that was their privilege. After it was sold the money was theirs to contribute in part or in its entirety.

What got them into trouble was trying to deceive Peter by having him think they had contributed all they could get for some surplus land they had sold, when they were actually holding back a substantial amount. As Peter said to Ananias, "Thou hast not lied unto men, but unto God."

The Bible says that after Peter had chastised Ananias the poor man immediately passed over into the spirit world to meditate on what he had done. When his wife came and told the same story she immediately joined her husband. The scripture says the bodies of both of them were carried out. No doubt the word rapidly spread among the saints, "Don't lie to Peter!"

Peter's explanation of the relationship between the saints and their property helps us to understand Bible commentaries such as the following:

> "The Church of Jerusalem recognized the principle of private property. A disciple's property really was his own, but he did not say it was his; he treated it as if it were common property." [63]

The Stewardship Principle

This meant that a Christian looked upon his property, his skills and his time as a stewardship from God; and that these resources should be multiplied

62. Acts 5:4.
63. Dummelow's Bible Dictionary under "communism," New York: The Macmillan Company, 1961.

as Jesus had taught in the parable of the talents. Each person was to strive to provide for himself and his family and then share any excess with those in need. When these principles were practiced the Lord promised that it would not be long before they would have no poor among them.[64]

Topics for Reflection and Discussion

1. Can you list five of the changes which occurred in the Judeo-Christian religious practices after the death and resurrection of the Savior?

2. Would they continue to celebrate passover? Would there be any more blood sacrifices? What kind of sacrifice would replace it?

3. After Israel insulted God by worshipping a golden calf, what was the purpose of adding all the tedious rituals Paul called the "schoolmaster law"?

4. Why was so difficult for the Jewish people to give up the ritual of circumcision? Can this operation still be performed for non-ritual reasons?

5. What about changing the sabbath day? Did the Christians still celebrate their sabbath "every seventh day" even though they counted their "seventh day" from the day of the Savior's resurrection?

6. What is "antinomianism?" Do we still have it today? What did Paul say which led some of his listeners to misinterpret his meaning? What did James say to try and correct it?

7. Did the Christians continue synagogue worship? Who presided over each Christian congregation? Was there a paid ministry? How did leaders of the church earn a living?

8. What was necessary to perform ordinances in the church? How were the women organized?

9. Can you name four of the officers in the Christian Church which were different than Jewish officers at the Synagogue?

10. Did the early Christians practice communism? Describe the "stewardship" principle which was practiced among the Christians.

---

64. Acts 4:34-35; Deuteronomy 15:4.

CHAPTER EIGHT

Jesus Adds Many Significant Refinements to God's Law

Now we come to the essence of Christianity which the Founders embraced and encouraged as the spiritual foundation for the American civilization operating under God's law. As Thomas Jefferson said:

> "I hold the precepts of Jesus, as delivered by Himself, to be the most pure, benevolent and sublime which have ever been preached to man. I adhere to the principles of the first age, and consider all subsequent innovations as corruptions of His religion, having no foundation in what came from Him." [1]

Benjamin Franklin said:

> "I think with you, that nothing is of more importance for the public weal, than to form and train up youth in wisdom and virtue. Wise and good men are, in my opinion, the strength of the state; more so than riches or arms." [2]

Samuel Adams, often called "the father of the Revolution," said:

> "If we would most truly enjoy the gift of Heaven, let us become a virtuous people; then shall we both deserve and enjoy it. While, on the other hand, if we are universally vicious and debauched in our manners, though the form of our Constitution carries the face of the most exalted freedom, we shall in reality be the most abject slaves." [3]

At the conclusion of the Revolutionary War, George Washington wrote the following message to the governors of each state:

> "I now make it my earnest prayer that God would have you, and the state over which you preside, in his holy protection; that he would incline the hearts of the citizens … to entertain a brotherly affection and love for one another … and to dispose us all to do

1. Allison, The Real Thomas Jefferson, op. cit., p. 366.
2. A letter from Franklin to Samuel Johnson, August 23, 1750; see Skousen, The Five Thousand Year Leap, p. 45. (visit: *www.skousen2000.com)*.
3. Wells, The Life and Public Service of Samuel Adams, op. cit., 1:22-23.

justice, to love mercy, and to demean ourselves with that charity, humility, and pacific temper of mind which were the characteristics of the Divine Author of our blessed religion, and without an humble imitation of whose example in these things we can never hope to be a happy nation."[4]

Trying to Teach the Gospel to the Jewish People

As we mentioned in the previous chapter, the apostles were left with two heavy burdens when Jesus ascended into heaven. In fact, it appears that a good many of the forty days after his resurrection were taken up with instructions concerning these two burdens.

The first task was to help the Jewish Christians forsake the schoolmaster law which every Pharisee had been trained to obey to the utmost perfection from the time he was a child.

The second task was to get all Christians—both Jew and Gentile—to sublimate their lives according to the Sermon on the Mount.

This sermon was not the mere mouthing of pleasant platitudes, but a forthright declaration of the Lord's expectations concerning the improved behavior of his disciples as he carefully itemized the things he wanted them to do. Altogether, counting the Beatitudes and the Ten Commandments, there are many significant areas of improvement which Jesus specifically called upon his followers to practice and preach as the Christian way of life.[5]

Righteous Leaders Are Always in Short Supply

To have a virtuous people Jesus knew he had to have virtuous leaders, and therefore the Savior told his disciples that he was depending upon them to be the salt of the earth. But he said they had to be valiant for the long haul. They must never lose their savor.[6]

In this same spirit Jesus told his disciples that they have the capacity and responsibility to spread the Savior's light throughout the world; not only to spread truth and the great message of hope that comes through the preaching of the Gospel but they were to be brilliant examples of righteous living and continually radiate their influence for good.[7]

---

4. Jay A. Parry and Andrew M. Allison, The Real George Washington, Washington, D.C.: The National Center for Constitutional Studies, 1991, p. 723.
5. Skousen, Days of the Living Christ, op. cit., volume 1, chapters 13, 14 and 15.
6. Matthew 5:13.
7. Matthew 5:14-16.

The Two Great Commandments

The great umbrella of divine law is encompassed by just two commandments.

It will be recalled that the rabbis had codified all of the commandments of God into 613 laws. A lawyer tried to trick Jesus by asking him which was the greatest of all these laws. Jesus replied:

> "Hear, O Israel: the Lord our God is one Lord: and thou shalt love the Lord thy God with all thy heart and with all thy soul, and with all thy mind, and with all thy strength: this is the first commandment. And the second is like [unto it], namely, thou shalt love thy neighbour as thyself." [8]

The lawyer was amazed. Jesus took the first commandment from Deuteronomy 6:5 and the second commandment from Leviticus 19:18. The lawyer exclaimed:

> "Well, Master, thou hast said the truth!" [9]

Two Commandments Expanded into Ten

All the people were encouraged to memorize the Ten Commandments. The first four commandments refer to the relationship between man and God. In their abbreviated form they are as follows:

1. Thou shalt love the Lord thy God and have no other gods before him.
2. Thou shalt not worship or attribute God's power to images or false gods.
3. Oaths in the name of God shall not be taken in vain.
4. Keep the sabbath day holy.

The remaining six commandments refer to relationships between people. In their abbreviated form they are as follows:

5. Honor thy father and thy mother.
6. Thou shalt not kill.
7. Thou shalt not commit adultery.
8. Thou shalt not steal.

---

8. Mark 12:29-31.
9. Mark 12:32.

9. Thou shalt not lie.

10. Thou shalt not covet and concoct schemes to take away thy neighbor's possessions.

If there were no other laws than these, think what a heaven on earth mankind could have and enjoy by honoring and obeying these divine injunctions.

Jesus Elaborates on Two of the Most Serious Offenses

Down through the ages the two most abominable offenses that have led God's people into apostasy and debauchery have been murder and moral decadence.

Murder very often comes about through harsh words and bitter quarreling, therefore Jesus said:

> "Ye have heard that it was said by them of old time, Thou shalt not kill. … But I say unto you, that whosoever is angry with his brother without a cause shall be in danger of the judgment: and whosoever shall say to his brother, Raca [vain fellow], shall be in danger of the council: But whosoever shall say, Thou fool, shall be in danger of hell fire." [10]

Jesus is simply emphasizing that in a godly society people should restrain themselves from using vile or provocative language that can lead to a homicide.

Then Jesus continued:

> "Ye have heard that it was said by them of old time, Thou shalt not commit adultery: But I say unto you, That whosoever looketh on a woman to lust after her hath committed adultery with her already in his heart." [11]

The Sin of Bitter Grudges

Jesus emphasized that those who come to him with their offerings and petitions, but who have bitter feelings against someone, are mixed up in their priorities. Therefore he said:

10. Matthew 5:21-22.
11. Matthew 5:27-28.

> "If thou bring thy gift to the altar, and there rememberest that thy brother hath ought against thee; leave there thy gift before the altar, and go thy way; first be reconciled to thy brother and then come and offer thy gift." [12]

Love and harmony are the qualities of heaven. Where grudges are cultivated and contention is nurtured, Satan revels in a situation which he can foment into contention and hatred.

Jesus said regardless of who is in the wrong, a righteous man will endeavor to restore harmony. If this fails, the Savior provided a procedure to get help from his brethren. If that fails, the curse of heaven rests upon the offender and he will pay in the next world "to the uttermost farthing." [13]

The Problem of Unrighteous Relatives and Friends

There is an old saying that "to get along you go along." However, Jesus knew the corrupting influence of one bad apple in the barrel and what it can do to a group of youths, to the members of a family, or even to close friends.

Jesus therefore talked about a right eye that becomes offensive or a right hand that offends. We now have a revised text which says:

> "And a man's hand is his friend and his foot also, and a man's eye, are they of his own household." [14]

Jesus goes on to say in another place that if a person has striven to help rebellious and unrighteous friends—or even relatives—who do not respond, the association should be terminated.[15]

The Sanctity of Marriage

The marriage relationship is of supreme importance to God. Not only is the family the nuclear unit of society but the sacred relationship between a husband and wife as "one flesh" has singular significance to the Lord.

Jesus said that because of the hardness of the hearts of the men in the days of Moses, an allowance was made for a bill of divorcement under certain conditions.[16] Nevertheless, divorce often creates far more problems than the parties would ever have guessed.

---

12. Matthew 5:23-24.
13. Matthew 5:26.
14. JST Matthew 18:9; see Skousen, Days of the Living Christ, op. cit., 1:249-250.
15. Ibid., p. 250.
16. Mark 10:2-6.

Jesus said as far as he was concerned, the only basis for a divorce should be adultery or fornication.[17] This sends the signal to married couples that the Lord wants them to work out their problems together if at all possible.

It is interesting that in all of the Savior's discussions about marital problems, Jesus puts the responsibility of working out a solution on the shoulders of the husband.[18]

But sometimes, even with the most strenuous patience and industry, the relationship does not work out. Therefore, the same God who said what he has joined together, "let no man divide asunder," also said to those in authority:

> "Whatsoever thou shalt loose on earth shall be loosed in heaven." [19]

Oath-taking and Profanity

From the beginning the Lord has made the taking of an oath very sacred because an oath is taken in the name of God. This commandment not only applies to sacred oaths or holy covenants but it is applicable where we swear to tell the truth in court, or when an oath is administered to those who are sworn into high and important offices. In the eyes of God an oath is not only very sacred, but God commands that it shall not be taken in vain.[20]

In the days of the Savior the Jewish people were accustomed to using oaths in their commercial transactions or to emphasize a casual commitment.

They would swear by the earth, or the heavens, by the heart or the head certifying that a particular product was of a certain quality or value, or that a specific service would be performed. It was this kind of swearing or oath-taking that led Jesus to say, "Swear not at all." [21] He said secular endorsements should simply be "Yea, Yea" and "Nay, Nay." [22]

Jesus was also concerned about speech pollution. This is acquiring the habit of replacing yea, yea, and nay, nay with expletives in the form of swearing, obscenities, or profanity. On one occasion Jesus emphasized his own feelings when he said:

> "But those things which proceed out of the mouth come forth from the heart; and they defile the man." [23]

17. Matthew 5:31-32.
18. See for example, Matthew 5:31-32.
19. Matthew 16:19.
20. Exodus 20:7.
21. Matthew 5:34.
22. Matthew 5:37.
23. Matthew 15:18.

He Who Hurts Shall Be Hurt Unless He Provides Full Satisfaction to His Victim.

This is the famous concept of "an eye for an eye, a tooth for a tooth," etc. In previous chapters we have provided a full explanation of this system of achieving justice through reparation to the victim (see page 66, and *Eye for an Eye* in *The Statutes–A List of God's Laws*, page 583-584). The dynamic piston rod behind this system of justice is the threat of the offender being injured in the same manner that he has injured his victim unless he makes full "satisfaction" or reparation.

This is a marvelous method of eliminating torts (an injury for which a civil action can be brought) and crimes in a very short time. It is recorded that the desire of some people to commit crimes may still remain but when they see what happens to them, "they stand more still." [24]

The Most Difficult of All the Commandments—Love Thine Enemy

There are four commandments in the Sermon on the Mount that defy the most rudimentary aspects of human nature. They might be lumped together under the general heading of "Love your enemies!" Individually, they are as follows:

1. "Whosoever shall smite thee on the right cheek, turn to him the other also." [25]
2. "Bless them that curse you." [26]
3. "Do good to them that hate you." [27]
4. "Pray for them that despitefully use you, and persecute you." [28]

It is indeed contrary to every instinct in human nature to be indifferent to injury, but the goal of a Christian relationship is peace, love, and harmony. Jesus was talking about the heart of this relationship when he said: "Blessed are the peacemakers for they shall be called the children of God." [29]

---

24. W. Cleon Skousen, "God's Covenant People," a speech given on December 18, 1991, copy in posession of the author.
25. Matthew 5:39.
26. Matthew 5:44.
27. Ibid.
28. Ibid.
29. Matthew 5:9.

To successfully bring about peace between enemies is God's goal, and cultivating this high level of human refinement is a supreme achievement in the eyes of God. Furthermore, the rewards and blessings match the effort.

When I was a young boy I told my father I found that I couldn't keep this commandment of loving my enemies. He replied: "Well, it's hard—even for prophets and apostles. But keep on trying."

Three Kinds of Enemies

The dictionary describes an enemy as one who cherishes harmful designs against another, one who is hostile or extremely unfriendly, a declared opponent or adversary, an assailant, a backbiter, a slanderer, a military antagonist, a stiff competitor, or a traitor.

Perhaps we could classify "enemies" in three groups.

The First Group

First, there is the human relations enemy. This is the most common kind. Such an enemy may arise from a personality conflict, an off-hand, unkind remark, spreading of gossip or tale-bearing, perceiving the individual as being a social or business threat, perhaps mutual resentment because of adverse political views or even different religious views.

This type of "enemy" can be approached with some act of kindness or friendship easier than the next two groups. Sometimes it simply requires getting better acquainted to make the hostile barrier diminish and eventually disappear. Watching for an opportunity to do a favor for an adversary nearly always alleviates tensions and opens doors for better relations. Seeking to develop a true sense of understanding and love can bring some surprising results.

The Second Group

The next group is more challenging. This is where you or your family have suffered a significant injury. The injury may be physical, economic, or even an injury to one's position in a profession or social status. Even wanting to love this kind of enemy takes a lot of prayer and introspection. But since this problem arises in every neighborhood or community, the Lord has suggested the following procedure to see if the feelings of those who have been injured can be resolved. The Savior said:

> "Moreover if thy brother shall trespass against thee, go and tell him his fault between thee and him alone: if he shall hear thee, thou hast gained thy brother.
>
> "But if he will not hear thee, then take with thee one or two more, that in the mouth of two or three witnesses every word may be established.
>
> "And if he shall neglect to hear them, tell it unto the church: but if he neglect to hear the church, let him be unto thee as an heathen man and a publican." [30]

Although this three-step attempt to reach or placate someone who has been an offender does not always work, it succeeds often enough to make the effort worthwhile.

The Third Group

Finally, we come to the third and most difficult group of all. These are the wretched wicked. They are the enemies of the community, sometimes preying upon the whole society.

This type of enemy is in a mental state of anarchy and revolt. We call it the criminal mind. This type of person enjoys his or her greatest satisfaction in getting away with deceit and treachery.

This type of enemy does not respond to kindness or love the way both of the other groups usually do. This last group considers kindness a weakness that deserves to be exploited by the criminal. To gain the love or even respect from this kind of enemy requires a different approach.

Professional penologists have learned that the criminal mind must first discover certain strict and undeviating barriers beyond which he or she cannot go. The criminal must discover that he or she cannot go beyond these limits without inviting serious consequences. This is called establishing fixed parameters with visible firmness.

The next step is to establish a sense of fairness—a feeling that he or she is being treated fairly even though the program is administered with firmness. The incorrigible criminal may not respond to the firmness-fairness therapy, but the majority do. Once the criminal has demonstrated a desire to cooperate and get back on track, then the element of love and kindness can be carefully administered in measured doses.

---

30. Matthew 18:15-17.

However, at no time must the criminal get the impression you feel sorry for him or her. Nor must the criminal get the impression that you accept any kind of excuse for what happened. It is very important that the offender face up to what was done. The Lord calls it "confession of sins." Penologists call it "reality therapy."

So we learn from the Lord what he means by loving our enemies. We must love them enough to want to help them. We must pray for them, and work with them. However, there is no requirement that we drown them with love. Wisdom must be used. Love is a very sacred and precious attribute and it must be administered carefully and wisely. It must not be cheapened or squandered. The best kind of love is reciprocal love, and this is the ultimate goal—to change an enemy into a loving friend.

Concerning Alms Giving

Jesus continually emphasized the need to be sensitive to the needs of the poor. He said:

> "Give to them that asketh thee, and from him that would borrow of thee turn not thou away."[31]

Of course, generosity must necessarily be tempered with prudence, and a person can neither lend nor give that which he does not already possess. Nevertheless, the Lord wanted those who loved him to be as generous as circumstances and good judgment permit. He also had another suggestion:

> "When thou doest alms, let … thine alms … be in secret: and thy Father which seeth in secret himself shall reward thee openly."[32]

Concerning Prayer

Jesus had three suggestions concerning prayer which need no explanation. For example:

1. Use the Lord's prayer as a pattern. Jesus said, "After this manner therefore pray ye."[33]
2. Pray in secret and the Lord will reward you openly.[34]
3. "When ye pray, use not vain repetitions."[35]

31. Matthew 5:42.
32. Matthew 6:3-4.
33. Matthew 6:9-13.
34. Matthew 6:6.
35. Matthew 6:7.

CONCERNING FASTING

Fasting is not a ceremony or an ordinance, but it is—in a manner of speaking—a "sacrifice." By going without food or water for a period of time and enduring both thirst and hunger it demonstrates in a physical way how much a blessing is needed or wanted. That is why fasting for spiritual purposes is always associated with prayer.

The duration of fasting is usually for twenty-four hours but forty-eight hours is the limit recommended by physicians. Long fasts such as that of Moses, Elijah and the Savior for forty days and forty nights require a "quickening" of the body by spiritual means through the Lord. In the absence of divine intervention, a person will begin to become delirious after seven days and after twelve days of fasting the consequence may be death.

Jesus wanted to emphasize that fasting is designed as a witness to the Lord. Therefore it is a form of hypocrisy if a person is fasting as proof of his or her piety. Therefore Jesus said:

> "Moreover when ye fast, be not, as the hypocrites, of a sad countenance: for they disfigure their faces, that they may appear unto men to fast. Verily I say unto you, they have their reward.
>
> "But thou, when thou fastest, anoint thine head, and wash thy face; that thou appear not unto men to fast, but unto thy Father which is in secret: and thy Father, which seeth in secret, shall reward thee openly."[36]

FORGIVING TRESPASSES

An important part of Christianity is forgiving one another. Therefore Jesus said:

> "If ye forgive men their trespasses, your heavenly Father will also forgive you. But if ye forgive not men their trespasses, neither will your Father forgive your trespasses."[37]

CONCERNING OUR TREASURES

God knows his children better than they know themselves, therefore he knew that one of the greatest satisfactions of life would be striving to achieve certain goals or attain certain things. These become our treasures. But earthly treasures are never long lasting nor secure. Therefore Jesus said:

36. Matthew 6:16-18.
37. Matthew 6:14-15.

> "Lay not up for yourselves treasures upon earth, where moth and rust doth corrupt, and where thieves break through and steal. But lay up for yourselves treasures in heaven, where neither moth nor rust doth corrupt, and where thieves do not break through nor steal. For where your treasure is, there will your heart be also."[38]

In another place Jesus said:

> "No man can serve two masters: for either he will hate the one, and love the other; or else he will hold to the one, and despise the other. Ye cannot serve God and mammon."[39]

He was simply saying, "Keep your priorities straight!"

What about "Take Ye No Thought of the Morrow"?

When Jesus gave his Sermon on the Mount to his disciples and twelve apostles he was talking to those who would be giving their full time to the service of the Lord. To these he said,

> "Therefore I say unto you, Take no thought for your life, what ye shall eat, or what ye shall drink; nor yet for your body, what ye shall put on … Your heavenly Father knoweth that ye have need of all these things. But seek ye first the kingdom of God, and his righteousness; and all these things shall be added unto you."[40]

However, when he came down from the mount the following day and gave practically the same sermon (called the Sermon on the Plain) he did not say this to the general membership of his followers.

It is this writer's feeling that the admonition to "take no thought of the morrow" is for the Savior's full-time servants and not the rest of his followers who would perish if they did not prepare for the morrow. In fact, they wouldn't even be able to help take care of the Lord's servants who might have to depend on the kindness of God's saints for their sustenance.

Judging Others

The scriptures concerning judging others is equated with "condemning" others. Most of the time we frail human beings tend to do this without having all the facts. But even if we did, Jesus said:

---

38. Matthew 6:19-21.
39. Matthew 6:24.
40. Matthew 6:25-33.

> "Judge not, that ye be not judged. For with what judgment ye judge, ye shall be judged: and with what measure ye mete, it shall be measured to you again."[41]

The Golden Rule

And now we come to the most perfect yet simple rule for Godly conduct ever devised. We often call it the Golden Rule. Jesus said:

> "Therefore all things whatsoever ye would that men should do to you, do ye even so to them: for this is the law and the prophets."[42]

This rule requires the most vigorous self-discipline. It is not an easy rule by which to live, but of all the rules it is the most rewarding. Any person who masters this mode of life is living on the level of the prophets of God.

The Broad Way and the Narrow Way

There are two roads that stand open before every human being of accountable age. Jesus made it very clear which road he hoped we would choose. He said:

> "Enter ye in at the strait gate: for wide is the gate, and broad is the way, that leadeth to destruction, and many there be which go in thereat: because strait is the gate, and narrow is the way, which leadeth unto life, and few there be that find it."[43]

Strive for Perfection

Only one person ever achieved perfection after the manner of our Heavenly Father, and that was the Savior himself. As the apostle Peter said:

> "Who did no sin, neither was guile found in his mouth."[44]

But the rest of us must strive toward that perfection as we go through mortal life. Jesus said:

> "Be ye therefore perfect, even as your Father which is in heaven is perfect."[45]

---

41. Matthew 7:1-2.
42. Matthew 7:12.
43. Matthew 7:13-14.
44. 1 Peter 2:22.
45. Matthew 5:48.

We take comfort from the fact that even the apostle Paul who was magnificently valiant had to confess that the struggle to perfect himself was indeed great. He said:

> "What I hate, that do I… The good that I would I do not: but the evil which I would not, that I do." [46]

Paul's message is simple: "Keep trying!"

THE HOUSE BUILT ON ROCK AND THE HOUSE BUILT ON SAND

Jesus concluded his sermon with the parable of the two houses. Concerning them, he said:

> "Therefore whosoever heareth these sayings of mine, and doeth them, I will liken him unto a wise man, which built his house upon a rock. And the rain descended, and the floods came, and the winds blew, and beat upon that house; and it fell not: for it was founded upon a rock.
>
> "And every one that heareth these sayings of mine, and doeth them not, shall be likened unto a foolish man, which built his house upon the sand. And the rain descended, and the floods came, and the winds blew, and beat upon that house; and it fell: and great was the fall of it." [47]

To follow God's commandments the best we can and keep the example of Jesus Christ central to our lives, is building on the rock. To a remarkable degree the founders built their lives on this rock and left our nation a fabulous legacy.

46. Romans 7:15-19.
47. Matthew 7:26-27.

Topics for Reflection and Discussion

1. Based on the quotations at the beginning of this chapter, how would you describe the feelings of the Founders toward the teachings of Jesus?

2. What are the two greatest commandments? Can you recite an abbreviated version of each of the Ten Commandments? In what way do you think it poisons a personality to carry bitter grudges? What is the ultimate objective of God insofar as human relations are concerned?

3. Based on the teachings of Jesus, what would help reduce the high rate of divorce? Why do you think Jesus puts the principal responsibility for maintaining the integrity of the marriage on the husband?

4. What did you learn from the discussion of the ancient law of "an eye for an eye and a tooth for a tooth?" How would the "law of reparation" curb crime and violence today?

5. Can you think of an incident where you were able to turn an enemy into a friend? Give your analysis of the way penologists try to straighten out confirmed criminals.

6. Have you ever helped the needy "in secret" ? On a scale of one to ten, how would you rate yourself on the practice of regular prayer? Do you sometimes find yourself using "vain repetitions" ?

7. Under what circumstances did Jesus say, "take no thought of the morrow" ? Did this apply to anyone other than those called into the top level of the Savior's ministry?

8. Why do you think there is a psychological satisfaction in condemning or judging others? When you are about to condemn someone do you have any mental device to help you postpone it until you get more facts?

9. Although we strive for constant perfection in our lives, what did Paul say by way of comfort when we find ourselves falling short of the mark?

10. Tell the parable of the two houses with which Jesus closed the Sermon on the Mount.

CHAPTER NINE

The Founders Search the Bible for the Keys to a Happy and Abundant Life

God's covenant society was specifically designed for happy and abundant living.

For each inhabitant it offers the essential ingredients for a life of freedom, prosperity, and peace. However, it obligated each citizen to honor, sustain, and promote a strict adherence to the values and inspired guidelines revealed by God for happy living. As the entire history of Israel demonstrates, it all begins with a virtuous people. That would be as true in modern times as it was during the previous five thousand years. As Isaiah warned the Israelites of his day:

> "There is no peace, saith the Lord, unto the wicked."[1]

In this chapter we will discuss many aspects of God's Law of the Covenant which provided exceptional promises to Israel. It included the promise that if they continued in righteousness, they could develop a divine commonwealth—called Zion—and become the most powerful, wealthy and blessed nation in the world. Let us remind ourselves once more of the Lord's promise:

> "Now, therefore, if ye will obey my voice indeed, and keep my covenant, then ye shall be a peculiar treasure unto me *above all people*: for all the earth is mine: and ye shall be unto me a kingdom of priests, and an holy nation."[2]

Just before the end of his mortal life, Moses reiterated the Lord's promise which is recorded as follows:

> "Wherefore it shall come to pass, if ye hearken to these judgments, and keep, and do them, that the Lord thy God shall keep unto thee the covenant and the mercy which he sware unto thy fathers:
>
> "And he will love thee, and bless thee, and multiply thee ... Thou shalt be blessed *above all people*."[3]

1. Isaiah 48:22.
2. Exodus 19:5-6.
3. Deuteronomy 7:12-14.

As we examine the numerous advantages of this Zion culture under the Law of the Covenant, there will be some supporting principles that apply in many different areas. It will therefore be understood why some of these need to be repeated as we discuss these various categories.

We will first discuss the advantages of citizenship in a nation living under the Law of the Covenant.

Citizenship under God's Law

A citizen of this commonwealth had a permanent inheritance in the land. If he had no inheritance the policy was to loan him money without interest and otherwise assist him until he became established.

Another great advantage of citizenship under the law of the covenant was the fact that no citizen could lose his land by taxation. No taxes were assessed against land.

A citizen could vote for the election of officers at all levels of the tribe or region to which he belonged.[4]

A citizen was entitled to full protection of his life, his property, and his rights, by an elaborate system of judicial officers.[5]

A System of Private Social Security

God's law was structured in such a way that social security was a private matter which revolved around the structure of the family.

It commenced with the owning of a home free and clear, and the acquisition of land as a permanent inheritance of the whole family. As the family expanded, so did its holdings. Within two or three generations, the immediate family was sufficiently secure in its financial stability to take care of any who were sick, disabled, temporarily unemployed, or old enough to retire. Until a family group was capable of sustaining its group needs, the burden was shared by the immediate community.

As with all insurance or security programs, this method was designed to "share the risks." Furthermore, by keeping the administration of the system within the family or community circle, there were few or very minimal overhead expenses, and funds appropriated for the benefit of the needy or the elderly went directly to those for whom it was intended. It did not have to pass

4. Deuteronomy 1:13-15.
5. Deuteronomy 1:16-17.

through numerous layers of bureaucratic distribution as required by a national or state social security system.

Family members and neighbors were also close enough to the recipients to observe any deliberate malingering or payments going to the disabled after they had recovered. No doubt this was the most efficient system of monitoring social services ever devised.

There was also a strict rule against laziness, and refusal to do one's fair share. Paul set forth the Lord's law when he wrote:

> "For even when we were with you, this we commanded you, that if any would not work, neither should he eat."[6]

The War Against Poverty

The ultimate goal of a godly society is to eventually achieve a dynamic economy with a well-trained constituency so that all can have an opportunity to work and become self-sustaining. In other words, the goal is to eventually attain the full maturity of a Zion society. The Lord said it would be when "there shall be no poor among you."[7]

But until that goal is attained, the Law of the Covenant set forth many provisions designed to ameliorate the conditions of the poor. It also provided positive programs to lift the poor substantially above the poverty level.

First of all, the poor could not be trapped in a syndrome of permanent debt. Every seventh year all debts were forgiven whether a person were poor or not. It was called "the year of release."[8]

Second, any poor person who had to borrow from his more affluent neighbors or relatives was not charged interest.[9]

Third, the farmers were required to leave corners of their fields and the gleaning of their crops to the poor. The same was true of the orchards and vineyards. The final picking of the fruit was to be left to the energetic poor to harvest.[10]

The Founders recognized that while this provision was primarily for an agrarian society, it laid down the guidelines of generosity and sharing which would assist the needy in any society.

---

6. 2 Thessalonians 3:10.
7. Deuteronomy 15:4.
8. Deuteronomy 15:1-3, 9-12; 31:10.
9. Exodus 22:25.
10. Leviticus 19:9-10.

Fourth, at least once in every generation there was a fifty-year Jubilee when all landed property was returned to its original owners. Thus, a poor family that had fallen on hard times and was compelled to lease their landed inheritance, might suddenly find itself in very favorable circumstances.[11]

Fifth, the poor were not supposed to be left to fight their battle for survival alone. Every person living under God's law knew that he or she had a special obligation to seek out and help the poor.[12]

The War Against Ignorance

Under the Law of the Covenant the primary responsibility for the education of children was placed on the parents. And it was to be a continuous system of training by day and by night:

> "And ye shall teach them [eternal truths] diligently unto thy children, and shalt talk of them when thou sittest in thine house, and when thou walkest by the way, when thou liest down, and when thou risest up." [13]

There was nothing casual about this responsibility to teach the children correct principles.

The teaching was also to include the historical background for the commandments, policies, and rituals which God required of the people.[14]

The Example of the Jews

Up until a child was six years of age, he or she was taught the basics of reading and writing in the home. The next six years were spent in training at the local synagogue under the Levite priests. The maximum number of students in one class was 25. Until the age of 10 no text book was studied except the scriptures themselves. Everyone was to know both the statutes and the commandments as well as the Bible stories which gave substance and meaning to the culture of the people.

It was in this spirit that William Holmes McGuffey wrote his six *McGuffey Readers* for American children beginning in 1836. This series became the most influential set of basic readers in the history of U.S. education. By the early twentieth century over 120,000,000 copies of these books had been used

11. Leviticus 25:9-10.
12. Leviticus 25:35; Deuteronomy 15:7-11.
13. Deuteronomy 6:7.
13. Deuteronomy 6:20-25.

to instruct four generations of Americans. The Bible, together with stories about morality and virtue were the central core of these readers.

At the age of twelve, the Jewish boys were taken to Jerusalem at one of the feasts and tested by one of the doctors of the law. When Jesus was examined he amazed the learned doctors, and he remained in Jerusalem three days conversing with them. His parents finally located him "sitting in the midst of the doctors, both hearing him and asking him questions. And all that heard him were astonished at his understanding and answers." [15]

National Defense

Moses was told to set up the military service so that it would be counted a great honor to serve in its ranks.

Battalions were formed from each of the twelve tribes which would make each contingent anxious to uphold the honor of its particular tribe.[16]

Then the purging began.[17]

All who were just completing their houses were sent home.

All who were just getting their vineyards planted were sent home.

All who had just recently married were sent home.

All who were the least bit faint-hearted or fearful about fighting were sent home.

Thus was the military defense of Israel forged into a blade of steel. As one of my students at the University exclaimed:

"Man, that only leaves the Marines!"

Nevertheless, all of those who returned home were part of the reserve to be called up if necessary. In fact every adult male over the age of 20 was subject to being called up if necessary. When Moses marched out of Egypt he numbered all of the men over 20 who were available for defense in case of attack, and found that the total was 603,550.[18]

This did not include the tribe of Levi. Because of their assignment in the civil service as well as the ministry, they were exempted from military duty.[19]

14. Luke 2:46-47.
15. Numbers, chapter 1.
16. Deuteronomy 20:5-8.
17. Numbers 1:46.
18. Numbers 1:47-50.

The Civil Service

There was one field which was completely unique to the culture of Israel. That was the national civil service.

Originally, the eldest son of every family was consecrated to the service of the Lord and the civil service of the nation.[20] Later the Lord assigned both of these tasks to the entire tribe of Levi.[21] They replaced the firstborn of the other tribes.[22]

The Founders recognized that a modern society would have to open the ranks of civil service to all applicants who could qualify. Nevertheless, they liked the idea of looking upon public service as a response to godly duty whether in the civil service or the ranks of the military.

Taxation

God's law provided three rules for the equitable taxation of the people.

1. The tax was directly related to the increased wealth of the individual. It consisted of a tithe or 10% of the "increase" of each individual,[23] and this ratio could not be changed to benefit the poor or denigrate the rich. It was a straight flat tax of 10% with no loopholes. Based on what a person made, he paid. God held each person individually responsible for the payment of an honest tithe. When the people held back or failed to pay an honest tithe, the prophet of that generation accused them of "robbing God."[24]

2. The tithe was levied against increased income only. That means an increase of herds, increase of grains, and an increase by means of wages or other income such as rents, or sale of goods. This left all property, both real and personal, free of all taxation and therefore free from confiscation by the government. Of course, if real estate or personal property, such as land, houses, jewels, clothing, etc. were sold, there would be a tithe on the profits.

3. One tenth of the tithe went to the Levites for collecting it.[25] The remainder represented the maximum the government could spend. This required the government to live within its income because it could not increase the taxes or initiate new taxes. The only way the government income could

19. Exodus 13:2; 22:29.
20. Numbers 3:12-13.
21. Numbers 8:18.
22. Deuteronomy 14:22; 2 Chronicles 31:5.
23. Malachi 3:8-18.
24. Numbers 18:26.

be increased was by adopting policies that would increase the income of the people.

The Money System

The Founding Fathers intended to use the same medium of exchange as that which was used under God's law. As the Constitution states in Article I, Section 9, paragraph 1:

> "No state shall… make anything but gold and silver coin a tender in payment of debts."

Today the people of the United States are extremely vulnerable because the present monetary system is operating in direct violation of this constitutional provision.

The Founders wanted the monctary system of the United States based on precious metals because they have an intrinsic value which fluctuates slightly—depending on the market—but less than any other commodity.

So far as we know, precious metals were always exchanged in terms of weight and purity. Eventually, coins of certified value were used to facilitate transactions.

The Law of the Covenant required that weights and measures must be honest. Therefore the Lord declared:

> "Ye shall do no unrighteousness in judgment, in meteyard, in weight, or in measure.
>
> "Just balances, just weights… shall ye have: I am the Lord your God."[26]

Lending

God's law makes a distinction between lending for commercial purposes, and lending to a person in desperate need. The scripture says:

> "And if thy brother be waxen poor, and fallen in decay … thou shalt relieve him …."[27]

Then it goes on to say:

---

25. Leviticus 19:35-36.
26. Leviticus 25:35.

> "If thou lend money to any of my people that is poor by thee, thou shalt not be to him as an usurer, neither shalt thou lay upon him usury [interest]." [28]

The Lord's restriction against charging interest is always in connection with loans to the poor. If a person wanted a loan for investment purposes, interest could be charged.

But in either case, the lender must keep in mind that the financial cycle under the Lord's law was every seven years, and on the seventh year all outstanding debts were wiped out.[29] However, this did not apply to a "foreigner," meaning a person who was not under the covenant.[30]

Employer-Employee Relations

Under the Law of the Covenant, the Lord holds employers responsible for the way they treat their employees:

> "Ye shall not therefore oppress one another; but thou shalt fear thy God." [31]
>
> "Thou shalt not rule over him with rigor; but thou shalt fear thy God." [32]

In both of these verses the emphasis is on the responsibility of the employer not only to his hired hands but to the Lord who will hold him accountable for the way he treats his employees.

There is a special word of caution to an employer who has workers who are poor and could easily be imposed upon because of their urgent necessity to keep a job:

> "Thou shalt not oppress an hired servant that is poor and needy, whether he be of thy brethren, or of thy strangers that are in thy land within thy gates.
>
> "At [the end of] his day thou shalt give him his hire, neither shall the sun go down upon it; for he is poor, and setteth his heart upon it: lest he cry against thee unto the Lord, and it be sin unto thee." [33]

---

27. Exodus 22:25; Deuteronomy 23:19.
28. Deuteronomy 31:10.
29. Deuteronomy 15:3.
30. Leviticus 25:17.
31. Leviticus 25:43.
32. Deuteronomy 24:14-15.

The advantage of these high standards for the worker was the fact that if he felt abused, or treated unfairly he could immediately present his case to the captain or judge having jurisdiction over the ten families to which he belonged. If he did not gain satisfaction he could appeal his case to the captain or judge of fifty, and after that to the captain or judge of one hundred who was usually over the immediate community.

It can be readily seen that a remedy was available to the worker without the necessity of a labor union.

Vacations

An important aspect of the abundant life under the Law of the Covenant was the fact that the people took time to enjoy themselves. They worked hard, but they took time at frequent intervals to rest from their labors, mingle with their families and friends, and enrich their spirits, minds and bodies.

It was traditional, of course, to rest every seventh day which was the sabbath.

Then, three times a year there were great feasts at the national capital in Jerusalem. Each of these feasts lasted a week. One was held in the spring, one in the summer, and one in the fall. On these occasions the people congregated together to renew their covenants at the temple, exchange news, make new acquaintances, and renew old ones. These were religious feasts but very festive celebrations.

Every seventh year, the entire population went on vacation for the entire year. Careful preparations of food, clothing and other supplies were laid up in store so that this special year would be long remembered. It was traditional to make this year a long season of special activities, doing the things they didn't ordinarily get to do. And in between there were days of complete relaxation.

After all of this the message to the Founders was simply that a well-ordered society under God's law was designed for a happy people with warm, satisfying human relations and abundant living.

Business Ethics

The competitive nature of business often leads individuals to excuse unethical tactics on the basis that it is all part of the game. They say, "I know this is wrong, but that's business!"

Here is what the Lord had to say:

> "Thou shalt not defraud thy neighbour." [34]

> "Ye shall do no unrighteousness in judgment, in meteyard, in weight, or in measure. Just balances, just weights, a just ephah, and a just hin, shall ye have." [35]

> "Thou shalt not have in thy bag divers weights, a great and a small … But thou shalt have a perfect and just weight, a perfect and just measure shalt thou have: that thy days may be lengthened in the land which the Lord thy God giveth thee. For all that do such things, and all that do unrighteously, are an abomination unto the Lord thy God." [36]

And God expected the judges to enforce the statutes against such rascals.

The Administration of Justice

Just to round out our discussion of the free and abundant society, let us summarize what we have already covered concerning the administration of justice.

There were two remarkable things about the administration of justice under the Law of the Covenant.

First, there was the policy of attaining true justice by demanding reparation to the victim. Fines and punitive damages did not go to the government, but to the person who had suffered injury or whose property had been damaged.

Secondly, there were many offenses which were destructive to the Zion society and therefore carried the death penalty. The reason for this was not the desire to inflict capital punishment for such relatively minor offenses, but to give the judges the means to force the offender to either reform or go into voluntary exile. In other words, if the culprit did not improve his ways, the judges could threaten his life so that he would leave the covenant society and go out to live with people whose lifestyle was more compatible with his own. It was simply a question of repentance or flight into exile. The probability is that in most cases the culprit would agree to mend his ways since exile would not only mean taking up an abode among strangers, but losing his portion of the family inheritance.

---

33. Leviticus 19:13.
34. Leviticus 19:35-36.
35. Deuteronomy 25:13-15.

By using this procedure, it provided an automatic self-cleansing device so that the covenant society would not lose the great promises which God had made to this people.

Under God's Law there was a strong emphasis on the high quality of those chosen to be judges. Moses was told:

> "Thou shalt provide out of all the people able men, such as fear God, men of truth, hating covetousness; and place such over them to be rulers ... And let them judge the people at all seasons." [37]

The judges were to be "wise men, and understanding, and known among your tribes." [38] This was so that they would have the confidence of the people.

The judges were to make decisions only after they had conducted a thorough investigation.[39]

Moses gave special instructions to the judges, saying:

> "Hear the causes between your brethren, and judge righteously between every man and his brother, and the stranger that is with him. Ye shall not respect [favor] persons in judgment; but ye shall hear the small as well as the great; ye shall not be afraid of the face of man; for the judgment is God's; and the cause that is too hard for you, bring it unto me, and I will hear it." [40]

> "Thou shalt not wrest judgment; thou shalt not respect persons, neither take a gift: for a gift doth blind the eyes of the wise, and pervert the words of the righteous." [41]

It is interesting that under the law of the Covenant, justice was the responsibility of the judges not merely the pleading and oratory of trained lawyers.

The Founders' Hope

It was the hope of the Founders that they could adopt those things from the Law of the Covenant which would contribute to a free, happy, and prosperous society in our own day.

Some may think that the Law of the Covenant was too idealistic for the materialistic, secular age in which we live, but that is not what the prophets

36. Exodus 18:21-22.
37. Deuteronomy 1:13.
38. Deuteronomy 19:18.
39. Deuteronomy 1:16-17.
40. Deuteronomy 16:19.

of God have said. Somehow, these great principles under the Law of the Covenant are going to have their hour of power again. Speaking of the "latter days," the great Isaiah who was allowed to see 2,700 years of future events, predicted:

> "And it shall come to pass in the last days, that the mountain of the Lord's house shall be established in the top of the mountains … And many people shall go and say, Come ye, and let us go up to the mountain of the Lord, to the house of the God of Jacob; and he will *teach us of his ways, and we will walk in his paths:* for out of Zion shall go forth the law, and the word of the Lord from Jerusalem."[42]

As we saw in an earlier chapter, the Founders believed this "Zion" would be established in America and that in God's own time, all of this would come to pass.

41. Isaiah 2:2-3.

Topics for Reflection and Discussion

1. If ancient Israel had diligently applied the principles of a covenant society, do you believe it might have become the most powerful nation in the world? What are your reasons?

2. Under the Law of the Covenant, how did a family gradually expand its inheritance from generation to generation? What prevented some spendthrift from wasting away the inheritance?

3. What would be the main advantages of a private family social security system? Would each family own the assets of their group security system or would it belong to community? Was this system designed to take care of the sick? The poor? The disabled? The elderly? The homeless?

4. Describe the system of taxation under the Law of the Covenant. Was it fair? Who paid the most? Could the leaders increase the taxes? How could they increase the tax receipts?

5. List some of the unique features for the lending of money under the Law of the Covenant. How about loans to the poor? What distinction was made with loans to non-Israelites or "strangers" ?

6. How did the Law of the Covenant eliminate the need for labor unions? If a laborer felt abused or unfairly treated, to whom would he appeal? Would he begin with the captain of ten or go higher?

7. Under the administration of justice, why did many offenses allow for the death penalty? Was it used extensively or was it merely a threat to secure conformity with the law?

8. Did the justice system need a system of lawyers to plead cases for offenders? Who had the responsibility to investigate each case and see that justice was done?

9. List three of the major qualifications for judges as outlined for Moses. In what way would this improve the quality of justice today?

10. If we admit that the Law of the Covenant was too idealistic, do we also admit it was impossible to achieve? What were the feelings of the Founders?

CHAPTER TEN

How Could the Founders Be Certain That God's Law Is the Best System?

The Laws of Babylon and Greece

This author knows of nothing that will make a person appreciate God's law or the Law of the Covenant to a greater extent than wading through the miasma of laws and constitutions which the ancient nations tried to invent.

To appreciate the contrast between God's law and the meager contributions of struggling humankind during the subsequent centuries, it is instructive to note that the Law of the Covenant was rather simple. It did not attempt to deal with most of the millions of different situations which arise in human relations. It painted its pattern of government and laws with a broad brush and left the details of human adjustment to the good sense of the people.

However, common sense often fails the human family unless they constantly keep in mind the good advice of their Heavenly Father. Notice how much of the Law of the Covenant is not "law," but just good practical advice. For example. "Love thy neighbor as thyself," and "Honor thy father and thy mother," are not true "laws." There are no penalties attached. This means they are standards of moral value to enrich our judgment and good sense when dealing with difficult human relations. This is a fundamental key to good legislation: Don't legislate too much.

It has always been extremely impressive to this writer, how much the Law of the Covenant left out. It is as though God were saying, "You can work out the vast majority of your problems if you just keep a few guidelines in mind." For example:

Show your love for God by obeying his commandments.

Be patient with others who express differing views.

Ignore slights and minor offenses—turn the other cheek.

You can do much good by mingling among those who are not good. Be with the world, but not of the world.

As long as people are trying, forgive them—even seventy times seven, forgive.

The Law of the Covenant emphasizes that human beings are not saved by good works. Salvation comes as a free gift of God. Nevertheless, without good works God withholds the gift and mankind reaps cursings instead of blessings.

God's Law Was Designed for Good People

To sum it all up, the Law of the Covenant was not designed for wicked people. It was designed for God's people—and that includes every human being who is willing to live under God's law.

The American Founders understood this. They knew that "righteousness exalteth a nation." [1]

Let us repeat what we quoted a little earlier from three of the Founders. John Adams warned:

> "Our Constitution was made only for a moral and religious people. It is wholly inadequate to the government of any other." [2]

Benjamin Franklin was equally emphatic when he said:

> "Only a virtuous people are capable of freedom. As nations become corrupt and vicious, they have more need of masters." [3]

Then Samuel Adams added a warning:

> "Neither the wisest constitution nor the wisest laws will secure the liberty and happiness of a people whose manners are universally corrupt." [4]

As we examine the efforts of ancient legislators to use strict and complex laws to force the people to be peaceful and decent citizens, we recognize the wisdom of the Founders and the diadem of brilliant reality in Job which says "they that plow iniquity and sow wickedness, reap the same." [5]

This is why the Founders followed the formula of God's law or the Law of the Covenant. If the people establish in their minds the basic guidelines

1. Proverbs 14:34.
2. Howe, The Changing Political Thought of John Adams, op. cit., p. 189.
3. Smyth, The Writings of Benjamin Franklin, op. cit., 9:569.
4. Wells, The Life and Public Service of Samuel Adams, op. cit., 1:22.
5. Job 4:8.

revealed from heaven, then they can enjoy peace, prosperity and happiness under a system of fairly simple laws and a constitutional pattern of sound government painted with broad, bold strokes.

In ancient times, as we shall see, this inspired approach to political science was almost entirely lacking. They tried to use external force as a substitute for internal virtue.

The Babylonian Code of Hammurabi

Let us first look briefly at one of the most ancient systems of law—the one developed by the Babylonians. This was the code of Hammurabi who lived from approximately 1955 to 1913 B.C. and issued the Babylonian code while he was king.

Hammurabi was a contemporary of Abraham. In fact Abraham lived the early part of his life in Ur of the Chaldees, a district adjacent to Babylon.

We first notice that the code of Hammurabi contains a number of elements from the Law of the Covenant. Both Noah and Abraham apparently possessed the Law of the Covenant in its original form. We assume most of the ancient nations would have been inclined to borrow some of their ideas from the Law of the Covenant since Noah's early descendants were all trained under this system.

As with Israel, the people were divided into tens and hundreds, but there is no mention of the intermediate group of fifty families.

Hammurabi Borrowed Some of His Best Ideas from God's Law

The code of Hammurabi[6] allowed for a reparation of damages as did the Mosaic code. It also provided heavy penalties in punitive damages for theft, robbery, or embezzlement. Also, as in the Mosaic code, the damages and fines all went to the victim rather than to the state.

To escape the death penalty, a convicted defendant could flee into exile, and a false witness received as a punishment the same penalty he was trying to impose on the defendant with his perjured testimony. The sacred oath was also a prominent part of the judicial system. As in Israel, each person pled his own case. There were no professional lawyers. However, the judges had to

6. For a comprehensive discussion of Babylonian law under Hammurabi, see the Encyclopedia Britannica, op. cit., under "Babylonian Law," 3:116-120.

know every detail of the law so it could be appropriately applied to the facts as presented and proved by the offended party.

Then He Added the Dregs of Pagan Culture

In contrast to these elements which were in the Law of the Covenant, the code of Hammurabi contained many additional provisions which were cruel and discriminatory.

First of all, the system of government was not a genuine republic but an aristocratic monarchy. There was no attempt to establish equal rights or equal political status.

The penalties for crimes and torts were neither consistent nor logical. Punishment was harsh and severe. In fact, the thirty or more offenses which carried the death penalty were often for relatively minor offenses.

The death penalty was invoked for false witnesses in cases where the defendant was charged with a capital offense. The same penalty applied to a person who broke into the king's palace or one of the temples to steal. The same also went for kidnaping, burglary, receiving stolen goods, harboring fugitive slaves, encroachment on the king's highway, fraudulent sale of drink, disorderly conduct, inciting a riot, mal-practice of medicine, or being a "bad" wife. Death penalties were by hanging, drowning, burning, or strangulation.

In addition to those mentioned above, there were certain crimes for which a person's ear could be cut off for listening to false rumors or confidential information; an eye could be put out for seeing confidential documents. The tongue could be torn out for speaking about government secrets to unauthorized persons. The eye of a Peeping Tom could be put out for lascivious conduct. The fingers of a thief could be cut off, and the hand of a surgeon could be chopped off for an operation or ministration of medicine to a person who died.

Political Science in Early Greece

Over 1,300 years after Hammurabi, there began to be a movement among Greek intellectuals to build a more just and efficient system of government. Unfortunately their progress was in jerks and jumps, but at least they put their minds to the task.

Up until 621 B.C. the Greeks had no written laws. They had provincial customs, but these were administered loosely and arbitrarily by the hereditary chiefs.

However, when Draco became Archon or chief magistrate of Athens in 621, he determined to draft a code of elaborate written laws.[7]

Draco decided that from here on there would be no sin in Athens. He wrote up his code designed to put the people of Athens in behavioral straight jackets. Furthermore, he felt it was the greatest affront to his personal dignity and the honor of Athens for a citizen to breach this code. To make sure the code would work he had just one punishment for all violators—death!

This meant that a man who was guilty of idleness, or stealing a cabbage or an apple, received the same punishment as someone who had committed murder. But the fear of being killed for the slightest offense virtually paralyzed any wrongdoing in Athens.

But Draco came to a very sad end. When wrongdoing of every kind disappeared overnight, the people began to think he had performed a miracle. As a result, when he appeared in the Athenian theater, there was such a rush to cover him with cloaks, robes, hats, and flowers that he was smothered to death![8]

But at least Draco added a new word to our vocabulary. It is "Draconian," meaning cruel and harsh.

Solon—The So-called Father of Democracy in Greece

Shortly afterward a new leader arose on the scene named Solon. He has been called one of the Seven Sages. He lived from 638 to 539 B.C. and came from wealthy, aristocratic parents who introduced him into the most influential circles of Athens.[9]

Two major problems plagued Athens at the time Solon began to attain prominence. The foremost problem was the bloody code of the dead Draco. The second problem was the great disparity between the rich and the poor. Gradually, the poor began to mobilize and joined the emerging middle class to elect Solon as a "reform" leader.

Solon did two things to entrench himself in power. First, he repealed all death penalties except for murder. Then he undertook to get the poor more thoroughly involved in the political system. He extended the vote to the unfortunate classes and expanded the assembly from 100 to 400 so as to

7. See the Encyclopedia Britannica, op. cit., under "Draco," 8:464.
8. Ibid.
9. Will Durant, The Story of Civilization, New York: Simon and Schuster, 1939, 2:112-119.

accommodate the newly franchised voters. It is from this that he gained his reputation as the "father of democracy" in Greece.

Solon's Economic Reform

The second thing he did was to stabilize the economy in favor of both rich and poor. Solon gave the people a new money system, passed laws allowing for the privatization of property, and legalized wills to insure a more orderly distribution of inheritances. He canceled all existing debts whether owing to private persons or the state, and with one blow cleared all lands in Attica of any mortgages. All persons in bondage for debt were released, and those who were sold into servitude abroad were reclaimed and freed.

He divided the people into four groups, depending on their income. He also introduced a graduated income tax with those belonging to the elite level paying twelve parts, the second level ten, and the third level five. The lowest level was exempt from any tax.[10]

On the community level, Solon made persistent idleness a crime, and no man, no matter how rich, who lived a life of debauchery could address the Assembly. He legalized and taxed prostitution, and licensed public brothels. He limited the size of dowries so that marriages would be based on affection rather than wealth, and he limited all women to three changes of clothing. He was asked to make gossip and slander a crime, but refused, saying both were an essential part of a free democracy!

Anyone who remained neutral during an attempt to overthrow the government, lost his citizenship. Children of those whose fathers died in war were to be educated at the expense of the government.

He condemned pompous ceremonies, expensive sacrifices, or lengthy lamentations at funerals. He also limited the articles that could be buried with the dead.

Solon virtually outdid himself trying to make a law for every conceivable situation. It was a cradle-to-grave legal code. He even provided for an unloved heiress who had been married for her money. Solon decreed that she was entitled to be loved three times a month whether her husband felt like it or not.

He was so popular that many wanted him to declare himself a dictator. He said that might be very appealing to a politician but, once a dictator "there is no way down." Meaning, except by assassination.

10. Ibid.

Five centuries later, Cicero could say that most of Solon's laws were still in force.[11]

Solon Goes to Egypt for Some Intensive Study

As with all politicians, there came a time when Solon grew weary of the constant bickering and bantering between contending interests, so he decided to leave Athens and travel for awhile. He was absent for ten years.

During this extended excursion, his most notable experience was in Egypt. He spent considerable time at the intellectual center of the world called Sais on the Canopic (western) branch of the Nile River.

Plato, a descendant of Solon on his mother's side, records in one of his dialogues[12] that this is where Solon was taught some amazing things by the priests of Egypt. They knew about the creation of the world, about the first man whom they called Phoroneus, about the Fall, about the city of Enoch, about the Great Flood and Deucalion and Pyrrha who survived it. There is also a discussion of the disappearance of Atlantis, a huge land mass west of Europe, which may have had reference to the "division" in the days of Peleg.[13] Solon even claimed the Egyptian scholars had elaborate genealogies from the first man down to their own time.

Returning to Athens, Solon found that Peisistratus had taken over the city. However, there was no serious friction between the two men. Peisistratus went out of his way to patronize Solon by retaining most of his laws and catering to Solon's approval before making important decisions.

Just a few years later, Solon died.

Pericles and the Golden Age of Greece

Pericles is believed to have been born around 487 B.C., just three years after the great battle with the Persians on the plain of Marathon. He was a descendant on his mother's side from Clesthenes, one of the major believers in democracy who followed the political philosophy of Solon.

Pericles was truly a man of the world. He was a brilliant military leader, a master of literary talents, extremely sensitive to artistic achievements of

---

11. Ibid., 3:118.
12. Plato, Timaeus, Great Books of the Western World, Chicago: Encyclopedia Britannica, 1952, 7:444.
13. Genesis 10:25.

various kinds, and a deep student of philosophy. It is said that he was the most completed man Greece ever produced.[14]

Pericles came into his prime at a most critical stage of Greek history. After the Persians were defeated in 490 B.C. on the plain of Marathon, they came back ten years later and almost wiped Athens out of existence. The entire population had to evacuate their homes, and the temples and shrines on the famous Acropolis overlooking Athens were put to the torch.

It was not until 466 B.C. that the Greeks were able to avenge themselves by invading the southern region of Asia Minor and smashing both the army and navy of the Persians at Eurymedon. A permanent peace treaty was signed in 449 B.C.

Pericles then proposed that all the Greek city states meet in Athens to show their appreciation to the Greek gods for their mighty victory by rebuilding the temples and shrines on the Acropolis. He also said he felt it would be better to transfer the defense funds from the small island of Delos to Athens under his administration.

Pericles was not above using public money for bribery in a good public cause, but those who knew him best said he was personally incorruptible. He never used his position to enrich himself as so many others had done, and he was so admired that during intervals spanning over forty years (467 to 428 B.C.) he was elected and re-elected as one of the ten commanders. This gave him a comfortable seniority in charge of the military and eventually gave him almost dictatorial authority over the nation.

At last he was ready to show what his version of "democracy" could do.

The Golden Age Begins

The so-called democracy of Athens was a microcosm of both the good and the evil of a system which depends on decision-making by the masses of the people. Of course, it is important to point out that the leaders of Athens only considered 43,000—out of its population of 315,000—to be free and equal citizens of the democracy. Of the remainder, over 115,000 were slaves, and the rest were women, workingmen, and 28,500 resident aliens.[15]

The good qualities of the Athenian experiment was primarily the result of the freedom it granted to the innovative talent of the people. In a brief period of approximately 20 years, Athens enjoyed a golden age which historians

14. Durant, The Story of Civilization, op. cit., 3:248.
15. Ibid., 3:254.

say has never been equalled before or since. In that brief period the high hill, called the Acropolis, was decorated with some of the most famous buildings in the world. Pericles used the defense funds from the Delian League to set up massive W.P.A.-type projects to reduce unemployment and provide the manpower to build the huge Parthenon, a beautiful theater, a huge entrance gate, and several elaborate shrines on the Acropolis.

The remains of these magnificent monuments are still the leading tourist attraction in all of Greece.

The American Founders saw the tremendous merit of the climate of freedom which gave Athens her golden age. However, they were equally impressed with the inherent weaknesses of its political structure based on people power rather than a republic—which soon led to its complete collapse. As James Madison, the father of the American Constitution, said:

> "Democracies [based on decisions by the masses of the people] have ever been spectacle to turbulence and contention; have ever been found incompatible with personal security or the rights or property; and have in general been as short in their lives as they have been violent in their deaths. Theoretic politicians, who have patronized this species of government, have erroneously supposed that by reducing mankind to a perfect equality in their political rights, they would at the same time be perfectly equalized and assimilated in their possessions, their opinions, and their passions." [16]

A terrible plague struck Athens in 429 B.C., and Pericles was one of the victims. He died in 428 B.C.

All of this forms the background for the rise of the next three famous Greek personalities who tried to grapple with the enigma of how to set up a sound system of government and economics.

The Strange Story of Socrates

When the rich in Athens conspired with Sparta to rescue them from the raid on their wealth by the democratic Athenians, Sparta responded. With Spartan backing, a totalitarian junta took over the government, called The Thirty Tyrants. They proceeded to carry out extensive purges which eventually erupted into a ferocious three-cornered civil war. It was not until 403 B.C. that sufficient political stability was established so that Sparta could be induced to withdraw her troops.

16. Madison, The Federalist Papers, op. cit., Number 10, p. 8.

But barely had some semblance of tranquility been restored when the democratic leaders decided to challenge what they considered to be a very dangerous old man of seventy for raising doubts about the Greek gods. Thus Socrates appears on the stage.

By any standard, Socrates was an anomaly. He never wrote a book. He was not an orator. He was not a politician. He was sort of a nobody. Even today, classical authorities are not quite sure what he stood for. However, he made it clear what he stood against—ignorance and bad decisions due to ignorance—and false gods. It was this last issue that cost him his life.

Socrates was born in Athens between 471 and 469 B.C.[17] He received the usual education and first started out as a sculptor. He is said to have carved a statue of the Graces which could be seen for many years on the road to the Acropolis. But suddenly he stopped this work. Socrates said he had a divine commission from God to go among the people—not to teach any doctrine—but to convince them of their ignorance. He said he had access to a "voice." It did not instruct him, but merely warned him when he was about to do something wrong.

The method Socrates used to uncover the ignorance of the public was to ask questions. Whatever answer was given would give Socrates an excuse for another question. And so it would go on for hours.

He went up and down the streets, barefoot, without a shirt, and wearing the same miserable coat summer and winter. His joy was picking out some individual who attracted his attention and pinning him to the wall with what was often rather impertinent and provocative questions. When people would ask him why he did this, he would say, "So you can learn how little you really know."

Socrates the Man

Socrates was not an attractive person. He was overly obese and short of stature. His face had a rather grotesque appearance with protruding eyes, "nose upturned and nostrils outspread, with a large mouth, and coarse lips, he seemed the embodiment of sensuality and even stupidity." [18]

But some of the leading intellectuals of Athens came to love him for his piety, sincerity, and good sense of humor. He believed there was one supreme God, and that all mankind are accountable to him for their actions. He also

17. Encyclopedia Britannica, op. cit., 25:331.
18. Ibid., 25:332.

believed in immortality. He looked upon himself as a world citizen rather than a Greek, but he was a patriot.

In his earlier life he had served as a good soldier, and for awhile he was a senator. He was not family oriented even though he was married and had two or more sons. He was extremely generous with any means that came into his possession, and gave freely without any inhibition as to race, sex, or social standing.

Socrates on Trial

The great sin of Socrates in the eyes of the recently restored democratic leaders was his proclivity for spreading doubt in the minds of the youth by asking them questions about the Greek pantheon of gods. His questions often led them to conclude that perhaps they were victims of superstition and fabricated stories about the gods.

At his trial Socrates gave his own defense, stating that he was sort of a "gadfly" with a commission from God to stir up the people to think for themselves. He said his work was important to Greece and "as you will not easily find another like me, I would advise you to spare me." [19]

He said he was well aware that they wanted him to recant and promise to stop asking questions, but, said he:

> "I shall obey God rather than you, and while I have life and strength I shall never cease from the practice and teaching of philosophy, exhorting anyone whom I meet, after my manner, and convincing him … Wherefore, O men of Athens, I say to you, do as Anytus bids [sentence him to death], and either acquit me or not; but whatever you do, know that I shall never alter my ways, not even if I have to die many times." [20]

There were 300 men on the jury, and the vote was "guilty" but only by a margin of 60 votes. His followers suggested they be allowed to pay a fine for him of thirty minas ($3,000) which might have satisfied enough jurors to change the final vote, but he would have none of it. He said he was ready to finish his mission and drink the hemlock.

Death came thirty days later as his followers stood around him weeping.

It is said that the Golden Age of Greece ended with the death of Socrates. Nevertheless, in death he made more of an impact than when he was alive.

19. Durant, The Story of Civilization, op. cit., 3:454.
20. Ibid.

Several academies sprang up to preserve his teachings. Although his followers never quite agreed as to what he taught, at least they agreed as to his method of making people think. It was called the Socratic method, and it is used extensively, even today. The dialectic of Socrates was to encourage the acquisition of knowledge but ask penetrating questions to make them realize they didn't know as much as they thought they knew.

Plato (427- 347 B.C.)

No disciple of Socrates was more devoted than Plato.

Plato was born in Athens in 427 B.C., and lived to the age of 80.[21] His father's name was Ariston, and he is said to have been a descendant of Codrus; and his mother's family, which claimed descent from Solon, included Critias, one of the Thirty Tyrants.

Being of aristocratic descent, Plato moved among the leaders of both major parties in Athens. In fact, it was some of his own relatives who engineered the execution of Socrates—for which Plato never forgave them. His mother's second marriage was to her uncle whose name was Pyrilampes. He was a prominent supporter of Pericles, and Plato was probably brought up for most of his life in his home.

Plato the Man

Plato's real name was Aristocles, but he was nicknamed "Plato" because of his exceptionally wide shoulders and his broad forehead. Plato means "wide."

Plato was an excellent wrestler, and during the civil war he fought in three battles. He wrote a lot of poetry in his youth but burned it after the death of Socrates. He was an articulate speaker but no orator. His voice was thin and high pitched.

Plato admired the Socratic dialectical approach to the discovery of truth by asking questions. Therefore he did nearly all of his writing in terms of dialogues. To give prestige to his line of argument in The Republic, he attributed his proposals to Socrates. However, all authorities seem to agree that there is nothing in the known writings or quoted statements of Socrates to support the thesis of *The Republic*. It is therefore assumed that Plato was simply using his old master's name to make his own ideas palatable.

21. Encyclopedia Britannica, op. cit., 21:808.

The Education of Plato

It is said that Plato was so horrified with the civil war and the subsequent execution of Socrates that he decided to get away from Athens. He traveled to Megara, then to Cyrene, and after that he is reported to have gone to Egypt to seek out the priests, no doubt, and review all of the things Solon was supposed to have learned there.

By 395 he was back in Athens, and a year later fought in the battle for the city of Corinth. Then, about 387, he studied at the Pythagorean school of Croton, the first university in Greece. He did not stay long. He proceeded to Sicily to see Mt. Etna. There he became acquainted with Dion of Syracuse and met Dionysius I. But there was a revolution and Plato found himself being sold into slavery. He managed to escape, however, and was back in Athens in 386.

Plato's Academy

Plato's friends had raised three thousand drachmas to pay for his ransom, but when he returned home without having to pay for his freedom, his friends took the money and bought a grove where he could teach. Plato's school was technically a religious fraternity. It was named after a local god, Academus, and it was there that Plato established his university which became the foremost intellectual center in Greece for the next nine hundred years.[22]

Plato did not charge any fees for attendance at his Academy. However, his students were often members of the foremost families of Greece, and they made generous contributions which kept the Academy alive.

The intellectual climate in Athens during the early years of the Academy was one of cynical criticism of democracy—government by the masses—or oligarchies—government by a few. The mood seemed to be pre-Solon when heroic rulers were supposed to have ruled as righteous dictators with justice and vigor. This was a pattern that Sparta had been developing and Plato undoubtedly reflected his bias toward this political philosophy when he wrote *The Republic*.

Plato's Republic

Reading Plato's *Republic* is not easy. This is because the ideas attributed to Socrates are intellectually obscured and strung out during complicated,

22. Durant, The Story of Civilization, op. cit., 3:510-511.

lengthy dialogues. This is true of all of Plato's Dialogues. As Will Durant, one of the foremost historians of modern times, says:

> "The Dialogues are cleverly and yet poorly constructed. They vivify the drama of ideas, and build up a coherent and affectionate portrait of Socrates; but they seldom achieve unity or continuity, they often wander from subject to subject, and they are frequently cast into a clumsily indirect mood by being presented as narrative reports, by one man, of other men's conversations."[23]

But a careful reading of *The Republic* leaves no doubt about Plato's ideas of a "just" society which he tries to sell through the words of his dead teacher. He says the goal is not individual happiness, but the greatest happiness of the whole.[24] How is this to be done?

The Republic to Be Ruled by Philosopher Kings

First of all, society will be divided into three groups. At the top will be the oligarchy or "philosopher kings." They will govern the people with vigor and strictness and "governing" will be their only occupation. They will live pure communism. They will own no property, but live in attractive houses with secluded privacy where they can study, think profoundly and write.

They will dine at a common dining hall, and the physical needs of food and clothing will all be provided by those they govern. The rulers will share the women communist style, and the women will share the men. Children will be raised by nurses and no one will know to whom the children actually belong.

The Three Levels of Society

The philosopher kings will have exclusive authority to decide on which level of the Republic each citizen will be assigned. Of course, the highest level is the exclusive commune of the philosopher kings.

The second level consists of the Auxiliaries or soldiers who guard the philosopher kings and keep them from being overthrown. This group also lives the communal life similar to the soldiers in Sparta. They own no property, live in barracks, and eat at a common table. They share the women as the women share the men, so they have no families as such. They have no other occupa-

---

23. Ibid., 3:513-514.

24. Plato, The Republic, Great Books of the Western World, Chicago: Encyclopedia Britannica, 1952, 7:319.

tion other than that of serving as "guardians," and all their needs are provided by the working people.

The third level consists of the masses of the common people. They are not allowed to live the communal life, but are to perform the tasks assigned to them. They live in either public or private housing, and live together as families. Whatever assignment each person receives is to remain his assignment for life.[25]

Plato's Dictatorship

Both the second and third group are to live under very strict discipline. No philosopher ever conceived of a more regimented society than Plato.

> "The greatest principle of all is that nobody," Plato said, "whether male or female should be without a leader. Nor should the mind of anybody be habituated to letting him do anything at all on his own initiative; neither out of zeal; nor even playfully. But in war and in the midst of peace—to his leader he shall direct his eye and follow him faithfully. And even in the smallest matter he should stand under leadership. For example, he should get up, or move, or wash, or take his meals… only if he has been told to do so. In a word, he should teach his soul, by long habit, never to dream of acting independently, and to become utterly incapable of it." [26]

But, of course the question immediately arises, how do you get the people on the two lower levels to accept the role to which the philosopher kings have assigned them? Suppose a person wants to be a philosopher king and he is assigned to be a common laborer?

In order to answer this question, Plato had Socrates say that the people would be told a huge religious lie. He emphasized that telling lies will be prohibited to all citizens except the philosopher kings. They may tell lies if they think it would be for the good of the people.

The Huge Religious Lie in Plato's *Republic*

So what is this religious lie? Plato has Socrates say:

> "I will speak, although I really know not how to look you in the face, or in what words to utter the audacious fiction which I

25. Ibid., 7:342.

26. Quoted by Eugene H. Methvin, The Rise of Radicalism, Arlington House, New Rochelle, New York, 1973, p. 30.

> propose to communicate gradually, first to the rulers, then to the soldiers, and last to the people … Citizens, we shall say to them in our tale, you are brothers, yet God has framed you differently. Some of you have the power to command, and in the composition of these he has mingled gold [in their souls]. Wherefore, also they have the greatest honor; others he has made of silver to be auxiliaries [soldiers], and others again who are to be husbandmen and craftsmen he has composed of brass and iron; and the species will generally be preserved in the children."[27]

He said the rulers would have the prerogative of assigning each new generation to their respective castes regardless of the class into which they were born. He said:

> "But as all are of the same original stock, a golden parent will sometimes have a silver son, or a silver parent a golden son, and God proclaims as a first principle to the rulers, and above all else, that there is nothing they should so anxiously guard, or of which they are to be such good guardians, as of the purity of the race. They should observe what elements mingle in their offspring; for if the son of a golden or silver parent has a mixture of brass and iron, then nature orders a transposition of ranks, and the eye of the ruler must not be pitiful towards the child because he has to descend in the scale and become a husbandman or artisan, just as there may be sons of artisans who have a mixture of gold or silver in them who are raised to honor and become guardians [rulers] or auxiliaries [meaning soldiers]."[28]

Selective Breeding, The Role of Women, and Sexual Practices

Plato proposed to improve the quality of the people by selective, compulsory mating as with farm animals.

> "The best of either should be united with the best as often [as possible], and the inferior with the inferior as seldom as possible; and that they should rear the offspring of the one sort of union, but not of the other, if the flock is to be maintained in first-rate condition."[29]

27. Plato, The Republic, op. cit., 7:340.
28. Ibid., 7:340-341.
29. Ibid., 7:362.

Notice how casually Plato refers to infanticide to destroy inferior children. Elsewhere he says they should not be murdered but put out on a rock to die of exposure and starvation while they are still infants.

He says the rulers will bring the best men and women together for mating by lotteries that are rigged.[30] If any of them mate without the approval of the rulers the relationship will be called unholy and licentious.[31]

Plato believes men and women should exercise together while naked, and that women should go to war and fight side by side with the men.[32]

Throughout the dialogues of Plato, including *The Republic*, there is continuous favorable reference to homosexuality.

The Republic Can Only Come after a Massive Revolution

Plato was a colorful writer. He was also an obscure writer. His words must be slowly and sometimes painfully digested to appreciate what he is saying. Nevertheless, he does make it clear that what he is proposing could only be undertaken after there had been a complete "rubbing out" of any previous society so that the philosopher kings could start with "a clean surface." He says:

"They [the philosopher kings] will begin by taking the State and the manners of men, from which, as from a tablet, they will rub out the picture, and leave a clean surface. This is no easy task. But whether easy or not, herein will lie the difference between them and every other legislator—they... will inscribe no laws, until they have either found, or themselves made, a clean surface."[33]

Classical scholars frequently praise Plato as a writer even though they may strongly disagree with what he is saying.

What the American Founders Had to Say about Plato

The American Founding Fathers who studied Plato had no illusions about his theories or his proposals. Thomas Jefferson was disgusted with Plato. In a letter to John Adams, he wrote:

30. Ibid.
31. Ibid., 7:361.
32. Ibid., 7:359-360.
33. Ibid., 7:382.

"I amused myself (recently) with reading seriously Plato's *Republic*. I am wrong, however, in calling it amusement, for it was the heaviest task-work I ever went through. I had occasionally before taken up some of his other works, but scarcely ever had patience to go through a whole dialogue.

"While wading through the whimsies, the puerilities, and unintelligible jargon of this work, I laid it down often to ask myself how it could have been that the world should have so long consented to give reputation to such nonsense as this.

"How the... Christian world, indeed, should have done it is a piece of historical curiosity. But how could Roman good sense do it? And particularly, how could Cicero bestow such eulogies on Plato? ....

"With the moderns, I think, it is rather a matter of fashion and authority. Education is chiefly in the hands of persons who, from their profession, have an interest in the reputation and dreams of Plato. They give the tone while at school, and few in their after years have occasion to revise their college opinions.

"But fashion and authority apart, and bringing Plato to the test of reason, take from him his sophisms, futilities, and incomprehensibilities, and what remains? In truth, he is one of the race of genuine sophists who has escaped the oblivion of his brethren, first by the eloquence of his diction, but chiefly by the adoption and incorporation of his whimsies into the body of artificial Christianity. His foggy mind is forever presenting the semblance of objects which, half seen through a mist, can be defined neither in form nor dimensions. Yet this, which should have consigned him to early oblivion, really procured his immortality of fame and reverence ....

"Socrates had reason, indeed, to complain of the misrepresentations of Plato, for in truth his dialogues are libels on Socrates."[34]

John Adams shot back a reply to Jefferson with these interesting observations:

"I am very glad you have seriously read Plato, and still more rejoiced to find that your reflections upon him so perfectly harmonize with mine.

34. Bergh, The Writings of Thomas Jefferson, op. cit., 14:147.

> "Some 30 years ago I took upon myself the severe task of going through all his works. With the help of two Latin translations, and one English, and one French translation, and comparing some of the most remarkable passages with the Greek, I labored through the tedious toil.
>
> "My disappointment was very great, my astonishment was greater, my disgust shocking ... His *Laws* and his *Republic*, from which I expected most, disappointed me most." [35]

The Older, Wiser Plato

In later years Plato wrote *The Laws* in which he took a much more sober look at the realities of what he had said in *The Republic* at the age of 52.

In his last writing, *The Seventh Letter*, Plato was 75 and as he reviewed his life, he soliloquized somewhat on various principles of government. His ideas in the *Seventh Letter* are so far removed from his musings in The Republic that one would not suspect it was written by the same author.

Unfortunately, it is not *The Laws* nor *The Seventh Letter* that has intrigued master planners in modern times. The dictators of the past three generations have all followed the main lines of Plato's earlier thinking with such intensity that hundreds of millions of lives have been sacrificed to the ideology of *The Republic* in hopes they could make it work. Only millions of graves, including that of the dictators, memorialize the effort.

Now we come to the third generation of Greek political philosophers who published their thinking during the fourth century.

Aristotle

Aristotle was 18 years of age when he entered Plato's Academy in 367 B.C. He stayed 20 years.[36]

Aristotle was born in the Macedonia region at Stagira in 384 B.C., and that is the reason he was sometimes called the "Stagirite." He came from a family whose ancestors had settled Stagira, and at the time of his birth his father was the physician to the king of Macedonia.

---

35. Howe, The Changing Political Thought of John Adams, op. cit., p. 382.
36. Aristotle, Great Books of the Western World, Chicago: Encyclopedia Brittanica, vol. 8, p. V of introduction.

The Education of Aristotle

Aristotle apparently studied medicine under the tutelage of his father and when his father died and he traveled to Athens, he knew enough about medicine to practice that profession even while he was studying under Plato.

From the beginning Plato observed that his brilliant young Stagirite was extremely self-confident and independent. Plato said he amusingly noticed that this new student spurned his teacher like young colts spurn their mothers.

Early in his residence in Athens, Aristotle plunged into the study of biology and nature in general. He made contact with the foremost astronomers in Athens and also studied rhetoric with great diligence. Before long, he was tutoring students of his own and was even writing his own books.[37]

Aristotle's Disgust with the Politics of His Day

Aristotle was very displeased with the way politics were being run in Greece. He saw the unjust expropriations of the leaders of the "democracy" as they pursued a policy to "soak the rich."

He also observed the dwindling population under the "oligarchy" at Sparta, and noted that throughout the Greek world there seemed to be a variety of tyrannies oppressing the people. Almost from the beginning, he decided that there ought to be a new constitution that would place the people under a monarch, but, of course, a monarch of pre-eminent virtue. Someone like Philip, the king of Macedonia.[38]

Aristotle Becomes the Tutor of Alexander

A major change occurred in 342 B.C. when the king of Macedonia summoned Aristotle to his palace in order to serve as the tutor of his son, Alexander. One day this 13-year-old student of Aristotle would grow up and become known as Alexander the Great.

Aristotle tutored Alexander for eight years, but after his student ascended the throne of Macedonia, Aristotle decided to return to Athens.[39]

37. Durant, The Story of Civilization, op. cit., 3:527-531.
38. Ibid., pp. 534-537; Encyclopedia Britannica, op. cit., under "Aristotle," 1:502.
39. Encyclopedia Britannica, op. cit., under "Aristotle," 1:502.

Aristotle's Lyceum

By that time Aristotle was 50 years of age and he decided to set up his own school at the Lyceum which was a gymnasium near the temple of Apollo in the suburbs.

Aristotle copied the lecture style of Plato in that he walked up and down while talking. His students did the same. They were therefore called the walking lecturers, or "peripatetic" teachers.[40]

When Alexander the Great suddenly died in 323 B.C., Aristotle found himself in a dangerous position because he was a friend of the new king of Macedonia. Athens wanted to regain her independence from Macedonia and went to war to achieve it. Aristotle therefore left his beloved academy and went across the gulf to Chalis in Euboea where he died in 322 B.C.[41]

The Writings of Aristotle

The writings of Aristotle demonstrate that he started with Plato but after weighing his philosophy in the balance found it wanting. He therefore shifted to a new philosophy and a new type of presentation.

He occasionally used the dialogue technique, but most of his lectures and writings were didactic presentations of his personal views. In other words, he taught organized facts and hypotheses much as they are taught in the best schools today.

Plato believed in reincarnation or the transmigration of the soul from one being who dies to another just born—either human or animal. But Aristotle rejected the whole idea of transmigration of souls. He felt God was a divine entity and that the intelligent soul was immortal. He believed that after earth life human beings return to God.[42]

Aristotle opposed Plato on other scores. Plato taught that God caused the universe to come into being simply by thinking what he wanted it to be like and it automatically came into existence—made out of nothing.[43]

Aristotle took the opposite view. He felt the universe was made of an eternal substance and that this eternal substance could be organized or disorganized, but it could not be destroyed. He considered matter eternal, just as God is eternal.

40. Ibid.
41. Ibid.
42. Ibid., 1:520.
43. Ibid., 1:203.

Aristotle also challenged Plato's "ideology." Plato developed the idea that nothing in this life is an ultimate reality. Rather, it is an imperfect and temporary form of that particular "thing" which merely reflects imperfectly the "idea" of that thing as it exists in the mind of God. Only the perfect visualized by God is an ultimate reality. So for Plato there was God's ultimate good, ultimate beauty, and ultimate reality of "things." Meanwhile, things in this life are merely "becoming" things. They are never true or ultimate reality.

Aristotle thought all of this was nonsense. He felt that whatever exists should be perceived as part of the real here and now. Things are not just "becoming" something. They are already something. They are a very real part of our present reality.[44]

Aristotle on Politics

As for government, Aristotle thought there ought to be a "right" government with a "right" constitution. As he lined up the different kinds of government, this is the way he perceived them:[45]

Monarchy—the government under one ruler who excels in virtue.

Aristocracy—the government under a class which excels in virtue.

Commonwealth—the government under a majority of the whole people who excel in virtue.

In the absence of sufficient virtue in any of these three categories, Aristotle thought it would be necessary to accept a less perfect system. He felt the outcome would be one of the following:

A democracy—aiming at the most good for the greatest number.

An oligarchy—aiming at the greatest good for the few.

A tyrant—aiming at the greatest good for the one who rules.

It can be seen that Aristotle was searching for something substantive in political philosophy. However, he never found it. He knew Plato didn't have the answer, but, in the end, neither did he. In fact, when Aristotle died, he was still grappling with the practical aspects of politics and since he didn't find it, he left his writings in a state of chaotic confusion.

Nevertheless, the application of the greatest brain power available was gradually leading toward a few of the most basic ingredients in God's law. It

44. Ibid., 1:519-520.
45. Ibid., 1:521.

would take something like two thousand years to mature, but at least it was the beginning.

The Contribution of Polybius (*circa* 205-125 B.C.)

The first glimmer of light came from Polybius, a brilliant Greek historian who allied himself with Rome.[46] His writings directed the political compass away from the impossible politics of Plato and back toward the separation of powers doctrine which was just beginning to take hold in the primitive republic of Rome.

Polybius felt there were two elements that should have a place in the law-making process. One would be those who represented the "established order." This would be the class which owned most of the property and wealth. In Rome this was the aristocracy which occupied the senate.

The second element would be those who represented the interests and will of the masses of the people or proletariat. This element of the government in Rome was eventually developed into the assembly of elected representatives.

Polybius also believed there must be an executive power (representing the monarchial principle) that could speak for the whole people in a time of emergency or a war.

As the Founders examined the writings of Polybius they thought they saw some basic elements of sound statesmanship which deserved further study as it developed in the early history of Rome. So we now turn to a brief review of the Roman system of government and law.

46. Encyclopedia Britannica, op. cit., under "Polybius," 22:18-19.

Topics for Reflection and Discussion

1. In what sense do you think it is accurate to say that God's law was not made for a wicked people? What kind of law do wicked people require?

2. What famous prophet lived about the time of Hammurabi? Did Hammurabi's code contain some of the same principles as the Law of the Covenant? Can you give two examples?

3. When Draco wrote up a code for the people of Athens, what was the principal punishment for almost any kind of violation? Ironically, what happened to Draco?

4. What did Solon do to involve more of the people in the political process?

5. A pure democracy requires major decisions to be made by the masses of the people. Why do you think James Madison said this type of "democracy is always a spectacle of turbulence and contention?" Can you think of three fatal weaknesses in "pure democracy" ?

6. Why did Socrates go around asking everybody questions? What was the main reason he was forced to drink hemlock?

7. What was Plato's huge "religious lie?" What was it intended to persuade the people to accept?

8. Under Plato's *Republic* what would be the status of the majority of the people? How strictly did he want the will of the philosopher kings to be enforced?

9. What was Plato's attitude toward women? What about unwanted infants? Name three important ways in which Aristotle completely opposed Plato. What did Jefferson and John Adams think about Plato?

10. Why were the American Founding Fathers impressed by Polybius? Why was this Greek—Polybius—impressed by what was happening in Rome?

CHAPTER ELEVEN

How Could the Founders Be Certain That God's Law Is the Best System?
(Continued)

The Romans

Having examined the Babylonian and Greek systems of government and law, let us now see how the Founders analyzed the history and philosophy of Roman law.

The Roman System of Government, Religion, and Law

The original tribes that settled the region which eventually became Rome, governed themselves by the "fathers" of the various major families and this evolved into what later became the Roman Senate.

This was a powerful body of men out of which grew the class known as the "patricians"—descendants of the fathers. All others were known as the "plebeians." Concerning the original Senate a modern historian, Will Durant, has this to say:

"When the three original tribes united, their clan heads made a senate of some three hundred members. They were not such lords of comfort and luxury as their descendants; often they put their own hands to the ax or the plow, lived vigorously on simple fare, and wore clothing spun in their homes." [1]

The Roman Senate

In the beginning, this Senate was all-powerful.

> "Membership was for life, but the Senate or a censor could dismiss any member detected in crime or serious moral offense. The august body convened at the call of any major magistrate ... The conduct of foreign relations, the making of alliances and

1. Durant, The Story of Civilization, op. cit., 3:25.

treaties, the waging of war, the government of the colonies and provinces, the management and distribution of the public lands, the control of the treasury and its disbursements—all these were exclusive functions of the Senate, and gave it immense power. It was legislature, executive, and judiciary in one."[2]

In time, however, this mighty concentration of power was challenged by the plebeians and some of the patricians. What happened strongly suggests a certain amount of influence from the threads of cultural tradition which had spread out from ancient Israel to the countries surrounding the Mediterranean basin.

As we saw earlier, the original Law of the Covenant given to Israel was a government of the people, by the people, and for the people. It structured the twelve tribes into communities of a hundred families and the word "ward" may have been identified with each of them. At least that is what happened in Rome. It is interesting that in the Bible the word "ward" is defined as an "oversight, a guarded" or watched over place.[3]

The Roman Transition from "Wards" to "Hundreds"

As the centuries went by, we find some of these Israelite elements emerging in the tribes which settled southern Italy. Concerning this development, Will Durant says,

"In the days of the kings, he [the citizen of Rome]... and other heads of families had come together in a gathering of the thirty *curiae*, or *wards*, into which the three *tribes* had been divided; and to the end of the Republic it was this Curial Assembly that conferred upon the elected magistrates the *imperium*, or authority to govern."[4]

With the passing of time, the Curial Assembly of wards shifted over to an assembly of hundreds to represent the communities of a hundred families in each ward and also a hundred military men in the army. Will Durant describes this transition as follows:

"After the fall of the monarchy the Curial Assembly [of the wards] rapidly lost its... powers to the *commitia centuriata* [co-MISH-a/cen-turi-ATA, council of the "hundreds"]—soldiers assembled in

2. Ibid., 3:27.
3. Hastings' Dictionary of the Bible, under "ward."
4. Durant, The Story of Civilization, op. cit., 3:25.

> 'centuries' originally of one hundred men. It was the Centurial Assembly that chose the magistrates, passed or rejected the measure proposed to it by officials of the Senate, heard appeals from the judgments of magistrates, tried all cases of capital crime charged to Roman citizens, and decided upon war or peace."[5]

How Many Presidents or Executives Should There Be?

When the Romans got rid of their kings and began their Republic in 509 B.C., they hesitated to have a single executive lest he use the army to make himself a monarch or otherwise abuse the people with his power. They therefore decided to have two presidents or executives and call them "consuls." They were elected annually by the council of the hundreds or the comitia centuriata. Either of these two Consuls could call the senate into session. However, the senate could only deal with matters which the two Consuls wanted discussed.

The Consuls had broad powers. They commanded the armies in time of war and often fought in the field. For this reason the Consuls were usually—but not always—chosen from the military elite. The Consuls presided at meetings of both the senate and the comitia centuriata (council of the "hundreds"). They exercised general supervision over the bureaus of the government, and in case of a national crisis they could appoint a "dictator" with absolute power for six months.

The Founders Study the Idea of Two Executives

The American Founders carefully reviewed the idea of a multiple executive similar to Rome but then decided against it. History demonstrated that there were six weaknesses in the dual executive which made it a dangerous device.

1. It created a built-in hostility between the two executives as they struggled for supremacy.

2. It made it difficult to fix responsibility for mistakes or even to make important decisions. The modern term is "buck passing."

3. It confused administrators and even the people as to just who was in charge.

5. Ibid., 3:25-26.

4. In a real crisis the two consuls could not coordinate quickly and efficiently. They therefore felt compelled to set up a temporary dictator to carry out a unified command until the crisis was over.

5. The senate had to wait on one of the consuls to call them into session and they were then restricted to the subject matter the consuls wanted them to debate.

6. By presiding over both the senate and the general assembly, the two consuls could dominate the legislative program of both bodies and destroy the independence of these law-making branches which were designed to represent the people.

At the Constitutional Convention in 1787, several Founders wanted two presidents while others wanted three—one to represent the New England states, one to represent the middle states and one to represent the southern states. However, after reviewing the experience of the Romans and the six elements cited above, it was agreed there should only be one executive to speak for the whole nation and serve as commander in chief in time of war.

The Censors

In the field of civil service, Censors were elected for five years to take the census, recruit the army, classify citizens by centuries (hundreds) and by tribes. They also kept the official lists of citizens and senators. They had the responsibility of granting public contracts, and acquired vast powers of appointment, even to the filling of vacancies in the senate. The censors were also given the duty to investigate the private lives of officials and candidates for office to make certain they were "worthy." This gave them an evil reputation of being spies and meddlers or snoopers.

The Tribunes

The plebeians were somewhat abused and downtrodden during the first 150 years of the Republic, but in 494 B.C. they succeeded in electing a body of officials called the *tribuni plebis*, or "tribunes of the people." As it turned out the tribunes acquired great power when it came to protecting the plebeians throughout the empire.

A special delegation of tribunes—first two and later ten—had the power to attend meetings of the senate, veto legislation which they considered hostile to the plebeian class, summon the senate to meet, propose laws, veto acts of the consuls, prosecute officials for malfeasance in office, and preside over the *comitia tribuna*—assembly of the tribes. We shall have more to say about this assembly in a moment.

They also had the distinction of being declared "sacrosanct," which meant that their persons were inviolable. Anyone injuring them or interfering with the performance of their duties, was automatically designated an outlaw, meaning he could be killed on sight.

Assembly of the Tribes

In addition to the Council of Hundreds and the assembly of the tribunes, there was another general assembly added around 287 B.C. called "The Assembly of the Tribes." This means that the Romans finally set up three competing legislative bodies in addition to the Senate.

There was the council or assembly of the hundreds to represent the interests of the various communities as well as the hundreds in the army; then there was the assembly of the tribunes to protect the interests of the plebeians against the patricians, and finally there was the assembly of the tribes to maintain the dignity and identity of the tribes who originally inhabited this territory. Only plebeians were allowed to be members of this body. The laws which it passed were called "plebiscites," meaning the laws passed by the plebeian assembly of the tribes.

The Roman Military Organization

The Roman system of government was closely associated with its military organization.

Originally the Latins fought haphazardly as they joined in an unorganized hand-to-hand combat with the enemy. At the same time their chieftains rode up and down the battlefield in their chariots challenging opponents to engage in a chariot fight. But the Etruscan kings played havoc with the Latins by using a new technique copied from the Greeks. To survive, the Latins soon copied it from the Etruscans.

Thereafter, the backbone of the Roman army consisted of a heavy-armed infantry. They marched into battle with foot soldiers in closed ranks and six to eight soldiers deep. This was called the phalanx and behind this solid front were the light-armed troops.

This system prevailed until the fourth century when the Romans developed a battle plan based on the techniques of their famous legions.

When a Roman army appeared in the field with its full complement it was a formidable sight. There were 193 companies of 100 soldiers each. The first 18 companies were made up of individuals who were wealthy enough to provide themselves with a horse and armor. These were called the equites or cavalry. Behind them marched eighty centuries or hundreds, equipped with heavy armor and forming the phalanx. Behind them came those who could afford only lighter weapons, and last of all came those equipped with only slings and stones. Since every soldier had to provide his own arms and equipment, his status in the army reflected his economic status at home.

The army was led by the highest magistrates of the state, who had been selected for their government positions while simultaneously keeping their military skill in mind. Subordinate commanders were called "military tribunes." Since every Roman citizen served in the army for ten seasons, the habits of military order and discipline were engraved deeply into the character, manners, and thinking of the Roman people.

The Romans Unite Church and State

The early Romans were an austere and puritanical people in which the family was the religious core with the father serving as priest. There were numerous spells and incantations that had to be recited in an ancient and often incomprehensible language. Different powers were invoked in the family worship, one for the kitchen, one for the entry way, one for the pantry and one for the hearth. Few people have had religion ingrained into their very souls more than the early Romans.

To the Romans there were good gods and bad. The bad spirits were called the Furies. Both kinds had to be placated.

It was the Etruscans who taught the Romans to build temples and fill them with figures representing their various gods. Thus they developed a pantheon of gods and a mythology to go with each of them. The patron god of Rome was Jupiter, inherited somehow from the old Nordic sky-god. The Romans equated him with Zeus, the supreme being of the ancient Greeks. In fact the Romans had a companion god for each of the pantheon of Greek gods. They even copied the Greek Sibylline Books which were consulted by the priests in time of distress to discover how to regain the favor of the gods. The Etruscans also taught the Romans to observe certain signs portending the future. Their priests or augurs claimed they could tell the future by examining the entrails of a sheep, the flight of the birds, a scanning of the heavens, or some other omen.

More important than any of these, however, was the role of organized religion in the national life of the people. They had a book of sacred laws (*ius sacrum*) drawn up in early times that were observed with strict literalness. "Colleges" of priests conducted public services according to the various cults dedicated to Jupiter, Mars, and the other gods.

In addition to the augurs who could predict the future, there were the pontiffs. The pontiffs were responsible for interpreting the sacred laws, and they had an important part in developing the Roman civil and criminal law. The pontiffs kept the records and regulated the calendar. There were twelve pontiffs and they were presided over by the *pontifex* maximus who was elected for life by his colleagues. After the emperors took over, the emperor was always elected to the office of *pontifex maximus*.

With the passing of time, the religion of the Romans became so debauched that thinking men like Cicero abandoned the whole collection of superstitions, meaningless rites and mythical gods. In a moment we shall see what was adopted in their place.

Ancient Roman ruins in the Bekka valley of Lebanon demonstrate the degradation of pagan worship in the late centuries of Rome. There is a huge temple to Jupiter with pillars 65 feet tall and roses carved at that height with exquisite delicacy which could be neither seen nor appreciated until the pillars fell down centuries later.

At the temple of Jupiter the devotee brought a sheep, a calf, or the fruits of the harvest as a gift to the priest along with some money for the upkeep of the temple. The worshipper then went next door to the temple dedicated to Bacchus, the Greek and Roman god of revelry and wine. There he made another contribution and proceeded to get himself sacramentally drunk. After showing his appreciation to Bacchus, the god of wine and revelry, he was now a fit patron to be taken to the temple of love where he hopefully had enough money for a contribution to Vesta, the love goddess. If so, he was then allowed to indulge in the favors of one of her Vestal Virgins.

I have seen modern tourists taken through a guided tour of the remains of these ancient Roman temples, and later exclaim, "What a racket!"

The Founders' Reaction to the Roman Political System

It will be appreciated that the trilateral legislative system of the Romans was not a product of design, but evolved as the need arose to check abuses. As a result, these three law-making bodies operated very unevenly and did not provide the symmetry or balance the American Founders were seeking. Nevertheless, it provided a courageous—though primitive—attempt to set up a republican system where the government operated to some extent through officers chosen by the people or their representatives.

The American Founders wrote into Article I of their Constitution a far superior system of law making. They set it up so that the House is balanced against the Senate and nothing becomes a binding law until both bodies have agreed upon it. Even then, the law becomes subject to the possibility of a Presidential veto unless a super-majority of at least two-thirds of both Houses can override the veto. And finally, the law is subject to a review by the courts to make certain that it conforms to the Constitution. This is the advantage of a carefully structured system of government provided by the Constitution.

The Roman Law

Like many primitive peoples, the early Romans had no written laws. The Anglo-Saxons also had no written laws, but memorized the laws of the Israelites and kept them simple so all of the people could memorize these provisions. It was not so with the Romans.

The patricians began to make the laws so complex that great injustices were perpetrated on the ignorant plebeians by their aristocratic officials.

About 451 B.C. the plebeians agitated until ten men were appointed to codify and publish the laws. These men were called the decemviri. The code they prepared was written on twelve tablets and set up in the Forum for all to read and study. This "Law of the Twelve Tablets" was thereafter regarded as the basic law of the Republic.

The *decemviri* were all politicians and therefore many prerogatives were reserved to the rich patricians. However, by 449 B.C. the plebeians had gained some substantial concessions, but, it was another 150 years before plebeians could be elected to the higher offices.

Nevertheless, the patricians shrouded the legal procedure with ritual and prescribed phrases without which a case could not be brought into court. This monopoly of the patrician lawyers was not broken until around 300 B.C. The next development in the law resulted from Roman conquests of foreign territories. Laws were passed to give Romans in these foreign territories the full protection of the Roman law. But when foreigners from these conquered countries came to Rome they wanted to be protected by their own law. Two systems of courts were therefore provided. One for Roman citizens and one for the "friendly allies" who had come to trade or study the Roman system.

Gradually the two systems began to blend together and a new and more elaborate judicial system emerged. Under this system the plaintiff simply came before the magistrate and stated his case. The magistrate or praetor weighed the plaintiff's allegations and if he thought the case had merit he assigned it to an arbitrator. He wrote up a writ or formula indicating the questions that needed to be decided and the redress to be given the plaintiff if the facts were found to be true as he or she had alleged.

It is interesting that these praetors or magistrates began legislating without authority by defining the law and the rights of the parties by judicial fiat. They then published the form of writ they would be willing to accept during the year they were in office. These writs then became the basis for what turned out to be the best in Roman law, even though these magistrates often usurped the authority of the legislature by formulating law through these edicts incorporated in their writs.

As Roman jurists became acquainted with other systems of law they began to realize that in human relations as in the relations between the elements, there must be a natural law—a law of God—a universal system of law, which could be applied to the whole world. Leaders such as Cicero began searching for this "divine science" of true law which would provide peace, justice and order for all mankind. If this system could be brought to light, they felt it would be a permanent, universal, and unchangeable system because it would be from God. Without knowing it, they were searching for God's Law of the Covenant.

Before leaving the law of the Romans we should mention that they never did develop a peaceful and secure way of transferring supreme power. For example, of the first 47 emperors, 24 were assassinated. They did not have a democratic method of removing unwanted rulers.

In the next chapter we will analyze the thinking of the man whom the Founders considered to be the greatest of the Romans.

Topics for Reflection and Discussion

1. The people who settled the region which became Rome divided into two classes. What were they? Which one became the core of the Roman Senate? How powerful did the Senate become?

2. What was the name of the first legislative assembly of the people to challenge the Senate? What influence might have caused the Romans to call their individual communities "wards" or "hundreds"?

3. Why did the Romans choose two executives or "consuls" instead of one? Can you recall three weaknesses in this arrangement? Nevertheless, did some of the Founders want two or more presidents for the United States? What dissuaded them?

4. Rome had censors. Describe the extent of their power. Were there any useful functions of the censors that could be an advantage today? Whom were the tribunes set up to protect? How powerful did they become?

5. What impressed you most about the Roman military organization? Why was it so frightening when it first came in sight of the enemy?

6. Why was it an unfortunate development when the Romans united the pagan religion and the state? Who was elected to preside over all the pagan churches and their celebrations? Who taught the Romans to build temples?

7. Describe the three pagan temples in Bekka Valley and the religious rituals associated with each.

8. What are two advantages of the American law-making system over that of the Romans?

9. To make the American system work, why do the law-makers have to respect the Constitution?

10. Can you think of two serious problems which have arisen when American leaders did not stay within the restrictions of the Constitution?

CHAPTER TWELVE

How Could the Founders Be Certain That God's Law Is the Best System?
(Continued)

Cicero

There was one Roman who impressed the Founders more than any other. His name was Marcus Tullius Cicero.

Cicero—The Roman Who Wanted to Save the Republic and Gave the Founders a Great Dissertation on Natural Law

Marcus Tullius Cicero was born in 106 B.C. If he had been born 1,400 years earlier, he would have made a great spokesman for Moses. If he had been born 1,700 years later he could have been one of the American Founding Fathers. He had a mind for it.

As it turned out, he was born a citizen of Rome, and he lived during that tragic century when the great Republic of Rome was on its death bed.

Cicero was one of those who wanted to save the Republic. He belonged to a wealthy and illustrious family and he received an exceptionally high-quality education. All of this assured him the opportunity to move socially and professionally among ruling circles of the Roman empire.

In 89 B.C., at the age of seventeen, he served in the military and saw action under two famous generals, Strabo and Lucius Sulla. By the age of 25 he was already in the limelight as a practicing lawyer. However, his health had never been good and he went abroad for two years, studying in Athens and Rhodes. When he came back he said he was "a changed man."

After his return, Cicero entered into marriage at the age of 30. His wife was a blue blood and rich, but the marriage was not a happy one.

Cicero's Rise to Power

By this time Cicero was an orator of note and received an appointment as a quaestor or officer of the treasury to go to Sicily and supervise the harvest of the wheat supply. While there he saw the Roman governor, Gaius Verres, committing robbery, fraud and extortion. Cicero later brought charges against him in Rome and was so powerful in his prosecution that Verres fled the country and went into exile even before he had heard the verdict. By this time Cicero was 36.

At the age of 40 he was made a judge—a praetor—and was assigned to hear cases involving extortion. He also continued handling major cases in the courts. At the age of 43 he was made a Consul in spite of the opposition of many patricians who didn't approve of "new men" when they were not part of their closed fraternity of the "rich and the well born." This was in 63 B.C.

During the next twenty years, Cicero plunged into writing and politics trying to find a solution to the spirit of dictatorship which was moving among several leaders of the senate. Cicero was an optimist and in the face of rampant conspiracies by several groups, he leaned first on one group and then another trying to find a combination that would save the Republic. For awhile he thought there might be some hope in Julius Caesar, but he was shocked when Caesar tried to make himself emperor, and this led some of Caesar's best friends to stab the would-be emperor to death on the senate floor.

Cicero Supports Octavian

It will be recalled that Julius Caesar was murdered in 44 B.C., just when Cicero—who had nothing to do with it—was making a herculean struggle to preserve the Republic.

Those who had murdered Caesar claimed it was to prevent him from becoming an emperor, but it turned out that Caesar's successor—named Octavian—and all those who had plotted Caesar's death—including Mark Anthony—were coveting the imperial crown themselves.

As between Octavian and Mark Anthony, it was a hard choice because both wanted to be emperor. Nevertheless, Cicero felt that Octavian—Caesar's natural heir—was the least dangerous and therefore gave Octavian his support. Cicero told the members of the Senate that if they would support Octavian instead of Mark Anthony he—Cicero—would pledge his entire fortune to guarantee the loyal integrity of Octavian in preserving the Republic.

As a result of this bold action by Cicero, Mark Anthony, Brutus, and their supporters immediately marked Cicero for assassination.

The Murder of Cicero

This leading defender of the Roman Republic felt compelled to flee for his life. He raced to his villa near Formiae and took ship to escape. However, the boat was forced back by contrary winds and Cicero reconciled himself to martyrdom. He refused to make any further attempt to escape, but said: "Let me die in the country I have often saved."

His villa was surrounded by the band of assassins and he was murdered on December 7, 43 B.C., barely twenty months after Caesar was slain. When Cicero's decapitated head was sent to Fulvia, the wife of Mark Anthony, she pulled the great orator's tongue out between his teeth and thrust it through with a hat pin. Then the head of Cicero as well as his hands were nailed on the rostrum or speakers platform of the Roman Forum where he had pleaded so many times for the preservation of the nation's ancient Republic.[1]

Of course, time was also running out for Mark Anthony. He consorted with Cleopatra (who bore him twins) and secured the support of her powerful navy in the great naval battle of Actium in 31 B.C. But the victory went to Octavian. He put sharp rams on smaller faster attack boats and they cut deep holes below the water line of the ships brought in by both Mark Anthony and Cleopatra. Mark Anthony and Cleopatra could scarcely believe the terrible reality of this fantastic defeat.

They barely escaped and then fled to Egypt. There they both committed suicide.

Octavian meanwhile became—what Cicero had hoped would never happen—the first emperor of Rome. He pretended modesty by asking the people not to call him "Emperor" but the august one—the first citizen of Rome. Thus we are introduced to the first emperor of Rome by the name of Augustus.[2]

Cicero Made a Powerful Impression upon the Founders

As we have already mentioned, it was Cicero who cut sharply through the political astigmatism and philosophical errors of both Plato and Aristotle to

1. Encyclopedia Britannica, op. cit., under "Cicero," 6:355.
2. Skousen, The Fourth Thousand Years, op. cit., p. 822.

discover the touchstone for good laws, sound government, and the long-range formula for happy human relations. In the Founders' roster of great political thinkers, Cicero was high on the list.

Dr. William Ebenstein of Princeton says:

> "The only Roman political writer who has exercised enduring influence throughout the ages is Cicero (106-43 B.C.) ... Cicero studied law in Rome, and philosophy in Athens ... He became the leading lawyer of his time and also rose to the highest office of state [Roman Consul] ... Yet his life was not free of sadness; only five years after he had held the highest office in Rome, the consulate, he found himself in exile for a year." [3]

In the last years of Cicero's life, he wrote frantically and furiously about the principles of law and justice he would liked to have seen adopted by Rome. Although Cicero was an incurable optimist, it finally became apparent, even to him, that the flood of evil in Rome was too big and too bad for him or anyone else to stem the tide. Therefore, he poured out his soul in writing, attempting to capture in his letters and books the ideals and principles which he hoped downtrodden humanity would some day discover and adopt.

Cicero's Writings

Those studies gave him the inspiration to write his two landmark books called The Republic and *The Laws*. Obviously these two titles had already become famous because Plato's two books carried these same names. However, Cicero used his books to repudiate practically everything Plato had said in his version of *The Republic* and *The Laws*. In fact, in Cicero's writings he captured some of the grandeur and promise of a great new society of the future which he believed could be based on Natural Law.

The American Founding Fathers obviously shared a profound appreciation of Cicero's dream because they also envisioned a commonwealth of prosperity and justice based on Natural Law or God's Law. In Cicero's writings they saw the necessary ingredients for that model society which they themselves eventually hoped to build.

Cicero's Fundamental Principles

To Cicero, the building of a society on principles of Natural Law was nothing more nor less than recognizing and equating the rules of "right

3. William Ebenstein, Great Political Thinkers, New York: Holt, Rinehart and Winston, 1963, pp. 122-123.

conduct" with the laws of the Supreme Creator of the universe. In other words, he hoped to have all human laws coincide with God's Law.

History demonstrates that even in those nations which are often described as "pagan" there were sharp, penetrating minds like Cicero's who reasoned their way through the labyrinths of natural phenomena to see behind the cosmic universe the brilliant intelligence of a Supreme Designer with an ongoing interest in both human and cosmic affairs.

Cicero's compelling honesty led him to conclude that once the reality of the Creator is clearly identified in the mind, the only intelligent approach to government, law, justice, and human relations is to state it in terms that are parallel with the cosmic laws which the Supreme Creator has already established in nature. That is why Cicero felt the Creator's eternal "order of things" should be called "Natural Law."

Man's Divine Endowment

It was clear to Cicero that a fundamental presupposition of Natural Law is that man's reasoning power is a special dispensation of the Creator and is closely akin to the rationale or reasoning power of the Creator himself. In other words, man shares with his Creator this quality of utilizing a rational approach to solving problems. He felt the reasoning of the mind will generally lead to common-sense conclusions based on what Jefferson called "the laws of Nature and of Nature's God."

Cicero saw that man's reasoning power is something over and above the survival instincts which we naturally inherit with all other living creatures. This is why Cicero concluded that since this marvelous gift of reason can often overcome our inborn instincts, it makes us more like God. The animals on the other hand survive by responding to each situation as their instincts dictate. Here is the way Cicero explains it:

> "That animal which we call man, endowed with foresight and quick intelligence, complex, keen, possessing memory, full of reason and prudence, has been given a certain distinguished status by the Supreme God who created him; for he is the only one among so many different kinds and varieties of living beings who has a share in reason and thought, while all the rest are deprived of it. But what is more divine, I will not say in man only, but in all heaven and earth, than reason? And reason, when it is full grown and perfected, is rightly called wisdom. Therefore, since there is

> nothing better than reason, and since it exists both in man and God, the first common possession of man and God is reason.
>
> "But those who have reason in common must also have right reason in common. And since right reason is Law, we must believe that men have Law also in common with the gods. Further, those who share Law must also share Justice; and those who share these are to be regarded as members of the same commonwealth. If indeed they obey the same authorities and powers, this is true in a far greater degree; but as a matter of fact they do obey this celestial system, the divine mind, and the God of transcendent power. Hence we must now conceive of this whole universe as one commonwealth of which both gods and men are members."[4]

No prophet of the Old Testament or the Gospel teachers of the New Testament ever said it any better.

Natural Law Is Eternal and Universal "Right" Reason

Let us now examine the major precepts of Natural Law which so profoundly impressed Cicero and the Founding Fathers.

First of all, Cicero defines Natural Law as "*true*" law. It is in harmony with divine thinking and God's order of things. Then he says:

> "True law is right reason in agreement with nature; it is of universal application, unchanging and everlasting; it summons to duty by its commands, and averts from wrongdoing by its prohibitions … *It is a sin* to try to alter this law, nor is it allowable to repeal any part of it, and it is impossible to abolish entirely. We cannot be freed from its obligations by senate or people, and we need not look outside ourselves for an expounder or interpreter of it.
>
> "And there will not be different laws at Rome and Athens, or different laws now and in the future, but one eternal and unchangeable law will be valid for all nations and all times, and there will be one master and ruler, that is God, over us all, for he is the author of this law, its promulgator, and its enforcing judge. Whoever is disobedient is fleeing from himself and denying his human nature, and by reason of this very fact he will suffer the worst punishment."[5]

4. Ibid., p. 133.
5. Ibid.

In these few lines the student encounters concepts which were repeated by the American Founders a thousand times. The Law of Nature or Nature's God is *eternal* in its basic goodness; it is *universal* in its application. It is a code of "*right reason*" from the Creator himself. It cannot be *altered.* It cannot be *repealed.* It cannot be *abandoned* by legislators or the people themselves, even though they may pretend to do so. In Natural Law we are dealing with factors of absolute reality. It is basic in its principles, comprehensible to the human mind, and totally correct and morally right in its general operation.

To Cicero and the Founding Fathers as well as to Algernon Sidney (1622-1683), John Locke (1632-1704), William Blackstone (1723-1780), Charles de Montesquieu (1689-1755), Frederic Bastiat (1801-1850) and Alexis de Tocqueville (1805-1859), this was a monumental discovery.

The First Great Commandment

Cicero comprehended the magnificence of the first great commandment to love, respect, and obey the all-wise Creator. He believed that for a nation to prosper it must put God in first place.

He fixed this precept in proper perspective by saying that God's law is "right reason." When perfectly understood it is called "wisdom." When applied by government in regulating human relations it is called "justice." When people unite together in a covenant or compact under this law, they become a true "commonwealth," and since they intend to administer their affairs under God's law, they belong to his commonwealth.

Thus Cicero conceived of what both Jews and Christians call the first great commandment.

As we mentioned earlier, a lawyer tried to discredit Jesus by asking him, "Master, which is the great commandment in the Law?" Of course, the rabbinical scholars had calculated that there were 613 laws or commandments, so the question was designed as a clever stratagem to discredit Jesus. No matter which commandment he selected, this lawyer thought there would be many who would disagree and thus he would embarrass Jesus. But Jesus was not embarrassed. He simply replied: "Thou shalt love the Lord thy God with all thy heart, and with all thy soul, and with all thy mind. This is the first and great commandment."[6]

The lawyer was amazed by this astute and ready response from the Galilean carpenter. But Jesus was not through. He added: "And the second is

6. Mark 12:30.

like unto it. Thou shalt love thy neighbor as thyself. On these two commandments hang all the law and the prophets."[7]

The astonished lawyer simply replied: "Well, Master, thou hast said the truth!"[8]

Jesus had picked out what he considered to be the foremost commandment from Deuteronomy 6:4-5, and then selected what he considered to be the second most important commandment clear over in Leviticus 19:18. The lawyer could recognize and appreciate better than most of the bystanders that this Jesus was a brilliant student of the law.

The Second Great Commandment

It is fascinating that Cicero, without being either a Christian or a Jew, was able to discover the power and fundamental significance of the first great commandment and then go on to discover the second great commandment as well. His mental ingenuity instinctively led him to comprehend the beauty and felicity of what Jesus meant when he said: "Thou shalt love thy neighbor as thyself."

Dr. William Ebenstein comments on this rather astonishing insight among Cicero's writings by saying:

> "There is another note, too, in Cicero that points forward, toward Christianity, rather than backward to Plato and Aristotle: Cicero's consciousness of love as a mighty social bond."[9]

Cicero raises this point in connection with his discussion of Justice. He points out that Justice is impossible except under the principles of God's just law. He said, "For these virtues originate in our natural inclination to love our fellow-men, and this is the foundation of justice."[10]

So Cicero felt that the glue which holds a social structure of human beings together in the commonwealth of a just society is love—love of God; love of God's great law of Justice; and love of one's fellow-men which provides the desire to promote true justice among mankind.

7. Mark 12:31.
8. Mark 12:32.
9. Ebenstein, Great Political Thinkers, op. cit., p. 124.
10. Ibid., p. 134.

All Mankind Can Be Taught God's Law

Cicero projected throughout his writings a particularly optimistic view of the potential improvement of human beings by teaching them the elements of virtue through education. He wrote:

> "Out of all the material of the philosophers' discussion, surely there comes nothing more valuable than the full realization that we are born for Justice, and the right is based, not upon men's opinions, but upon Nature. This fact will immediately be plain if you once get a clear conception of man's fellowship and union with his fellow-men … However we may define man, a single definition will apply to all. This is a sufficient proof that there is no difference in kind between man and man … *In fact, there is no human being of any race who, if he finds a guide, cannot attain to virtue.*" [11]

What about Legislation in Violation of God's Law?

We cannot complete our review of Cicero's discourse on Natural Law without including his warning against legislators who undertake to pass laws which violate the "laws of Nature and of Nature's God." Cicero wrote:

> "But the most foolish notion of all is the belief that everything is just which is found in the customs or laws of nations … What of the many deadly, the many pestilential statutes which nations put in force? These no more deserve to be called laws than the rules a band of robbers might pass in their assembly. For if ignorant and unskillful men have prescribed deadly poisons instead of healing drugs, these cannot possibly be called physicians' prescriptions; neither in a nation can a statute of any sort be called a law, even though the nation, in spite of being a ruinous regulation has accepted it." [12]

All Law Should Be Measured by God's Law

Cicero then set forth the means by which people may judge between good and evil laws. All laws must be measured according to God's law, which is described by Cicero as follows:

---

11. Ibid.
12. Ibid.

"Therefore Law [of the Creator] is the distinction between things just and unjust, made in agreement with that primal and most ancient of all things, Nature; and in conformity to Nature's standard are framed those human laws which inflict punishment upon the wicked and protect the good." [13]

Cicero also emphasizes that the essence of an evil law cannot be mended through ratification by the legislature or by popular acclaim. Justice can never be expected from laws arbitrarily passed in violation of standards set up under the laws of Nature or the laws of the Creator. Here is his argument:

"But if the principles of Justice were founded on the decrees of peoples, the edicts of princes, or the decisions of judges, then Justice would sanction robbery and adultery and forgery of wills, in case these acts were approved by the votes or decrees of the populace. But if so great a power belongs to the decisions and decrees of fools that the laws of Nature can be changed by their votes, then why do they not ordain that what is bad and baneful shall be considered good and salutary? Or, if a law can make Justice Injustice, can it not also make good out of bad?" [14]

Cicero's Conclusion

It was clear to Cicero as he came toward the close of his life that men must eliminate the depravity that had lodged itself in society. He felt they must return to the high road of Natural law. They must pledge obedience to the mandates of a loving and concerned Creator. What promise of unprecedented grandeur awaited that future society which would undertake it! He wrote:

"As one and the same Nature holds together and supports the universe, all of whose parts are in harmony with one another, so men are united in Nature; but by reason of their depravity they quarrel, not realizing that they are of one blood and subject to one and the same protecting power. If this fact were understood, surely man would live the life of the gods!" [15]

The American Founders believed this. They embraced the obvious necessity of building a highly moral and virtuous society. The Founders wanted to lift mankind from the common depravity and chicanery of past

13. Ibid., p. 135.
14. Ibid., pp. 134-135.
15. Ibid., p. 135.

civilizations, and to lay the foundation for a new kind of civilization built on freedom for the individual and prosperity for the whole commonwealth. This is why they wanted to build their system on Natural Law.

Examples of Natural Law

It may be surprising, even to Americans, to discover how much of the Founders' Constitution and their life-style was based on principles of Natural Law. For example:

Unalienable Rights

The concept of *unalienable rights* is based on Natural Law. Twenty-two of these unalienable rights are listed in *The Five Thousand Year Leap.*[16] Every unalienable right is based on right reason, genuine morality and true justice.

Unalienable Duties

The concept of unalienable duties is based on Natural Law. Twenty of these unalienable duties are also listed in *The Five Thousand Year Leap.*[17] Each one of these is based on obligations which are just and morally right in a godly commonwealth where duties are performed for the welfare of all.

Habeas Corpus

No one should be held in prison without some specific charge against him. Therefore there should be a device to release the person from incarceration. This is called a writ of *habeas corpus* which orders the jailer to bring the individual before the court. He cannot send his attorney. The court says, "Habeas corpus"—have the body brought forth. This whole concept is based on Natural Law.[18]

Limited Government

No government official should be allowed to impose any authority over the people unless that power has been specifically granted to the government by the people or their representatives. Therefore the concept of *limited government* is based on Natural Law.[19]

---

16. Skousen, The Five Thousand Year Leap, op. cit., pp. 122-123.
17. Ibid., pp. 134-135.
18. W. Cleon Skousen, The Making of America, Washington, D.C.: National Center for Constitutional Studies, 1987, p. 474.
19. Ibid., pp. 712-713.

Separation of Powers

The Founders knew that the moment the power to make the law, interpret the law and enforce the law is deposited in the hands of the same person, it is tantamount to setting up a potential tyranny. Therefore the Founders knew that the concept of separating the legislative, executive and judicial powers is essential to the preservation of freedom and therefore based on Natural Law.[20]

Checks and Balances

The Founders also knew that each branch of government must have authority to check the abuses committed by other departments. Therefore the concept of *checks and balances* written into the Constitution to provide the correction of abuses by peaceful means are based on Natural Law.[21]

Self-Preservation

Since the right to live or exist is the most precious of all divine prerogatives granted to man by God, the right of *self-preservation* is based on Natural Law.[22]

The Right to Contract

Since human beings need to be able to assist one another by entering into agreements of performance and payment, the Founders knew the right to *contract* is based on Natural Law.[23]

The Family

Because the most sacred and enduring human relationships occur within the boundaries of the family, the Founders knew that the laws protecting and perpetuating family relationships are based on Natural Law.[24]

Torts and Crimes

Because no person should be allowed to deprive another of his security, property or physical well-being, the Founders knew that Natural Law requires a full reparation or adequate "satisfaction" for any injury or loss. Under Natural Law this is called "justice" or "due process of law."[25]

20. Skousen, The Five Thousand Year Leap, op. cit., pp. 198-202.
21. Ibid., pp. 205-215.
22. Skousen, The Making of America, op. cit., pp. 694-700.
23. Ibid., pp. 499-500.
24. Skousen, The Five Thousand Year Leap, op. cit., pp. 281-288.
25. Ibid., p. 136.

The Right to Bear Arms

The right to protect one's life and property mandates the need to have the means to provide such protection. Therefore the right to *bear* arms is based on Natural Law.[26]

No Taxation Without Representation

The Founders knew that the power to tax is the power to destroy, therefore no tax can be imposed without the consent of the people. For this reason they said it was a principle of natural law to say "no taxation without the consent of the people or their representatives". In other words, taxation without representation is an offense against both God and man.[27]

Conclusion

These few examples from the most basic principles of our system of law will illustrate how extensively the entire American constitutional system is grounded on Natural Law. In fact, Natural Law is the foundation for everything we call "People's Law." These are just different words for God's law.

This is precisely what Thomas Jefferson was talking about when he wrote in the Declaration of Independence: "We hold these truths to be self-evident, that all men are created equal, that they are endowed by their Creator with certain unalienable [or inalienable] rights, that among these are Life, Liberty and the Pursuit of Happiness."

These well-remembered phrases from America's initial charter of liberty are all primary pre-suppositions under the principles of Natural law.

---

26. Skousen, The Making of America, op. cit., pp. 694-700.
27. Ibid., p. 782.

Topics for Reflection and Discussion

1. What was the name of the only Roman political writer who had a lasting effect on the thinking of the Founders? About when did he live? He served in what high office of the Roman Empire?

2. Briefly outline the circumstances that led to Cicero's death. He was murdered by the henchman of what famous Roman? Then what happened to that famous Roman? What did the wife of this Roman do with the head and hands of Cicero? What did she do to the tongue of this great orator?

3. Is it accurate to say that Natural Law is God's law? In what way does Natural Law set forth "rules of right conduct"? What makes Natural Law eternal and universal?

4. What intellectual quality does mankind possess which is similar in a finite way with that same quality possessed by God? If other creatures do not enjoy this high quality of mind, by what means are they governed in order to survive?

5. Give an example of reason overcoming instinct. Explain why Natural Law is "eternal" and "universal right reason." Can this law be changed or amended? Can it be abandoned or repealed? Why is Natural Law easy to interpret?

6. Cicero discovered the first two great commandments of God. What are they? What quality of the heart did Cicero say demands "justice"? Is this the same quality that binds man to God? Should it also bind mankind to one another?

7. Why should laws which violate the principles of Natural Law be declared null and void? What does Cicero say about legislatures that pass laws contrary to Natural Law? Therefore by what eternal and universal criteria should all legislation be measured?

8. Can you give two examples of legislation that fails to pass the Natural Law test? Does Natural law protect our unalienable rights?

9. Explain how "separation of powers" is based on Natural Law. Explain how habeas corpus is based on Natural Law. Explain how "self-preservation" is based on Natural Law. Why is the principle of "no taxation without representation" based on Natural Law?

10. What is People's law? In what way is People's law identical with Natural Law or God's law? Can you think of two laws under which we are now living that violate God's Law?

CHAPTER THIRTEEN

AFTER THE APOSTLES MANY CHANGES OCCURRED IN CHRISTIANITY

As far as the historical records show, John was the last of the Apostles, and he disappeared from the scene toward the end of the first century. Once the divinely appointed spokesmen for God were no longer available to provide guidance and also to correct erroneous doctrines, a deadly plague of root-rot began gnawing away at the foundation of the church.

Like ancient Israel, the Christians lost the blessing of heavenly guidance just as the descendants of Jacob had done.[1] Therefore, as in former ages, the Christian saints were left to their own devices, and gradually significant changes began to appear.

CAREFUL STUDIES OF MANY CHANGES

Few people have time available to read the hundreds of books and manuscripts which describe the many changes which gradually took place in Christian doctrines and practices. Therefore we have taken advantage of Dr. James O. Barker who spent his lifetime discovering these changes and documenting the details for students of ecclesiastical history.

In order to qualify himself, Dr. James O. Barker studied all of the basic background sources and then spent eight years in the major centers of learning in Europe carefully examining the writings of both Catholic and Protestant authorities, always reading them in their original languages. The summary of his life's studies in this field is entitled, *Apostasy from the Divine Church*.[2]

200 YEARS OF MASSACRES, PERSECUTION AND BOOK BURNING

Dr. Barker traces the ten cycles of bitter persecution of the Christians by the Roman emperors. Two of the worst scenes of atrocities were committed by Emperor Decius (249-251 A.D.) and later by Emperor Diocletion (300-305 A.D.).

1. See, for example, 1 Samuel 28:6, and the 400 years of darkness which followed the ministry of Malachi.
2. James O. Barker, Apostasy from the Divine Church, published by Kate Montgomery Barker, Salt Lake City, 1962.

The *modus operandi* of these two emperors was to raid the centers of worship in Christian communities and carry the prisoners to Rome or one of the major cities of a Roman province. There the hapless martyrs were torn to pieces by ravenous beasts that had been deliberately starved, or the Christians were covered with oil and set afire to illuminate the horrible orgy of torture and death taking place in the arena.

Besides all the human suffering, one of the most disastrous consequences of these cruel persecutions was the loss of the libraries of hand-written Christian literature wherever these attacks took place. Roman raids played havoc with the sacred epistles of the apostles as well as the precious manuscripts being prepared by church leaders at the time of the assault.

It is also clear that once the apostles were no longer available and heavenly revelation had ceased, the absence of the original writings of the apostles and prophets impelled the people to turn to the bishops of the larger metropolitan cities for guidance.

Bishops of Major Christian Centers Gradually Gained Preeminence

It will be appreciated that it was an awesome responsibility to be a bishop over a community of saints in these extremely difficult times. It is also understandable why the bishops of the smaller communities would turn to the bishops of the metropolitan centers when questions of doctrine and administrative procedures arose. Over a period of several decades the bishops in the following major cities rose to preeminence:

1. *Antioch*. This was originally the capital of the Greek kingdom of Syria. During the days of the Romans it was an important province governed by a Roman administrator. It was located on the bend of the Orontes river, 300 miles north of Jerusalem and 16 miles inland from the Mediterranean Sea.

2. *Alexandria*. This city is located at the mouth of the western branch of the Nile river along the coast of the Mediterranean Sea. For many centuries it was considered the most important intellectual center for both Christians and Jews. It was named to honor Alexander the Great shortly after his death in 323 B.C., and when his General Ptolemy took over Egypt after Alexander's death, he made this city the capital of Egypt.

3. *Ephesus*. This was the capital of the entire Roman province of Asia. It was located about one-third of the way up the coast of Asia Minor on the Mediterranean Sea. Here the Greeks built their largest theater with a capacity

for 21,000 people. When Paul was preaching in Ephesus with such great success, his opponents seized him and carried him to this theater. Later, Paul wrote several of his epistles from this city. Today, it lies in ruins.

4. *Corinth.* This was one of the two most celebrated cities in the days of Greece. The other city was Athens located 40 miles east of Corinth. Corinth became a famous port because the gulf of Corinth nearly cuts southern Greece completely off from the mainland to the north. Therefore hundreds of ships brought their cargoes to this port and then hauled them over the small land bridge to waiting ships on the other side. The wealth of Corinth was celebrated in the ancient world and so was its licentiousness and debauchery. Paul established a Christian church in Corinth and later wrote two of his most famous epistles to the people of that city.

5. *Rome.* This was the city built on seven hills located near the Tiber river. Rome is 15 miles inland from the Mediterranean Sea. On the map Rome is nearly half way up the west side of the Italian boot. For about 300 years the bishop of Rome had little influence but when Constantine made Christianity the official religion of the empire it changed Rome into the central core of the Christian church.

6. *Constantinople.* This city is called Istanbul today. The emperor Constantine set up the city as the capital of the Eastern Roman Empire in 330 A.D. When the eastern branch of the Christian church took strong exception to the doctrines and policies coming out of Rome, an independent branch of Christianity was set up in Constantinople and was called the Greek Orthodox Church. The popes of the Roman and Greek Orthodox Churches excommunicated each other with delightful satisfaction at regular intervals.

With all of these various bishoprics promulgating their own inurisdiction and doctrinal supremacy would soon create serious conflicts.

Eusebius Attempts to Save the Remnants of the Original Christian Faith

Eusebius (approximately 260-340 A.D.) was the first scholar to attempt to put together the history of the Christian Church.

His objective was to record the development of Christian doctrine as well as the history of the church itself. He was greatly disturbed by the effort of some bishops to preach and defend doctrines which Eusebius felt were contrary to the fundamental teachings of the apostles. However, it is clear from his writings that after two centuries and without the guidance of the apostles, he, himself, was having trouble sorting it all out.

Just a word about Eusebius, the man. His biography—which is cited in many writings—no longer exists, but we know he lived from about 260 to 340 A.D. To distinguish him from others with the same name, he has been identified by historians as Eusebius of Caesarea. He lived in this famous port city of Palestine most of his life and was made bishop of Caesarea in 313 A.D. He continued in that office until his death around 340 A.D.[3]

Eusebius was remarkably well educated and knew the philosophers of Greece as well as he knew the writings of the apostles.

When Emperor Diocletian launched his bloodbath on the Christians in 303 A.D., Eusebius lived through those seven brutal years of terror that followed. Several of his closest friends became martyrs but Eusebius was conciliatory with the Romans and somehow managed to escape.[4]

After Constantine became the supreme emperor of Rome he virtually made Christianity the official religion of the empire in 313 A.D. It was his hope that Christianity would unite the disintegrating provinces of Rome and he therefore insisted that the Christians unite themselves. To accomplish this, Constantine called a conference at Nicea in 325 A.D. to settle all disputes concerning the Godhead and other matters of doctrinal controversy. Professor Barker has an interesting observation concerning this conference:

> "In the Council of Nicea… guidance [was] by the emperor, as yet unbaptized, and still the *pontifex maximus*, the supreme pontiff or head of the pagan worship.
>
> "The emperor was not greatly concerned with religious truth, and still less with questions discussed by the council. He desired unity in the church as a means of furthering unity in the empire. How the unity was secured mattered but little; and he used force to secure it."[5]

Eusebius was in the midst of all this but managed to stay out of the fury of the hurricane during the debates and quarrels between the bishops and prelates present.

---

3. The Nicene and Post-Nicene Fathers, op. cit., 1:10.
4. Ibid., 1:8-10.
5. Barker, Apostasy from the Divine Church, op. cit., p. 271.

Some Interesting Statements by Eusebius as a Defender of the Faith

In his ten books covering the history of Christianity, Eusebius makes a number of significant doctrinal statements which arc of interest.

1. Eusebius admits that he is approaching the writing of the history of the Christian church with considerable timidity. He began by saying:

> "It is my purpose to write an account of the succession of the holy apostles… and since I am the first to enter upon the subject, I am attempting to traverse as it were a lonely and untrodden path. I pray that I may have God as my guide and the power of the Lord as my aid, since I am unable to find even the bare footsteps of those who have traveled the way before me …."[6]

2. He refers to a Psalm and interprets it (compare KJV Psalms 110:3) to mean that Jesus, as a spirit, was begotten of a mother before the world was made. The Psalm says: "Out of the womb, before the morning star, have I begotten thee."[7] He then says, this means "he came into existence from God himself before the morning star, that is before the organization of the world."[8] This is one of the rare documented references to the Savior's birth by a heavenly mother in the pre-existence.

3. Eusebius presents Christianity as the oldest religion in the world, pointing out that it was the religion taught to men from the beginning. He then says:

> "Our doctrines of religion, have not been lately invented by us, but from the first creation of man, so to speak, having been established by the natural understanding of divinely favored men of old."[9]

4. Eusebius then says the God of the Old Testament—or Jehovah—was actually Jesus Christ as he existed in the spirit before his birth to Mary. He cites many instances of the Lord's appearance to the Old Testament prophets. For example: "Moses most clearly proclaims him second Lord after the Father, when he says, 'The Lord rained upon Sodom and Gomorrah brimstone and fire from the Lord.' The divine scripture also calls him God, when he appeared again to Jacob in the *form of a man* and said to Jacob, 'Thy name

6. The Nicene and Post-Nicene Fathers, op. cit., 1:81.
7. Ibid., 1:86.
8. Ibid., 1:87.
9. Ibid.

shall be called no more Jacob ....' Wherefore also Jacob called the name of that place 'Vision of God,' saying, 'For I have seen God face to face, and my life is preserved.'"[10]

5. Concerning all of the Old Testament prophets, Eusebius says:

> "They also clearly knew the very Christ of God; for it has already been shown that he appeared unto Abraham, that he imparted revelations to Isaac, that he talked with Jacob, that he held converse with Moses and with the prophets that came after."[11]

In many respects Eusebius makes extremely interesting reading for the modern student of the Bible.

Augustine, the Bishop Who Split Christianity in Two

If Eusebius was the bishop of Caesarea who wanted to unify the church, Augustine was the bishop of Hippo whose strange doctrines ultimately split the church and culminated in ferocious wars that raged up and down the continents of Europe, Africa and Asia.

Augustine was born in Tagaste near ancient Carthage, Algeria, of Northern Africa. The date of his birth was 354 A.D., which would be approximately 14 years after the death of Eusebius. His mother (Saint Monica) was a Christian, his father was a pagan.

In his famous autobiography entitled *Confessions*, Augustine describes his profligate youth and his subsequent spiritual vacillations. Finally, in 387 A.D. he was baptized at the age of 33 after his long struggle with unchastity. His conversion was not based on any profound study of Christianity but a scrap of scripture which said:

> "Not in rioting and drunkenness, not in chambering [harlotry] and wantonness, not in strife and envying. But put ye on the Lord Jesus Christ, and make not provision for the flesh to fulfil the lusts thereof."[12]

Later Augustine wrote a book entitled, *The City of God.* Since all manmade cities reflect the wickedness of the human race, he described an ideal city on a spiritual plane which would be acceptable to God.

---

10. Ibid., 1:83.
11. Ibid., 1:87.
12. Romans 13:13-14.

Augustine's training was in teaching rhetoric. He was in Rome for awhile and also Milan but in 388 Augustine finally returned to his hometown of Tagaste with his illegitimate son who died shortly thereafter. Augustine then formed a religious community which later became the inspiration for his order of Augustinian monks. Martin Luther later belonged to this order.

In 391 A.D. he traveled to Hippo where the Christians induced him to make his home. Hippo was located just south of the modern city of Annaba which is west of Carthage in Algiers. Augustine was ordained a priest that year and later became the bishop of Hippo in 396 A.D. In spite of his many activities in Rome and elsewhere, he remained the bishop of Hippo until his death in 430 A.D.

The Dogmas and Doctrines Invented by Augustine

Augustine became famous for certain dogmas which he either initiated or defended with such vigor that they became the foundation of theological doctrine throughout the Christian world. In fact it was primarily the dogmas of Augustine that were so reprehensible to most of the American Founding Fathers and gained for some of them the epithet of "atheist" when they resisted the non-biblical opinions of this famous prelate of the fourth century.

A summary of Augustine's basic dogmas might be stated as follows:

1. Augustine believed that when Adam and Eve fell, they imposed a curse on all their posterity. This is his doctrine of "original sin." He believed all humanity inherited the "sin" of Adam and Eve.

2. Augustine believed the sin of the first parents resulted in the entire human family being doomed forever.

3. However, Augustine claimed that God decided to demonstrate his supremacy over Satan by electing a few to be saved no matter what they did. This is known as the doctrine of "election."

4. Whether a person was elected to be saved or elected by God not to be saved, Augustine believed it was all pre-determined before we were born. This meant our fate was fixed and unalterable regardless of what kind of life we lived. This is called Augustine's doctrine of "Predestination."

5. Augustine also believed in a "purgatory" or hell where mankind suffer the most extreme tortures forever unless they are released by baptism or the prayers of the Saints.

6. Since baptism was supposed to get a person released from purgatory, Augustine reasoned that little children should be baptized shortly after birth or as soon as possible thereafter, since otherwise—without baptism—they would remain in purgatory forever.

But even with baptism and a release from purgatory, it did not provide complete redemption unless one were among the elect.

The Theological Resistance to Augustine

Anyone acquainted with the original Biblical scriptures would have a multitude of questions for Bishop Augustine. However, about the only people who had copies of the scriptures were those who were leaders of the various churches. Nevertheless, the resistance not only came from scholars but from the many Christians relying on pure reason and the simple doctrines of their faith as they understood it.

Augustine's Dogma of "Election"

Augustine's invention of the doctrine of "original sin" sprouted two other mistaken concepts that have afflicted mankind from then until now.

Dr. Bruce L. Shelley summarizes how Augustine visualized the fall of man.

> "In Augustine's view Adam's [original] sin had enormous consequences. His power to do right was gone. In a word, he died, spiritually—and soon physically. But he was not alone in his ruin. Augustine taught that the whole human race was 'in Adam' and shared his fall. Mankind became a 'mass of corruption,' incapable of any good act. Every individual, from earliest infancy to old age, deserves nothing but damnation." [13]

But God is all powerful and to prove his power over Satan he "elected" to choose a few to be saved. Dr. Shelley continues his summary of the thinking of Augustine:

> "Since man of himself can do nothing good, all power to do good must be the free gift of God, that is, 'grace.' Out of the mass of the fallen race God chooses some to receive this grace, which comes to them from the work of Christ, and ordinarily through the church, and especially through the sacraments ....

---

13. Bruce L. Shelley, Church History in Plain Language, Waco, Texas: Word Books, 1982, pp. 145-146.

> "As Williston Walker explains, 'Those to whom God does not send his grace are lost. Nor can any man be sure, even if he now enjoys God's grace, that he will be saved. Only those to whom God gives the added grace of perseverance, that is, who have the divine aid to the end of life, will be redeemed.' Man, therefore, has no power or worthiness of himself, his salvation is fully from God." [14]

It will be immediately perceived that Augustine had virtually obliterated the concept of free choice or free will. If one is elected he or she is automatically saved. If not, he or she is automatically damned. And, as Williston Walker points out, neither can be sure until the end whether or not they made it. But Augustine said God knows already who will be saved and who will be damned.

Augustine's Doctrine of Predestination

Augustine explains how certain ones are predestined to be saved whether they like it or not:

> "And those whom he has predestined them he has also called; and those whom he has called, them he has also justified, and those whom he has justified, them he has glorified. Of their number no one perishes, because they are all chosen; and they are chosen because they are called according to the purpose—not their own purpose, but that of God." [15]

Augustine wrote:

> "I have said all this about those who have been predestined to the kingdom of God, whose number is so fixed that not one can be added to it, or taken from it ... The number of the elect is fixed, not to be increased or diminished." [16]

He also wanted to make it clear that no individual can alter the course which God has predestined for that person. He wrote:

> "Nor can the human will prevent Him from doing what He will, seeing that even with the wills of men, He does what He will when He wills to do it. Accordingly, there is no doubt that human

14. Ibid., p. 146; see also Barker, Apostasy from the Divine Church, op. cit., pp. 451-452.
15. Quoted by Barker in Apostasy from the Divine Church, op. cit., p. 453.
16. Ibid., p. 452.

will cannot resist the will of God, who hath done whatsoever He pleased in heaven and on earth."[17]

The Whole Concept of Baptism for the Remission of Personal Sins Was Twisted to Mean Adam's Sin

The student will realize that once Augustine, the bishop of Hippo, had invented the dogma of "original sin" and had sanctified it by the sword of Rome, the concept of getting rid of Adam's sin became more important than the remission of personal sins. Infant baptism had been growing in the Church and Augustine's dogma of all mankind being under the "original sin" cemented the idea in the minds of parents that if a child had not been baptized to get rid of the "original sin" the baby was damned to hell regardless of the virtue of his or her personal life.

Election and Predestination Made God an Arbitrary, Capricious Being

We also recall that the pernicious and unscriptural doctrine relating to the fall of Adam and Eve completely missed the fact that it was the divinely designated gateway to human progress and the only way to learn for themselves the difference between good and evil.

But Augustine's mind set was quite different. He claimed that partaking of the fruit of the Tree of Knowledge damned them for all eternity. This laid the foundation for Augustine's invented theory that God decided to prove his supremacy over Satan by "electing" to save some who would be predestined to salvation no matter what they did, while the remainder would be damned even though they lived the lives of saints.

All of a sudden God became the arbitrary, whimsical creature Plato had claimed he was. The loving and just God of the Bible had disappeared into the labyrinth of an apostate miasma filled with philosophical darkness and confusion which launched the Dark Ages.

Augustine's Doctrine of Grace Made Free Agency Virtually Irrelevant

To the inquiring mind, the complicated argument put forth by Augustine concerning God's gift of grace defies rational comprehension. Let me therefore turn to the summary of this doctrine in two short paragraphs from Dr. Barker:

17. Ibid., p. 453.

> "The loss of the true conception of man as a child of God, free to make choices between good and evil, and the substitution of the idea of man as a machine created out of nothing and unable of himself to choose the good, resulted in Augustine's original conception of salvation. For him, salvation was not the outgrowth of character development, but was a salvation independent of character development—at least of character development which is the result of the action of a free will—and is wholly arbitrary… on the part of the Almighty. His idea of salvation has dominated the thinking of the historical Christian churches.
>
> "Augustine made of man only a puppet, impelled by God to do good or left as an imperfect automatic machine to do unavoidable evil. According to Augustine in order for man to do good, his will must be impelled by 'irresistible grace.' Therefore, there can be no real development of character, for character growth could come only by the exercise of free will, wholly free. The idea of man as a child of God… had been lost, and the 'Be ye perfect as your Father in heaven is perfect' could be no part of the work of them to whom the command was given, but only the result of the action of God on passive man incapable of 'resisting divine grace'." [18]

The people in the last analysis, have neither choice nor voice.

For hundreds of years the wars in Europe were the vehement struggles to resist the non-Biblical theories of Augustine. Eventually, the sword of Rome was used in a sweeping determination to wipe out any resistance to these doctrines. It was called the "Inquisition."

Pelagius—The Missionary from Britain

A logical place to begin the study of the theology of Augustine might be when Pelagius—a Christian from Britain—came to Rome and began teaching three things that outraged Augustine, the bishop of Hippo.[19]

At the outset, Pelagius attacked Augustine's doctrine of Original Sin. In summary he declared that:

1. Adam's sin was purely personal, and affected none but himself. In other words, Augustine's doctrine of "original sin" which he said was

18. Barker, Apostasy from the Divine Church, op. cit., p. 455. For clarity, I have reversed the order of these two paragraphs.
19. Encyclopedia Britannica, op. cit., under "Augustine," 1:909.

inherited by all mankind was his own invention and violated the scripture which said:

> "Neither shall the children be put to death for the fathers: every man shall be put to death for his own sin."[20]

Pelagius also attacked Augustine's doctrine of infant baptism, explaining that:

2. When little children are born they are innocent before God and only fall into sin under the force of temptation or evil example by others. Once again Pelagius was accusing Augustine of inventing a false doctrine when he said little children are guilty of the "original sin" of Adam and must be baptized and cleansed of that sin or they will be condemned to hell forever.

Pelagius emphasized that:

3. Children who die in their infancy—being untainted by sin—are saved without baptism. This declaration cut to the very heart of Augustine's radical idea that terrified parents for centuries. The bishop of Hippo preached that children who die in their infancy and have not been baptized are beyond redemption. Pelagius said this was palpably false.

As might have been expected, Augustine became so agitated by the teachings of Pelagius that he conjured up his most vehement rhetoric to denounce this Christian fundamentalist from Britain. Then he went further. He demanded that the doctrines taught by Pelagius be officially denounced and declared rank heresy.

How Augustine Made the Bishop of Rome the Final Authority

To accomplish this, Augustine forced Pelagius through two separate hearings and after getting favorable results in each of them, he exercised his authority as bishop of Hippo to appeal the question to the bishop of Rome. The object was to have Pelagius excommunicated so that his doctrines would be declared anathema. And that is exactly what happened.

To complete his victory, Augustine then pronounced a dictum that became the precedent for making the bishop in Rome the final authority for ultimate decisions on doctrinal questions. Augustine declared: "Rome has spoken, *the cause is finished*."[21]

20. Deuteronomy 24:16.
21. Barker, Apostasy from the Divine Church, op. cit., p. 477.

As time went by, those pontifical words conclusively settled many hotly debated issues for a number of centuries.

Babies in Purgatory?

But there was one trailing cloud of dissent that would not die. It was the resistance to the abhorrent idea that a loving God would condemn an infant to purgatory forever just because the child had not been given a sprinkling-type "baptism" by a priest before it died. In spite of numerous edicts out of Rome confirming this doctrine, many parents and priests on three continents continued to question this obscurely reasoned Augustinian dogma.

Finally, nearly a thousand years after Augustine's original pronouncement, the Council of Trent (1545-1563) flatly declared that if anyone taught that Adam's sin was not inherited by all mankind, he should be declared "anathema" and excommunicated. That being the case, it followed that babies must continue to be baptized shortly after birth to save their souls.

And any who resisted could be imprisoned, tortured and mutilated, or sentenced by the Court of Inquisition to be burned at the stake.

What about the Bible?

Augustine had built his gospel on the shaky, wobbly foundation of Plato's speculative thinking. The whole structure of the Bible cried out against him.

Around 1400 B.C. Joshua had said:

> "Choose you this day whom ye will serve... as for me and my house, we will serve the Lord."[22]

Nearly a thousand years later, Elijah said to Israel:

> "How long halt ye between two opinions? If the Lord be God, follow him: but if Baal, then follow him."[23]

Then came Jesus and the apostles. Jesus said to his disciples:

> "Go ye into all the world and preach the gospel to every creature. He that believeth and is baptized shall be saved; but he that believeth not shall be *damned*."[24]

---

22. Joshua 24:15.
23. 1 Kings 18:21.
24. Mark 16:15-16.

Did Augustine ever read this scripture? If so, his mind must have been distracted by some perplexing mystery of Plato or Aristotle because he obviously missed it. And what could be his excuse for missing this magnificent message of Peter when he explained to the Jews how they could attain salvation:

> "Repent, and be baptized … And with many other words did he testify and exhort, saying, Save yourselves from this untoward generation. Then they that gladly received his word were baptized: and the same day there were added unto them about three thousand souls."[25]

And where was Augustine the day his Bible Study class read Paul's statement to the Romans:

> "The righteous judgment of God; who will render to every man according to his deeds."[26]

Or to the Corinthians:

> "For we must all appear before the judgment seat of Christ; that every one may receive the things done in his body."[27]

Or to the Galatians:

> "Be not deceived; God is not mocked: for whatsoever a man soweth, that shall he also reap."[28]

The Founders' Reaction to These Dogmas

The dogmas of Augustine continued to be warmly debated right down to the time when America began to be settled. It is interesting that most of the Founding Fathers had read the New Testament in Greek and the Old Testament in Latin. Some had even read the Old Testament in Hebrew. They decided they knew their scriptures better than Augustine and were capable of drawing their own conclusions. Most of them were revolted by Augustine's dogmas on "election" and "predestination."

The Founders describe in their writings how they continued attending Church because they believed in the teachings of Jesus but they secretly

25. Acts 2:38-41.
26. Romans 2:5-6.
27. 2 Corinthians 5:10.
28. Galatians 6:7.

repudiated these dogmas which remained prominent in most of the Christian churches and had often been enforced at the point of the sword.

Franklin said he doubted these Augustinian dogmas as early as age fifteen. John Adams said he never did believe them. Jefferson was of the same opinion but said he kept his religious convictions hidden in his heart. Nevertheless, all of these men continued to attend a Christian church of their choice. They looked beyond the creeds of the day and went to church to ferret out the golden nuggets of Bible-based Christianity on which they hoped to build the American civilization.

Opposition from Mainstream Churches

Under these circumstances, it was risky business for a group of political leaders to resist many of these doctrines and even go so far as to say that taxes should not be used to support various denominations.

This was particularly reprehensible to the seven states that had already adopted "official" churches. Those states were all supporting their favorite denominations with tax money.

In the final analysis, the Founders instinctively felt a profound responsibility as they undertook to structure a government for the first free people in modern times. John Adams called their work a "divine science."[29] As they approached history, philosophy and the Bible, they felt it was their special challenge to sort out and eliminate the doctrines and practices which were identifiable as alien to God's law and the teachings of God's servants.

The Founders Were Distinguished Scholars in Their Own Right

The unique quality of the Founders as an assembly of truly virtuous men, was the fact that they were highly qualified to do their own thinking and make educated decisions as they went along.

J. Reuben Clark, the noted constitutionalist, exclaimed:

> "What a group of men of surpassing abilities, attainments, experience, and achievements! There had not been another such group… [in] our history… that even challenges the supremacy of this group."[30]

29. Skousen, The Making of America, op. cit., p. 195.
30. The Improvement Era magazine, June, 1957, p. 397.

Concerning their training and experience, he said:

> "The Framers were deeply read in the facts of history; they were learned in the forms and practices and systems of the governments of the world, past and present; they were, in matters political, equally at home in Rome, in Athens, in Paris, and in London; they had a long, varied, and intense experience in the work of governing their various Colonies."[31]

Against what did the Framers measure all of this learning and experience? They measured it in terms of the Bible.

As we have already mentioned, when Dr. Donald S. Lutz and Dr. Charles S. Hyneman studied 2,200 speeches and articles in the days of the Founders from 1760-1805, it was discovered that they and their friends supported their arguments for the new system of government with quotations from the Bible 34% of the time—more than from any other source.

The Founders had access to comprehensive studies of ecclesiastical history in English, French, and German. In all of these works it was emphasized that down through the centuries large segments of the Christian population had resisted many of the radical changes which they felt were in violation of basic Biblical teachings. They also observed that in nearly every instance this opposition was suppressed either by the sword or by church councils that had sufficient authority to drown out and suppress the opposition.

This left the American Founders—as it does the modern student—with the need to compare each of these changes with a reliable frame of reference. This is obviously the Bible and the writings of the Christian leaders during the first century.

---

31. Ibid.

Topics for Reflection and Discussion

1. Who was the last of the twelve apostles to survive? About when did the Christians cease to have any apostles among them? During the ten persecutions of the Christians by the Romans, what were the names of the two emperors who committed the worst atrocities?

2. Why was the destruction of the Christian libraries considered such a tremendous loss? Do we presently have any of the original manuscripts of the Gospels and the letters of the Apostles?

3. Can you turn to your Bible maps and locate Antioch, Alexandria, Ephesus, Corinth, Rome, and Constantinople? Why did the bishops of these cities become so prominent?

4. What famous history book did Eusebius write? Where did he serve as bishop? About when did he live? What were two of the doctrines emphasized by Eusebius that impressed you the most?

5. Where did Augustine become bishop? This place was not far from ancient Carthage. Can you locate it on the modern map? Why did he delay getting baptized? In what skill was he trained?

6. What did Augustine say would happen to a person who had been elected by God to be saved if he or she were wicked? What did he say would happen to a person who had not been elected but lived a saintly life? Did Augustine believe in free agency?

7. Can you explain Augustine's doctrine of "election?" Can you explain his doctrine of "predestination"? Name three scriptures which show that Augustine was teaching false doctrines.

8. Why is it illogical to have babies baptized even if it is just by sprinkling? What did Augustine say would happen to a baby that died without being baptized? This doctrine was given universal application by the Council of Trent. Why had it taken nearly a thousand years to get this doctrine accepted on a world-wide basis?

9. When Pelagius came to Rome from Britain what three principles of the gospel did he preach that outraged Augustine? Can you explain the thinking of Augustine that led him to believe in "original sin"?

10. Can you cite two scriptures which clearly indicate that Augustine's denial of free will is a false doctrine? What was the reaction of the Founding Fathers to Augustine's dogma? But even though many of the denominations were giving lip service to these doctrines, why did the Founders continue going to church services? What were they looking for?

CHAPTER FOURTEEN

CHRISTIANITY AND GOD'S LAW ENTER THE DARK AGES

As we saw in chapter 12, if the high ideals of the Roman statesman, Cicero (106-43 B.C.), had survived they could have changed the history of the world. Unfortunately, Cicero's dreams did not survive, and the iron-studded boots of the Roman legions continued to march over Europe, Asia, the Middle East, and Africa.

With the marching Roman Legions came the Roman law. It left its brand on the whole western world thereby perpetuating itself in most of the European nations as well as other regions the Romans conquered.

In the process Rome carried the remnants of Christianity with it. In fact, the worst thing that could have happened was when Christianity was adopted as the official religion of Rome. Beginning with the edict of Constantine in 313 A.D., a totally distorted and changed Christianity was being proclaimed at the point of Roman swords as the only means by which mankind could attain salvation.

The apostle John—in his apocalyptic vision—had seen this tragic epoch of human history. He described how the beautiful, glorious Church of Jesus Christ would be like a woman who had to be carried away into the wilderness to protect her while the ravages of a wicked, satanical host of evil spewed its venom upon mankind for several centuries.[1]

In the ensuing war between good and evil, God has made it clear that individual denominations should not be attacked but encouraged and commended for whatever good they are able to achieve. This became the policy of the Founding Fathers. The enemy of society and all churches is the diabolical conglomerate of organized evil. In a sense, that is Satan's "church." His priesthood include the hosts of spirits who were defeated in the war in heaven and cast out into the earth.[2] His converts are the hapless creatures who fall prey to his treacherous schemes to ensnare and destroy the essence of human happiness and the fabric of society.

1. Revelation, chapter 12.
2. Revelation 12:7-9.

Jesus and His Apostles Would Never Have Recognized the Remnants of Christianity

During the 200 years of persecution and book burning following the apostles, the fabric of gospel theology and ordinances under Biblical Christianity had been mutilated almost beyond recognition. For example, here are ten important characteristics of Roman Christianity which had forced the true Church of Jesus Christ into the wilderness:

The Majority of the People Were Without Any Scriptures

It would be over a thousand years before the printing press would be invented (1440 A.D.). Meanwhile, the scriptures had to be copied by hand on manuscripts that were both expensive and tedious to provide.

The development of monasteries in recent times had encouraged religious devotees to take strict vows and gather in cloistered quarters to devote themselves to religious service. One of the most important assignments was to carefully write out scriptural manuscripts.

Constantine ordered fifty copies of the scriptures prepared with highly decorated margins. These were distributed to the principal bishops as a guide to the churches. However, this policy of keeping the scriptures in the hands of the principal prelates of the church prevented the people from challenging any doctrines or practices which they felt were wrong.

When the reformation began in the sixteenth century one of the first weapons which the reformers used against false doctrines and unchristian practices was the printing and distribution of tens of thousands of Bibles among the people.

The People Didn't Know Who or What They Worshipped

Jesus had talked about his loving Heavenly Father, and Paul had described him as a glorified person whose attributes were identical with those of Jesus after the resurrection. Paul wrote:

> "God [the Father]... hath in these last days spoken unto us by his Son... who being in the brightness of his [the Father's] glory, and the *express image of his person*... sat down on the right hand of the Majesty [of the Father] on high."[3]

3. Hebrews 1:1-3.

By the fourth century God had become identical with Plato's "first cause," which was a vast omniscient essence of divine mind without body, parts or passions[4] and who made everything out of nothing.[5]

Even Jesus had been hypothesized into a being of mysterious qualities. He had been made part of a Godhead where the three members of that heavenly presidency had been converted by some strange formula of spiritual arithmetic into three in one and one in three. Among the vast number of lost doctrines was the Savior's clear scriptural declaration that he and his Father were one only in purpose—not one in identity. He said he wanted his disciples to be "one" in the same sense.[6]

The theology of fourth century Christianity wasn't even certain whether Jesus was all divine or just half divine. They quarreled bitterly as to whether he was the Father manifest in the flesh or a separate divine creature who acquired a mortal nature by being born of Mary.

Revelation and Ministering of Angels were No Longer Part of God's Gospel

As we mentioned in the last chapter, it became an established doctrine that revelation and the ministering of angels ended with the last apostle. The head bishop of the church could be expected to interpret existing scriptures to be certain they were properly understood but the people were not to expect new revelations or the ministering of angels.[7]

And this, of course brings us back to Augustine and the Inquisition which was eventually employed to enforce confession of faith and commitment to the authority of Rome.

This became the foundation for nearly a thousand years of abysmal dark ages.

Constantine

As we have already pointed out, Constantine himself was still a pagan when he decided Christianity might serve as a unifying element in his disintegrating empire. The adoption of Christianity as the principal religion of Rome

4. Quoted in "First Book of Common Prayer," Article 1, in Barker, Apostasy from the Divine Church, op. cit., pp. 229-231.
5. Barker, Apostasy from the Divine Church, op. cit., p. 436.
6. John 17:21-23.
7. Barker, Apostasy from the Divine Church, op. cit., pp. 650-654.

was purely a political ploy and had nothing to do with the genuine conversion of either the emperor or the people.

There are a variety of stories about Constantine having had visions—including an appearance of Jesus—and after seeing a flaming cross in the sky being told, "By this sign, thou shalt conquer."

After a lifetime of study, James L. Barker concluded that these stories were fictitious fabrications. He says:

> "But in view of his [Constantine's] life, it is difficult to believe that Constantine received a vision. However, he immediately pursued a policy favorable to the Christians although *he was not baptized until twenty-five years later, shortly before his death.*"[8]

It would seem the wily emperor-politician took advantage of the cohesive forces of Christianity to neutralize the centrifugal forces that were tearing the empire apart. His deathbed repentance and baptism twenty-five years later was no doubt urged upon him by some well-meaning church prelate.

Roman Law Virtually Obliterated God's Law

It is rather amazing that when Christian churchmen became Roman emperors they practically demolished the remnants of God's law. Justice was totally commercialized and decisions often went to the highest bidder. Political and church positions were also auctioned off in the same manner and the whole corrupt structure of church and state were amalgamated together in a massive juggernaut of oppression and injustice.

The Theodosian Code

The former American Under-Secretary of State, J. Reuben Clark, Jr., discusses how this whole tragic view of life and law merged into a virtual dictatorship beginning with the Theodosian Code. He writes:

> "Following the pattern of the somewhat earlier private codification of Gregorious and Herogenes (at the time of Constantine), the Emperor Theodosius II and Valentinian III on March 26, 429 A.D., appointed by Imperial Edict (the people were not consulted either directly or through representatives), a committee of jurists to prepare an official code. They prescribed what it was to contain.

8. Ibid., p. 204.

"This code was prepared and presented to the Roman Senate some nine years and nine months later [December 25, 438 A.D.]. That Senate which had long since lost its power and was almost menially subservient to the Emperor, received the Code with shouts of approval: 'It is right! So be it!' accompanied by loud exclamations of oriental flattery for the Emperor.

"There was no debate on the Code by the Senate, no objection, question, or dissent; the Senate did not so much as dot an 'i' or cross a 't.' The Code was wholly the offspring of the Emperors; the people had no part whatever in it.

"We should understand that everything connected with the Emperor was divine or sacred—there was the sacred imperial palace, the sacred imperial bed chamber, the sacred imperial wardrobe, the sacred laws, etc.

"The government was an absolute autocracy, the state was thoroughly militarized, the Emperor in supreme Command. The Emperor was the sole source of law. By the simple issuance of a new law, the Emperor could modify or repeal any previous law. All imperial utterances were considered divine or sacred, the contravention of a given law, as was often proclaimed, was sacrilege, and the punishment for sacrilege was death. The laws, issued and codified, were designed to keep secure this absolute, unchallenged power and authority of the Emperor.

"It is interesting to note that these laws, proclaimed over 1,500 years ago, had provisions covering so-called modern concepts, which our emigres [from the Soviet Union] and fellow travelers would have us believe are new inventions, as price fixing, black markets, excessive taxation, socialized medicine, conscription of labor, anti-Semitism, inflation, corruption in government bureaus, the relationship between Church and State—all phrases familiar to our ears.

"Under these laws, 'the entire population was organized as in one vast army. All, including the highest officials, were strictly classified, and even the least had a station.' In substance, this meant that everyone did what he was told, and did not act without permission.

"There was a great body of secret police to report disobedience; there was a 'special' secret police appointed to watch the ordinary secret police.

"These laws were framed to provide security. We of today have heard that same kind of security talk. But, in fact, all this bred not security, but scarcity of grain, of materials, of men.

"The mere making of laws, even in an absolute despotism, does not change the great laws of nature and economics—neither then nor now, for there can be no permanent stability where men are not free.

"In fewer than forty years from the issuance of the Theodosian Code [i.e. 476 A.D.], the Empire of the West fell, notwithstanding the operation under complete autocratic power, of economic devices enacted to promote the welfare of the people and preserve the empire. Some of these devices were the same ones that we have been told would rebuild our economic structure and preserve our free institutions. These devices failed with Rome; they will ultimately fail with us." [9]

The Code of Justinian

"Ninety years later, in 528 A.D., Justinian, Emperor of the Roman Empire of the East, struggling to preserve and build his empire by complete autocratic authority, called a noted jurist named Tribonian to collect about him a group of other jurists (there were nine others) and with them to compile the laws issued since the time of Constantine, nearly 200 years before (306-337 A.D.).

"The accumulations of laws were said to be so voluminous as to fill 2,000 books and some 3 million verses, estimated to equal 580 volumes of 400 pages to a volume." [10]

Tribonian's compilations were in four parts:

"*A Code*, containing all the imperial statutes thought worthy of preserving from Hadrian (117-138 A.D.) to Justinian.

"*The Institutes*, which contained the great elements of the Civil Law, but none of them embodying the principles of a free government.

9. An address by J. Reuben Clark given November 21, 1952, and quoted in his book, Stand Fast By Our Constitution, Salt Lake City: Deseret Book Company, 1973, pp. 139-147.

10. Ibid.

> "*The Pandects*, declared to be 'the greatest repository of sound legal principles, applied to the private rights and business of mankind, that has ever appeared in any age or nation.' (Justinian called it 'the temple of human justice.')
>
> "*The Novels*, a collection of new laws passed subsequent to the compilation of the Code, to correct errors and supply omissions in the Code.
>
> "The new Code was published in 534 A.D. All of the sources on which the Justinian compilations were based, except the Theodosian Code, disappeared after the publication of Justinian's Code, Institutes, and Pandects.
>
> "The works were composed and written in Latin and later translated in Greek." [11]

The Emperor's Arrogant Declaration of Total Supremacy

J. Reuben Clark, Jr., was amazed at the crass arrogance of Justinian in boldly declaring that all political, religious, social and economic power was centered in his divine personage. Clark says:

> "While the absolute power of the Emperor was implicit in the Theodosian Code, it was boldly announced in the Justinian compilations. The Emperor had all legislative, judicial, and executive power in himself. Some affirm this principle had its origin during the reign of Augustus Caesar, some trace it back to Romulus and the founding of Rome in 753 B.C.
>
> "This principle seems to have been basic to Roman law in the West, for over 1,200 years, with almost a thousand years more in the East, or until 1453 A.D., when the Turks captured Constantinople ....
>
> "Thus it was inevitable that this principle of the autocratic power of the Emperor, the executive, which was basic in the laws of Western and Southern Europe and portions of the Near East for over 2,000 years... should be a vital portion of the warp and woof of the law of continental Europe ...." [12]

---

11. Ibid.
12. Ibid.

The Code of Napoleon

[At this point J. Reuben Clark includes one other code which attempted to repair the obvious weaknesses of both the Theodosian and the Justinian codes.]

> "One other code may be mentioned here—a modern one—the Code of Napoleon.
>
> "Having been appointed Consul, Napoleon assigned a committee to make a codification of new laws. Napoleon assisted in the deliberations.
>
> "Here again the people were not consulted. It was compiled in four months, and is said to be the product of the Roman and customary laws, the ordinances of the kings, and the laws of the Revolution.
>
> "This Code is firmly entrenched in most of the countries of Europe and prevails among most of the Latin races.
>
> "The Code of Napoleon, like the Theodosian and Justinian Codes, did not originate with the legislative branch of government, nor on the initiative of the people. All these codifications originated with the ruler of the nation; their provisions were dictated by him.
>
> "The rigors of this system were at times mitigated by a benign sovereign, but only to the extent that he desired; legislative bodies might at times be set up and function as he permitted; but any attempt by those bodies to go contrary to his will was somehow made ineffective; sometimes such efforts were treasonable and so treated.
>
> "The people under this system have those rights, powers, and privileges, and those only, which the sovereign considers are for their good or for his advantage. He adds or takes away as suits his royal pleasure.
>
> "All residuum of powers [remained] in the Emperor. Under this system, the people look into the law to see what they may do. They may only do what the Emperor has declared they may do.
>
> "It may be noted in passing, that under our [English] common law system, we look into the law to see what we may not do, for we may do everything we are not forbidden to do ….

> "We must always remember that despotism and tyranny, with all their attendant tragedies to the people, as in Russia... come to nations because one man, or a small group of men, seize and exercise by themselves the three great divisions of government—the legislative, the executive, and the judicial.
>
> "For now a score of centuries the nations and peoples of Western and Southern Europe—the bulk of the civilized world... have lived under this [Roman Civil Law] concept... and, when the concept has been operative, have suffered the resulting tragedies—loss of liberty, oppression, great poverty among the masses, insecurity, wanton disregard of human life, and a host of the relatives of these evil broods." [13]

The American Founders Saw What Had Happened

In the Founders' search for the correct principles of government and law, it was apparent to them that Roman Civil Law had largely obliterated the essential elements of God's Law.

The original proclamation of liberty had been smothered under the debris of oppression and tyranny.

The concern for the poor, the sick, the elderly, the widows and orphans had been replaced by greed and conquest that had created poverty, widows, orphans, and human suffering on a monumental and pervasive scale.

The statutes of God's law that provided reparation to the victims of crimes or torts had been forgotten by powerful potentates who perpetrated these crimes themselves and used their religious or secular power to escape unscathed.

The moral code of the commandments and the statutes had been debauched to the point where Edward Gibbon in his *Decline and Fall of the Roman Empire*, describes immorality, and depravity as major factors in bringing about the collapse of the Roman civilization.

For centuries reformers both inside and outside the church endeavored to cleanse the church and the government of all the numerous aberrations that had taken place since the Roman emperors and their appointed surrogates had united church and state.

---

13. Ibid.

As we have seen, the divine organization of the people both under the Mosaic pattern as well as the Apostles, had been completely altered by the gradual adoption of a dictatorial hierarchy structured after the political dominion of Rome.

The formalized creed demanded by Constantine created theological confusion and sometimes open warfare in the centuries that followed.

It was apparent to the Founders that God's Law, in its historical and prophetic sense, had lost its opportunity to radiate the bright human hope for freedom, prosperity and peace which it had produced for the City of Enoch and might have produced for ancient Israel.

In its place the Dark Ages had taken over.

A Valiant Effort to Preserve the Ancient Records

It is interesting that for centuries those who believed they had the true records of the gospel and the teachings of the prophets, hid up their records in hopes they could come forth in some later, brighter day. Sometimes they were hidden in water-proof jars and buried in the earth. Sometimes they were hidden away in caves. When a surprise attack occurred, the family scriptures were often thrown back into caves helter skelter with no protection whatever. However, the urine and accretions of birds and animals that used these caves over the centuries encased these scrolls with an organic protection and scholars have been able to carefully unroll thousands of them for a special kind of photography that would preserve their contents.

Today a Flood of Ancient Records Is Supplementing Our Understanding of the Sacred Scriptures

Dr. Hugh Nibley, one of my former associates at Brigham Young University, is one of the world authorities on these ancient manuscripts. He points out that in the past, these lost manuscripts were found one at a time and many years apart. However, today they are being discovered "in whole libraries of multiple volumes."

As a result, we now have literally thousands of precious portions of the ancient scriptures to study and compare. These are the writings of the Essenes, the Coptic Christians, and other important record-keeping people.

Here are some of the principal finds so far:

1. *The Dead Sea scrolls*. The first of these was discovered in a cave by a Bedouin shepherd boy in 1947. The cave was located in Qumran Valley on the northwestern shore of the Dead Sea. Later ten more caves were found to contain literally hundreds of scrolls and fragments comprising hundreds of documents. They dated from around 300 B.C. to 135 A.D. A complete copy of Isaiah was found and major portions of every book in the Old Testament except the book of Esther. Most of the documents were leather or papyrus. When the nearby headquarters of the Essenes was uncovered, archaeologists found a table and materials used in writing manuscripts.

2. *The Nag Hammadi manuscripts*. Dr Hugh Nibley writes:

> "Nag Hammadi is Arabic for the old monastery … about sixty miles north of Thebes where the Nile takes a big bend, [and] about ten miles off the river in the eastern desert. In the same year [1947] and under the same circumstances in which the Dead Sea Scrolls were found, a peasant, while digging for fertilizer, found a special cache just like the Dead Sea Scrolls.
>
> "It contained thirteen volumes, beautifully bound in leather. They weren't scrolls at all, but volumes, marvelously preserved, as if they had been written yesterday. They were regular books with pages, whose wrappings and bindings we still have. The leather bindings contained forty-nine different works, five of them repeated works. One of these thirteen volumes is in the Jung Museum in Zurich … The other twelve are in the Old Cairo Coptic Museum in Cairo. These … works [were] written and preserved and put away in an early church, many of them going back to the First Century A.D., others to the Fourth Century A.D. Most of them are Coptic translations of Greek documents that are lost today ….
>
> "This library is a marvelous thing. Van Unnik says that the books were written in a little local country church in Egypt before the apostasy ever took place—before there was any Gnosticism … These documents are very numerous and can be correlated with others—for example, the Mandaean texts." [14]

3. *The Mandaean texts*:

> "We know something of the very secretive Mandaean religion, a last holdover of the people who came from the Dead Sea. Their

14. Hugh Nibley, Old Testament and Related Studies, Salt Lake City: Deseret Book, 1986, pp. 124-125.

traditions and their ancient writings describe them as possibly leaving the Qumran people (the Dead Sea Scroll group) at the fall of Jerusalem [70 A.D.]. They first went up to Haran [Abraham's home for a number of years at the upper regions of the Euphrates River], then went down river.

"Some two thousand or so Mandaean people remain today. They have their own language and preserve the marvelous records they've kept for all this time. Originally, [around 600 B.C.], the Mandaeans went down to Qumran [on the Northwestern region of the Dead Sea] ... going out into the desert to live the gospel in its purity, setting up their own churches and communities ... then practicing their baptism. These doctrines were taught in those communities. The Mandaean writings relate very closely to the Nag Hammadi, and the Dead Sea Scrolls people too, because the Mandaeans came from there." [15]

4. *The Odes of Solomon*:

"Up on the Tigris, quite far north, were found in 1906 the forty-two Odes of Solomon, viewed as the earliest most valuable Christian collection of writings known ... One of the Odes turns up in the Dead Sea Scrolls and in the Nag Hammadi collection way down in Egypt ....

"The point is that all these writings come together. We have a large collection from the East, a large collection from Qumran, from Palestine, and a huge collection from southern Mesopotamia—all discovered since World War II, all sitting together, showing early isolated Christian and Jewish communities, all teaching very much the same thing." [16]

Now that we are enriching our store of knowledge concerning the scriptural treasures which once existed among ancient peoples, we appreciate more than ever the anxiety of the ancient religious people to preserve their sacred records so the Romans or other predators would not destroy them.

15. Ibid., pp. 125-126.
16. Ibid., p. 126.

Topics for Reflection and Discussion

1. Why would Cicero's concepts of "Natural Law" have been a great advantage to the apostles in spreading Christianity? What did the apostle John predict would happen to the Christian Church to save it from the ravages of Roman law and Roman culture?

2. By the fourth century, can you identify five things which would have prevented Jesus from recognizing the Church which carried his name and was being forced upon whole nations at the point of Roman swords?

3. Why would it be important to you to have access to the scriptures? How important is it for the masses of the people to have access to the scriptures?

4. Is it vital to a person's faith to know who or what to worship? In what way does "election" and "predestination" make God an arbitrary and capricious being?

5. How did Augustine's doctrine of "grace" make human free agency virtually irrelevant? Why was it a major calamity for Christianity when the Romans adopted Christianity as their official religion?

6. What aspects of Roman law virtually obliterated God's law?

7. How much influence did the people have in the adoption of the Roman Theodosian code? Did the Roman senate offer any opposition whatsoever when this code was presented to it for approval nine years later? How were the people organized under this code?

8. Was the method of adopting the Justinian code any more democratic than the procedure followed in adopting the Theodosian code? What did Emperor Justinian tell the people concerning his divine nature and authority?

9. The code of Napoleon required four months to compile. Were the people consulted in its preparation or ratification? Today, what large body of nations is living under the basic provisions of the Napoleonic code?

10. What was the reaction of many of the Founders to the doctrines of Augustine? Did they continue going to some church? What were they looking for?

CHAPTER FIFTEEN

After a Thousand Years God's Law Finally Began to Emerge in England

After carefully studying European history by a wide variety of authors, it became entirely apparent that the spring waters of freedom under God's law finally surfaced in England before they pooled their strength in America and created the first free people in modern times.

Very briefly, here is the story.

During the first thousand years of England's history, the people lived under three separate societies of pagan culture. The earliest culture belonged to the Celts who occupied the entire British Isles and most of Europe for several centuries before the Christian era. However, the Celts in England were eventually subjugated by Julius Caesar around 55 B.C. The Romans stayed for a little over four centuries and during this time they referred to this island tributary as "Britain." The Romans did not withdraw from the British Isles until around 400 A.D. when Rome needed all of her legions to fight the invading Goths migrating down from northern Europe.

The departure of the Romans left the original native Celts to govern themselves and it was not long before they were violently attacking one another to determine who would be the new rulers of the island.

One of the kings of a Celtic tribe in Southern England—called Kent—found his people being attacked by a fierce Celtic tribe from Scotland known as the Picts. The king of Kent looked desperately around for help. Earlier he had observed some tall, yellow-haired Anglo-Saxon pirates from Scandinavia who were ferocious fighters. He therefore invited two of these Anglo-Saxons who were brothers—named Hengist and Horsa—to bring their people across the channel to Kent and help him drive out the Picts from Scotland.

Hengist and Horsa agreed to assist the king of Kent and came across the English channel leading their people as they embarked in hundreds of Viking boats. They assaulted the Picts in a wave of violent fury and a great victory was won. Then the king of Kent wanted to reward the Anglo-Saxons and send them back to the continent. But they didn't want to go. They liked England. Hengist and Horsa—together with their Viking hordes of tens, fifties and hundreds—announced that they planned to stay in England and make it their home.

This outraged the king of Kent and it was not long before open conflict erupted between the people of Kent and their erstwhile Anglo-Saxon allies.

The Anglo-Saxon Conquest of England

As it turned out, the Anglo-Saxons not only occupied Kent but within a few generations they had brought over more of their tribes from the continent and pushed the native Celts all the way west to the region now known as Wales. In fact, many Celts fled across the Irish sea to Ireland or migrated north from Wales to Scotland.

The dominant tribe among the Anglo-Saxons were the Engels or Yinglings and it was not long before they had changed the name of the island from Britain—as the Romans had called it—to Yingling-land or Engel-land and eventually it took on the modern name of England.

How the Pagan Anglo-Saxons Became Christians

The story is told that Gregory I, while still a young priest and long before he became Pope in 590 A.D., happened to see some youths in the slave market of Rome who had long blonde hair and were strikingly handsome. When he learned that they were prisoners from England who were being sold as slaves, he determined to send missionaries to convert these beautiful people.[1]

The first missionary was named Augustan and he went directly to King Ethelburt who ruled all of England up to the Humber River. Father Augustan said he was a messenger from Rome and he had come to tell the king how he could have "everlasting joy in heaven, and a kingdom that should never end."[2] The king was very impressed, but the Anglo-Saxon pagan priests were violently opposed to the Christian missionary and his message about a heavenly kingdom. Nevertheless, by patient persistence Augustan gradually gained the confidence of the people and established a foothold of Christian believers who began to spread their influence throughout the region in spite of Druid opposition.

The Anglo-Saxons Found Their Law Recorded in the Bible

As some of the Anglo-Saxons were taught Latin so they could read the Bible, they were amazed to find that their own traditional laws were recorded

1. Turner, The History of the Anglo Saxons, op. cit., 1:335-336.
2. Ibid., 1:339.

by Moses in the Biblical books of Exodus, Leviticus, Numbers and Deuteronomy. The pagan Anglo-Saxons had never written these laws down but had memorized them from generation to generation right along with their poems and traditional stories that described their earliest history.

It was the Anglo-Saxon King Alfred who later recorded these laws in his native language and said: "The law was first revealed in the Hebrew tongue ...."[3]

How Nations Practicing God's Law Became the Envy of Rome

The Anglo-Saxons were not the only ones who had preserved God's law. All over northern Europe this code of Hebrew law was widely practiced even though its provisions were memorized rather than written. Historians tell us these elements of God's Law were not only practiced among the Anglo-Saxons but also among the "Lowland Scotch, Normans, Danes, Norwegians, Swedes, Germans, Dutch, Belgians, Lombards and Franks."[4]

It is interesting that according to their historical traditions, all these nations were descendants of the Scythians or Goths who originally migrated from the region of the Black Sea where the lost Ten Tribes were located just before they disappeared into the north.

We read that after the Ten Tribes were captured and led off into the heathen cities of the Assyrians, they reformed themselves and decided that:

> "... they would leave the multitude of the heathen, and go forth into a further country, where never mankind dwelt, that they might keep their statutes, which they never kept in their own land."[5]

It was for this reason many scholars have suspected that the descendants of the Goths or Scythians in northern Europe were actually remnants of the Ten Tribes and that the code of laws which they handed down from generation to generation was basically the same charter of commandments and statutes which Moses had received on Mount Sinai.

Meanwhile, the cousins of the Anglo-Saxons—the Goths—had sacked the city of Rome and taken over portions of the Roman Empire. It is interesting that even though the Anglo-Saxons, the Goths, the Scythians, etc. were fierce warriors in time of conflict, they were the best governed people in

3. Ibid., 2:19.
4. Ibid., 2:95.
5. 2 Esdras 13:40-47, The Apocrypha According to the Authorized Version, Merrimac, Mass.: Destiny Publishers, 1946, pp. 56-57.

the world once peace was reestablished. We now know that they organized themselves in tens, fifties, hundreds and thousands and maintained order and justice under the principles of the Hebrew code even though they had lost the Hebrew faith and become pagans.

This Hebrew code was far superior to anything in the ancient world and historians point out that during the last days of Rome, many were willing to give up their highly prized Roman citizenship in order to live in areas where the Goths or other relatives of the Anglo-Saxons had established their system of government. As one Roman writer asks:

> "Can we then wonder why the Goths are not conquered by us, when the people would rather become Goths with them than Romans with us?"[6]

The Widespread Practice of God's Law in Northern Europe

Traditional history books tell the following story about these pagans who practiced God's Law:

> "These tribes all called themselves *Deutsch*, which meant the people; indeed most of them do so still, though we English only call those Dutch who live in Holland. Sometimes they were called Ger, [War], or Spear-men just as the Romans were called Qurites [after Quirinus—god of war]; and this name, Spear-men or Germans, has come to be the usual name that is given to them together, instead of Deutsch as they call themselves, and from which the fine word Teutonic has been formed ....
>
> "The men were either freemen or nobles ... Their villages were formed into what were called hundreds [just like ancient Israel], over which, at a meeting of the freemen from all of them a chief was elected from among the nobles; and many of the tribes had kings, who always belonged to one family, descended, it was thought, from their great god Woden [or Odin]."[7]

In his classical three-volume work on the Anglo-Saxons, Sharon Turner points out that there is no doubt but that "Odin" who heads up all of the memorized genealogies of these northern people, was not a mythical personality but a very real, historical individual who led a host of people—called the Scythians by Herodotus—into the northwest corner of Europe from which

6. Turner, The History of the Anglo Saxons, op. cit., 1:187.
7. Charlotte M. Yonge, Germany, Boston: D. Lothrop Company, 1878, pp. 13-15.

the Norwegians, Danish, Swedes, Icelanders, Germans, Dutch, Belgians, English, and some of the French have descended.[8]

One of these genealogies traces every generation from Odin to Hengist and Horsa who brought the ancient culture of the Anglo-Saxons to England around 450 A.D.[9] It is also through this series of genealogies that the English line of George Washington is traced back through the royal Scandinavian line to Odin.[10]

How the People Who Practiced God's Law Became Pagans

It is interesting that during the passing centuries all of these nations lost their traditional religious background and became pagans. Even though they had the remnants of God's law to govern themselves, they had completely forgotten about the Lord God Jehovah and Moses. It was not until they were converted to Christianity and had carefully read the Bible that they began to realize that their system of commandments and statutes actually came by direct revelation from God.

When the famous Alfred became king of the Anglo-Saxons (877-899 A.D.), Christianity was already well entrenched. Alfred had not only become a comprehensive linguist in order to study the Bible, but he had become a diligent student of the Greek and Roman classics. His writings also demonstrate that he was amazingly well informed about European geography and history.[11]

King Alfred Used the Bible and Common Sense to Challenge Some of the Doctrines Coming out of Christian Rome

Alfred translated a number of books into Anglo-Saxon. One of these was the writings of Boethius (Bow-EE-thias), the Roman philosopher, who had raised some serious questions concerning certain doctrines taught by the church in Rome. King Alfred had wondered about these doctrines himself and when Boethius confessed he could not explain them, Alfred proceeded to provide his own conclusions that these teachings were contrary to the Bible and therefore wrong. For example:

8. Turner, The History of the Anglo Saxons, op. cit., 1:275-279.
9. Ibid., 1:276.
10. Ida M. Ferguson, Heraldry and the United States of America, Vancouver, B.C., Canada: The Covenant People, p. 22.
11. Turner, The History of the Anglo Saxons, op. cit., 2:34-71.

King Alfred rejected Saint Augustine's doctrine of "original sin" and emphasized that mankind will not be punished for Adam's sin. Men are only responsible for their own sins. He said:

> "God had appointed freedom to be given to men … If they sin in any thing through this freedom, they shall, by penitence, compensate for it, to recover that freedom; and if any of them will be so hard-hearted that he will do no repentance … he shall then have a just punishment." [12]

In numerous statements along these lines King Alfred emphasized human responsibility and personal accountability. Contrary to Augustine's doctrine of "election" and "predestination," he insisted that God is not an arbitrary, whimsical deity who rewards or condemns without a cause. Men are judged according to their deeds. Contrary to Augustine's doctrine of "predestination," King Alfred emphasized that God's omniscience and foreknowledge of things to come is not predestination. Here is what he wrote:

> "He seeth all our works, both good and evil, before they are done … But he compels us not to … necessarily do the good; nor prevents us from doing evil; because he has given us freedom." [13]

Historian Sharon Turner compliments King Alfred for his penetrating insight concerning Augustine's confusing doctrine and says:

> "Alfred has hit upon the real wisdom of opinion on this contested subject, which many theologians and metaphysicians have failed to attain. He could not have left a more impressive instance of the penetrating sagacity of his clear and honest mind." [14]

This same purity of theological insight is reflected in his understanding of the attributes of God. Here are samples of his views concerning the Creator:

> "God is the beginning of all good things, and the governor of all creatures. He is the supreme good." [15]

> "All is present to him … He never remembers any thing, because he never forgets aught; He seeks nothing … because … he knows it all. He searches for nothing, because he loses nothing … He dreads nothing because he knows no one more powerful than himself … He is always giving and never wants. He is always

12. Ibid., 2:66-67.
13. Ibid., 2:69.
14. Ibid., 2:68-69.
15. Ibid., 2:72.

> Almighty, because he always wishes good, and never evil. To him there is no need of any thing. He is always seeing. He never sleeps … There never was a time that he was not, nor ever will be. He is always free."[16]

The Most Moral and Best Educated King England Ever Had

We have already noted the remarkable intellectual development and advanced scholarship of King Alfred, and Sharon Turner makes a passing note concerning King Alfred's determination to live a moral life of the highest Christian quality. He even prayed that God might alleviate his temptations to commit any unrighteous sexual act by afflicting him with some physical debilitation sufficient to help him control this powerful instinct.

Indeed, when the affliction did come he thanked God that while it debilitated his sexual urge it did not inhibit his powers in the field of battle or his capacity for wisdom in governing the people.[17]

Highlights of the Anglo-Saxon Law

For several centuries the Anglo-Saxon system of government flourished in England and the people prospered. However, as a result of the conquest of England in 1066 by William the Conqueror from Normandy, France, the English lost their great legacy of Anglo-Saxon law and found themselves struggling to survive under Roman civil law. As we proceed it will become plain that after 1066 the primary goal of the English people for a thousand years was to regain the inspired Hebrew law which had given them a high degree of prosperity, justice and domestic tranquility.

So What Were Whey Trying to Recover?

For the record here are the highlights of the Anglo-Saxon principles which had proved so successful:

1. The English Anglo-Saxons considered themselves a common-wealth of freemen who had inalienable rights that could not be taken away by their rulers. This meant that the source of sovereign power to govern was in the people, not the rulers.

2. Any powers granted by the people to their rulers were specifically described and strictly limited in scope.

16. Ibid., 2:77.
17. Ibid., 2:131.

3. Government was by freely elected representatives to their general assembly. No law or assessment of taxes could be imposed upon the people unless they or their representatives had consented to it.

4. The king was surrounded by a council of wise men called the Witenagemot (or Witan) who could remove the king if he was incompetent or did not abide the law. In other words, the ruler was not above the law of the people. The Witenagemot is Old English for "Wita" or councilor and "gemot" or assembly.[18]

5. The people were divided into small manageable groups of one hundred families which constituted a community and they were further divided into groups of ten families under an elected "tithingman." Each group was held responsible for the good conduct of its members. Five of these groups constituted a "vil" or village of fifty families and the elected leader was called a vil-man. Two vils comprised a hundred families which elected a "Hundred-man" and this was the nodal unit for an Anglo-Saxon community. The elected leader of each group was a judge and an administrator, and in time of war he served as a military commander over his group.

6. Anglo-Saxon law also gave strong emphasis to local self-government with very strict limitations on the powers given to the elected leaders.

7. The entire code of justice was based on "reparation to the victim" for any injury to his person or property. God's law was enforced with firmness and fairness. However, any person charged with a crime could demand a trial by a jury of his peers. Some historians believe the jury system can be traced back to King Alfred and the Anglo-Saxons.[19]

8. Under Alfred the Great there was freedom of religion which required separation of church and state and a spirit of tolerance between people of different faiths.

Efforts of the Anglo-Saxons to Civilize the Pagan Vikings

Alfred the Great was a magnificent warrior and eventually drove the invading Danish Vikings to the northern part of England above the Humber river. However, after a tribe of invaders were conquered it was the policy of the Christian Anglo-Saxons in England to offer arable land to the conquered invaders and teach them the art of farming so they would no longer have to carry out raids in order to make a living.[20]

18. See the International Dictionary of the Houghton Mifflin Company, Boston, 1979.
19. See "Petit Jury," Encyclopedia Britannica, Micropedia Ready Reference, Chicago, 1974, 7:912.
20. Turner, The History of the Anglo Saxons, op. cit., 1:570.

It was also the goal of the English Anglo-Saxons to convert these former enemies to Christianity.[21]

After settling down, these primitive rustics also saw that Alfred was very efficient. In spite of constant peril of invasion, he saved time to study, translate and write. He set up schools, encouraged the building of churches and continually encouraged the extended establishment of new settlements with sturdy homes, gardens and cultivated fields. He even initiated the university at Oxford.[22]

He kept time with candles. He used six candles of equal length, each one twelve inches long and separately marked. When the candles were used successively they covered the entire twenty-four hours. However, to avoid room breezes that would cause the candles to burn unevenly, the lighted candle was encased in a white horn which eventually became almost transparent, thereby allowing the light to radiate into the room. This Anglo-Saxon device eventually led to the invention of lanterns.[23]

The quality of Alfred's mind and philosophy is vividly demonstrated in his final instructions to his son who would be the next king:

> "My days are almost done. We must now part. I shall go to another world, and thou shalt be left alone in all my wealth. I pray thee … strive to be a father, and a lord to thy people. Be thou the children's [orphan's] father, and the widow's friend. Comfort thou the poor, and shelter the weak; and, with all thy might, right that which is wrong. And son, govern thyself by law; then shall the Lord love thee, and God above all things shall be thy reward. Call thou upon him to advise thee in all thy need, and so shall he help thee …."[24]

In his classical three-volume work on the Anglo-Saxons, Sharon Turner devotes 150 pages to the life and writings of King Alfred. At one point he pauses to pay him the following tribute:

> "We can scarcely believe that we are perusing the written thought of an Anglo-Saxon of the ninth century, who could not even read till he was twelve years old; who could then find no instructors to teach him what he wished; whose kingdom was overrun by the fiercest and most ignorant of barbarian invaders; whose life

21. Ibid., 1:570-571.
22. Ibid., 2:148.
23. Ibid., 2:127-128.
24. Ibid., 2:124.

> was either continual battle or continual disease; and who had to make up both his own mind and the minds of all about him. How ardent must have been Alfred's genius, that, under circumstances so disadvantageous, could attain to such great and enlightened conceptions!"[25]

In another place he praises Alfred's skill in writing and says:

> "It is clear, easy, animated, attractive, and impressive. It comes the nearest to our preset best English prose style of all the Anglo-Saxon prose writings … and entitles Alfred to be considered as the venerable father of our best English diction, as well as our first moral essayist … Has any country, within so short a period, produced in itself an intellect amongst its sovereigns, that combined so many excellencies?"[26]

Anglo-Saxons Miss Having a Moses and an Aaron

The Bible indicated that the ancient Israelites had the advantage of a spokesman for God in administering justice. Moses said:

> "Hear the causes between your brethren, and judge righteously between every man and his brother, and the stranger that is with him … The cause that is too hard for you, bring it unto me, and I will hear it."[27]

But what if the case was too hard for Moses and his brother, Aaron?

God gave them an instrument called the Urim and Thummim by which they could appeal directly to God for a correct ruling.[28]

The Anglo-Saxons operated with the advantage of the basic principles of God's law but without the divine advantage of a prophet with a Urim and Thummim to provide judgment directly from God when it was beyond the capacity of human wisdom.

How the English People Lost Their Freedom

As we have already mentioned, it was in 1066 A.D. that England was invaded and conquered by the Normans from France. The Normans were actually Northmen (like the Anglo-Saxons) but they had completely lost their

25. Ibid., 2:78.
26. Ibid., 2:120.
27. Deuteronomy 1:16-17.
28. Exodus 28:30.

cultural legacy. William the Conqueror and his Norman barons brought to England a whole new philosophy of government based on Roman law with all power in the ruler.

Roman law included the union of church and state and the doctrine of divine right of kings which gave the king power over all property as well as the life or death of every citizen. Instead of ministering justice under people's law or God's law as practiced by the Anglo-Saxons, the Normans ruthlessly imposed the statutes of Roman civil law upon the people according to the Justinian and Theodosian codes. Under these codes government and justice were ministered from a totalitarian or dictatorial perspective with no questions asked.

With this kind of power, William immediately confiscated vast tracts of land and Anglo-Saxon wealth so he could lavish them on his own people as a reward for their participation in the invasion. He replaced many of the bishops with his own bishops and thereby changed the political, social and religious climate of the whole English environment.

The Magna Charta

The original inhabitants of England knew a great tragedy was occurring but it was not until 1215 A.D. that the indignation of the people—particularly the families of former Anglo-Saxon barons—reached the boiling point. Their armed knights came to King John (the seventh Norman ruler down from William) and compelled him, with sword in hand, to sign the Magna Charta.

This document was designed to restore many of the ancient Anglo-Saxon rights, but when King John signed it he must have had his fingers crossed because he was violating the charter almost before the ink was dry. In fact, from century to century the various kings signed similar documents and then scrapped them the moment they had the power and supporting circumstances to do so. The whole history of England until recent times has been the struggle of the English people to restore the golden age of Anglo-Saxon rights.

In 1265 the barons forced King Edward I to set up the primary elements of an Anglo-Saxon Witenagemot which became known as a parliament. Later, in 1295, the king felt compelled to allow a "model" Parliament to be established, and in 1297 he was forced to agree that henceforth no taxes could be assessed against the people without the consent of the Parliament.

Henry VIII Declares Independence from Rome

Under the "divine right of kings" doctrine there was continual warfare trying to decide whether the various governments were under the Pope or whether the Pope and the various churches were under the political power of the Christian rulers in each country.

This contest rocked along until 1534 when Henry VIII decided to liberate the English people from the political and spiritual control of the Roman Papacy. He declared himself the spiritual father of the church rather than the Pope. Nevertheless, Henry retained the Catholic ritual and made no attempt to reform any doctrinal weaknesses that had accumulated during the centuries. His only major change was to cut the link with Rome and hold back the donations of the English churches instead of sending a substantial portion to the Pope as in the past.

After the death of Henry VIII in 1547, his sickly son was crowned Edward VI at the age of ten and his appointed guardians or regents officially adopted Protestantism as the doctrine of the Church of England. When he died of tuberculosis at the age of sixteen, his frail half-sister Mary took over in 1553 and ruled during five terrible years in which every form of torture and execution was employed to force the nation back to Roman Catholicism. When she died in 1558, another daughter of Henry VIII then became the famous Queen Elizabeth I who restored the independent Church of England under the Protestant faith.

During all of this religious vacillation, English politicians were trying to stay politically correct by changing their religion when the king or queen changed. Thus, Dr. Andrew Perne of Cambridge was a Catholic by choice, then became a Protestant under Edward VI, reverted to Catholicism under Mary, and then frantically embraced Protestantism under Elizabeth. But at least he kept his job![29]

Elizabeth was no marshmallow queen. As George F. Willison writes:

> "She was certainly not pious and loathed solemn moralists, possessing in large measure the love of pomp and show, the wit and gaiety, the high animal spirits of the lust age to which she gave her name. She openly dallied with one lover after another, had a taste for beer and 'strong waters,' swore like a trooper on occasion, and delighted in telling bawdy stories that left hardened men of the world gasping."[30]

29. George F. Willison, Saints and Strangers, New York: Reynal and Hitchcock, 1945, pp. 25-26.
30. Ibid., p. 23.

> "As Church and State were one, Elizabeth [as the spiritual head of the Church] demanded absolute uniformity of belief. No one could preach without a license. Above all there was to be no unlicensed printing ... Machinery to enforce uniformity already existed in the Court of High Commission, a counterpart of the Court of the Holy Inquisition. Dominated by the bishops, it shared the latter's supreme faith in the stake and gallows as the surest means of spiritual conversion ...."[31]

> "If suspects hesitated to answer from fear of incriminating themselves, punishment was even more certain. The kingdom's vile and stinking prisons, incredible sinkholes of disease and vice, were filled with innocent people lying helplessly awaiting the bishop's pleasure or displeasure, with no recourse whatever at law. The writ of habeas corpus [forbidding imprisonment without a cause] had yet to be devised ...."[32]

Although Elizabeth took a variety of lovers to her bed, she never married nor even left an illegitimate offspring to claim the throne. The next in line to inherit the crown of England was Mary Queen of Scots, but she became a scandalous disgrace and fled from Scotland to save her life. She crossed over into England and pleaded with Elizabeth to give her asylum. Elizabeth consented, but once Mary was safely established in one of the English estates, she immediately began plotting with France and Spain to invade England, overthrow Elizabeth and make England a Catholic nation with herself as queen.

When the plot was uncovered, Mary was arrested but given fairly comfortable quarters in the Tower of London. Nevertheless, she foolishly continued to send secret messages abroad plotting for the overthrow of England by one of the Catholic countries that would make her queen. Finally, as though her sanity had been completely consumed by her ambition, she tried to bribe certain nefarious individuals to assassinate Queen Elizabeth so Mary could be crowned in her stead. As this treasonous and ungrateful conduct eventually became known, the Parliament insisted that Mary be executed for blatant treason.

Mary, the fallen queen of Scotland, was beheaded February 8, 1587. Witnesses say that when her severed head toppled to the ground, her wig fell

---

31. Ibid., p. 24.
32. Ibid., p. 25.

away and revealed that her natural hair had turned snow white. She was only forty-four years old at the time.[33]

James I (1567-1625)

After Mary had been disgraced and fled from Scotland the mandate of monarchial government required that her thirteen month-old son James be crowned king of Scotland on July 29, 1567. He was only ten months old when he saw his mother for the last time. Four regents acted successively as proxies to rule the country until James officially became the king of Scotland at the age of seventeen.[34]

Four years later, the mother of James was executed and this made him next in the royal line for the crown of England. However, Queen Elizabeth continued to wear that crown until 1603, but when she passed away without heirs the 37 year-old James of Scotland triumphantly transferred his residence to London where he was crowned James I of both England and Ireland in 1603.

In his younger years James was force-fed a classical education and surprised the English peers with how much he knew. But he was completely ignorant of the Magna Charta and the Anglo-Saxon principles it contained. In fact, he had only contempt for Parliament and looked upon himself as the supreme ruler of all his domain and this meant he expected his subjects to obey without question. Historian Will Durant capsulated his attitude which was reflected in a speech which the king gave to Parliament:

> "The state of monarchy is the supremest thing upon earth. For kings are not only God's lieutenants on, and sit upon God's throne, but even by God Himself are called gods ... Kings are justly called gods, for that they exercise a man or resemblance of divine power on earth; for if you will consider the attributes of God, you shall see how they agree in the person of a king. God hath power to create or destroy, make or unmake at his pleasure, to give life or send death, to judge all and be judged nor accountable to none ... *And the like power have kings*."[35]

By these words King James disdainfully rejected the Magna Charta and three hundred years of slow progress during which the English had struggled to restore the remnants of God's law as practiced by the Anglo-Saxons.

33. Durant, The Story of Civilization, op. cit., 7:130.
34. Ibid., 7:131.
35. Ibid., 7:138.

These words also shocked the English people into the alarming realization that James I not only claimed to be king by "divine right" but that he expected the people to embrace his royal declarations as the inspired and infallible will of God. Not even the Pope had proclaimed more than this.

And it was the Catholics who decided to do something about it.

The Gunpowder Plot

A small group who had suffered severe persecution under the anti-Catholic laws of England, decided "to blow up Westminster Palace while the King, the royal family, the Lords and the Commons were assembled there for the opening of Parliament." [36]

They leased a house adjacent to Westminster and labored sixteen hours a day to dig a tunnel from the leased house to the cellar of Westminster. Then they hauled in thirty casks of gunpowder and placed them directly under the meeting chamber of the House of Lords.

By warning certain friends not to attend the opening of Parliament, suspicions were aroused, and when the king's agents entered the cellar they not only found the casks of gunpowder but arrested one of the leaders named Guy Fawkes. He confessed their intent to blow up Westminster the following day which would be November 5, 1605. Even today England celebrates "Guy Fawkes Day" with fireworks and bonfires and parading "guys" or effigies of Fawkes up and down the streets.

Even though Fawkes was subjected to extreme torture he refused to disclose his accomplices but two were apprehended and executed with Guy Fawkes on January 27, 1606. The identity of the others finally came out and while two escaped to the continent the other two were apprehended. One turned collaborator and the other was hanged, drawn and quartered.[37]

The persecution of Catholics which followed these events was so oppressive that it became virtually impossible to avoid violating the technicality of the strict anti-Catholic statutes passed by Parliament. As a result, twenty-two priests were arrested and put to death.[38]

---

36. Ibid., 7:141.
37. Ibid., 7:142.
38. Ibid.

Two Notable Things for Which James I is Remembered

Eventually, one of the notable things attributed to James I was a new translation of the Bible. Of course, he merely authorized it. The gargantuan task was actually undertaken by Dr. Laurence Chaderton and his associates at Cambridge University.[39] It is my opinion that no translation has been as accurate or as beautiful since it was published in 1611 A.D. An occasional word or phrase has been improved upon but the overall accomplishment of this monumental work has never been equalled.

It can also be said to the credit of James I that he had the wisdom to authorize a group of businessmen to undertake the establishment of settlements along the Atlantic seaboard of North America. The first settlement was in 1607 and was named Jamestown. The details of this adventure will be covered in a later chapter.

Strange Aspects of England's First Stuart King

Historians tell us that after James became king of England "he ceased marital relations with his wife."[40] However, in 1615 he established a romantic liaison "with handsome, dashing, rich George Villiers, twenty three. He made him Earl, then Marquis, then Duke of Buckingham and, after 1616, allowed him to direct the polices of the state."[41]

Although a homosexual by choice, James had married Anne, the daughter of Frederick II of Denmark while he was the king in Scotland,[42] and she had given him two sons. The eldest was named Henry, but he died in 1612 and that left Charles, the second son, as the king's heir.[43]

Under James I the Church of England continued to sell indulgences, and preach that children should be rescued from Adam's original sin by being baptized as infants.[44] Many of the bishops had further discredited the church by purchasing the right to receive the offerings from numerous parishes while neglecting to provide any services to these parishes whatever; not even sermons, funerals, or marriages.[45]

---

39. Willison, Saints and Strangers, op. cit., p. 29.
40. Encyclopedia Britannica, 1974 (15th edition), op. cit., 10:22.
41. Durant, The Story of Civilization, op. cit., 7:156.
42. Ibid., 7:131.
43. Encyclopedia Britannica, op. cit., 10:22.
44. Ibid., 10:27.
45. Ibid., 10:26.

The worst part of all this religious disintegration was the fact that it was worth a person's life to openly protest against it. Some had spent years in prison for the slightest objection. The growing sentiment among many outraged Englishmen was to abandon the Church of England and set up independent congregations. Thcse became known as "Separatists" or "Independents." Others thought the national church should be retained but purified from within. These became known as Puritans who were eventually considered by James to be as evil as the Separatists.

King James could not believe anyone would want to leave "his" Church or try to "purify it". He particularly objected to the Separatists and looked upon them as virtually committing treason against the Crown. Heresy was already considered a capital crime and King James thought the setting up of a separate church seemed even worse. Wherever "separatists" could be found he ordered a heavy dose of imprisonment in rat-infested prisons, the slitting of noses, the cutting off of ears and the confiscation of property. In some cases execution.

Charles I (1600-1649)

James I died at Theobalds, his favorite country residence in Herfordshire, on March 27, 1625. Perhaps he never quite realized it, but the throne of England had become the eye of a hurricane and that is what his son, Charles I, inherited. It would be during the reign of Charles I that the critical showdown would occur between those who wanted to restore Anglo-Saxon principles and the house of the Stuarts who wanted the king to be treated like a god.

Charles I is described as follows:

> "He had begun the struggle of life by fighting a congenital weakness of physique; he could not walk till he was seven. He overcame this defect by … vigorous sports, until … he could ride and hunt with the best. He suffered from an impediment of speech; until ten he could hardly speak intelligibly … Charles gradually improved, but to the end of his life he stammered … He became proficient in mathematics, music and theology, learned something of Greek and Latin, spoke French, Italian, and a little Spanish ….
>
> "He inherited his father's conception of the royal prerogative as absolute, with power to make as well as administer laws, to rule without Parliament, and override laws enacted by parliament."[46]

46. Durant, The Story of Civilization, op. cit., 7:200.

It was inevitable that Charles would clash with Parliament. He called his first Parliament June 18, 1625, a few months after his father died. There were 100 in the House of Lords and 500 in the House of Commons. Three-fourths of them were Puritans.[47]

The meeting came to an impasse when the king was not given the money he demanded and refused to agree to an annual meeting of Parliament and an annual examination of his expenses. The king dissolved the Parliament August 12 after meeting less than two months.

In the spring of the following year the king was under heavy expenses because of military commitments and felt compelled to call a second Parliament. The members of Parliament demanded removal of a corrupt and inefficient minister in the king's council. The king was outraged and dissolved the Parliament again June 15, 1626.

The Petition of Right

France declared war on England in 1627 and the king called his third Parliament. However, he was so insolent in making huge demands for funds that the Parliament retaliated by demanding that he accept a new "Petition of Right."

Actually it was not new. It was a plea similar to the Magna Charta asking for the restoration of fundamental Anglo-Saxon rights. The people were to be treated and respected as "freemen." There were to be no taxes without the consent of Parliament. There were to be no forced loans, no holding of prisoners without a charge, no criminal judgments without a trial by jury, martial law was to be terminated, soldiers were to be removed from the homes of the people, and the king's officers would take no action against the people except that which was specifically authorized by law.[48]

At first the king balked. This repudiated the very things his father had proclaimed from his very first Parliament. But the times were desperate. Finally, Charles gave his consent.

The Parliament immediately demanded the removal of the Duke of Buckingham, the favorite of both James I and Charles, who was accused of flagrant abuses of his power. The matter was settled when John Felton, a lieutenant in the army who felt he had been egregiously wronged, stabbed Buckingham to

47. Ibid., 7:201.

48. For the complete text see John Richard Green, A Short History of the English People, New York: A. L. Burt Company, 1900, 2:54-55.

death and then voluntarily surrendered. The king was almost out of his mind with anger and grief.

In the feverish excitement of the day, Parliament began to pass laws dealing with religion and other sensitive matters, whereupon the king ordered the Parliament to be dissolved. It refused to do so but when the Parliament heard the armed forces were at the doors, it adjourned on its own initiative.

Eleven Years Without a Parliament

Charles now assumed totalitarian control of the government and ruled England for eleven years (1629-1640) without calling a single assembly of the Parliament. He began by "levying unsanctioned taxes, forcing loans, billeting soldiers on citizens, making arbitrary arrests, denying prisoners the rights of habeas corpus and trial by jury, extending the tyranny and severity of the Star Chamber in Political [matters], and of the Court of High Commission in ecclesiastical [matters]." [49]

During those eleven years Charles I should have learned for himself that his father was wrong. There is no such thing as a divine right of kings. Nor is there any divine right in any particular family to rule a nation.

If Charles had been taught God's law he would have known that the Almighty has delegated the unalienable right of sovereign government to each individual and that if a host of those individuals combine to form a nation, the sovereign authority of those individuals is delegated to rulers on a specific and limited basis. Just as this sovereign power can be delegated, there is an unalienable right to suspend or withdraw it.

Charles I never realized that a king who has lost the respect and support of the people is nothing. As we shall see in the next chapter, the failure of Charles I to understand this basic principle of God's law cost him his life.

49. Durant, The Story of Civilization, op. cit., 7:204.

Notes for Reflection and Discussion

1. When did the Romans leave Britain? Why did the king of the Celts invite the Anglo-Saxons to come to England? Why did the Celts end up in Wales and Ireland?

2. How did the pagan Anglo-Saxons become Christians? Which of their customs did they find in the Bible? What nations had been practicing God's law in northern Europe? How could they have God's law and still be pagans?

3. Name at least two doctrines being taught by the church in Rome which King Alfred refuted. What is the basis for the statement that King Alfred was the best educated and the most moral king England ever had?

4. List four of the fundamental beliefs which the Anglo-Saxons adopted from God's law. How did King Alfred try to civilize the pagan Vikings he had conquered?

5. Name two things King Alfred emphasized in his final instructions to his son who would succeed him. Why did the writings of King Alfred astonish historian Sharon Turner?

6. How did the English lose their legacy of God's law? What did the Magna Charta seek to restore in 1215 A.D.? Why did King John sign the Magna Charta? Why was the establishment of a Parliament important? What did the English kings have to do before they increased taxes?

7. What significance do we attach to King Henry VIII's break with Rome? Did he reform any of the doctrine? How strict was his daughter, Queen Elizabeth, in the enforcement of church ritual? Why did she feel compelled to execute Mary, Queen of Scots?

8. Summarize the doctrine of "divine right of kings" as explained to the Parliament by James I. How did this promote the "Gunpowder Plot?" Name the two notable things for which James I is credited.

9. Why did James I object to the Separatists? Why did he eventually turn against the Puritans? What did James I teach his son Charles that led to the English civil war?

10. What childhood weaknesses did Charles I have to overcome? What happened to his first Parliament? The Second? the Third? What was the "Petition of Right" which he signed? How long was it before he called another Parliament? In trying to rule England alone, what lesson did he fail to learn that ultimately cost him his life?

CHAPTER SIXTEEN

What Americans Learned from the Failure of the First English Constitution

Sometimes Americans forget that it was England, not the United States, that first tried to escape from a monarchy and set up a written constitution based on republican principles.

But it failed. The question is, "Why?"

The Founding Fathers carefully studied the English civil wars and the "Instrument of Government" set up in 1653. This was the first written constitution in England and it might have made the English the first free people in modern times. It was extremely important to the Founders to discover all the reasons why Cromwell failed and why the English retreated back to a corrupt monarchy.

At the end of this chapter we will itemize all the lessons the Founders learned from these 60 years of tragic English history.

It all began in 1640 under the reign of King Charles I.

After calling and dissolving three different Parliaments, Charles displayed his utter contempt for Parliament by refusing to call up another one for eleven years. During this period he tried to rule England, Scotland and Ireland without any input from the people or their representatives.

One of his worst offenses was allowing Archbishop Laud to install Episcopalian bishops over the churches of all other faiths. In fact, no individual could even preach without getting permission from the Episcopalian bishop in charge of his particular district.[1]

Episcopalians even wanted the death penalty for Puritans or independents who no longer professed to believe in the whole doctrine of election and predestination.[2] That proclamation would have sent the famous Alfred the Great to the gallows if he had still been alive.

1. Durant, The Story of Civlization, op. cit., 7:205.
2. Ibid., 7:203.

As a result of this persecution, 20,000 Puritans had followed the Pilgrims to America and settled mostly in New England.[3] Meanwhile, those who remained in the mother country were so outraged that their wrath reached the boiling point of open revolution.

The First Civil War

It was Scotland that started the revolt against Archbishop Laud's "Canons" which imposed Episcopal bishops over all other faiths.

It began on February 28, 1638, when all the Presbyterian ministers signed a National Covenant at a huge General Assembly in Glasgow.[4] They repudiated every Episcopal bishop who had taken over one of their congregations and declared that henceforth the Presbyterian churches were completely independent of the king and his ministers.

King Charles immediately ordered the General Assembly in Glasgow to disperse or he would charge them with treason. To enforce this threat he needed an army and to raise an army he needed money. That meant calling up a new Parliament. It was a bitter pill but after eleven years he finally called for a new election and the Parliament met April 12, 1640. In history this is called the "short parliament."

This was because it only lasted three weeks. It would not vote for new money and without it there would be no army to punish the Scots.

In total frustration, the king dissolved the Parliament and decided to depend on his faithful royalists to help him raise an army. The effort was a failure. Few royalists responded and when the Scots heard he was coming they scattered the king's army in a furious attack and took possession of all northern England.

Charles suddenly realized that this defeat sent a signal to the whole kingdom that his authority was on the verge of collapsing. He therefore frantically returned to London to call up a new Parliament. It convened at Westminster on November 3, 1640 and remained throughout the oncoming civil wars. This is why it became known as the "Long" Parliament.

Oliver Cromwell (1599-1658)

Sitting in this new Parliament was a "country gentleman" representing the town of Cambridge in eastern England. His name was Oliver Cromwell.

---

3. Ibid.
4. Ibid., 7:206.

By all standards Cromwell was no aristocrat. He was just a country gentleman with a limited education, a small landed estate and nine children. Nevertheless, he was elected to the last two Parliaments and had a feeling for the rising indignation of the English people. Cromwell's greatest asset was his skill as a horseman. He later gave the Parliament its fincst cavalry.

The Parliament's Drastic Demands of the King

This fifth Parliament was visibly angry with the king. Before they would think of voting money for a war against the Scots, all the Puritans and Presbyterians in Parliament combined to demand the arrest of the king's chief advisors who were blamed for the wretched policies the king had imposed upon the people.

One was the Earl of Strafford and the other was Archbishop Laud whom we have already mentioned. Parliament was in an ugly mood. Strafford was arrested, tried for treason and executed.

Parliament then went after the churchmen who were suspected of being allies of the Papacy. This included Archbishop Laud. In due time he was also executed.

Bills were also passed abolishing the king's horror-inspired Star Chamber Court and the Court of High Commission. It also ended monopolies granted by the king to his favorite supporters, and terminated the illegal levy of so-called ship money. It was plain that eleven years of Parliamentary suspension had allowed a tidal wave of anger and resentment to accumulate in the hearts of the people.

Parliament's Grand Remonstrance Against King Charles

On December 1, 1641, the Parliament passed and presented to the king its ultimatum called "The Grand Remonstrance" or protestation. Everything the people held against the king was in that document.

However, by this time the Parliament was beginning to split apart. One party eventually became known as the Tories (who sympathized with the king) while the other party became known as the Whigs (who supported the views of Parliament). Because of the split the Grand Remonstrance passed by only 11 votes.

In a fit of rage the king took the Grand Seal and fled toward the north to somehow raise a royalist army while the queen—who was Catholic—took the crown jewels and rushed forth to raise funds from the Catholic countries where she had friends.[5]

The Parliament raised funds for a "new model army" of 22,000 men and Cromwell was assigned to train them. Historian Durant says this about Cromwell:

> "He had no military experience before the war, but his force of character, his steadiness of purpose and will, his skill in playing upon the religious and political feelings of men, enabled him to mold his regiments into a unique discipline and loyalty. The Puritan faith equaled the Spartan ethic in making invincible soldiers.
>
> "These men did not 'swear like a trooper'; on the contrary, no oaths were heard in their camp, but many sermons and prayers. They stole not, nor raped, but they raided churches to rid them of religious images and 'papistical' [pro Catholic] clergymen. They shouted with joy and fury when they encountered the enemy."[6]

They were called "round heads" because they cropped their hair to show their disdain for the long curls of the fancy Cavaliers under King Charles. Cromwell's "butched" troops looked like a battalion of modern Marines.

The End of the First Civil War

The Scots decided to throw in their lot with Parliament so the next thing the king knew he was being attacked by a newly mobilized army of Scots, strengthened by Cromwell's cavalry. They came roaring out of the north and shattered the king's forces at the battle of Marston Moor near York. A little later the king was crushed at the battle of Naseby near Coventry. In this last battle King Charles lost all his infantry, all his artillery, half his cavalry and all of his personal baggage and correspondence.

It was in this correspondence that the king's treasonous letters to other countries revealed that he had openly invited them to invade England and conquer his own subjects.

The king surrendered.

Thus concluded the first civil war. The king was taken as a prisoner to London and placed in the Hampton Court Palace. The more radical elements

5. Ibid., 7:212.
6. Ibid., 7:215.

in Parliament clamored for the king's head, but Cromwell insisted that an effort be made to see if the king would agree to some kind of peaceful arrangement which today would be called a "limited" monarchy.

King Charles Escapes

But the guard at Hampton Court must have grown careless, because Charles escaped and managed to reach the coast of England and then the Isle of Wight where friends protected him.

During the next two years (1646-1648) Charles took advantage of his temporary security by entering into treasonable negotiations with anyone who would put him back on the throne. He promised to make England a Catholic country if the Irish helped him. He promised to make England a Presbyterian country if the Scots helped him.

The Outbreak of the Second Civil War

As the second civil war broke out, everyone knew it was a fight to the death.

Cromwell proved his military skill in every encounter. Although outnumbered most of the time, he won every battle and even when many of the Scots decided to gamble making England Presbyterian by siding with the king, Cromwell suppressed hostilities in Scotland and brought the second civil war to a conclusion by winning the final battle at Pontefract.

Cromwell would have been further amazed if he had known that while he was doing all of this fighting, certain friends of the king in the House of Lords and others in the Commons were planning to have Cromwell charged with treason against the king and condemn him to be executed![7]

Colonel Thomas Pride's Purge of Parliament

To the army and those who had carried the burden of both wars, these maneuvers by the royalists in the house of Lords and the house of Commons were equated with blind, brazen treason against the people of England. It aroused a sudden sense of extreme emergency among the minority in Parliament who had risked their lives and carried the real burden of the war.

Therefore, while Cromwell was still in the field, his closest friends supported Col. Thomas Pride in bringing to Westminster a substantial platoon of soldiers on December 8, 1648, and selectively throwing out of Parliament

7. Green, A Short History of the English People, op. cit., 2:142.

all those who had demonstrated strong sympathies for the king. This is known in history as "Pride's Purge."[8]

Of the original 500 members of Parliament, only 56 remained in Westminster. The ousted members were helpless but they sent up a roar of protest and began calling the survivors of the purge a "Rump Parliament." But whether considered a "rump" or a cabal of radical rebels, this body of survivors had control of Westminster and generated a vigorous plan of action. They demanded that the king should be immediately arrested, brought to London, and tried for treason. Should he be found guilty, they proposed that he be promptly executed.

Execution of Charles I

Charles was arrested and the "Rump Parliament" appointed 150 commissioners to hear the case against the king with John Bradshaw, an eminent London lawyer, acting as the presiding officer.[9]

As the fragmentary Parliament expected, the king was found guilty as charged and sentenced to death. The scaffold was built in front of Whitehall which was the king's banqueting palace, and on January 30, 1649, a hooded executioner raised his broad axe and with one stroke Charles was decapitated.

In all of this there was a feeling of anguish among the English people because they had been taught to revere their royal rulers. Nevertheless, there was also a sense of complete finality as the curtain was rung down on a most important epoch in English history.

What Kind of New Government?

But who would take charge? There was no doubt that Cromwell was the hero of the war, but should he replace the king or should Parliament take charge as the remnant of the people's representatives?

Although more than a century apart, Oliver Cromwell found himself in exactly the same spot as George Washington at the end of the Revolutionary War. In both cases the people had been liberated from the prevailing monarchy and they were free to set up a new commonwealth with freedom, liberty and justice for all.

But both men were confronted by a baffling dilemma. In each instance Cromwell and Washington were urged by their loyal followers to continue in

8. Durant, The Story of Civlization, op. cit., 7:219.
9. Green, A Short History of the English People, op. cit., 2:144.

power at the head of the military until order was established and the fruits of their victory secured.

Washington recognized the peril of this suggestion, but he had the advantage of knowing what happened to Cromwell. Washington determined not to make the same mistake. Therefore, to the amazement and alarm of the Continental Congress, he promptly resigned his commission and went home.

For Washington this was a soul-wrenching decision.

For several tumultuous years he had cringed as he watched the convulsions of the American states. There were riots, threats of civil war, monetary inflation, economic depression and violent quarrels continually erupting between the states. At times these destabilizing upheavals threatened to tear the whole confederation to pieces.

Nevertheless, with firm determination, Washington restrained himself and resisted all the massive pressures to use his popular prestige and intervene in order to establish martial law and take command. Instead, he handed his commission back to Congress and went home.

If Cromwell had done this, the subsequent history of England might have been entirely different.

Washington was determined to keep the civilian control in the hands of Congress whether they liked it or not. By going home, Washington left the Congress with no alternative. They had to take charge.

In 1787, the Continental Congress felt compelled by the force of threatening circumstances to set up a constitutional convention and attempt to find a better way to govern the commonwealth.

To Washington, the important thing was that Congress—representing the states—did it, not the commander in chief. He had successfully resisted the temptation that comes to all military leaders in a time of crisis. History and thousands of years of human experience clearly confirm that he had made the right choice.

Cromwell Makes a Different Choice

With no historical precedent to guide him, Cromwell decided to accept the challenge and see if he could save the country.

Oliver Cromwell had great plans for England. He wanted to set up a new commonwealth with a written constitution. As a Puritan he wanted to establish freedom of religion as well as a permanent restoration of the Anglo-Saxon rights as set forth in the Magna Charta.

But Cromwell had to postpone all these constructive plans because of a threatened invasion by Scotland on the north and Ireland on the west.

In Scotland the plan was to bring over the son of the dead king from the continent and install him as Charles II.

At the same time many Royalists in Ireland wanted to raise up a powerful army to invade England. As an inducement to the Irish, the royalists promised the Catholics of Ireland complete religious freedom, plus an independent Irish Parliament and a gift of sufficient money to raise an infantry of 15,000 men and a cavalry of 500.[10]

All they had to do was march into England and help put Prince Charles on the throne.

Cromwell first started putting down the opposition in Ireland, but after a few months he learned that Charles II had landed in Scotland. Cromwell therefore left—what was to be a three-year war in Ireland—to his son-in-law, Henry Ireton.

With his customary efficiency, Cromwell returned to England, mobilized a new army and led them into Scotland July 22, 1650.

In spite of being outnumbered, Cromwell vanquished the main Scottish army at Dunbar within five weeks and took 10,000 prisoners. During a time when Cromwell was ill, Charles led the Scots triumphantly into England. As soon as Cromwell had recovered he caught up with them.

Cromwell once again found himself outnumbered, but by superior strategy and superb courage he defeated 30,000 Scots. Charles II escaped by using a peasant's disguise and sleeping in attics, barns or the woods and living on a near-starvation diet. After 40 days he made his way to the coast and found a sympathetic captain who sped him away to France October 15, 1651.

Cromwell Assumes Political Leadership of England, Ireland and Scotland

Cromwell returned to London to find that the "Rump Parliament" had passed the Navigation Act in 1651 which required all foreign imports to be shipped to England on English ships. This had significantly improved the

10. Durant, The Story of Civilization, op. cit., 8:186.

economy, but other than this Cromwell found the Parliament little more than a cluster of fighting hornets.

What about the plans for the new commonwealth? Nothing was happening. The winnowed-down Parliament was malingering. Coming fresh from the battle field the disgusted Cromwell brought with him a company of soldiers and forced the "Rump" Parliament to dissolve itself and depart.

But now what?

Instead of risking exposure to another nest of hornets by electing a new Parliament, Cromwell and the army officials decided it would be safer to appoint a new Parliament of 140 "God-fearing men" and thereby provide some semblance of traditional government. One of these "appointed" members had the singular name of Praisegod Barebone so the people picked up on this and began jeering this newly appointed assembly as the "Barebone Parliament."

The Instrument of Government

This was the setting in 1653 when a group of men in this "appointed" Parliament undertook to compose England's first and only written constitution. They called it "The Instrument of Government." Having submitted the document to Cromwell on December 12, the "appointed" parliament abdicated or dissolved itself so a new Parliament could be elected.

This Instrument of Government contained 42 articles. Cromwell who was already the lord general of the army, was also named by this new charter to be the "lord protector" of England, Scotland and Ireland. However, this office was not made hereditary.

The lord protector was provided with a council of fifteen and each member was appointed for life to insure a continuity of government in case the lord protector died and the Parliament was not in session. There were fifteen in the original council and the lord protector and the council were authorized to add six more.

The power to make new laws was assigned to "one person—the lord protector—and the new Parliament." This meant the lord protector could make laws with the consent of the council until the Parliament was elected, but after that the new Parliament was exclusively responsible for new laws. However, it was provided that if the lord protector did not happen to like a particular law, he would have twenty days to lobby for a change before the law went into effect.

To avoid having a self-perpetuating Parliament, a new election had to be held at least once in every three years. Each election would provide 400 representatives from England, 30 from Scotland and 30 from Ireland, making a total of 460. Roman Catholics and the Irish who had fought against the Parliament forces in Ireland were ineligible to sit in Parliament or exercise the privilege of voting.

The lord protector's council was to see that only men were elected to Parliament who were "persons of known integrity, fearing God, and of good conversation." This provision allowed the council to exclude any elected member from taking his seat who was judged to be lacking in these qualities.

In case of war, Parliament had to be summoned immediately.

The Parliament could not be dissolved by the lord protector in less than five months.

The lord protector was given power to raise two hundred thousand pounds to operate the government in addition to the cost required for the building of the navy and maintaining thirty thousand men in the army.

It was generally agreed at the time that this Instrument of Government was rather brilliant and seemed to cover all the requirements for a sound system of republican (representative) government. The test would come with the passing of time.

Testing the Instrument of Government

When the first Parliament assembled on September 3, 1654, Oliver Cromwell, as the lord protector, asked the newly elected members to accept all of the ordinances that he and the council had passed while waiting for the Parliament to assemble. But the members had their own ideas. They immediately took over the floor and demanded complete control of the army and asked for numerous changes in the Instrument of Government. Cromwell was outraged by this obvious disrespect and arrogant, sophomoric display of immature statesmanship. By January, 1655, Cromwell declared the required five months had passed and he had authority to dissolve the Parliament, which he did.

He and the council then went back to the task of governing the country as before. Whether they liked it or not the lord protector and the council were the temporary governors of England, Ireland and Scotland.

Launching Numerous Reforms

Cromwell now undertook to build England into a great world power. The base of that power was an impregnable new navy and a fleet of sturdy vessels in England's merchant marine. As historian Will Durant describes it:

> "He had proposed to make the name of [an] Englishman as great as ever that [of a] Roman had been, and he came close to realizing his aim. The mastery of the seas had now fallen to England; consequently it was only a matter of time until England would dominate North America and extend her rule in Asia. All Europe looked in awe upon this Puritan who praised God but built a navy, who preached sermons but won every battle, who founded the British Empire by martial force while invoking the name of Christ. The crowned heads who had counted him an upstart now sought his alliance, making no fuss about theology." [11]

The End of England's Only Written Constitution

In July, 1656 Cromwell decided to take a chance on a new Parliament which might be more responsible and would treat the new Instrument of Government with greater respect.

The new Parliament met in September, but as the members assembled, the Council proceeded to exercise its presumed authority and exclude all the representatives whom they considered lacking in "integrity, fear of God, or good conversation." This produced some harsh complaints and deep resentment.

But even those who passed muster did not come up to Cromwell's expectations. Finally, Cromwell and the council decided they had done a better job without a Parliament.

But the Parliament also felt Cromwell could do a better job if he acted alone. The members therefore passed a "Humble Petition and Advice" which terminated the whole Instrument of Government and gave Cromwell the powers of a virtual dictator. He was even allowed to designate his successor. Then the Parliament dissolved itself.

The Liabilities of Being a Dictator

At first Cromwell probably thought the Parliament had paid him a great compliment by conferring so much power upon him, but under a one-man rule Cromwell soon found himself being blamed for anything that went wrong.

---

11. Ibid., 8:200.

For example, England had become deeply involved in several wars on the continent and taxes had risen to unprecedented heights. Cromwell was blamed. In addition, emergency pressures led the army and political bureaucrats to neglect traditional rights of citizens. There was taxation without representation, arrests without due process of law, trials without juries, and government by naked force.

Without a constitution to limit the power of the various departments of government, Cromwell was blamed for the abuses and became so hated it required 160 bodyguards to keep him from being assassinated.

The End of England's Experiment

But in the summer of 1658 Cromwell became deathly ill from what modern medical authorities believe was malaria. Toward the end, as his condition became terminal, Cromwell's judgment failed him. He appointed Richard, his soft natured son, to succeed him and died September 3, 1658.

Within six months Richard realized he was completely inadequate to meet the demands of the role of a "lord protector" which his father had imposed upon him. In a spirit of dignity and humility he humbly abdicated.

Prince Charles received the news of Cromwell's death and Richard's abdication while he was in Flanders and his spirits skyrocketed. He knew his moment of triumph was near.

Over in England the feelings of the royalists also rose to a fever pitch. They agitated vigorously on every level of the populace and set up a wild clamor to have the royal family return to London immediately. Before the end of 1660 the so-called "Restoration" had taken place and the man whom Cromwell had defeated was sitting on the throne of England, Ireland, and Scotland.

Charles II (1630-1685)

But it wasn't long before the people of England realized that their smart-alecky new king was not really a royal prize. At great expense he restored all the pomp and ceremony as well as traditional immorality of the courtly ways he had learned in France. Puritans were especially offended and even the prelates of the official church had to turn their heads so they wouldn't seem to notice many of the abominable things that were happening.

In 1662 Charles married a Portuguese Catholic princess but they had no children. However Charles maintained a bevy of mistresses all about him and by them he had numerous illegitimate children.

Charles reigned from 1661 to 1685. On his death bed he made his confession to a priest and asked to be accepted into the Catholic Church. His wish was granted and he died February 5, 1685.

The major events during the reign of Charles II were two wars with the Dutch, a deadly devastation during the great plague, the leveling of much of London during the great fire, the Rye House Plot, and the triumph of Parliament in forcing through the famous Habeas Corpus Act in 1679. This act outlawed the practice of holding prisoners without any violation being charged against them.

In 1683 the king ordered Algernon Sidney beheaded for teaching that God had vested all sovereignty in the people and there was no such thing as "divine right of kings." The dead Algernon Sidney was immediately pronounced a "martyr to the cause of freedom" by advocates of liberty in both England and America.

One of these was John Locke, an English scholar who was already preparing what would become his famous *Essay Concerning Civil Government*. In it he had declared there is no such thing as divine right of kings because God had vested all sovereignty in the people. In the light of what had happened to Algernon Sidney he decided to move immediately to Holland.

James II (1633-1701)

The Parliament had done everything in its power to keep the king's Catholic brother from being next in line for the English throne, but Charles had held his ground and thwarted the law Parliament repeatedly tried to pass. When Charles II died everyone realized that the next king would be a Catholic, and there was nothing they could do about it. The brother of Charles ascended the throne as James II in 1685.

James was born at the St. James Palace in London on October 14, 1633, the son of Charles I and was eventually made a peer as the Duke of York. During the first civil war he escaped to Holland and later to France and did not return to England until 1660 when he became part of the "Restoration" with his older brother Charles.

In 1664 the English took New Amsterdam away from the Dutch and renamed it New York in honor of James, the Duke of York.

In spite of Parliament's earlier protests against the possibility of a Catholic king, most of the people accepted James because they didn't want another civil war and they did not want the illegitimate son of Charles II—the Duke of Monmouth—to ascend the throne. Nevertheless, Charles had admitted that the Duke of Monmouth was his bastard son and when Monmouth laid claim to the throne, hand-to-hand combat had to be waged to keep him from getting it.

The first wife of James II bore him two daughters—Mary and Anne—who were raised Protestants. Mary later married her cousin, William of Orange in Holland, whose mother was the sister of Charles II but Mary had no children. Anne married Prince George of Denmark and succeeded Mary as Queen of England in 1702.

After becoming king in 1685, James made himself very unpopular by giving appointments to Catholics wherever possible. He also favored the Catholics as an official policy. His second wife then gave birth to a son who was christened a Catholic and the Parliament immediately saw the prospects of a Catholic hierarchy becoming established over the kingdom.

The Parliament thereupon invited Mary and her husband, William of Orange, to immediately replace James II as co-rulers of England. Under these circumstances James II abdicated and fled to France.

It was a bloodless revolution.

The English Bill of Rights

Before William and Mary were allowed to take over the throne they agreed to accept the English Bill of Rights which was being drawn up by Parliament. This Bill of Rights was finished and presented to William and Mary on February 13, 1689 and thereafter it was enacted into law by the Parliament during December of that year.

This document actually contained nothing that was particularly new but simply reiterated the Anglo-Saxon basic rights set forth in the Magna Charta and the Petition of Right.

It included the right of free speech, the right of petition, the elimination of Church courts, the stipulation of free elections, the prohibition against a standing army in peacetime, the prohibiting of excessive fines or the inflicting of cruel or unusual punishment. It guaranteed free elections, and frequent meetings of Parliament as needed.

The United States Constitution incorporated most of these provisions as did the individual states. In the minds of the American Founders, the English Bill of Rights as well as the Magna Charta, the Petition of Right and the

Bill of Habeas Corpus all became cornerstones in the legacy of American freedom.

American Founders Glean Important Lessons from These Sixty Years of English History

Since The English Instrument of Government in 1653 was the first attempt among the English people to write a constitution, the American Founding Fathers scrutinized both its merits and weaknesses.

Probably no one understood the profound lessons to be gained from this period of English history better than John Locke. He lived through this entire period and became the classical authority quoted by the Founders to demonstrate the authoritative substance and reliability of the principles underlying the Constitution of the United States.

In his writings John Locke reflected how much he had learned from England's first attempt to write a constitution. Let us close this chapter by listing some of the political truths which were of particular interest to the Founders.

How to Be Well Governed and Still Remain Free

The following profound concepts became part of the American legacy:

1. By divine mandate, the inalienable right of sovereignty for any nation is vested in the whole people. There is no such thing as a "divine right of kings" nor is the right of sovereignty vested in a particular family nor any oligarchy of the rich or people of aristocratic birth.

2. No nation can violate the inalienable rights of its people without facing the judgment and eventual wrath of God.

3. A sovereign nation should be governed by a *written* constitution which carefully delineates the separation of powers and defines the checks and balances assigned to each.

4. The Constitution should clearly set forth the fundamental rights of the people.

5. Powers granted to the central government should be specified with clearly defined limitations.

6. Powers not granted should be strictly reserved to the people or the states.

7. The powers of the central government should be separated into the legislature to make the law, the executive to administer the law, the judiciary to interpret the law and make certain the states and national government stay within the parameters of the Constitution.

8. No king should ever rule in America. The lure of having a king was not easy to erase even from the minds of some American Founders. It will be recalled that many revolutionary soldiers wanted Washington to be king. He blistered them with his reply.

9. The military must always remain subject to the civil authorities. As we mentioned, at the end of the Revolutionary War, Washington was just where Oliver Cromwell was at the end of the English civil war. They were both heroes but there was great instability in the country. The soldiers in both cases insisted that their general must take over and restore order. Cromwell did so and ended up a hated dictator. Washington refused. He resigned and thereby forced the Congress to work out a better system of government.

10. The government must allow religion to operate freely among the people. Religion should be encouraged but no denomination should become the "established order" of religion. The American colonies were so accustomed to having the government set up the church, appoint the bishops, presbyters or prelates, that seven of the states adopted a denomination as their official religious establishments. The Founders held up the ideal of freedom for all religions and then left it up to each state to gradually phase out those establishments of "official" religion they had adopted. The last state to phase out its official church was Massachusetts around 1827.

11. All men are created equal which means equal before God, equal in their rights, and equal before the bar of justice. In our own day, America is finally getting around to making its people equal regardless of race, color or sex.

12. All mankind were designed by God to be free. This meant that eventually America had to deal with the issue of slavery.

13. The central government must never be allowed to take away from the people the arms required to defend themselves.

14. The President as the commander in chief of the armed services should never be allowed to enter a foreign war without the consent of the people's representatives.

15. People charged with any crime shall have the right:

To be informed of the charge being made against them.

To have legal counsel.

To cross examine accusers.

To have access to a writ of Habeas Corpus (cannot be held without a charge).

To refuse to testify against one's self.

To not be deprived of life, liberty or property without due process of law.

To a fair and speedy trial.

To a trial by jury.

To be allowed reasonable bail.

To be protected from cruel and unusual punishment.

To be charged with treason only for levying war against the country or giving aid and comfort to its enemies.

16. The congress should meet automatically every year.

17. The representatives of the people should stand for election at least every two years.

Topics for Reflection and Discussion

1. By 1640 how long had King Charles tried to govern the people without a Parliament? What was so offensive about the conduct of Archbishop Laud? Because of persecution, what had happened to thousands of Puritans from England?

2. Who were the first people to revolt against Archbishop Laud? What was the National Covenant of the Presbyterians? What did the king call this? What was the punishment for this offense? What did the Scots do about it? Whom did the Tories support? Whom did the Whigs support?

3. What kind of military background did Oliver Cromwell have? Was he an aristocrat? What skill had he developed that eventually made him a leader during the English civil war? Which religious faith did he represent? What was unique about the soldiers he trained?

4. Why were Cromwell's soldiers called "round heads?" After Charles escaped, what did he do to provoke the second civil war?

5. Out of the 500 members of Parliament, how many were left after Pride's Purge? What did the ousted members call the dwarf-sized Parliament? Nevertheless what did this remnant in Parliament decide to do? Where was Cromwell? Did he return in time to sign the king's death warrant?

6. Did historian Will Durant think the execution of Charles I was just? Why? Had Charles prevailed what would have probably happened to Cromwell and his associates? At what point were the circumstances of George Washington and Oliver Cromwell almost identical? Did Washington make the right decision?

7. Why were Cromwell's circumstances far more difficult? From what two directions did the royalists plan to invade England? As a result, what did Cromwell have to do before he could settle down to reform the commonwealth according to republican principles?

8. What was your estimate of the "Instrument of Government," which was intended as England's first Constitution? Did the newly elected Parliament like it? Did Cromwell and his council prove efficient as administrators without the Parliament? Why did the "appointed" Parliament eliminate the Instrument of Government and make Cromwell a dictator?

9. Was it a mistake for Cromwell to appoint his son Richard to succeed him? After "the Restoration," were the people as happy with King Charles II as they had expected? Why was James II so unpopular?

10. After the "Bloodless Revolution" of 1688 who became king and queen? What did they have to sign? Name eight things the American Founders learned from this tragic period of English history. Why did the Founders quote John Locke so often?

CHAPTER SEVENTEEN

THE ENGLISH STRUGGLE TO PLANT THE SEEDS OF FREEDOM IN VIRGINIA

Sometimes we forget that nearly all of the early Europeans who originally came to America were seeking easy riches, even the English. Nevertheless, the English finally had to face the grim reality that in taming the western wilderness, the rough and rugged planting of settlements for survival had to take priority over the accumulation of riches.

Those who came over with jubilant enthusiasm soon learned the terrible reality of seeing thousands dying from starvation while others were forced to beg for a few handsful of corn from the Indians. Eventually, the newcomers became reconciled to the threatening dangers of life on the frontier and the price they had to pay to survive. It meant hard work from dawn to dusk, extremely careful preserving and storing of resources, living frugally, even austerely, and above all, keeping their powder dry and risking life itself at a moment's notice for the protection of life and loved ones from the tomahawks, raping and looting of wild savages.

It took just over 125 years (1607-1733) to establish the original thirteen American colonies. Virginia was the first permanent English settlement followed by the gradual setting up of eleven other colonies during the next seventy-five years. Georgia was the last to be established and she did not become a full fledged colony until 1733. That was just forty-three years before the Declaration of Independence. The stories of each of these thirteen colonies are uniquely different and unless their histories are carefully studied it is impossible to fully understand the monumental problems which confronted the Founding Fathers when they tried to mold all of these segments of English colonial life into the United States of America.

In this study we will sample just a few of these diverse experiences that rose up like dragons to destroy the earliest settlers in this hostile wilderness of North America.

JAMESTOWN

The first English settlement to survive in America began as a business venture, but not a very good one.

Sir Walter Raleigh had induced a friend named Richard Hackluyt to write a book. It was entitled, *Discourse of Western Planting*. In this book the author gave six important reasons why Queen Elizabeth should invest the wealth of the crown in the setting up of English colonies in North America. However, the queen prudently declined, knowing that the same investment-minded men who had just set up the English East India Company in 1600 would probably be tempted to do the same for North America.[1]

And eventually that is precisely what happened.

As we have mentioned earlier, right after Elizabeth's reign, James, the son of Mary, Queen of Scots—whom Elizabeth had beheaded—stood next in line to become the king of England.

In many ways he was a strange, slovenly character, but there was one thing he firmly believed in until the day he died. That was the doctrine of divine right of kings. He considered himself the king of England and all her domain by the divine personal selection of the Almighty himself. Therefore, when he heard that Spain was planning to move up the coast of North America and plant a permanent Spanish settlement, James decided to open the territory to English settlements before the Spanish adventure got under way.

A group of investors in London had wanted to launch a group of settlements in America even though three earlier efforts by Sir Walter Raleigh and his friends had totally failed.[2] The king therefore issued a charter in 1606 authorizing English settlements from the 34th to the 45th latitude—which meant from about Wilmington, North Carolina of our own day, up to Canada.

However, the king's charter only extended inland 100 miles. Four years later the James issued another proclamation stating that the new charter would extend from "sea to sea," meaning from the Atlantic to the Pacific ocean. Amazingly, geographers of that time thought this extended the chartered territory inland by about 200 miles. Because the English had made no exploration of North America beyond the Atlantic Seaboard, the mapmakers of that day assumed that the east coast which extended up to Canada was merely a long, narrow strip about as wide as Central America in the region of Panama. They actually believed the Pacific Ocean was only about 200 miles away![3]

Originally, the king granted charters to two joint-stock companies to start English settlements in America. The First Company—the London

1. John Fiske, Historical Writings, Boston: Houghton Mifflin Co., 1902, 4:49-52.
2. Ibid., 4:187.
3. Ibid., 4:71-72.

Company—included some of the leading political and financial figures of the kingdom. Another group became known as the Plymouth Company but it turned out to be of minor consequence.

In 1607, the London Company targeted for its first settlement the arca between the 34th and the 38th parallels. Three ships were equipped and outfitted to make the journey.

The council of the London Company sent some of its leaders along as supervisors, and they were given a sealed "casket" which was not to be opened until they had located a place of settlement. The secret box contained instructions from the council in London as to the manner in which the settlement should be set up, and it also contained the names of the leaders who were to govern the settlement after they arrived in Virginia.[4]

One of the names for the governing body in Virginia was to be John Smith. However, midway across the ocean Smith was giving the leaders a lot of trouble because of the way they were managing the voyage. John Smith thought it was ridiculous that Captain Christopher Newport had not taken the most direct route from England to Virginia but had gone all the way down the coast of Europe to the Canary Islands off the bulge of North Africa before he headed west.

Actually, this was the route Columbus had followed but it nearly doubled the distance for the English venture and required four months to reach Virginia. The second in command, Captain Gosonold, had made the direct route from the English Channel to Cape Cod in a single month the year before. Nevertheless, Gosonold deferred to the captain's judgment.

But not John Smith. He was the most experienced traveler on the captain's flagship, and he could not resist expressing his total exasperation that the voyage was not only taking too long but that the 105 settlers were consuming much of the precious food which had been stored aboard for their first winter in the new land.

One of the officials of the London Company—who had come along as sort of a corporate overseer—was Captain Edward Wingfield. He interpreted John Smith's criticism of captain Newport as "mutinous" and when the three ships finally reached Dominica, Wingfield had this obstreperous passenger arrested and put in chains. John Smith remained imprisoned in a stifling lockup below deck for the rest of this monotonous journey.[5]

4. Ibid., 4:84-98.
5. Ibid., 4:107-108.

As circumstances developed, it turned out that John Smith was certainly no ordinary passenger. We can be quite certain that Captain Wingfield would never have suspected that the well-known historian, John Fiske, would later describe Smith as one of the greatest Englishmen of that generation.[6]

John Smith (1580-1631)

Because John Smith figures so prominently in the story of Virginia, we will briefly highlight his early biography.

He was born in Willoughby, Lincolnshire, and received infant baptism January 9, 1580. In his youth he had an irrepressible craving for adventure and went to France where he served as a soldier for awhile and afterwards spent three years in the Netherlands, fighting against the Spaniards. He was still only twenty years old when he returned to Willoughby in 1600 and decided to immerse himself in study. He went to a wooded pasture far from town and built himself a pavilion of tree branches. There he read Machiavelli's *Art of War* and Marcus Aurelius. He had a good horse for exercise and practiced using the lance with his horse plunging ahead at top speed. During this brief hermitage hideaway he lived mainly on venison.[7]

It bothered young John Smith that so many Christians were engaged in deadly wars and killing each other, so he decided to try his fortune against the infidels—the Turks. In his biography he says that while traveling through France he was robbed of everything he owned, including his clothes. His life was saved by a peasant who found him half dead, lying in the forest where he was starved and nearly frozen.[8]

After regaining his strength, young Smith made his way to Marseille where he joined a company of pilgrims headed for Palestine where the latest Crusade was being waged against the infidels. However, enroute the Christian crusaders discovered that Smith was somewhat of a heretic and when a terrible storm threatened to drown them they threw him overboard thinking that gesture might appease God and save their lives. For John Smith it was the Jonah story without the whale.

Fortunately, Smith had always been a good swimmer and made his way to a small island where a boat later picked him up. The captain who rescued him knew some of Smith's friends in France and treated him kindly. The rescue boat went to Crete and then to Egypt. As they were returning to Greece

6. Ibid., 4:185-188.
7. Ibid., 4:96-97.
8. Ibid., 4:97.

a Venetian ship fired on them and a fierce fight ensued, but the Venetian ship finally struck its colors and John Smith joined the commander in seizing a huge treasure of silks, velvets, gold and silver. After the looting, the Venetian vessel was allowed to continue on its way. Young Smith received his share of the loot in the form of a bag of coins and a box of expensive goods which later brought him a handsome sum.

The commander put Smith ashore in Italy and he began a leisurely tour from Naples to Rome. In that city he met a famous English Jesuit and had the opportunity of visiting Pope Clement VIII. After his sightseeing in Rome, Smith travelled on to Florence and Bologna, then to Venice.[9]

John Smith Becomes a Captain

Smith eventually made his way to Syria where the battle with the Turks was in progress and there he enlisted in the service of Emperor Rudolph II of the Holy Roman Empire. He was put in command of a company of 250 cavalry with the rank of captain, and very shortly developed some crude missiles which he called the "fiery dragons" that alarmed the Turks terribly by setting fire to their camps.[10]

During the years 1601 and 1602, John Smith encountered some very rough campaigning, and his troops finally passed into the service of Sigismund Bathori, Prince of Transylvania.

The city of Regal was occupied by the Turks, and the Transylvanians put it under heavy siege but nothing decisive seemed to be happening. One day a Turkish captain sent a challenge to the Transylvanian army which said, "... in order to delight the ladies, who did long to see some court-like pastime, he did defy any captain that had command of a company, who durst combat with him for his head."[11]

Here was a challenge with life as a forfeiture for the loser. John Smith was the captain chosen from the Christian army and he was given a lance to meet the Turkish challenger. As the two horses charged toward each other, Smith plunged his lance into the challenger, instantly impaling him. He then dismounted, removed the Turk's helmet and cut off his head. The gruesome trophy was triumphantly presented to the Christian general.

The Turks were so chagrined and anxious for revenge that one of the captains shouted a personal challenge to Smith for another round. So the

9. Ibid., 4:97-98.
10. Ibid.
11. Ibid., 4:99.

next day the jousting tournament was repeated. This time both lances were shattered and the combatants were allowed to resort to pistols for the finale. The Turk was hit and thrown to the ground. Smith immediately dismounted and rushed upon him with his sword. A moment later the Turk had been decapitated.

Smith then decided to issue a bold challenge to any Turkish captain who wanted to come out and win back both heads in a final duel. The challenge was accepted. This time the Turks were given a choice of weapons and they chose battle-axes. The Turkish challenger came charging down with such a ferocious attack that Smith's axe became dislodged and flew out of his hand. A loud cheer rose from the Turks on the city wall but a moment later when the challenger turned to charge again, Smith dodged the oncoming blow and then—by quickly turning his horse while withdrawing his sword—he plunged the sharp blade completely through his Turkish opponent. A moment later, Smith had his head.

The reputation of this daredevil Englishman spread throughout the ranks of the crusading forces and eventually came to the attention of Prince Sigismund. The grateful emperor granted Smith a special coat of arms showing the decapitated heads of three Turks on a shield.[12]

But Smith's good fortune was not to last forever.

Slavery

On November 18, 1602, Smith was taken prisoner at the disastrous battle of Rothenthurm, and sold into slavery. His new master was abusive and severely mistreated him. Smith had only the skin of a wild animal for warmth and an iron collar was fastened around his neck to identify him as a captive slave in case he escaped.

However, on one occasion while Smith was threshing wheat the Turkish Pasha came upon him and began to brutally abuse him. In a sudden rage Smith knocked the Pasha down and used his threshing stick to crush the man's skull. He then dressed in the dead man's clothes, mounted his horse with a sack of grain tied to his saddle and galloped off into the Scythian desert.[13]

For sixteen days he fled until he came to a Russian fortress on the Don where he got rid of his badge of slavery, the iron collar. He then took a roundabout course until he could reach Prince Sigismund and obtain a letter of safe

12. Ibid., 4:100.
13. Ibid., 4:104-105.

conduct. By the time he finally reached England he had travelled over most of Europe and arrived in London just in time to sign up for the expedition to America with the London Company.[14]

Reflecting on Smith's recent maelstrom of dangerous, death-defying adventure, perhaps we can better understand his impatience and easily-aroused rancor against the badly managed voyage across the South Atlantic which lasted four months. But, as we have already mentioned, Smith's protests resulted in his being arrested and confined below deck for the last several weeks of the trip.

The James River

It was April 26th, 1607, when Captain Newport brought his three ships into the mouth of the river which was named after James I. A party of the more adventurous passengers briefly ventured on shore, but they were viciously attacked by Indians and two of the company were wounded with arrows. Hauling the wounded with them, they hurriedly reboarded the ship and proceeded further up river.

As they maneuvered up the stream they saw a site which most of them felt would be satisfactory for a settlement. This was named Jamestown in honor of the English king. That evening the members of the Council opened the secret box and saw for the first time the names of those who would govern the new settlement. Here, on May 13th, they set up their encampment. For a church they nailed a board between two trees to serve as a reading desk and stretched a canvas awning over it. There Reverend Hunt solemnly read the Episcopal service for the first time in Virginia and then preached the first sermon.

Because of the Indian attack, a fort was commenced immediately with a mounting for two cannons. Meanwhile Captain Newport sailed up the river as far as the present city of Richmond and found that the Indians had their main headquarters at this location and seemed friendly. They were called the Powhatans and belonged to the Algonquin tribe.

As Captain Newport sailed back down the river he was alarmed to find that their settlement had been attacked by about two hundred Indians and although Wingfield, the new president, finally drove them off, one settler was killed and eleven settlers were wounded. No matter how friendly the Indians seemed when the settlers gave them trinkets, the Jamestown leaders realized they had planted their village in enemy territory.

14. Ibid., 4:105-106.

Up to this time, the members of the council who were hostile to John Smith had refused to let him sit on the council because he had been suspected of provoking a mutiny during the voyage. Smith demanded a jury trial and when all the evidence was presented and debated, the jury said he was not guilty. Consequently, Smith promptly assumed his place on the council in spite of the reservations of Wingfield and several others.

Compulsory Communism

The London Company had agreed to provide the means for the launching of the Virginia colony; however, it was stipulated that no wages would be paid. The Company promised that houses would be built for everyone but stipulated that when the crops were harvested they would be divided among the settlers equally. The Company was to receive its share of the profits and after several years the settlers would receive a division of the proceeds and enough land for farming and the building of private dwellings.

Today we would call this scheme "voluntary" communism. However, it did not take long to discover that human nature does not adapt itself to working voluntarily when it is known that all will share equally in the harvest whether they worked or not. Not only is this arrangement an open invitation for the lazy to engage in malingering, but those who actually do the work feel cheated when they see the lazy settlers getting as much as those who performed the labor. Before long this voluntary communism became compulsory communism.

Jamestown Is Left Stranded

The system was already producing anger and unrest when Captain Newport prepared to return to England. The Fort was finished on June 15th, 1607, and Captain Newport sailed on the 22nd, but this time he took the direct route to England. Before leaving the captain promised to return in twenty weeks with supplies and more settlers.

The 105 settlers had been left with all the supplies Captain Newport could spare, but it was soon apparent that it was not enough to last more than a short time and therefore everyone had to be put on strict rations. On a daily basis there was only a half pint of wheat and a half pint of barley per person, and no salted meat to go with it. Furthermore, the grain had been stored for 26 weeks in the ship's hold, and loud complaints arose when the settlers discovered it "contained as many worms as grains." [15]

15. Ibid., 4:113.

There was little or no game to be had and even the attempt to catch fish produced only a few crabs and an occasional sturgeon from the river. The poor diet, unfamiliar kinds of labor for many of the settlers and the stifling heat of an American summer began to take its toll. Furthermore, malarial fever broke out and by the end of September, 1620, fifty of the settlers had died and been consigned to their graves. All the rest were sick and if the Indians had chosen to attack, John Smith speculated there would not have been even five men strong enough to man the bulwarks.[16]

At this point John Smith began making overtures to the Indians and developing a friendly dialogue which allowed him to beg sufficient corn from them to keep the survivors alive. He thought that if they could eke out an existence until fall the cooler weather would bring back the wild fowl and they could then have enough meat to save their lives.

Pocahontas Saves the Life of John Smith

But foraging for corn among the Indians had its risks. On January 5, 1608, John Smith was negotiating with some Indians for corn when he was suddenly taken captive and hauled off before Powhatan, chief of all the tribes in that region. He was first taken into the chief's long house and there an extensive consultation transpired. Finally the chief made a decision and two stones were placed close together. Smith's head was placed in the crevice between the two stones and the tribal warriors stood around with clubs in hand ready to beat his head to a pulp.

Smith knew that in spite of all of his narrow escapes in the past, this crisis undoubtedly marked the end of his life. However, everything changed when the chief's thirteen-year-old daughter threw herself across John Smith and begged for his life. There was a brief moment when time stood still, then the chief ordered John Smith released.[17] Some time later Chief Powhatan told Smith he would like to adopt him as a son.

John Smith thankfully returned to Jamestown on January 8, the very day that Captain Newport arrived from England with supplies and more settlers. Only thirty-eight of the original one hundred and five were still alive.[18]

The Starving Time

The London Company was shocked when they heard Captain Newport's account of the first phase of the Virginia adventure but they voted to send over

16. Ibid., 4:114-115.
17. Ibid., 4:121.
18. Ibid., 4:132.

more people and more supplies at regular intervals to assure its survival. But it was never enough.

Under the denigrating system of communism—whether voluntary or compulsory—the colony could not sustain itself. John Smith was put in charge and he had to place the whole settlement under martial law to provide enough for even a bare subsistence. About forty men did the work while two hundred malingered and shirked. Smith finally called them together and declared that any who did not work would not eat. And he said it with a musket in his hand so they knew he meant it.[19]

However, in September, 1609, John Smith was arranging to move Jamestown to a more healthy site when an explosion of gunpowder severely wounded him and he had to be taken to England for surgery and a gradual recovery. He took with him a very carefully drawn map of Virginia which he subsequently published. Modern students marvel at the skill with which this work was executed.[20]

Meanwhile, the population of Jamestown had grown to five hundred, and the London Company felt assured that the colonists would dig in and finally become self sustaining. However, when the supply ships arrived in May, 1610, there were only sixty people left alive out of the five hundred. Jamestown was a vista of grave mounds in every direction. It had been a severe winter and many just simply froze to death because they were too weak to get out and cut wood and take care of themselves. A further calamity occurred when one of the leaders and thirty of the men were caught unawares and brutally massacred by Indians.[21]

It was so discouraging that the sixty survivors decided to completely abandon the settlement and return to England. It was agreed that they would completely dismantle the settlement and leave for home on June 7, 1610. It was not until the forlorn and broken-hearted refugees were already leaving the mouth of the James River that they sighted on the distant horizon the first of three ships sponsored by Lord Delaware who had come to save them. He had brought both food and people. Hopefully, the survivors returned to the abandoned Jamestown to rebuild it and try once more.[22]

But it is impossible to save people from themselves. More people and more supplies continued to pour in from England to rescue the Virginia

19. Ibid., 4:167.
20. Ibid., 4:138.
21. Ibid., 4:179.
22. Ibid., 4:181-183.

investment; but starvation, death and disease continued its toll the rest of the year. By spring, 150 more graves had been dug.[23]

Free Enterprise Saves Virginia

Finally—by 1611—the London Company realized it had made a terrible mistake by refusing to allow the settlers to have private property and operate on their own initiative. Sir Thomas Dale was sent as the new ruler of the colony and carried the title of High Marshal of Virginia. Under his direction communism was abandoned and replaced with a plan that gave each settler three acres of cleared land to cultivate and reap the harvest thereof. In return, each colonist had to pay six bushels of corn per year as a tax and then he could call the land his own.

Amazingly, not everyone liked the idea of private ownership and the opportunity to improve their lot under a system of free enterprise. Nor did they like the new order of things and the strict discipline initiated by the new High Marshal. Jeffrey Abbott and five henchmen secretly plotted to assassinate Sir Thomas Dale, but the devious plot was discovered and all of the would-be assassins were executed.[24]

Meanwhile, some astonishing things began happening at the Jamestown settlement. All those who eagerly accepted the new regime commenced to improve their situation so remarkably that word spread to England that Virginia was going to survive after all.

John Fiske writes:

> "Six months after Dale's administration had begun, a fresh supply of settlers raised the whole number to nearly eight hundred and a good stock of cows, oxen, and goats were added to their resources. The colony now began to expand itself beyond the immediate neighborhood of Jamestown."[25]

The settlers said it would not be long before Virginia would be declared a royal commonwealth.

Pocahontas Goes to England

After John Smith was injured and returned to England, Pocahontas left her own tribe and went to live with the Potomac tribe. In 1612 one of the

23. Ibid., 4:191.
24. Ibid., 4:194.
25. Ibid., 4:197.

leaders from Jamestown found her there and bribed the Potomac chief with a copper kettle to let him take her to the English settlement.[26] So far as we can tell she would then be around eighteen years of age.

It so happened that a recent emigrant to Jamestown was a colonist named John Rolfe whose wife died shortly after they reached Virginia. Within a year Rolfe had suggested to the chaplain of the settlement that he approach Pocahontas about the possibility of accepting the gospel of Jesus Christ. Apparently this suggestion was well received, and Pocahontas became a Christian. At her baptism she was given the Bible name of Rebekah.[27]

Not long afterward John Rolfe approached Pocahontas and asked her to marry him. She consented and in April, 1614, with a large crowd of both Englishmen and Indians present at the ceremony, Pocahontas became Mrs. John Rolfe. By that time she is thought to have been between nineteen and twenty years old.

Because the commonwealth of Virginia was beginning to thrive, it was thought appropriate to make a good will tour to England in order to encourage more settlers to migrate to America. The leaders of Jamestown observed that Pocahontas had developed into a very attractive and dignified young woman, and it was decided that no better good-will ambassador could be chosen to accompany the expedition than the Indian princess.

By this time Pocahontas had an infant son, so John Rolfe took both of them with him to England. The baby's name was Thomas Rolfe.[28]

Pocahontas Becomes a Celebrity

Jamestown's former governor, Thomas Dale, introduced John Rolfe and his wife into the highest circles of English Society. Pocahontas was a sensation. The Indian princess "was entertained with banquets and receptions, she was often seen at the theatre, and was watched with great curiosity by the people."[29]

A humorous touch for the modern student occurred when John Rolfe introduced his wife to King James as Princess Pocahontas. The king is said to have become quite indignant. He looked down his long nose and said in effect, "Sir, how dare you marry into royalty without my permission!"[30]

26. Ibid., 4:198.
27. Ibid., 4:200.
28. Ibid., 4:200.
29. Ibid., 4:202.
30. Ibid.

Pocahontas was so popular that she was asked to sit for a portrait by the celebrated artist, Simon Van Pass. Dressed in London's latest style, she makes a very pretty picture.[31]

She was received and entertained royally by the bishop of London. She was also visited by John Smith who was fully recovered and delighted to see her. But Pocahontas was hurt when she was told that she shouldn't call him her "father" and have him call her "my child" the way they both did in Virginia.

In March, 1617, as John Rolfe and his wife prepared to return to Virginia, Pocahontas suddenly became deathly ill. Some say it was small pox. In any event, when she realized she was dying, Pocahontas placed her little son in the care of Sir Lewis Stuckeley who raised him in England. The death of the Indian princess came as a great shock to those English people who had come to know her or had heard about her. Pocahontas was lovingly buried in the cemetery of the Gravesend Church.

At this juncture, John Rolfe was appointed secretary of the Virginia Colony and therefore returned immediately to Jamestown. Tragically, however he was killed four years later by a band of Indians led by the uncle of Pocahontas.[32] But the record does not indicate that the attack was related in any way to Pocahontas or her marriage to John Rolfe.

Just as a final note, we might mention that when young Thomas Rolfe grew up he moved from England to Virginia where he married and raised a large family. In due time his sons and daughters intermarried with some of the finest names in Virginia, and as a result the blood line of Pocahontas was perpetuated in the families of the Bollings, the Eldredges, the Murrays, the Gays, the Whittles, the Robertsons, as well as a branch of the Randolphs and the Jeffersons.[33]

Virginia Organizes the First Legislative Body in America

By 1619 the population of Virginia was around 2,000 and its plantations and villages were scattered up and down the James and York rivers.[34] In Anglo-Saxon days the people were divided into "hundreds" or "wards", meaning communities that could provide a hundred military men if necessary

31. Ibid., next to 4:204.
32. Ibid., 4:204.
33. Ibid.
34. Ibid., 4:218.

for defense. In Virginia the "hundreds" were called by that name for awhile and then changed to "boroughs" where the town was a fortified place. People who were inhabitants of a borough were called "burgesses."[35]

In 1619 the people of each political division in Virginia were allowed to elect representatives and on the 30th of July, 1619, the first legislative body of free Englishmen in America was called together in the wooden church in Jamestown. Eleven local constituencies were represented under the various designations of city, plantation, or hundred, and each constituency was allowed to elect two representatives who were called "burgesses." They continued to meet as Virginia's House of Burgesses until 1776.[36]

It was also in 1619 that the Company began inviting boatloads of young women over to Virginia. Prospective husbands were required to pay 120 pounds of tobacco to cover the cost of the voyage from England. This delightful procedure immediately reflected itself in the growth of Virginia's population. By 1622 the population of Virginia was up to 4,000.[37]

A Tragic Event That the Settlers Hoped Would Never Happen

It was at this point in the history of Virginia that the optimistic spirit of good relations between the Indians and the English came to a blood-curdling halt. Many had hoped that the marriage of Pocahontas to John Rolfe signalled the birth of a new age when the natives would accept the English as friends and carefully consider their message of Christianity. But it was not to be.

Stirred up by haunting visions of the white man spreading his fields and towns throughout their ancestral hunting grounds, the Indians took to their war paint and wild dances. It may have been sparked earlier in 1622 when an Indian chief named Jack of the Feather killed a white man and was captured and killed in return. Whatever the cause, a short time later the whole Indian population descended on the white settlements from Chesapeake Bay to the present site of Richmond.

Many of the women and girls were raped, children were tomahawked and scalped, men were scalped and sometimes tortured to death by roasting. Altogether 347 Virginians were killed. If this had happened two years earlier it would have no doubt closed down the entire settlement, but by the spring of 1622 the survivors were sufficiently strong to rise in a rage and begin hunting

35. Ibid., 4:219-220.
36. Ibid., 4:219.
37. Ibid., 4:223

down the Indians as though they were predatory beasts. Nothing would satisfy the agonizing of the whites over the massacre of their people but the complete eviction or extermination of all the Indians in Virginia.

This was a tragic scenario that was eventually repeated in nearly all of the thirteen colonies. Every formula for peaceful coexistence between the Indians and the whites failed to endure. As an extreme experiment the Quakers in Pennsylvania allowed hundreds to be massacred without retaliation in hopes that kindness and capitulation would satisfy the savage lust for blood, but finally the non-Quakers had to rise up and purge the entire colony of the Indian population just as Virginia had done.

A Final Note on Virginia

In spite of her rugged birth pangs, Virginia began to expand and prosper with a quality of life that became the paradigm for all of the other southern states.

By 1776 when the thirteen colonies declared themselves to be free and independent, Virginia had the largest population of any state in the Union.

Topics for Reflection and Discussion

1. List some of the qualities the early settlers in America found necessary in order to survive. Why did it take so long to develop these qualities?

2. When the Virginia settlers set out from England what two important things were in their sealed box?

3. Why was John Smith upset with the route chosen by Captain Newport? What happened to Smith? How long did the voyage take?

4. Name three things in the early life of John Smith which impressed you the most. Can you think of any reason why historian John Fiske would call John Smith one of the greatest Englishmen of his generation?

5. Explain the system of compulsory communism imposed on the Jamestown colony by the London Company. Why didn't it work? Out of the one hundred and five settlers, how many survived?

6. About how old was Pocahontas when she saved the life of John Smith? How was her father going to have him killed?

7. What was the Biblical name given to Pocahontas when she became a Christian? Who married her? What was the name of her first son? How was Pocahontas received when she accompanied her husband to England?

8. When Pocahontas was introduced to King James why did the king criticize John Rolfe? What is believed to have caused the death of Pocahontas? What happened to her son? Did he ever return to Jamestown?

9. What year was the first legislative body established in America? When the London Company sent young women to Jamestown, how much did the prospective husbands among the settlers pay for the cost of their transportation?

10. When the first major Indian massacre occurred in Virginia during 1622, what reprisal did the settlers take against the Indians? Did any of the other colonies work out a successful policy of peaceful coexistence with the Indians? What policy did the Quakers try? What happened?

CHAPTER EIGHTEEN

NEW ENGLAND—LAND OF THE PILGRIMS AND THE PURITANS

It is interesting that the first permanent English settlement in New England was an accident. A ship load of Pilgrims seeking religious freedom had intended to land in the upper or northern part of what was originally called "Southern Virginia." This would have meant that their first settlement was intended to be in what we now call Delaware or New Jersey. Unfortunately, violent storms blew the ship completely off course and the Pilgrims ended up in Plymouth Bay, about 34 miles south of modern Boston.

As this story unfolds, it will help us to get a little better background on these Pilgrims.

THE DIFFERENCE BETWEEN THE PILGRIMS AND THE PURITANS

From a religious standpoint the Pilgrims were called "Separatists" which meant they wanted to set up a church completely independent of the Church of England where King James was the spiritual father. The Pilgrims thought the Church of England was too much like the Catholic Church in its theology as well as its ordinances. So they wanted to set up a new church more like the one they felt existed in New Testament times.

King James could not believe anyone would want to leave his church. He objected strenuously to the Pilgrims or Separatists as though they were committing treason against the Crown. Heresy was already considered a capital crime and King James thought the setting up of a separate church was almost worse than treason. Wherever Separatists could be found he ordered a heavy dose of punishment. It might be imprisonment in rat-infested prisons, the slitting of noses, the cutting off of ears and the confiscation of property. In some cases he ordered outright execution.

In contrast to the Separatists (which included the Pilgrims), the situation with the so-called Puritans was quite different—at least, in the beginning. The Puritans wanted to reform the Church of England but do so by purifying it from *within*. They therefore boldly rejected the idea of separation from the Church—which at first was pleasing to the king—but when he learned they were also laying plans to radically change the doctrines and ceremonies of the Church from the inside, he was furious. By 1620 the king got around to persecuting the Puritans as fiercely as he had the Pilgrims or Separatists.

In fact, by the time the Puritans got to America they had suffered sufficiently to turn them into "separatists." But first, let us go back to the Pilgrims.

The Flight of the Pilgrims

We should point out that originally there were two groups of Pilgrims who approached the London Company for a settlement in America. Both wanted to settle considerably north of the Jamestown settlement—perhaps near the mouth of the Hudson River where New York later became established. Both groups were granted permission to settle in the chartered territory of the London company but they were told to seek financial help from some independent source since the London Company was struggling to keep the Jamestown settlement alive. Both groups agreed.

Unfortunately, the first group of Pilgrims encountered continual tragedy almost from the beginning because of poor planning.

This group had fled to Amsterdam, Holland, for safety, but their pastor, Mr. Francis Blackwell, became so anxious to depart for America that he impulsively chartered a small ship in 1618 so he could immediately set out for Virginia. Blackwell herded 180 people onto this relatively tiny boat where they were "packed together like herrings." In reckless haste it took off without adequate preparations for any kind of emergency should the voyage be delayed by storms, fog, contrary winds or other unforeseen mishaps.

The worst possible scenario transpired and the crowded boat nearly capsized several times as the mountainous waves continually crashed across its decks. Not only was the length of the voyage disastrously prolonged to six months, but starvation, lack of fresh water, and disease began to take their toll. When the battered hulk of the ship crept into the welcomed protection of Virginia's Chesapeake Bay, there were only 50 of the 180 passengers still alive. Even Pastor Francis Blackwell had died and been buried at sea.[1]

In 1620 the Second Group Decided to Risk it

It will be recalled that this second group of Pilgrims had tried to escape the persecution of the king by taking refuge in a huge old Manor House in Scrooby which belonged to their minister, William Brewster. Scrooby was

1. John Fiske, Historical Writings, op. cit., 6:95-96; George F. Willison, Saints and Strangers, op. cit., p. 110.

a small town which was located about half way between London and the Scottish border, not far from Sherwood Forest of Robin Hood fame. William Brewster was not only the pastor but had the honor of serving as the local postmaster.

As with the previous group, the Scrooby congregation became intensely frightened as the king's officers began to close in on them. They therefore fled to Amsterdam where the first group of Pilgrims had sought refuge and William Brewster sold the old Manor House in order to pay for the transportation of his flock.

At that time Amsterdam was one of the most flourishing industrial cities in Europe, but after several years of bare subsistence, these Pilgrims grew restless and decided to sail south a few miles to a branch of the Rhine River and then go inland to a smaller industrial city named Leydon.

But even this move proved economically disappointing, so William Brewster felt it was time to attempt an ocean-crossing voyage to Virginia. Good fortune came their way when the famous John Smith offered to be their guide.

It will be remembered from the previous chapter that John Smith had suffered severe powder burns at Jamestown and had been forced to return to England. However, when he recovered he did not go back to Jamestown but decided to carefully explore the part of the Virginia charter which extended from what is now Rhode Island to the Canadian border. He was a careful explorer and drew immaculate maps of this northern section of the Virginia charter and gave it a new name. It was John Smith who named the whole region "New England."

After finishing his New England expedition, John Smith returned to England just as William Brewster obtained a patent to build a settlement in "Virginia." This immediately aroused John Smith to the possibility of going with them and serving as their guide. But of course these religious refugees had no idea they were going to end up in "New England" or no doubt they would have leaped at the good fortune of having John Smith accompany them. No man alive knew more about that barren, rock-bound coast than he did. Smith could have shown them how to get into the lumber industry for masts and clapboard and how to exploit the rich fishing treasures along the teeming Newfoundland banks.[2]

But that was not to be.

---

2. Willison, Saints and Strangers, op. cit., p. 145.

William Brewster rejected the generous offer of John Smith to go with them and serve as guide and advisor on the journey.

The Speedwell and the Mayflower

But rejecting John Smith was just the first of their bad judgment calls. Immediately afterwards they had the misfortune to get involved with a rather unscrupulous promoter named Thomas Weston from London. He convinced William Brewster that Weston's "stock company" would be the most reliable way to finance this great new adventure. The name of Thomas Weston would haunt the Pilgrims until he died.

The Weston stock company had signed on two "noble ships" to take Brewster's flock to America, and the launching point was to be the port of Southampton. Those coming from Holland reached the rendezvous port in the Speedwell where it docked beside the *Mayflower*. There the Pilgrims were shocked to discover that Thomas Weston had put eighty work recruits on the *Mayflower* to make sure the investment of his stock company would make a profit from the new settlement. This meant the Brewster congregation on the *Mayflower* was substantially outnumbered by these eighty "strangers."

There was much haggling and heated discussion which caused extended delay, but finally, on August 5, 1620, the two ships sailed down the coast toward the open sea. Their holds were filled with huge barrels of water, beer, biscuits and cod, as well as sacks of smoked beef and tubs of pickled eggs.

Unfortunately, they were barely out to sea when the Speedwell began to leak so badly the two vessels were forced to return to the port of Dartmouth for caulking and repairs. After another costly delay they once again set forth and had gone nearly 300 miles into the North Atlantic when the captain of the Speedwell said his boat was once again shipping water and he would have to turn back. This time the two vessels went back to Southampton and everything from the Speedwell was hauled on board the *Mayflower*. However, when the passengers saw how congested the *Mayflower* would be, about one-sixth of them elected to remain behind. Twenty of these were among the "strangers" Weston had recruited. The remaining passengers totalled to one hundred and two "saints and strangers" who crowded aboard the *Mayflower* and on September 6, 1620, a stiff breeze carried them out onto the billowing ocean toward their destiny.[3]

3. Fiske, Historical Writings, op. cit., 6:126-128; Willison, Saints and Strangers, op. cit., p. 127-128.

THE CROSSING

By the end of September the *Mayflower* had reached the mid-Atlantic and the captain prayed mightily that the weather would hold steady. But it was not to be. In October the notorious "westerlies" hit the boat with waves fifty feet high and turned everything below deck into a scene of total pandemonium.

Furthermore, a near disaster occurred when the ship was twisted violently and the huge beam running from stem to stern was cracked and threatened to break. Had this occurred, every soul aboard the ship would have drowned. However, someone remembered that he had brought a huge screw jack from Holland capable of lifting the corner of a house. There was a mad scramble among the jumbled baggage until it was found. As the screw was turned and the jack moved up under the sagging beam, there was a breathless moment to see if it was strong enough to lift the load. Then the jack took hold and the mighty beam creaked back into its original position. Timbers were brought up to further brace the beam and the captain said he felt certain that the ship could now survive.[4]

During the storm the *Mayflower* was blown hundreds of miles off course. When land was finally sighted the captain was amazed to find that he was approaching the snow-covered coast of Cape Cod (which is now part of Massachusetts).

Once the "strangers" realized they were far beyond the region granted by the charter, there was talk of mutiny against the saints.

Elder William Brewster took the matter in hand and ordered all the men to meet as a body to hear him read a document on which the authority of the new colony would be established. It was a covenant "in the presence of God" to obey all just and equal laws "which would be drawn up for the general good."

Every man signed, even the "strangers." The threat of mutiny was thereby averted, and this is known in history as the famous Mayflower Compact.[5]

THE FIRST WINTER

Once the *Mayflower* was safe inside the cape, exploring parties scrutinized the maps which were finally given to them by John Smith and found a place he had designated as "Providence." After a couple of Indian skirmishes and several other disquieting escapades, the Pilgrim colony was settled at this

4. Willison, Saints and Strangers, op. cit., p. 136.
5. Ibid., pp. 142-143.

place which John Smith had thought would be a good location. They could tell it had been an Indian settlement, but what they didn't know was the fact that the tribe which previously lived there had been wiped out three years earlier by a plague.

Members of this Plymouth settlement worked feverishly to get houses built and a common hall constructed, but before they could get out of the weather a plague of influenza struck down the whole population. It was devastating.

Thirty-four men with families died and twenty of the twenty-four mothers perished. Spring found less than half of the company still alive. The first Indian to help them was named Samoset from Pemaquid Point, Maine, where English fishermen had taught him their language. Samoset later brought the principal chief, Massasoit, with whom they made a treaty of peace, and he also brought an Indian named Squanto who joined the Pilgrims because it was his tribe that had been wiped out by the plague at this very site three years previously.

It was this friendly Indian named Squanto who taught them how to put two or three herring in each hill of Indian corn as fertilizer. He also assured them that by the middle of April the nearby brook would contain all the herring they needed for their entire corn planting.

John Carver had been elected the original governor, but he died of a stroke in April, 1621, and young William Bradford was elected to take his place. However, it was not a pleasant assignment.

Another Round of Compulsory Communism

In spite of the bitter experience which the investors had endured under communism at Jamestown, Thomas Weston and the stockholders insisted that the Pilgrims practice compulsory "Communism" for seven years and have "all things in common." After seven years the fruits of their efforts were to be divided up according to the number of shares each person had acquired either through investment or labor.

This system was predictably inefficient but there were enough hard workers among them to put together a fairly good harvest by fall. Therefore they decided to celebrate with three days of thanksgiving. Chief Massasoit came with 90 of his braves and five deer, freshly killed. Bradford sent four men out and they killed enough turkeys, ducks and geese to provide food for a week.

The Revolt Against Communism

Even though this first American "Thanksgiving" was a happy event, the memory of it faded as the workers returned to the dull routine of their communal struggle. Each year became more arduous as the Pilgrims tried to survive in a self-defeating routine of bare subsistence rations. For many it was just too much and in nearly every family there were those who succumbed to disease and the rigors of this hostile climate. Finally, Governor Bradford wrote:

> "This community … was found to breed much confusion and discontent and retard much employment that would have been to their benefit and comfort. For the young men that were most able and fit for labor and service did repine [complain] that they should spend their time and strength to work for other men's wives and children without recompense. The strong … had no more in division of victuals and clothes than he that was weak and not able to do a quarter the other could; this was thought an injustice … and for men's wives to be commanded to do service for other men, as dressing their meat, washing their clothes, etc., they deemed it a kind of slavery, neither could many husbands well brook it."[6]

The production level under this system was so low that ultimately the colonists faced complete extinction by starvation. Therefore Governor Bradford says:

> "At length, after much debate … the governor, gave way that they should set corn every man for his own purpose, and in every regard trust to themselves … and so assigned to every family a parcel of land according to the proportion of their number."[7]

The basic slogan which seemed to emerge from this new arrangement was "root hog or die." Of course the sick and the helpless had to have the benefit of Christian charity but every healthy worker began to see the results of a strong competitive free society where he could enjoy the fruits of his labor.

---

6. William Bradford, History of Plymouth, 1606-1642, Collections of Massachusetts Historical Society, Fourth Series, 1856, pp. 160-162.
7. Ibid.

The Fruits of Free Enterprise

After one year the governor was able to report:

> "This had very good success; for it made all hands very industrious, so that much more corn was planted than otherwise would have been … The women now went willingly into the fields, and took their little ones with them to set corn, which before would allege weakness and inability; whom to have compelled would have been thought great tyranny and oppression." [8]

Years later Governor Bradford reflected on this experience and wrote:

> "The experience that was had in this common cause and condition, tried sundry years, and that amongst godly and sober men, may well evince [demonstrate] the vanity of that conceit of Plato and other ancients—applauded by some in later times—that taking away of property, and bringing it into a commonwealth, would make them happy and flourishing as if they were wiser than God." [9]

For several centuries economists among the Christians had been advocating the communal life as a principle of the Bible, but Governor Bradford disagreed with their interpretation of the New Testament. He thought these men felt they were "wiser than God" and had twisted the scriptures to fit their communal dreams of a Christian utopia. As we learned in an earlier chapter, Governor Bradford was right and the promoters of "Christian communism" were in error.

What Happened to Plymouth?

Before leaving the Pilgrims we should point out that eventually they were able to buy out their joint stockholders in England and branched out to establish ten small satellite towns. However, Plymouth itself never became a metropolis. Even by 1637 it had only 549 residents. Nevertheless, the experience of this community became a miniature laboratory in which the later lessons of the entire American economy were mirrored. Plymouth and her neighboring communities were eventually absorbed into the Massachusetts Bay colony which grew up around Boston just a decade after the founding of Plymouth.

---

8. Ibid.
9. Ibid.

New England Is Flooded with Puritans

Here at the beginning we should mention that before either the Pilgrims or Puritans arrived in New England there had been earlier groups who had tried to establish colonies up and down the coast of what is now Massachusetts and Maine. It was their intent to accommodate the fishing and fur trading business which thrived during the summer months as ships arrived from England, Holland, France and Spain to fish the Newfoundland banks and trade with the Indians.

However, none of these earlier settlements survived except a small one called Naumkeag which became known as Salem. It was the only established settlement when the first boatloads of Puritans began to arrive in 1630.

The New Charter for Massachusetts

The Puritan businessmen who laid the foundation for the colonizing of Salem purchased the land from the Council of New England—the former Plymouth company. In 1629 they sent over the good ship Abigail with forty men aboard to build houses and prepare Salem for settlement. This was followed by another body of workers in five boats, one of which was the *Mayflower* that had brought over the Pilgrims.

Meanwhile, the Puritan businessmen in England were successful in obtaining a royal charter in the name of the Massachusetts Bay Company. This charter was especially significant since it gave the members of this colony the right to virtually govern themselves.

This charter encouraged John Winthrop and a group of prosperous Puritans to seize this opportunity of escaping from the persecution of Charles I and taking a large contingent of their people to Salem. This was the beginning of the big Puritan migration in 1630. John Winthrop brought over seventeen ships carrying a thousand colonists. He also brought over the company's charter so it would not be confiscated by the king in case he became displeased with the Puritan project.[10]

It turned out that Salem was not as attractive as most of the immigrants had hoped, so many of the recent arrivals began to spread abroad and establish a number of separate colonies around the bay. First they set up Charleston on the Charles River opposite modern Boston, and then they went on to establish Medford, Watertown, Roxbury, and finally Boston. Boston was built on a segment of land which jutted out into the bay and except for a narrow neck

---

10. Donzella Cross Boyle, Quest of a Hemisphere, Boston: Western Islands, 1970, p. 60.

of connecting land was almost an island. This made it an ideal port and merchandising center.

But this was no place for marshmallow colonists. "Plows were scarce, and those used were of the most primitive pattern. What was reaped with a sickle was threshed with a flail. Four-wheeled wagons were unknown and the only kind of vehicle used in farm work was a rude cart. In Higginson's Catalogue of 'needful things' for the New England planter he enumerates … 1 broad hoe; 1 narrow hoe; 1 broad axe; 1 felling axe; 1 steel hand-saw; 1 whip saw; 1 hammer; 1 shovel; 1 spade; 1 hatchet."[11]

But in spite of the hardships, all of these Puritan settlements prospered so that between 1630 and 1640 some 200 ships carried more than 20,000 settlers to the Massachusetts Bay. This is known in history as the "Great Migration."

Shift to the Congregational Church Pattern

Not all of the emigrants were Puritans, of course, but most of them were non-conformists of some sort. Almost from the beginning the Puritans abandoned the idea of purifying the Church of England and turned instead to the Separatists' policy of allowing each congregation to independently enter into a mutual covenant and then select a minister of their own choosing. They therefore became known as the Congregational churches.

A block of around ten families was called a tythe, and a tything-master or block warden was in charge. A group of around a hundred families was called a "ward" or township.

While the first Puritans were crossing the ocean, John Winthrop had declared that their Puritan society would be like "a city on a hill." It would exemplify Christian ideals on the highest level. As a result, rules and regulations were very strict, especially concerning the sanctity of the sabbath day. Frivolous parties and worldly behavior were severely frowned upon.

The work ethic was both preached and practiced. It applied to household chores and work in the field. Anyone caught loitering around town ran the risk of being charged with "idleness" and suffering the consequences. Heads of families were expected to supervise their families with careful rigor. All young men were required to live with their families under the discipline of their fathers until they married.

---

11. Daniel Waite Howe, The Puritan Republic, Indianapolis: The Bowen-Merrill Company, 1899, p. 132.

The Combining of Church and State

From the beginning, however, the Puritans made the mistake of combining church and state. In fact, they violated their own charter in 1631 by ruling that no man could be accepted as a "freeman" and vote in elections unless he was "saved" and a member of one of the Congregational churches. This made it impossible for Quakers and many others to vote.

In order to qualify as a "saved" Christian it was necessary to testify openly in one of the church meetings that by an inner divine manifestation the individual knew that he or she had been predestined by God for salvation. The idea that only certain people are "predestined" to be saved is often referred to as "Calvinism," but it is really based on the teachings of St. Augustine (354-430 A.D.) who said that the fall of Adam subjected all mankind to damnation but that God extends to a few the gift of salvation to demonstrate that he is all-powerful. In other words, God has arbitrarily predestined certain ones to be saved through his grace while all others are precluded forever from redemption because of the fall.

Since the leaders of the Massachusetts Bay Colony sincerely believed this doctrine, they determined to have only the "sanctified" participate in government, thereby assuring the people the best of all possible administrations in their public affairs. This is the reason that originally the right to be a "freeman" and have the privilege of voting was restricted. The requirement of sanctification was also necessary in order to run for public office.

It took Massachusetts nearly two hundred years to achieve a genuine separation of church and state; but from the beginning, the people resisted and resented the self-appointed concentration of power in these religious leaders. There was a revolt even among the sanctified in 1636 when John Winthrop was temporarily voted out of office as governor and replaced by Henry Vane. However, Winthrop subsequently regained his position and ousted or brought to heel all major opposition. The struggle of the people to regain their traditional rights extended over several generations.

The Problem of Religious Bigotry

Meanwhile there was a bitter persecution of Quakers (especially 1656-1662) and strong legislation against Baptists (lasting from 1644 to 1678). Official action partook of the brutality of the time, including scourging, boring of tongues, cutting off ears, banishment, and in rare cases, capital punishment. During the witchcraft scare a total of thirty-two persons were executed (according to W.F. Poole) but this was only a pittance compared to the wholesale persecution of alleged witches in England, Scotland and Ireland during the same period. In Scotland alone, fourteen courts were kept busy handling "witch cases."[12]

Many people sensed that these manifestations of bitter intolerance were inherently wrong, and on a number of occasions mobs gathered to rescue Quakers or Baptists from the brutality of the authorities. By 1641 Rev. Nathaniel Ward of Ipswich, Massachusetts, had drawn up a code of laws called "The Body of Liberties" which was adopted by the council deputies from the various townships. These ninety-eight stipulations launched the beginning of a long march back toward religious freedom which could be traced back to the traditions of the early Anglo-Saxons beginning with Alfred the Great around 850 A.D.

The Settling of Rhode Island

The situation in Massachusetts was bound to create friction.

The first crisis occurred when one of the leading ministers in Salem named Roger Williams began preaching that the governing officials of the Massachusetts Bay Company had no right to impose a particular creed of religious belief on the colonists. Roger Williams was well-to-do, well-educated and soon became very popular because of his plea for greater tolerance among the colonies. A significant number of families moved to Salem so they could be members of his congregation.

Eventually the leaders of the Massachusetts Bay Company and the church court officially condemned Williams and gave him just six weeks to leave the region. However this still gave the condemned minister a little time to circulate among the various churches and preach against the "state" religion, particularly in Boston, Plymouth and Salem.

To the astonishment of the church leaders Roger Williams was using the brief interlude they had allowed him, to build up a goodly number of converts. The authorities therefore decided to kidnap Williams and ship him back to England. He escaped, however, and fled to a tribe of friendly Indians called the Narragansetts. He stayed with them during the winter of 1635 and wrote: "I was unmercifully driven from house to a winter's flight, for fourteen weeks, in a bitter winter season, I knew not what bread or bed did mean."[13]

When spring came Williams purchased some land from the Indians and sent for his wife and children. He called the site "Providence" after the name

12. Durant, The Story of Civilization, op. cit., 8:482.
13. Boyle, Quest of a Hemisphere, op. cit., p. 62.

originally given to Plymouth by John Smith. He invited any who were being persecuted to join him in what finally became known as the colony of Rhode Island.

Some of the first to come were the persecuted Baptists who did not believe in infant baptism but held that people should be baptized when they are old enough to understand the Bible and covenant with God to obey his will.

Roger Williams felt good about the doctrines of the Baptists and for a short time they looked upon him as their Baptist leader. However, he was not comfortable in this role and his independence soon carried him off to a non-denominational position where he remained the rest of his life.

Ann Hutchinson

Another notable refugee who fled from Massachusetts to Rhode Island was Ann Hutchinson, a mother of fourteen children.

She was born in Lincolnshire, England, around 1600 A.D. where her father was a clergyman. After reaching maturity and getting married, she migrated with her husband, William Hutchinson, to Boston in 1634. She became a great admirer of Rev. John Cotton and gained considerable influence among the women of the colonies, especially in Boston, because of her competence as a nurse.

Nevertheless, she had a deep concern about some of the doctrines the Puritan preachers were expounding. Before long she began holding meetings in her home where she analyzed the sermons being taught in the churches. She said that she, Rev. John Cotton, and her brother-in-law, Rev. John Wheelwright, were under a "covenant of grace," with a "peculiar indwelling of the Holy Ghost." By way of comparison, she accused Rev. John Wilson and certain other ministers of being under a "covenant of works" which the Puritans had always attributed to the Catholics. Because of her disdain for works and complete reliance on grace she and her supporters became known as "Antinomians" which meant they believed in salvation by grace alone and were opposed to relying on the works of obedience to commandments as the means of gaining salvation.[14]

She must have been very persuasive because she was supported by Governor Vane, Rev. John Cotton, Rev. John Wheelwright and the majority of the Boston Church. Nevertheless, she was bitterly opposed by the Dep-

14. See chapter 11 for a more detailed discussion of Antinomianism.

uty-Governor, John Winthrop, and the leaders of the churches in the other colonies.

After Winthrop defeated Vane for the governorship, Ann Hutchinson was excommunicated from the Boston church and was then tried and convicted of heresy in 1637. The judges ordered her banished from Massachusetts forever. Former Governor Vane was so upset by the whole proceeding that he returned to England in disgust. Her brother-in-law, John Wheelwright, was also tried and banished. He went to New Hampshire and established a church at Exeter. John Cotton made submission and suffered certain minor penalties to retain his church membership.

Another dissident who supported Ann Hutchinson was William Coddington. He followed Roger Williams to Rhode Island and Williams helped Coddington to buy enough land from the Indians to set up the community of Portsmouth in 1639.

The End of a Tragic Trail for Ann Hutchinson

Ann Hutchinson lived with her family in Portsmouth, Rhode Island, for four years but after her husband died she decided to move her family to Long Island and set up her home near the place which is now known as New Rochelle in Westchester County.

It was during August of 1643 that the Indians went on a rampage. Ann Hutchinson and her family were all massacred along with many other settlers during this Indian attack. American historians remember Ann Hutchinson for the independence of her spirit and her willingness to suffer persecution and eventual martyrdom for her beliefs.

Connecticut—Where America's First Constitution Was Written Based on God's Law

The strong suppression of dissent in the Massachusetts Bay Colony led a number of the "sanctified" as well as the open dissenters to move to the fertile valley of the Connecticut River.

One of the leaders of this movement was the well-known pastor of the church in New Town (Cambridge). His name was Rev. Thomas Hooker. He and his congregation were not only dissatisfied with the way the affairs of the colony were being governed, but they felt severely handicapped by the authorities restricting the amount of land which they were allowed for farming.

Finally, in 1636 they petitioned for the right to settle somewhere in Connecticut and the General Court in Boston grudgingly granted it. Rev. Hooker and his congregation took all their possessions and marched through the wilderness to what is now the heart of the state of Connecticut. Two other dissenting congregations came to the same area in 1637 and as a result three communities were established—Hartford, Windsor, and Wethersfield.

Confederating Connecticut under God's Law

These three towns confederated and formed the "Fundamental Orders of Connecticut" which were adopted in 1639. This was largely the work of Rev. Thomas Hooker who had given a famous address to the General Court of the three towns on May 31, 1638. His talk was based on Deuteronomy 1:13 where Moses told the Israelites:

> "Take you wise men, and understanding [men], and known among your tribes, and I will make them rulers over you."

Rev. Hooker felt this scripture struck down the tactics of the arrogant leaders in Massachusetts. He pointed out that this passage plainly taught that the people are to nominate and elect those who are to rule over them and that they should select only the best known and most trusted among them to be their magistrates, judges, and rulers.

He further pointed out that since God has indicated that the foundation of political authority is in the free consent of the people, they have the right to set bounds and limitations to the powers granted to those who rule over them.

Based on these principles the people entered into a "Plantation Covenant," and attempted to organize and govern themselves according to God's law. They saw that the Massachusetts Bay colony had been scripturally correct in organizing themselves into "wards [or townships] and counties" and therefore followed—at least to this extent—the pattern of the colony they had just left. Nevertheless, they wanted the *people* to determine who should govern them, not the church or the general court in Boston.

Historian John Fiske Praises God's Law

Modern historians tend to denigrate or ignore the remarkable break-through of the confederation in Connecticut, but not John Fiske. In his notable work on the history of New England he says:

> "This little federal republic was allowed to develop peacefully and normally; its constitution was not violently wrenched out of shape

like that of Massachusetts at the end of the seventeenth century. It silently grew till it became the strongest political structure on the continent, as was illustrated in the remarkable military energy and the unshaken financial credit of Connecticut during the Revolutionary War; and in the chief crisis of the Federal Convention of 1787 Connecticut, with her compromise which secured equal state representation in one branch of the national government and popular representation in the other, played the controlling part." [15]

No other colony was successful in sorting out these principles until more than a century after Connecticut had successfully launched them. Finally, Rhode Island saw what was happening and copied the "Fundamental Orders of Connecticut" for their own constitution. When the Declaration of Independence created the United States of America, there were only two states that did not have to completely restructure their constitutions to fit the new order of things.

These two were Connecticut and Rhode Island.

The Settling of New York

It was the Dutch—not the English—who first established a permanent settlement in what is now known as New York, but the Dutch called it New Netherlands.

England immediately protested that this violated her claim to the Atlantic seaboard under the Virginia and Plymouth charters, but the Dutch ignored the protest and went right ahead building the harbor into a magnificent commercial port called New Amsterdam.

The Dutch also began building settlements up along the Hudson valley which—to a certain extent—virtually separated New England from the English colonies to the south. However, in 1664 the British invaded New Amsterdam and seized the Dutch colony in the name of Charles I. There were only 8,000 Dutch in the colony at the time and they quickly made their peace with the English. Charles I then turned over New Amsterdam as well as the larger region of New Netherlands to his brother, the Duke of York, and the area thereupon became known as New York.

During its first hundred years, this English colony had a boisterous, topsy-turvy history. The royal governors from England were as arrogant and vindictive as the governors in the other colonies. There were uprisings followed

15. John Fiske, Historical Writings, op. cit., 7:156.

by hangings. There was the administration of the notorious Edmund Andros which is a drama all by itself.[16]

By the time of the Revolutionary War, New York was only seventh in population compared with the other states. Furthermore, her government was in the hands of loyalists and there were more Tories in New York than anywhere in the new confederation of states. When the Constitution came around for ratification, New York came within three votes of remaining outside of the Union.

Laying the Foundation for a Future World Power

It was 180 years (1607-1787) before all thirteen Americans states were firmly in place and anxious to declare to the world that they were ready to become a major world power. Here is the roll-call of the colonies as they originally appeared on the scene:

Virginia	1607
Massachusetts	1628
(Plymouth—1620)	
Maryland	1634
Rhode Island	1636
Connecticut	1636
Maine	1641
North Carolina	1663
South Carolina	1663
New York	1664
New Jersey	1664
New Hampshire	1680
Pennsylvania	1681
Georgia	1732

16. John Fiske, The Beginning of New England, Boston: Houghton Mifflin Co., 1902, pp. 334-340.

Topics for Reflection and Discussion

1. In England the words, "Puritan" and "Separatist" meant two different things. Can you explain the difference? What did they both become after their arrival in America?

2. What happened to the first group of Pilgrims? Why did the second group nearly drown in mid-ocean? What saved them?

3. Who was Squanto? Why was he a life-saver for the Pilgrims? Why did Governor Bradford say communism nearly destroyed the colony? What saved them? Why did he think their proprietors thought they were "wiser than God?" Did the early Christians practice communism?

4. What caused 20,000 Puritans to flee to New England? Were they poor or fairly well-off? Instead of setting up the Church of England, what church pattern did they follow? What was their attitude toward idleness?

5. Why did combining church and state almost prove fatal for the Puritans? How did their religious beliefs exclude many voters? How brutal was the bigotry in Massachusetts? What famous religious refugee set up Rhode Island? Who followed him?

6. What was the name of the minister who wrote America's first constitution? Can you describe the elements of political structure which this minister took from God's law as revealed to Moses?

7. What state copied this constitution a hundred years later? In what way did both states become superior to all the other states?

8. Who were the first people to settle New York? What did they call New York City? What did they call New York state? What changed everything in 1664?

9. By the time of the Revolutionary War how did New York compare in population with the other states? Which state had the most Tories (supporters of England?) By how many votes did New York nearly miss being in the Union?

10. How many years did it take the thirteen colonies to get established. Which colony was the last to receive official recognition? When did that occur?

CHAPTER NINETEEN

Sweat, Blood and Tears—
The Price of Freedom

The famous revolution which exploded in America in 1775 was caused by precisely the same arrogant abuses of power that produced the violent English Civil War in 1642 and England's so-called Glorious Revolution of 1688.

In America the power of the English crown was exercised through a royal governor in each colony. A major task of the royal governor was to collect taxes—for which the people had never voted—and to collect revenue from tariffs on all imported goods. To do this the royal officers often ransacked the homes of the colonists for secretly smuggled products and did so without a traditional search warrant. What was worse, offenders were then tried in an Admiralty court where juries were not allowed.

The Stamp Act

This was the setting when Parliament passed the Stamp Act in 1765. A mighty roar of protest went up because it was "taxation without representation." The colonists raised such a ruckus that the Parliament finally decided it would be prudent to repeal the act. But this respite did not last long.

The Townsend Acts

Then the Townsend Acts were passed imposing a tax on most imports. Once more a mighty roar went up, but this time the king and the Parliament stubbornly resisted the pressure and not only refused to repeal the act but sent British troops across the Atlantic to enforce the law and collect the tax.

The Boston Massacre

The bitter resentment of the colonists boiled over on the night of March 5, 1770, when a Boston mob provoked the guards at the State House until they fired into a crowd of protesting civilians. This became known as the Boston Massacre and even though an American jury decided that the mob was more to blame than the soldiers, a wave of flaming indignation swept up and down the Atlantic seaboard.

The Notorious Boston Tea Party

But the development that finally tipped the scales toward open, violent warfare was a shrewd trick by the king's bureaucrats that backfired. This was a sneaky little tax on tea.

Americans had been buying so much smuggled tea from Holland that the English warehouses belonging to Britain's India Tea Company were filled to the rafters. It occurred to some bright master planner among the king's advisors that it might be smart to drastically slash the price of English tea so it would be cheaper than the tea smuggled in from Holland. It was also part of the scheme to have the price slashed so deep that a tea tax could be added and still have the total cost less than the price of the smuggled tea. The basic strategy was to establish a popular precedent for a tax without the approval of the colonists. The talk around London was "The Americans will buy anything so long as it's the cheapest."

The shipments of the cut-rate tea had barely left England when the word got out that the price of the tea included a tax. Consequently, the captains of the tea ships had a big surprise waiting for them when they arrived at each of the American ports. The wharfs were crowded with armed colonists who forced the captains to turn their boats around and take the tea back to England. In one or two instances the tea was unloaded but stored in damp, musty cellars where it would spoil quickly and therefore be unfit for sale.

Up in Boston, however, it was a different story. The royal governor refused to let the ships return to England until the tea was unloaded, and the armed patriots refused to allow it to be unloaded.

During the heated debate with the royal governor, Sam Adams learned that he was playing a waiting game. Adams found out that under admiralty law the cargo of any ship that was not unloaded in twenty days became the property of the crown and the royal governor could auction it off. Sam Adams believed the strategy of the governor was to wait for the required twenty days and then seize the cargo and auction it off cheaply *with the tea tax added.*

This would give the governor the precedent he needed for future taxes "without representation" which meant without the approval of the people. For centuries, English wars had been fought over the issue of "taxation without representation."

On the eve of the governor's nineteenth or final day, Sam Adams organized his "Sons of Liberty" and assembled them at Boston's Old South Church. Sam Adams patiently made a final plea to the governor to return the ships to England with the condemned tea, but when the governor haughtily refused, Adams gave the fatal signal for what became known as "The Boston Tea Party." The date was December 16, 1773.

The Sons of Liberty quietly moved from the church to the wharf and solemnly performed an act which they knew was tantamount to a declaration of war. History students are often surprised when they read a detailed account of the Boston Tea Party and learn that it was not a "party" at all. It was a very solemn affair. At the very least they knew they would have to pay damages for the tea and at the worst it could mean a shooting war. A large assembly of women and older men stood silently along the wharfs as the tea was dumped into the bay. They knew they were throwing the gauntlet down at the feet of their king and everyone realized this could have monumental consequences.

Reaction of King George III to the Boston Tea Party

When word reached London that the colonists had completely sabotaged the whole tea tax scheme, the king was furious. He took out most of his rage on the colony of Massachusetts. The charter of Massachusetts was repealed and the people's elected assembly dissolved.

A price was put on the head of Sam Adams dead or alive.

A new royal governor was appointed for Massachusetts—none other than the head of the king's military forces in the American Colonies, General Thomas Gage.

The Boston Harbor was closed to all shipping and the city of Boston was placed under martial law.

All town meetings were suspended unless authorized by the new military governor.

At the discretion of the king, any future offenders could be brought to England for trial.

The American Colonies Hold Their First Congress

By the summer of 1774 it was becoming very evident that the consequences of the Boston Tea Party were rolling up like a dark, threatening cloud of imminent disaster. Leaders of the thirteen English colonies realized that at any moment they might very well become involved in a shooting war with the largest army and most powerful naval power in the world. It was time to hold an emergency meeting.

The First Continental Congress met in Philadelphia from September 26 to October 22, 1774. Twelve colonies sent 56 delegates. Only Georgia—because of its sparse population and internal instability—did not participate.

This Congress issued a "Declaration of Resolves" proclaiming the colonists' loyalty to Britain but setting forth the rights of the colonists as English citizens and declaring their intent to defend those rights even if it meant war.

Only two of the delegates were sufficiently angry to demand outright independence from England. These were Samuel Adams and his younger cousin, John Adams. Most of the other delegates were shocked with this suggestion. Nevertheless, they favored the use of arms to protect their property and their fundamental English rights if it became necessary.

To demonstrate their earnestness they declared an embargo on all English imports, and since Massachusetts was the principal target of the crown, the Congress instructed Massachusetts to carry out its "Suffolk Resolves." These resolves called for the election of a provisional government to replace their revoked charter and provided that each county should have a militia ready to fight at a minute's notice. Thus the famous "Minutemen" of New England came into being.

The Congress then agreed to adjourn for the year but meet again in 1775 if the king and the Parliament did not agree to conciliate their grievances peacefully.

1775—The Year That Changed the Colonists from Loyal Englishmen to Patriotic Americans

Unfortunately, the king treated the petition of the Continental Congress as a contemptible document written up by a crowd of treasonable rebels. When the colonists learned of the king's pompous derision of their petition, they knew a bloody showdown might be coming soon.

The two leaders of the outlawed provisional government of Massachusetts were Samuel Adams and John Hancock. It was not long before John Hancock—as well as Samuel Adams—had a price on his head "dead or alive."

It so happened that General Thomas Gage had a gun shed next to his headquarters and he was outraged when he found that some of Sam Adam's Sons of Liberty had stealthily succeeded in hauling off both powder and cannon from right under his nose. It was rumored that this military loot was being concealed at Concord, and it was also whispered about that illegal meetings of the new provisional government of Massachusetts were convening at Concord.

The Attack on Lexington and Concord

On April 19, 1775, General Gage dispatched a task force of 700 men to conduct a raid on Concord where they were to arrest Samuel Adams and John Hancock. They were also to recover or destroy the stolen munitions.

Paul Revere learned of the plan and made his famous midnight ride to warn the patriots along the way.

At Lexington the British troops were confronted by two companies of colonial militia. However, when the colonists saw how badly they were outnumbered they started to take cover. In the process, someone fired on the king's troops, and the British immediately returned the fire. Eight Americans were killed.

At first there was temporary pandemonium until the British officers finally got their men under control and continued the four-mile march toward Concord. An order was also sent back to Boston for more reinforcements.

At Concord there was immediate resistance as the British redcoats tried to cross the bridge and enter the town. It was later said that when the Minutemen fired, it was "the shot heard round the world." Nevertheless, the British forcefully subdued the opposition, burned whatever armaments they discovered, and searched everywhere for Samuel Adams and John Hancock. But they never found them. They were actually hiding in Lexington when the redcoats came marching through.

The British Shedding of American Blood Changed Everything

As the British retreated back toward Boston, the farmer-militia fired at them from behind trees and rocks all the way to Boston. The redcoats had to carry back 72 of their comrades who were killed and a great many more who were wounded.

As soon as word spread that American blood had been shed in Massachusetts, the temperature of colonial war-fever rose precipitously throughout the colonies. It stimulated enough anger among the Green Mountain Boys of

Vermont to provoke a group of them to rally under Ethan Allen and attack the British fort at Ticonderoga. In the early morning hours of May 10, 1775, the patriots roused the redcoats out of their beds and burned the fort to the ground. In the ashes were 59 cannon and pieces of artillery which would become a great boon to Washington a year later.

The Second Continental Congress

On May 10, 1775—the very day Ethan Allen and his Green Mountain Boys burned the British fort at Ticonderoga—some of the men who later bore the most illustrious names in early American history assembled in Philadelphia for the Second Continental Congress.

The conflict with mother England had developed into a shooting war and emergency measures had to be taken. Massachusetts requested the Congress to set up a "Grand American Army" under a single commander in chief. It also asked the Congress to set up a central government to run the affairs of all the colonies during this emergency.

George Washington, an officer in the Virginia militia, was nominated by John Adams of Massachusetts to be the commander in chief. Washington was about to nominate someone else as commander when his name came to the fore. He therefore stepped outside so the Congress could discuss his qualifications without concern for his feelings.

There were many questions. How could a Virginian take over an army in Massachusetts when he scarcely knew the territory? Shouldn't someone be chosen who had demonstrated his courage and leadership among the Minute Men? Some loyal Puritans even questioned appointing a Church of England southern aristocrat when they had available staunch Congregationalists who were heroes at Concord. Nevertheless, after two days of debate and a thorough discussion of all the alternatives, Washington was designated the new commander in chief.

Washington was no novice at warfare. During the French-Indian wars he had served as a British officer under General Edward Braddock. In the assault against Fort Duquesne, Braddock ignored Washington's advice and marched his troops into a ravine which was a perfect trap for an Indian ambush. When the slaughter began, it was Washington who saved as many British soldiers as possible and dragged the wounded Braddock to safety where he later died.

How George Washington Became Part of an Indian Prophecy

All of this happened long before on July 9, 1755. While Washington was trying to save the remnants of Braddock's army he had two horses shot from under him. One bullet went through his hat and two others went through his cloak. He later wrote that he survived only by the "miraculous care of providence."[1]

It was not until 1770 during a trip to the Ohio Valley that Washington learned from an old Indian chief how miraculous his "care of providence" had actually been. Dr. James Craik was with Washington on the trip to Ohio and later recorded the words of the old chief. According to Craik's report, the old Indian said:

> "I am a chief, and the ruler over many tribes. My influence extends to the waters of the great lakes, and to the far blue mountains. I have traveled a long and weary path that I might see the young warrior of the great battle."[2]

The old chief continued:

"It was on the day when the white man's blood mixed with the streams of our forest that I first beheld this chief. I called to my young men and said, Mark yon tall and daring warrior? He is not of the red-coat tribe—he hath an Indian's wisdom, and his warriors fight as we do—himself is alone exposed. Quick, let your aim be certain, and he dies. Our rifles were levelled, rifles which but for him knew not how to miss—'twas all in vain; a power mightier far than we shielded him from harm. He cannot die in battle.

> "I am old, and soon shall be gathered to the great council fire of my fathers in the land of shades; but ere I go, there is something bids me speak in the voice of prophecy. Listen! The Great Spirit protects that man, and guides his destinies—he will become the chief of nations, and a people yet unborn will hail him as the founder of a mighty empire."[3]

Later, when the American patriots saw Washington risk his life time after time, Dr. Craik would tell the soldiers about this prophecy of the old chief that Washington would never die in battle. He called upon the soldiers to witness the literal fulfillment of this remarkable prediction.

---

1. Parry and Allison, The Real George Washington, op. cit., p. 47.
2. Ibid.
3. Ibid., p. 49.

The Battle of Bunker's (Breed's) Hill

While the Second Continental Congress was in session, the Massachusetts militia succeeded in forming a circle around Boston to prevent General Gage from sending out foraging parties to purchase milk, vegetables or other supplies from the surrounding villages. Trenches were dug along the summits of two hills.

On June 17, 1775, General Gage assigned 2,300 men to form ranks at the foot of these two hills for the purpose of destroying the entrenched Americans. Although this is popularly known as the Battle of Bunker's Hill, the assault by the British actually took place on the adjacent slopes of Breed's Hill.

The redcoats went up the hill in three separate lines with one line following a few steps behind the other, but the Americans did not fire until the front line was within about fifteen paces and each American had fixed a deadly aim on some nearby redcoat. When the Americans did fire, about 500 British soldiers were killed or wounded. The remainder ran frantically down to the bottom of the hill where their officers ordered them to regroup and attack again. The second assault was just as disastrous as the first. Another 500 redcoats fell. Once again the remnants fled to the bottom of the hill and were forced into line by their officers for a third attack.

But this time things went differently. The Americans were almost entirely out of ammunition, and when the redcoats reached the top there was only a sputtering of fire. With fixed bayonets the British went over the summit and into the trenches where they killed or wounded 500 Americans. It was a terrible loss for the patriots, but General Gage had lost 1,054 of his soldiers which amounted to a fifty percent casualty rate for the British.

This devastating encounter cost General Thomas Gage his job. The king angrily replaced General Gage with Sir William Howe.

Washington Takes over the Siege of Boston

On July 3, 1775, Washington arrived in Cambridge, Massachusetts, and took over the Continental Army as well as the siege of Boston.

On August 23, 1775, King George lashed out at the Colonists with a dispatch in which he declared that the Colonies were henceforth to be considered "enemies of the king" whom he considered to be in open rebellion against the crown. Therefore they should be treated accordingly. On December 22, he followed this up with an instrument of war called the Restraining Act. It prohibited any further British trade with the Colonies and declared that all

American ships were open to seizure. This meant that the cargoes of any captive ships would become the legal booty of any raiders that captured American vessels.

The Invasion of Canada

Congress ordered Washington to send a branch of the army into Canada to capture Montreal and another by a separate route to capture Quebec. The effort nearly succeeded under the heroic assault of the American forces, but disease and Canada's bitter winter cold turned the prospect of victory into an overwhelming loss. This was the first great defeat of the war.

1776 Begins with an Order to Capture Boston

In the early winter of 1776, Congress asked Washington to perform a miracle—liberate Boston from Sir William Howe.

Boston is located on an island with a narrow neck leading to the mainland. This made the city virtually impregnable from any direct assault either by sea or by land. But Congress gave Washington his orders: "Capture it!"

History verifies that the genius of Washington thrived on tackling the impossible. His first decision was to call in a Boston bookstore owner named Henry Knox. He weighed about 300 pounds and a lot of it was muscle. He had no military experience but he spent all his spare time reading every available book on the nature and utility of the artillery.

In the dead of winter, Washington sent Knox with a company of men up to Fort Ticonderoga on Lake Champlain. They were instructed to dig out of the ashes all of the cannons they could find from the burned out fort.

After digging out a total of 59 separate pieces of artillery, Knox commandeered the local farmers to build sleds and loan him the oxen to pull these ponderous loads of iron across many miles of wilderness to Boston. At the start some of the cannon slid off into the water and had to be hauled up by heavy ropes. During the journey across Vermont and New Hampshire as well as a corner of Massachusetts, some of the hills were so steep that Henry Knox strapped himself into a harness to add his 300 pounds to the pulling power of the oxen as they struggled to get over some of the slippery summits.

Meanwhile, Washington waited anxiously back at his military headquarters. At the moment he was heartsick. Most of his army had gone home for Christmas when their enlistments expired. That was bad enough, but many of the remainder came down with dysentery. Then the basic food supplies began to run out. Two miraculous things happened to change the picture.

First of all, large numbers of Washington's soldiers whose enlistments expired in December suddenly came back. They had gone home for Christmas, rested up, ate the goose, and returned for re-enlistment. On top of this, Washington's daily prayers were answered when Henry Knox suddenly came over the hill with teams of borrowed oxen dragging sleds through the snow with their precious burdens of 59 heavy cannons. Washington now had the two essential ingredients for liberating Boston—his impossible task.

Of course, all this time General Howe and his British soldiers were tucked comfortably in the warm cozy homes of the Boston colonists waiting for the end of winter.

Unexpectedly, on the night of March 4, 1776, a whole army of patriots crept up the wintry slopes of Dorchester Heights which overlooks the bay and the town of Boston. The men worked all night digging into the frozen ground and hauling up the heavy artillery to be fixed in place.

On the morning of March 5, the British commander awakened to see Dorchester Heights bristling with heavy guns, fully manned, and securely dug in with a sweeping position which made the further occupation of Boston impossible. One can well imagine Sir William Howe contemplating the ingenuity of Washington in completely out-maneuvering him.

At first, the British general contemplated a strong offensive to break out across the bay, but a hurricane swept in from the sea and smashed his hopes. Finally he felt compelled to evacuate the city and flee north aboard British ships to Halifax. But a host of Tories thought they would be massacred if they stayed behind so William Howe had to stack them in like sardines aboard his already overloaded vessels.

Washington marched triumphantly into Boston on March 17 and found stockpiles of supplies which the British had been forced to leave behind. Washington told his men to go to church and thank God they had taken the city without the shedding of blood.

The Declaration of Independence and the Articles of Confederation

Four months later, Washington and his cheering troops learned that the Congress in Philadelphia had swept forth to a political position out beyond the point of no return. They had proclaimed a Declaration of Independence on July 4. The die was cast. There was no turning back. Everyone knew the American Revolutionary War had now begun in deadly earnest.

In addition to the Declaration of Independence the Congress had also undertaken to write up a compact of perpetual union. This was America's first attempt to provide some kind of written constitution. After several modified drafts an approximation of a national charter was adopted by the Congress on November 15, 1777, and was designated "The Articles of Confederation." Most of the states ratified it immediately, but Maryland held out until March 1, 1781. Nevertheless this frail and somewhat faulty instrument was the structure of government under which Washington fought the Revolutionary War and which more or less held the United States together until the famous and inspired Constitution of the United States went into effect June 21, 1788.

The Tragic Loss of New York and Two American Forts

After the liberation of Boston, Washington knew General Howe would probably come down from Halifax and strike the main port of New York. What he didn't suspect, however, was the plan of Parliament to have Howe's British transports from Halifax met at New York with the largest fleet of ships ever seen in America. Furthermore, the admiral in charge of that fleet would be Richard Howe, a brother of General William Howe.

Washington had no navy and realized immediately that he would not be able to hold New York City without one.

First the British gathered around Staten Island, then troops and ships moved in and took Long Island. Moving quickly across the East River they occupied Manhattan and New York City. Somebody set the city on fire and Washington was forced to retreat clear up to White Plains. Fort Lee and Fort Washington were bastions of strength on opposite sides of the Hudson, but both of these forts were eventually taken by the British.

So the year that began triumphantly with the liberation of Boston ended with a colossal defeat and the loss of New York followed by the retreat of George Washington and his decimated army across the snow fields to the south.

The Retreat into New Jersey

Washington retreated into New Jersey after leaving around 7,000 men with his second in command who was Charles Lee. Little did he know that this former British Officer would leave him stranded with a much smaller force hoping to embarrass Washington in the eyes of Congress and perhaps acquire his command.

Meanwhile, Washington led the British under General Howe and Lord Cornwallis on a cat-and-mouse chase. When the British commanders ranged out across the snow fields of New Jersey, Washington sauntered back in retreat, but when the British returned to their main base, Washington followed them so closely it was a temptation to chase him again. No doubt General Howe spluttered, "Doesn't Washington know you don't fight in winter?"

Finally both General Howe and General Cornwallis made a determined march and forced Washington and his American patriots to flee out of New Jersey and cross the Delaware River into Pennsylvania just a few miles upstream from Philadelphia. Washington immediately gathered all the boats for miles up and down the river so that when the British came charging up to the shore line they found no way to ferry their army across. Dejectedly they turned back to their main camp.

Up north the traitorous Charles Lee who had ignored the orders of Washington to join him, assumed Washington must have become exhausted and discouraged by this time so he took the main body of the American army and drifted down toward New Jersey. Just south of Morristown he took a few intimates and completely left the body of his army to enjoy the comforts of a tavern four miles away. A Tory saw him, sent word to the English, and an excited troop of British cavalry joyfully captured their former English compatriot.

When General John Sullivan, the next in command, learned what had happened to Lee, he immediately took charge of the orphan army and hastened down to join Washington further south.

The Battles of Trenton and Princeton

One of the great battles of the war took place the day after Christmas, 1776. The night before—on Christmas night—Washington moved his army back across the Delaware to the New Jersey side. The river was choked with ice floes and the crossing was both dangerous and slow. It was so cold two men froze to death. Then in the dark with his scantily clad army shivering against the sleet and the snow, Washington marched these loyal patriots nine miles to Trenton. At dawn the weary, ragged, hungry American army attacked.

It was a complete rout. Trenton was being held by Hessian soldiers loaned to the British by the king's royal cousins in Germany. Over 1,000

Hessian troops were captured and 115 were killed. No Americans were killed but two were wounded. One was James Monroe who later became President of the United States.

On January 2, 1777, Cornwallis left Princeton and marched on Trenton to punish Washington and recover the prisoners. When he arrived after dark he saw huge fires on the east side of the river which meant that he had Washington trapped and could wait until the following morning to attack. But when he led his redcoats toward the river the following morning he found nothing but ashes. There was no camp. It was a ruse. While Cornwallis and his troops were asleep, Washington had taken a circuitous route to Princeton and captured the town Cornwallis had just left!

If Congress had furnished him with fresh reserves, Washington could have gone another eighteen miles to New Brunswick and captured the main British headquarters. But with a ragamuffin army that had gone two nights without sleep and fought two battles, it was impossible.

The British Attempt to Cut off New England

In London the king's ministers decided this war could be concluded much more quickly by adopting a strategy of divide and conquer. They therefore ordered General Burgoyne in Canada to come across the border and take Fort Ticonderoga on Lake Champlain. He was then to move down the Hudson river to Saratoga where General Howe could meet him with troops from New York and they would thereby cut off Washington from New England with all its resources and reserves.

However, General Howe had a different plan. He argued with the king's ministers that it would be much more decisive if the British captured Philadelphia which was the headquarters for the Congress and served as the provisional capital of the United States.

While London was debating over which strategy was best, General Burgoyne in Canada went ahead preparing for an invasion of the United States on the assumption that General Howe would meet him at Saratoga on the Hudson.

Burgoyne's thrust out of Canada worked very well at first. When he crossed the Canadian border to attack Ticonderoga, it fell almost without resistance on July 2, 1777. However, when the Canadian infantry started down the Hudson to reach Saratoga they encountered huge trees, ditches and hundreds of other encumbrances which blocked their way. They also had to fight several pitched battles with the Americans, and Burgoyne advanced only at the expense of heavy losses among the Canadian, Hessian and Indian ranks. Not until the middle of September did Burgoyne get within striking distance of Saratoga.

The Battle of Saratoga

But there was no General Howe with thousands of British and Hessian troops from New York to meet him. Instead, he was met by the American Northern Army under the command of an ex-British officer named Horatio Gates who had joined the American cause. Even more important, Gates had under his command Benedict Arnold, the finest field commander in the American ranks at that time.

There was a furious series of battles and in the end the Americans won, primarily through the brilliant and daring leadership of Benedict Arnold. Over 5,000 British prisoners were captured, and this victory was so impressive to the king of France that Benjamin Franklin—who was serving as the American envoy in Paris—used it as the means of persuading the French to declare war against England as an ally of the Americans.

Eventually, as we shall see, this resulted in France providing America with thousands of soldiers, a strong fleet of ships and tons of blankets, tents, and clothes for Washington's poverty-stricken soldiers.

The Duplicity of Horatio Gates

However, all of this good news of a French alliance was nothing but sour pickles for Benedict Arnold who had fought so brilliantly at Saratoga. Horatio Gates had written a report making himself the hero and in the process completely obscured the magnificent part Benedict Arnold had played in achieving this monumental victory and receiving a serious wound in the process. It was later discovered that Gates had perpetrated this tissue of lies in hopes it would induce Congress to appoint him the commander in chief to replace Washington.

Although this deliberate and despicable deception failed to get Gates the high command for which he had been lusting, it definitely planted a malignant and bitter hatred in Benedict Arnold's heart toward Congress, and laid the foundation for his subsequent attempt to betray West Point to the British.

Congress had relied on General Gates' report to promote five of Arnold's junior officers while ignoring the courage and superb brilliance of Arnold because they knew nothing about it. All this forms the background for the fatal day when Benedict Arnold under the pestering temptation of his Tory wife turned traitor and accepted a bribe to become a commander for the British.

The Howe Brothers Capture Philadelphia

Meanwhile, we finally learn why General Howe did not go up with an army to Saratoga as Burgoyne had originally requested. It appears that while London was still debating their best future strategy, General Howe and his brother—Admiral Howe—were working on their own road to glory.

On July 23, 1777—months before Burgoyne had reached Saratoga—the Howe brothers set out with 260 ships and 15,000 fully equipped soldiers to capture Philadelphia.

They originally thought they could achieve this by sailing up the Delaware River to the point where Philadelphia could be cannonaded by their boats, but when this proved impractical they went on down around the cape of Chesapeake Bay and came up on the inside. This allowed General Howe to land the British troops at a port called Head of Elk in Maryland, putting the invading British force within fifty miles of Philadelphia.

Washington made two attempts to stop the British from reaching the provisional capital of the United States, once at Brandywine, Maryland, on September 11, 1777, and once at Germantown in Pennsylvania—just outside of Philadelphia—on October 3. In both battles the Americans were driven off and Washington was forced to retire to Valley Forge for the winter. Meanwhile the Howe brothers were welcomed by the incipient Tories in Philadelphia who thought this would undoubtedly mark the end of the war.

Of course, the coming of the British forced the Congress to flee from Philadelphia and set up this final fragment of the American government in several different cities as they tried to find security and get relocated.

The Death Camp at Valley Forge

With the members of Congress fleeing for their lives and the government in a temporary state of disarray, Washington found himself literally abandoned. The quartermaster ceased to function and the supplies of food, tents, clothing, bedding and recruits dwindled to a trickle and then stopped altogether.

What was most disgusting and aggravating to Washington was the report that the states were extremely indifferent and dilatory in contributing assessments of money and supplies as well as militia recruits. He knew the states were actually prospering and some of them were allowing their farmers to make excessive profits by selling grain and other supplies at high prices directly to the British. Everywhere there was a spirit of profiteering and graft. From Washington's perspective this was a brazen betrayal of the American cause. It was treasonable to the country, disloyal to those who had volunteered to fight and abhorrently dishonest by every measure of common decency.

At Valley Forge soldiers were cold, ragged, and on the verge of starvation. Those who had coats were put to work chopping down trees to build cabins, but there were never enough. As the winter storms increased, hundreds were without any shelter whatever except the soggy, wet blankets which they wrapped around them as they sat shivering around the log fires. Their staple diet was flour, water and salt, called fire cakes, and while it lasted they got it morning, noon and night.

A rough estimate of the critical situation at Valley Forge may be drawn from Washington's numerous reports to Congress. In one of them he said a foraging party of British soldiers was observed in the area but when an attempt was made to mobilize a defense force it was discovered that three thousand of his American patriots were unfit for service because they had no shoes to trek through the snow and their clothes were nothing but rags that barely covered their nakedness.

Fortunately, no direct encounter withly described the horrors of that winter at Valley Forge. Within six months three thousand soldiers deserted and went home or enlisted with the British in order to get food. Two hundred officers resigned their commissions and left. Of those soldiers who stayed with Washington, two thousand froze to death or died of starvation and disease.

As one suffering American wrote home: "Poor food—hard lodging—cold weather—fatigue—nasty clothes, nasty cookery—vomit half the time—smoked out of my senses—the Devil's in it—I can't endure it—why are we sent here to starve and freeze ….?"[4]

The coming of spring was never more welcomed than at Valley Forge. In addition word had come that a powerful French fleet was heading for America with soldiers, guns, ammunition, tents, and clothes. Washington thanked God for those who had stood by him. At least there would be a semblance of an army to welcome the French when they arrived.

---

4. Robert Leckie, The Wars of America, New York: Harper and Row, p. 181; quoted by Skousen in The Making of America, op. cit., p. 91.

The British Abandon Philadelphia

A shock wave went up and down the American states in May of 1778 when it was learned that both General William Howe and Admiral Richard Howe were resigning their commands in America. Sir Henry Clinton took over the British command and promptly ordered the evacuation of Philadelphia. If the British were to match strength with the French it had better be from New York.

A brief exchange of prisoners between Americans and the British resulted in Charles Lee returning to his old role of second in command. But he hadn't changed. British files later revealed that Lee had spent much of his time as a prisoner with General Howe plotting on how best to betray Washington into British hands. This was the situation when the British prepared to leave Philadelphia.

As the British packed up and headed toward New York, their ranks of marching soldiers and baggage trains stretched out for a dozen miles. This was too great a temptation for Washington. He ordered his half-healed army out of winter quarters and led his troops across New Jersey in hot pursuit.

They caught up with the British near Monmouth, New Jersey, where Washington held a war council. To his amazement Charles Lee argued against any attack on the straggling, stretched out British entourage. But Lee suddenly changed his mind when he heard that young Lafayette would replace him and have the honor of leading 5,000 men to make the initial attack. It was agreed that Washington should bring up the rear with the remainder of the army and prevent any regiments of the British from escaping.

But Lee's attack was a disorganized disaster. At the most critical point of the assault, Lee gave up completely and ordered a hurried retreat. Washington could scarcely believe his eyes as he saw his 5,000 advance guard scurrying back from their assigned battle station. Washington angrily ordered Lee to the rear and tried to regroup his army, but it was too late to capture the main body of the British troops. Had Lafayette been in command of the initial attack Washington knew he could have captured the whole British army and perhaps ended the war. As it was, the remnants of the two forces fought themselves into exhaustion and then camped at dark with the outcome undecided.

But the battle was not renewed at sunup. Clinton had awakened his camp at midnight and they had quietly stolen away in the darkness and marched double time to get safely out of reach so they could proceed on to New York. Washington had Charles Lee court-martialed and then moved his army into the vicinity of New York where he could monitor the movements of the British while he awaited the arrival of the French.

The British Strategy in the South

Sir Henry Clinton, the new British Commander, heard there were many Tories in the South who would support an invasion by the British. The first British experiment occurred in Georgia the last of 1779 and the beginning of 1780. Just as General Clinton had hoped, the American Tories rallied to the British colors. Both Savannah and Atlanta were captured and the British literally took over the state of Georgia. Greatly encouraged, Clinton moved up to South Carolina and took Charleston.

Meanwhile, nothing was happening up in New York. Washington pleaded with the French to unite with him in a joint attack on New York, but they declined to participate. The French preferred to make great sweeping sails up and down the Atlantic seaboard as though they could win the war by merely threatening the British. Without a joint attack on New York by both Americans and the French, the whole northern campaign came to a halt. Furthermore, one of the worst winters of that entire century suddenly swept down on the Atlantic seaboard and that forced Washington to make hasty preparations in the hills of Morristown, New Jersey, to somehow survive the winter.

The Winter at Morristown

In the midst of this situation Washington once more discovered that he and his army had been abandoned by Congress and the states. The winter at Morristown was in every respect a duplication of Valley Forge, some say it was even worse.

Congress forsook its responsibilities by ordering Washington to go out among the people and confiscate food for the soldiers and hay for the horses. Washington was revolted by the idea but his officers wanted to give it a try. Farmers and other civilians were paid for the food and confiscated hay with Continental dollars that weren't worth the paper on which they were printed. Alexander Hamilton wrote:

> "We begin to hate the country for its neglect of us. The country begins to hate us for our oppression of them."[5]

With all the starving, dying and desertion going on in Morristown, it would have been a symptom of lunacy for one of Washington's soldiers to

5. John C. Miller, Triumph of Freedom, Boston: Little Brown and Company, 1948, p. 483; quoted by Skousen in The Making of America, op. cit., p. 96

have prophesied that within eighteen months the war would be over and the American people would be recognized by all of Europe as a free and independent sovereign nation. But the powers of heaven knew it was just about to happen.

It all came about because Washington outsmarted the British strategy in the South.

The British Try to End the War with Overwhelming Victories in the South

After Clinton's initial success in the south, he turned over the entire British command in Georgia and South Carolina to General Charles Cornwallis. To meet this challenge Congress decided it would also set up an overall commander in the South. Washington needed to monitor the British forces around New York so he recommended Nathaniel Greene for the southern command. Almost defiantly, Congress appointed this key command to Horatio Gates—the boastful deceiver from Saratoga.

The first major clash came at the battle of Camden, South Carolina, where General Gates had the largest army and intended to win brilliant new honors for himself. But a series of misfortunes overtook the Americans, and their infantry began to retreat. In the turmoil that followed nobody retreated faster nor further than the ex-British officer Horatio Gates. He fled 240 miles in three days of hard riding before he finally came to a stop. No general in history is known to have abandoned his army and fled so far and so fast as General Gates following his defeat at Camden. He resigned from the army in disgrace.

But though the Americans had run away, they came back to fight another day. The atrocities of the British and their Tory allies in the South caused the resistance of the patriots to stiffen.

The Battle of King's Mountain

One of those who had pillaged and ravaged civilian towns and outlying settlers was Major Patrick Ferguson. The American forces hoped that some day there would be an opportunity to confront the Major. That opportunity came when Ferguson was discovered on the top of King's Mountain near the border between South and North Carolina. The date was October 7, 1780.

Ferguson was so secure at the top of King's Mountain that he said neither the demons of hell nor God Almighty could dislodge him. But about a thousand frontiersmen from the mountains of that region closed in on Ferguson and after a pitched battle sent him and a host of his men to kingdom come.

This was a tremendous victory which shocked the British and marked the beginning of the end for Cornwallis in the south.

The British Retreat Toward Yorktown

Clinton, prior to leaving for New York had told Cornwallis that if the campaign in the south bogged down he should head for Yorktown at the mouth of the York River where the British fleet could come in and rescue him. As Cornwallis began to lose one battle after another and Tories began to slough away, Cornwallis decided it was prudent to take Clinton's advice.

We should mention that after the disgrace of Horatio Gates at Camden, it was General Nathaniel Greene—whom Washington had wanted in the first place—that dislodged Cornwallis from his moorings in the south. Greene divided his forces and was reconquering South Carolina from the Tories while Cornwallis gradually maneuvered his British army toward Yorktown, Virginia.

By the early part of 1781 Cornwallis had captured Yorktown and set up his British headquarters. However, there were no boats to meet him because the English fleet had been seriously damaged by a hurricane. However, it was being hurriedly repaired. Cornwallis felt confident he could survive at Yorktown until the British navy arrived to carry his entire army away to safety.

But he hadn't counted on a secret American ally that Washington called "the divine intervention of Providence." Washington worshipfully mentioned his dependence upon God in all his prayers night and morning. In his letters to Congress he pointed out 67 different times where there had been a sudden turn of events in favor of the Americans because of the obvious intervention of the Almighty. During the remainder of his life he would thankfully acknowledge that throughout the Revolutionary War, God had saved them in many of their most critical situations.

And Yorktown was one of those critical situations.

How the British Were Caught Totally off Guard

However, the British felt quite certain Washington was not thinking about Yorktown. Their spies related that he and the French commander, Rochambeau, were plotting with the admiral of the French fleet to launch a massive attack on New York. But Washington learned that the French admiral had deceived him. He was not bringing his fleet in from the West Indies to attack New York, but intended to set up his main base in Chesapeake Bay.

But maybe this was providential.

Suddenly Washington saw a miraculous opportunity. He would let the French admiral continue his deceptive plan to sail his fleet into Chesapeake Bay instead of New York and when it was fully in place Washington would use the French fleet to help him take Yorktown. Meanwhile he continued his pretended stratagem with what appeared to be elaborate plans for an attack on New York City.

The Battle of Yorktown

As soon as Washington was assured the French fleet was on the way to Chesapeake Bay, Washington gave the British their first surprise. He quietly pulled most of the New York troops out of their barracks and—with several thousand French soldiers under Rochambeau—force-marched them south at top speed. They reached Philadelphia before the British even knew Washington and Rochambeau had departed. This large force then continued its march to the upper end of Chesapeake Bay and there the boats from the French fleet provided transportation to a site near Yorktown.

It was obvious to the British that Washington had devised a brilliant strategy to capture Cornwallis. They therefore rushed the newly repaired English fleet down to rescue the beleaguered general and his army of around 8,000 men. But as the British war vessels neared Yorktown, the French fleet pounced upon them and drove them out to sea with so much damage that the English fleet had to limp back to New York for further repairs.

When Cornwallis learned what had happened he knew he and his army had been abandoned to their fate.

As Washington and Rochambeau combined their strength with the American army of the south it came to more than seventeen thousand men at arms. Once this vast force was in their assigned positions, Commanding General George Washington fired the first cannon. By the following night fifty-two guns were belching fire and balls of iron on the besieged town. But Cornwallis stiffened his troops to endure the holocaust. For three weeks the bombardment continued until Cornwallis knew he must try one last desperate avenue of escape.

On the night of October 16, 1781, he assembled around 6,000 British and German mercenary survivors along the banks of the York River where boats had been gathered. Barely a mile across the mouth of this river was Gloucester. His soldiers were told to row for their lives. If they reached Gloucester there was a possible chance they could race northward and somehow escape.

And for a breathless interval it looked like they might make it. In the darkness the boats were scattered across the water only half a mile from Gloucester when a virtual hurricane came in from the sea and blew the whole contingent back into the arms of their enemy. The exasperated Cornwallis clenched his teeth and said: "Even God wants Washington to win!"

It was not long before it was all over. The formal surrender was set for 2 P.M. October 19. Cornwallis felt so completely disgraced he declined to attend the ceremony but sent General Charles O'Hara to attend. Then, a historian tells us:

> "Out marched the British in their red coats and the Hessians in their blue and green, striding between the long lines of smartly dressed French soldiers on one side and the more ragged Americans on the other. The Germans grounded their arms neatly, but the British, many of whom were weeping, smashed their muskets down and marched sullenly off. Through it all the British fife-and-drum corps played a doleful tune called 'The World Turned Upside Down.'"[6]

Aftermath of the Surrender at Yorktown

George III was so devastated when he learned of the disaster at Yorktown that he prepared to abdicate and even wrote his formal message of abdication, but was finally dissuaded at the last moment.

In terms of military reality, the surrender at Yorktown had only wiped out a fourth of the British strength in America, but the English fighting spirit was crushed. Nevertheless, Washington had to endure eighteen more months of constant anxiety and tension before he could announce to his troops on April 18, 1783 that a formal peace treaty had been signed and Britain had acknowledged the independence of the United States of America.

In spite of this welcomed development, however, it did not settle the ferment that began boiling up among the citizens of the new nation.

Soldiers were threatening to march on Philadelphia to compel Congress to give them the wages and land they had been promised. The states were quarreling over trade disputes, boundary lines, tariffs and fishing rights.

6. Parry and Allison, The Real George Washington, op. cit., p. 365.

The problems of some kind of sound money system had to be resolved. The terrible burden of debt ensuing from the war by both the nation and the states had to be addressed. The cloud of threatening insurrection and civil strife was growing continually, as explosive inflation and post-war elements of economic depression thundered over the land.

Washington's Dilemma

Some of Washington's own military leaders had urged him to accept the title of king and restore some semblance of order among the people and the states. They received a tongue lashing for their suggestion.

Washington saw what was coming. He was being caught in the same vice that trapped Oliver Cromwell. He must resign before they tried to make him a king or military dictator. He must take formal action so the people would be willing to turn their political and economic problems over to their elected representatives.

Through bitter experience Washington knew the Articles of Confederation was an extremely weak instrument of government, and for many months he had been urging the Congress to call a convention to consider a new and stronger form of government. But they were delaying, postponing, deferring and neglecting their sworn course of duty. Whether consciously or unconsciously they were still leaning on Washington as they had done throughout the course of this terrible war.

He knew it was time to resign.

Washington Takes Affirmative Action

The British boarded their ships to depart from America on November 25, 1783. Washington thereupon called his officers and comrades together at Fraunces' Tavern in New York to thank them and bid them farewell. Many of the officers wept as their commander embraced them. Then he boarded a barge which took him to Philadelphia. On December 23, Washington rode to Annapolis, Maryland, and presented himself at the State House where the Congress was then meeting.

One historian calls this a "bittersweet" meeting for Washington.[7] Here was a congress of both friends and enemies. These were the men to whom he had pleaded for food, clothes, blankets and soldiers and had so many times been ignored. Sometimes he felt virtually abandoned. There were some who

---

7. Ibid., p. 434.

had fought valiantly to support him in every way they could but there were some who had seriously considered replacing him with the traitor Charles Lee or the deceptive coward Horatio Gates.

But at least the war was over. And they had won.

Washington completely broke down at one point in his prepared statement as he read it to the Congress. They saw his emotions overwhelm him as he said:

> "I consider it an indispensable duty to close this last solemn act of my official life by commending the interest of our dearest country to the protection of Almighty God, and those who had the superintendence of them, to his holy keeping."[8]

Washington knew he had been on God's errand. So had all those thousands who had suffered, starved, frozen, bled and died. Now he prayed God to help those who must carry on.

8. Ibid.

Topics for Reflection and Discussion

1. How would you describe your innermost feelings after reading this chapter? Why did the American colonists resist the Stamp Act? Describe the strategy that made the Parliament think they could get away with a tax on tea. After the Boston Tea Party, name three things King George III did to avenge himself on the people of Massachusetts.

2. Why was the First Continental Congress considered an emergency meeting? Why didn't Georgia participate? Who were the two delegates who wanted an immediate declaration of independence? List three of the things the Congress did to show England it meant business.

3. Why did the attack on Lexington and Concord seriously damage the colonists' feeling of loyalty toward England? What direct action did Ethan Allen and the Green Mountain Boys take on May 10, 1775? On that same day who met in Philadelphia? List two things that came out of this meeting.

4. Describe the circumstances that led to the Battle of Bunker's Hill. About how many British were killed or wounded? How many Americans? What was Washington's biggest problem when he was ordered to liberate Boston? What two things happened to help him solve it?

5. What did Washington lack which made it impossible for him to save New York? One of the great stories of early American history was Washington's victories at Trenton and Princeton. Can you give the highlights of this story? What future President was wounded at Trenton?

6. Why did General Howe and his brother, Admiral Howe, ignore the plan of General Burgoyne to isolate New England and decide to capture Philadelphia instead? What two battles did Washington lose trying to protect Philadelphia? Describe Washington's conditions at Valley Forge. About how many died? How did the victory at Saratoga bring the French into the war on the side of America?

7. Why did the British abandon Philadelphia? Why did the British think they would have better success in the South? Who were the Tories? Why did Cornwallis finally lead his army he English fleet from rescuing him? Describe Washington's brilliant strategy that resulted in the surrender of Cornwallis.

8. What kind of impact did the British defeat at Yorktown have on King George III? What did he threaten to do? What percentage of the British army was still intact in America? Why didn't the British use it?

9. Why were the American soldiers so angry with Congress? What did they threaten to do? Why were the states quarreling over so many different things? What was the economic situation? To restore domestic tranquility what did some of Washington's soldiers urge him to do? What was his reaction?

10. Why did Washington think this was the right time to resign? What had he learned from Oliver Cromwell's experience? Why could it be described as a bittersweet experience when Washington met with Congress who were meeting at Annapolis? What caused him to break down emotionally when he was reading his resignation to the Congress?

CHAPTER TWENTY

PROBING THE MINDS OF THE FOUNDING FATHERS

Before proceeding with the next sequence of historical events, we need to pause and examine some of the sweeping and progressive ideas that were beginning to congeal in the minds of the Founding Fathers.

We need to remind ourselves that they were extremely well-trained in history, philosophy, economics, political science and religion. As the constitutional scholar, J. Reuben Clark, has said:

> "What a group of men of surpassing abilities, attainments, experience, and achievements! There has not been another such group of men in all … our history, no group that even challenged the supremacy of this group ….
>
> "The Framers were deeply read in the facts of history; they were learned in the forms and practices and system of the governments of the world, past and present; they were, in matters political, equally at home in Rome, in Athens, in Paris, and London; had a long varied, and intense experience in the work of governing their Colonies; they were among the leaders of a weak and poor people that had successfully fought a revolution against one of the great powers of the earth; there were among them some of the ablest, most experienced and seasoned military leaders of the world."[1]

The Founders had also learned from experience that there are some popular ideas concerning government that seem attractive in theory but which turn out to be catastrophic when put into practice. As we have already seen, both Jefferson and John Adams pointed to Plato's *Republic* as an example. Many classical scholars called Plato's political philosophy the best theoretical approach to sound government, but these two American scholars called it the worst.

1. "The Inspired Constitution and J. Reuben Clark, Jr.," The Freemen Digest, Salt Lake City: The Freemen Institute, March, 1978, p. 15

Historical Developments Needed Before the First Free People in Modern Times Could Be Established

Looking back through the history of the past 500 years, the Founders recognized that certain monumental events had to transpire before the world was ready for the first free people in modern times. Here is a suggested list of those important developments which had to come to pass before mankind was prepared to embrace the miracle of America.

1. First of all, *America had to be discovered* so people with an instinct for freedom could escape from the oppression and corruption of Europe and get a fresh start.

2. Furthermore, *religious freedom* had to be cultivated so freedom of thought could flourish.

3. For this to happen, there needed to be a spiritual *reformation* both inside and outside of the "universal church."

4. This would not occur unless there was a widespread *study of the Bible* by Christians all over the world.

5. To do this the *printing press* had to be invented in 1440 so Bibles and other important books could be widely published and economically distributed.

6. The expanding *Holy Roman Empire* needed to be dismantled so political freedom could begin to manifest itself in a variety of nations. By 1800 the Holy Roman Empire had been reduced to virtually one country and the last emperor ended his reign in 1806.

7. There also needed to be a *revolution in social and economic principles* to allow prosperity, education, and a higher standard of living to flourish as the radiant new climate of freedom and human self-fulfillment spread across the earth.

8. Then, of course, there had to be a strong collection of hard-working *scholars who knew what to do* to set up a powerful free people in modern times.

The Amazing Diversity of the Founding Fathers

One of the most amazing aspects of the American story is the fact that while the nation's founders came from widely diverse backgrounds, their fundamental beliefs were virtually identical. They quarreled bitterly over the most practical plan of implementing those beliefs, but rarely, if ever, disputed about their final objectives or basic convictions.

These men came from several different churches, and some from no churches at all. They ranged in occupation from farmers to presidents of universities. Their social background included everything from wilderness pioneering to the aristocracy of landed estates. Their dialects included everything from the loquacious drawl of South Carolina to the clipped staccato of Yankee New England. Their economic origins included everything from frontier poverty to opulent wealth.

Then how do we explain their remarkable unanimity in fundamental beliefs?

Perhaps the explanation will be found in the fact that they were all remarkably well-read, and mostly from the same books. Although the level of their formal training varied from spasmodic doses of home tutoring to the rigorous regimen of Harvard's classical studies, the debates during the constitutional convention and the writings of the Founders reflect a far broader knowledge of religious, political, historical, economic, and philosophical studies than would be found in any cross section of American leaders today.

By 1787 the Founders were at the crossroads. Which of the many brilliant minds of the past discovered the precious principles that would provide the most ideal government for the first free people in modern times? Here are the principal fountains of wisdom from which they drank deeply:

Polybius (*circa* 205-125 B.C.)

To appreciate Polybius we must remind ourselves that a most popular pastime among political writers during ancient times was attempting to decide which *form* of government was the best.

Some argued for a *monarchy* with a single, powerful ruler. Others preferred an *aristocracy* where the "best families" of the nation were allowed to rule. Yet a third favored a pure *democracy* (as in Athens) where all important decisions were made by the whole people. Unfortunately none of these systems had proved successful.

> "Even more keenly than Aristotle, he [Polybius] was aware that each form carried within itself the seed of its own degeneration, if it were allowed to operate without checks and balances provided by opposing principles. Monarchy could easily become tyranny, aristocracy would sink into oligarchy [oppressive government by

> a few rich families], and democracy would turn into mob rule of force and violence."[2]

Polybius was a Greek who lived from approximately 205 to 125 B.C. Next to Herodotus and Thucydides, Polybius is recognized as the greatest of all Greek historians.

When Greece was conquered by the Romans, Polybius was taken to Rome and soon became an ally of these people who had structured an amazing system of law by which they ruled millions of people in their vast empire. In due time he began to write history for his new rulers. They allowed him to accompany military campaigns and diplomatic missions to Europe, Asia, and Africa. He became a prolific writer concerning the things he saw and the lessons he learned. These valuable records eventually grew into a priceless library of forty volumes of hand-written history.

Before he was through, Polybius began to develop some deep convictions about the possibility of a new kind of government that he didn't think any nation had ever tried. Here were some of his meditations:

In an ideal government the people ought to have a say in government because they constitute the majority. At the same time the wealthy or aristocratic elements representing the established order of society and business interests—the ones who will end up paying most of the taxes—must have a place in government. Then the executive—whether he is a king, emperor or consul—should have a voice since he will have to carry out the laws and sometimes act on behalf of the whole nation, especially in time of war or a national crisis.

Polybius Raises a Vital Question

But since all three systems represented unique and essential elements for the governing of a people, why not combine them into a single system?

Polybius saw the synthesizing process of all three ingredients beginning to develop in the Roman system, but shortly after Polybius died, the Romans abandoned their principles of a republic and eventually set up an emperor. Thus came to an end what Polybius had hoped would be the first three department constitution in history.

He visualized the strength of a monarchy being assigned the executive duties of government; the interests of wealth and the "established order" would be represented in the Senate; the interests of the general populace would be

2. Ebenstein, Great Political Thinkers, op. cit., p. 110.

represented in the popular Assembly. Polybius felt that if these three departments were set up as coordinated equals they could perform their necessary functions, but at the same time counter-balance one another as a restraining mechanism so that no one of them would acquire oppressive power and abuse the people.

The Death of a Dream

This new inspired concept of government was called a "mixed" constitution. It was a brilliant idea, but it virtually dissolved and disappeared when Polybius died.

It was not until the early 1700s that a scholarly French genius by the name of Baron Charles de Montesquieu undertook to resurrect the inspired potentialities of a "mixed" constitution and publish it in his classical study called, *The Spirit of the Laws*.

Baron Charles De Montesquieu (1689-1755)

Montesquieu became one of the best-educated scholars in France. Although his mother died when he was seven, and his father died when he was twenty-four, a wealthy uncle left him a title, a judicial office, and his whole fortune.

Montesquieu traveled extensively and spent considerable time in England where thought he saw the first sprouting buds of a "mixed" constitution emerging.

After twenty years of intensive research in his massive study (sixty by forty feet) with books from floor to ceiling at his palatial residence in La Brede, he finally brought forth the manuscript for his famous book, *The Spirit of the Laws*, in 1748.

This has been described as "one of the most important books ever written," and certainly ranks as "the greatest book of the French 18th century."[3]

The book was full of praise for the English system but it was never popular in France and was scarcely read. Nevertheless, it became famous elsewhere and was greatly admired by the American Founders. It carefully documented the practical possibility of a government based on "separation of powers" and a "mixed" constitution.

---

3. George Saintsbury, Encyclopedia Britannica, under "Montesquieu," op. cit., 18:776.

Montesquieu's "Model Constitution"

Beginning with Book XI in *The Spirit of the Laws*, Montesquieu actually began the presentation of what he hoped might be a model constitution based on a "mixed" system of government.

Montesquieu saw the separation of powers developing under the English system somewhat differently than Polybius had seen it in Rome.

Instead of the three departments of government being the executive, the senate, and the people's assembly as visualized by Polybius, Montesquieu saw the powers of government developing along the lines of an executive, a legislature (of both an upper and a lower house), and an independent judiciary. This last element was something Polybius had missed.

Montesquieu saw the legislature enacting the laws and the executive administering them. But he felt it was just as important to have an independent judiciary to interpret and enforce the laws; but it must not be part of the legislature or the executive branches of government. He said:

> "Again, there is no liberty, if the judiciary power be not separated from the legislative and executive. Were it joined with the legislative, the life and liberty of the subject would be exposed to arbitrary control, for the judge would then be the legislator. Were it joined to the executive power, the judge might behave with violence and oppression."[4]

Because many of the Founders were equally as profound as Montesquieu in their study of history and political science, they immediately caught the vision of his book. The Founders admired it enough to use many portions of it as a guide in their own work in 1787. However, the joint efforts of the Founders in working out the complexities of the American Constitution greatly excelled that of Montesquieu.

Nevertheless, to Montesquieu must go the well-deserved credit for illuminating the minds of the Founders with the exciting possibilities of a government based on "separate" but "coordinated" powers.

Since reading many of the same books proved to be some of the strongest glue that held them together, let us briefly remind ourselves of some of the great secular books they read in addition to the Bible.

---

4. Montesquieu, The Spirit of the Laws, Great Books of the Western World, Chicago: Encyclopedia Britannica, Inc., 1953, p. 70.

JOHN LOCKE (1632-1704)

The Founders were particularly attracted to the writings of the English political philosopher, John Locke, who was a devout monarchist in his youth, but ended up writing two famous essays on government, the first of which shattered the whole foundation of the "divine right of kings." His second essay on civil government was extremely congenial to the convictions which the Founders were also beginning to accept.

However, original thinking about government was dangerous business. Locke's contemporary and close friend, Algernon Sidney, was beheaded in 1683 for saying what John Locke was already privately thinking. Locke decided it would be entirely prudent for him to immediately flee to Holland to complete his writings. He did not return to England to publish his writings until 1689, a year after the overthrow of James II by William of Orange.

Locke also wrote an "Essay on Human Understanding," in which he said, "Everyone can know there is a God." He was already beginning to sound like Cicero.

A small sample of Locke's principles cited by the Founders will demonstrate the high regard they held for his thinking. They quote him on such varied topics as the following:

Natural law is the same as God's law and it cannot be superseded by any manmade law.[5]

The supreme and sovereign power to govern is vested by the Creator in the whole people. In other words, there is no such thing as "divine right of kings."[6]

Anyone who has suffered a wrong is entitled to complete reparation by the offender.[7]

Orderly government requires that political decisions must be made by majority rule.[8]

It is important that the money system be based on gold and silver.[9]

---

5. John Locke, Second Essay on Civil Government, op. cit., 35:56, paragraph 135.
6. See Locke's First Essay on Civil Government which is devoted to this subject. It is presumed to be an established and proven fact throughout his Second Essay on Civil Government," Ibid., 35:25 ff.
7. Ibid., 35:26-27, paragraphs 8-9.
8. Ibid., 35:47, paragraphs 96-98.
9. Ibid., 35:35, paragraphs 46-50.

No man can transfer to government power to do that which would be wrong if he did it himself.[10]

Parents are primarily responsible for the education and welfare of their children.[11]

The legislature cannot transfer its law-making powers to any other branch of government.[12] A major weakness in government today is the mass of regulations pouring out of the executive Bureaus of the government in violation of Article I, section 1 of the Constitution.

Legislatures cannot exempt themselves from laws they have made for everybody else.[13] One of the greatest offenses of the Congress in this century has been to exempt its members from many laws they have imposed on the rest of the nation.

The government cannot take from any person his property without his personal consent or that of his representative.[14]

Locke explains why the seizure of land under eminent domain does not violate this provision.[15]

It is obvious from this comprehensive sampling that the Founders looked upon John Locke as a profound scholar and dedicated constitutionalist.

William Blackstone (1723-1780)

When it came to the scholarly ability to understand the laws of England, no authority was more respected among the Founders than William Blackstone.

He became disgusted with the practice of law because neither the judges nor the lawyers really knew the structure for a comprehensive system of sound legal principles. He therefore went back to Oxford and launched the first law school in English history. Prior to that time, a student of the law served as an apprentice of some lawyer until he could pass the bar. Blackstone undertook to improve the qualifications of the entire legal profession by publishing his *Commentaries on the Laws of England* between 1765 and 1769.

10. Ibid., 35:56, paragraph 135.
11. Ibid., 35:36-42, especially paragraph 58.
12. Ibid., 35:58, paragraph 142.
13. Ibid., 35:58, paragraph 143.
14. Ibid., 35:58, paragraph 142.
15. Ibid., 35:52-53, paragraph 119-122.

He began his commentaries with a long introduction concerning the supreme excellence of God's law. He said that all laws, both criminal and civil, must be compatible with divine principles because all provisions of God's law were rational and morally right. It is surprising how many modern complex laws of our own day cannot pass the simple tests laid down by William Blackstone in his *Commentaries*.

Blackstone, like George Wythe—America's first professor of law—did not think a lawyer was competent to practice his profession until he had a thorough knowledge of history, both ancient and modern, and the Bible.

John Calvin (1509-1564)

The Founders were admirers of the reformers who undertook to rediscover the essential elements of Biblical Christianity. However, none of the reformers came up with the whole formula. Instead each of them caught the light of some important facet that gave brilliance to the glories of the Christian past, but made no further effort to explore the field. As a result of this limited perspective each reformer made a contribution but not a restoration.

One of these was John Calvin.

The French theologian, John Calvin, was born in Noyon, fifty miles north of Paris, on July 10, 1509. He soon came under the influence of the disciples of Martin Luther whose Ninety Five Theses against the sale of indulgences had been nailed on the door of the Wittenburg Castle, October 31, 1517. But that courageous act of Luther occurred when Calvin was barely eight years old.

Calvin received an excellent education, first with the idea of entering the ecclesiastical field, but soon his academic tastes switched to jurisprudence and the humanities. He broke away from the Church of Rome some time between 1528 and 1532. Persecution of all Protestants forced him to take to the underground, and for several years he lived under a number of pseudonyms to escape detection and the wrath of the inquisition.

By 1536 he had completed and published the first edition of his famous book on evangelical Christianity entitled, *Institutes of the Christian Religion*. In his book, Calvin followed many of Martin Luther's precepts as set forth in the Lutheran catechism. One of the appealing aspects of his book was his declaration that all Christians were entitled to political freedom.

As he matured in his theological studies and convictions, Calvin decided to settle in Strassburg on the French-German border, but the reformers in

Geneva, Switzerland, induced him to come and teach the Bible in Geneva so he could help them strengthen the Reformed Church. In his eagerness, he undertook to restructure the entire city and aroused so much resistance that he was compelled to flee back to Strassburg for three years (1538-1541). There he came across a popular church that was set up along evangelical lines, and he promptly adopted the evangelical structure as his own.

Like all the reformers, Calvin's theology made him highly controversial, particularly after he finally returned to Geneva and began to enforce his ideas on the city with harsh discipline and extreme strictness.

Calvin's Ideas Received a Mixed Reaction from the Founders

However, those whom we now call the Founding Fathers viewed the teachings of Calvin from their own Biblical perspective. They had a tendency to sort out the ideas which they considered reasonable and more or less disregarded the residue.

Of course, many of the Founders were very critical of the doctrines and practices of some of the main stream churches because they felt their creeds and ritual were neither Biblical nor Christian. Jefferson and Franklin were among this group. Nevertheless, both of them continued to attend church regularly because they felt that even with their defects, each denomination deserved support for the good they did.

Here are some of the doctrines attributed to Calvin which became popular among those who ultimately structured the framework for the first free people in modern times:

1. *God created men politically free.* Calvin taught that no government can legitimately exist without the consent of the people.[16]

2. Furthermore, the people should *enter into a covenant with one another and with God for their mutual welfare and the protection of their rights.*[17]

3. *Limited government.* Since God delegated to the people the authority to choose their own leaders, they are also entitled to limit the authority of those leaders. Furthermore, the people have the right to recall or discharge any officer who violates his covenant with the people by trespassing beyond the limits of his authority.[18]

---

16. John Eidsmoe, Christianity and the Constitution, Grand Rapids: Baker Book House, 1987, p. 24.
17. Ibid.
18. Ibid., pp. 25-26.

4. *The universal priesthood.* This was interpreted to mean that every individual is entitled to read the scriptures and gain a personal understanding of God's teachings under the influence of the Holy Spirit without being required to accept the dictates of a priest, a pastor or church council as to the meaning of God's word. Calvin said every plowboy should be able to read and interpret the scripture for himself. Among Calvinists education became mandatory at an early age so that all could read their Bible.[19]

5. *The depravity of human nature.* Calvin held to the position that man is by nature sinful and the government must be structured with legally enforceable chains on the elected leaders in order to prevent them from indulging in reckless and greedy exploitation of the people by graft, oppression, excessive taxation, and the usurpation of power.[20]

6. *Local self-government.* Calvin held that local elders should govern each congregation. If there were several local congregations, they could then be organized into local synods. Both the Presbyterian and Congregational churches developed a strong tradition of local self-government. Local meetings at the church developed into town meetings and these became a hallmark of New England political structure which exists down to the present time.[21]

7. *The system of law and government should be based on God's law.* As we have pointed out earlier, nearly every institution of higher learning in colonial America was set up to train ministers and encourage an intensive study of the government, commandments, statutes, and judgments under God's law.[22]

Regardless of whether one's denominational theology harmonized with John Calvin, it can be readily seen why these seven precepts provided rich soil in which the seeds of American freedom could sprout and grow.

Two-Thirds of the American Colonists Were Calvinists

The widespread influence of these Calvinistic precepts is better appreciated when we stop to recall that of the 3,000,000 Americans at the time of the Revolution, around 900,000 were of Scotch or Scotch-Irish origin, around 600,000 were English Puritans, and 400,000 were German or Dutch Reformed. Even the Episcopalians had a Calvinistic confession in their

19. Ibid., pp. 21-23.
20. Ibid., pp. 20-21.
21. Ibid., p. 26.
22. Ibid., pp. 23-24.

Thirty-nine Articles, and many French Huguenots were Calvinists who had fled to the western world. From this we are able to appreciate that about two-thirds of the entire colonial population had been trained in the philosophy of Calvin.[23]

It is interesting that non-Calvinist George Bancroft, probably the foremost historian in America during the nineteenth century, called John Calvin the ideological "father of America." Bancroft then added, "He who will not honor the memory, and respect the influence of Calvin knows but little of the origin of American liberty." [24]

Thomas Jefferson Discovers a Remarkable Link Back to Moses

One of the highly significant developments that occurred in connection with the American resurrection of individual rights and human freedom was the discovery of a people that linked America back to Moses.

These people were the Anglo-Saxons.

Looking back, it seems almost providential that people suddenly became highly interested in the Anglo-Saxons right at the time the American passion for independence was coming to a boil. And no American found the Anglo-Saxons more significant and exciting than Thomas Jefferson.

Jefferson not only studied everything he could find out about these people—who were the ancestors of most of the colonists—but he devoted many months to learning how to read the Anglo-Saxon language so that he could study their ancient principles of law and government in the original text.[25]

It was his intention to graft these principles into the basic charter for the first free people in modern times. As we have mentioned earlier, Professor Gilbert Chinard, one of the distinguished biographers of Jefferson states:

> "Jefferson's great ambition at that time was to promote a renaissance of Anglo-Saxon primitive institutions on the new continent. Thus presented, the American Revolution was nothing but the reclamation of the Anglo-Saxon birthright of which the colonists had been deprived 'by a long train of abuses,' nor does it appear that there was anything in this theory which surprised or shocked

23. Ibid., p. 19.
24. Ibid., p. 18.
25. Allison, The Real Thomas Jefferson, op. cit., pp. 74-75.

> his contemporaries; Adams apparently did not disapprove of it, and it would be easy to bring in many similar expressions of the same idea in documents of the time."[26]

Jefferson's intense interest in the Anglo-Saxons was shared by a notable English historian and lawyer named Sharon Turner who subsequently published a three-volume work that became the outstanding classic on the history and culture of these people.

Sharon Turner's Classic on the Anglo-Saxons

Since we have already quoted extensively from the writings of Sharon Turner, we will just summarize his notable career to better appreciate why he was working in close proximity to the research and conclusions of Thomas Jefferson.

He was born in London in 1768, and as a boy he became infatuated with the poem entitled, "Death Song of Ragnar Lodbrok." This created in his youthful mind an undying interest in the Anglo-Saxons, particularly after their immigration into Britain around 450 A.D. He engaged in an intensive study of these people from documents in England, Europe, and Iceland. His research and writing on this life-long interest continued right up to the time of his death in 1847.

As a result of his studies, he not only published his three-volume work on the Anglo-Saxons, but several other works including *A History of England During the Middle Ages, A Modern History of England, A Sacred History of the World*, and a volume on Richard III.

His first volume on the Anglo-Saxon roots in early English history came out under the title of *History of England from the Earliest Times to the Norman Conquest*. Of course it was the Norman Conquest in 1066 A.D. that shattered the rich Anglo-Saxon culture among the English.

Turner's first volume came out in 1799, the year before Jefferson was elected President of the United States. What Turner published with elaborate documentation, was what Jefferson had discovered long before through his own research.

Why the Anglo-Saxon Link with Moses Was Important

Thomas Jefferson had already learned that it was not sufficient to learn from the 30th chapter of Deuteronomy that modern man was expected to

26. Charles Chinard, Thomas Jefferson, The Apostle of Americanism, Ann Arbor, Mich.: University of Michigan Press, 1964, pp. 86-87.

restore the "perfect law" given to Moses, but the monumental problem was finding out how it originally worked and how to put it into operation.

Consider, for example, the "statutes" given to Moses. They had never been codified in a simple, readily available text for ready reference. After 3,200 years they still remained scattered among the books of the Pentateuch which Moses had written.

And that was not the only problem. Even if these statutes had been codified, there were no treatises or instructions on the manner in which the jurisprudence of the Israelites operated. There was also no background on the way the political system worked. When a serious student of the Bible pursued an in-depth understanding of the Lord's statutes and divine system of government, he was likely to come away with some extremely puzzling problems.

Jefferson was right at this stage himself when he was astonished and thrilled to discover that just a few centuries before he was born there were still people living on the earth who had practiced the principles of government and Biblical law that God gave to Moses. Perhaps these people had the key to the interpretation and application of the divine law that Moses said would be restored "in the latter days."

Once Jefferson had learned that the Anglo-Saxons had this great heritage or legacy from the past, nothing would satisfy him until he had learned the Anglo-Saxon language and studied their Mosaic "statutes" in their native texts.

Where Did the Anglo-Saxons Come From?

According to the *Saga of the Norse Kings*, which were transcribed from the Anglo-Saxon oral history in Iceland, this people had originally lived in large numbers around the Black Sea until the first century B.C. (This is the general area where the lost Ten Tribes of Israel lived until they disappeared.)

According to Anglo-Saxon tradition, they migrated en masse to the north about 65 B.C. which was the time Pompey and his Roman legions began to conquer the Black Sea region. Their oral history, songs and traditions say that as a result of this migration they eventually settled in Germany and in the Scandinavian countries.

Whether or not the details of this history could be thoroughly established from a historical standpoint was not as important to Jefferson as the exciting fact that for centuries these people had been practicing many of the principles of government and law which God had given to Moses.

How Did Some of the Anglo-Saxons Migrate to England?

These principles had been introduced into the English culture during the fifth century A.D. when the king of Kent saw these huge "Viking" pirates with their long blonde hair waving in the wind, and thought they might make excellent ground troops to fight off the Scots and other Celtic tribes that were trying to invade the south of England. He therefore hired two brothers, Hengist and Horsa, to bring over their followers to fight for him.

The Anglo-Saxons proved to be everything the king of Kent had expected of them. They cleared out the invading tribes with an organized fury that was amazing to behold. But then the king had a problem. The Anglo-Saxons wouldn't go home. They liked England. In fact, it wasn't long before the Anglos or Engels had taken over the coastal region of Britain and called it East Anglia. The Saxons, meanwhile, were establishing themselves in Essex (East Saxon land), Sussex (South Saxon land), and Wessex (West Saxon Land).

The aboriginal Celtic tribes who had invited the Anglo-Saxons over in the first place were horrified with this development. They fought with all their might but were gradually driven west into Wales and Ireland. According to tradition, the last great battle by the Celts was fought under King Arthur as he valiantly struggled to resist the advancing tide of Anglo-Saxons.

During all of this, the thing which impressed Jefferson the most was the fact that everywhere the Anglo-Saxons went, they established the highest order of government and law the islands of Britain had ever known. Eventually, the Anglo-Saxons were converted to Christianity, and it was then that they discovered in the Bible nearly the same laws and organizational structure which they had inherited from their ancestors.

Jefferson learned from Sharon Turner—one of the foremost authorities on the Anglo-Saxon culture mentioned above—that the famous Saxon ruler, King Alfred the Great, was thrilled to find the traditional Saxon law in the Bible. He therefore copied into the Anglo-Saxon law, not only the Ten Commandments, but several chapters of the Old Testament which so closely harmonized with traditional Saxon laws and social structure.

The English Law Compared with the Law of the Anglo-Saxons

Jefferson was one of the best legal minds in America. He was trained by George Wythe as were several other of the foremost intellectual leaders among the Founders. He knew that ever since the French Normans had conquered England in 1066 A.D. the best elements of Anglo-Saxon law had been seriously decimated with many elements of Roman civil law, canon law and feudal law. As professor Chinard pointed out, one of the urgent ambitions of Thomas Jefferson was to get back to the "primitive" Anglo-Saxon law which he felt would help the Founders understand how to administer God's law.

The Founders were very Critical of English Common Law

One of the most serious weaknesses of English law in the days of the Founders was the fact that disputes between litigants were administered through various writs that had been cast in concrete generations before, and a case that could not fit into one of these official writs was beyond legal remedy. The only hope was to appeal to the conscience of the king through the courts of equity.

Another weakness of the English legal system in the days of the Founders was the fact that criminal violations were considered a breach of the king's peace. Therefore, fines went to the king and his courts, not to the victim of the crime. In order to attain any kind of true "justice," the victim of a crime had to initiate a suit in civil court which was often too expensive to even think about. Or, as we mentioned, he might appeal to the "court of the king's conscience," the Court of Equity, which was also expensive and the outcome unpredictable.

Furthermore, to supplement the treasury of the king, a vast number of acts were called "crimes" for which heavy fines could be assessed as breaches of the king's peace. Of course, theoretically, a crime is supposed to be an offense against the whole people, but Parliament had passed a host of violations with heavy fines which related only to the king and his royal prerogatives such as the "king's peace."

So a very important aspect of "primitive" Anglo-Saxon law was the emphasis on reparation to the victim, not to the king or to the courts. To Jefferson this concept of "reparation to the victim" carried with it the very essence of justice.

Law of the Anglo-Saxons Compared to the Bible

Many have suspected that the Anglo-Saxons must have included a branch of the ancient Israelites because they came from the territory of the Black Sea (where the Ten Tribes disappeared) and because they preserved many of the unique features of law and government which had been revealed to Moses.

To Jefferson, this was exciting.

Here are some examples of the Anglo-Saxon culture which closely paralleled that of the ancient Israelites:

1. The Anglo-Saxons considered themselves a commonwealth of freemen as did the ancient Israelites.

2. They organized themselves into units identical with those of the Israelites—tens, fifties, hundreds, thousands, etc.[27]

3. Among the Anglo-Saxons the head of 10 families was called a Tithing-man.

4. The head of 50 families was called a Vil-man or head of a village.

5. The head of 100 families was called a Hundred-man.

6. The head of 1,000 families was called the Ealdorman, later shortened to earl. The territory occupied by 1,000 families was called a shire, and the administrative assistant to the earl was called the "shire reef," which later became "sheriff."

7. All laws, as well as the election of leaders, had to be by the common consent of the people.

8. Authority granted to a chieftain in time of war was extremely limited and was taken away from him as soon as the emergency had passed.

9. Their system of justice was based on reparation to the victim rather than calling offenses a violation of the king's peace and having fines go into the king's coffers.

Jefferson Encouraged Anglo-Saxon Reforms in Virginia

Jefferson was so impressed by the possibility of using the Anglo-Saxon system to make a gargantuan leap forward toward the laws revealed to ancient Israel, that he advocated stringent and immediate reforms.

On August 13, 1776, Jefferson wrote to Edmund Pendleton of the Virginia legislature to urge him to help abolish the remnants of feudalism, and return to the "ancient principles" which carry with them a promise from God.[28]

27. Deuteronomy 1:15.
28. Bergh, The Writings of Thomas Jefferson, op. cit., 1:492.

But, of course, Jefferson was far ahead of his time—perhaps a couple of centuries or more. But eventually, he knew it had to happen. He had implicit faith that someday the prophecy of Moses concerning the modern establishment of God's law would be fulfilled.

Meanwhile, the urgent task was to educate the people, and get a segment of the nation ready for the big change when time and circumstances made the adoption of God's law a radiant reality.

One of the most immediate needs was developing a more tolerant attitude among people of different faiths.

The Need for Greater Religious Harmony

Thomas Jefferson believed the political and social stability of the new American culture would be facilitated by greater religious tolerance and understanding. He was well aware of the wars which had lacerated Europe for several centuries because of religious differences.

Bigotry and religious intolerance had left ugly scars on the pages of early colonial history. Three of the colonies—Rhode Island, Pennsylvania and Maryland—had been specifically created to provide a refuge for non-conformists, Quakers and Catholics.

In an effort to better understand some of the various religious factions, Jefferson made a profound study of Christian history and defined the various heresies which he felt were devastating to the beauty of the original teachings of Jesus Christ.

Here is a summary of brief notes written up for his personal use and rounded out to facilitate reading:

> "*Sabellians*: Christian heretics. [Believed] that there is but one person in the Godhead. That the 'Word' and Holy Spirit are only virtues, emanations or functions of deity."[29]

> "*Sorcinians*. Christian heretics. [Believed] that the Father is the only one God. That the Word is no more than an expression of the godhead and had not existed from eternity; that Jesus Christ was God but not otherwise than by his superiority above all creatures who were put in subjection to him by the Father. That he was not a mediator, but sent to be a pattern of conduct to men. That the punishments of hell are not eternal."[30]

---

29. Padover, The Complete Jefferson, op. cit., p. 937.
30. Ibid.

"*Arminians*: [Note that Jefferson does not classify this group as 'heretic.'] They think with the Roman Catholic church (as against the Calvinists) that there is a universal grace given to all men, and that man is always free and at liberty to receive or reject grace. That God creates men free, that his justice would not permit him to punish men for crimes they are 'predestined' to commit. They admit the existence of God, but distinguish between fore-knowing and predestination. All the Christian fathers before St. Augustine (354-430) were of this opinion. The Church of England founded her article on predestination on St. Augustine's authority." [31]

"*Arians*: Christian heretics. They avow there was a time when the Son was not, that he was created in time, was mutable in nature, and like the angels, liable to sin. They deny the three persons in the trinity to be of the same essence. Erasmus (1466-1583) and Grotius (1583-1645) were Arians." [32]

"*Apollinarians*. Christian heretics. They affirm there was but one nature in Christ, that his body as well as soul was impassive and immortal, and that his birth, death, and resurrection was one in appearance." [33]

"*Locke's system of Christianity is this*: [Once again, Jefferson does not refer to Locke's ideas as heretic.] Adam was created 'happy and immortal;' but his happiness was to have been *Earthly* and his immortality was to have been *Earthly*. By sin he lost this—so that he became subject to total death (like that of brutes) and subject to the crosses and unhappiness of this life. At the intercession, however, of the Son of God this sentence was in part remitted. And moreover, to them who *believed* their *faith*, was to be counted for righteousness. But this did not mean that faith without works would save them. Saint James, chapter 2, says expressly the contrary; and all the original Christian fathers stress faith and *repentance* ...." [34]

Jefferson Tries to Sort out Some of His Own Basic Beliefs

Any student of the Bible and ecclesiastical history cannot help but be impressed by Jefferson's careful analysis of the New Testament in an attempt

31. Ibid.
32. Ibid.
33. Ibid.
34. Ibid., p. 938.

to define and therefore understand the basic elements of Christianity. In the following paragraphs we have in his own words the results of this research.

The Gospels

> "The fundamentals of Christianity were to be found in the preaching of our Saviour, which is related in the gospels," i.e. Matthew, Mark, Luke and John.[35]

Epistles of the Apostles

> "These fundamentals are to be found in the epistles dropped here and there, and promiscuously mixed with other truths. But these other truths are not to be made fundamentals. They serve for edification indeed and explain to us matters in worship and morality, but being written occasionally, it will readily be seen that their explanations are adapted to the notions and customs of the people they were written to."[36]

Basic Principles

> "The fundamentals of Christianity as found in the Gospels are 1. faith, 2. repentance. That faith is every[where] explained to be a belief that Jesus was the Messiah who had been promised. Repentance was to be proved sincerely by good works. The advantage accruing to mankind from our Savior's mission are these:
>
> "1. The knowledge of one God only.
>
> "2. A clear knowledge of their duty, or system of morality ....
>
> "3. The outward forms of religious worship wanted [needed] to be purged of the farcical pomp and nonsense with which they were loaded.
>
> "4. An inducement to a pious life, by revealing clearly a future existence in bliss, and that it was to the reward of the virtuous."[37]

It is obvious Jefferson is searching for a foundation of religious peace. He is avoiding quarrels about creeds, ordinances and sacraments over which cruel and terrible wars had been fought.

35. Ibid.
36. Ibid.
37. Ibid.

He commends the idea of *each* congregation choosing its own ministers and being locally controlled. He quotes the New Testament to show that bishops were "elders" or ministers of the gospel "elected by the hands of the whole church" and not geographical authorities.[38]

He emphasizes that no church has authority to minister physical punishment for heresy or misconduct. The most it can do is to excommunicate.[39]

Then he adds: "Each church, being free, no one [church] can have jurisdiction over another one ... Every church is to itself orthodox; [but] to others [is] erroneous or heretical."[40]

To Have Freedom of Religion, the Government Must Not Adopt Any Particular Church

Jefferson felt that the worst thing the colonial governments could do was to adopt a particular religion. By 1776 eight of the colonies had made a particular faith its "official" establishment of religion. These were:

Virginia (Episcopal)

Massachusetts (Congregational)

Connecticut (Congregational)

New Jersey (Protestant)

South Carolina (Protestant)

New Hampshire (Protestant)

Maryland (Christian)

Delaware (Christian)

In 1779 Jefferson and Madison undertook to disestablish the Episcopal Church in their own state of Virginia and trust that the other states would soon follow by adopting complete freedom of religion and "disestablishing" whatever religion they had previously proclaimed to be "official."[41]

But Jefferson and Madison found that rock-ribbed religionists were not going to roll over and give up so easily. They fought back as though

38. Ibid., pp. 940-941.
39. Ibid., p. 942.
40. Ibid.
41. Ibid.

their soul's salvation depended upon the preservation of their "official" state religion.

It required ten years before the Virginia legislature finally acknowledged the wisdom of allowing all religions to have a free and equal opportunity to promote their faiths in that state.

The last of the states to relinquish its official religion was Massachusetts around 1827.

Throughout the debates over the freedom of religion it becomes apparent that the Founders were men who had studied the Old Testament in Latin or Hebrew and the New Testament in Greek. Most of them had been equally diligent in studying ecclesiastical history.

But debating creeds and catechisms was not Jefferson's primary concern. He was yearning for the time when there would be a restoration of classical Biblical Christianity so that the various denominations could be more united under a common doctrine. He felt confident the restoration of Biblical Christianity would happen in America, but not in his day.[42]

42. Allison, The Real Thomas Jefferson, op. cit., p. 366.

Topics for Reflection and Discussion

1. List four things that had to happen before the Founders could set up the first free nation in modern times.

2. In spite of the strong differences between the Founders on some issues, what factors would tend to unite them?

3. What was there about the writings of Algernon Sidney and John Locke that would make it dangerous for them to be in England? What happened to Algernon Sidney?

4. Blackstone believed a law had to satisfy two things to be legitimate. What were they?

5. Did Baron Charles de Montesquieu actually write a draft for a model constitution? Were many of his ideas compatible with the thinking of the Founders?

6. Where did John Calvin say political freedom originated? What did he say about a political covenant? Who has the primary responsibility to interpret the scripture?

7. Why did Calvin think political leaders should be chained down so that their powers would remain under the legal control of the people?

8. What did the Calvinistic churches contribute to the concept of self- government and local control that made a lasting impression on the Founders?

9. Why did Thomas Jefferson feel the study of the Anglo-Saxon culture could be a great advantage to the American leaders? In what way was the Anglo-Saxon system of justice superior to the English system?

10. Why did Jefferson feel the eight states that adopted official establishments of religion had made a serious mistake? What did he do in Virginia to reverse the trend? Was he eventually successful?

CHAPTER TWENTY-ONE

Preparing for the Birth of a New Nation

One of the most astonishing aspects of the American historical development is the providential manner in which the right people were at the right place and inspired at the right time to do the right things.

How Jefferson Gradually Learned to Write a Sound Constitution

While the Founders were in the midst of the Revolutionary War, Thomas Jefferson became extremely agitated that no one was devising a plan for the government of a free people after they had won the war. Of course, he was not yet thinking of a national government but merely wondering how the individual states would govern themselves after they became free and independent.

Up to that time the desperate anxiety of the people was to win the war. It was generally felt that afterwards there would be plenty of time to leisurely determine what kind of government the people wanted. But Jefferson felt there would be an interval at the end of the war when the nation would teeter back and forth between chaos and a military dictatorship. He felt the entire future of the nation depended upon having the states work out the structure of government which could be adopted by each of the states even while the war was in progress.

It turned out that there were others with the same concerns. Virginia was the largest state in the union and its leaders decided to bring together their most capable leaders to write a constitution for the state. Jefferson saw this announcement as a great opportunity and he immediately resigned from Congress in hopes he could help.

In terms of propitious circumstances, conditions could not have been worse.

The Americans had just lost the great battle of New York City and shortly afterwards lost the two forts on each side of the Hudson. At that moment the Americans were in full retreat across the snow-covered plains of New Jersey. When Jefferson resigned, the members of Congress could not imagine why he would leave for Virginia at this extremely critical stage of the war. But Jefferson felt the colonies were eventually destined to win this war. What worried him was the fact that not one of the states knew how to govern itself as a free people after the war was won.

Experiments in Drafting a Sound Constitution

Jefferson had read several preliminary drafts of Virginia's proposed constitution and they were revolting to him. They were filled with British political philosophy at its worst.

So Jefferson wrote three different drafts of a constitution for Virginia, each one better than the last, but the British-trained Virginia legislature rejected all of them. Apparently undaunted, he wrote a fourth draft and when Congress sent him to France on a diplomatic assignment, he took the fourth draft with him for further refinement.

Even in France, Jefferson's anxieties were primarily back home in Virginia. Since Virginia was one of the leaders in structuring a new constitution, he was fearful a defective document would be copied by the other states. This was the principal reason why Jefferson had felt compelled for several years to somehow dislodge his fellow Virginians from their British mind set.

Much earlier Jefferson had submitted to the Virginia legislature a whole roster of proposals to completely change the Virginia statutes dealing with torts and crimes. He restructured them to conform with God's law as set forth in the Bible and the Anglo-Saxon code of law. As we mentioned in an earlier chapter, he wrote to a leader of the Virginia state legislature saying:

> "Are we not better for what we have hitherto abolished of the feudal system? Has not every restitution of the ancient Saxon laws had happy effect? Is it not better now that we return at once into that happy system of our ancestors, the wisest and most perfect ever devised by the wit of man, as it stood before the eighth century?" [1]

Of course, the Anglo-Saxons had not originated their system of law and government. They had simply preserved the Mosaic code of ancient Israel. So, in spite of Jefferson's compliment to the Anglo-Saxons, it was really ancient Israel that had originated the "wisest and most perfect [law] ever devised by the wit of man," and Moses had received it from God.

---

1. Boyd, The Papers of Thomas Jefferson, op. cit., 1:492.

1776—The Year America Decided to Tie its Destiny to the Roots of Ancient Israel

It will be recalled that in 1774 when the first Continental Congress was held, only two delegates wanted an immediate declaration of independence from England. These two zealots for freedom were Samuel Adams and John Adams, the two cousins from Massachusetts.

A year later when the Second Continental Congress was held everything had changed. Americans had been killed. Some at Lexington, some at Concord, over 500 killed or wounded at the Battle of Bunker's Hill, and after heavy casualties at Quebec the American expedition had been driven out of Canada.

By this time Tom Paine had written Common Sense, demanding independence from England, and both the press and the public were asking, "If we cut ourselves loose from England, what kind of government will each of the colonies have?"

It was a great compliment to John Adams—who was in Philadelphia at the Second Continental Congress—when leaders from both the north and south asked for his suggestions on how best to organize the new state governments.

How to Convert a Theocracy into a Democratic-Republic

Ever since 1639 when Connecticut first undertook to set up its government according to the first chapter of Deuteronomy, there had been an inclination to look to the Bible for political guidelines. But the principal roadblock was the fact that Moses had set up a theocracy—a government under the immediate direction of God and his prophets. How could the Founders take the principles of God's law in the Bible and set them up without the divine guidance of either God or his prophets?

In a sense, they already had the needed guidance in the Bible itself. The scripture describes exactly how to set up God's law. But could it be administered justly? Could its various powers be kept in balance? Charles de Montesquieu had already written about the genius of setting up the functions of government in three separate branches—the legislature, the executive and the judiciary—but who would keep these powerful departments separated? And who would prevent them from abusing one another or having one department usurping authority over the other departments?

It was John Adams who came to grips with these questions in January, 1776.

"Thoughts on Government" by John Adams

John Adams recognized the arduous task of learning how to govern the "United Colonies." He said it would take:

> "... the meekness of Moses, the patience of Job and the wisdom of Solomon added to the valor of David."[2]

However, as Solomon had said, there is a right time for everything, and John Adams thought this was the year of destiny for America. He wrote:

> "But on such a full sea are we now afloat that we must be content to trust to winds and currents with the best skill we have under a kind Providence to land us in a port of peace, liberty and safety."[3]

John Adams envisioned a government with a legislature of two independent houses, then a strong executive and an independent judiciary. This did not set well with the Congress which was a single body of delegates representing each of the provinces. Nevertheless, John Adams warned:

> "A government cannot be long free nor ever happy whose government is one assembly ... for a single assembly is liable to all the vices, follies and frailties of an individual; subject to fits of humor, starts of passion, flights of enthusiasm, partialities, or prejudice, and consequently productive of hasty results and absurd judgments."[4]

He also believed a single assembly would develop a lust for power. He felt it would be:

> "... at first elective, then for life, and finally self-perpetuating."[5]

He also wanted to get around the problem of a theocracy by having the supremacy of the government divided into its three fundamental functions just as Charles de Montesquieu had suggested:

> The legislature to make the law.
>
> The executive to administer the law.

---

2. Page Smith, John Adams, Garden City, New York: Doubleday & Company, 1962, 1:241.
3. Ibid., 1:242.
4. Ibid., 1:246-247.
5. Ibid.

The judiciary to interpret and enforce the law.

In addition, John Adams wanted the powers of each of these departments subjected to constitutional checks in case one of them became abusive in exercising its powers or strayed from the boundaries of its assigned powers.

Genius Without Justice

The genius in the separation of powers with a self-reparation device to get around the absence of theocracy in the modern version of God's law, met with strong opposition at first. In a letter to Dr. Benjamin Rush on April 12, 1798, John Adams describes what happened:

> "I call you to witness that I was the first member of Congress who ventured to come out in public, as I did in January 1776, in my 'Thoughts on Government,' ... in favor of a government with three branches and an independent judiciary. This pamphlet, you know, was very unpopular. No man appeared in public to support it but yourself. You attempted in the public papers to give it some countenance, but without much success ....
>
> "Paine's wrath was excited because my plan of government was essentially different from the silly projects that he had published in his 'Common Sense.' By this means I became suspected and unpopular with the leading demagogues and the whole constitutional party in Pennsylvania."[6]

But two years later, John Adams had his moment of triumph when he put all of these ideas into the new constitution for the state of Massachusetts. He says:

> "Upon my return from France in 1779, I found myself elected by my native town of Braintree a member of the Convention for forming a Constitution for the State of Massachusetts. I attended that Convention of near four hundred members. Here I found such a chaos of absurd sentiments concerning government that I was obliged daily, before the assembly, and afterwards in a Grand Committee, to propose plans and advocate doctrines, which were extremely unpopular with the greater number. Lieutenant-Governor Cushing was avowedly for a single assembly, like Pennsylvania. Samuel Adams was of the same mind. Mr. Hancock kept

6. John Adams' letter to Benjamin Rush, April 12, 1809; see Koch, The American Enlightenment, op. cit., p. 763.

> aloof in order to be governor. In short, I had at first no support but from the Essex junto who had adopted my ideas in the letter to Mr. Wythe [back in 1776] … They made me, however, draw up the Constitution, and it was finally adopted, with some amendments very much for the worse."[7]

The Ingenious Contribution of John Adams Became Lost

As the ideas of John Adams gradually found their place in the minds of the Founders, they adopted them without remembering where they came from. The separation of powers with checks and balances even worked their way into the national Constitution when it was adopted in 1787. Nevertheless, when James Madison carefully wrote the five *Federalist Papers* (47 to 51) explaining how this brilliant combination of checks and balances operates, the name of John Adams was never mentioned.

Madison does acknowledge that the Constitution of the State of Massachusetts has these qualities embodied in it, but there is no reference to it as an original contribution, nor that John Adams had to overcome strong opposition to get it adopted.

In the five *Federalist Papers* mentioned above, Madison gives appropriate accolades to Baron Charles de Montesquieu for his promotion of the separation of powers, but he completely neglects to mention John Adams who developed the device of checks and balances which made the separation of powers workable.

And nowhere do we see an acknowledgement of the inspired device by which John Adams changed the theocracy of God's law in the days of Moses to a democratic-republic in our own day.

As John Adams saw the praise and glory for the inspired American federal systems slipping away from his own brow to enhance the illustrious reputation of others, he ignored the neglect of his own inspired role and said:

> "Mausoleums, statues, monuments will never be erected to me. Panegyrical romances will never be written, nor flattering orations spoken to transmit me to posterity in brilliant colors."[8]

Historian Adrienne Koch says this is precisely what happened:

> "... for something like a century after his death, these purple predictions appeared to be virtually self-fulfilling. Neither historians

7. Ibid., pp. 163-164.
8. Ibid., p. 154.

> nor the American people he had so paternally looked after paid him tribute for his great statesmanship and his indispensable contribution to the logic of independence and republican government in the states. One could not find a statue to him in Washington, the city over which he had presided as the first occupant of the White House, nor in his native Massachusetts for whose interests he had fought as fiercely as a mother lion guards her cubs."[9]

Setting the Stage for a Declaration of Independence

Now we return to equally notable events which were occurring at precisely the same time that John Adams was performing his noble service. His work would have been aborted had not the American colonies girded up their loins and declared themselves completely separate from the king and Parliament of England.

It is interesting that no one deserves more credit for bringing this separation about than John Adams and his immediate Whig associates in the Congress. Beginning in 1776 they worked day and night and used every conceivable political strategy to get to the point where Richard Henry Lee of Virginia could introduce a resolution on June 7, 1776, calling for a declaration of independence.

There was an immediate uproar in the Congress with noisy delegates from several of the colonies claiming they had no authority to vote on such a radical proposal until they had the approval from their respective colonial assemblies back home. It was therefore agreed to postpone the vote until July 2nd.

Meanwhile, a committee was appointed to draft the Declaration of Independence and present it to the Congress on the same date as Richard Henry Lee's resolution. The five members of the committee in order of their ages were Benjamin Franklin (70), Roger Sherman (55), John Adams (41), Thomas Jefferson (33) and Robert Livingston (30).

How Thomas Jefferson Happened to Write the Declaration

When the committee convened, Jefferson immediately proposed that John Adams be authorized to prepare the initial draft. John Adams describes what happened:

> "Jefferson proposed to me to make the draft. I said: 'I will not. You should do it.'

9. Ibid.

"Jefferson: 'Oh no! Why will you not? You ought to do it.'

"Adams: 'I will not!'

"Jefferson: 'Why?'

"Adams: 'Reasons enough.'

"Jefferson: 'What can be your reasons?'

"Adams: 'Reason first—You are a Virginian, and a Virginian ought to appear at the head of this business. Reason second—I am obnoxious, suspected, and unpopular. You are very much otherwise. Reason third—You can write ten times better than I can.'

"Jefferson: 'Well, if you are decided, I will do as well as I can.'"[10]

The Ancient Principles

Thomas Jefferson labored over the Declaration of Independence seventeen days. It is generally assumed he took most of that time writing out the long catalog of crimes by the king and the Parliament which justified the separation of the colonies from the mother country. However, this does not appear to have been the case. Here is the reason why.

Jefferson had already written three successive drafts for a proposed constitution for Virginia. He had planned to present the latest version to the Virginia legislature in Williamsburg; however, his trip was interrupted when a dispatch arrived instructing him to go to Philadelphia as Virginia's delegate to Congress.

He obediently set out on his journey and arrived at his new post on May 14, 1776, with the third constitutional proposal in his pocket. This draft contained the lengthy list of offenses which he felt was a full justification for Virginia setting up a separate government.

In his new committee assignment at the Congress, it would have taken Jefferson only a day or two to copy this list of offenses into the Declaration of Independence and then use it as a full justification for all of the colonies to demand their independence.

Assuming this to be the case, we are led to conclude that Jefferson spent the rest of the fifteen or sixteen days poring over the ancient principles that

10. Charles Francis Adams, ed., The Works of John Adams, Boston: Little, Brown and Co., 1850-56, 2:51 note.

he wanted incorporated in the first two paragraphs of the new Declaration of Independence.

These ancient principles constitute eight of the foundation stones of the newly contemplated American system of government and were carefully enunciated by Jefferson with classical brevity in these opening paragraphs. A brief discussion of these eight principles can be found in *The Making of America.*[11]

Jefferson Offers His Draft to the Committee and the Congress

When Jefferson presented the draft of the Declaration to the whole committee they were very pleased with it and only minor suggestions were made by John Adams and Benjamin Franklin.

On July 2 when the draft was presented to the Congress there was a lively discussion for two days. Some of the delegates from Tory states—such as New York—felt the list of offenses were too harsh and needed to be toned down for diplomatic reasons. In the end over sixty changes were made in the document, but not one of the ancient principles was deleted.

It was a glowing tribute to the skill of Thomas Jefferson as a writer and to the patient molding of the Congress by John Adams that finally brought this highly diversified body of delegates to the crowning summit of unity where each of the new United States of America finally ratified the Declaration of Independence. It was July 4, 1776, which John Adams said he hoped Americans would celebrate from generation to generation as the birth date of the nation.[12]

The First Proposed Seal Gave Credit to Ancient Israel for the Inspiration of the Founders

A short time after the Declaration of Independence was adopted, Thomas Jefferson, John Adams, and Benjamin Franklin were the fore-most leaders assigned to formulate an official seal for the new nation.

As mentioned earlier, Jefferson—and several of the other Founders, including the Reverend Thomas Hooker, who wrote the constitution for Connecticut in 1649—had discovered that the most substantive principles of representative government were those practiced by ancient Israel under the

11. Skousen, The Making of America, op. cit., p. 28.
12. A letter from John Adams to Abigail Adams without a date except for 1780; quoted in Koch, The American Enlightenment, op. cit., p. 187.

leadership of Moses. Jefferson had also studied the institutes of government of the Anglo-Saxons and had found that they were almost identical to those of the Israelites.

After a brief discussion it was decided that both of these ancient peoples should be represented on the great seal of the United States.

Here is Franklin's description of the way he thought the Bible's ancient Israel should be portrayed:

> "Moses standing on the shore, and extending his hand over the sea, thereby causing the same to overwhelm Pharaoh who is sitting in an open chariot, a crown on his head and a sword in his hand. Rays from a pillar of fire in the clouds reaching to Moses, to express that he acts by command of the Deity. Motto: Rebellion to tyrants is obedience to God." [13]

John Adams described what Jefferson proposed:

> "Mr. Jefferson proposed: The children of Israel in the wilderness, led by a cloud by day, and a pillar of fire by night, and on the other side Hengist and Horsa, the Saxon chiefs, from whom we claim the honor of being descended and whose political principles and form of government we have assumed." [14]

Professor Gilbert Chinard, one of the distinguished biographers of Jefferson, states:

> "Jefferson's great ambition at that time was to promote a renaissance of Anglo-Saxon primitive institutions on the new continent. Thus presented, the American Revolution was nothing but the reclamation of the Anglo-Saxon birthright of which the colonists had been deprived by 'a long train of abuses.' Nor does it appear that there was anything in this theory which surprised or shocked his contemporaries; Adams apparently did not disapprove of it, and it would be easy to bring in many similar expressions of the same idea in documents of the time." [15]

As we mentioned earlier, on August 13, 1776 (about the time the committee was trying to design an official seal), Jefferson wrote to Edmund Pendleton to

---

13. Richard S. Patterson and Richardson Dougall, The Eagle and the Shield A History of the Great Seal of the United States, Washington, D.C.: U.S. Department of State, 1976, p. 16.
14. Ibid., p. 18.
15. Gilbert Chinard, Thomas Jefferson, The Apostle of Americanism, op. cit., pp. 86-87.

convince him that Virginia must abolish the remnants of feudalism and return to the "ancient principles." He wrote:

> "Are we not better for what we have hitherto abolished of the feudal system? Has not every restitution of the ancient Saxon laws had happy effects? Is it not better now that we return at once into that happy system of our ancestors, the wisest and most perfect ever yet devised by the wit of man, as it stood before the eighth century?" [16]

A Different Seal Eventually Adopted

Congress did not immediately adopt any official seal, and as time went by other committees were appointed. Eventually Congress adopted a simpler seal. It consisted of an American eagle on one side and an unfinished pyramid of thirteen steps on the other (representing the thirteen original colonies).

The pyramid insignia was copied from the fifty-dollar bill of the Continental currency used during the Revolutionary War. At the bottom of the pyramid were inscribed the Roman numerals for 1776, and the popular all-seeing eye of the Creator was implanted over the pyramid, symbolizing the providential power which the Founders had observed interceding in their behalf during the war for independence.

There were also two classical Latin mottoes inscribed on the seal. One was *Annuit Coeptis*—He (God) hath favored our undertaking. The other was *Novus Ordo Seclorum*—the New Order of the Ages, or the Beginning of a New Age.[17]

How the Congress Was Forced to Call a Constitutional Convention

It will be recalled that the nation was in a state of desperate confusion as the Revolutionary War came to a conclusion and the peace treaty was signed in 1783.

During June, 1783, a body of around a hundred soldiers of the Pennsylvania line stormed the seat of Congress in Philadelphia and so terrified the members that they fled to Princeton and then to Annapolis for safety. They never restored the seat of government to Philadelphia again.

---

16. Boyd, The Papers of Thomas Jefferson, op. cit., 1:492.
17. Skousen, The Making of America, op cit., p. 33.

Meanwhile, all of the states were involved in serious economic pressures from inflation, depression, resistance to taxes and occasional riots.

At one point some of the foremost business interests in the country seriously considered uniting with the army to set up a military dictatorship to restore order. But this required the leadership of George Washington. This was exactly the situation Oliver Cromwell had found himself being pressured to establish after the two civil wars in England. Cromwell made the mistake of allowing the Parliament to make him a military dictator and the results were totally disastrous.

As we pointed out earlier, Washington knew this history and before the conspiracy had come to a head in America, the General hurriedly rode to Annapolis where the Congress was meeting and resigned his commission. It will be recalled that an officer had offered to make Washington "king" of America and the General had angrily chastised him for his outrageous suggestion.

Washington announced to the soldiers who had faithfully served under him and to the public that he was returning to Mount Vernon and entering into permanent retirement on his plantation there.

Nevertheless, Washington was extremely sensitive to the disintegration of the economy and the bitter quarreling among the thirteen states. There was no doubt the nation was on the verge of total collapse.

In a letter to his fellow Virginian, James Madison, he wrote:

> "No day was ever more cflection ... What stronger evidence can be given of the want of energy in our government than these disorders?... A liberal and energetic constitution, well guarded and closely watched to prevent encroachments might restore us." [18]

On December 26, 1786, the following sentiments were expressed by Washington to General Henry Knox:

> "I feel, my dear General Knox, infinitely more than I can express to you, for the disorders, which have arisen in these states. Good God! Who ... could have foreseen, or ... predicted them?" [19]

Washington also wrote a letter in which he said:

---

18. Fitzpatrick, The Writings of George Washington, op. cit., 29:51-52; quoted by Skousen in The Making of America, op. cit., p. 118.
19. Ibid.

> "If ... any person had told me that at this day I should see such a formidable rebellion ... as now appears, I should have thought him a bedlamite, a fit subject for a madhouse."[20]

Steps That Led to the Calling of a Constitutional Convention

About this time Washington became aware of a bitter quarrel between the officials of Virginia and the officials of Maryland over certain fishing rights in the Potomac River and the Chesapeake Bay. The contestants were about ready to come to blows.

Washington saw what was happening and invited the parties from both states to meet with him on the porch of Mount Vernon. After sipping some appropriate refreshments and talking things over, they settled the fishing rights dispute in one afternoon.

In fact, they developed such a cordial feeling with one another that they went back to their respective authorities and suggested that all of the states ought to be invited by Congress to send representatives to a general trade conference in Annapolis. It was hoped that at this conference the delegates could settle their various boundary disputes and trade disagreements once and for all.

Unfortunately, only five states responded to the invitation and that was not enough to constitute a quorum that could conduct business. Nevertheless, the delegates could see the advantage of sitting down together, and therefore Alexander Hamilton—who had been one of the most aggressive advocates of a Constitutional Convention—urged the Congress to call a convocation of delegates from all of the states as soon as possible.

The members of Congress were relieved to have a suggestion that might reduce the explosive pressure that was building up around the country. Therefore, on February 21, 1787, the Congress officially extended an invitation to all of the states to send special delegates to Philadelphia on May 14, 1787—just three months hence.

Congress said the convention was for the sole and express purpose of revising the Articles of Confederation, thereby rendering the federal constitution "more adequate to the exigencies of the government and the preservation of the Union."[21]

---

20. Ibid.
21. Skousen, The Making of America, op. cit., p. 135.

Topics for Reflection and Discussion

1. Why was it shocking to the members of Congress when Jefferson suddenly resigned and went back to Virginia to help write its new constitution? Why did he feel the constitution of Virginia was so important? How many drafts did Jefferson write? Were any of them accepted by the legislature in Williamsburg?

2. What law did Jefferson consider to be the most perfect law ever devised by the wit of man? Where did this perfect law originate? What year did Americans decide to tie their destiny to the roots of ancient Israel?

3. What is a "theocracy?" What is a "democratic-republic?" Who devised the best plan to convert Israel's theocracy into America's democratic-republic? Did all of the states adopt it for their respective constitutions? Was it incorporated into the Constitution of the United States?

4. What are the five *Federalist Papers* that explain this unique system of government? Was any credit given to the Founder who put it in his pamphlet called "Thoughts on Government?" How much honor was he paid during the following century?

5. Which of the Founders worked the hardest with the Whigs in Congress to reach a point where the Congress would vote for a Declaration of Independence? Explain how Jefferson finally got the assignment to write the Declaration.

6. How many days did Jefferson take to write the Declaration of Independence? Was most of the time required to list the numerous offenses committed by the Parliament and the king? What did take most of the time?

7. Did the Congress make any changes in Jefferson's draft? Did the Congress eliminate any of the ancient principles incorporated in the first two paragraphs?

8. What three Founders were on the committee that prepared the first plans for the official seal of the United States? What two peoples were honored as the founders of the American system of government? How did a different seal happen to be adopted later on?

9. Who took the first initiative to settle the dispute between Maryland and Virginia over fishing rights? Why was it successful? What conference was subsequently called at Annapolis to settle disputes among all the states? How many states responded?

10. Who was the Founder at the Annapolis trade conference who suggested a new convention to be held at Philadelphia to amend the Articles of Confederation and try to mold it into a genuine constitution? What date was set for the meeting? How long did the states have to get ready?

CHAPTER TWENTY-TWO

SETTING UP A CONSTITUTION FOR THE FIRST FREE PEOPLE IN MODERN TIMES

When the Constitutional Convention convened in Philadelphia on May 14, 1787, nobody knew how it was going to turn out. Our purpose in this chapter is to look for the elements in the Founders' original formula which were not only inspired but which provided the genius for the building of the greatest nation on the face of the earth.

We are also stimulated by the realization that the most valuable features of the original Constitution have been shredded and eventually they will have to be restored. In other words, the structuring of the original constitution requires our closest attention since someday a modern generation of Americans will have to do it all over again.

It is interesting that Thomas Jefferson and John Adams—the two best prepared constitutionalists of that time—were not at the Convention. Jefferson was in France serving as a diplomatic representative of the United States, and Adams was in England serving in a similar capacity.

Fortunately, Adams had published his Thoughts on Government some twelve years earlier which most of the Founders had read. Furthermore, Jefferson had carefully tutored James Madison and he became recognized by most of the delegates as the foremost political scientist at the Convention. Nevertheless, even though Madison is often referred to as the "father of the Constitution," he gives Thomas Jefferson full credit for being the original architect or "chief magistrate" responsible for the structuring of the Constitution of the United States.[1]

Jefferson also did everything possible to see that James Madison had access to the finest political writings of the ages. He sent over a hundred books from France so that Madison could prepare himself even before anyone knew there would be a Convention.

And in fairness to John Adams, we must continually remind ourselves that—as we mentioned earlier—it was his concept of checks and balances

1. Madison, The Federalist Papers, op. cit., Number 48, p. 310.

that made the Constitution with its separation of powers the functioning miracle which it became.

Did Anyone Have an Agenda for the Convention?

Although the Congress had instructed the convention in Philadelphia to "amend the Articles of Confederation," there was no concrete bill of particulars concerning the specific improvements which were to be addressed. This meant the convention was being called without any particular agenda, and a convention without an agenda could be a disaster. Fortunately, the delegates from Virginia were able to come up with one, and this is how it happened.

On May 14th when the Convention was called to order, only Virginia and Pennsylvania had a quorum of delegates present. This was not enough to officially conduct any business, so the delegates had to wait for nearly two weeks before a quorum had arrived.

This was a godsend to James Madison who rallied the Virginia delegation around him so they could anticipate what would be best to include in the new Constitution. These suggestions could then be presented at the opening session of the Convention as a proposed agenda. Madison's planning meetings with the Virginia delegates extended over approximately thirteen days before the Convention finally got under way.

What about Scrapping the Defective Articles of Confederation and Starting All over Again?

At one of the first Virginia caucus meetings, Madison presented a major question: "Why not scrap the Articles of Confederation and start over?"

Of course, the Congress had only authorized the delegates to amend the Articles of Confederation which was like patching a pair of worn out breeches. Madison argued that the basic structure of the Articles was so defective that it almost caused them to lose the Revolutionary War. Why not start over again and do it right?

George Washington immediately saw the wisdom of Madison's suggestion. He was impressed by Madison's rationale that they could excuse the irregularity of presenting a new Constitution on the ground that legally speaking the Convention was only designed to propose something to correct the weaknesses of the Articles. A completely new constitution—containing their best thinking—would be such a proposal, and it would not be binding on anyone until after it had been approved by the Congress and the individual states.

The Virginia delegates finally agreed and set about preparing a list of important principles to propose to the Convention as soon as a quorum was present.

The Most Famous Political Convention in History

It will be recalled that the Convention was held in the Pennsylvania State House where American Independence had been declared. For the sake of secrecy all the windows and doors were locked shut and a guard was placed at the door. Unfortunately, however, this was the hottest summer in the memory of man, and the deadly humidity along the Delaware River was suffocating. Four months under these conditions—with the delegates sitting there in woolen broadcloth suits—was enough to make heroes out of all of them.

The Convention opened on May 25, 1787, and George Washington was immediately and unanimously elected president.

A secretary by the name of Major William Jackson of South Carolina had been employed, but he was not sufficiently detailed to satisfy James Madison. It therefore turned out that Madison was the real secretary who took minutes from the perspective of a historian. He sat up front and took copious notes on everything that was said. After each session, Madison would work far into the night filling in details. He occasionally made himself ill from overwork trying to capture every detail of the debates. These notes of Madison were kept secret for 30 years, but they were finally published by an act of Congress in 1843. They constitute the most authoritative record available on the Convention.

A Strict Code of Rules

A strict code of rules was prepared under the direction of America's first professor of law, George Wythe:

1. The proceedings were to be conducted in secret.

2. Each state was to be allowed one vote, and the majority of the delegation from a state had to be present and in agreement in order to have its vote counted.

3. Many times during the proceedings a poll was taken of the individual delegates to see how they stood, but the rule was adopted that none of

these votes were to be recorded lest delegates be embarrassed if they later changed their minds after hearing the debate. (In spite of this restriction, Madison nearly always made a record of how Washington voted as the various issues were polled prior to the official vote.)

4. Each delegate could speak only twice on each issue until after everyone else had been given the opportunity to speak. And no one could speak more than twice without special permission from the Convention members.

5. Everyone was expected to pay strict attention to what was being said. There was to be no reading of papers, books, or documents while someone was speaking.

6. All remarks were to be addressed to the president of the convention and not to any particular delegate or group of delegates. This was to avoid heated polemics between individuals engaging in direct confrontation.

The Fifteen Resolves

It was on Tuesday, May 29, that Governor Edmund Randolph of Virginia arose and introduced the "Fifteen Resolves" (containing 41 propositions) which had been prepared by the delegation from his state.

The Convention then followed a procedure which greatly facilitated an informal discussion of each issue. It resolved itself into a "committee of the whole." George Washington stepped down from the chair and Nathaniel Gorham replaced him as chairman of the Committee of the Whole. The discussion then continued on the basis of an informal "committee" meeting instead of the official, formal "convention." At any time the members could resolve themselves back into the "Convention" and formal vote on the matter previously decided in the committee. Whenever this happened, George Washington once more resumed the chair.

This was only one of several parliamentary devices employed by the Convention to encourage extensive discussion and conduct numerous straw ballots to see how they were progressing in reaching a consensus. As indicated earlier, no record was officially kept of the straw ballot vote, but James Madison felt it was important to indicate in his own notes how Washington voted.

Striving for Consensus

The Founders were most anxious to get general agreement whenever possible rather than proceed after merely getting a majority vote. In the Anglo-Saxon meetings the freemen did not take a vote, but kept "talking it out" until everyone, or practically everyone, felt satisfied. Many of the Founders were aware of this policy and followed it wherever possible.

This was illustrated when they tried to decide who should select the members of the Senate. The Virginia Resolves had proposed that this should be the responsibility of the House of Representatives, but apparently the Virginia delegates changed their minds because after "talking it out," the record says the vote in favor of having Senators appointed by the state legislatures rather than the House of Representatives was approved "unanimously."

On June 14, the proceedings were suddenly interrupted by William Paterson of New Jersey, who asked to have the day free for the preparation of a completely new plan which the smaller states wished to present the following day.

The New Jersey Plan was laid before the Convention on Friday, June 15. William Paterson said the smaller states wanted to scrap the Virginia Resolves and go back to patching up the original Articles of Confederation. He then presented the New Jersey Plan.

The following day, James Wilson of Pennsylvania compared the Virginia Plan with the New Jersey Plan point by point:

The Virginia Plan

1. Two branches for the legislature.
2. The legislative powers derived from the people.
3. A single executive.
4. A majority of the legislature can act.
5. The executive can be removed by impeachment.
6. Provision was made for the establishment of inferior federal courts.

The New Jersey Plan

1. A single legislative body.

2. Legislative power derived from the states.

3. More than one executive share supreme authority.

4. A small minority could control the legislature.

5. The President could be removed upon application of a majority of the states.

6. No provision concerning inferior courts to be established.

Hamilton's Plan

While the Convention was contemplating the two different plans, Alexander Hamilton suddenly arose and presented an entirely different plan of his own. He said it was too dangerous to tread untried waters. It would be best to go back to the British system of government. He recommended:

1. A single executive chosen for life by electors from the states. He wanted the President to have an absolute veto over any legislation, similar to the veto power of the king of England. In the notes for his speech, Hamilton referred to the executive as the "Monarch," and said the office "ought to be hereditary." [2]

2. Senators were also to be chosen for life similar to the English House of Lords.

3. The House of Representatives, like the British House of Commons, would be chosen for a limited term. Hamilton recommended three years.

4. Governors of the states would be appointed by the federal government, just as the king of England appointed governors for each of the colonies before the Revolution.

Hamilton had carefully structured this speech even though he did not give it with his usual flourish. Nevertheless, his listeners knew he was trying to arouse in them the old fervor for crown and country they had felt as loyal Englishmen in a bygone quarter of a century. For the effort he received polite but adequate applause. However, William Samuel Johnson from Connecticut said the oration had been "praised by everybody" but "supported by none." [3]

Hamilton was deeply disappointed. His plan was not even discussed, let alone presented for a vote. Hamilton left the convention in a dark mood, and

---

2. Noemie Emery, Alexander Hamilton, An Intimate Portrait, New York: G. P. Putnam's Sons, 1982, p. 98.
3. Forest McDonald, Alexander Hamilton, New York: W. C. Norton & Company, 1979, p. 105.

except for a couple of "drop-by" visits did not return to the Convention until the last few days when it was time to sign the finished document. As a result, he missed the debates on all of the vital issues and we will have more to say about his actual feelings toward the Constitution later on.

Madison's Plea

On June 19, a moving speech was given by James Madison in which he said the Convention must come up with a "Constitution for the ages." He felt only the Virginia Plan would stand the test of time because it had been grounded on time-tested principles. Immediately afterwards, the New Jersey Plan was voted down and the Virginia Plan therefore continued to serve as the agenda for the rest of the Convention.

The following day the Convention began to probe some of the more delicate questions which had previously been postponed. This is known as the "Crisis Period" and lasted clear up until July 26. It was during the strong polemics and heated debating of this period on June 28 that 81-year-old Benjamin Franklin made his famous plea for prayer.

This fervent plea for prayer contained some of the most eloquent statements during the entire Convention which we will discuss later.

Sixty Ballots on One Issue

Another valley of shadow enveloped the Convention while it was trying to decide how the President and Vice President should be elected. It required more than 60 ballots to reach an agreement. During this dark period, Washington wrote:

> "I almost despair of seeing a favorable issue to the proceedings of the Convention, and do therefore repent having had any agency in the business."[4]

Observers said he looked as grim as he did at Valley Forge.

It was on July 10 that Lansing and Yates—who were the two remaining delegates from New York—left the Convention and never returned.

The Founders Decided God's Law Had the Best Method of Selecting Qualified Leaders

The Convention finally decided to follow the procedure under God's law and set up a council of special electors or "wise men" to select their leaders

4. Fitzpatrick, The Writings of George Washington, op. cit., 29:245.

who were leaders of "understanding" and "known" among the people. The candidates would be "called to serve" or drafted by their respective areas as the most qualified and respected people available, and would agree to serve if elected. As with Washington, most candidates would be deeply involved in business or other activities and asked to be excused but agreed to serve as a matter of civic duty if elected.

After the electors had interviewed, investigated, and evaluated each candidate, they would mark their ballots on a certain date and send them to Washington. There the ballots would be opened by a joint session of Congress and counted to determine who had been chosen. There would be no political party campaigning, expensive conventions or candidates trying to get themselves elected.

It was this procedure which the Founders felt would give them the best available talent to serve the people.

We should mention that the number of delegates from each state would be weighted in favor of the smaller or disadvantaged states. This compromise was granted to the smaller states so they would not leave the convention.

It is important to remember that if this "equalization plan" had not been adopted, probably six of the smaller states would have never come into the Union.

How the "Equalization Plan" Operates

Notice how much weight one of the smaller states such as Utah has in comparison with Arizona which has *twice* the population.

Utah has three Representatives and two Senators for a total delegation of five. Arizona has six Representatives and two Senators for a total delegation of eight. In other words, Arizona has only three-eighths more representatives than Utah even though Arizona has twice the population.

Of course, the comparison is less dramatic when Utah is compared with large states such as California or New York, but the fact remains, that this formula was definitely designed by the Founders to give a greater advantage to the smaller or less advantaged States.

Before leaving the subject of the Electoral College, let us ask one more question.

Why Don't We Use the Electoral College Today?

The whole concept of the Electoral College lost its meaning when the political party system began to evolve around 1800. It not only shattered the Founders' original plan to get our best leaders into top position but it destroyed any inclination to go back to the original Electoral College system.

Nevertheless, in chapter 31 of this text, we will talk about the coming restoration of the Constitution, and it will be readily seen that the Electoral College will be restored right along with it.

The Connecticut Compromise

A big breakthrough came on July 16 when the Convention finally agreed to a formula for a balanced allocation of representatives in Congress.

The small states had been determined to have one vote for each state as provided in the Articles of Confederation.

The larger states had insisted that representation should be according to population. Georgia argued that if the population formula were used a big state such as Virginia would have sixteen times more representatives than Georgia. But Madison argued right back that if each state had only one vote, then a person from Georgia would have sixteen times more representation than a citizen from Virginia.

Both sides finally agreed to accept the suggestion of Roger Sherman of Connecticut that each state should have equal representation in the Senate, but that the House of Representatives should be apportioned according to population but subject to the weighting which we have already discussed.

Many Singular Aspects of the Constitution

There are 248 provisions in the Constitution as it came from the hands of the Founders up to the Twelfth Amendment. Nothing more was added to the Constitution until after the Civil War. Today there are 286 provisions in the Constitution and not all of the recent ones have been an improvement. All 286 of the present Constitutional structure are covered point by point in the book we were asked to prepare for the Bicentennial in 1987. It is called *The Making of America*.

The Founders addressed scores of intricate questions and provided some ingenious answers. For example:

1. Who could pass laws under the original Constitution?

Nobody but the United States Congress. The President could suggest laws, but he cannot pass laws by executive order. All that came later and without a Constitutional amendment. Nor can the Supreme Court lay down new laws. That also came later without a Constitutional amendment.

2. Could the President veto any law?

Yes. Any law except a joint resolution by the House and the Senate to withdraw the President's war powers. That happened to President Truman.

3. Could the Congress override a Presidential veto?

Yes. A two-thirds vote of both the House and the Senate can still override the President's veto.

4. If the people of a state elect a reprehensible character to sit in the House or the Senate, must that individual be admitted as a product of the democratic process?

No. The House and the Senate each have the right to exclude any person whose proven record is of a reprehensible nature. Nevertheless, the basis for the ruling must be verifiable in a federal court if it is challenged.

5. Why shouldn't Senators be elected by popular vote the same as Representatives?

Because the Founders wanted them to be appointed by the individual state legislatures to watch over states rights and resist radical legislation emanating from the House of Representatives. However, the Fifteenth Amendment reversed the Founders' design by requiring Senators to be elected by a popular vote. Now the states do not have any appointed representatives to specifically watch over states rights.

6. How can federal officials from the President on down be removed from office for misfeasance or malfeasance?

The House of Representatives holds a hearing and where the charges warrant it, they go before the Senate and seek an impeachment which removes the offender from office.

7. Should an official be suspended from office during impeachment proceedings?

   No. It could then be used as a tactic to remove a Congressman or Senator from action during a very critical legislative situation.

8. If an impeached official committed criminal acts which led to his or her impeachment, can that person be prosecuted after being removed from office?

   Yes.

9. Did the Founders intend to allow appropriations for farmers, teachers, the poor or the elderly under the guise of "general" welfare?

   No. These are all cases of "special" or "private" welfare which were forbidden until 1936 when the Supreme Court suddenly handed down a dictum in the Butler Case which no longer required appropriations to be for "general" welfare. This change—which was virtually an unconstitutional amendment—opened the floodgates to almost unlimited welfare appropriations from which the country has never recovered.

10. Why didn't the Founders want the federal government to participate in "private" welfare?

    Because these are matters reserved to the states. Experience had demonstrated that federal welfare corrupts both the government and the people.

11. Why did the Founders require all treaties and agreements with other nations to be ratified by the Senate?

    Because secret agreements by heads of state could involve us in war or other dangerous commitments without the people knowing anything about it.

12. Why does the Constitution state that the income of judges cannot be reduced nor can they be discharged unless they have committed an impeachable offense?

    This was so the judges could make honest and independent decisions without suffering reprisal from officials who did not like the decision.

These are just a few examples of the numerous, tangled complexities of government with which the Founders had to deal before the 248 provisions (eventually 286) of the Constitution had been carefully evaluated and finally cast into legislative concrete.

The Committee on Detail

Finally, by July 26, the principal issues had been sufficiently settled so that they could be organized in an orderly pattern and a rough draft of the Constitution could be presented to the delegates for review. A Committee on Detail was therefore appointed with instructions to have its report completed by August 6.

After receiving the rough draft on August 6, the delegates worked until September 8 hammering out some of the more important details which still needed refining.

By this time 11 of the 55 delegates had departed and gone home. However, Hamilton had returned but could not vote because Yates and Lansing did not return. Hamilton would have needed at least one of them to form a quorum before a ballot could have been cast for New York.

The Committee on Style

On September 8, the amended rough draft from the Committee on Detail was turned over to a special Committee on Style to do the final rewrite. Most of the rewrite was done in four days by a highly skilled lawyer and writer who was a delegate from Pennsylvania. His name was Gouverneur Morris.

When the new draft was read to the Convention, some of the delegates raised 18 new issues during the next three days. However, the vast majority of the delegates were satisfied with the draft as written, and therefore the Constitution was turned over to a skilled penman to be inscribed in its final form.

Signing the Constitution

On Monday, September 17, 1787, a total of 41 of the original 55 delegates solemnly met in the east room of Independence Hall for the signing. Because a few delegates still had some significant reservations, Franklin asked that the Constitution be signed by the majority of each delegation so they could say it was by "unanimous consent" of all the "states" represented. This was done. It is interesting that four new delegates signed for New York. The following delegates were present but declined to sign:

1. Elbridge Gerry of Massachusetts
2. George Mason of Virginia
3. Governor Edmund Randolph of Virginia

Their main objection was that the Constitution did not include a Bill of Rights.

The other delegates came forward, however, and affixed their names. It is recorded that when Benjamin Franklin signed, "the old man wept."[5]

Later, as the last delegates were signing, Franklin referred to a picture of the sun on the back of George Washington's chair. He said:

> "I have ... often, in the course of the session ... looked at that [sun] behind the president without being able to tell whether it was rising or setting. But now at length I have the happiness to know that it is a rising and not a setting sun."[6]

As the famous Convention came to a close it was as though a great battle had been won. But the Constitution still had to go to the Congress and the people. This meant that the great intellectual battle to get the American charter of liberty established in the hearts and minds of the American people still had to be fought.

What about a Bill of Rights?

Nevertheless, on September 17, 1787, the Constitution was almost unanimously approved, and Washington prepared a letter to dispatch with it to the Congress which was meeting in New York City. The Congress took very little time to discuss the Constitution because a number of the delegates from the Convention were members of Congress and could respond to any questions.

The Constitution was then sent on to the States.

At first many of the states refused to ratify the Constitution because they wanted a Bill of Rights. Eventually, George Washington had to promise them that a Bill of Rights would be added at the first session of Congress if they would just go ahead and accept the original text for the present. He even invited the states to submit suggestions of the rights they would like to have

5. Catherine Drinker Bowen, Miracle at Philadelphia, London: Hamish Hamilton, 1967, p. 263.
6. Max Farrand, The Records of the Federal Convention of 1787, New Haven: Yale University Press, 1974, 2:648.

included. On this basis the Constitution was ratified and went into effect June 21, 1788 with the ratification of New Hampshire, the ninth state.

At the first session of Congress, James Madison insisted that one of the first orders of business should be the adoption of a Bill of Rights. The states submitted a long list of rights they wanted to have included. Of course, there were many duplicates. Madison reduced the number of proposed amendments for the Bill of Rights to 17, Congress then reduced the number to 12, and the states ratified 10. These then became America's famous Bill of Rights.

There are many books covering the details of the Constitutional convention, but one of the most enjoyable to read is *The Miracle at Philadelphia*, by Catherine Drinker Bowen which we have cited a number of times.

For a day-by-day account of the debates, the best compilation is *The Records of the Federal Convention of 1787*, edited by Max Farrand in four volumes.

The Founders Knew They Had Accomplished Something Monumental

When James Madison wrote to Jefferson in France, he said the spiritual elements of a genuine "miracle" were present in the final hours which made the adoption of the Constitution possible.[7]

Washington later wrote to Lafayette in France and also said that the convention had accomplished what was "little short of a miracle."[8]

The latter part of 1787, Washington wrote to Catherine Macauley Graham the following:

> "The United States enjoys a scene of prosperity and tranquility under the new government that could hardly have been hoped for."[9]

The following day he wrote to David Humphrey:

> "Our public credit stands on that high ground which three years ago it would have been considered as a species of madness to have foretold."[10]

7. Robert A. Rutland, The Papers of James Madison, Chicago: University of Chicago Press, 1962, 10:208.
8. Fitzpatrick, The Writings of George Washington, op. cit., 29:409.
9. A letter dated July 19, 1791, to Catherine Macaulay, and quoted by Skousen in The Miracle of America, Salt Lake City: Freemen Institute, 1981, p. 63.
10. A letter written to David Hymphrey on July 20, 1791; quoted by Skousen, Ibid.

Washington saw this as an unfolding of the will of God. He wrote to Benjamin Lincoln as follows:

> "No one can rejoice more than I do at every step the people of this great country take to preserve the Union ... The great Governor of the Universe has led us too long and too far on the road to happiness and glory to forsake us in the midst of it." [11]

Americans weren't the only ones that knew something wonderful had happened. The Prime Minister of England, William E. Gladstone, later said:

> "It is the greatest piece of work ever struck off at a given time by the brain and purpose of man." [12]

Later, the first Prime Minister of Canada, Sir John A. Macdonald, said:

> "I think and believe that it is one of the most perfect organizations that ever governed a free people." [13]

Was the Constitution of the United States Divinely Inspired?

A number of the Founders expressed the conviction that they received a tremendous amount of help from a higher power or they would never have come up with such a perfect structure of government.

Is it possible that God might have had a hand in structuring the Constitution of the United States? Nobody talks about visions and ministering angels, but is it possible?

A Vital Lesson from the History of Cyrus of Persia

In our search for an answer to this question we might turn to the history of King Cyrus. Cyrus was the king of the Medes and Persians who conquered Babylon in a single night. That notable event occurred in 539 B.C.

It is highly significant that Cyrus was known by name to the Prophet Isaiah around 175 years before he was born.[14]

Isaiah said Cyrus would be "called" by the Lord to accomplish his righteous purposes. The year after Cyrus conquered Babylon he suddenly felt inspired to release the Jews who had been captured by the Babylonians

11. Fitzpatrick, The Writings of George Washington, op. cit., 30:11.
12. Harry Atwood, Our Republic, Merrimac, Mass.: Destiny Publishers, 1974, p. 62.
13. R. MacGregor Dawson, The Government of Canada, Toronto: The University of Toronto Press, 1970, p. 36.
14. Isaiah 44:28; 45:1.

and send them back to Jerusalem to rebuild the Temple of Solomon which the Babylonians had demolished.

This is an interesting situation. Here is a pagan king who, without visions or ministering angels, receives a direct heavenly shower of diamond dust inspiring him to do something important for God's people. Cyrus probably thought he conjured up this whole idea by himself but, as a matter of fact, God was discussing the whole situation with Isaiah nearly two centuries earlier. At that time God spoke as though he were addressing Cyrus and said:

> "For Jacob my servant's sake, and Israel mine elect, I have even called thee by thy name: I have surnamed thee, though thou hast not known me." [15]

Thus it was in 538 B.C. that Cyrus released 50,000 Jews and told them to return to Jerusalem and rebuild the temple. As he addressed these Jews, he said:

> "The Lord God of heaven hath given me all the kingdoms of the earth; and he hath charged me [put it into my mind] to build him an house at Jerusalem, which is in Judah. Who is there among you of all his people, his God be with him, and let him go up to Jerusalem, which is in Judah, and build the house of the Lord God of Israel." [16]

Cyrus said God had "charged" him to do this. Cyrus was like many people who have received a sudden inspiration and recognized that it was not part of their own mental processes. It came from an outside source. Many artists, musicians, inventors and scientists have left testimonies of experiences similar to this.

The Gift of Revelatory Diamond Dust

Thus the Bible brings us to the illuminating medium by which God fulfills his righteous purposes by showering certain selected individuals with what we might call God's revelatory diamond dust. Notice that it was not the purpose of God to convert Cyrus at this time but simply have him release the Jews and get them started on their own divine destiny.

When the Jews were ready to leave, Cyrus brought forth 5,400 vessels of gold and silver which were captured from the temple during the earlier conquests of Judah. The Persian king turned over this sacred temple treasure

15. Isaiah 45:4.
16. Ezra 1:2-3.

to the Jewish leaders so that it could be returned to the holy house where it belonged. He then added—no doubt to everyone's astonishment—that all the expenses for the restoration of the temple should be paid out of the king's personal account.[17]

If a person were looking for concrete evidence that Cyrus was inspired by God, he need search no further. This generosity was so out of keeping with the habits and training of oriental rulers that the Jewish leaders must have equated it with a miracle.

Some of the Founders Sensed the Presence of Diamond Dust at the Constitutional Convention

As we have already mentioned, a great many of the Founders confessed their dependence on God for the success of the Constitutional Convention. This was especially true of Franklin, Washington and Madison.

Once a person such as Benjamin Franklin had become familiar with the fact that on occasion he would receive a sudden endowment of pure intelligence from an outside source, he undoubtedly understood a lot more about what must have happened to Cyrus.

We have ample evidence that during his long life, Benjamin Franklin had come to depend upon this outside intelligence in a time of crisis. We have reason to believe this was precisely why Franklin wanted the convention to have regular prayers. They needed help from a higher source. He saw them wrestling with problems so complex that solutions were completely beyond the experience and intellectual capacity of the delegates.

Franklin's Plea for Prayer at the Convention

Notice that he gives this as his main reason for the suggestion that they start having regular prayers at the convention. Here are Franklin's words:

> "The small progress we have made, after four or five weeks' close attendance and continual reasonings with each other … is, methinks, a melancholy proof of the imperfection of the human understanding." [18]

This tells us two things about Franklin. First of all, he recognized the human limitations of every person at the convention, including himself.

17. Skousen, The Fourth Thousand Years, op. cit., p. 768.

18. Andrew Allison, The Real Benjamin Franklin, Washington D.C.: National Center for Constitutional Studies, 1987, pp. 455-456.

Secondly, he quite obviously knew from experience where to go to ask for a gentle sprinkling of inspiration. Therefore, he said:

> "In this situation of this assembly, groping, as it were, in the dark to find political truth, and scarce able to distinguish it when presented to us, how has it happened, Sir, that we have not hitherto once thought of humbly applying to the Father of Lights to illuminate our understanding?" [19]

Franklin then pointed a finger of shame at the members of this convention by reminding them that in their great struggle with Great Britain during the Revolutionary War the meetings of the Continental Congress were always opened with prayer. Then why haven't prayers been held now? Just to refresh their memories he said:

> "Our prayers, Sir, were heard—and they were graciously answered. All of us who were engaged in the struggle must have observed frequent instances of superintending Providence in our favor." [20]

The record shows that on at least 67 occasions General Washington stated in his reports to the Congress that except for the intervention of God the consequence of those contests would have been different. Every man in that convention knew that these were sometimes manifest in a most spectacular way.

As we mentioned earlier, when Cornwallis put 6,000 men in boats to cross the York River and escape from Washington, a tremendous storm came up and blew the boats right back to the shore where the British could be taken prisoner. Cornwallis was led to exclaim, "Even God wants Washington to win!" [21]

There were many such instances.

Franklin concluded his plea—which is one of the most eloquent speeches of the entire convention—with a proposal. He said:

> "I therefore beg leave to move, that henceforth prayers, imploring the assistance of Heaven and its blessing on our deliberations, be held in this Assembly every morning before we proceed to business; and that one or more of the clergy of this city be requested to officiate in that service." [22]

19. Ibid., p. 456.
20. Ibid.
21. Skousen, The Making of America, op. cit., p. 104.
22. Allison, The Real Benjamin Franklin, op. cit., p. 456.

The Difference Between Diamond Dust and Plain, Ordinary Dust

At this point in our account we have a dramatic demonstration of the difference between precious, inspired diamond dust and common, ordinary dust.

After Franklin's moving plea for prayer, certain members of the convention rose with all kinds of reasons why prayers should not be held. They completely missed the inspired guidance from one of God's wisest of the "wise men" at that convention.

They thought it might make the public think the delegates had lost confidence in themselves and were now seeking divine help in desperation—which was exactly their situation. Others thought the wide disparity of denominational membership among the delegates might be divisive and create feelings as they selected ministers from different churches. The worst of all the arguments—and the one which finally prevailed—was the fact that the convention had no budget and they didn't want to ask ministers to pray without compensating them.

Of course, there were more than a dozen ministers sitting in the convention who could have prayed, but the immediate response was that they would be depriving some minister of his living.

The bottom line was simply that *they never held prayers*! Washington prayed twice a day out loud, but that was a private matter. Many of the others prayed daily, but the "plain-dust" people prevailed at the convention.

All through this historic conference these plain-dust people got in the way of the wise men that knew what to do. They not only engaged in conniving, procedural delays, but wasted time with hour-long windbag oratory. Washington accused them of having frustrated a number of brilliant suggestions because they seemed to enjoy being against anything that would give them an excuse to orate.

"Wisdom" and "Foolishness" Depend on the Issue

Of course, having said this, we quickly add that nobody has a monopoly on wisdom nor do others have a monopoly on stupid foolishness. These qualities tend to shift from one person to another as the issues change. Both common dust and the diamond dust will settle first on one and then on the other.

When it comes to the common dust of foolishness, we have an interesting example in Alexander Hamilton who has as many admirers as he has detractors. Hamilton was one of the wisest advisors in George Washington's council during the Revolutionary War. Furthermore, he demonstrated the courage of a lion when he led the assault on a British redoubt at Yorktown and forced it to surrender in bare-fisted, hand-to-hand combat.

Nevertheless, Jefferson considered Hamilton extremely foolish when it came to genuine political science. Nowhere is this better illustrated than at the Constitutional Convention when—as we have previously pointed out—Hamilton tried to press his love affair with the British system on the members of the convention rather than adopt a new American Constitution. His speech was so eloquent it aroused the admiration of the delegates, but it will be recalled that Madison wrote in his notes that it was applauded by all and approved by none.[23]

Another example of plain-dust foolishness was when Alexander Hamilton decided to recruit a certain aristocrat from a European royal family and make him king of America!

This happened in 1786—one year before the constitutional convention—when Hamilton joined with several friends to ask 50-year-old Prince Henry of Prussia if he would be the king of the United States. Prince Henry was the brother of Frederick the Great.

Hamilton and his friends felt this would be such a superb political coup that they kept the plan secretly cloistered within their group. The idea was to get Prince Henry's consent and then pop this sensational political surprise on the rest of the country.

But Prince Henry hesitated and that was a providential blessing. It gave the group sufficient time to discover to their dismay that Henry was one of the most debauched and notorious homosexuals in Europe.[24]

In the End, Divine Inspiration Prevailed

Probably the most amazing aspect of the United States Constitution is the fact that fifty-five delegates survived through four months of heavy intellectual debate and then came up with a structure of government which completely repudiated practically everything they had been taught to believe in as loyal Englishmen. For example:

23. Skousen, The Making of America, op. cit., pp. 167-168.

24. David Wallechinsky and Irving Wallace, Peoples Almanac, New York: William Morrow and Company, 1978, 2:400.

1. In spite of Hamilton's eloquent plea they wanted nothing to do with a monarchy, not even a *limited* monarchy. They saw what happened to the Israelites when they demanded a king so they could be "like all the other nations." The Israelites never recovered from that fatal political blunder.

2. They rejected the idea of a prime minister selected from the members of Parliament.

3. They rejected the idea of the cabinet being selected from among the members of Parliament.

4. They rejected the idea of having the members of Parliament serve as the executive administrators in charge of various departments of government.

5. They rejected the British idea of an "unwritten constitution."

6. They rejected the idea that the acts of Parliament would automatically become the supreme law of the land even though they may violate some of the most fundamental provisions of their unwritten Constitution.

7. They rejected the idea of the upper chamber of the legislature being a House of Lords occupied by a body of lifetime aristocrats.

8. They rejected the British idea of a "unitary" republic where all power was concentrated in the central government.

9. They rejected the idea of the national government being allowed to nullify the laws of the local governments even when there was no constitutional issue involved.

10. They rejected the idea of the national executive being allowed to dissolve the legislature before it had finished its session.

11. They rejected the British coinage system and chose a system based on the dollar instead of the pound.

12. They rejected the doctrine of *primogeniture*—an old feudal law—which required a parent to bestow his entire estate on the eldest son whether he was competent or not.

13. They rejected the doctrine of *entail estates*—another old feudal law—which required large tracts of land (sometimes millions of acres) to be maintained intact by the same family because of important feudal obligations to the king or some high ranking lord or baron. This was designed

to preserve the English feudal society and prevent a father from dividing his estate among his children and grandchildren.

14. They eventually got around to rejecting the authority of the legislature to select a certain religious denomination as the official church of the state or the realm, and then tax the people to support that church whether they were members or not.

15. The Founders also tried to get rid of serfs and slaves, but the circumstances in two states (Georgia and South Carolina) forced them to postpone this decision. As everyone knows, that was the biggest mistake the Founders ever made. The inspiration was right but they allowed themselves to be talked out of it.

We mention these examples of the Founders' forthright rejection of the most fundamental aspects of the British theory of government to demonstrate the gargantuan leap which they made under the inspiration of a higher power. They didn't achieve perfection, but they came closer than any nation in more than 5,000 years.

Topics for Reflection and Discussion

1. Why didn't John Adams or Thomas Jefferson attend the Constitutional Convention? To whom does James Madison give credit for being the real architect of the Constitution? How many preliminary constitutions had Jefferson written for one of the states?

2. Why did James Madison want to completely scrap the Articles of Confederation? On what basis did Madison suggest that they could explain to Congress why they were proposing a completely new Constitution?

3. Had Congress suggested an agenda for the Constitutional Convention? What happened to the Virginia delegates which allowed them to develop an agenda? Had they not taken this initiative to work up an agenda, what do many authorities believe would have happened to the Convention?

4. Why didn't the small states like the Virginia proposal? What did they offer as an alternative? What did Roger Sherman suggest on three different occasions that was finally accepted as a compromise?

5. Explain the "equalization plan" to accommodate the smaller or disadvantaged states. Approximately how many states would have stayed out of the Union if there had not been an equalization plan?

6. Were you surprised by the plan which was submitted by Alexander Hamilton? What was the reaction of the Convention delegates? Why did Hamilton leave the Convention? Did he miss nearly all of the important debates? When did he return? Did he sign the Constitution?

7. Why did Benjamin Franklin say the delegates should open their meetings with prayer? What did he say they needed? Does Franklin appear to have been familiar with dispensations of inspiration which he recognized as coming from outside of himself? In view of this, why didn't the delegates start holding prayers? What impressed you most about the story of Cyrus, the pagan king of Persia?

8. After the Constitution was finished, what two committees processed it before it was finally signed by the delegates? Three prominent delegates declined to sign the Constitution and some of the states hesitated to ratify it. What did they give as their reason?

9. What promise did Washington make to the delegates if they would immediately go ahead and sign the Constitution? Was the promise kept?

10. What did James Madison say happened to Benjamin Franklin when he signed the Constitution? What did he tell the delegates about the carving of a sun on the back of George Washington's chair?

CHAPTER TWENTY-THREE

LAUNCHING THE CONSTITUTION

Many of the states could scarcely wait until they received copies of the Constitution so they could ratify it.

Some of the small states who had been so fearful that the Constitution would not protect them, now read the new federal charter with complete satisfaction and were among the first to step forward—three of them without a single dissenting vote. The first was Delaware on December 7, 1787, then New Jersey on December 18, and Georgia followed on January 2, 1788.

A week later Connecticut ratified on January 9, but it was a different story across the border in Massachusetts. After a hard-fought contest between 187 delegates there was only a spread of 19 votes between those who favored and those who opposed. If 10 more delegates had voted against ratification the great state of Massachusetts would have been left out of the Union.

Maryland ratified April 26, 1788, with a vote of 63 to 11.

South Carolina ratified May 23, 1788, with a vote of 149 to 73.

The Constitution provided that as soon as nine states had ratified it, the new charter could begin operating. New Hampshire was expected to come up for a vote in June and would be the ninth state if the Constitution was ratified. However, there was fierce opposition to the Constitution in that state. It was said that this new national government would rob the people of all their basic rights as citizens of New Hampshire.

The likelihood of defeat was so threatening that the legislature and state officials were called into a solemn assembly where they listened to one of the greatest political sermons in the history of the United States. The speaker was Reverend Samuel Langdon, and he called his talk: "The Republic of the Israelites—An Example to the American States."

A VOTE FOR THE CONSTITUTION IS A VOTE FOR THE BIBLE

Taking a strong biblical—but non-denominational—stance, Reverend Langdon quoted Moses from his great last sermon to the children of Israel. In this final discourse Moses had declared in Deuteronomy 4:5-8 that God had given them the greatest system of law in existence. Then he went on to say:

> "When first the Israelites came out from the bondage of Egypt, they were a multitude without any other order than what had been kept up, very feebly, under the ancient patriarchal authority ... Yet in the short space of about three months ... they were reduced into ... civil and military order ... Able men were chosen out of all their tribes, and made captains and rulers of thousands, hundreds, fifties and tens: and these commanded them as military officers and acted as judges in matters of common controversy." [1]

Reverend Langdon pointed out that from this point on the structure of the government of Israel began to take on many aspects which had their counterpart in the Constitution of the United States. They had a senate of seventy select men, also a general assembly where all the tribes were represented.

It was also significant that Moses installed an elaborate system of courts where the people could obtain justice or be required to repair any damage to another's property or compensate a person who had been wronged.

God's Law under a Theocracy Provided Justice and Efficiency

Reverend Langdon continued:

> "A government thus settled on republican principles, required laws ... But God did not leave a people—wholly unskilled in legislation—to make laws for themselves. He took this important matter into his own hands, and beside the moral laws of the two tablets, which directed their conduct as individuals, gave them ... a complete code of judicial laws.
>
> "They were not numerous ... but concise and plain and easily applicable to almost every controversy which might arise between man and man, and every criminal case which might require the judgment of the court." [2]

In the early part of this book we have gone over the entire code of laws revealed to Moses, and it is easy to agree with Reverend Langdon when he said:

> "... the judicial laws were founded on the plain immutable principles of reason, justice, and social virtue, such as are always necessary for civil society. Life and property were well guarded, and punishments were equitably adapted to the nature of every

1. Langdon's sermon is set forth in Cherry's God's New Israel, op. cit., this quotation is from p. 94.
2. Ibid., p. 95.

crime. In particular, murder stands foremost among capital crimes, and is defined with such precision, and so clearly distinguished from all cases of accidental and undesigned killing, that the innocent were in no danger of punishment and the guilty could not escape."[3]

A God-centered Society Can Attain Superlative Excellence

"Let us now consider the national worship which God established among this people on which their obedience to the moral law very much depended ... For unless they paid constant reverence and homage to their God, agreeable to his nature and will, they would soon break loose from all other obligations to morality ....

"How unexampled was this quick progress of the Israelites from abject slavery, ignorance, and almost total want of order to a national establishment perfected in all its parts far beyond all other kings and States: from a mere mob to a well regulated nation, under a government and laws far superior to what any other nation could boast."[4]

Then Why Did They Lose it All?

Reverend Langdon felt the United States could learn an impressive lesson from this rise and fall of a great nation after being so highly favored by God. In explaining the reason the Israelites lost it all, he said:

"They never adhered in practice ... to the principles of their civil polity ... They received their law from God, but they did not keep it. They neglected their government, corrupted their religion, and grew dissolute in their morals, and in such a situation no nation under heaven can prosper."[5]

A Prediction and a Promise to America

The same thing could apply to America:

"Instead of the twelve tribes of Israel, we may substitute the thirteen States of the American union and see this application plainly offering itself, *viz*. That as God in the course of his kind providence hath given you an excellent constitution of govern-

3. Ibid., pp. 95-96.
4. Ibid., pp. 96-98.
5. Ibid., p. 98.

ment, founded on the most rational, equitable, and liberal principles by which all that liberty is secured which people can reasonably claim, and you are empowered to make righteous laws for promoting public order and good morals; and as he has moreover given you by his son Jesus Christ, who is far superior to Moses, a complete revelation of his will and perfect system of true religion, plainly delivered in the sacred writings; it will be your wisdom in the eyes of the nations, and your true interest and happiness, to conform your practice in the strictest manner to the excellent principles of your government, adhering faithfully to the doctrine and commands of the gospel and practice every public and private virtue."[6]

Then came Reverend Langdon's promise with a warning:

"By this you will increase in numbers, wealth, and power, and obtain reputation and dignity among the nations; whereas, the contrary conduct will make you poor, distressed and contemptible."[7]

God's Hand Clearly Manifest in American History

Reverend Langdon did not want Americans to miss the dramatic demonstration of God's influence in the events of recent years. He said:

"The God of heaven hath not indeed visibly displayed the glory of his majesty and power before our eyes, as he came down in the sight of Israel ... Nor has he written with his own finger the laws of our civil polity, but the signal interpositions of divine providence in saving us from a powerful irritated nation ... in giving us a Washington to be captain-general of our armies ... and making us twice triumphant over numerous armies ... and finally giving us peace with a large territory and acknowledged independence; all these laid together fall little short of real miracles and a heavenly charter of liberty for these United States."[8]

God's Minister Makes His Final Plea

Reverend Langdon seems to have realized that he might never have another opportunity to say what God needed to have said to these American

6. Ibid.
7. Ibid.
8. Ibid.

leaders. He therefore spoke with both courage and boldness as he opened his heart to give them the advice of a loving and deeply concerned religious leader:

> "Preserve your government with the utmost attention and solicitude, for it is the remarkable gift of heaven. From year to year be careful in the choice of your representatives and all the higher powers of government.
>
> "Fix your eyes upon men of good understanding and known honesty; men of knowledge, improved by experience; men who fear God and hate covetousness; who love truth and righteousness, and sincerely wish the public welfare.
>
> "Beware of such as are cunning rather than wise; who prefer their own interest to everything; whose judgment is partial or fickle, and whom you would not willingly trust with your own private interests.
>
> "When meetings are called for the choice of your rulers, do not carelessly neglect them or give your votes with indifference ... but act with serious deliberation and judgment, as in a most important matter, and let the faithful of the land serve you.
>
> "Let not men openly irreligious and immoral become your legislators; for how can you expect good laws to be made by men who have no fear of God ... and who boldly trample on the authority of his commands?... If the legislative body are corrupt, you will soon have bad men for counsellors, corrupt judges, unqualified justices, and officers in every department who will dishonor their stations ...."[9]
>
> "Therefore be always on your guard against parties and the methods [of] unworthy men, and let distinguished merit always determine your vote. And when all places in government are filled with the best men you can find, behave yourselves as good subjects; obey the laws, [be] cheerfully subject to such taxation as the necessities of the public call for. Give tribute to whom tribute is due, custom to whom custom, fear to whom fear, and honor to whom honor [is due] as the gospel commands you.

9. Ibid., pp. 100-101.

"Never give countenance to turbulent men, who wish to distinguish themselves and rise to power by forming combinations and exciting insurrections against government. For this can never be the right way to redress real grievances ...."[10]

"I call upon you also to support schools in all your towns, that the rising generation may not grow up in ignorance ... It is a debt you owe to your children and that God to whom they belong ...."[11]

"I call upon you to preserve the knowledge of God in the land and attend to the revelation written to us from heaven.

"If you neglect or renounce that religion taught and commanded in holy scriptures, think no more of freedom, peace, and happiness ...."[12]

"May the general government of these United States, when established appear to be the best which the nations have yet known, and be exalted by uncorrupted religion and morals! And may the everlasting gospel diffuse its Heavenly light and spread Righteousness, Liberty, and Peace through the whole world."[13]

New Hampshire Casts its Critical Vote

At the very next meeting of the state legislature—June 21, 1788—the people waited breathlessly to see if the sermon of Reverend Langdon had diminished the opposition.

It had, but not overwhelmingly. The vote was 57 to 46. A switch of six votes would have reversed the outcome.

But even with nine state ratifications, no formal action was taken to inaugurate the government because New York and Virginia were on the verge of voting and the other states wanted to make sure these two important partners were part of the team.

Within a week after the New Hampshire vote, Virginia finally ratified on June 26 with a tally of 87 to 79. A switch of four votes would have meant defeat.

10. Ibid., p. 101.
11. Ibid.
12. Ibid., p. 102.
13. Ibid., p. 105.

Furthermore, New York had one of the most bitter battles of all. To promote ratification, Alexander Hamilton, John Jay and James Madison had combined to write 85 newspaper articles using the name of Publius. These became known as the *Federalist Papers* and constitute the first comprehensive commentary on the principles of the Constitution. Even so, New York barely squeaked through with a tally of 30 to 27. A switch of 2 votes would have changed the outcome.

North Carolina had to hold two conventions before the vote was final. It was sixteen months after the New York convention that North Carolina ratified with a tally of 194 to 77.

Rhode Island was a case all by itself. Her leaders seemed perfectly content to stay aloof and remain completely independent of the rest of the states. As a result, they made no attempt to even hold a convention. The Senate became so disgusted with "Rogue" Island that it voted to cut off all commercial relations with the obstinate rebel and treat her like a foreign country. That's when her leaders woke up. The Rhode Island convention was held May 29, 1790, nearly two years after the Constitution had been in full operation. But its ratification was a skimpy 34 to 32. One more opposition vote could have kept Rhode Island out of the Union.

The Birth of the Nation

To get the Constitution functioning, each state was instructed to pick its Presidential electors so they could cast their secret ballots for President and Vice President on January 7, 1789. These sealed ballots were then to be shipped to New York, the temporary capital. Each state was also instructed to have its legislature appoint two Senators.

The new House of Representatives and the United States Senate met in joint session on April 6, 1789, to open the ballots and see who would be President and Vice President. As might have been expected, George Washington was unanimously elected President and John Adams was next in line with 34 votes which made him Vice President.

On April 30, George Washington was inaugurated in the Senate Chamber of the Federal Hall in New York City. However, his estate was still suffering from the ravages of the Revolutionary War and his absence for 10 years, so he was compelled to borrow money in order to buy a suit and attend his own inaugural.

On September 11, President Washington appointed Alexander Hamilton as the Secretary of the Treasury and hefty General Henry Knox as Secretary of War.

On September 24, the federal court system was set up with a federal district court in each state and a Supreme Court to preside over them. Two days later John Jay was appointed the Chief Justice.

It was also on September 26 that Edmund Randolph, former governor of Virginia, was appointed the first Attorney General.

On September 29, 1789, President Washington created the United States Army. However, he was only allowed to muster 1,000 soldiers in the beginning. The Congress was taking no chance on a "large standing army in peacetime."

Alexander Hamilton—The Man Who Wanted to Be Prime Minister of America

It meant a lot to Hamilton to have the President ask him to serve as Secretary of the Treasury.

It will be recalled that he had given a five-hour speech during the opening days of the Convention in which he urged the adoption of a strong, centralized system of government patterned after the monarchy of England. He was offended that scarcely anyone took him seriously, and he left the Convention a few days later. However, he did return in time to sign the Constitution but let it be known that he felt it was a weak instrument. As historian Carl Van Doren wrote:

> "Hamilton did not even like the Federal government which had been chosen instead of the consolidated national government he preferred." [14]

Nevertheless, he wrote most of the *Federalist Papers* urging the adoption of the Constitution and commented that it was at least a beginning and "better than nothing." [15] This suggested that he had in mind something much more vigorous as time went by.

All during the Revolutionary War, Hamilton saw the agonizing of Washington and his troops because the new-born United States did not have a dependable financial structure. For eight years, Hamilton wrestled

14. Carl Van Doren, The Great Rehearsal, New York: The Viking Press, 1948, p. 192.
15. Emery, Alexander Hamilton, An Intimate Portrait, op. cit., p. 103.

with various ways he felt they might remedy this weakness once peace was restored.

In studying the history of England a generation earlier, Hamilton was intrigued by the role of Sir Robert Walpole, Prime Minister of England under George II. George II, like his father, was a German elector who spent nearly all his time in Germany with his mistresses. This left Walpole free to practically run the government as he saw fit. His twenty years of peace and prosperity were unprecedented.

It seemed highly significant to Hamilton that Walpole was "chancellor of the exchequer" (or Secretary of the Treasury) while functioning as Prime Minister. As Hamilton entered on his new duties as the U.S. Secretary of the Treasury, one biographer writes:

> "Hamilton contemplated an American adaptation of the British scheme of things—with Washington as George II and himself as Sir Robert Walpole." [16]

Hamilton Undertakes Three Dangerous Enterprises

Even though September 11 was a Sunday, Hamilton went to work immediately. He had three important papers to write in hopes he could sell President Washington and the Congress on the following devices copied from England:

1. Monetize the national debt. Hamilton knew this was Washington's biggest worry since the Revolutionary War had left the nation with the burden of a huge debt and some of the payments to France and Holland were already overdue.

2. Set up a privately controlled central bank which would handle the government's finances similar to the operation of the Bank of England.

3. Start subsidizing various industries with tax money to build America into a great industrial nation rather than continue as an agricultural society.

Why These Enterprises Were Dangerous

In England each of these enterprises was held together by granting substantial "favors" to key people in Parliament, the landed gentry, among certain investors and among certain centers of political power.

---

16. McDonald, Alexander Hamilton, op. cit., p. 126.

Instead of outright bribes, these special favors usually came in the form of substantial considerations—inside investment tips, lucrative contracts, prestigious appointments or nominations to high offices in the government.

During Hamilton's eight years of planning, he had tentatively decided how he could spread favors around various power centers in the United States and accomplish the same thing.

To get the support of the states he would offer to have the federal government assume all of the state debts resulting from the war. And in case the actual documents supporting such claims were unavailable, he would be willing to accept "estimates" of those debts.

To get the support of Congress for the chartering of a private bank to handle the government's business, he would see that a comfortable majority of the Congressmen were stockholders in the new bank. And to make the rest comfortable he would have the government own two-fifths of the remaining stock—but of course, not enough to control the board.

To get the worry of the national debt off the mind of President Washington, he would monetize the debt and let people buy up some of the debt so they would receive annual interest payment as long as the debt lasted—and national debts nearly always lasted forever.

To attract the leaders of industry, shipping and commercial enterprises, he would use tax money from various sources to set up a "sinking fund" for subsidies. There would also be special tax breaks or even bounties for high risk enterprises.

In all of this spreading around of favors and considerations, Hamilton had no intention of feathering his own nest. The record is very clear that he was immaculate in administering his personal affairs.

Nevertheless his ambitions to make America a great industrial nation "after the manner of England," ran the extreme risk of being exposed as an elaborate scheme of "political corruption."

Hamilton's First Serious Mistake

It is difficult to understand why Hamilton would hire William Duer, his cousin by marriage, as the Assistant Secretary of the Treasury. William Duer had a very questionable reputation when Hamilton hired him, and it became worse by the month. His accounts were $200,000 short when he left the Bank of North America at the close of the Revolutionary War. The moment he learned of Hamilton's plan to pay soldiers and suppliers full value for their Continental money or government certificates, he spread the word among his friends and they began scouring the country trying to buy up as much of this paper as possible at ten or fifteen percent of its value.

Duer's activities went unchecked until the Congress threatened a full-scale investigation and he was forced to resign after barely six months as Assistant Secretary of the Treasury.

But amazingly, no censure or warning came from Hamilton.

During the next two years Duer promoted all kinds of schemes that consistently collapsed and took trusting investors down with him. At one point he barely escaped being lynched, and died soon after in a debtor's prison.

Hamilton Pays Bribes to Cover Adultery

It was during the same period that Hamilton was extremely worried over threats of exposure by the husband of Maria Reynolds with whom he had established extra-marital relations soon after the government offices were moved from New York to Philadelphia in 1790.

Mrs. Reynolds had gained Hamilton's sympathies by claiming her husband had deserted her, but after their liaison had continued for some time, the husband suddenly returned and threatened Hamilton with exposure if he did not provide immediate satisfaction. At first Hamilton paid $600, then $400, and apparently other payments from time to time. By 1797 the scandal broke in the press and Hamilton eventually issued a public confession setting forth a complete recitation of the whole sordid affair.[17]

However, by this time Hamilton had long since resigned as Secretary of the Treasury and was practicing law.

Hamilton had also gone through a bitter and long-standing dispute with Thomas Jefferson who considered Hamilton one of the foremost enemies of the Constitution as it was originally designed by the Founders.

Thomas Jefferson as Secretary of State

As we have mentioned earlier, Thomas Jefferson had been serving as a special diplomatic minister to France for several years, but in the fall of 1789 he decided to return for a "visit" to Virginia in order to check on his farms as well as his family home at Monticello.

17. Emery, Alexander Hamilton, An Intimate Portrait, op. cit., pp. 163-164.

But he had barely set foot on American soil when he was handed a dispatch from President Washington asking him to be the new Secretary of State. He immediately communicated his acceptance but asked that he be granted a couple of months to visit his home and settle his personal affairs before reporting for duty in New York.

His arrival at Monticello was a memorable event. Some idea of the affection which Jefferson's black servants had for their master is indicated by his daughter's description of what happened. She wrote:

> "The negroes discovered the approach of the carriage as soon as it reached Shadwell, and such a scene I never witnessed in my life. They collected in crowds around it, and almost drew it up the mountain by hand ….
>
> "When the door of the carriage was opened, they received him in their arms and bore him to the house, crowding around and kissing his hands and feet—some blubbering and crying, others laughing. It seemed impossible to satisfy their anxiety to touch and kiss the very earth which bore him." [18]

It was not until the spring of 1790 that Jefferson reported for duty in New York as the new Secretary of State.

His first shock was discovering that nearly all of the officials were talking about the need to replace the Constitution with a monarchy as soon as possible.[19]

His second shock was discovering—as we have already mentioned—that it had been leaked from the office of the Secretary of the Treasury that all outstanding currency and government drafts issued to the soldiers and suppliers during the Revolutionary War were to be redeemed at face value. Most people had watched these government IOUs and bills of currency depreciate to a fraction of their stated value. However, as soon as the Secretary of the Treasury had decided to redeem these papers at face value, the word leaked out almost immediately. Jefferson later described how the insiders had been tipped off and launched a mad scramble to buy up as much of this paper as possible:

> "Couriers and relay horses by land, and swift sailing pilot boats by sea, were flying in all directions. Active partners and agents were associated and employed in every State, town, and country

18. Allison, The Real Thomas Jefferson, op. cit., pp. 151-152.
19. Padover, The Complete Jefferson, op. cit., pp. 1207-1208.

> neighborhood, and this paper was bought up at five shillings, and even as low as two shillings [to] the pound before the holder knew that Congress had already provided for its redemption at par."[20]

Jefferson never forgave Hamilton for this loose talk in his office which had resulted in the organized cheating and betrayal of the veterans, farmers and business houses who had sacrificed so much to support the war effort.

Jefferson was further scandalized to learn that Hamilton had won the support of the President by monetizing the huge war debt and he had also gained the praise of the states by agreeing to absorb their unpaid debts as well.

Jefferson took the first opportunity to sit down with Washington and carefully explain to him what the monetizing of the debt meant to future generations. Instead of paying off this debt, Jefferson explained that Hamilton and his moneyed friends were buying the right to receive interest on this debt for generations to come.

But Washington told Jefferson that high finance was something he didn't entirely understand but he was impressed with the fact that when he first took office, the government was caught in a series of terrible financial straits, but since the monetizing of the debt took place, the credit of the country was first rate.

Jefferson sadly returned to his office and later recorded:

> "Unversed in financial projects ... his [Washington's] approbation of them was bottomed in his confidence in the man [Alexander Hamilton]."[21]

How shocked Washington would have been if Jefferson could have shown him our own day—two hundred years hence—when the national debt would be over five trillion dollars and the interest payments would exceed 300 billion dollars per year, with a lot of it going to foreign investors.

In fairness to Alexander Hamilton, we should say that before he left office, he proposed a debt-liquidation plan that would have paid off the war debt in thirty years. However, Congress predictably wanted to spend the money rather than pay the debt, so they rejected Hamilton's proposal. As a result, when Jefferson became President in 1801 he tried to start paying off the debt by selling public lands. During his eight years as President he wiped

20. Ibid., p. 1208.
21. Ibid., p. 1211.

out half of this huge liability. He insisted that each generation of Americans should pay off its own debts and not pass them on to their descendants.

Buying Political Power with Special Favors

Hamilton was very gratified when his special favors to members of Congress had won him the necessary support to put through the monetizing of the national debt and the creation of the quasi-private bank of the United States to handle the future finances of the country.

Thomas Jefferson had arrived before the bank bill had passed, and he exerted his strongest persuasive powers to convince Congress that the bank was completely unconstitutional. He pointed out that the federal government is restricted to the twenty-five powers listed in Article I, section 8. There is nothing in this provision to suggest that Congress could charter a bank.

However, Hamilton pointed out that this same article concludes by saying that Congress can do anything "necessary or proper" to put these twenty-five powers into operation, and that by giving the Constitution a "loose" interpretation the Congress might consider a bank "necessary and proper."

Jefferson shot back that this was a complete misreading of the provision. It says the Congress can only do things which are "necessary and proper" to put these twenty-five specific powers into operation. He insisted that the Constitution must be "strictly" interpreted according to the original intent of the Founders and no additional powers could be exercised without violating the Tenth Amendment.

But now an interesting thing happened. This important constitutional question was not referred to the Supreme Court but since the Congress favored the view of Hamilton, it simply voted that the bank would be chartered for twenty years.

However, the Supreme Court followed Jefferson's line of argument whenever this issue came up later on, and the Court insisted that Congress could only do what was "necessary and proper" to carry out the twenty-five powers listed in section 8 of Article I. This remained the rule until 1936—during the New Deal days—when the Court arbitrarily reversed itself and took Hamilton's "loose" interpretation to open the floodgates of the U.S. Treasury from which we have never recovered.

An Interesting Dialogue Between Hamilton and John Adams

Alexander Hamilton pounced on every opportunity to emphasize the superiority of the British political system over that of the United States and the Constitution.

One day John Adams, the Vice President under Washington's regime, apparently intended to placate or at least humor the Secretary of the Treasury, so he said:

> "Purge that [British] constitution of its corruption, and give to its popular branch [House of Commons] equality of representation, and it would be the most perfect constitution ever devised by the wit of man."

Hamilton immediately picked up on this comment and said:

> "Purge it of its corruption and give to its popular branch equality of representation, and it would become an *impracticable* government; as it stands at present, with all its supposed defects, it is the most perfect government which ever existed."[22]

Thomas Jefferson, who recorded this conversation, said:

> "Hamilton ... [was] so bewitched and perverted by the British example, as to be under thorough conviction that corruption was essential to the government of a nation."[23]

Jefferson, Franklin, Madison, John Adams and the majority of the Founders were of a completely different stripe. They felt that for political science to be honorable, it had to be honest. When men or women accept favors and then vote contrary to their honest best judgment, the Founders called it "corruption."

Washington's Farewell Address

By 1793 Jefferson felt that Hamilton was adopting policies so out of tune with the original vision of Constitutional government that he resigned in protest and returned to Monticello.

In 1795—after a bout with yellow fever—Hamilton also resigned. He was in low spirits. The Congress had declined to pass his legislation designed to subsidize business enterprises, which was the first of his projects to falter.

22. Ibid.
23. Ibid.

Furthermore, he couldn't support his family on the $3,500 salary paid by the government, so he decided it was a good time to return to New York and once more take up the practice of law. He was always a brilliant practitioner and within a year Hamilton had become the foremost attorney in the city.

Meanwhile, Washington was drawing toward the close of his second term and wanted to leave his best advice to the nation's leaders of the future. This famous treatise became known as Washington's Farewell Address.

After he had sketched out the principal points, he sent the draft to Hamilton who was skillful in preparing documents of this kind.

Of course, Hamilton couldn't resist the temptation to put in a few ideas of his own, but Washington carefully removed anything that wasn't completely in harmony with his own thinking. As James Flexner, Washington's foremost biographer, has said:

> "Almost all of them [Hamilton's personal ideas] came out. Washington also cut out almost all the 'egotisms' which Hamilton ... had inserted in the new manuscript ... The Farewell Address could be considered Hamilton's had it expressed Hamilton's ideas [but] it expressed Washington's. It was as much Washington's as any presidential paper was likely to be that had been drafted by an intimate aide ... The famous paper is correctly called Washington's Farewell Address."[24]

No Political Parties

One of the most significant doctrines set forth in the Farewell Address was Washington's extremely insightful warning concerning the peril of allowing candidates to be nominated and national policies to be promoted by competing political parties. In fact, he prophesied exactly what would happen if the American leaders ever fell into the seductive trap of trying to run the nation with opposing parties. He said:

> "They serve to organize factions ... to put in the place of the delegated will of the nation the will of a party, often a small but artful and enterprising minority ....
>
> "Let me ... warn you in the most solemn manner against the baneful effects of the spirit of party ...."[25]

---

24. James Thomas Flexner, Washington, The Indispensable Man, Boston: Little, Brown and Company, 1974, p. 349.
25. The Annals of America, 1796, Chicago: Encyclopedia Britannica, 1968, 3:610-611.

Washington then went on to predict that if party politics ever became the established way of life in America, we would find that as soon as an election was over the winning party would undergo continual harassment from the losing party, and the losing party would employ every trick and conniving device to prevent the winning party from carrying out the will of the people.

It is interesting that most modern political scientists have shut their eyes to Washington's warnings. They have painted in rose-colored hues the great merits of the two-party system which Americans have struggled to make respectable for over two hundred years. From a well-known college textbook we read:

> "The Founding Fathers ... were unable to see clearly that such organizations, especially if highly competitive, can improve the function of democracy. Parties define the policy alternatives between which voters must choose; they identify, even if vaguely, the will of the majority, they provide a measure of discipline with which to implement majority wishes, and finally, when evenly matched, they tend to keep government reasonably honest, efficient, and responsive to popular will." [26]

The entire history of the political party system in the United States completely repudiates every major premise set forth in this amazing statement. If the best minds in America had been drafted into service around 1835-1850 they could have prevented the Civil War. The two-party system did not.

If our best men with the best minds could have been called to serve and placed in positions of power in time, the United States could have very probably stayed out of two terribly wasteful world wars, and at least two completely unconstitutional wars in Korea and Vietnam. The two-party political system did not avert the political blunders which proved so costly in national treasure and American lives in these wars. In their anxiety for power political leaders deliberately deceived the people. They propagandized the nation into believing "facts" which later proved to be totally false.

George Washington knew precisely how greedy and perniciously ambitious men would exploit the political party system to lead the nation down these crooked paths. He said:

> "The alternate domination of one faction over another, sharpened by the spirit of revenge ... has perpetrated the most horrid enormities ....

26. Norman A. Graebner, et al., A History of the American People, New York: McGraw-Hill Book Company, 1970, p. 243.

> "It [the contention between the parties] serves always to distract the public councils and enfeeble the public administration. It agitates the community with ill-founded jealousies and false alarms, kindles the animosity of one party against another, foments occasional riots and insurrection ... [Party politics] is a spirit not to be encouraged ... there being constant danger of excess ... A fire not to be quenched, it demands a uniform vigilance to prevent its bursting into a flame, lest instead of warming, it should consume."[27]

Party Politics Thrive on Political Spoils

Washington was well aware that political parties are conspiratorial in the sense that they build their power on political spoils. In fact, it is called the "spoils system."

Under the spoils system political leaders try to build up a cadre of supporters by promising jobs, contracts, or other political favors in case they win. But what if there were a change in leadership without any massive vacating of jobs or revolutionary changes in policies and personalities, or payoffs to supporters? That is the way it would be under the Electoral College system set forth in the Constitution.

Political spoils always include an alluring assortment of highly paid political positions. But why should public service positions be so attractive to ambitious and venal-minded individuals?

The Founders' Advice Concerning Compensation Policies

The problem of professional salaries for governmental officials was thoroughly discussed at the Constitutional Convention, and Benjamin Franklin made a powerful speech on the subject. When it came to positions of trust, he felt the high honor should serve as the principal reward. In fact, he said it was his experience that high salaries usually attract scoundrels! He then asked:

> "What kind are the men that will strive for this profitable preeminence, through all the bustle of cabal, the heat of contention, the infinite mutual abuse of parties, tearing to pieces the best of characters?
>
> "It will not be the wise and moderate, the lovers of peace and good order, the men fittest for the trust. It will be the bold and

27. The Annals of America, op. cit., 3:611.

> the violent, the men of strong passions and indefatigable activity in their selfish pursuits. These will thrust themselves into your government, and be your rulers. And these, too, will be mistaken in the expected happiness of their situation; for their vanquished competitors, of the same spirit, and from the same motives, will perpetually be endeavoring to distress their administration, thwart their measures, and render them odious to the people." [28]

While in Europe in 1777, Franklin explained to a friend the widespread feeling of Americans that compensation for civil servants should be modest and that high officials should simply have the "honor" of serving without being paid large salaries. He said:

> "In America, salaries, where indispensable, are extremely low, but much of public business is done gratis. The honor of serving the public ably and faithfully is deemed sufficient. *Public spirit* really exists there, and has great effects." [29]

Long before the Constitutional Convention, Pennsylvania had put the following provision in their State Constitution:

> "As every freeman, to preserve his independence, (if he has not a sufficient estate) ought to have some profession, calling, trade, or farm, whereby he may honestly subsist, there can be no necessity for, nor use in establishing offices of profit; the unusual effects of which are dependence and servility, unbecoming freemen ... Wherefore, whenever an office ... becomes so profitable, as to occasion many to apply for it, the profits ought to be lessened by the legislature." [30]

Can Qualified Volunteers Be Recruited to Accept Positions under the Founders' Original Plan?

Those who are unacquainted with Deuteronomy, chapter 1, and the Mosaic type of political efficiency, may be inclined to doubt that competent, professional people would be willing to serve under such a modest, parsimonious policy of compensation. However, Benjamin Franklin pointed to the High Sheriffs administering the various counties in England, and said:

---

28. Smyth, The Writings of Benjamin Franklin, op. cit., 9:591, and quoted by Allison in The Real Benajmin Franklin, op. cit., p. 447.
29. Ibid., 7:4.
30. Ibid., 6:409.

> "It may be imagined by some that this is a utopian idea, and that we can never find men to serve us in the executive department without paying them well for their services. I conceive this to be a mistake. Some existing facts present themselves to me, which incline me to a contrary opinion.
>
> "The high sheriff of a county in England is an honorable office, but it is not a profitable one. It is rather expensive, and therefore not sought for. But yet it is executed and well executed, and usually by some of the principal gentlemen of the county ....
>
> "I only bring the instance to show that the pleasure of doing good—and serving their country, and the respect such conduct entitles them to—are sufficient motives with some minds to give up a great portion of their time to the public, without the mean inducement of pecuniary satisfaction."[31]

Franklin then went on to point out that in America he, and his associates among the Founders, were all serving without compensation and that the kind of people needed in public service were those who had proven through industry and frugality that they knew how to manage their own affairs and were therefore more likely to be proficient in managing the affairs of the people.[32]

For the Founders, the bottom line was simply "Beware of those who seek public office just because they need a job." To a scandalous extent, those who enter public office poor, retire rich.

Were the Founders' Ideas Too Idealistic to Be Realistic?

In the past two centuries the curse of party politics has fulfilled to the dregs the prophecies of both Washington and Franklin.

Today, every loyal American trying to serve his country in a political office knows how much time and energy must be squandered trying to fend off the avaricious conniving of the opposition party.

Tragically, politics will continue along this dark and dismal pathway until circumstances create such a hopeless crisis that the people will be humbled sufficiently to consider taking the high road under God's law and restoring the original Constitution.

31. Ibid., 9:591; and quoted by Allison in The Real Benajmin Franklin, op. cit., p. 448.
32. Ibid.

What would it be like? We shall talk about it in chapter 31 of this book.

Meanwhile, we must never forget that the divine destiny of America includes the prospects of a brighter day when councils of wise men elected at every level of our society will have the assignment of selecting governors, mayors and other public officials who have proven themselves and feel honored and duty-bound to serve both God and country.

When that happens party politics that have had such a denigrating impact on America will disappear into oblivion. Furthermore, the quality of those who are drafted to serve like the sheriffs of England (cited by Franklin) will serve voluntarily for the most part and become the most efficient public administrators in the world.

How Did Political Parties Get Started in America?

As we have already observed, the Founders emphasized from the beginning that there would be no political parties under the new Constitution. In fact, they set up the Electoral College (discussed in chapter 22) to make political parties unnecessary.

Nevertheless it turned out to be well nigh impossible to prevent competing parties from rising up and taking over the political process.

The Founders themselves had divergent feelings as to the best way to make the new government work. One group wanted to give the central government strong regulatory powers over the states as well as the Union. This group became known as the "Federalist Party."

As we have seen, however, when Thomas Jefferson returned from Europe and saw what was happening, he became so alarmed that he felt compelled to set up the "Democratic Republican Party" to oppose the Federalists and protect the rights of the states.

In the election of 1796, John Adams became President, but Thomas Jefferson got enough votes to be made Vice President. By the next election in 1800, the Federalist party had lost ground so completely it appeared to be headed for extinction. In fact there was a tie vote for two "Republicans." They were Jefferson and Aaron Burr. In this case the Constitution said the House of Representatives should make the final decision. The House voted 36 times without being able to break the tie, and therefore when Hamilton saw what was happening he encouraged some of his friends to withhold their votes so Jefferson would win.

And all of this came just a year after George Washington wrote his famous Farewell Address in which he warned America that it must not split apart into several competing political parties. But the die was cast, and everything Washington predicted concerning opposing political parties literally came to pass.

Perhaps no one quite realized it at the time, but this emerging phenomenon of competing political parties completely doomed the brilliant conception of the Founders' Electoral College and laid the foundation for the abominable spoils system. By the time Andrew Jackson became President, the accepted slogan was "to the victor belong the spoils."[33]

Someday the Electoral College Will Be Restored

As we shall see in the latter part of this study, the day will come when the original Constitution will be restored, and the people will see the tremendous advantage of electing a council of wise men to interview, investigate and evaluate the candidates. A functioning Electoral College will give the people the wisest and most experienced leaders to govern rather than the off-scouring of the competing political party system which very rarely gives the people the quality of leaders they deserve.

33. Marquis James, The Life of Andrew Jackson, New York: Garden City Publishing Co., Inc., 1940, pp. 489-522; Speech of Senator William L. Marcy, John Bartlett, Familiar Quotations, Boston: Little, Brown and Co., 1968, p. 553.

Topics for Reflection and Discussion

1. How many states had to ratify the Constitution before it became operational? Which state fulfilled that requirement? Why did the leaders of that state fear the Constitution would be rejected? Why did Reverend Samuel Langdon say a vote for the Constitution was a vote for the Bible?

2. The Americans didn't have divine manifestations like ancient Israel, but why did Reverend Langdon say the hand of God was clearly manifest in American history? Name three things that impressed you most in Reverend Langdon's final plea.

3. On what date did the United States become a functioning government under the Constitution and open the ballots to see who had been elected President? Who was the Vice President? Whom did Washington appoint Secretary of the Treasury?

4. On what basis did Hamilton consider himself the new Prime Minister of America? What corruption of the political system did he feel was necessary to make government function efficiently? How did he intend to win the support of the states? Whom did he plan to favor in order to set up a bank to handle the finances of the country?

5. How did he plan to win over the leaders of business and industry? Which of the three plans failed to win the support of Congress? Why did Hamilton make a serious mistake hiring William Duer as the Assistant Secretary of the Treasury?

6. Why was Washington delayed in appointing Thomas Jefferson as the new Secretary of State? What was the first shock that Jefferson encountered when he first took over his new job? What was the second? What was Washington's reaction when Jefferson tried to explain why Hamilton had made a serious mistake in monetizing the national debt?

7. Why did Jefferson insist that Hamilton's bank bill was unconstitutional? Whose position did the Supreme Court favor until 1936? What happened to the national debt after the Court reversed itself in favor of Hamilton's interpretation?

8. Why did Washington say political parties would be a handicap to the American people? What did he predict concerning political parties that literally came to pass during the past 200 years? Explain why party politics are so dependent upon political spoils.

9. Why do you think many of the Founders felt the honor of holding a position of trust should be more important than the salary? Was Hamilton able to support his family on the prevailing salary of $3,500 per year for the Secretary of the Treasury?

10. After Hamilton worked up a plan to pay off the national debt in 30 years, why didn't Congress support it? What did Thomas Jefferson do to pay off half of the national debt after he became President? How much is the national debt today? How much interest do we pay every year?

CHAPTER TWENTY-FOUR

Did the Founders Leave Us a Book of Instructions?

Throughout the Constitutional Convention and during the ratification debates there were eloquent declarations concerning the policies that would make the Constitution a success. In fact, throughout their lives, Thomas Jefferson, John Adams, George Washington, James Madison, and certain of the other Founders also took occasion to refer to those moments of inspiration which seemed to give them advance inspiration of how to make the Constitution function successfully.

Unfortunately, these inspired declarations were never codified and published in a formal "book of instructions" or statements of perpetual political policies.

In this chapter we will try to identify some of those instructions, including some we have already discussed. It is not our purpose to provide extensive essays or explanations of these instructions but simply provide a brief statement of the principals they left us and perhaps include a statement or two from the Founders themselves.

Let us begin with a question which profound students of God's law have been asking for over two centuries.

When Should God's Law Be Put into Operation?

The Declaration of Independence was only three months old when Thomas Jefferson proposed to the Virginia Legislature that they adopt a new system of laws. The proposal was adopted October 24, 1776, and a committee was appointed to "revise the laws." The members elected to serve on the committee were Thomas Jefferson, Edmund Pendleton, George Wythe, George Mason and Thomas Ludwell Lee. Jefferson was made chairman and this led Dr. Julian P. Boyd to comment as follows:

> "To be chosen, at the age of thirty-three, head of so important a committee and in competition with some of the finest legal minds in America … agrees with all other surviving evidence as to his leadership and fitness for the work of reform." [1]

1. Boyd, The Papers of Thomas Jefferson, op. cit., 2:314.

The most challenging decision of the committee was to decide whether the people were ready "to abolish the whole existing system of laws, and prepare a new and complete Institute" or whether—at this early stage—they should "preserve the general system and only modify it to the present state of things."[2]

Like most committees, there was hesitation, but Jefferson plunged in and spent many months working with interested members of the committee in rewriting state laws to reflect Biblical principles such as "reparation to the victim" in criminal and tort cases. But the tedious effort was not appreciated by the main body of the legislature. The various proposals failed to pass. Only James Madison seemed to catch the vision of it.

Jefferson was also aware that there were several social problems which had to be solved before God's law could be put into effect. Here were some of the existing road blocks.

Social Requirements for God's Law

Moses had been required to set up a structured society with families divided into tens, fifties, hundreds, thousands, etc.—and with elected captains over each division—before he initiated God's law. There was a serious question in the minds of the Founders whether divine law would even work in a loosely-knit pluralistic society.

As we shall see in a future chapter, Jefferson had diligently tried to structure the states into a system of "wards" or townships—similar to those in New England—but with little success and sometimes with strong resistance. God's law requires a structured society.

God's law also requires a "virtuous" people. What the Founders meant by "virtuous" was far more comprehensive than the way we use that word today. Professor Gordon S. Wood describes what the Founders meant:

> "Each man must somehow be persuaded to submerge his personal wants into the greater good of the whole. This willingness of the individual to sacrifice his private interest for the good of the community—such patriotism or love of country—the eighteenth century termed *public virtue* ... The eighteenth century mind was thoroughly convinced that a popularly based government 'cannot be supported without virtue.'"[3]

2. Ibid.
3. Gordon S. Wood, The Creation of the American Republic, Chapel Hill, N.C.: The University of North Carolina Press, 1969, p. 68.

But of course this is expecting the whole country to have the same spirit of dedication and service as the Founding Fathers. This description fits most of them but what about a nation of ordinary people?

The Founders expected everybody to shape up. In fact, they didn't even think the Constitution would endure without a virtuous people. John Adams said:

> "Our Constitution was made only for a moral and religious people. It is wholly inadequate to the government of any other."[4]

Benjamin Franklin said:

> "Only a virtuous people are capable of freedom. As nations become corrupt and vicious, they have more need of masters."[5]

The Need for Greater Religious Affinity

Then there was the problem of religion. Jefferson suspected that perhaps God's law would not be established until after Biblical Christianity had been restored. This would mean a restoration of Christianity in its original purity. He said:

> "I hold the precepts of Jesus, as delivered by himself, to be the most pure, benevolent, and sublime which have ever been preached to men … If the freedom of religion guaranteed to us by law in theory can ever rise in practice … truth will prevail over fanaticism, and the genuine doctrines of Jesus … will again be restored to their original purity. This reformation will advance with the other improvements of the human mind, but too late for me to witness it."[6]

So the practice of God's law was coming but sometime in the future—after the restoration of Biblical Christianity.

What Would Prevent God's Law from Being Adopted Now?

Sometimes when I lecture on the coming epoch of God's law, people will say, "But trying to inaugurate so many changes is too idealistic. In fact its unrealistic. The country would never vote for it. The political parties wouldn't

4. Howe, The Changing Political Thoughts of John Adams, op. cit., p. 189.
5. Smyth, The Writings of Benjamin Franklin, op. cit., 9:569.
6. Bergh, The Writings of Thomas Jefferson, op. cit., 15:288.

allow it. The big banks wouldn't allow it. The major corporations wouldn't allow it. Hollywood wouldn't allow it. The liberal medial wouldn't allow it."

To all of this, I simply say, "They would in a time of extreme crisis."

All down through history, God has succeeded in humbling great nations when it was necessary to achieve his righteous purposes. When the time is right, it will happen to America.

The most important thing for America—when the crisis strikes—is to have enough people who know what to do.

It will be as it was with the Sons of Issachar during a crisis described in the Bible. The scripture says the Sons of Issachar were the smallest of the tribes but they "had understanding of the times, to know what Israel ought to do."[7]

Even though there were only 200 ready to take charge, it was enough to restore the confidence of the other tribes and the whole people of approximately three million Israelites "were at their commandment."[8]

In the thirty-first chapter of this book we will discuss what America will be like after the Constitution is restored. That is the first step in preparing for the setting up of God's law.

Sound Economics

Having the people trained in sound economic principles is also a preliminary requirement for God's law.

In *The Making of America* there is a section devoted to the Founders' basic policies on "Prosperity Economics."[9] From the Founders' perspective Adam Smith of Scotland and England could not have chosen a better time to publish his comprehensive study of economics. The book was called, *Inquiry Into the Nature and Causes of the Wealth of Nations* and it was published in 1776.

Adam Smith undertook to set forth a technical analysis of various economic systems and also describe ways to encourage free enterprise and individual initiative.

This was interpreted by the Founding Fathers to mean the government intervention should be minimal. But at the same time government policy

7. 1 Chronicles 12:32.
8. Ibid.
9. Skousen, The Making of America, op. cit., pp. 203-220.

should protect the four main freedoms for a healthy, progressive economy. These are:

1. Freedom to *try* so that new products and markets are continually developed.

2. Freedom to *buy* so that as new products are invented and developed they can be welcomed into the market.

3. Freedom to *sell* so that there is a continuous incentive to enlarge the market.

4. Freedom to *fail* so that poor products and inefficient management cannot get subsidies but will be compelled to improve that sector of the market or automatically disappear from the scene.

The past two centuries have demonstrated the wisdom of these four freedoms wherever they have been allowed to flourish. However, a continuous war has often been waged against them by vested interests clamoring to secure some illegal or unethical advantage.

Adam Smith taught that whenever the free market is being invaded by these illegitimate elements, the government has the responsibility to intervene and protect the integrity of the market. The power of the government is needed in these situations to:

1. Prevent the use of force in the market place. In other words, to intervene wherever legitimate buyers and sellers are intimidated by certain political or economic power structures which attempt to interfere with the normal operation of the free market. Organized labor, business cartels, or government agencies operating outside of the legitimate sphere of influence come under this category.

2. Prevent fraud which is misrepresenting the quality, location, or ownership of goods and services which are being bought or sold.

3. Prevent monopoly of goods or resources so that the advantages of normal competition is smothered or new enterprises are being stifled.

4. Prevent the debauchery of society by those who use vice, drugs, alcohol, pornography, gambling or any other commercial channels to exploit human weakness or promote degradation of society.

It is interesting that when Alexander Hamilton became Secretary of the Treasury and based his policies on England's philosophy of using political favors to manipulate the economic and political structure of the United

States, his sister-in-law, Angelica Schuyler Church, gave him a copy of Adam Smith's classical book in hopes it would influence his thinking.[10] He is said to have read the book, but obviously it had no influence over his policies.[11]

Hamilton's policies became an American hallmark during the past two centuries, particularly after the Civil War when widespread intermeddling—both politically and economically—was virtually thrust upon the United States as she rose to become the most powerful nation in the world. On occasion ambitious political leaders have involved America in unconstitutional wars, and borrowed billions to provide massive foreign aid to military dictatorships. These reckless adventures into foreign alliances have propelled the United States in horrible world wars, and numerous mini-wars which the Founders would never have contemplated.

When the Constitution is restored, the United States will no longer be taxing its people and spending the next generation's legacy to be the Santa Claus of the world and the policeman of the world, nor will it be treading along a precipice of imminent bankruptcy. It will have minimal taxes, a much less complicated society, and exist as a strong exemplary member of the community of nations, helping where it can, but otherwise minding its own business.

The Policy of Making All Americans Free and Equal

When Thomas Jefferson was twenty-five years old he was elected to the legislature of Virginia, and from then on throughout his life he tried to conjure up some kind of plan to get rid of slavery.

Eventually, Jefferson had the opportunity to write his first draft for the new constitution of Virginia. In that draft he provided that from the very day this new constitution was ratified, every child born in Virginia would be born free.[12]

Had the Virginia legislature accepted this suggestion it could have set an example for the rest of the states and changed the history of the country. Within one generation slavery would have been erased. It would have been accomplished without a war, and without any expense to the taxpayers to buy the freedom of the slaves as some had suggested. Furthermore, it would have given the free-born children time to be trained and get educated so they could find their place in the competitive work force of an agricultural society.

---

10. Emery, Alexander Hamilton, An Intimate Portrait, op. cit, p. 143.
11. Ibid.
12. Skousen, The Making of America, op. cit., p. 466.

But Virginia hesitated. Some said the plan had to have time to gestate, but at least the idea had been planted. Somehow there had to be a way to solve this, the most aggravating problem in the nation.

By the time the Constitution of the United States was being written it was assumed that since all of the states had accepted the declaration that all men are created equal it would not be long before slavery would be outlawed. The Founders book of instructions definitely pointed in that direction, and except for three states it could very well have happened at the time the Constitution was adopted.

Here is the story.

Slavery in America

Originally all of the colonies had slaves and bond servants. The slave market in Boston was located on the Boston Common.

The first slaves arrived in Jamestown in 1619 on a Dutch boat and were sold to the settlers who were just learning how to cultivate a new sweet variety of tobacco. But as time went on, it was the British who virtually monopolized the importation of slaves to America.

Nevertheless, almost from the beginning religious leaders of nearly all faiths had bitterly campaigned against slavery. It is interesting that when some of the states, including Virginia, tried to terminate any further importation of slaves it was the British Parliament that prevented it. The Declaration of Independence specifically mentions this in its bill of particulars against the British.

Of course, the agricultural South had the major population of slaves but it was also in the South that some of the foremost leaders arose who wanted to root it out. Thomas Jefferson was one of them.

It is also interesting that more slaves were given their freedom in the South than in the North, and this was by the voluntary initiative of their owners rather than by legislation. By 1760 the Southern States had 53% of the freed slaves throughout the country and the percentage would have been much higher if it had included the large number of freed slaves in the South who had gone north.[13]

Pulitzer-prize winning historian Fred A. Shannon adds a surprising note when he says:

---

13. Fred Albert Shannon, Economic History of the People of the United States, New York: The Macmillan Company, 1934, p. 318.

> "Many of the Negroes, especially in Louisiana, Virginia, South Carolina and Maryland, were well-to-do or rich, some had plantations, and thousands of them were owners of slaves ... Other accounts tell of a South Carolina Negro in 1790 who owned 200 slaves and had a white wife and [white] son-in-law ... Cyrpien Richard, a Louisiana Negro, bought a plantation and 91 slaves for about a quarter of a million dollars." [14]

The Northwest Ordinance Outlaws Slavery in That Region

While the Constitutional Convention was sweating it out in Philadelphia, the members of Congress were convened in New York where they passed the Northwest Ordinance on July 13, 1787. This ordinance provided that there would be no slavery allowed in this north eastern region or in the future states carved out of this territory.[15]

Only one congressional delegate voted against the ordinance and he was from New York.[16]

So what about the rest of the country?

The Constitutional Convention Wrestles with the Slavery Issue

There seemed to be a general consensus at the Constitutional Convention that since outlawing slavery for the entire nation would immediately divide north and south, it would prevent the adoption of the Constitution. Therefore abolitionists realized they must tread lightly and take it a step at a time.

It was decided to start out by simply outlawing the further importation of slaves. Perhaps the complete abolition of slavery could come later. But the two "swamp" states, South Carolina, and Georgia vehemently objected. They said rice and indigo were the heart of their economy and unless they had cheap labor in the form of newly imported slaves they could not compete.

These two states were adamant in their position and said they would stay out of the union if this provision passed. North Carolina said she would join them if they were forced into this extreme position.

Madison felt the union of all thirteen states was imperative and he therefore invited the two states to propose a compromise. They said that

14. Ibid., p. 325.

15. Samuel Eliot Morison, The Oxford History of the American People, New York: Oxford University Press, 1965, pp. 300-301.

16. Ibid.

if they were allowed twenty years to adjust their economy then they could absorb this restriction without committing economic suicide. In other words, they would accept the restriction on importation of slaves providing no action was taken by Congress until 1808.[17]

So that's the way it reads in the Constitution.[18]

It is clear from the record that this compromise not only preserved the union of all thirteen states but it was considered by many delegates to be the constitutional authority by which the Congress would get jurisdiction over slavery by 1808 and not only outlaw the importations of slaves but eventually outlaw the "whole abominable institution" of slavery.

As James Madison said:

> "It were doubtless to be wished that the power of prohibiting the importation of slaves had not been postponed until the year 1808 … but … it ought to be considered as a great point in favor of humanity that a period of twenty year may terminate forever … a traffic which has so long and so loudly upbraided the barbarism of modern policy … within that period it may be totally abolished." [19]

James Wilson, along with others,[20] hoped 1808 would bring about the end of slavery in the United States. He said:

> "Yet the lapse of a few years, and Congress will have the power to exterminate slavery from within our borders." [21]

One of the Worst Tragedies in American History

But by 1808 the Founding Fathers were no longer running the Congress. The most recently elected Congress obediently passed a law prohibiting any further importation of slaves as the Constitution had stipulated, but the states had already done this.

What the Congress failed to do—as Madison, Wilson and other had expected—was to take its jurisdiction over the issue of slavery and terminate "the whole abominable institution" as the Northwest Ordinance had done.

---

17. Farrand, The Records of the Federal Convention of 1787, op. cit., 2:436.
18. Article I, Section 9, clause 1.
19. Madison, Federalist Papers, op. cit., Number 42, p. 266.
20. Elliot, Jonathan, ed., The Debates in the Several State Conventions, Philadelphia: J. B. Lippincott Co., 1901, 2:484, and quoted by Skousen in The Making of America, op. cit., pp. 468-469.
21. Ibid., 10:284.

At the very least it could have followed Jefferson's moderate approach and declared that henceforth every child born in the United States would be born free. As mentioned earlier, that would have eliminated slavery in one generation and would have done it without war, without any expense to the taxpayers, and would have allowed the new generation of free-born Blacks to follow George Washington Carver's example by seeking an education and integrating themselves in the competitive American work force.

But the Congress of 1808 did nothing. It was one of the most tragic mistakes in the history of the United States. Fifty-two years later the United States began paying for this blunder with the blood of hundreds of thousands of lives.

The Difficult Policy of "No Entangling Alliances"

If there was any one thing on which the Founders all appeared completely united it was the iron-clad determination to stay free of any entangling alliances with foreign nations.

They didn't mind trade alliances but becoming entangled in any kind of diplomatic, political, or military alliance was equated with a lethal dose of Constitutional cyanide. These few quotes from the Founders themselves will make their position clear.

George Washington said:

> "It is our true policy to steer clear of permanent alliances with any portion of the foreign world."[22]

Europe had been in constant military turmoil for over a thousand years, and therefore he said:

> "I hope the United States will be able to keep disengaged from the labyrinth of European politics and war."[23]

Thomas Jefferson said:

> "I have ever deemed it fundamental for the United States never to take part in the quarrels of Europe. Their political interests are entirely distinct from ours. Their mutual jealousies, their balance of power, their complicated alliances, their forms and principles of government are all foreign to us.

22. Parry and Allison, The Real George Washington, op. cit., p. 687.
23. Ibid., p. 685.

> "They are nations of eternal war. All their energies are expended in the destruction of the labor, property, and lives of their people.
>
> "On our part, never had a people so favorable a chance of trying the opposite system of peace and fraternity with mankind, and the direction of all our means and faculties to the purposes of improvement instead of destruction." [24]

The Monroe Doctrine

But the Founders had barely laid down these strict resolutions of virtual isolationism when some hard questions arose.

What happens when Latin American countries begin to gain their independence and European nations get ready to retaliate or even expand their holdings?

Responding to this challenge, President Monroe delivered a message to Congress on December 2, 1823, announcing that the United States would not interfere with those colonies which had not struck for independence, but any effort by any foreign nation to regain or expand its influence on the American Continent would be treated as a threat to the peace of the United States.

Thus the Monroe Doctrine was born.[25]

Thomas Jefferson had also said:

> "Although we have no right to intermeddle with the form of government of other nations, yet it is lawful to wish to see no emperors nor kings in our hemisphere ...." [26]

But widespread intermeddling both politically and economically was virtually thrust upon the United States as she rose to become the most powerful nation in the world. Wars of intervention, foreign aid, and the defense of democratic nations against massive, rapidly expanding dictatorships propelled the United States into horrible world wars and numerous mini-wars the Founders would never have contemplated.

How the American leaders wished there had been something in the Founders' book of instructions to help them deal wisely with all of these crises.

---

24. Allison, The Real Thomas Jefferson, op. cit., p. 440.
25. Graebner, A History of the American People, op. cit., p. 335.
26. Allison, The Real Thomas Jefferson, op. cit., p. 443.

When the Constitution is restored the United States will no longer be taxing its people and spending the next generation's legacy to be the Santa Claus of the world and the policeman of the world, nor will it be treading along a precipice of imminent bankruptcy. It will have minimal taxes, a much less complicated society, and exist as a strong, exemplary member of the community of nations, helping where it can, but otherwise minding its own business.

National Debt

As the infant United States came out of the Revolutionary War she found herself burdened by a mountain of indebtedness—at least, a huge indebtedness for those days.

Of course, since it was a new government, the Europeans expected the Americans to abrogate or cancel their past debts as other countries did when they had a revolution or set up a new government.

But the Founding Fathers did not follow that European example of fraudulent behavior. Instead, they assured the world that the United States would accept full responsibility for the payment of all its war debts, and even assume responsibility for the war debts of the states. They put it right in the Constitution.[27]

This brings us to the Founders' philosophy of paying off its national debts. Thomas Jefferson said:

> "We shall all consider ourselves unauthorized to saddle posterity with our debts, and morally bound to pay them ourselves; and consequently within what may be deemed the period of a generation or life of the majority."[28]

George Washington was just as emphatic:

> "As a very important source of strength and security, cherish public credit. One method of preserving it is to use it as sparingly as possible … avoiding likewise the accumulation of debt, not only of shunning occasions of expense, but by vigorous exertion in time of peace to discharge the debts which unavoidable wars may have occasioned."[29]

27. Article VI, Section 1.
28. Edwin Morris Betts and James Adam Bear, Jr., ed., The Family Letters of Thomas Jefferson, Columbia, Mo.: University of Mississippi Press, 1966, p. 43, and quoted by Skousen in The Making of America, op. cit., p. 394.
29. Parry and Allison, The Real George Washington, op. cit., p. 742.

And a final thought from Jefferson:

> "The principle of spending money to be paid by posterity, under the name of funding, is but swindling futurity on a large scale."[30]

When Jefferson became President in 1801, he knew Congress had passed new taxes in hopes of paying something on the national debt. But, as usually happens, Congress spent the money on other things as fast as it accumulated. But Thomas Jefferson not only preached, he practiced. Immediately upon becoming President he repealed several obnoxious taxes and promptly announced he would start paying off the war debt.

How could he do it?

His plan was to sell large tracts of public land and use the proceeds to apply to the debt. By this means during the eight years he was in the White House, Jefferson paid off half the national debt. When Andrew Jackson became President he picked up where Jefferson left off and paid off the rest of the debt by selling public lands.

The Founders Advice: Don't Transact Government Business Through Private Banks

Of course, the big question concerning massive government borrowing arises when an emergency faces the nation such as an impending war. What is the best course of action? In the beginning there was a wide disparity of opinion between Hamilton and Jefferson, particularly on the subject of banks.

Hamilton adored the institutions of England including the Bank of England which was incorporated by Parliament in 1694. It was a privately-owned bank—in spite of its name—and the British government leaned heavily upon it when major loans were necessary. Hamilton felt this was just what the United States needed and he therefore sponsored the Bank of the United States—also a private bank—and offered stock to the members of Congress if they would vote for it.[31]

Jefferson strongly protested and even resigned as Secretary of State because he considered the Bank of the United States an unconstitutional blunder.

The bank began pouring out vast quantities of paper money—far more than could be redeemed in gold and silver. Jefferson felt Hamilton had

30. Bergh, The Writings of Thomas Jefferson, op. cit., 15:23, and quoted by Skousen in The Making of America, op. cit., p. 394.

31. Allison, The Real Thomas Jefferson, op. cit., p. 166.

deceived the President in getting him to sign the bank bill and feared the nation was facing an impending calamity. In 1796 he said:

> "We are completely saddled and bridled, and the bank is so firmly mounted on us that we must go where they will guide."[32]

The following year as Washington was approaching the end of his second term, Jefferson wrote:

> "It was impossible the bank and paper mania should not produce a great and extensive ruin. The President (Washington) is fortunate to get off just as the bubble is bursting, leaving others to hold the bag."[33]

But by this time even Alexander Hamilton recognized that the bank and its "paper money mania" was a grave mistake. On August 22, 1798, he wrote to Oliver Wolcott, the Secretary of the Treasury, urging the United States to abandon the plan he had concocted and return to the original idea expressed at the Constitutional Convention.[34]

Jefferson ventured to suggest that the country immediately go back and do it right. He said:

> "... could we not make a beginning towards our own bank [the U.S Treasury], and letting the treasurer give his draft or note … which in a well-conducted government ought to have as much credit as any private draft, or bank note?..."[35]

However, most of the country did not feel the same degree of anxiety as Jefferson. Both businesses and individuals had become accustomed to the operation of the Bank of the United States and so it was allowed to run out its legally allotted term of twenty years.

Jefferson's Advice: Borrow from the People, Not the Banks

Meanwhile, Jefferson had been trying to teach the people how the government could borrow in an emergency without having to get the money from private banks and pay them exorbitant interest rates. Here is what he wrote in 1813, after the Bank of the United States had ceased to exist and Jefferson had paid off half of the national debt during his two terms as President:

---

32. Ibid., p. 354.
33. Ibid.
34. Henry Cabot Lodge, ed., The Works of Alexander Hamilton, New York: G.P. Putnam's Sons, 1904, 10:317.
35. Allison, The Real Thomas Jefferson, op. cit., p. 355.

> "It is a wise rule, and should be fundamental in a government disposed to cherish its credit … never to borrow a dollar without laying a tax in the same instant for paying the interest annually and the principal within a given term ….
>
> "On such a pledge as this, sacredly observed, a government may always command, on a reasonable interest all the lendable money of their citizens ….
>
> "But the term of redemption must be moderate, and at a rate within the limits of their rightful powers ….
>
> "The period of a generation, or the term of its life, is determined by the laws of mortality … In seeking then for an ultimate term for the redemption of our debts, let us rally to this principle, and provide for their payments within the term of nineteen years at the furtherest."[36]

When the Constitution is restored, the U.S. Treasury will be the official national bank with branch banks in the states. Top-rated loans with substantial collateral will be granted at extremely low interest rates and profits will go to the general fund of the Treasury to cut down on taxes. Branch banks will give their profits to the states in which they operate for the purpose of reducing state taxes.

Higher risk loans can be made through private banks but the interest rate will be correspondingly higher.

To Be Constitutional, Money must Be Based on Gold and Silver

The Founders' book of instructions is very specific about the need to have an honest money system based on gold and silver. The Constitution specifically states:

> "No state shall make anything but gold and silver coin as tender in payments of debts."[37]

This provision automatically made all transaction throughout the United States payable in gold and silver. Thomas Jefferson explained why this protected the people in ways that no other medium of exchange could accomplish:

36. Ibid., pp. 394-395.
37. Article I, Section 10, clause 1 of the Constitution.

> "Specie [gold and silver] is the most perfect medium because it will preserve its own level; because having intrinsic and universal value, it can never die in our hands; and it is the surest resource of reliance in time of war." [38]

The standard of gold and silver as the base for our monetary system deteriorated completely over the past sixty years. We now know it was actually part of the plan of those who sponsored the Federal Reserve System, but they knew it violated the Constitution and would be resisted by the people. Therefore they carefully planned to make the changes very gradually in times of crises so the people would accept it more readily as a response to the prevailing emergency. Here, then, is the story of what happened to our money.

1. From 1914 to 1934 every Federal Reserve note was redeemable in gold and silver.

2. April 5, 1933, one month after his inauguration, President Franklin D. Roosevelt declared a national emergency and ordered all gold coins, gold bullion, and gold certificates to be turned into the Federal Reserve banks by May 1. This did not apply to foreigners living abroad.

3. As all forms of gold and gold certificates were surrendered to the Federal Reserve, people received their value in silver certificates.

4. On January 30, 1934, the Gold Reserve Act was passed giving the Federal Reserve—a consortium of private banks—full title to all the gold which had been collected. This act also changed the price of gold from $20.67 per ounce to $35 per ounce which meant that all of the silver certificates the people had received for their gold had lost 40 percent of their value.

5. On June 24, 1968, President Johnson issued a proclamation that henceforth Federal Reserve silver certificates could not be redeemed in silver. That meant that if you surrendered a silver certificate you received a Federal Reserve note in exchange.

6. On March 16, 1973, Congress set the American dollar completely afloat with nothing to back it up except the declaration on the face of each note that it was "legal tender." Since that time the value of the dollar has fluctuated up and down depending on how much confidence the foreign exchanges have in the stability of the American economy. Should the economy go into a slump, the value of the dollar could rapidly fall.

38. Allison, The Real Thomas Jefferson, op. cit., pp. 551-552.

Today, the American economy operates under a monetary system which is completely outside the Constitution. Its fiat money is continually manipulated both in value and in quantity.

This has had a devastating impact on the purchasing power of the dollar since 1933. It will now buy only 8% of what it would purchase in 1933 when we first began the process of forsaking constitutional money. Some of us still remember those days when ten cents would buy a loaf of bread, fifteen cents would buy a quart of milk and twenty-five dollars would buy a Brooks suit.

This process of depriving Americans of constitutional money has unconscionably and immorally eroded the value of savings, insurance policies, retirement funds and the fixed incomes of the elderly.

The Senate Was Set up under the Constitution to Protect States Rights

The Tenth Amendment reads:

> "All powers not specifically delegated to the Congress of the United States by this Constitution, nor prohibited to the states by the Constitution, are reserved to the states or to the people."

Congress specifically designated the United States Senate to be the watchdog over states rights and enforcement of this amendment.

This was achieved by having the state legislatures appoint the Senators who would represent them. Each one is appointed for a term of six years, and it was expected that these senatorial representatives would mature into astute statesmen both for the state they represented and the government in general.

That is why the Founders gave the Senate certain executive responsibilities in addition to its legislative duties. The Constitution states that before major appointments by the President can take effect they must be approved by the Senate. This is also true of treaties. Before they become law they must be subject to the "advice and consent" of the Senate.

It has been observed down through history that the masses of the people, and consequently their surrogates in the House of Representatives, tend to propose legislation of the more sensational and impulsive variety which is momentarily popular with their constituents but which a careful study and additional experience will prove undesirable if not downright dangerous.

It was therefore the intent of the Founders to set up the Congress so the House of Representatives would be sensitive and responsive to the needs of the people while the Senate would have a "cooling effect" and insist on testing the validity of impulsive legislation before it was approved and sent to the President for his signature.

This analytical and restrictive quality of the Senate rendered inestimable value through the years but after the Civil War there was a continuous drive to have the Senate elected as a representative body of the people rather than appointed by the state legislatures.

Although this proposal seriously unbalanced the original inspired and evenhanded distribution of power as envisioned by the Founders, the Seventeenth Amendment was finally passed and became part of the Constitution on April 8, 1915.

Since that time, the State legislatures have had no direct representation in Congress. Instead, we have the people of each state with double representation—once in the House and once in the Senate. So the Senate no longer represents the legislatures of the states but merely the people just like the House of Representatives.

When the Constitution is restored the Senate will once more be answerable to the state legislatures and the original constitutional balance will be restored.

Elected Officials Should Be Allowed to Serve as Long as the People Wish to Re-Elect Them.

During the Constitutional Convention there were several attempts to put limitations on the length of time a particular official could serve. In each case the proposal was rejected. However, after President Franklin Delano Roosevelt was elected four times and finally died in office, the twenty-second amendment was passed which said:

> "No person shall be elected to the office of President of the United States more than twice."

At the time this seemed to be a reasonable provision but when President Ronald Reagan was serving he found that right at the time he was fighting to end the Cold War with the Soviet Union, his effectiveness during his second term was seriously impeded by the fact that he was a "lame duck" President and his presidency would soon be over.

He reported that even though he did not want to run for a third term, the possibility that he could run—and might have run—would have kept many forces in line that undertook to thwart the important work he was trying to accomplish.

When the Constitution is restored, there will be no term limits on any elected officer of the United States government.

Conclusion

After more than two hundred years of experience with the legacy of the American system we can look back and historically analyze what we have done to ourselves. We need to get back on track.

It reminds me of one time when I ordered a bicycle for one of my boys from a Sears catalogue. It came unassembled and inside was a large sheet of paper which said:

"Having any trouble?

When all else fails, read the instructions."

That's where we are today. Our instructions are in the original Constitution and the writings of the Founding Fathers.

Topics for Reflection and Discussion

1. Can you think of three things that must occur before God's law can be put into operation? What has happened in the past to humble nations and make them a "virtuous" people? What are the four economic freedoms Adam Smith said each country should try to preserve?

2. How was the Electoral College designed to select a better quality of public servant than the political party system? List two reasons why Washington said competing political parties were a threat to the future welfare of the nation.

3. When did Thomas Jefferson first try to eliminate slavery? What did he propose which would have eliminated slavery in one generation and accomplish it without a war or any expenses to the taxpayer?

4. When did the first slaves arrive in the American colonies? Who prevented the colonists from outlawing the importation of slaves? Were more slaves set free in the South or in the North? Did many of the freed slaves have plantations and slaves of their own?

5. How many states voted to outlaw slavery when the Northwest Ordinance was passed in 1787? Why were the Founders so opposed to foreign entangling alliances? Why was it difficult to avoid them? What is your understanding of the Monroe Doctrine?

6. Give two of Jefferson's main objections to the government accumulating a heavy national debt. When Jefferson became President, what steps did he take to cut the national debt in half?

7. Why did Jefferson want the government to conduct its fiscal affairs through the U.S. Treasury rather than private banks? In case of an emergency, how did Jefferson propose to borrow from the people instead of the banks?

8. Which President confiscated the people's gold in 1933 and gave them paper certificates in return? The gold was then turned over to whom? What does the Constitution say about gold and silver as a medium of exchange in the United States? Is our present money system completely outside of the requirements of the Constitution?

9. How does the current buying power of tith the U.S. dollar of 1933? How much was bread back then? Milk? A Brooks suit?

10. Were the Founding Fathers in favor of term limitations? What was their reason? What did President Reagan say about it?

CHAPTER TWENTY-FIVE

America's Manifest Destiny Grounded on 28 Principles

In addition to the specific instructions left by the Founders concerning the Constitution, there were certain basic principles scattered among their writings which they described as "indispensable" for America's future survival.

By carefully noting each of these principles it became apparent that these guidelines were the Founders' inspired roadmap by which they hoped to attain America's divine or "manifest destiny."

These principles also turned out to be the perfect litmus test by which to judge any new legislation. If an act or a legislative proposal violates any of these principles it is defective. For this reason, people going into politics or public service will find these 28 principles the best advice—the most "indispensable" advice—the Founders Fathers could leave with them.[1]

Principle Number One

The only basis for sound government is Natural Law.

Natural law is God's law. There are certain laws which govern the entire universe, and just as Thomas Jefferson said in the Declaration of Independence, there are laws which govern in the affairs of men which are "the laws of nature and of nature's God."

The Founders agreed with Cicero who felt that the first and most important law is to recognize the supremacy of God in the universe. The second law is to treat all others as one would like to be treated. Cicero was a pagan but he couldn't have said it better as a prophet or apostle.

Cicero said since God is universal, his law is universal. It cannot be amended and if it is violated there are unavoidable consequences.

1. These principles were compiled into a book by the present author entitled, The Five Thousand Year Leap. (visit: *www.skousen2000.com*).

He said a principle of God's law is easy to recognize because it is reasonable and morally right. Man's gift of reason was given to him to reflect God's capacity to reason. It is a divine quality which man and God share in common.

Principle Number Two

A free people cannot survive under a republican constitution unless they remain virtuous and morally strong.

As we previous quoted Benjamin Franklin as saying:

> "Only a virtuous people are capable of freedom. As nations become corrupt and vicious, they have more need of masters."[2]

Washington warned that the Constitution could only survive so long as there was public virtue in the people.[3]

Professor Gordon S. Wood gives us a good definition of public virtue. He says:

> "[Each person] must somehow be persuaded to submerge his personal wants into the greater good of the whole. This willingness of the individual to sacrifice his private interest for the good of the community—such patriotism or love of country—the eighteenth century mind termed public virtue ... A popularly based government cannot be supported without virtue."[4]

The Founders were praying people, but Samuel Adams, the "Father of the Revolution," said:

> "If we would most truly enjoy the gift of Heaven, let us become a virtuous people; then shall we both deserve and enjoy it."[5]

Principle Number Three

The most promising method of securing a virtuous people is to elect virtuous leaders.

Samuel Adams pointed to a sobering fact concerning political survival as a free people when he said:

> "Neither the wisest constitution nor the wisest laws will secure the liberty and happiness of a people whose manners are univer-

2. Smyth, The Writings of Benjamin Franklin, op. cit., 9:569.
3. Saul K. Padover, ed., The Washington Papers, New York: Harper & Brothers, 1955, p. 244.
4. Wood, The Creation of the American Republic, op. cit., p. 68.
5. Wells, The Life and Public Service of Samuel Adams, op. cit., 1:22-23.

> sally corrupt. He therefore is the truest friend to the liberty of his country who tries most to promote its virtue, and who … will not suffer a man to be chosen into any office of power and trust who is not a wise and virtuous man."[6]

He then went on to say that public officials should not only be virtuous but they should have demonstrated that they have the experience and training to fulfill the office effectively.

All of this is set forth under God's law as described in Deuteronomy, chapter 1, verse 13.

PRINCIPLE NUMBER FOUR

Without religion the government of a free people cannot be maintained.

In Washington's famous Farewell Address he said:

> "Of all the dispositions and habits which lead to political prosperity, religion and morality are indispensable supports … And let us with caution indulge the supposition that morality can be maintained without religion."[7]

The emphasis of the Founders was primarily on the Bible rather than creeds. When Benjamin Franklin was asked by Ezra Stiles, President of Yale University, to enunciate his religious beliefs, he wrote:

> "I believe in one God, the Creator of the universe. That he governs it by his providence. That he ought to be worshipped. That the most acceptable service we render to him is in doing good to his other children. That the soul of man is immortal and will be treated with justice in another life respecting its conduct in this. These I take to be the fundamental points in all sound religion."[8]

When the Northwest Ordinance was pass by Congress in 1787, it required that "religion, morality and knowledge" be taught in the schools. The "religion" was to emphasize universal principles rather than the creed of any particular denomination. Based on Franklin's "fundamental points in all sound religion," we find the schools teaching five major religious principles:

1. There exists a Creator who made all things, and mankind should recognize and worship Him.

---

6. Ibid.
7. The Annals of America, op. cit., 3:612.
8. Smyth, The Writings of Benjamin Franklin, op. cit., 10:84.

2. The Creator has revealed a moral code of behavior for happy living which distinguishes right from wrong.

3. The Creator holds mankind responsible for the way they treat each other.

4. All mankind live beyond this life.

5. In the next life mankind are judged for their conduct in this one.

Thomas Jefferson said these basic beliefs are the principles "in which God has united us all."[9]

Principle Number Five

All things were created by God, therefore upon him all mankind are equally dependent, and to him they are equally responsible.

In his Essay Concerning Human Understanding, John Locke said everyone can know there is a God. All a person has to do is think.

To begin with, each person knows that he or she exists. With Descartes each person can say, "Cogito ergo sum" ("I am a conscious thinking being, therefore I know that I am.") With God each person can say, "*I am*!"

Furthermore, each person knows that he or she is *something*. And each person knows a *something* could not be produced by a *nothing*. Therefore, whatever brought mankind and everything else into existence also had to be *something*.

It follows that this *something* which did all of this organizing would have to be all-knowing to the full extent required for such an achievement.

This *something* would therefore have to be superior to everything which it organized. This superiority makes this *something* the ultimate "good" and in the Anglo-Saxon language, the word for supreme good is "God."

We can get to know God by analyzing ourselves.

The Creator would have to be a reasoning being with a sense of compassion and love for he gave mankind these sublime qualities.

The Creator would also have a sense of right and wrong and feel indignation or anger when "right conduct" is violated. Since mankind were made in the "image of God" we know the Creator has a sense of humor, and a sense of

9. Bergh, The Writings of Thomas Jefferson, op. cit., 14:198.

beauty. The Creator has organized everything according to fantastic qualities of form, color and contrasts.

The American Founding Fathers agreed with Locke. They considered the existence of the Creator as the most fundamental premise underlying *all* self-evident truth. They felt a person who boasted he or she was an atheist had just simply failed to apply his or her divine capacity for reason and observation.

Principle Number Six

All mankind were created equal.

Everyone knows that no two human beings were created exactly alike in any respect. Each one is born with different looks, different tastes, different skills. They are different in physical strength, mental capacity, emotional stability, in their inherited social and economic status, their opportunities for self-fulfillment and scores of other ways.

Then how can they be equal?

They can't except in three ways, and in these three ways they are treated as equals. The Founders knew that all mankind are theoretically treated as:

1. Equal before God.
2. Equal before the law.
3. Equal in the protection of their rights.

The highest goal of any society is to see that these principles of equality become a reality.

Principle Number Seven

The proper role of government is to protect equal rights, not provide equal things.

The Founders recognized that the people cannot delegate to their government any power except that which they have the lawful right to exercise themselves.

For example, every person is entitled to the protection of life, liberty and property. Therefore it is perfectly legitimate to set up a police force to protect these unalienable rights.

But suppose a kind-hearted man saw that one of his neighbors has two cars while another neighbor has none. What would happen if, in a spirit of benevolence, the kind-hearted man went over and took one of the cars from his prosperous neighbor and generously gave it to the neighbor in need? Obviously, he would be arrested for car theft. No matter how kind his intention, he is guilty of flagrantly violating the natural rights of his prosperous neighbor who is entitled to the protection of his property.

Of course, the two-car neighbor could donate a car to his poor neighbor if he liked, but that is his decision to dispose of his property, not that of his well-meaning neighbor who wanted to make things a little more equal in the neighborhood.

But suppose the kind-hearted man decided to ask the mayor and city council to force the man with two cars to give one to his pedestrian neighbor? Does that make it any more legitimate? Obviously, that makes it worse, because the mayor and the council are assigned to make the law and if they start redistributing people's property as a matter of law, the owner of two cars not only loses one of his cars, but "the law" would have destroyed his right to get his property back.

One of the worst sins a government can commit against God's law is to get the idea that it is more "just" to take from the haves and give to the have-nots. It is equally sinful for a government to think it has a duty to make everybody equal in "things." I have a neighbor with thirty cows. Under no circumstances do I want one of his cows. I would rather buy milk from him in a carton. I have a library of several hundred books. I am sure my neighbor doesn't want all those books to clutter up his house.

Each of us has the right to decide what "things" are desirable. The government has no such right.

Principle Number Eight

Mankind are endowed by God with certain unalienable rights.

No one has defined unalienable rights better than William Blackstone in his *Commentaries* when he said:

> "Those rights, then, which God and nature have established, and are therefore called natural rights, such as are life and liberty, need not the aid of human laws to be more effectually invested in every man than they are; neither do they receive any additional strength when declared by the municipal [or state] laws to be inviolable. On the contrary, no human legislation has power to abridge or

> destroy them, unless the owner [of the right] shall himself commit some act that amounts to a forfeiture."[10]

In other words, an unalienable right is one given to us by God when we are born. This mean that a person's unalienable rights cannot be violated without coming under the judgment or wrath of God. If that judgment does not come in this life the Bible says it will come in the next.[11]

In the Declaration of Independence, Thomas Jefferson says that "*among*" these unalienable rights are "life, liberty, and the pursuit of happiness." What are some of the other unalienable rights?

The right of self-government.

The right to bear arms in self-defense.

The right to own, develop, and dispose of property.

The right to make personal choices.

The right of free conscience.

The right to choose a profession.

The right to choose a mate.

The right to beget one's kind.

The right to assemble.

The right to petition.

The right of *Habeas Corpus*—meaning that a person cannot be held against his will when he or she has not been charged with an offense.

The right to have government *limited* to those powers delegated to it by the people.

Separation of powers is based on God's law because *if* the power to make the law, administer the law and interpret the law all rest in the same hands it is the definition of tyranny or dictatorship.

Justice by reparation is based on God's law. It says he who hurts shall be hurt or must apologize and make reparation to his victim.

---

10. William Blackstone, Commentaries on the Laws of England, William Carey Jones, ed., San Francisco: Bancroft-Whitney Company, 1916, vol. 1, p. 54 in the original at the top of the page; in Jones ed. p. 93 at the bottom of the page.
11. Galatians 6:7.

The rule that there shall be no taxation without the consent of the people or their representatives is based on God's law.

Laws protecting the family and the institution of marriage are all based on God's law.

All these are unalienable rights.

Principle Number Nine

To protect human rights, God has revealed a code of divine law.

William Blackstone points out that the Creator is not only omnipotent or all-powerful,

> "But as he is also a Being of infinite wisdom, he has laid down only such laws as were found in those relations of justice that existed in the nature of things ... These are the eternal, immutable laws of good and evil, to which the Creator himself in all his dispensations conforms, and which he has enabled human reason to discover, so far as they are necessary for the conduct of human actions. Such, among others, are these principles that we should live honestly, should hurt nobody, and should render to everyone his due."[12]

Blackstone said it was necessary to reveal these laws by direct revelation:

> "The doctrines thus delivered we call the revealed or divine law, and they are to be found only in the Holy Scriptures. These precepts, when revealed, are found by comparison to be really a part of the original law of nature, as they tend in all their consequences to man's felicity."[13]

Principle Number Ten

The God-given right to govern is vested in the sovereign authority of the whole people.

As we noted earlier, Algernon Sidney was one of the first to openly declare that there was no such thing as a "divine right of kings" to govern. He said God had vested the right to rule in the whole people. King Charles II was horrified with such a doctrine and had Algernon Sidney beheaded in 1683.

---

12. Blackstone, Commentaries on the Laws of England, op. cit., p. 40 in the original at top of the page; in the Jones ed. pp. 59-62 at the bottom of the page.
13. Ibid., p. 42 in the original at the top of the page; in the Jones ed., p. 64 at the bottom of the page.

John Locke was teaching the same doctrine so he immediately left for Holland where he could denounce the "divine right of kings" without losing his head. After the Revolution of 1688 he returned to England on the same boat that transported the new Queen Mary. In 1690 he published two famous essays on *The Original Extent and End of Civil Government*. The doctrine set forth by John Locke was expressed by Alexander Hamilton in the following words:

> "The fabric of American empire ought to rest on the solid basis of *the consent of the people*. The streams of national power ought to flow immediately from that pure, original fountain of all legislative authority." [14]

The divine right of the people to govern themselves and exercise exclusive power of sovereignty in their official affairs was expressed by the Commonwealth of Massachusetts in its first official Proclamation of January 23, 1776:

> "It is a maxim that in every government, there must exist somewhere a supreme sovereign, absolute, and uncontrollable power, but this power resides always in the *body of the people*; and it never was, or can be, delegated to one man, or a few. The great Creator has never given to men a right to vest others with authority over them, unlimited either in duration or degree." [15]

Madison confirmed this doctrine when the ratification of the Constitution was being debated:

> "The adversaries of the Constitution seem to have lost sight of the *people* altogether ... They must be told that the *ultimate authority* ... resides in the *people alone*." [16]

Principle Number Eleven

The majority of the people may alter or abolish a government which has become tyrannical.

The Founders were well acquainted with the vexations resulting from an abusive, autocratic government. Thomas Jefferson therefore stated the following in the Declaration of Independence:

---

14. Hamilton, Federalist Papers, op. cit., Number 22, p. 152.
15. Quoted by Hamilton Albert Long in Your American Yardstick, Philadelphia: Your Heritage Books, Inc., 1963, p. 167.
16. Madison, Federalist Papers, op. cit., Number 46, p. 294.

> "Prudence, indeed, will dictate that governments long established should not be changed for light and transient causes ... but when a long train of abuses and usurpations, ... evinces a design to reduce them under absolute despotism, it is their right, it is their *duty*, to throw off such government, and to provide new guards for their future security." [17]

However, John Locke emphasizes that there is no right of revolt by individuals or a minority. They must seek their remedy in the courts. It is only when a clear majority of the people have been seriously abused—so that there is a united spirit of determined action by practically the whole people—that rebellion against the government has any chance of success.

This was the thinking behind the "Virginia Declaration of Rights" when it expressed the belief:

> "That government is, or ought to be, instituted for the common benefit, protection, and security of the people ... And that, when any government shall be found inadequate or contrary to these purposes, a *majority of the community* hath an indubitable, inalienable, and indefeasible right to reform, alter, or abolish it, in such manner as shall be judged most conducive to the public weal." [18]

Principle Number Twelve

The United States of America shall be a republic.

This principle is highlighted in the pledge of allegiance when it says:

"I pledge allegiance to the flag

Of the United States of America

And to the *republic*

For which it stands ...."

There were many reasons why the Founders wanted a republican form of government rather than a democracy.

Theoretically, a democracy requires the full participation of the masses of the people in the passing of laws or in the decision-making procedures of the government.

---

17. The Annals of America, op. cit., 2:447-448.
18. Ibid., 2:432.

This has never worked because the people always become so occupied with their daily tasks that they will not properly study the issues nor will they take the time to attend the hearings or participate in the public discussion designed to test the merits of the issues under consideration.

The Greeks tried to use the democratic system of mass participation but each time the people would leave everything to a small group called an oligarchy and that always ends up in outright tyranny.

The American Founders wanted to use the democratic method of mass participation in electing representatives, but after the election they wanted to be governed by these representatives. And that is what "republican" means—government by elected representatives.

When the people lose confidence in those they have elected there is a temptation to insist that the people be allowed to decide. This may work sometimes when the entire populace is agitated and studying the issue at hand, but if this becomes a habit, it eventually degenerates into some form of dictatorship.

Principle Number Thirteen

A Constitution should protect the people from the frailties of their rulers.

The big question at the Constitutional Convention in Philadelphia during 1787 was this: "How can you set up an efficient system of government and still protect the freedom and unalienable rights of the people?"

Human nature being what it is, the Founders felt it was a serious mistake to blindly trust their elected leaders. As Madison put it:

> "If angels were to govern men, neither external nor internal controls on government would be necessary ... [But lacking these] you must first enable the government to control the governed; and in the next place oblige it to control itself." [19]

And this is what a constitution is supposed to do.

The genius of the Constitution of the United States is that it was specifically designed to keep government in the balanced center with enough power to maintain order and justice but not enough power to abuse the people. It further provides for a peaceful remedy if the government drifts toward anarchy (too little government) or tyranny (too much government).

19. Madison, Federalist Papers, op. cit., Number 51, p. 322.

This was achieved by a Constitutional separation of powers among the three branches of government and with power in each of those branches to check the powers of the other two, thereby keeping the system in the balanced center.

There was also a specific list of powers (twenty-five in Article I, Section 8) which the people delegated to the federal government and the Tenth Amendment made it unconstitutional for any branch of government to usurp or try to exercise additional powers.

However, the problem with all of this was not the Constitution, but the failure of the people and the states to maintain vigilance and keep the federal government within its designated parameters. As Madison said during the ratification debates:

> "I believe there are more instances of the abridgement of the freedom of the people by *gradual and silent encroachments* of those in power, than by violent and sudden usurpations … This danger ought to be wisely guarded against."[20]

In 1785, Madison vigorously warned his own state of Virginia as follows:

> "It is proper to take alarm at the *first experiment on our liberties*. We hold this prudent jealousy to be the first duty of citizens and one of the noblest characteristics of the late Revolution. The *freemen of America* did not wait till usurped power had strengthened itself by exercise and entangled the question in precedents. They saw all the consequences [of government abuses] in the principle, and they avoided the consequences by denying the principle [on which the abuses were based]. We revere the lesson too much … to forget it."[21]

The great sin of Americans since the days of the Founders is that they were not diligent in standing up to government abuses when they originally appeared. As a result, many aspects of the Constitution of the United States have now been shredded.

PRINCIPLE NUMBER FOURTEEN

Life and liberty are secure only so long as the rights of property are secure.

20. Elliot, The Debates in the Several State Conventions, op. cit., 3:87.

21. Rivers and Fendall, eds., Letters and Other Writings of James Madison, Philadelphia: J. P. Lippincott, 1865, 1:163.

The three foremost unalienable rights mentioned in the initial constitution of Massachusetts were: "Life, Liberty and Property."

This raises an important question. Why is it an unalienable right to own, develop and dispose of "property?" Justice George Sutherland of the U.S. Supreme Court summarized his answer to this question as follows:

> "It is not the right of property which is protected, but the right to property. Property *per se*, has no rights, but the individual—the man—has three great rights equally sacred from arbitrary interference: the right to his *life*, the right to his *liberty*, the right to his *property*.
>
> "These three rights are so bound together as to be essentially one right. To give a man his life but deny him his liberty, is to take from him all that makes life worth living. To give him his liberty but take from him the property which is the fruit and bade of his liberty, is to still leave him a slave."[22]

But at what point does something become somebody's "property?"

John Locke reasoned that God gave the earth and everything in it to the whole human family as a gift. Therefore the land, the sea, the acorns in the forest, the deer feeding in the meadow belong to everyone "in common." However, the moment someone takes the trouble to change something from its original state of nature, that person has added his ingenuity or labor to make that change. Herein lies the secret to the origin of "property rights."[23]

For example, let us say an Indian gathers acorns or wild apples in the forest or shoots a deer. John Locke says:

> "That labour ... added something to them [the apples or acorns] more than nature, the common mother of all, had done, and so they became his private right. And will any one say he had no right to those acorns or apples ... because he had not the consent of all mankind to make them his? ... If such a consent as that was necessary, [the] man [would have] starved, notwithstanding the plenty God had given him ... It is the taking any part of what is common, and removing it out of the state of nature ... which begins the [right] of property, without which the common [gift of God] is of no use ....

22. George Sutherland, "Principle or Expedient?", annual address to the New York State Bar Association, January 21, 1921, quoted by Skousen in The Five Thousand Year Leap, op. cit., pp. 172-173.
23. John Locke, Second Essay Concerning Civil Government, op. cit., 35:31.

> "Thus this law of reason [which is natural law or the law of God] makes the deer … [the property of the Indian] who hath killed it; it is allowed to be his goods who hath bestowed his labour upon it, though, before, it was the common right of every one."[24]

Locke described property as an extension of a person's life, energy and ingenuity. A person who has worked diligently to cultivate a farm, obtain food by hunting, carved a beautiful statue, or secured a wage by his labor, has projected the essence and substance of his very being into that labor. Therefore, under God's law or natural law, it has become that person's property in which the individual enjoys certain unalienable rights. This is why John Locke maintained that a threat to one's property is a threat to the essence of life itself.

It is obvious that if there were no such thing as "ownership" in property—which means legally protected exclusiveness—there would be no subduing or extensive development of the resources of the earth. This would defeat God's command to "subdue" the earth.[25]

Furthermore, without "private rights" in developed or improved property, it would be perfectly lawful for a lazy, covetous neighbor to move in as soon as the improvements were completed and take possession of the fruits of his industrious neighbor. And even the covetous neighbor would not be secure, because someone stronger than he could take it away from him.

The Primary Purpose of Government Is to Protect Property

The spark that ignited the Revolutionary War was the attempt of the Parliament and the king to extort from the colonists their property by various kinds of taxation without their consent. They quoted John Locke to prove this was a violation of the English constitution and the English common law. He said:

> "The supreme power cannot take from any man any part of his property without his own consent. For the preservation of property being the end of government, and that for which men enter into society, it necessarily supposes and requires that the people should have property, without which they must be supposed to lose that

24. Ibid.
25. Genesis 1:28.

> [property] by entering into society, which was the end for which they enter into it."[26]

Should Government Take from the "Haves" and Give to the "Have-Nots?"

As we have pointed out earlier, one of the worst sins of government, according to the Founders, was the exercise of its coercive taxing power to take property from one group and give it to another.

Early in the history of the United States the Supreme Court clearly proclaimed that any attempt by the government to "redistribute the wealth" was unconstitutional. It said:

> "No man would become a member of a community in which he could not enjoy the fruits of his honest labor and industry. The preservation of property, then, is a primary object of the social compact … The Legislature, therefore, had no authority to make an act divesting one citizen of his freehold, and vesting it in another, without a just compensation. It is inconsistent with the principles of reason, justice and moral rectitude; it is incompatible with the comfort, peace and happiness of mankind; it is contrary to the principles of social alliance in every free government; and lastly, *it is contrary to the letter and spirit of the Constitution*."[27]

Caring for the Poor Without Violating Property Rights

Of course, the question always arises, if it corrupts a society for the government to take care of the poor, who will take care of them? The answer of those who built America seems to be: "Anybody but the federal government."

Americans have never tolerated the suffering and starvation which have plagued the rest of the world, but until the present generation, help was given exclusively by the generosity of the people of the community. President Grover Cleveland vetoed legislation in his day designed to spend federal taxes for private welfare problems. He wrote:

> "I can find no warrant for such an appropriation in the Constitution, and I do not believe that the power and duty of the General Government ought to be extended to the relief of individual

---

26. John Locke, Second Essay Concerning Civil Government, op. cit., 35:138.
27. 2 Dall 394, 310 [Pa. 1795]; quoted by Skousen in The Five Thousand Year Leap, op. cit., pp. 175-176.

suffering which is in no manner properly related to the public service or benefit. A prevalent tendency to disregard the limited mission of this power and duty should, I think, be steadfastly resisted, to the end that the lesson should be constantly enforced that though the people support the Government the Government should not support the people.

"The friendliness and charity of our countrymen can always be relied upon to relieve their fellow-citizens in misfortune. This has been repeatedly and quite lately demonstrated. Federal aid in such cases encourages the expectation of paternal care on the part of the Government and weakens the sturdiness of our national character, while it prevents the indulgence among our people of that kindly sentiment and conduct which strengthens the bonds of a common brotherhood."[28]

28. "Why the President Said No," in Essays on Liberty, 12 vols., The Foundation for Economic Education, Inc., 1952-1965, 3:255.

Topics for Reflection and Discussion

1. What is Natural Law? Who was the Roman historian-philosopher who first emphasized its importance? What is the source of Natural Law? Is it universal? Is it based on "sound reason?" Is it always "morally right?" Can it be repealed by a legislature?

2. Name two ways in which a free society is weakened by its people becoming immoral. Was Benjamin Franklin exaggerating when he said, "Only a virtuous people are capable of freedom?" How did Professor Gordon S. Wood define "public virtue?"

3. What did the Founders recommend as one of the most successful ways to develop public virtue in a society? Will a well-structured constitution and admirable code of laws succeed if the people become corrupt?

4. How did John Locke support his claim that "Everyone can know there is a God?" In what three ways are "all men created equal?"

5. What is an "unalienable right?" What makes it unalienable? In what way has God provided that no unalienable right can be violated without punishment? Name five unalienable rights.

6. How did Blackstone say we came into possession of God's law? Why is that significant?

7. What happened to Algernon Sidney when he proclaimed in England that there is no such thing as "divine right of kings?" What did John Locke do to protect himself while advocating the same thing?

8. What is the basis of government by "majority rule?" Is there any practical alternative? Can a minority legitimately revolt? What is their remedy?

9. What is a republican form of government? What is a democracy? What did the Founders design the United States to be?

10. In what way did the Founders believe a written constitution gave them an advantage over England? Why is the right to possess, develop and dispose of property an unalienable right? How did John Locke say property rights originated? What is one of the greatest sins of government with reference to property rights in our day?

CHAPTER TWENTY-SIX

THE FOUNDERS' INDISPENSABLE PRINCIPLES—PART II

PRINCIPLE NUMBER FIFTEEN

The highest level of prosperity occurs when there is a free-market economy and a minimum of government regulations.

The Founders wondered if there were any principles of natural law for prosperity economics.

As we have mentioned, a set of five books was published in 1776 by a professor in Scotland named Adam Smith. These writings fitted into the thinking and experience of the Founders like a hand in a glove. It was called *The Wealth of Nations*.

Concerning this study, Thomas Jefferson said:

> "In political economy, I think Smith's *Wealth of Nations* is the best book extant."[1]

The United States was the first country to undertake the structuring of a whole national economy on the natural law principles recommended by Adam Smith. Among other things, the formula called for the following:

1. Specialized production—let each person or corporation of persons do what they do best.

2. Exchange goods in a free-market environment without government interference in production, prices, or wages.

3. The free market will provide the basic needs of the people on the basis of supply and demand, with no government interference or imposed monopolies.

4. Prices are regulated by competition on the basis of supply and demand.

---

1. Bergh, The Writings of Thomas Jefferson, op. cit., 8:31.

5. Profits are necessary as the means by which the production of goods and services are made worthwhile.

6. Competition is the means by which quality is improved, the quantity of products and services increased, and the prices of products and services reduced.

As we have mentioned earlier, prosperity depends upon a climate of wholesome stimulation with four basic freedoms in operation:

1. The Freedom to *try*.
2. The Freedom to *buy*.
3. The Freedom to sell.
4. The Freedom to *fail*.

By 1905 the United States had become the richest industrial nation in the world. With only 5 percent of the earth's continental land area, and merely 6 percent of the world's population, the American people were producing over half of almost everything—clothes, food, houses, transportation, communications, even luxuries. It was an economic miracle.

However, a successful economy must depend upon the government to prevent four corrosive elements from destroying the open, free-enterprise market. The government must prevent:

1. The use of illegal *force* in the market place to compel buyers or sellers to violate their free will.

2. The use of *fraud* in misrepresenting the quality, location or ownership of items being bought and sold.

3. The greedy exploitation of *monopoly*. This eliminates competition and results in the restraint of trade.

4. *Debauchery* of the moral fiber of society by commercial exploitation of vice, pornography, obscenity, drugs, liquor, prostitution or commercialized gambling.

Principle Number Sixteen

The government should be separated into three branches.

For centuries political thinkers argued over the best form of government. Some said a monarchy was the only way to go. Others preferred an aristocracy of the "best families" ruling the nation. Still, the Greeks and others favored a pure democracy where decisions were made by the whole people.

Then came Polybius.

Polybius was a Greek who lived from 204 to 122 B.C. Next to Herodotus and Thucydides, Polybius is recognized as the greatest of all Greek historians. His writings encompass forty volumes.

Polybius said each of the three systems of government under consideration contained its own self-destruction. A monarchy readily degenerated into some form of tyranny. An aristocracy would degenerate into an oligarchy where the nation would be oppressed by a few rich families. Democracy would disintegrate into mob rule and rule by force and violence.

Polybius said the solution was a system of "mixed government." Some of the powers of government should be in an executive who could act in an emergency for the whole people. Then there needed to be a popular assembly where elected representatives of the people could have a major voice in new laws. However, the people are often greedy and want to destroy property rights and the established order of things. Polybius felt the senate should represent property rights and the constitutional order of things to keep the people's assembly from destroying the whole structure.

In this mixed political formula we find certain powers in the executive to be exercised as needed; certain powers in the elected representatives of the people to express the desires of the masses; and certain powers in the senate to prevent the abuse of power by either the executive or the people's popular assembly.

Nobody knew for certain whether the ideas of Polybius would work because no nation was willing to try them.

It was not until the mid-1770s that Baron Charles de Montesquieu resurrected the ideas of Polybius and after twenty years of careful study wrote them up in a book called *The Spirit of the Laws*. Book XI of this massive tome outlined a model constitution which has many elements which were included in the United States Constitution in 1787.

Baron de Montesquieu improved on Polybius by not merely having a roughly mixed government but a highly refined and beautiful balance between the instruments of government.

He said there should be a single executive, a legislature of two houses—one to be the elected representatives of the people and the upper house to represent the states. He also felt there should be an independent judiciary to see that the other departments of government did not violate their constitutional parameters.

John Adams was the first American statesman to begin promoting the ideas of Montesquieu. In a letter to Dr. Benjamin Rush, he said:

> "I call you to witness that I was the first member of the Congress who ventured to come out in public, as I did in January 1776, in my *Thoughts on Government* ... in favor of a government with three branches and an independent judiciary. This pamphlet, you know, was very unpopular. No man appeared in public to support it but yourself."[2]

In later years, Adams was successful in getting his ideas incorporated in the U.S. Constitution, but he was never able to gain a genuine acceptance by the people. Even though he was elected the first Vice President of the United States and the second President, he very shortly disappeared into history with scarcely a ripple.

A hundred years later neither Washington, D.C., nor Massachusetts had erected any kind of monument to John Adams.[3] Nevertheless, he insisted that what he had proposed was part of the "divine science" that was needed to allow the United States to attain her manifest destiny.

Toward the end, John Adams left a prophetic utterance. He said it was his aspiration "to see rising in America an empire of liberty, and the prospect of two or three hundred millions of freemen, without one noble or one king among them."[4]

It demonstrated that in God's scheme of things, one man can make a difference.

Principle Number Seventeen

A system of checks and balances should be adopted to prevent the abuse of power by the different branches of government.

James Madison had to spend five issues of the *Federalist Papers* (47 to 51) to explain the genius of the separation of powers and then turn around and explain why they all had to be carefully laced back together to provide

2. John Adams' letter to Benjamin Rush on April 23, 1809, and quoted by Koch in The American Enlightenment, op. cit., p. 163.
3. Ibid., p. 154.
4. John Adams' letter to Count Sarsfield, February 3, 1786, and quoted in Ibid., p. 191.

the necessary checks and balances so that no department of government could become abusive. As he explained:

> "It will not be denied that power is of an encroaching nature and that it ought to be effectually restrained from passing the limits assigned to it."[5]

As it turned out, the American Founding Fathers achieved a system of checks and balances far more refined and complex than Montesquieu ever envisioned. Unfortunately, down through the years the political leaders of the United States failed to respect these checks and vigorously enforce them. Had they done so, the American system would be far more just and efficient than it is today. Here is what the Constitution originally provided:

1. Only Congress can pass laws. If the Executive or Judiciary attempt to pass laws or regulations they are unconstitutional.

2. The House of Representatives serves as a check on the Senate since no statute can become law without the approval of the House.

3. At the same time the Senate serves as a check on the House of Representatives since no statute can become law without its approval.

4. The President can restrain both the House and the Senate by using his veto to send back any bill he does not approve.

5. The Congress, on the other hand, can restrain the President by passing a bill over the President's veto with a two-thirds majority in each house.

6. The Congress has a further check on the President through its power of refusing to appropriate funds for the operation of the Executive branch.

7. The President must have the approval of the Senate in filling important offices of the Executive branch.

8. The President must also have the approval of the Senate before any treaties can go into effect.

9. The Congress has authority to conduct investigations of the Executive branch to determine whether or not funds are being properly expended or the laws properly enforced.

10. The Executive branch has a discretionary power over the Congress by deciding where federal funds will be expended for military bases, building dams, improving navigable rivers, building interstate highways,

5. Madison, Federalist Papers, op. cit., Number 48, p. 308.

etc. Unfortunately, after the system of political parties developed, these discretionary powers were usually allocated in terms of Senators and Congressmen who favored the President's policies.

11.The Judiciary has a check on the Congress by having authority to review all laws and determine their constitutionality.

12.The Congress, on the other hand, has a restraining power over the Judiciary by having the constitutional authority to restrict the extent of its jurisdiction.

13.The Congress also has the power to impeach any of the judges who are guilty of treason, high crimes or misdemeanors.

14.The President also has a check on the Judiciary by having the power to nominate new judges subject to the approval of the Senate.

15.The Congress has further restraining power over the Judiciary by having the control of appropriations for the operation of the federal court system.

16.The Congress is able to initiate amendments to the Constitution which, if approved by three-fourths of the states, could seriously effect the operation of both the Executive and Judiciary branches of the government.

17.The Congress, by joint resolution, can terminate certain powers granted to the President (such as war powers) without his consent.

18.The people can exercise their voting power to check on their representatives every two years (and since the 17th Amendment) on the Senate every six years, and on the President every four years.

Principle Number Eighteen

The unalienable rights of the people are most likely to be preserved if the principles of government are set forth in a written Constitution.

England still does not have a written constitution and therefore the latest act of Parliament is enforced as part of its constitutional structure.

The structure of the American system is set forth in the Constitution of the United States and the only weaknesses which have appeared are those which were allowed to creep in despite the Constitution.

Principle Number Nineteen

Only limited and carefully defined powers should be delegated to government, all others being retained by the people.

It will be recalled that one of the reasons many of the states would not adopt the original draft of the Constitution was because there was no specific bill of rights. The first ten amendments were therefore added to include the ancient unalienable rights of Anglo-Saxon freemen.

The Ninth Amendment is the catchall provision which states:

> "The enumeration in the Constitution of certain rights shall not be construed to deny or disparage *others* retained by the people."

The Tenth Amendment is the most widely violated provision of the bill of rights. If it had been respected and enforced America would be an amazingly different country than it is today. This amendment provides:

> "The powers not delegated to the United States by the Constitution, nor prohibited by it to the States, are reserved to the States respectively, or to the people."

The abuses of this amendment also include violations of many of the indispensable principles we have been discussing.

Principle Number Twenty

Efficiency and dispatch require that the government operate according to the will of the majority, but constitutional provisions must be made to protect the rights of the minority.

The theory of majority rule was explained by John Locke as follows:

> "Every man, by consenting with others to make one body politic under one government, puts himself under an obligation to every one of that society to submit to the determination of the majority, and to be concluded [bound] by it."[6]

Locke then proceeds to demonstrate why there is no way to have orderly government except on the basis of this principle. He says:

> "For if the consent of the majority shall not in reason be received as the act of the whole ... nothing but the consent of every individual can make anything to be the act of the whole, which, consider-

6. Locke, Second Essay Concerning Civil Government, op. cit., 35:46-47.

> ing the infirmities of health and avocations of business which … will necessarily keep many away from the public assembly; and the variety of opinions and contrarity of interest which unavoidably happen in all collections of men, it is next [to] impossible ever to be had."[7]

But to accept majority rule as a practical necessity puts the minority at risk unless their basic rights are protected in spite of the majority. This is a monumental task and while considerable progress has been made in achieving this goal in the United States, much remains to be accomplished.

For Americans, the greatest triumph was in eliminating slavery. The second was in eliminating any "established" religion. The major task of providing equal civil rights for minorities is an ongoing struggle. However, Colin Powell made a very insightful statement when he announced he would not be a candidate for President. As a brilliant military leader and Afro-American he said:

> "[My being here] says more about America than it does about me. In one generation we have moved from denying a black man service at a lunch counter to elevating one to the highest military office in the nation and to being a serious contender for the Presidency."[8]

Only a few decades ago, most Americans would have doubted this could ever happen.

Principle Number Twenty-One

Strong local self-government is the keystone to preserving human freedom.

Thomas Jefferson probably said it better than anyone when he declared:

> "The way to have good and safe government is not to trust it all to one, but to divide it among the many, distributing to every one exactly the functions he is competent [to perform best].
>
> "Let the national government be entrusted with the defense of the nation, and its foreign and federal relations; the State government with the civil rights, laws, police and administration of what concerns the State generally; the counties with the local concerns

7. Ibid., 35:48.
8. New York Times, November 9, 1995, p. A10.

of the counties, and each ward [township] direct the interests within itself.

"It is by dividing and subdividing these republics, from the great national one down through all its subordinations, until it ends in the administration of every man's farm by himself; by placing under every one what his own eye may superintend, that all will be done for the best.

"What has destroyed liberty and the rights of man in every government which has ever existed under the sun?

"The generalizing and concentration of all cares and powers into one body, no matter whether of the autocrats of Russia or France, or the aristocrats of a Venetian senate."[9]

Principle Number Twenty-Two

A free people should be governed by law and not by the whims of men.

Plato was one of the ancient philosophers who did not believe in a code of fixed laws. He felt that wise men like himself could make better on-the-spot decisions that would be more fair and more likely to be "just."

On the other hand, the American Founders and their Anglo-Saxon forebears looked upon law as a "rule of action" to guide the people in their daily behavior. They felt that the law was of divine origin and therefore as binding on the ruler as it was on the people.

The Founders agreed with John Locke that where there is no law there is no freedom. They looked upon law as the guardian of freedom. Here is the way John Locke said it:

"The end of law is not to abolish or restrain, but to preserve and enlarge freedom. For in all the states of created beings, capable of laws, where there is no law there is no freedom. For liberty is to be free from restraint and violence of others, which cannot be where there is no law."[10]

Nevertheless, people have confidence in the law only to the extent that they can understand it and feel that it is so well stated it will not have to be continually amended. James Madison emphasized both of these points when he said:

---

9. Bergh, The Writings of Thomas Jefferson, op cit., 14:421.
10. Locke, Second Essay Concerning Civil Government, op. cit., 35:37.

> "It will be of little avail to the people that the laws are made by men of their own choice if the laws be so voluminous that they cannot be read, or so incoherent that they cannot be understood; if they be repealed or revised before they are promulgated, or undergo such incessant changes that no man, who know what the law is today, can guess what it will be tomorrow. Law is defined to be a rule of action, but how can that be a rule which is little known and less fixed.[11]

Principle Number Twenty-Three

A free society cannot survive as a republic without a broad program of general education.

John Adams stated that from the earliest colonial days, Americans considered education the main-sail for freedom and human progress. He said:

> "They made an early provision by law that every town consisting of so many families should be always furnished with a grammar school. They made it a crime for such a town to be destitute of a grammar schoolmaster for a few months, and subjected it to a heavy penalty. So that the education of all ranks of people was made the care and expense of the public, in a manner that I believe has been unknown to any other people, ancient or modern.
>
> "The consequences of these establishments we see and feel every day [written in 1765]. A native of America who cannot read and write is as rare ... as a comet or an earthquake.
>
> "It has been observed that we are all of us lawyers, divines, politicians, and philosophers. And I have good authorities to say that all candid foreigners who have passed through the country and conversed freely with all sorts of people here will allow that they have never seen so much knowledge and civility among the common people in any part of the world ....
>
> "Liberty cannot be preserved without a general knowledge among the people ... They have a right, an indisputable unalienable, indefeasible, divine right to the most dreaded kind of knowledge—I mean, of the *character and conduct of their rulers*."[12]

11. Madison, Federalist Papers, op. cit., Number 62, p. 57.

12. John Adams, Dissertation on the Canon and the Federal Law, February 1765, and quoted by Koch in The American Enlightenment, op. cit., p. 239.

Gradually the zeal for universal education spread from new England to all of the other colonies. By 1831, when Alexis de Tocqueville of France visited the United States, he was amazed with the fruits of this effort. He wrote:

> "In New England every citizen receives the elementary notions of human knowledge; he is taught, moreover, the doctrines and the evidences of his religion, the history of his country, and the leading features of its Constitution. In the state of Connecticut and Massachusetts, it is extremely rare to find a man imperfectly acquainted with all these things, and a person wholly ignorant of them is a sort of phenomenon." [13]

Principle Number Twenty-Four

A free people will not survive unless they stay strong.

It was the philosophy of the Founders that the kind hand of providence had been everywhere present in allowing the United States to come forth as the first free people in modern times. They further felt they would forever be blessed with freedom and prosperity if they remained virtuous and well-armed. Benjamin Franklin said:

> "Our security lies, I think, in our growing strength, both in numbers and wealth … which will make us more respectable, our friendship more valued and our enmity feared; thence it will soon be thought proper to treat us not with justice only, but with kindness, and thence we may expect in a few years a total change of measures in regard to us; unless, by a neglect of military discipline we should lose all martial spirit, and our western people become as tame as those in the eastern dominions of Britain [India] when we may expect the same oppressions; for there is much truth in the Italian saying, 'Make yourselves sheep, and the wolves will eat you.'" [14]

Washington's position on national defense was in terms of grim realities experienced on the field of battle. No man wanted peace more than he, but no man was willing to risk more in life and property to achieve it. In nearly the same words as Franklin, he declared:

---

13. Alexis de Tocqueville, Democracy in America, Rochelle, New York: Arlington House, 1840 Heirloom Edition, 1:326-327.
14. Smyth, The Writings of Benjamin Franklin, op. cit., 2:347.

> "To be prepared for war is one of the most effectual means of preserving peace." [15]

PRINCIPLE NUMBER TWENTY-FIVE

"Peace, commerce, and honest friendship with all nations—entangling alliances with none."

These are the words of Thomas Jefferson, given in his first inaugural address.[16]

This was the Founders' original doctrine of "separatism." It was far different from the modern term of "isolationism." The latter term implies a complete seclusion from other nations, as though the United States were to be detached and somehow incubated in isolation from other nations.

In point of fact, the policy of the Founders was just the opposite. They desired to cultivate a wholesome relationship with all nations, but they wished to remain aloof from sectional quarrels and international disputes. They wanted to avoid alliances of friendship with one nation which would make them enemies of another nation in a time of crisis.

The Founders' original policy was similar in many ways to that of modern Switzerland, which has successfully remained neutral and aloof from entangling alliances during two world wars and numerous European quarrels besides. During these periods of intense military action, Switzerland did not follow a policy of "isolationism," but maintained universal diplomatic relations with all who might wish to come to Switzerland to buy, sell, borrow, or bank. She took no hostile posture toward any country unless it threatened Switzerland.

In general terms, this is the doctrine of "separatism" envisioned by the early American Founding Fathers. In his Farewell Address, George Washington outlined his concept of "separatism" when he said:

> "Observe good faith and justice toward all nations. Cultivate peace and harmony with all. Religion and morality enjoin this conduct; and can it be that good policy does not equally enjoin it? It will be worthy of a free, enlightened, and, at no distant period, a great nation, to give to mankind the magnanimous and too novel [rare] example of a people always guided by an exalted justice and benevolence." [17]

15. Fitzpatrick, Writings of George Washington, op. cit., 30:491.
16. Bergh, The Writings of Thomas Jefferson, op. cit., 3:321.
17. Fitzpatrick, Writings of George Washington, op. cit., 35:231.

To emphasize this policy, he said:

> "The great rule of conduct for us, in regard to foreign nations, is in extending our commercial relations to have as little political connection as possible."[18]

Principle Number Twenty-Six

The core unit which determines the strength of any society is the family; therefore the government should foster and protect its integrity.

The family-centered culture which developed in America was not the austere pattern which characterized England or the profligate pattern which developed in France. Alexis de Tocqueville compared the American family with that of Europe in the following words:

> "There is certainly no country in the world where the tie of marriage is more respected than in America, or where conjugal happiness is more highly or worthily appreciated. In Europe almost all the disturbances of society arise from the irregularities of domestic life. To despise the natural bonds and legitimate pleasure of home is to contract a taste for excesses, a restlessness of heart, and fluctuating desires.
>
> "Agitated by the tumultuous passions that frequently disturb his dwelling, the European is galled by the obedience [to moral standards] which the legislative powers of the state exact.
>
> "But when the American retires from the turmoil of public life to the bosom of his family, he finds in it the image of order and peace. There his pleasures are simple and natural, his joys are innocent and calm; and as he finds that an orderly life is the surest path to happiness, he accustoms himself easily to moderate his opinions as well as his tastes. While the European endeavors to forget his domestic trouble by agitating society, the American derives from his own home that love of order which he afterwards carries with him into public life."[19]

It is interesting that under God's law the husband and wife have their respective roles but otherwise share all rights in common. Dr. H. Carlton Marlow described it as "differential" equality.[20]

---

18. Ibid., 35:233.
19. de Tocqueville, Democracy in America, op. cit., 1:315.
20. H. Carlton Marlow and Harrison M. Davis, The American Search for Women, Santa Barbara, California: Clio Books, 1976, chapter 5.

John Locke emphasizes the same theme of equality between husband and wife under Bible law. As the apostle Paul pointed out:

> "Neither is the man without the woman, neither the woman without the man, in the Lord."[21]

Locke goes on to say:

> "We see the positive law of God everywhere joins them [both husband and wife] together without distinction, when it commands children to 'Honor thy father and thy mother,'[22] 'whosoever curseth his father or his mother' etc.,[23] 'Ye shall fear every man his mother and his father,'[24] 'Children, obey your parents,'[25] is the style of the Old and New Testament."[26]

Let us close this segment with Benjamin Franklin's earnest plea to a young friend to choose marriage rather than his plan for what he thought would be a happy, promiscuous bachelorhood. Franklin said:

> "Marriage is the proper remedy. It is the most natural state of man, and therefore the state in which you are most likely to find solid happiness. Your reasons against entering into it at present appear to me not well founded.
>
> "The circumstantial advantages you have in view by postponing it are not only uncertain, but they are small in comparison with that of the thing itself, being married and settled [emphasis by Franklin].
>
> "It is the man and woman united that make the complete human being. Separate, she wants his force of body and strength of reason; he, her softness, sensibility, and acute discernment. Together they are more likely to succeed in the world.
>
> "A single man had not nearly the value he would have in that state of union. He is an incomplete animal. He resembles the odd half of a pair of scissors. If you get a prudent, healthy wife, your

21. 1 Corinthians 11:11.
22. Exodus 20:12.
23. Leviticus 20:9.
24. Leviticus 19:3.
25. Ephesians 6:1.
26. Locke, The Second Essay Concerning Civil Government, op. cit., 35:36.

> industry in your profession, with her good economy, will be a fortune sufficient [for you both]."[27]

Principle Number Twenty-Seven

The burden of debt is as destructive to human freedom as subjugation by conquest.

Slavery is involuntary servitude and it can be inflicted by conquest or self-inflicted by debt.

Debt, of course, is simply borrowing against the future. It exchanges a future obligation for the enjoyment of a present advantage. It will require not only the future return of the original advance but also a substantial compensation to the creditor for the use of his money.

The Founders knew that borrowing can be an honorable procedure in a time of emergency, but they deplored it just the same. They looked upon it as a temporary handicap which should be paid off at the earliest possible moment.

The Founders knew that excessive debt greatly curtails the freedom of the debtor. It also obscures his search for happiness. There seems to be a perpetual burden every waking hour. There is a constant threat to his sense of security as he rides the razor's edge of potential disaster.

There is also the sense of waste—much like the man who has to make payments on a dead horse. His debt is money spent for pleasures or even needs that are long since past. It often means sleepless nights as the debtor recoils under the burden of a grinding weight which is constantly increasing its interest payments with every tick of the clock, and sometimes at usurious rates.

Thomas Jefferson understood this and said:

> "The maxim of buying nothing without the money in our pockets to pay for it would make our country one of the happiest on earth. Experience during the war proved this, and I think every man will remember that, under all our privations, it obliged him to submit to during that period, he slept sounder and awoke happier than he can do now [with the current wave of speculative debt]."[28]

---

27. A letter to a young friend on June 25, 1745, and quoted by Koch in The American Enlightenment, op. cit., p. 70.

28. Paul Leicester Ford, The Writings of Thomas Jefferson, New York: G. P. Putman's Sons, 1892, 4:414.

The Founders also looked upon a national debt as a curse, particularly where it might have to be paid off by subsequent generations. Jefferson said:

> "I, however, place economy among the first and most important of republican virtues, and *public debt* as the greatest of the dangers to be feared."[29]

Where the national debt was made necessary by an emergency such as a war, he said:

> "We are bound to defray expenses [of the war] within our own time, and are unauthorized to burden posterity with them ... We shall all consider ourselves morally bound to pay them ourselves and consequently within the life [expectancy] of the majority."[30]

One cannot help but stand in amazement as we contemplate the present national debt of over five trillion dollars. Obviously, those last two generations never read or gave respect to the warnings of the Founders.

Principle Number Twenty-Eight

The United States has a manifest destiny to eventually become a glorious example of God's law under a restored Constitution that will inspire the entire human race.

The Founders sensed from the very beginning that they were on a divine mission. Their great disappointment was that it didn't all come to pass in their day, but they knew the prophet Moses had promised that someday it would.[31]

John Adams wrote:

> "I always consider the settlement of America with reverence and wonder, as the opening of a grand scene and design in Providence for the illumination of the ignorant, and the emancipation of the slavish part of mankind all over the earth."[32]

Thomas Jefferson looked upon the development of freedom under the Constitution as "the world's best hope," and in 1801 he wrote that what had been accomplished in the United States by 1801 would be "a standing monument and example for the aim and imitation of people of other countries."[33]

29. Bergh, The Writings of Thomas Jefferson, op cit., 15:47.
30. Ibid., 13:357-358.
31. Deuteronomy 30:1-8.
32. Quoted by Cherry in God's New Israel, op. cit., p. 65.
33. Bergh, The Writings of Thomas Jefferson, op. cit., 10:217.

Alexander Hamilton made this statement at the time the Constitution was being ratified:

> "It has been frequently remarked that it seems to have been reserved to the people of this country, by their conduct and example, to decide the important question whether societies of men are really capable or not of establishing good government from reflection and choice or whether they are forever destined to depend for their political constitutions on accident and force."[34]

James Madison summed up the feelings of the Founders when he said:

> "Had no important step been taken by the leaders of the Revolution for which a precedent could not be discovered, no government established of which an exact model did not present itself, the people of the United States might at this moment have been numbered among the melancholy victims of misguided councils, must at best have been laboring under the weight of some of those forms which have crushed the liberties of the rest of mankind."

Then he continued:

> "Happily for America, happily we trust *for the whole human race*, they pursued a new and more noble course. They accomplished a revolution which had no parallel in the annals of human society. They reared the fabrics of governments which have no model on the face of the globe. They formed the design of a great Confederacy, which it is incumbent on their successors to *improve and perpetuate*."[35]

And therein lies the challenge to modern Americans. At some point we are obligated by divine injunction to "improve and perpetuate" what the Founding Fathers began.

Topics for Reflection and Discussion

1. Who was the principal authority quoted by the Founders on free-enterprise economics? What nation was the first to adopt these principles? Although a small part of the world's population, how much of the world's goods was this country producing by 1905?

---

34. Hamilton, Federalist Papers, op. cit., Number 1, p. 33.
35. Madison, Federalist Papers, op. cit., Number 14, pp. 104-105.

2. A famous Greek historian developed the idea of a "mixed" system of government with certain elements of a monarchy, an aristocracy and a democracy all blended into a new kind of government. What was his name? Who was the Frenchman who revived these ideas? What was the name of his book? Who was the first American to promote these principles in modern times? Did it make him popular?

3. After setting up a separation of powers, why did the Founders have to weave checks and balances back into the system? Can you identify five checks in the Constitution to prevent the abuse of power? Why did the Founders feel it was important to have a written Constitution? Does England have a written constitution?

4. Does the Bill of Rights contain the unalienable rights of the Anglo-Saxons? Can you name five of them? What does the Ninth Amendment provide? What does the Tenth Amendment provide? Of all the Bill of Rights, which one is violated the most?

5. On a scale of one to ten, how far up the scale of equal civil rights do you think America has attained? How much progress did General Colin Powell think we had made?

6. Why did the Founders put so much stress on strong local self-government? Why does government, especially the national government, have such a poor reputation for efficiency and economy where it has been assigned major tasks? Can you name two examples?

7. How important is education in the preservation of the American culture? What did de Tocqueville say school children were learning in 1831 that is being neglected today? Why did Washington believe that to have peace we must stay strong? To what extent do you think he would agree to some kind of disarmament?

8. Why were the Founders against "entangling alliances?" How important is the family in preserving America? What specific problems come to your mind as the family has seriously deteriorated in the last two generations? What impressed you most in Benjamin Franklin's discourse on marriage?

9. Name four significant advantages in staying out of debt. Why do you think the Founders were so strongly opposed to the accumulation of a national debt? Who did they say should pay off the debt accumulated by each generation? The interest on our national debt today is a third of a trillion dollars per year. In view of the fact that this annual interest exceeds the cost of all the wars since America became a nation, why would the Founders have called this a form of slavery?

10. Can you describe the Founders' original conception of America's "manifest destiny?" In what particular areas do you feel future generations must make up for lost ground?

CHAPTER TWENTY-SEVEN

Eventually the People Must Be Organized in God's Own Way

Thomas Jefferson's Great Treatise on "Wards"

In the first chapter of Deuteronomy, Moses describes how God wanted to have the people organized. This became an important part of God's law.

It is very apparent from this scripture that God never intended human beings to become lost souls among the faceless multitudes of the millions who constitute the crowded masses of modern congested cities.

People are precious and each individual should be an integral part of a community hierarchy where he or she is recognized and appreciated as someone of importance and worth.

God accomplished this by organizing the entire population under God's law "by families." The administration of the government, particularly in times of famine or crises, was "by families."[1] Handling emergencies is always tremendously facilitated when the people are properly organized.

Strength Through Orderly Procedures and Voluntary Discipline

The genius of God's law is orderly procedure and voluntary discipline. Even the Romans borrowed some of these principles when they organized themselves according to "hundreds." However, Thomas Jefferson knew that the only people who practiced the broad ramifications of God's law were the Anglo-Saxons. They memorized the code of around a hundred principles as taught by Moses and organized themselves in tens, fifties and hundreds. Eventually, the Anglo-Saxons became pagans, but they continued to elect their captains and adhere to the traditional code of laws given to Moses even though they couldn't remember their origin.

These cultural qualities actually became the trademark by which they were known half-way round the world.

1. Numbers 1:2.

We might also mention in passing that after the Romans were defeated by the Goths—who were cousins of the Anglo-Saxons—many Romans gave up their highly prized Roman citizenship to enjoy the security and prosperity that existed among the Goths.[2] It is amazing to learn that even the remnants of God's law exceeded the appeal of *Pax Romana*.

Thomas Jefferson Became the Recognized Authority on God's Law and the Anglo-Saxon System of Organization

As we mentioned earlier, Thomas Jefferson was a devoted student of the Anglo-Saxon culture and even learned the Anglo-Saxon language so he could study their laws in the original tongue.

When New England began setting up a system of "wards" or "hundreds" Jefferson immediately visualized this as the foundation for God's law which Moses had promised in the "latter days."[3] He wanted the whole nation to be organized on this basis. Jefferson wrote:

> "These wards [of approximately 100 families], called townships in New England, are the vital principle of their governments, and have proved themselves *the wisest invention ever devised by the wit of man* for the perfect exercise of self-government, and for its preservation."[4]

It was representative government at its best.

Jefferson knew that in the Anglo-Saxon structure, ten families were called a "tithing" and the elected leader of this group was called a "tithing-man," or captain of ten families.[5]

Five tithings grouped together, comprised approximately fifty families. These fifty families were called a "vill" (village) and the elected leader was called a "vill-man."[6]

Two vills, or approximately a hundred families, were called a "hundred," and the elected leader was called a "hundred-man."[7]

2. Turner, The History of the Anglo Saxons, op. cit., 1:187.
3. Deuteronomy 30:1-8 plus 31:29.
4. Thomas Jefferson, The Autobiography of Thomas Jefferson, New York: The Library of America, 1984, p. 74-75.
5. Henry Campbell Black, Black's Law Dictionary, 4th ed., St. Paul: West Publishing Company, 1968, under "tithing" and "tithing-man," p. 1655.
6. Ibid., under "vill," p. 1730.
7. Ibid., under "hundred," pp. 874-875.

The Advantage of Dealing with Someone Who Belonged to a "Ward"

In England the Anglo-Saxons began to call the section of a city which comprised approximately a hundred families, a "ward," or "watched over place." [8] It is used in the Bible with the same meaning.[9]

It is thought that the word, "ward" gradually replaced the term "hundred" because in the Anglo-Saxon language the word "ward" meant "warrant guarantee." In other words, one of the principal appeals in dealing with someone who belonged to a ward was the fact that if he failed to fulfill an obligation, his hundred or "ward" was supposed to make it up for him.[10]

A region containing many hundreds of wards was called a shire or county. For example, in the shire of southeast England, called Kent, there were 60 "hundreds" or wards.

Jefferson Wanted the Whole Nation Organized into Wards

Thomas Jefferson felt that before God's law could be realistically put into operation, the whole nation needed to be organized into wards. He said:

> "Were not this great country already divided into states, that division [into states] must be made, that each might do for itself what concerns itself directly, and what it can so much better do than a distant authority. Every state again is divided into counties, each to take care of what lies within its local bounds; each county again into townships or wards, to manage minuter details; and every ward into farms, to be governed each by its individual proprietor." [11]

He described each ward as being similar to a tiny republic with full authority to perform all of the functions of an independent township. When asked how to set up the counties of the state, he said:

> "Divide the counties into wards of such size as [so] that every citizen can attend, when called on, and act in person. Ascribe to them the government of their wards in all things relating to themselves exclusively:

8. Ibid., under "ward," p. 1754.
9. Hastings' Dictionary of the Bible, under "ward."
10. Ibid.
11. Jefferson, Letters, op. cit., p. 1308.

"A justice, chosen by themselves, in each, a constable, a military company, a patrol, a school, the care of their own poor, their own portion of the public roads, the choice of one or more jurors to serve in some court, and the delivery, within their own wards, of their own votes for all elective officers of higher sphere, [this] will relieve the county administration of nearly all its business, will have it better done, and by making every citizen an acting member of the government, and in the officers nearest and most interesting to him, will attached him by his strongest feelings to the independence of his country, and its republican constitution." [12]

This paragraph deserves careful analysis, but it contains, along with those that follow, more pure political science than any popular textbook dealing with local self-government.

A Ward Allows Prompt Determination of the Will of the People

To intelligently administer the affairs of a state or a nation, Jefferson saw the ward as a perfect microcosm to quickly sample the feelings of the people on critical issues. He said:

"Here, then, would be one of the advantages of the ward divisions I have proposed. The mayor of every ward, on a question like the present, would call his ward together, take the simple yea or nay of its members, convey these to the county court, who would hand on those of all its wards to the proper general authority; and the voice of the whole people would be thus fairly, fully, and peaceably expressed, discussed, and decided by the common reason of the society." [13]

Jefferson Began to Legislate for the Adoption of Wards

"My proposition [in the legislature] had for a further object, to impart to these wards those portions of self-government for which they are best qualified, by confiding to them the care of their poor, their roads, police, elections, the nomination of jurors, administration of justice in small cases, elementary exercises of militia, in short, to have made them little republics, with a Warden at the head of each, for all those concerns which, being under

12. Ibid., pp. 1399-1400.
13. Ibid., pp. 1402-1403.

their eye, they would better manage than the larger republics of the county or state." [14]

How the People Could Effectively Exercise Their God-Given Sovereign Power

> "A general call of ward-meetings by their Wardens on the same day throughout the state would at any time produce the genuine sense of the people on any required point, and would enable the state to act in mass, as your people have so often done [in Massachusetts], and with so much effect, by their town meetings. The law for religious freedom, which made a part of this system, having put down the aristocracy of the clergy, and restored to the citizen the freedom of the mind, and ... [provided] an equality of ... education [and] ... raised the mass of the people to the high ground of moral respectability necessary to their own safety, and to orderly government." [15]

On another occasion he said something very similar:

> "The elementary republics of the wards, the county republics, the States republics, and the republic of the Union, would form a gradation of authorities, standing each on the basis of law, holding every one its delegates share of powers, and constituting truly a system of fundamental balances and checks for the government.
>
> "Here every man is a sharer in the direction of his ward-republic, or of some of the higher ones, and feels that he is a participator in the government of affairs, not merely at an election one day in the year, but every day; when there shall not be a man in the State who will not be a member of some of its *councils*, great or small, he will let the heart be torn out of his body sooner than his power be wrested from him by a Caesar or a Bonaparte." [16]

No political writer has ever risen to greater heights in contemplating the glorious emanations of patriotic fervor which rises in the breasts of human beings who are made active participants in the daily affairs of their government. In fact, it would be difficult if not impossible to find a writer with a deeper appreciation of the beauty of participatory democracy than Thomas Jefferson.

---

14. Ibid., p. 1308.
15. Ibid.
16. Ibid., p. 1380.

In a Time of Crisis the Ward System Is Superb

Even during the early colonial period, Jefferson saw the united strength of the wards exceeding that of the rest of the country. He said:

> "How powerfully did we feel the energy of this organization [of wards] in the case of [the] embargo [prohibiting imports from England]?
>
> "I felt the foundations of the government shaken under my feet by the New England townships [wards]. There was not an individual in the State [Massachusetts] whose body was not thrown with all its momentum into action; and although the whole of the other states were known to be in favor of the measure, yet the organization of this little ... minority [of Massachusetts] enable it to overrule the Union.
>
> "What would the unwieldy counties of the middle, the south, and the west do? Call a county meeting, and the drunken loungers at ... the court houses would have collected, the distances being too great for the good people and the industrious generally to attend. The character of those who really met would have been the measure of the weight they would have had in the scale of public opinion. As Cato, then, concluded every speech with the words "Carthago delenda est," so do I [conclude] every opinion, with the injunction, "divide the counties into wards!" [17]

The Wards Provide Parent-Centered Education

There were few subjects closer to the heart of Thomas Jefferson than parent-center education. He knew from experience the key to good education, especially in the primary grades, was schools under the management of parents. He said:

> "If it is believed that these elementary schools will be better managed by the governor and council, the commissioners of the literacy fund, or any other general authority of the government than by the parents within each ward, *it is a belief against all experience*." [18]

17. Ibid., pp. 1380-1381.
18. Ibid., p. 1379.

Wards Far More Effective than Large Political Rallies

Jefferson had a low opinion of the larger precincts where they depended upon community or county rallies to generate political enthusiasm. Concerning political leaders who depend upon these rallies, he said:

> "If invited by private authority, or county or district meetings, these divisions are so large that few will attend; and their voice will be imperfectly or falsely pronounced. Here, then, would be one of the advantages of the ward divisions I have proposed." [19]

Congress Finally Agreed to Divide the Nation's Public Land into Townships Six Miles Square

Although the rich cultural legacy visualized by Jefferson was not immediately adopted, the idea of dividing the public lands into plots six miles square was presented to Congress.

On May 20, 1785, (even before the Constitution was adopted) Congress passed a law providing that all of the unoccupied public lands would be divided into townships six miles square. Each township was to contain 36 sections of land, each section being one mile square with 640 acres.

Today, anyone flying over the vast regions of America's open landscape cannot help but notice the beautiful symmetry of the carefully surveyed townships (or wards) that extend from horizon to horizon. It is like an expanded checkerboard. Tourists seldom realize that they are looking down at Thomas Jefferson's "ward" system.

If Americans had followed the brilliant concept of wards or townships as visualized by Thomas Jefferson and many of the early founders, the pioneering and cultural development of the United States could have been far more peaceful and orderly than history subsequently recorded it. This would have been particularly true if each ward was granted to the new settlers with the understanding that they would be expected to live according to the statutes of God's Law as outlined by Moses and the Anglo-Saxons.

Jefferson Was Eager to Have it Done the Right Way

But early on, Jefferson speaks of his attempt to get such a plan adopted by his own state. He says:

---

19. Ibid., pp. 1402-1403.

> "A plan was formerly proposed to the legislature of this State [Virginia] for laying off every county into hundreds or wards of five or six miles square, within each of which should be a school for the education of the children of the ward, wherein they should receive three years' instructions gratis, in reading, writing, arithmetic as far as fractions, the roots and ratios, and geography." [20]

To friends in New England he wrote:

> "I hope they will adopt the subdivision of our counties into wards. The former may be estimated at an average of twenty-four miles square; the latter should be six miles each, and would answer to the hundreds of your Saxon Alfred." [21]

The reference to King Alfred (around 870 A.D.) demonstrates how thoroughly Jefferson was acquainted with the Anglo-Saxon culture.

Jefferson's Vision of an Agricultural Aristocracy

From his early writings it is clear that Jefferson felt the best hope of America was in promoting the ward system and developing what he called an "agricultural aristocracy" of good and great people who loved the soil. One author describes his early point of view as follows:

> "In contrast to Hamilton's zeal to foster manufacturing, Jefferson wanted to foster agriculture. 'Those who labour in the earth,' he had written in his *Notes on Virginia*, 'are the chosen people of God.'
>
> "He favored assistance to commerce so that surplus agricultural commodities might be sold abroad, but rather than aid manufacturing, he believed Americans should 'let our workshops remain in Europe' and thus avoid the growth of cities whose mobs he considered a menace to 'pure government.'
>
> "To serve the interest of ordinary farmers, Jefferson believed, as they did, that what was needed was not Hamiltonian mercantilism but 'a wise and frugal government, which shall restrain men from injuring one another, shall leave them otherwise free to regulate their own pursuits.'
>
> "In particular Jefferson wished to limit the role of the federal government. He considered state governments 'the most competent

20. Ibid., p. 1348.
21. Ibid., p. 1402.

administrators for our domestic concerns and the surest bulwark against anti-republican tendencies.'"[22]

Jefferson's Answer to Those Who Wanted a Strong Central Government

"No, my friend, the way to have good and safe government, is not to trust it all to one, but to divide it among the many, distributing to every one exactly the functions he is competent to.

"Let the national government be entrusted with the defence of the nation, and its foreign and federal relations; the State governments with the civil rights, laws, police, and administration of what concerns the State generally; the counties with the local concerns of the counties, and each ward direct the interests within itself.

"It is by dividing and subdividing these republics from the great national one down through all its subordinations, until it ends in the administration of every man's farm by himself; by placing under every one what his own eye may superintend, that all will be done for the best."[23]

The Cultural Refinements Required for Life in the Ward System

No environment for the successful operation of a ward was more propitious than the one the apostles generated when they began setting up their congregations which were about ward-size. Luke describes the circumstances which Jefferson had in mind when he talked about the need for a "virtuous people" in order to make the ward system work. The Book of Acts says:

"And the multitude of them that believed were of one heart and of one soul; neither said any of them that ought [any] of the things which he possessed was his own; but they had all things in common."[24]

This was the stewardship principle where each person looked upon his property or resources as a gift of God which must be cultivated and multiplied as in the parable of the talents so there would be more to share with those in need. And as we mentioned earlier, the Christians did not have their property

22. Graebner, A History of the American People, op. cit., p. 251.
23. Letter to Joseph C. Cabell, Feb. 2, 1816, Jefferson, Letters, op. cit., pp. 1388.
24. Acts 4:32.

"in common" but rather their problems. They shared one another's problems as though each person considered them his own and wanted to help in any way possible.

We have already described the disaster which occurred in Jamestown and Plymouth when their stockholders wanted the colonists to practice "Christian communism." This was later challenged by William Bradford who said the stockholders had misinterpreted the scriptures and there was no such thing as "Christian communism." It was only as they turned to private ownership of property and the exercise of free enterprise that they saved themselves.

Luke also describes the spirit of the people as they generously undertook to make their ward or congregation a heavenly association of "virtuous people." He says:

> "Neither were there any among them that lacked: for as many as were possessors of [excess] lands or houses sold them, and brought the prices of the things that were sold, and laid them down at the apostles' feet; and distribution was made unto every man according as he had need."[25]

The Apostles Had Several Advantages in Their Wards

The remarkable spirit of godly charity exhibited by the early Christians was the genius of the ward system. However, these people were new converts who still felt the zeal of repentance and radiant covenant-making in their souls.

Furthermore, they were all of one faith, one Lord, one baptism and one belief. In a certain sense this was also true of the Anglo-Saxons.

But what about a mix of many faiths? Could a ward of multiple faiths and multiple religions unite sufficiently to overcome the frailties of human nature and the wide variety of creeds?

Jefferson recognized the challenge but he felt this impediment of traditional antagonism could be overcome if their survival was at stake and the leaders emphasized the great common denominators of all Christian faiths as Franklin had done in his famous "creed."[26] In fact, Jefferson achieved this same ecumenical spirit at the University of Virginia. This encouraged him to feel that this spirit of mutual respect and interdependence could be ultimately spread to all the wards throughout the country.

25. Acts 4:34-35.
26. Smyth, The Writings of Benjamin Franklin, op. cit., 10:84.

The whole process would be facilitated as people began to recognize the supreme advantage of living in a ward.

The Appealing Advantages of Living in a Ward

The bristly briars of human nature which many people cynically concluded would make the operation of a theoretical "ward" a practical impossibility, overlook the fact that human nature might also be motivated to see some tremendous advantage of "life within a ward" system. For example:

1. A ward, when properly organized, would provide an astonishing degree of security for both the individual and family. It is one thing to go out into the wilds and try to survive, and quite another thing to be surrounded by a body of fairly decent people who are anxious to make "life in the ward system" a success.

2. The goal of the ward leaders is to see that everyone has adequate employment and the security of a decent home. If a person demonstrates a willingness to be industrious it is possible to obtain a loan, at no interest (one of the advantages of God's law), and have the backing of the ward if unforeseen circumstances make it temporarily impossible to keep up the payments.

3. The ward constitutes a support group of decent people—the Founders called them "virtuous people"—which makes it remarkably easier to raise and educate a family in a wholesome, happy environment. The elected leaders have a responsibility to immediately deal with behavioral problems and when a bronco youngster is being loved and supervised by captains of tens, fifties and the hundred, it really makes a difference in ameliorating the worries and stress of parenthood.

4. The entire operation of a ward is structured to carry out the will and aspirations of the people themselves. There is no dictatorial authority from above to manipulate them, deceive them or politically propagandize them. They not only get to elect their captains of tens, fifties, and their own hundred, but they also have a voice and a vote in choosing every leader above them—the captains of thousands, tens of thousands and even the leaders of the whole nation.

5. The close-knit social structure of a ward greatly reduces the risks of life which are inherent in this mortal existence. In a mature, well-developed ward a person would enjoy the benefits of affordable:

   Health insurance.

Hospital insurance (in a cooperative hospital built and sustained by a consortium of wards).

Disability insurance.

Unemployment insurance.

Old Age retirement insurance with an opportunity to continue in some kind of useful service.

Plus the opportunity to change jobs.

The opportunity to change to another ward if desired.

Exceptional opportunities for varied recreational facilities and generous vacations each year.

Spiritual growth and training in the church of one's choice.

A Vision of the Future

It is important to remember that the Founding Fathers had their eyes on the future, and none of them more so than Jefferson.

They anticipated the day—predicted by Moses—when the people in the new Zion would have an opportunity to "obey the voice of the Lord, and do all the commandments [under God's law] which I command thee this day. And the Lord thy God will make thee plenteous in every work of thine hand, in the fruit of thy body, and in the fruit of thy cattle, and in the fruit of thy land for good: for the Lord will again rejoice over thee for good, as he rejoiced over thy fathers." [27]

It will be recalled that the last two Founding Fathers—Thomas Jefferson and John Adams—died on the same day. It was July 4, 1826, exactly fifty years after the adoption of the famous Declaration of Independence.

As John Adams was dying he seemed to be thinking of the only other living founding father survivor as he roused himself from a coma long enough to say, "Thomas Jefferson survives ...."

But 500 miles to the south, at Monticello, Virginia, the valiant Jefferson had already crossed the veil just a few hours before John Adams. These two great vanguards of God's Law had been compelled to leave their unfinished work to others hands.

27. Deuteronomy 30:8-9.

Dr. Thomas Chalmers Experiment with God's Law

It is not likely that Rev. Thomas Chalmers (1780-1847) had come to the attention of either John Adams or Thomas Jefferson, but they would have rejoiced if they had known what God's law was accomplishing in a faraway corner of Scotland. I am indebted to Vicki Joe Anderson—a fellow researcher and writer—who furnished me with the following account just in time to be included in this present book. Here, in part, is what she wrote:

> "The biography of Thomas Chalmers began with his birth on March 17, 1780 in Anstrutyher, Scotland. He was the sixth of fourteen children ....
>
> "At the age of fifteen he entered divinity school ... and at the age of nineteen Thomas Chalmers received his doctor of divinity [with additional recognition for his distinguished contribution in chemistry and mathematics] ....
>
> "Chalmers maintained that it was essential for a Christian church to possess the right of self-government, undisturbed by the intrusion of secular government. This lead to a great disruption with Chalmers and others separating from the Church of Scotland and forming the Free Church of Scotland.
>
> "Following Chalmers, four hundred and seventy ministers resigned their livings and joined the Free Church."[28]

The Experiment Begins

The account relates:

> "In 1820, the chance came for Chalmers to implement his belief. He transfered to the largest and poorest parish in Scotland. He convinced the town council to give him the right to administer the welfare funds raised by the church rather than those collected by the town through compulsory taxation.
>
> "Dividing the parish into districts and sub-districts, much like the Law of the Covenant under Moses, he chose laymen of Christian character ... There were twenty-five districts with 50 to 100 families and over each was placed an elder and a deacon. The elder worked with the families' spiritual needs and the deacon addressed their physical needs.

28. From a manuscript in the possession of the author.

"Chalmers personally supervised the whole program making an effort to visit every family in the entire parish. His efforts were highly successful.

"Chalmers believed that 'compulsory assessment,' or taxation for welfare—as we know it today—only resulted in the swelling of the welfare rolls and that relief funds should be raised and administered by voluntary means. He felt taxation created the very monster it was trying to eliminate ....

"It was the job of the deacon to interview every family residing in this district, who were making application for help. Every effort was made to help enable the poor to help themselves. Once the system was in operation it was found that a deacon, by spending an hour a week among the families committed to his charge could keep himself acquainted with their character and condition. And by analyzing their resources and sharing with others within their district, many got by where they had been unable to before.

In the End the Bureacrats Won

"In the beginning, the poor of the parish were costing the city 1400 per anum, and in four years, through the adoption of Chalmers method, the welfare cost to the city was reduced to 280 per anum. The results were not only accompained by an economic success, but by an increase of morality as well. Drunkeness decreased, and parents took an increased interest in the welfare of their children.

"Chalmers pleaded with the city to allow him to continue, but a new council had taken over and a law was passed taking the control out of the church's hand and placing it back into the hands of the government." [29]

Nevertheless, what all of this illustrated was the fact that God's law is wiser than man's law and when it is administered by those who understand it, the results are remarkably successful.

Until God's Law Is Established What Can a Family Do to Achieve Some of These Goals?

It will be obvious that it is a tremendous advantage to a family to be a participating member of a ward or some other organized group designed for

29. Ibid.

mutual protection and assistance. However, the risks of life being what they are, certain additional steps should be taken by a family to soften the blow of any unexpected emergency. Here are some suggestions:

> The family should have on hand a carefully planned one-year's supply of food, savings, clothes, and a trustworthy vehicle.
>
> The stability of the entire family can be fortified by getting completely out of debt. This takes frugality and sacrifice, but it will bring more satisfaction and peace of mind than a debt-ridden person could even imagine. Being out of debt and having a high credit rating is a major asset in a time of unexpected emergency.
>
> "Togetherness" is also a key characteristic of a high quality family. They talk together, watch good programs together, take trips together, and go to church together.

Togetherness is strengthened by holding weekly home evenings. It is an ideal time to discuss future plans, major expenditures, family problems, studies of the scriptures, and a discussion of God's law and its application to the problems of everyday life.

There should be a pooling of risks (by way of insurance) to protect family health and protect property against fire, theft, and automobile accidents. Liability insurance is also important as well as a certain amount of life insurance.

We should also mention the supreme importance of reinforcing the moral stability of the family. Under God's law there should be complete sexual abstinence before marriage and genuine fidelity after marriage. Think of the avalanche of heartbreaks and divorces which would be prevented if each family followed a strict adherence to God's moral code.

Topics for Reflection and Discussion

1. What nation besides the Anglo-Saxons borrowed some of their ideas from God's law? Name three advantages in a society that depends on orderly procedures and voluntary discipline. Which of the Founders knew the most about the Anglo-Saxons?

2. What was a "tithing?" What did they call the person in charge? What was a "vill?" What did they call the person in charge? What was a "Hundred?" What did they call the person in charge?

3. What was the advantage in dealing with a person who belonged to a ward? In England what did they call a region with several hundred wards? In what way was a ward like a tiny republic?

4. How did the ward system allow the leaders to promptly determine the will of the people? In a time of crisis why was the ward so efficient?

5. Why did Jefferson feel it was an advantage to have parent-centered schools in each ward? By what means did Jefferson, John Adams and others get the unoccupied public lands divided into six miles square? What was each square designed to become?

6. In your opinion, to what extent would it have changed the settling of the United States if it had been based on the ward system? What advantage would it have been if the United States had emphasized a dominance of the agriculture life rather than large industrial centers?

7. Describe the ideal separation of powers as Jefferson visualized it. In what way did the Christian apostles achieve the cultural refinements and social bonding which Jefferson visualized for life in the ward system?

8. But what advantages did the apostles have which a secular ward of many faiths might find extremely challenging? How did Jefferson expect to overcome these problems?

9. Name three attractive advantages which could be used in persuading people to enter into a ward? Name two ways it would be advantageous to parents seeking to raise a creditable family? Do you see any advantage to parents in the way the ward was structured?

10. In what specific ways did the life-style of the ward take a great deal of the stress out of the ordinary risks of life? What was the ultimate expectation of the Founders concerning the ward system? Who had predicted it?

CHAPTER TWENTY-EIGHT

STRONG WARNINGS FROM THE FOUNDERS AND EARLY AMERICAN LEADERS

When the Founders set up the first free people in modern times they knew it was risky business. They all realized that any man-made institution—even under the inspiration of the Almighty—would be subject to foibles and human weaknesses of those who worked under its canopy. Nevertheless, these men who master-minded the United States of America had the highest aspirations for the great nation they were founding. It was only in their quiet, more somber moments that their apprehensions concerning the future of America came out in concrete phrases and words.

THE WARNING OF BENJAMIN FRANKLIN

Next to Washington, probably no American did more to serve the United States and bring about the final victory over England than Benjamin Franklin.

Not only did he secure the first shipment of arms from France, but eventually he induced Louis XVI to enter the war on the side of the United States and provide both troops and a fleet of ships.

After the Revolutionary War was won, Franklin became the principal negotiator, backed up by John Jay and John Adams. Not only did the Americans gain their complete independence from England, but Franklin pushed the British to double the territory of the United States by acquiring title to practically all of the territory between the Atlantic seaboard and the Mississippi River.

Later, Franklin served as one of the foremost architects in structuring the Constitution, and while most of the Founders were congratulating one another on their remarkable charter of liberty, Benjamin Franklin injected this note of prophetic insight.

WHAT HAPPENS WHEN THE PEOPLE BECOME CORRUPT?

Franklin said:

> "I agree to this Constitution … and I believe, further, that this is likely to be well administered for a course of years, and can only end in despotism, as other forms have done before it, when the people shall become so corrupted as to need despotic government, being incapable of any other." [1]

All of this went along with Franklin's basic philosophy of sound government; namely, that no people can remain free if they become wicked and immoral.

When a society decays to the point where people begin to fear for their lives and their property, the demands for a police state have always been inevitable.

The Warning Voice of President George Washington

When the Constitution was adopted, no one could have been more elated than George Washington as he contemplated the rise of a free, prosperous and magnificent new nation.

However, after he had served two terms as President, he had some insightful and sobering thoughts about the future.

It was September 19, 1796 when President Washington formally announced that he was retiring at the end of his second term, thus bringing to a conclusion forty-six years of public service by one of the greatest Americans that ever lived.

In addition to announcing his retirement, Washington took this occasion to issue his famous Farewell Address. In this address he offered a number of carefully calculated warnings based on the wisdom of a brilliant mind and the experience of a lifetime as a soldier and a statesman.

In chapter 23 we mentioned his vociferous warning against political parties and political spoils.

We should also mention the warning of Washington concerning the insidious and subtle forces which he felt were creeping into the structure of government which could destroy the very foundation of constitutional government.

---

1. Smyth, The Writings of Benjamin Franklin, op. cit., 9:569.

Warning Against One Branch of Government Devouring the Others

Almost prophetically he anticipated the encroachment of one branch of government over the others. He said:

> "It is important ... that ... those entrusted with its administration ... confine themselves within their respective constitutional spheres, avoiding in the exercise of the powers of one department any encroachment upon another ... The spirit of encroachment tends to consolidate the powers of all the departments in one, and thus to create ... a real despotism."[2]

Imagine the indignation of Washington if, in our day, he could see the Congress meddling in foreign affairs all around the globe with committee investigations, special missions, foreign excursions, etc. The Constitution gave these responsibilities to the President and the State Department.

At the same time he would be equally shocked to see the President and the Executive Branch issuing more laws and regulations than Congress, and all of which is in direct violation of Article I, Section 1 of the Constitution. It reads:

> "All legislative powers herein granted shall be vested in a congress of the United States which shall consist of a Senate and House of Representatives."

Today, we see the President proclaiming administrative and regulatory laws through a whole army of administrative agencies in direct violation of this provision.

To add insult to injury, the Supreme Court rises up to issue rules and regulations to both the Executive and the Legislative branches of government as well as all fifty states. Many of these decrees relate to matters never mentioned in the Constitution.

Changing the Constitution by Usurpation Rather than by Amendment

Nothing aroused the wrath of Washington more than arrogant bureaucrats actually changing the fundamental structure of government by sheer despotic assertion of administrative power. He said:

---

2. Fitzpatrick, The Writings of George Washington, op. cit., 35:225.

> "If, in the opinion of the people, the distribution or modification of the constitutional powers be in any particular wrong, let it be corrected by an amendment in the way which the Constitution designates. But let there be no change by usurpations; for though this, in one instance, may be the instrument of good, it is the customary weapon by which free governments are destroyed."[3]

We could easily make a list of a hundred changes in the overall structure of government today which was done by usurpation rather than amendment.

Major examples would include the setting up of a worthless currency system rather than using gold and silver as required by Article I, Section 10, clause 1.

Then there is the setting up of the so-called Federal Reserve System which allowed trillions of dollars in debt to accumulate with nothing behind the debt but federal bonds which are simply IOUs on the American taxpayer.

Washington's warning went unheeded in the Supreme Court allowing the federal usurping of jurisdiction over labor unions, the meddling with intra-state commerce under the theory that it indirectly affected inter-state commerce, etc.

And so it has gone down through the years.

Washington's Vigorous Denunciation of Immorality and Irreligion

On these two important subjects, he said:

> "Of all the … habits which lead to political prosperity, religion and morality are indispensable supports. In vain would that man claim the tribute of patriotism who labors to subvert these great pillars of human happiness … It is substantially true that virtue and morality is a necessary spring of popular government … Who … can look with indifference upon attempts to shake the foundation of the fabric?"[4]

Washington Would Severely Chastise the Supreme Court of Our Day

It is obvious that the Founders would have totally disowned a Supreme Court that outlawed prayer in school, eliminated reading of the Bible in

3. Ibid.
4. Ibid.

the classroom and made schools tear out plaques from the walls of school buildings setting forth the Ten Commandments.

Notice that Washington says these "supports" are the very things that are "indispensable" to the well-being of the nation. He calls a person devoid of the very essence of genuine patriotism who undertakes to subvert these great pillars of human happiness.

So, from Washington's own words, the Supreme Court and thousands of school administrators should have no doubt as to how this great Founding Father would have felt about the way American children are being mis-educated today.

John Adams Says the Constitution Will Never Work for an Immoral and Irreligious People

Among the warning voices of the Founders none was more forceful in proclaiming the need for a virtuous people to make the Constitution function than John Adams. He said:

> "Our Constitution was made *only* for a moral and religious people. It is wholly inadequate to the government of any other." [5]

This coincided with the warning of Benjamin Franklin who said:

> "Only a virtuous people are capable of freedom. As nations become corrupt and vicious they have more need of masters." [6]

Franklin is simply emphasizing that whenever a nation becomes so lawless and decadent that life and property cease to be secure, the people will demand that the government mobilize its police powers to maintain order and provide protection. In the process, these forces of government become the "masters" Franklin was talking about. He had seen such demands of the people for masters evolve into despots all over Europe.

The Role of Jefferson as the Architect of the Constitution

Although James Madison is often called "the father of the Constitution," he tells us in the *Federalist Papers* that it was Thomas Jefferson who was

---

5. Howe, The Changing Political Thought of John Adams, op. cit., p. 189.
6. Speech at the Constitutional Convention, Sept. 17, 1787, Smyth, The Writings of Benjamin Franklin, op. cit., 9:607.

really the great architect or "chief magistrate" of the American constitutional structure.[7]

This is important since we have Jefferson's constant warning that the American system cannot survive unless it continues to be grounded on those sound precepts which Jefferson considered to have come from a divine origin.

For example, Jefferson spent nearly sixteen days making certain that the "ancient principles" of Anglo-Saxon law or God's law were stipulated or implied in the first two paragraphs of the Declaration of Independence.[8]

He also worked with Benjamin Franklin and John Adams to make certain that the official seal of the United States illustrated that its constitution and laws came from God. This committee had ancient Israel portrayed on one side of the seal and the Anglo-Saxons—who preserved God's law for centuries—portrayed on the other.

Unfortunately, this proposal for the original seal was temporarily misplaced and when the Congress found itself under pressure to come up with something immediately available, they chose the pyramid design which now appears on the back of the dollar bill. This was copied from the Continental currency and did not carry the powerful message of the more symbolic seal proposed by Jefferson, John Adams, and Benjamin Franklin.[9]

Jefferson—Even in His Day—Called the Supreme Court the Foremost Enemy of the Constitution

During his two terms as President, Jefferson detected some evil and subversive trends which were luring the American people away from the original Constitution. Notice how direct he was in pointing the finger of accusation at the judiciary for corrupting the original constitutional plan:

> "Our government is now taking so steady a course as to show by what road it will pass to destruction, to wit, by consolidation first, and then corruption … The engine of consolidation will be the federal judiciary; the two other branches the corrupting and corrupted instruments." [10]

In other words, the Supreme Court uses its judicial mandates to draw more and more power to Washington; then the Congress and the Executive

7. Madison, Federalist Papers, op. cit., Number 48, p. 310.
8. See Skousen, The Making of America, op. cit., p. 28.
9. Ibid., pp. 32-33.
10. Bergh, The Writings of Thomas Jefferson, op. cit., 15:331-332.

use this new power to shatter the Constitution and corrupt the dual federalism which was designed to balance the political powers between the government and the states.

Thomas Jefferson—One of America's Foremost Lawyers—Saw the Federal Courts Destroying States Rights

Once Jefferson's distant cousin, John Marshall, became chief justice of the Supreme Court, Marshall set himself and his associates up as the "final arbiter" on all constitutional issues. Nowhere in the Constitution was the federal judiciary given the power to enforce its will on the states or the other two federal departments. Jefferson had the Supreme Court in his gun sights when he wrote:

> "The great object of my fear is the federal judiciary. That body, like gravity, ever acting with noiseless foot and unalarming advance, gaining ground step by step and holding what it gains, is engulfing insidiously the [state] governments into the jaws of that [federal government] which feeds them." [11]

On another occasion he explicitly pointed to the courts as the major villain in the corruption of the whole American system:

> "It has long … been my opinion, and I have never shrunk from its expression … that the germ of dissolution of our federal government is in the constitution of our federal judiciary; an irresponsible body (for impeachment is scarcely a scarecrow), working like gravity by night and by day, gaining a little today and a little tomorrow, and advancing its noiseless step like a thief over the field of jurisdiction, until all shall be usurped from the states, and the government of all be consolidated into one.
>
> "To this I am opposed, because when all government, domestic and foreign, in little as in great things, shall be drawn to Washington as the center of power, it will render powerless the checks provided of one government on another, and will become as venal and oppressive as the government from which we separated [Great Britain]." [12]

---

11. Ford, The Writings of Thomas Jefferson, op. cit., 10:189.
12. Bergh, The Writings of Thomas Jefferson, op. cit., 15:331-332.

Jefferson Greatly Feared Precisely What Has Happened

Jefferson was relentless in his campaign to awaken the American people to the collectivization policy of the Court. He said:

> "There is no danger I apprehend so much as the consolidation of our government by the noiseless, and therefore unalarming, instrumentality of the Supreme Court." [13]

And again:

> "The judiciary of the United States is the subtle corps of sappers and miners constantly working underground to undermine the foundations of our confederated fabric.
>
> "They are construing our Constitution from a coordination of a general and special government to a general and supreme one alone. This will lay all things at their feet." [14]

Originally the Supreme Court Decided Cases But was "Helpless and Harmless" when it Came to Governing America

Jefferson felt the Supreme Court had lost its vision of how it was supposed to function in the constitutional scheme of things. He said:

> "At the establishment of our constitutions, the judiciary bodies were supposed to be the most helpless and harmless members of the government. Experience, however, soon showed in what way they were to become the most dangerous; that the insufficiency of the means provided for their removal gave them a freehold and irresponsibility in office; that their decisions, seeming to concern individual suitors only, pass silent and unheeded by the public at large; that these decisions nevertheless became law by precedent, sapping by little and little the foundations of the Constitution, and working its change by construction, before anyone has perceived that the invisible and helpless worm has been busily employed in consuming its substance in truth, man is not made to be trusted for life if assured against all liability to account." [15]

---

13. Ibid., 15:421.
14. Ibid., 15:297.
15. Ibid., 15:486-487.

Jefferson Proposed an Amendment to Control the Judiciary Before it Was Too Late

To curb the tidal wave of power gravitating to Washington, Jefferson felt a solid "separation of powers" amendment was required before it was too late. He said:

> "There was another amendment of which none of us thought at the time [when the Constitution was being framed], and in the omission of which lurks the germ that is to destroy this happy combination of national powers in the general government for matters of national concern, and independent powers in the states for what concerns the states severally ....
>
> "I deem it indispensable to the continuance of this government that they [the judges] should be submitted to some practical and impartial control; and that this, to be impartial, must be compounded of a mixture of state and federal authorities [to enforce it].
>
> "It is not enough that honest men are appointed judges. All know the influence of [special] interest on the mind of man, and how unconsciously his judgment is warped by that influence ....
>
> "I do not charge the judges with willful and ill-intentioned error, but honest error must be arrested where its toleration leads to public ruin. As for the safety of society, we commit honest maniacs to bedlam [an insane asylum], so judges should be withdrawn from their bench whose erroneous biases are leading us to dissolution.
>
> "It may, indeed, injure them [the Supreme Court judges] in fame or in fortune; but it saves the Republic, which is the first and supreme law." [16]

So much for the warnings of Thomas Jefferson. He did not get his amendment, but there is no doubt that he was very angry with what he saw happening. He could not have been more pointed if he had been arguing his points before a jury with his cousin, John Marshall, on trial for treason (for giving aid and comfort to the enemy).

---

16. Ibid., 1:120-122.

The Warnings of James Madison

As a modern American reads the prophetic words of James Madison, the master technician at the Constitutional Convention, we would almost think he was living among us today and describing what we are experiencing.

Madison was known to be the philosophical soul-mate of Thomas Jefferson, but sometimes his contemporaries considered him somewhat paranoid and suffering from fears for the nation that would never happen. But the passing of time was to prove him more insightful than many of his contemporaries had thought. He said:

> "If Congress can employ money indefinitely, for the general welfare, and are the sole and supreme judges of the general welfare, they may take the care of religion into their own hands; they may appoint teachers in every state, county, and parish, and pay them out of the public treasury; they may take into their own hands the education of children, the establishing in like manner schools throughout the union; they may assume the provision of the poor … Were the power of Congress to be established in the latitude contended for, it would subvert the very foundations, and transmute the very nature of the limited government established by the people of America." [17]

In a future sixth edition of *Prophecy and Modern Times*, we shall discuss how this potential nightmare became a stark reality and changed the whole economic system of the United States. In the process, it pulled down several of the most important pillars of the Constitution.

Samuel Adams Declared Socialism and the Welfare State Totally Unconstitutional in America

It was the purpose of the Founders to completely outlaw socialism or the welfare state in the United States. Sam Adams who is sometimes called the "father of the Revolution," had this to say:

> "The utopian schemes of leveling [redistribution of the wealth] and a community of goods [communism] are as visionary and impracticable as those which vest all property in the Crown. [They] are arbitrary, despotic, and, in our government, unconstitutional." [18]

17. Quoted by Thomas James Norton, Undermining the Constitution -- A History of Lawless Government, New York: Devin-Adair Co., 1950, p. 188.
18. Wells, The Life and Public Service of Samuel Adams, op. cit., 1:154.

Thomas Jefferson is also frequently quoted on this subject of the welfare state when he said:

> "If we can prevent the government from wasting the labors of the people under the pretense of taking care of them, they must be happy." [19]

Samuel Adams Also Warned That a Sound Constitution Will Not Save a Wicked Nation

There have always been some who say, "Give us a sound system of government and the morals will take care of themselves." To this Sam Adams replied:

> "Neither the wisest constitution nor the wisest laws will secure the liberty and happiness of a people whose manners are universally corrupt." [20]

Abraham Lincoln Warns Against the Destruction of the United States by Suicide

At the age of twenty-eight, Abraham Lincoln gave one of the great speeches of his life.

He had been asked to speak at the Young Men's Lyceum at Springfield, the capital city of Illinois. He chose as his subject, "The Perpetuation of Our Political Institutions." The date was January 27, 1837.

Lincoln deplored the spirit of lawlessness that was increasing among the people. He said:

> "There is even now something of ill omen amongst us. I mean that increasing disregard for law which pervades the country—the growing disposition to substitute the wild and furious passion in lieu of the sober judgment of courts, and the worse than savage mobs for the executive ministers of justice. The disposition is awfully fearful in any community; and that it now exists in ours … it would be a violation of truth to deny." [21]

He was not afraid of invasion from without, but he saw the ominous possibility of self-destruction from within. He said:

---

19. Bergh, The Writings of Thomas Jefferson, op. cit., 10:342.
20. Wells, The Life and Public Service of Samuel Adams, op. cit., 1:22.
21. Nicolay and Jay, Complete Works of Abraham Lincoln, New York: Francis D. Tandy Co., 1894, 1:36-37.

> "At what point, then, is the approach of danger to be expected? I answer, if it ever reaches us, it must spring up among us. It cannot come from abroad. If destruction be our lot, we must ourselves be its author and finisher. As a nation of freemen, we must live through all time or die by suicide." [22]

Daniel Webster Warns Against Disintegrating Poison in the American Culture

Daniel Webster was one of the most eloquent orators the United States ever produced.

He was born in New Hampshire three months after the British surrender at Yorktown which virtually ended the Revolutionary War. After graduating from Dartmouth and being admitted to the bar at the age of 23, he spent the next five years learning how to turn ordinary words and phrases into polished jewels.

He had a rich, resonant voice, and a great dignity in his bearing, but the power of his delivery was facilitated by his ability to memorize the entire text of his public addresses.

As the slavery issue threatened to divide the nation he would often close each speech with this thundering declaration:

> "The Union, one and inseparable, now and forever!"

But one of his most memorable statements concerning the troubled country was his contemplation of what had made America great followed by his contrasting anxiety that it may not survive. He said:

> "Unborn ages and visions of glory crowd upon my soul, the realization of all which, however, is in the hands and good pleasure of Almighty God; but, under his divine blessing, it will be dependent on the character and virtues of ourselves and our posterity ....
>
> "If we and they shall live always in the fear of God, and shall respect his commandments ... we may have the highest hopes of the future fortune of our country ... It will have no decline and fall. It will go on prospering.
>
> "But if we and our posterity reject religious instruction and authority, violate the rules of eternal justice, trifle with the injunc-

---

22. Ibid.

> tions of morality, and recklessly destroy the political Constitution which holds us together, no man can tell how sudden a catastrophe may overwhelm us, that shall bury all our glory in profound obscurity.
>
> "Should that catastrophe happen, let it have no history! Let the horrible narrative never be written." [23]

One of the Most Significant Warnings of All Was by Alexis De Tocqueville

In 1830 a young judge from France arrived in America. His name was Alexis de Tocqueville. He was accompanied by a young lawyer named Gustave de Beaumont, a grandson of the Marquis de Lafayette, who was the noted French hero of the American Revolutionary War.

These two French travelers soaked up more information about the great American experiment in ten months than most scholars absorb in a lifetime.

Much of this was due to the fact that they were both unusually well-educated in history and political science. They travelled extensively up and down the Atlantic seaboard, asking thousands of questions and taking careful notes. Then they crossed the Alleghenies and probed the hearts and minds of those living on the frontier.

Returning to France, Alexis de Tocqueville wrote a two-volume work entitled, *Democracy in America*. De Tocqueville saw the people of the United States passing through several distinct stages.

First of all, he saw the strength of character and moral integrity that would make them prosperous.

But as they became self-sufficient he saw that they would be less concerned about each other and much less concerned about the principles that made them a great people.

This would leave them vulnerable to the manipulation of clever politicians who would begin to promise them perpetual security if they accepted certain schemes contrived by some of their leaders. He then described what modern students have been led to identify as "democratic socialism."

23. Delivered before the New York Historical Society, February 22, 1852, quoted by Skousen in The Making of America, op. cit., pp. 687-688.

The Lure of Democratic Socialism

The fascinating aspect of democratic socialism is that while the people lose their inherent freedoms in exchange for promises of security, they think they still have their freedom because they get to choose their leaders at the polls. But their leaders are always those who believe in the rapid centralization of political and economic power. Of course, as de Tocqueville points out, they plan to do it gently and gradually so as not to arouse any alarm. But the goal is ultimate despotism over the whole nation, and once the people have lost their freedom, nothing but revolution and bloodshed will bring it back.

The Despotic Elements of Democratic Socialism

De Tocqueville knew both the greedy science and nefarious art of spinning the web of socialism. He describes how very gradually the economic and political choices of the people are circumscribed by a network of regulations, rituals and rules which the people begin to accept as the normal pattern of life. Thus, the people lose their freedom without ever realizing exactly when it happened. He says:

> "That power is absolute, minute, regular, provident, and mild. It would be like the authority of a parent, if, like that authority, its object was to prepare men for manhood; but it seeks on the contrary to keep them in perpetual childhood; it is well content that the people should rejoice, provided they think of nothing but rejoicing.
>
> "For their happiness such a government willingly labors, but it chooses to be the sole agent and the only arbiter of that happiness; it provides for their security, foresees and supplies their necessities, facilitates their pleasures, manages their principal concerns, directs their industry, regulates the descent of property, and subdivides their inheritances—what remains, to spare them all the care of thinking and the trouble of living."[24]

De Tocqueville Described How America Could Be Taken over and Lose its Freedom

De Tocqueville even visualized how a whole people could be captured in this kind of sociological miasma. Here is how he thought it would be done:

24. de Tocqueville, Democracy in America, op. cit., 2:336.

> "After having thus successively taken each member of the community in its powerful grasp, and fashioned them at will, the supreme power then extends its arm over the whole community. It covers the surface of society with a network of small complicated rules, minute and uniform, through which the most original minds and the most energetic characters cannot penetrate, to rise above the crowd.
>
> "The will of man is not shattered, but softened, bent, and guided—men are seldom forced by it to act, but they are constantly restrained from acting. Such a power does not destroy, but it prevents existence; it does not tyrannize, but it compresses, enervates, extinguishes, and stupefies a people, till [the] nation is reduced to be nothing better than a flock of timid and industrious animals, of which the government is the shepherd."[25]

Of course, this does not go on forever, because eventually the bribery, cheating, conniving and internal conspiratorial forces operating in such a system initiate a cancerous rot of social self-destruction. That is when a nation either disintegrates or generates sufficient fire in its soul to reach up once more for the glory of its past.

The Founders' Long-Range Perspective

In spite of everything we have read in this chapter, every student of the writings of the Founders will recognize their expectation that even though the legacy they gave the United States might falter, there was a divine or manifest destiny for America that would cause her to rise, Phoenix-like, from the ashes.

Jefferson said Biblical Christianity would be restored, though not in his time, and he looked forward to the day when God's law would be raised up and practiced exactly as Moses had predicted.

To make this possible he knew the inhabitants of America would have to be humbled and become a virtuous people. He also knew that some day the inspired, original Constitution would have to be restored in all of its pristine simplicity and beauty.

---

25. Ibid., 2:337.

Topics for Reflection and Discussion

1. If the coming American crisis is not inevitable, what could prevent it from happening?

2. What did Benjamin Franklin mean when he said Americans would demand a "despotic government" if they became corrupt? Can you think of any other countries where this happened?

3. Do you feel comfortable with Franklin's statement that, "Only a virtuous people are capable of freedom" ? Name three ways in which the three branches of the federal government have encroached on one another just as George Washington feared.

4. Name three ways in which the Constitution has been amended by usurpation instead of following the constitutional procedure. Up to this point has the elimination of religion and morality "shaken the foundations of the nation"? What are some examples?

5. Thomas Jefferson said the destruction of America could come from two major factors. What were they? Which department of the federal government did Jefferson say had done the most to consolidate political and economic power in Washington?

6. Why did Jefferson emphasize that in the beginning the courts were weak and helpless compared to the other departments? Whom did Jefferson blame more than any other single person for the trend to exercise massive power in the Supreme Court?

7. How would you define a "welfare state?" What trends in the United States during the past century have developed in spite of the warnings of James Madison? Have any of Madison's predictions been fulfilled so far?

8. What did Samuel Adams say the Constitution had done to the idea of socialism, communism and the welfare state? What accompanies the spirit of lawlessness which Abraham Lincoln said could lead to national suicide?

9. Who was Alexis de Tocqueville? Who was the man who came to America with him and was related to a great American hero? What is so remarkable about the two-volume set of books de Tocqueville wrote after returning to France? Give his description of what we have now come to call "democratic socialism." What has it been doing to the United States.

10. How would you describe the Founders' long range perspective? What are some of the changes our survival will require? Will the original Constitution have to be restored?

CHAPTER TWENTY-NINE

Preparing America for the Adoption of God's Law

The Founders knew that some day America would pick up where Moses left off and bring back the splendid order of God's law which would lay the foundation for the glorious political kingdom of God described by Daniel.[1] But of course they also knew this could not happen until the people had been prepared in a very special way to enjoy that great blessing.

The strong warnings of the Founding Fathers indicate that they were aware that before God's law could be initiated, the people of America might have to go through a monumental reform or even a thorough cleansing of the nation.

From the very beginning there have been leaders such as Jefferson, Washington, Madison and Franklin who saw the original Constitution and the principles of God's law as the golden bench mark or the straight and narrow path for the building of an independent, free, happy, prosperous people.

At the same time—as we have seen—there have been those enterprising, ambitious people like Alexander Hamilton who possessed ability and ingenuity but sought every opportunity to do things their way even if it involved dangerous manipulating or even distorting of the original, inspired system in order to achieve their objectives.

Over the years I have tried to carefully study the lives and careers of those who were of Hamilton's talent and temperament, and it has been astonishing to discover how far off the track they have led America. It was also shocking to find out how many unconstitutional twists and turns have been justified because of some emergency or trying to cope with a depression, or attempting to "improve on the Founders' formula," or "to help the poor."

But the bottom line is that our majestic ship of state has ended up on a sand bar, far outside the Constitution in so many different areas that as a teacher of constitutional principles I was astonished with the audacity of those who thought they could get away with it.

1. Daniel 2:44.

Could the Preparation for God's Law Be by Massive Reformation?

As our years of research demonstrated, the adoption of God's law does not depend so much upon restructuring of the Constitution and the passage of new legislation as it does on the elimination of the moral and social decay among the people themselves. Until this is achieved no amount of legal reformation will help. In fact, with the reformation of the people a very simple and much less complex system of law will function admirably.

So the massive reformation of the people *could* definitely provide the wholesome environment for the adoption of God's law.

But what if the masses of the people reject the call to reform and continue reveling in the decadence of degradation which Jesus said would prevail in the latter days just as it did in the days of Noah?[2]

In that case, a whole new set of rules apply.

The History of Nations That Have Angered God

Thomas Jefferson knew there was such a thing as Americans becoming so depraved they could lose the privilege of living in America. He said:

> "I tremble for my country when I reflect that God is just, that his justice cannot sleep forever."[3]

The Apostle Paul also knew that a nation which mocks God stands in dire peril. He said:

> "Be not deceived; God is not mocked: for whatsoever a man soweth, that shall he also reap."[4]

The Apostle Peter added his warning:

> "For if God spared not the angels that sinned, but cast them down to hell, and delivered them into chains of darkness to be reserved unto judgment; and spared not the old world [from the Great Flood], but saved Noah the eighth person, a preacher of righteousness, bringing the flood upon the world of the ungodly; and turning the cities of Sodom and Gomorrah into ashes condemned

---

2. Matthew 24:37.
3. An inscription on the wall of the Jefferson Memorial, Washington, D.C.
4. Galatians 6:7.

> them with an overthrow, making them an ensample unto those that after should live ungodly [lives]." [5]

The chief of the apostles is simply saying that when an extremely patient and long-suffering God has watched a people degrade themselves until they have reached the point of no return, the hedonistic existence of that nation will suddenly grind to a shuddering halt through divine intervention.

No nation is immune from the administration of God's justice.

The Cleansing Can Come in Numerous Ways

As any student of history knows, when God's judgment cleanses a nation, it often comes as an unmitigated disaster. In some cases this has been by a surprise attack from a powerful enemy, with burning, looting, devastation and bloodshed. At other times it has come by flood, hurricanes and earthquakes. But the most devastating of all has been by the massive affliction of an irresistible scourge of an incurable plague.

Biblical prophecy suggests that a massive, widespread affliction of consuming plagues will be the principal means by which major regions of the earth will be cleansed in the latter days.[6]

Consider some of these plagues of the past. The bubonic plague cleared out nearly half the population in some parts of the earth in a matter of months. There were 25,000,000 deaths in Europe alone.[7]

In 1918 the influenza plague brought the United States to a standstill.[8] This spread worldwide and took the lives of more than 12,000,000 people.

I was only a small boy at the time, but I can remember being virtually house-bound, with no one going to church, no one going to school, no public meetings being held, and only a few wearing heavy masks going to the stores where the shelves were practically stripped bare. Sometimes for weeks there were not enough healthy workers available to bury the dead. In midwinter my father helped a neighbor bury two little girls.

But plagues of the past have usually been short-lived; often within eighteen months they may have disappeared.

---

5. 2 Peter 2:4-6.
6. Zechariah 14:1-19; Revelation 9:20; 11:6; 15:1.
7. Will Durant, The Reformation, New York: Simon and Schuster, 1957, p. 64.
8. The Worst Pestilence in Modern Times," Scribner's, January 1938; "Fate Joins the Flu Fighters," American Medical Association, Hygeia, March, 1941.

Two Lessons from the Pages of History

History has taught us two things about great nations of the past that have been cleansed or have crumbled and disappeared into oblivion.

It appears that in each case there was a strong core of God-fearing or decent citizens—traditionally called "the remnant"—who held the shaky timbers of the collapsing nation in place much longer than the overall structure deserved. Nevertheless, the evil eventually prevailed and the inevitable collapse took place in spite of the remnant's heroic effort.

The second lesson of history tells us that when a dying political colossus collapses through a combination of war, plague, moral decay, pestilence or gigantic terrestrial disturbances, the remnant tends to survive. And even though the nation is terribly depopulated and its social structure ravaged, the loyal remnant often forms the nucleus for the new nation.

This is the prophetic destiny of the "remnant" in America.

The Founders knew that after America is cleansed the surviving remnant will have a divine mandate to raise up a revitalized nation that will fulfill the prophecy of Moses in Deuteronomy 30:1-8.

This means the remnant will launch an urgent campaign to adopt God's law, restore the original Constitution, organize the people into secular wards with captains of tens, fifties and hundreds, and teach the people the satisfying efficiency and rich rewards of an America built according to the original vision of the Founders under God's law.

The Cleansing Process Will Change Everything

A disaster goes through five major stages. The shock stage comes first when there is a sudden realization that a terrible and deadly thing is apparently happening to everybody.

The second stage is the "rescue and hunting" phase. All are involved in trying to help those immediately around them and then there is the frantic hunting for relatives and friends to make certain they are safe.

The third stage is mobilizing emergency resources by way of medical supplies and services, temporary shelters, food, water, clothing, bedding, etc.

The fourth stage is the deployment phase. This consists of getting people out of care centers and temporary shelters into homes or more permanent facilities.

The fifth stage is getting the people organized and permanently settled where they can become self-sustaining and self-governing.

This will be covered extensively in our next chapter.

The Cleansing Will Be a Monumental Watershed

The cleansing of America will change everything.

As we shall see later, those leaders in charge will know this is the time anticipated both by God and the Founders to restructure America. The speed with which changes are inaugurated will probably come as a surprise to the general populace, and especially to those who are refugees or part of the massive migration to the mountain west.

There will be a completely new system of law.

There will be a completely new system of community life.

There will be a new system of money.

There will be a new system of government.

The original Constitution will be restored.

Leaders will be selected without involving politics.

There will be an amazingly efficient system of justice.

There will be a remarkable new spirit of cooperation and tolerance among people of various faiths.

Even Alvin Toffler in his national best-seller, *The Third Wave*, anticipated that everything would be better after the new order of things is established. He said:

> "There are powerful reasons for long-range optimism, even if the transitional years immediately ahead are likely to be stormy and crisis-ridden."[9]

The Rise of a Virtuous People

The people who survive the cleansing will have endured a terrifying, soul-searing experience. Whether they were among the righteous who tried "to do all things" whatsoever the Lord had commanded, or whether they were

9. Toffler, The Third Wave, New York: Bantam Books, 1981, p. 3.

among the rebellious and wicked who were fortunate enough to escape, they will all feel an overwhelming sense of complete dependence on God.

This writer has witnessed the phenomenal change in wicked and rebellious people who suddenly came face to face with the threat of impending death and destruction.

They suddenly find themselves pleading with God for mercy, and because of their inclination to humbly seek the approbation of God, they promise from the depth of their souls to obey the commandments of the Almighty. After the cleansing, this miracle of a changed attitude and humble obedient behavior will be a demonstrated phenomenon superior to anything this generation will have ever seen.

And out of this new spirit of humility in a God-centered society there will rise the phenomenon of a truly "virtuous people." The Founders knew this was the most important single ingredient required to insure the smooth administration of a society seeking to practice the principles of God's law.

Topics for Reflection and Discussion

1. What has to happen to the people of America before they can practice God's law? Of the two options which, in your opinion, appears to be the most likely to occur? If so, is it likely to last long?

2. Did Thomas Jefferson fear the people of the United States might become so depraved they could lose the privilege of living in America?

3. In what way did Alexander Hamilton reflect a different attitude toward the Constitution than most of the other Founders? (See page 458.)

4. What was his favorite model for an ideal structure of government? (See Hamilton's plan, page 433.)

5. What are some of the ways America could be cleansed?

6. What is the "remnant?"

7. How does a remnant help the nation even before the cleansing? What is their principal opportunity after the cleansing?

8. What are four of the major changes that will occur after the cleansing? Which two seem the most significant to you?

9. How would you describe a "virtuous people?" Why would the Founders say the Constitution was made only for a virtuous people?

10. Why would the cleansing of America tend to make the wicked and rebellious assume the demeanor of a virtuous people?

CHAPTER THIRTY

SETTING UP THE NEW ORDER OF THINGS

This chapter is about the rebirth of America.

We observed in the last chapter, when the cleansing has reached the fifth stage—and the people are anxious to get settled down—they will be ready for the new era under God's law.

At the very beginning this might be called the "settling in" stage.

Many thousands will be temporarily accommodated in homes of survivors. Isaiah also saw that great numbers would cleanse and occupy the desolated homes of the gentiles who had lost their lives by pestilence, tempests and earthquakes.[1]

There will also be a pressing need to set up townsites where tens of thousands of new migrants and dislocated families can be resettled and begin helping themselves.

Then comes the crucial step of carefully setting up the new form of community organization.

ORGANIZING EVERYBODY INTO WARDS

The whole population must be organized into wards of approximately one hundred families each. At first there may be a few who refuse to participate in the "ward system" and desire to "make it on their own." Of course, they are entirely free to do this, but very shortly any kind of difficulty or emergency will dramatically demonstrate to them the marvelous advantages of the ward system.

The agriculture families will occupy a township of six miles square but business and suburban families will occupy a section of a city or town where approximately 100 families have located.

Temporary captains will be elected until the people get better acquainted with one another and then a more permanent "official" election will be held. A new election will be held every year.

1. Isaiah 54:3.

There will be captains elected over each group of ten families, then two captains will be elected—each one over fifty families—and finally a captain will be elected over the entire community of around 100 families.

At every level leaders will be elected after being nominated by a search committee of "wise men." Jefferson says there is a "natural aristocracy" of leadership in any concourse of people who always seem to emerge in a critical situation and provide a semblance of guidance until a more permanent order of things can be established.

In certain emergency situations, temporary leaders will be appointed from the trained corps of those who knew this crisis was coming and have been preparing themselves to organize the people and thereby facilitate the distribution of food and emergency supplies.

Among the Founders Thomas Jefferson was the most advanced student of the art of setting up the "ward system"—after the manner of the Anglo-Saxons. Referring back to Jefferson's teachings in chapter 27 will be helpful. The Anglo-Saxons had kept alive the ward culture from generation to generation and Jefferson gained many practical ideas from examining the manner in which the County of Kent (in England) handled its 60 wards.

Regional and National Channels of Leadership

To facilitate the distribution of food and other necessities there will have to be a network of county and state officers. Although appointed leaders can serve temporarily, within a few months the "search" committee will no doubt have assembled a roster of natural leaders who are willing to be drafted into service if elected by the people at each level of government.

The selection of these state and national leaders will not be accompanied by a lot of political hoopla. The candidates did not seek these offices but agreed to serve as a matter of duty if elected. It involves tremendous sacrifice on their part but the early Founders proved this was the way to get top quality leaders.

So for the first time since the days of George Washington, Americans will have a national election as originally contemplated by the Constitution. It will be quiet, dignified, and full of surprises.

There will be no political campaigns.

There will be no political parties.

There will be no political spoils.

Every captain at each level of government is asked to serve for a period of time as a matter of duty—and without compensation except for minimal expenses.

The Initial Challenge of a Decentralized Society

Right at the beginning, one of the biggest adjustments in the daily lives of the people will be the lack of grocery stores, department stores, pharmacies, hardware stores, utility suppliers, service stations, garages, doctors, dentists, etc. All of a sudden all of the things that previously could be taken for granted are temporarily suspended and the people are reduced to their own basic resources.

The free enterprise economy—which will soon go into operation—will eventually begin supplying all of these conveniences, but it will take the better part of a year or more to get supplies in place just as it did after World War II.

Those who have their basic supply of food and clothing will no doubt get through the stress of this period with nothing more than an occasional inconvenience, but those who made no preparations will have to depend upon the generosity of others in their new ward system in order to survive.

At the height of this challenging period people will think back on the luxury of living in an economy where mass production, mass transportation, mass communication, and a vast network of specialization made everything so common it was all more or less taken for granted.

But it certainly won't be taken for granted during the year or more when shortages prevail and readjustments have to be made almost every day. Children who once demanded expensive cereals will be thankful for a bowl of plain oatmeal mush. Parents who spent most of their lives eating the delicacies shipped in from all over the world will learn to like beans, homemade bread, cheese, sprouted grains, roots, water cress, and other pioneer-day diets.

Some of us have experienced such crises and they are not soon forgotten. It is like a special course in cultural appreciation.

The New Order of Things

The captains must not only take care of their own affairs but see that there is order in their group and that the needy are not neglected. Most problems are settled on the level where they occur and only extremely difficult matters are referred to a higher level.

The principal leader or captain over approximately a hundred families serves as mayor. He holds weekly meetings with the heads of families and coordinates relations with other wards. He is responsible for roads and bridges, sanitation, the trucking of culinary water until wells can be dug and the water tested. He is responsible for the building of a community hall where school can be taught during the week and church services can be held at different times on Sunday for the various denominations.

The ward must also have a health care center and eventually cooperate with approximately nine other wards in the county to set up the county hospital. He will also work with the county leaders to provide gas and electricity for each ward. Finally, he heads a committee to see that there are recreation activities in the ward each week.

The mayor presides over the ward council and delegates to specific individuals the job of being a steward over certain projects mentioned above. This greatly alleviates much of his burden by wisely delegating tasks to responsible people.

Should some wards lack competent leaders the captain and council over ten wards (the county) may call talented men to move their families into a particular ward to help out. The goal of God's law is to have everybody succeed.

As the people are trained to live under the ward system it is important to stress that the ward takes responsibility for the debts or obligations of its members and therefore each member should faithfully perform his obligations so the general public will continue to trust the integrity of the ward and all of the people who are proud to be its inhabitants.

An illustration reputation for integrity would be the situation where an individual wants to build or buy a home on credit.

In a Zion society the poor are allowed to secure such a loan without interest. However, the creditor—whether it is an individual or a bank—must be confident that the borrower or the members of his ward will be good for the principal of the loan in case the debtor defaults.

The Advantage of Having the Captains Serve as Judges

The administering of God's law requires that captains of each ward to not only function as mayors or executives but also as judges whenever there has been a disturbance of the peace or of good order in the community.

There are some very substantial advantages in having the captains serve in this dual capacity.

In the first place, the mayor or captain was elected by the people to preside over the ward. The very nature of his office gives him the prestige and respect which is needed in settling disputes or administering justice where offenses have occurred. The fact that he has to continue living and getting along with the people he judges (or even punishes) will encourage a sense of compassion as well as discipline.

The reciprocal feelings of offenders toward the captain are also tempered by the fact that the captain is recognized as trying to serve the people under arduous circumstances and therefore deserves cooperation rather than hostility when he is trying to do the best he can.

Furthermore, members of the ward know that if their captain becomes overbearing or seems unjust in a particular case, the entire matter can be reviewed by appealing the case to the higher judges which could be either the captain of ten wards or county level or even the highest judge who presides over the state.

The very fact that the captain of the ward knows his decisions can be appealed is likely to make him more temperate and long-suffering. Nevertheless, he will learn not to be over-indulgent or too lenient in his discipline lest the more aggressive youth of the ward who have already defied the discipline of their parents may arrogantly strike out and destroy the peace and tranquility of the entire ward.

Of course, if someone has been hurt the fundamental rule of God's law is that the offender must also be hurt or apologize and try to make it up to the offended person. In some extreme cases the offender may agree to accept or otherwise be sentenced to received an appropriate number of "stripes" with a three-inch flat strap to somehow even the score. When this procedure was followed in Canada for misdemeanor cases it was found to have remarkable therapeutic value and the recidivism rate of repetitive offenders was practically zero.[2]

Everybody over Eight must Know God's Law

God's law—as revealed to Moses and outlined in the early chapters of this book—is neither technical nor difficult to understand. If possible, this law should be taught in the various congregations of the churches. Those who

2. Skousen, The Third Thousand Years, op. cit., p. 360.

belong to a religion which is too small to have a congregation, may join with any other congregation of their choice.

The most important reason for having God's law taught by the various churches is to emphasize the fact that God's law is sacred and not merely the secular rules and standards set up by the government.

During this study course it would no doubt be helpful to divide the classes according to ages so the discussion can be aimed at the interests and level of understanding of each group.

The Law Should Be Reviewed and Discussed at Least Once Every Year

In ancient Israel, the king had to go through the law continually to refresh his memory on the requirements of this sacred code of conduct.[3] In a Zion society the review of the law at least once each year would no doubt become traditional for all the people, not just those who happen to be leaders.

Everyone Should Make a Covenant with God to Honor and Obey the Law

At the conclusion of the course of study the local officials should administer the oath of the covenant so that in a Zion society everyone agrees to honor, obey and study this law just as God had commanded.[4]

The People Should Be Taught the Great Advantage of Having God's Law to Guide Them

It is one of the greatest blessings of heaven to have a system of government and law which produces freedom, justice, peace and prosperity.

During one brief moment in the history of Greece the people had adopted enough of the divine principles which we called "God's law," to allow the Greeks to enjoy their greatest epoch of progress. In fact, it was called "The Golden Age of Greece."

At the height of this rare moment, their leader—named Pericles (490-429 B.C.)—gave a famous oration describing what they had achieved. He said:

> "Our government is called a democracy because it is in the hands of the many and not of the few. Our laws secure equal justice for

3. Deuteronomy 17:19.
4. Deuteronomy 11:19.

all in their private disputes, and our public opinion welcomes and honors talent in every kind of achievement, not for any sectional reason, but on grounds of excellence alone. And as we have free play to all in our public life, so we carry the same spirit into our daily relations among ourselves. We are not angry with our neighbor if he does what he likes, nor do we put on sour looks at him which, though harmless, are unpleasant.

"Open and friendly in our private relations, in our public acts we keep strictly within the law. We recognize the restraint of reverence; we are obedient to officials and laws, especially to the laws that protect the oppressed and to the unwritten laws whose violation brings admitted shame.

"Yet ours is no work-a-day city only. No other provides so many recreations for the spirit—contests and sacrifices all year round, and beauty in our public buildings to cheer the heart and delight the eye day by day. Moreover, this city is so large and powerful that the wealth of the whole world flows into her, so that our own products seem no more homelike to us than those of other nations.

"We love beauty without extravagance, and wisdom without unmanliness. We employ wealth, not as a means to vanity and ostentation, but as an opportunity for service. To acknowledge poverty is no disgrace: the true disgrace is in making no effort to overcome it.

"An Athenian citizen does not neglect public affairs because he is too concerned with his private business. We regard a person who takes no interest in public affairs, not as 'quiet' but useless.

"If few of us are originators, we are all sound judges of a policy. The great impediment to action is, in our opinion, not discussion, but the lack of full information which is gained by discussion prior to action." [5]

But all of this did not last long because the people forgot what had made them great. Modern Zion must never forget the principles of God's law which will help them fulfill the prophecy of Daniel when he said:

---

5. William Ebenstein, Two Ways of Life, New York: Holt, Rinehart and Winston, 1962, pp. 10-11, and quoted by Skousen in The Fourth Thousand Years, op cit., pp. 810-811.

> "The God of heaven [shall] set up a kingdom which shall never be destroyed: and the kingdom shall not be left to other people, but … it shall stand forever."[6]

The Gradual Elevation of Competent Leaders

As time goes on, the most successful captains of the wards are elevated by the people to be captains of the counties and one eventually presides over the whole state.

However, there are elected councils of wise and trusted individuals who serve respectively under the captains of the counties and the captain of the state.

One of the principal responsibilities of those who serve on these councils is to constantly watch for natural leaders who can be developed for major assignments throughout the system.

These councils also have the task of making certain God's law is taught to all of the people from the age of eight and upward. After the latest contingent of trainees has passed rigorous qualifying tests, a special assembly might be called where parents and friends can hear them take the oath to honor, obey, and sustain God's law.

Subsequent assemblies would be appropriate to honor those who have attained superior knowledge of God's law and learned how the judges should apply the law in different situations. The advanced courses would be especially helpful in setting up standards and assisting the captains at various levels who serve as judges.

The higher captains as well as the councils of counties and the state will settle problems relating to highways, economical transportation, water, sanitation, electricity, and fuel. They will also take steps to encourage the development of industries, hospitals and higher education in the state.

The States must Not Lose the Power to Protect Themselves

Under the restored Constitution which we will discuss in the next chapter, the states will be able to protect themselves from ambitious political leaders or federal bureaucrats.

---

6. Daniel 2:44.

The states must never forget what happened in America during the epoch just before the cleansing. The states lost the power to protect themselves. For example:

A state could *not* have an honest system of money based on gold and silver.

A state could not educate its children in universal religious principles as the Founders recommended in the Northwest Ordinance of 1787.

A state could not take over the federal lands which have been retained by the government in violation of Article I, Section 8, clause 17.

No state could return to the original taxing structure which made *income* taxes unconstitutional.

No state could disallow the federal government's program of *withholding* the amount of taxes from a paycheck before they are actually due.

No state would be allowed to use a number of the penalties outlined in God's law to compel a wrongdoer to provide *reparation* to his victim for injury and damages. (This will become immediately apparent by referring back to the topic of "Penalties" in the chapters covering God's law.)

No state could replace the federal laws relating to wilderness areas, pollution, minimum wages, child labor, prayers in school, Bible reading in school, the court-protected civil rights of AIDS carriers, the price of steel, eliminate the subsidizing of favored enterprises, and a hundred other issues which may have been based on good intentions in the beginning, but for which there is absolutely no authorization in the Constitution and already most of them have miserably failed to accomplish the gigantic promises which were made by the sponsors hundreds of billions of dollars ago.

These are merely illustrations of the tentacles of usurpation and miserably obnoxious intrusion by the federal government which had broken the chains of the Constitution and confused or obliterated the division of responsibilities between the federal government and the states.

This must never happen again.

The Original Philosophy of the Founding Fathers

James Madison, sometimes called the "father of the Constitution," described the philosophy of the Founders in the *Federalist Papers* which gave the states the full power to manage their own affairs and highly restricted the powers of the federal government. We quoted Madison earlier when he said:

> "The powers delegated by the proposed Constitution to the federal government are *few and defined.* Those which are to remain in the State governments are *numerous and indefinite*. The former [powers of the federal government] will be exercised principally on external objects, as war, peace, negotiation, and foreign commerce ... The powers reserved to the several States will extend to *all* the objects which, in the ordinary course of affairs; concern the lives, liberties, and properties of the people and the internal order, improvement, and prosperity of the State." [7]

That statement proclaimed by James Madison was the official policy of the Constitution of the United States. If it had been suddenly enforced just before the cleansing, it would have wiped out a couple of million federal jobs, scores of unconstitutional agencies, and created an opportunity for new jobs and prosperity that would have astonished the world.

The Miracle of the Water in the Wilderness

Some wonderful things will happen in America as the Zion society begins to flourish and spread out across the land. The population growth will make the wilderness area valuable real estate.

In our day, Western America is known for two things—its fantastic beauty and its desolate deserts. However, after the cleansing there will be a surge of population that will overwhelm the resources of the whole western region. The land is rich but it lacks the most precious resource to make it flourish—the indispensable element of abundant water.

Hidden away in the writings of divinely inspired men who were allowed to see a vision of modern times, we read some remarkable promises concerning water in the western wilderness. Isaiah says:

> "For in the wilderness shall waters break out, and streams in the desert. And the parched ground shall become a pool, and the thirsty land springs of water: in the habitation of dragons, where each lay, shall be grass with reeds and rushes." [8]

7. Madison, The Federalist Papers, op. cit., Number 45, pp. 292-293, emphasis added.
8. Isaiah 35:6-7.

> "The wilderness and the solitary place shall be glad for them; and the desert shall rejoice, and blossom as the rose. It shall blossom abundantly, and rejoice even with joy and singing."[9]

There has always been a little water on the desert but in the latter days there will be gushing streams of abundant water. Isaiah says:

> "Ho, everyone that thirsteth, come ye to the waters, and he that hath no money; come ye ...."[10]

This miracle of the water seeping up through the barren ground in the wilderness of the west will permit millions of acres to be inhabited by the gathering multitudes and allow extensive rural development where former desolation prevailed.

And because it is by divine intervention, we call it a "miracle."

Ruined Cities to Be Rehabilitated

As we have already mentioned, Isaiah says the multitudes will be so great that eventually they will "break forth on the right and on the left" and the people will find it necessary to clean up and inhabit the great cities that were depopulated during the cleansing process. As though he were seeing it in vision, Isaiah says:

> "Enlarge the place of thy tent, and let them stretch forth the curtains of thine habitation; spare not, lengthen thy cords, and strengthen thy stakes; For thou shalt break forth on the right hand and on the left ... and make the *desolate cities* to be inhabited."[11]

Some have thought the cleansing would be by nuclear destruction, but the reclaiming of these cities and the inhabiting of vacated houses would suggest a cleansing primarily by plague rather than extensive nuclear explosions.

The Miracle of Law, Order and Peace

One of the most gratifying surprises for thousands of these refugees will be the phenomenon of settling down into a peaceful and orderly life. It, too, is the result of a pattern through divine instruction and therefore listed among our miracles.

After their immediate necessities are provided, these refugees of all faiths will be invited—along with their friends and relatives—to settle and establish

9. Isaiah 35:1-2.
10. Isaiah 55:1.
11. Isaiah 54:2-3.

themselves in the ward system at some appropriate place. Finally, they and their families will be safe.

In this environment of orderly security the administration of the law will provide a perfect system of justice under judges or captains elected by the people themselves. Here indeed will be an ideal opportunity to practice the Lord's basic formula for peace on earth, good will toward men.[12]

The Miracle of Eliminating Poverty

God's law requires that each community share one another's problems "in common."[13] This does not mean sharing property in common, but it does mean sharing one another's needs, especially in an emergency. There will be a strong emphasis on volunteerism as it was in early America. If a person's barn burned down the whole community turned out to build a new one.

The object is to support and help one another until everyone is "settled in" and there is no poverty among them.[14] This means that even though the standard of living may be somewhat modest in the beginning, everyone will have the basic necessities. It is up to the captains of tens, fifties, and hundreds to see that no one is neglected.

With the passing of time, everyone will gradually move from tents to cabins, and from cabins to comfortable homes with gardens, vines and fruit trees.

The Miracle of Eliminating Crime

The suppression of crime is almost automatic under God's law. Those with dishonest tendencies soon learn that crime does not pay under God's law.

Reparation and punitive damages all go to the victim and the enforcement of the law is based on the principle we have already mentioned that he who hurts must be hurt unless he or she "makes satisfaction" in terms of fines or services to the injured person.

This is a far more satisfactory way to repair the damages and injuries suffered by the victim than having a person locked up or merely pay fines to the court. At the same time it gives the offender some solid therapeutic training in character building that he or she is not likely to forget.

---

12. Luke 2:14.
13. Acts 2:44-45; 4:32.
14. Acts 4:34.

The Miracle of Complete Religious Tolerance

Brigham Young, one of America's greatest pioneers, set up 350 successful communities in the West after 1847. He emphasized that a government under God's law promotes and protects the rights of all faiths so they can live harmoniously together. He is reported to have said to the members of his own church:

> "If the Latter-day Saints think, when the Kingdom of God [government under God's law] is established on the earth, that all the inhabitants of the earth will join the church called Latter-day Saints, they are egregiously mistaken. I presume there will be as many sects and parties then as now."[15]

An official LDS Church bulletin was sent out in 1847 which said:

> "The Kingdom of God [which is government under God's law] consists in correct principles; and it mattereth not what a man's religious faith is; whether he be a Presbyterian, or a Methodist, or a Baptist, or a Latter-day Saint ... or a Catholic or Episcopalian ... If he will bow the knee and with his tongue confess that Jesus is the Christ, and will support good and wholesome laws for the regulation of society—we hail him as a brother ...."[16]

So here we have a civic brotherhood and sisterhood of many faiths united in a community—clearly a secular community—and faithfully practicing God's law.

The Miracle of Universal Prosperity

We have already mentioned many of the factors which are the underlying requirements for a prosperous community, but it all begins with a spirit of mutual concern.

As we have already pointed out, an important aspect of the responsibility of the captains or heads of each community is to see that no one is neglected.

Furthermore, any community living under God's law is expected to be a very industrious population with full employment and everyone doing his or her share. All who can work are expected to work, and the rapidly rising standard of living and prosperity will bear eloquent witness to the supreme excellence of a godly society.

15. Journal of Discourses, 11:275.
16. Hyrum Andrus, Doctrines of the Kingdom, Salt Lake City: Bookcraft Publishers, 1973, p. 396.

Importance of the Principle of Simplicity

It will no doubt come as an astonishing surprise to those who are new to the wonders of God's law to realize how much more simple life can be compared to former days when corrupt and venal scoundrels were in charge of things.

While this writer was studying law in Washington D.C., I was appalled to discover how confused and complex our whole society had been allowed to become. By way of contrast, the genius of God's law is its simplicity in every aspect of life. It provides:

1. A sound and much more simple system of government where everybody has a voice and a vote.

2. A sound money system based on a medium of exchange with inherent value (gold or silver). This means currency is redeemable in gold or silver—immediately upon demand at any government bank.

3. A sound system of law and justice based on God's law where an offender has to completely compensate his victim and pay him additional (punitive) damages to remind the culprit not to do it again.

4. A sound economic system where the Golden Rule will demonstrate that honesty and fairness are good for business and both parties can walk away from an exchange better off than they were before.

5. A sound social structure based on righteous principles which are reflected in the lives of virtuous people.

6. A sound system of cultural education where everyone is taught the same basic principles of hard work, acquiring extensive knowledge, living honestly, and promoting a spirit of peace and good will toward all races, cultures and faiths.

Jefferson Visualized Each of the Wards Becoming Almost Entirely Self-Sufficient and Self-Contained

Not only was it intended that each of the wards or townships would be self-governing, but each one was to look to its own resources for its progress and development as well as its economic independence. This was "community building" of the highest order and the way Moses originally designed it.

Thomas Jefferson pointed out that each ward should have its own schools under the exclusive control of its own parents.[17] Then he went on to say:

> "My proposition had for a further object to impart these wards those portions of self-government for which they are best qualified." [18]

Jefferson said this would include:

> "1. An elementary school.
>
> "2. A company of militia, with its officers.
>
> "3. A justice of the peace and constable.
>
> "4. Each ward should take care of their own poor.
>
> "5. Their own roads.
>
> "6. Their own police.
>
> "7. Elect within themselves one or more jurors to attend the courts of justice.
>
> "8. Give in at the Folk-house [town hall] their votes for all functionaries reserved to their election.
>
> "Each ward would thus be a small republic within itself, and every man in the State would thus become an acting member of the common government, transacting in person a great portion of its rights and duties … entirely within his competence. The wit of man cannot devise a more solid basis for a free, durable, and well administered republic." [19]

Jefferson called these small, solid, self-governing wards "the keystone of the arch of our government," [20] and stated that if each community conscientiously performed its assigned tasks it would not only become a prosperous, independent entity, but it would leave very little on the local level for the counties or the state to worry about.[21]

---

17. Jefferson, Letters, op. cit., p. 1379.
18. Ibid., p. 1308.
19. Ibid., pp. 1492-1493.
20. Ibid., p. 1309.
21. Ibid., p. 1339.

Teaching the 28 Principles

It will be on the ward level where God's law will be taught and this is the ideal level to teach the 28 principles which the Founders considered "indispensable" if America is to fulfill her manifest destiny.

Since these principles constitute the Founders' divinely inspired road map, it is entirely appropriate that the 28 principles be taught right along with God's law.

Duties of Counties and States

The primary responsibility of the counties and the state is to concentrate on coordinating the development and encouragement of all types of utilities including water, electricity, fuel, and channels of communication and transportation.

The genius of leadership on the county and state levels is to encourage the development of all these services on a competitive, free-enterprise basis.

To achieve this there must be a pooling of private capital and the harnessing of the spirit of volunteerism wherever possible. The business aspect of building these various projects and services is greatly facilitated by a constant emphasis on the practice of the "golden rule" in financial transactions and cooperative enterprises. This quality of "virtue" reflected in the lives of the people after the cleansing will pay wonderful dividends just as it did in early pioneer days.

The County, State and National Network of Roads and Highways

The prosperity and welfare of the individual wards depend to a great extent on good roads and an efficient system of communication and transportation.

Jefferson emphasized the responsibility of the wards to provide good thoroughfares within their respective boundaries, but the connection between wards and the major centers of industry and shipping will depend upon the counties and the various states.

In a free enterprise economy it does not take long until there are enterprising cooperatives to fill the need for rapid transit highways and thoroughfares. By using the "toll" system the finances can be raised to build strong bridges and paved expressways.

The new national banking system can provide immediate funding where the state and counties are able to demonstrate that they can make regular payments on the principal. Under the new national banking system interest rates are minimal as a matter of policy.

What about Moving from One Ward to Another?

Under the restored Constitution complete freedom of movement to any area is guaranteed.

However as people get settled into a ward where there is a wholesome culture of caring and sharing, family membership in that ward will become a prized legacy.

Nevertheless, economic and social factors being what they are, there will always be a certain amount of mobility as families decide to move from one region to another.

Under the ward system a departing family will take a letter of recommendation with them. When they have selected a new place to settle this document will be invaluable in gaining acceptance and respect in any new ward.

However if a family has become culturally alienated and cannot get a letter of recommendation they will find this will be a serious handicap as they seek to plant roots in a new community. There are tremendous economic and social advantages to living in a well-ordered ward, but the leaders of such a ward will be careful not to grant admission to a family with a disagreeable, contentious reputation—and no letter of recommendation.

This will be particularly true if the renegade family has been banished from their former ward. Part of the discipline of the ward system will require this family—when they have been sufficiently humbled—to seek out the leaders of a new ward and ask for permission to join the ward on a probationary basis or until they have proved themselves.

In such cases there will be an inquiry of their former ward to determine the seriousness of their problem and the new ward will then make a decision as to whether it is believed this unattached family has reformed and deserves another chance. In serious cases there may be a considerable period of extensive probation or even non-acceptance before they have gained trust required to be incorporated in a new ward.

The policy is striving for "inclusion, not exclusion." Everybody needs a place where they are respected, trusted and loved.

Nevertheless, it will be noted that God's law is not unconditional. Even in a loving environment, each person knows he or she is accountable for their conduct. As the scripture says:

> "Thus saith the Lord: if ye will not hearken to me, to walk in my law which I have set before you … then will I make this house like Shiloh, and will make this city a curse to all the nations of the earth."[22]

Financing the New Order of Things

The original Constitution did not authorize the national government to impose any direct taxes on the people. This would include income taxes, unemployment taxes, disability taxes, social security taxes, or retirement taxes. Before these taxes could be extracted from the people, the leaders knew there had to be an amendment to the Constitution and that is why both political parties combined to pass the Sixteenth Amendment.

Under the new order of things and the restored Constitution all of these taxes will be repealed.

However, the Constitution does allow for excise (or sales) taxes[23] and these, plus import taxes,[24] will probably provide the principal source of income under the new order of things. The Founders considered sales taxes (excise taxes) to be the most equitable way to raise revenue. Under this system everybody pays the same rate but the rich pay more because they buy more. This was the Founders' intention when they provided in the original Constitution that all taxes must be "uniform."[25] However, the Supreme Court completely ignored this interpretation in order to allow the socialists to set up the graduated income taxes which is a direct violation of this provision.

The law of ancient Israel required a payment of a "tithe" (or 10%) on all "increases." This would include increase in flocks, capital gains, and net profits on business transactions.

---

22. Jeremiah 26: 4, 6.
23. Article I, Section 8, clause 1.
24. Ibid.
25. Ibid.

It is interesting that according to economic studies a 10% sales tax would meet all the requirements of America today, especially if we had a Balanced Budget Amendment and eliminated deficit spending.[26]

Topics for Reflection and Discussion

1. Can you think of three important reasons why the people must be quickly organized into wards as soon as the cleansing is over? In the beginning, why would the appointment of leaders from the ecclesiastical wards be useful as an emergency measure?

2. Why would it be important to stress that this is not a "church" project? When things have settled down sufficiently for the temporary selection of leaders on the ward, county and state levels, why is this done through a "search committee" or council of highly trusted individuals rather than a popular election?

3. How do you visualize the "culture shock" immediately after the cleansing? What system of economics is most likely to restore the necessities of life quickly? Couldn't the government do it better? In what way do the captains of the wards become the heroes of the day?

4. Under God's law what unique advantages result from having the captains of the wards serve as judges? Why is it so important to have everybody know the statutes of God's law? Who should teach it? Would you consider it important to have everyone make a covenant to obey the law?

5. What happened to the people of Athens after they forgot what made them great? What happened to the rights of the states in America after they forgot to stay within the boundaries of the Constitution? Name four things states could not do before the cleansing.

6. James Madison neatly defined the proper distribution of power between the national government and the states. In a single sentence can you define the formula he gave us?

7. How would you define a "miracle?" Describe the predicted "miracle of the water." In what way would "law, order, and peace" be a miracle? Why would it be a miracle to eliminate poverty? Would it be a miracle to eliminate crime?

8. Under God's law, how is religious tolerance promoted? How would that be a "miracle?" What is the basic principle of justice under God's law? How is it possible leaving one ward for another, how important is it to have a letter of recommendation?

---

26. The Constitution magazine, Washington, D.C.: National Center for Constitutional Studies, July, 1987, p. 2.

9. What are the most important features of a sound education? Why did Jefferson feel it was so important for each ward to be as self-sufficient as possible? Who is expected to promote the development of water, electricity, communications and transportation in each state?

10. Who is responsible for developing a network of roads and highways? What is a "toll" road? Do we have any today? Can counties and the states borrow from the national banking system to finance major projects? Are interest rates high? What must the state demonstrate before the loan is granted? What is the tax system under God's law?

CHAPTER THIRTY-ONE

THE RESTORATION OF THE ORIGINAL CONSTITUTION

The original Constitution was a dream that never came true.

Only in this coming century will Americans have a chance to see what they missed. The genius of the Constitution shines when it is governing the right kind of people. As we have mentioned several times before, John Adams said:

> "Our Constitution was made only for a moral and religious people. It is wholly inadequate to the government of any other." [1]

And Benjamin Franklin added:

> "Only a virtuous people are capable of freedom. As nations become corrupt and vicious, they have more need of masters." [2]

And it will be corruption and cultural corrosion in our great nation that will eventually lead to a day of cleansing.

After the cleansing of America, the primary difference will be the quality of the people. The traumatic scouring during the cleansing will produce a virtuous people—humble, teachable, and God-centered. Virtuous people don't need so many laws. They will be able to show how efficient and just God's law can be.

THE TASK AHEAD

The Founding Fathers would never recognize the mutilated Constitution in operation today. It is almost completely outside the parameters—Jefferson called them the "chains"—of the American charter which was designed to build and preserve the greatest nation on earth.

Furthermore, the people of our day who are accustomed to the deformed and crippled Constitution of this generation would be amazed if they could see what life will be like in that bright and beautiful day which will follow

1. Howe, The Changing Political Thought of John Adams, op. cit., p. 189.
2. Smyth, The Writings of Benjamin Franklin, op. cit., 9:569.

America's cleansing and the restoration of the Constitution. But will it really happen?

It is part of the divine destiny of America to have God's law in operation and the original Constitution restored.[3]

The Cleansing of America Will Level the Playing Field

It would appear from the cataclysmic nature of the cleansing of America that for a brief period of time the struggle for individual, family or community survival will be the immediate challenge facing the whole nation.

There will be no collection of taxes, no mailing out of Social Security checks, no massive commercial exchanges of food, goods and supplies by trucks, trains or planes. The complexities of modern America will be reduced to the most primitive requirements of early pioneer life.

But as order is restored and the survivors recognize that now is the time to adopt God's law and restore the Constitution, the whole American culture will rapidly begin to take on the image which the Founders had originally envisioned.

From the very beginning, the genius of the restructuring of the country will be precisely the way Jefferson had planned it—the organizing of the people into hundreds, or wards, where everyone has a voice and a vote. Food, tents, medicine and supplies will be distributed in an orderly fashion through these channels during the emergency. Before long the people will begin to see why Jefferson was so anxious to build America into a solid national pyramid of wards, counties and states with comparatively little responsibility assigned to the central government at the top.[4]

Fulfilling Washington's Wish to Eliminate Political Parties

There is nothing Washington emphasized more firmly in his Farewell Address than the need to eliminate political parties and run the government by representatives elected directly from the people.

How this is done is described in Deuteronomy 1:13-15. The process begins at the grass roots level.

3. Deuteronomy 30:1-8.
4. See Skousen, The Making of America, op. cit., pp. 41-61.

Ten families elect a leader, then five of these groups join to elect a leader of fifty families, two groups of fifty combine to elect a captain of a hundred families. The "Hundred" became the basic community unit in ancient Israel and later among the Anglo-Saxons which Jefferson studied so diligently. When America is restructured, the same carefully structured ward system will be inaugurated.

The captain on each level presides as a matter of civic duty over the group that has chosen him, and for a certain period of time he accepts the responsibility as:

1. An administrator over the group.
2. A judge to settle disputes within the group.
3. A military commander in time of war.

On occasion certain wise and greatly admired women were appealed to in judging a dispute,[5] however the captains elected by the people were chosen from among the men since they had to serve as their military leaders in time of war.

As we have described throughout this study, the structuring then continues upward from the "hundred" to have the people elect a captain over a thousand families (a county), then ten thousand families and so forth (for the state). All the way up the line everyone had a voice and a vote.

Choosing the President and the Vice President

However, the Founders knew the choosing of the national leaders was too far removed from the people for them to make a knowledgeable and insightful selection.

The element of inspiration is evident in the Constitution where the Founders set up a completely separate council chosen by the states to elect both the President and the Vice President. Let us review how the Founders wanted the Electoral College set up and how it will be revived under the restored Constitution.

First of all, each state selects either by its state legislature or a convention of the people, a designated number of electors or representatives to interview, investigate and evaluate each of the candidates for these two high offices.

5. For example, Deborah in Judges 4:4.

Since there are no political parties, one might ask where does the list of candidates come from? The very first election in 1789 answered that question.

Each state put forward the names of its most trusted, experienced and admired leaders as possible candidates for these high offices. When first approached, these distinguished citizens probably vigorously protested just as Washington did, but eventually they allowed their names to be entered for consideration as a matter of civic duty.

But, like Washington, each of them realized that if he were elected, the "winner" would be expected to sacrifice his private life, perhaps some of his private fortune, and he would have to forego many of his anticipated pleasures that he had planned in connection with his business, his professional career, and his family life.

Making the Final Choice

Nevertheless, no greater compliment could be paid to a leading citizen than to be drafted or "called to serve" in the highest office in the land. In the first election George Washington of Virginia was elected President and John Adams of Massachusetts became Vice President. One glitch in the process was corrected by the Twelfth Amendment so the Vice President is drafted for that office rather than use the runner up among the presidential candidates for Vice President.

It was thus that the Founders had tried to carry out in a general way the method of selecting their leaders as Moses described it in the first chapter of Deuteronomy. They recognized that this was God's way of securing the very best available talent to lead the nation. This was strongly emphasized at the constitutional convention when they discussed the importance of selecting their leaders by a council of wise men and thereby eliminate the mediocrity which so often results from a popular election.[6]

The genius of the Electoral College is the fact that the delegates not only interview, investigate and evaluate each of the candidates, but then, as required in the Twelfth Amendment, they meet on a certain day—presumably in their respective capitals—and cast individual votes for President and Vice President. A certified list of the outcome of their balloting is then sent to the President of the Senate.

---

6. Charles Callan Tansill, The Making of the American Republic, New Rochelle, N.Y.: Arlington House, 1987, pp. 412-414.

A joint session of congress convenes at a designated time and the president of the Senate opens the ballots in the presence of the entire congress, and after counting the votes, announces the President elect.

If no candidate for President has a majority, the top candidates—not to exceed three—are voted on by the House of Representatives with each state having one vote. If no candidate for Vice President has a majority, then the two top names will be submitted to the Senate and the one receiving the most votes will be declared the winner.

No Longer Will There Be Wars Between Political Parties Grasping for Political Spoils

By restoring the Electoral College as the Founders originally envisioned it, there will no longer be political campaigns with candidates trying to raise millions of dollars for advertising and obligating themselves to huge corporations and special interest groups in order to raise the funds.

There will no longer be any national political conventions with nationwide television presenting charismatic candidates theatrically reading professionally written orations loaded with meaningless promises and frequently weaving a web of carefully designed deception in order to entice support from the millions of unsuspecting and often ill-informed masses of voters.

Neither will there be tens of thousands of jobs in the form of political spoils going to the winners. Nor will the winning Congressmen or other leaders be in a position to pay off obligations to lobbyists and special interest groups with jobs or other special favors.

But What Happened to Old-fashioned Democracy?

Some will say, "But where is the element of democracy in this procedure?"

The answer is simple. The democracy factor is right down on the grassroots level where it belongs. Every step of this procedure involves the expressed will of the whole people. They all have a voice and a vote in selecting those whom they consider to be the wisest and most trustworthy to serve on the councils and choose those considered to be the best leaders. This is democracy of the highest order.

Of course there are elements of risk in any procedure where the factor of human frailty is involved, but Moses knew that as long as the people remained virtuous and conscientious, this pattern of government would be as close to a heavenly procedure as mankind is likely to enjoy until after the second coming of the Son of God.

How Are the Members of the House of Representatives Elected?

Everything we have said about the election of the President and Vice President involves the same principles in electing the members of the House of Representatives.

Each state sets up a search committee or electoral council to interview, investigate, and evaluate the best citizens whose names have been put forward by the respective counties. On a certain date they meet together and cast their ballots for the number of representatives that state is allowed to send to the House of Representatives. Those selected must have a majority vote so the council may need to have a runoff until that is achieved.

The Value of Carefully Selected Councils

Once the councils have demonstrated their fairness and ability for hard work, the community and state leaders may want to use them for elections in the future. The longer they are on the council the more expertise they will develop in spotting the right people for each kind of elected office.

However, the leaders must be very sensitive to the possibility of a faction forming, very much like a clique or political party. Should this occur the entire council should be dissolved and a new council drafted into service.

How Are Senators Elected?

Under the restored Constitution two Senators are selected by the state legislature to represent the long-range interests of the states, and also watch for any questionable legislation passed by the House of Representatives. The Senate was specifically set up by the Founders to represent their state legislatures in protecting the rights and prerogatives of the states.

Changes in the Congress

One of the big surprises under the restored Constitution will be the lifting of the gigantic burden from the Congress which—before the cleansing—had become almost unbearable. The fatal mistake in our day has been the abandonment of the Constitution and accepting to a regrettable extent the possibility that "socialism" is the new hope of the world. Scarcely any assignment can be more miserable for a congressman than trying to keep all of his constituents happy during a socialist regime. In our own day, some members of Congress have up to 25 assistants and still can't keep up with the complaints.

It will be recalled that socialism is defined as "the *government* ownership or control of all the means of production and all the means of distribution."[7]

Of course, it is an impossible task to satisfy everyone, and this whole approach is diametrically opposed to the most fundamental aspects of the Constitution. When the Constitution is restored, all of this illegal clutter will be eliminated.

This means 40% of the land which the government unconstitutionally acquired through the years will be returned to the states. And it means that those 26,000 government-owned (or government-operated) businesses we discussed earlier will be privatized or phased out.

Congress will no longer be allowed to spend taxpayers' money for huge projects not authorized by Article I, Section 8 of the Constitution. This further means that the Tenth Amendment will come back into full force and effect. What a difference this will make in the profile of the federal government.

How about Congressional Sessions Lasting Only Three Months?

It was never contemplated by the Founders that Congress would be in session all year round.

It was the transfer of decision-making from the states to Washington that made it necessary for Senators and Congressmen to acquire permanent homes and actually live in hot, crowded Washington or its environs. They had to have their offices open and running almost continually in order to watch over the problems of their constituents who continually ran afoul of the numerous government master planners and the complex spider web of government regulations and political handouts (entitlements).

Of course, the Constitution required that they also retain a home and office in the state they represented.[8]

It wasn't long before the people's representatives couldn't make a living back home because they were compelled to be in Washington so much of the time on a meager salary—which originally started out at $6 per day. Nevertheless, the Constitution allowed them to set their own pay schedule

7. Skousen, The Five Thousand Year Leap, op. cit., p. 30.
8. Article I, Section 2, clause 2; Section 3, clause 3.

(which Madison thought was "indecent") so salaries began to climb and soon exceeded what most of them could have earned if they had stayed at home and worked full time.

To provide for their old age security the members of the House and Senate gave themselves very substantial retirement benefits. Then there were all the perks and generous inside tips which allowed many of them to leave Washington as multi-millionaires.

Under the restored Constitution the Socialist structure will be entirely dismantled so the members of Congress will have time to read their own mail and make decisions under much more congenial circumstances than at present. They will be able to have short sessions the way the Founders planned it—something like three months.

Lifting a Burden from the Shoulders of the President

After the Constitution is restored, a vast array of government departments will be completely eliminated while those that remain will be greatly reduced in both responsibilities and power.

Using the original Constitution as our frame of reference, here is what we can expect:

The President's cabinet will be substantially reduced. There will be no Secretary of Labor, no Secretary of Education, no Secretary of Agriculture, no Secretary of Health and Human Services, and no Secretary of Housing and Urban development. Perhaps two or three others will be eliminated.

All of these national advisory officers in the cabinet were largely expensive bureaucratic brokers distributing the political spoils of the winning party. They pretended to provide much needed services to the whole national structure, but experience demonstrated that they were for the most part simply arbitrary, and often unfair distributors of billions to the heavy contributors or supporters of the winning party. For nearly two centuries it had all become an accepted part of the corrupt political spoils system.

Elimination of Unconstitutional Administrative Agencies

Beginning primarily with the New Deal, it became popular to completely ignore the first paragraph of the Constitution which says:

> "*All* legislative powers herein granted shall be vested in a Congress of the United States, which shall consist of a Senate and House of Representatives."[9]

This provision gave every American the right *not* to be subjcct to any federal law unless it had been reviewed and approved by a majority of the House and the Senate. In other words *nobody* can write a law for the people of the United States except the Congress.

With the restoration of the Constitution the vast array of unconstitutional administrative agencies will be eliminated and the President will no longer be answerable for them. Consider how this will change the Executive Branch of the government:

There will be no welfare or social services to administer.

There will be no foreign aid to administer or monitor.

There will be no domestic federal insurance programs to administer or monitor.

There will be no social security to administer.

There will be no disaster funds to administer.

Who Will Pass the Laws for the Nation?

Under the restored constitution only one agency of the federal government will be allowed to pass laws governing the whole nation. That one agency is the Congress.[10] Of course, they will pass on their laws to the President for any suggestion, but even he cannot prevent the will of the Congress from going into effect if two-thirds of the Congress override his veto.[11]

This will change the whole structure of law making as we know it today.

The President cannot pass a law or issue executive orders except to manage the departments of government under his immediate direction.

The Secretary of the State cannot pass laws.

The Secretary of the Treasury cannot pass laws.

The Secretary of Defense cannot pass laws.

9. Constitution of the United States, Article I, Section 1.
10. Article I, Section 1.
11. Article I, Section 7, clause 3.

The Attorney General cannot pass laws.

The Secretary of the Interior cannot pass laws or issue regulations.

The Secretary of Agriculture cannot pass laws or issue regulations.

The Secretary of Commerce cannot pass laws or issue regulations.

The Secretary of Labor cannot pass laws or issue regulations.

The Secretary of Health and Human Services cannot pass laws or issue regulations.

The Secretary of Housing and Urban Development cannot pass laws or issue regulations.

The Secretary of Transportation cannot pass laws or issue regulations.

The Secretary of Energy cannot pass laws or issue regulations.

The Secretary of Education cannot pass laws or issue regulations.

The Secretary of Veteran's Affairs cannot pass laws or issue regulations.

This represents the entire cabinet of the President. Under the new order of things, many of these departments will not even exist. Those departments that remain must submit any needed legislation to the Congress for review and possible action. The new order of things will require very little federal legislation. Once in place, it will require few changes.

But the New Deal was barely off the ground when clever lawyers contrived the idea of "administrative law." It had been experimentally tried earlier but now it flooded the bureaus of Washington.

Elimination of Administrative Law

All this began happening while I was in law school and I recall the words of Professor Davidson, a visiting professor from Harvard, who said, "For all practical purposes administrative law undoubtedly marks the end of the Constitution as it was originally designed."

As socialistic services began to be provided, the burden of writing all their rules and regulations was more than Congress could handle, therefore the strategy was to have Congress pass an "enabling act" which created an administrative agency or assigned the social services to one already in existence. In the bill it stated that the agency was authorized to write its own regulations, and these usually went into effect as an executive order from the President but without Congressional review or debate.[12]

Furthermore, on occasion the President created administrative agencies on his own initiative without even an enabling act. In these cases thc agency also was unilaterally empowered to write its own regulations. President Roosevelt created fifteen of these administrative agencies during World War II.[13]

When the Constitution is restored, all of these illegal agencies will be eliminated. The restored charter has no place for this vast web of Socialist programs. As of this writing there are 81 such agencies with hundreds of thousands of federal employees operating under multi-billion-dollar budgets.[14]

Concerning Executive Orders and Executive Agreements

The President has always had the authority to issue orders of an administrative nature to the various departments of the executive branch of the government. However, the President has never had the constitutional authority to issue executive orders (except as Commander-in-Chief in a wartime emergency) which would operate as laws affecting the nation as a whole.

Today there are thousands of these Executive Orders which lie beyond the scope of Presidential authority and are enforced in the courts as "laws." Many of these are remnants of the New Deal days when the official policy—even in the courts—considered constitutional restrictions outmoded and old fashioned.

Under the restored Constitution all of these "expanded" executive orders will be repealed since they violate Article I, Section 1 of the Constitution which we cited above.

We should also mention that Presidents—particularly in this present century—have been entering into secret agreements with leaders of foreign nations and hiding them from the people by calling them temporary "executive agreements" rather than treaties.

Of course this is a fraudulent procedure because the Constitution provides that all agreements with foreign nations must be approved by the Senate.

12. Corwin, Constitution of the United States, Washington, D.C.: U.S. Government Printing Office, 1964, pp. 99-104.

13. Ibid., p. 442.

14. The U.S. Government Manual, National Archives and Records Administration.

The notorious Yalta agreement was secretly made in 1945 between FDR, Winston Churchill and Joseph Stalin. The Senate has never been able to force the State Department to reveal many details of that agreement. Nevertheless, the State Department has continued to follow the requirements of the Yalta "executive agreement" as though it were treaty law. And many of the Yalta agreement policies have turned out to be very damaging to the best interests of the United States.

Under the restored Constitution there will be no secret executive agreements.

No Federal Reserve but a New Banking System

We have already mentioned that under the restored Constitution there will be no Federal Reserve System.

The Federal Reserve Act provided that it would only require a majority of Congress to repeal the system. It also provided that if that should happen, all of the assets of the Federal Reserve would be turned over to the United States Treasury.

This would mean that instead of Federal Reserve notes, the people will have "honest" money based on gold and silver, or currency which can be redeemed in gold or silver "on demand."

In place of the Federal Reserve there will be an official bank of the United States and it will advance money on fully collateralized loans at very low interest rates. Any profits from the national bank will go to the general fund of the U.S. Treasury to reduce taxes.[15]

Branches of the official bank of the United States will operate in each of the states on the same basis as the national bank except that their profits will accrue to each of the states to reduce their taxes.[16]

What about Private Banks?

Strictly interpreted, the original Constitution has no authority to charter banks, however, the states could charter closely supervised private banks. These would be commercial and investment banks which make their profits by taking somewhat higher investment risks than the national bank but requiring the people to pay higher interest rates.

15. See Skousen, The Urgent Need for a Comprehensive Monetary Reform, Salt Lake City: Freemen Institute, 1982, pp. 22-24.

16. Ibid., p. 24.

More than two hundred years experience with fractional banking suggests that this practice should be considered a criminal act. No bank should be allowed to loan money it doesn't have.

The Advantages of a Private Social Security System

One of the biggest boondoggles of the New Deal master planning was the Social Security Act passed in 1935. We will not take the time to point out its many deficiencies except to say that one out of every six Americans is presently receiving benefits from this system and studies show that they are receiving very mediocre returns in comparison with that same amount of money invested in a private social security program.

For example, in 1995 a national financial letter pointed out the disparity between the two approaches to retirement benefits. It said:

> "Today a retired American gets a maximum $1,200 a month from Social Security.
>
> "Social Security taxes have been increased 17 times … [but] too many people depend on Social Security to finance their retirement. They are in for a rude awakening.
>
> "Recently, I read about a 76-year-old retired man in Florida who said his $1,200-a month Social Security check is a lifesaver.
>
> "Well, how would he like to be collecting a guaranteed lifetime annuity of $4,000 a month? That's how much he would be getting if his Social Security taxes had been invested in conservative stocks during his working years." [17]

To suggest that the amount paid into Social Security could build a personal investment retirement fund that would provide a lifetime annuity of $4,000 per month may seem incredible. Nevertheless, the author goes on to give a concrete example of why this is true:

> "A 20-year-old earning $10,000 a year (the minimum wage) pays $23.85 a week, or $1,240 a year, into Social Security.
>
> "Suppose that $23.85 were invested in a money market fund and earned an average of 5% per annum. Even investing only in a

17. Mark Skousen, Forecasts & Strategies, Phillips Publishing, Inc., September, 1995, p. 5.

> money market, our fabled worker would be a millionaire when he retires at 65." [18]

Here is the advantage of a private Social Security program. A person who never earns more than minimum wage can save what the government is taking out of his pay check and invest it in a very secure money market at 5% and retire at 65 with a lifetime annuity of $4,000 per month.

Chile Had More Farsighted Leaders than the United States

This financial report continues:

> "In 1981, under the influence of free-market economists, Chile privatized its failing Social Security system and replaced it with *private pension fund accounts* for new workers ... Those within a few years of retirement remained untouched. Middle-aged workers were given the option of using the new privatized pensions or remaining in the state system.
>
> "The results have been astounding. Today 93% of the labor force is enrolled in 20 separate private pension funds. Annual real returns on pension investments averaged 13% from 1981 to 1993.
>
> "Chile's private pension fund deepened the nation's capital market and stimulated economic growth.
>
> "Its domestic savings rate has climbed to 26% of the gross domestic product ....
>
> "In short, Chile provides a role model for a successful privatization of the U.S. Social Security system." [19]

Why the Founders Made Government Social Programs Unconstitutional

A study of Article I, Section 8 of the Constitution will reveal that the federal government was never authorized to spend money for social programs.

If the states wished to develop social programs they could do so, but not the federal government. One advantage of the states doing it would be the fact that they are closer to the problem and could determine whether abuses were occurring or there were cases of malingering.

---

18. Ibid.
19. Ibid., p. 6.

Think how many billions of the taxpayers' money have been squandered in our present generation for social programs that sometimes spent nine-tenths of the appropriation trying to deliver the one-tenth to the needy.

For this very reason the restored Constitution will have no social security tax, no unemployment tax, and no disability tax.

Congress caught the government sending out checks for disability to people, some of whom had completely recovered from their ailments many years earlier. When the bureaucratic administrators were asked why they were so foolish, they said, "It is cheaper to send out the checks than hire the monitors to check on people!"

After the wards are set up, there will be quick relief for the unemployed or the disabled but the people furnishing the help will be close enough to know when the relief is no longer needed.

Facing up to Abortion, Gambling and Alcohol

During our day the Supreme Court has been running fast and loose to satisfy a host of socialist provisions which have no legal basis. In Roe vs. Wade, the court manufactured a right that doesn't even exist. The Court declared that women have the "private right" to destroy their unborn babies. After destroying an estimated 30 million American children in one generation, we suspect this will be a major factor in bringing about the judgment of an angry God who will demand a cleansing of the whole country.

Meanwhile, what about abortion? After the Constitution is restored, the Tenth Amendment will put the whole issue right back into the jurisdiction of the states where it should have been left in the first place.

Even the common law allowed abortions in cases of rape, incest or to save the life of the mother. If the medical profession is to be allowed to go further—such as terminating the gestation of a fetus where ultra-sound reveals serious defects—that decision must be left to the independent legislation of each state.

The same principle holds true in the control of gambling and alcoholic beverages. The Twenty-First Amendment which repealed prohibition specifically stated that:

> "The transportation or importation ... of intoxicating liquors into any state ... in violation of the laws thereof, is hereby prohibited."

So it is a federal violation for anyone to transport or import alcohol within a state contrary to its laws. That is as far as the federal law should go. Under the Constitution the federal government only has authority to prosecute instances of "interstate" crime—stolen cars, interstate transportation of prostitutes, interstate fraud, crossing state lines with kidnap victims, interstate transportation of stolen goods, etc. And under the Twenty-First Amendment it has no control over alcohol unless it is shipped into a state in violation of its laws.

Why the Restored Constitution Will Make the Economy Virtually Depression-Proof

Depressions are primarily caused by one thing: people just simply stop spending their money.

People do this when they are afraid. Under fractional banking the fear of a run on the bank will paralyze the economy.

When the money system can be manipulated by banks or politicians, the slightest rumor that there will be a tightening up of the money will create a panic.

The threat of war can cause a depression when men know they will probably be drafted and families know they may be broken up.

Even when the money system is based on gold and silver the rumor that someone has acquired a monopoly on either of the precious metals will create economic pandemonium.

However, the restoration of the Constitution and the organizing of the whole country into wards will either eliminate or sharply curtail any of the above situations which trigger depressions.

An honest money system based on gold and silver where no one is allowed to monopolize precious metals will be a strong stabilizing factor.

The close interdependence of families in the wards will also mitigate against panics and the element of fear which destabilizes the economy.

The absence of fractional banking and the close regulation of the state-chartered banks will further insulate the economy and secure the savings of the people.

The Genius of an Economy Based on Competitive Free Enterprise

The restored Constitution will allow the whole American economy to operate on the basis of an honest, free, competitive system.

As we stated earlier, it was Adam Smith of Scotland who first solved the mystery of why a free society succeeds and becomes wealthy whereas a government-controlled society always seems to remain stagnant with its people stewing around in confused frustration.

But first, a word about Adam Smith whom we mentioned earlier.

He was born June 5, 1723, which would be seventeen years after the birth of Benjamin Franklin and nine years before the birth of George Washington. In other words, he was a contemporary of many of the Founders, and did not die until 1790, one year after the United States had become established.

Smith's father died before Adam Smith was born, and his mother devoted the remaining 61 years of her life anxiously caring for this precious son.

At the age of three some gypsies kidnapped Adam Smith, but he was rescued by his uncle.

Smith graduated from the University of Glasgow and then spent six years at Oxford. Later he was at the University of Edinburgh and then he taught at the University of Glasgow. It was there that he converted the business leaders to a policy of free trade. Meanwhile he had become a close friend of David Hume and had given popular lectures on economic liberty which were beginning to attract attention.

He spent nearly two years in France and there met Voltaire. Later he spent several years in London where he became a close associate of Edward Gibbon and Edmund Burke. He also sought out Benjamin Franklin and had many productive conversations with him.

By 1776 he was able to publish his famous book, *The Wealth of Nations*, and it sold out in six months. Before he died in 1790 it had gone through five editions.[20] The best and most readable treatment of the economic thinking of Adam Smith and Thomas Jefferson can be found in the national best-seller of a few years ago, *Free To Choose*, by the noted economist Milton Friedman and his wife, Rose Friedman.

---

20. Adam Smith, The Wealth of Nations, Great Books of the Western World, Chicago: Encyclopedia Britannica, 1952, vol. 39, p. v-vi.

Among the leaders of the American colonies Adam Smith was looked upon as "one of their own" in mind and spirit. His ideas concerning "economic liberty" or competitive free enterprise were widely discussed and the United States was the first nation to put these principles into practice.

Smith's Four Great Economic Freedoms

Adam Smith began as a mathematician and ended up as a moral philosopher who believed in whatever does the greatest good for the greatest number.

As we have emphasized earlier, his studies demonstrated his complete, unalterable conviction that prosperity and economic progress in any nation requires four radiant principles of freedom operating in the lives of the people. These are:

1. The freedom to try.
2. The freedom to buy.
3. The freedom to sell.
4. The freedom to fail.

Nevertheless, he was quick to point out that there are four situations where the government *should* intervene:

1. To prevent the use of force (criminal invasion of the market place to control market operations).
2. To prevent the practice of fraud (invasion of the market with trickery, deception and confidence schemes).
3. To prevent monopoly (which blunts or destroys the capacity of legitimate merchants to compete).
4. To prevent debauchery (the exploitation of the vices to the detriment of the community—drugs, gambling, liquor, prostitution, pornography, etc.).

Isn't 'Profit' a Form of Robbery?

Adam Smith was not an unkind man but he could have run a rapier through economic philosophers who thought it was immoral to add a profit to the actual cost of a product. In reality profit is the engine that makes the economic system run. Profit makes it all worthwhile. The production system depends on profit, the distribution system depends on profit, even the original invention that represents an improvement in the nation's standard of living, depends on profit.

Of course, "gouging" is not a legitimate profit but a flagrant way of violating the eighth commandment.

Adam Smith felt that in a virtuous society—a "godly society"—it would be possible to eliminate this aspect of shady business by following the golden rule.

Of course, it is natural for the buyer and seller to each come to the bargaining table with a different perspective. The seller may think the car he is selling is worth a little more, and the buyer may think the car should cost a little less. In the bargaining process Adam Smith said one must always make allowance for a reasonable margin of difference which can be negotiated and still be within the parameters of an honest, just and acceptable deal by both parties.

If they finally reach an agreement so that each has improved his economic position to meet specific needs, then Adam Smith would say they have both "made a profit." A free market economy is set up so that if each person deals honestly and fairly with his neighbor, everybody wins.

How the Free Enterprise System Makes Things Abundant and Cheap

One of the marvels of the free enterprise economy is that it succeeds to a remarkable degree in doing just what Adam Smith said it would do—it makes things abundant and cheap.

Let us consider the "parable of the ballpoint pen."

This glamorous little piece of writing equipment came on the market at the close of World War II at $12.95 each. In the beginning the sales were relatively few but the profit on each pen was considerable.

I have a copy of an advertisement from Gimbel's Department Store in New York which describes its $12.50 ballpoint pen as:

> "Fantastic ... miraculous fountain pen guaranteed to write for two years without refilling."[21]

Competition and improved methods of production brought the price down to $4.95 and that is when I got my first ballpoint pen. In fact, many people

21. New York Times, December 26, 1964.

began enjoying the luxury of owning one of these marvelous "two-year, non-refilling pens," and while the profit was less per pen, the accumulated profits seemed to skyrocket. The ballpoint next came down to $2.95, then $1.98, and eventually it came all the way down to 10 cents. In fact, if you knew a real estate salesman you could get one free.

By that time millions of pens were being purchased, and while the profit per pen was minuscule, the accumulated profits were enormous. By the time the inventor of the ballpoint pen died in 1985 the glamorous little piece of writing equipment numbered in the billions and the profits in the hundreds of millions.[22]

As Adam Smith had said, a free economy tends to make things abundant and cheap.

Is Competition Wasteful?

In a highly centralized socialistic economy it is often claimed that competition is wasteful. It is argued that it is a waste of resources to build two railroad tracks when one can carry the traffic.

But that is not the way it works out. If there is only one track and only one company providing the service, an economic tragedy occurs. The track gets in disrepair, the service is abominable, and before long it is not handling the traffic.

On the other hand, if there are two or more systems competing for the business, the tracks are constantly improved, the equipment gets faster, safer, and more comfortable; the people get better service, therefore more people ride the train, more profits are made, and the system expands to areas which a monopoly system would refuse to serve.

Adam Smith figured all of this out over two hundred years ago. He believed that competition is the most frugal and economical way to provide an abundance of goods at cheap prices with the highest quality of service.

He said it is the *monopoly* that wastes, decays, and degenerates into a miasma of disappointing results.

What about Price Controls?

Price controls are a political gimmick which are often recommended as a panacea for high prices when there are extremely vociferous consumer

22. Salt Lake Tribune, October 26, 1985.

complaints. This becomes a popular theme for many politicians who unitedly demand price controls for the sake of the poor.

But price controls always inflict inestimable damage to the market and especially to the poor.

Let us take a specific example. A few years ago the potato crop was very meager and the prices shot up so high that many people found it difficult to get potatoes. But the government rushed forward with a remedy—price controls.

There doesn't happen to be any constitutional authority for price controls in peacetime—and they don't work in wartime—but they had a highly popular political appeal, so the Washington bureaucrats rushed forward with a "courageous price-control program."

The results were interesting. At suppressed prices, the whole potato supply disappeared in a couple of weeks. Thereafter, no potatoes could be had at any price. Now what would the poor do; or anyone else for that matter?

Had the government let things rock along, everyone could have had a few potatoes and the high prices would have made it worthwhile for potato farmers to bring in a substantial new crop within a few months and the new supply would automatically force the price back down again.

But with price controls it was not worthwhile or profitable for farmers to go to all that trouble, so there would have been a scarcity of potatoes for another year unless the government lifted the controls after seeing they had failed.

It should also be mentioned that the high price of potatoes will greatly accelerate the purchase of rice, macaroni, spaghetti and noodles!

The Baling Wire Famine Creates a Flourishing Black Market

Let us take another example. One year the government decided the price of steel was too high and so it imposed stiff price controls. Almost immediately a number of essential products disappeared from the market. Baling wire was one of them. It was no longer worthwhile to produce it.

Baling wire ordinarily sold for $12.95 a reel, but when the farmers and ranchers found they could not buy baling wire at any price, a cry went out, "We *have* to have baling wire!" The government did not respond, but someone else did—the black marketeers.

The wire was smuggled in from foreign countries or a high tariff was paid to get it through customs. In either event the retail price of baling wire went up 400%. Furthermore, the black market developed a chain of bribery and corruption all along the distribution channels.

So here is the story of price controls.

1. They wipe out the margin of profit.

2. This results in a scarcity of the product.

3. This in turn results in a powerful black market enthusiastically bootlegging the product.

4. And this results in skyrocketing prices and a rash of corruption all along the channels of distribution to capture the excess profits.

Adam Smith believed these problems are best solved by allowing the market to run its course. High prices without controls will promptly promote new production and in a very short time the problem will be solved and prices will drop back to normal.

To put it another way, a free market tends to be self-regulating if the government does not intervene except to prevent monopoly and artificial price fixing.

There Are Better Days Coming for America

At this point we can summarize the promise of a brilliant new order of things which is coming to America.

1. *A virtuous people.* The cleansing will be so rigorous that the whole people will turn back to God in a spirit of humility and prayerful dependence which is the first requirement for a virtuous people.

2. *Equality.* The cleansing will definitely create a more level playing field. Everyone acquires a new sense of being "little people" who desperately need one another.

3. *Unity.* The cleansing will also produce a universal sense of crisis and interdependence that will draw the people closer together than ever before. In our own day the people who live in the Third World have already developed this feeling far superior to that of the prosperous nations.

4. *Individuality*. As the people are organized into wards where everyone has a voice and a vote, there is a wonderful new sense of "belonging" in a "participatory democracy."

5. *Order*. God's law creates a climate of responsibility and accountability. It provides guidelines and inward-motivated discipline that makes self-government and good order practically automatic.

6. *Freedom*. The restored Constitution under God's law provides the atmosphere for unlimited creative expression. A person can face the universal opportunities which flash green lights in every direction and choose the course which seems most desirable at the moment. After all, that is all freedom is—the chance to choose.

7. *Prosperity*. In a truly free society, natural law and a willingness to work always produces prosperity. A people may start out with tents and rude cabins but in one generation there will be a broad vista of fields, orchards and comfortable homes—some of lumber, others of brick and stone. A spirit of industry, commerce, transportation and communication soon spreads in all directions like a spontaneous network with a life of its own.

When all of these principles are in operation simultaneously it is called a Zion society and the system under which it operates is what the Apostle James called "*the perfect law of liberty*."[23]

23. James 1:25.

Topics for Reflection and Discussion

1. Can you think of three things the government is doing which the Founders would call "unconstitutional"? Describe how the election of the President and Vice-President would be conducted under the restored Constitution.

2. What will happen to political parties? What will happen to political spoils? How does the restored Constitution change the President's cabinet?

3. What is the classical definition of Socialism? How will the restored Constitution change the role of Congressmen? Why would the sessions of Congress be much shorter?

4. Why would many administrative departments be eliminated or sharply reduced in authority and manpower? Explain why the Yalta agreement was an "Executive agreement." What did it lack to make it constitutional?

5. What would replace the Federal Reserve System? What would replace the Federal Reserve notes? What would happen to fractional banking? In what way would this help to prevent depressions?

6. What is the main argument for private pension funds in preference to government Social Security? Why is the private Social Security Program in Chile working out better than our own?

7. What steps could be taken to handle abortion better and more fairly than the prevailing system? On what level should gambling be controlled? How about alcoholic beverages?

8. Did Adam Smith know any of the Founders personally? What was their attitude toward his idea on economics? What were his four great ideas of Freedom that must be preserved to make a prosperous people?

9. What was there about the development of the ballpoint pen that shows that free enterprise makes things abundant and cheap? Could we do away with profits and still prosper? How would you answer a person who claims competition is wasteful?

10. Why haven't price controls worked successfully? In the long run have they helped the poor? Can you name the seven qualities of a Zion Society after the cleansing?

CHAPTER THIRTY-TWO

Striving for a Higher Level of Civilization

Our review of the principles contained in the Constitution and its amendments makes it clear that the Founders were striving mightily to attain a higher order of civilization than mankind has ever known. They knew that freedom, peace, and prosperity could be America's greatest export—and that the principles embodied in our Constitution could enrich the lives of all mankind. This is our greatest challenge today: to help America climb to the summit, so the rest of the world can follow.

Certainly it is a slippery pathway, just as it has been a hazardous adventure to reach our present level. Nevertheless, even in their upward struggle during the past two hundred years, the American people have been able to lead the world in several remarkable ways. And we can continue, if we will only stay true to the vision of the Founders.

Consider, for example, the effort to produce an adequate supply of food. The American farmer has taken advantage of technology, machinery, fossil fuels, fertilizers, pesticides, and nutritional feed additives for dairy and meat production, until today each American farmer is able to feed his own family and some seventy-eight other people in the United States and around the world. To produce this much food in 1918, before the widespread use of tractors, would have required around 61 million horses and mules. To feed this many work animals today would require about 180 million acres of cropland—almost half of the American cropland now in cultivation.

When Freedom Fails, Famine Follows

In contrast to this we have the approach of dictatorships, such as we find in Ethiopia. To appreciate what happened in Ethiopia, it is helpful to remember that Emperor Haile Selassie ruled Ethiopia for forty-five years and was considered a benevolent ruler in comparison to the present regime. He tried to use education and modern methods to gradually prepare his people for a more advanced society with a greater degree of self-determination. However, radical forces used extravagant promises, which made the people impatient and stirred them into rebellion. As a result, on September 12, 1974,

Haile Selassie was seized by the radicals and thrown into a dungeon, where he died. The radical element then launched its "reform," destroyed thirty thousand people to terrorize the general population into submission, and imported twenty thousand troops to "keep the peace." Almost immediately thousands of foreign "advisors" arrived to establish the new order. This order included, among other things, the collectivization of agriculture.

Suddenly, Ethiopia, which had been the breadbasket of Africa, ceased to be a breadbasket. The peasant farmers were no longer free to use the food-raising methods of the past. Traditionally, Ethiopian farmers had saved food in good years to prepare for possible bad years. The new regime outlawed this practice by calling it "hoarding." Peasants had also traditionally followed a practice of reinvesting their surplus in their own farms so as to expand production. The new regime denounced this as "capitalist accumulation" and "private investment," which was no longer allowed. Historically, Ethiopian tradesmen engaged in food distribution had bought products in the food-surplus areas to sell in food-deficient areas. The new regime outlawed this practice as "exploitation," and thereupon replaced the entire free market system of Ethiopia with numerous tightly supervised government commissions.

The next step was a so-called land reform, where peasants were assigned a few acres from land appropriated from large landowners—but these were entirely too small to justify cultivation by mechanical equipment. Large commune farms were also established under the government, but these immediately suffered the same disastrous crop failures and the same drastic drop in production that have characterized commune farms all over the world.

The results were sadly predictable. Within a few years Ethiopia was suffering widespread famine, with several million people starving. In less than a decade, Ethiopia had gone from the breadbasket of Africa to a bleak land of desolation and unfulfilled promises.

The Freedom Formula

The tragedy in Ethiopia is not significantly different from that which has occurred in other nations and in other times when statist dictatorships or monarchial rule has crowded out man's instinct for freedom. Historically, dictatorships and other forms of tyranny have always compounded human problems. Conversely, it has been people thriving in a climate of freedom who have somehow found the best solutions.

This was the important lesson which Adam Smith emphasized in his famous book of 1776, *The Wealth of Nations*. It was he who advocated a system of strong private enterprise and a system of free marketing which no nation of that period had yet dared to try. But the Founders decided to try it. They determined to combine the teachings of Adam Smith with the long list of freedom-based political principles they set forth in the Constitution. And not only was freedom to be the watchword for their new republic, but eventually they hoped it would spread around the world.

America's Upward Reach

A careful study of the Founders' writings will reveal that many aspects of their success formula yet remain to be fulfilled, and where these elements are lacking, the United States still reflects weaknesses the Founders knew we could overcome through continuous perseverance. Nevertheless, even at this stage, it has become apparent that the American people have accomplished something in human relations which has never been achieved before. They have demonstrated that over 250 million people from Europe, Asia, Africa, the Orient, Latin America, and the islands of the sea can be united and live in a free society in relative harmony—and receive mutual benefits which none of them could have found in isolation or without freedom.

America has been called a gigantic melting pot, which indeed she is. But more importantly, she has demonstrated that these widely varied cultures can be blended together in a free society and can prosper as a nation.

Small, Free Republics must Unite to Survive

It is interesting that, in order to accomplish this, the Founders felt the American republic had to be large, both geographically and in population. They also felt that as small nations gained their freedom they must combine together in great unions as the United States had done.

During this study we have noted that the Founders saw many serious disadvantages in small republics trying to face the world alone. They said small republics would be more easily corrupted by ambitious leaders. They would be susceptible to insurrections internally and military assaults externally. They would also be too small and too weak to provide an economy capable of supporting an adequate military defense, public services, and the necessary machinery of government. Since their own tiny republics and states were so weak and vulnerable, the Founders set out to make the United States a broad-based coalition of many states. As individual states united together they could still have all the advantages of local self-government, but, as a union, they could combine their strength in national defense, supply a coordinated system of central services, and present a united front in foreign relations.

They noted a further advantage in having a large population under a union of states: if any radical movements or insurrections erupted, they would tend to burn themselves out before they destroyed the whole nation. Furthermore, a larger nation is too diverse to be easily suppressed under the control of an ambitious tyrant. Additionally, they perceived a great advantage in establishing a national common market among all the states, where they could exchange goods freely and could assist one another in case of drought or disaster in particular areas of the country.

The Founders' advice to other suppressed nations was to struggle for freedom and then to unite with some larger coalition of free states for their mutual protection and economic development.

The Western Hemisphere Seen as the First Bastion of Freedom

When it came to freedom, the Founders were expansionists, but not imperialists. They talked about having Canada, Cuba, and other neighboring regions join them and become a part of the United States of North America. They also favored the liberation of Central and South America, as well as Mexico, and encouraged both Simon Bolivar and Jose de San Martin in their aspiration to set up a union to be called the United States of Latin America. Although these efforts failed initially, it does not eliminate the possibility that this could be achieved in the future.

The Founders were determined that while the rest of the Western Hemisphere was liberating itself, there should be no further incursions into this continent by the imperialistic powers of Europe or Asia. It is interesting that the British Foreign Office eventually encouraged this same policy. King George III finally died in 1820 after several years of complete insanity, and by 1823 the new British administration was actually encouraging the United States to issue its Monroe Doctrine to preclude France, Spain, and all other European imperialistic powers from expanding their dominions in the Western Hemisphere.

An American Pledge

The Monroe Doctrine also contains a pledge which modern American leaders might well remember, and that is the promise that even though the United States would look upon any foreign invasion of the Western Hemisphere as a threat to her own security, she would not use her military power to interfere in the domestic or internal affairs of any other nation. Of course, any defensive action to protect the Western Hemisphere would affect the internal affairs of some nations indirectly, but such action must not have the intent of advancing any imperialistic ambitions of the United States. This was the promise.

The Founders' Policy Against Entangling Alliances

For hundreds of years the more advanced nations of Europe and Asia tried to maintain a "balance of power" in an effort to promote peace. The fact that these various alliances led more often to war than peace is a matter of record in the more tragic annals of world history.

The Founders advocated an approach different from that of the Europeans. Jefferson clearly articulated their future hopes when he said, "Peace, commerce, and honest friendship with all nations, entangling alliances with none."[1]

The Founders' position on foreign relations has been frequently misinterpreted. Their policy was not one of "isolationism" but one of "separatism." They looked upon the United States as the cornerstone of a mighty fortress providing security, freedom, and prosperity. Using the United States' formula, other nations could be invited to join into a union of free states which could survive without alliances and without entangling themselves in the quarrels of other nations.

Through "separatism," without "isolationism," the Founders wanted America to maintain cordial relations with all while having entangling alliances with none. They intended to become strong and independent, but not the policeman of the world.

Switzerland Followed the Founders' Original Policy

The Founders' original policy was similar in many ways to that of modern Switzerland, which has successfully remained neutral and aloof from entangling alliance through two world wars and numerous European quarrels. During these periods of intense military action, Switzerland did not follow a policy of "isolationism," but rather one of universal diplomatic relations with all who might wish to come to Switzerland to buy, sell, borrow, or bank. She took a hostile posture toward none unless threatened. In general terms, this

1. Bergh, The Writings of Thomas Jefferson, op. cit., 3:321.

is analogous to the doctrine of "separatism" practiced by the early American leaders.

Dealing with Interdependence

The Founders were well aware that no nation is an island. This is especially true in our own age of modern technology where a widespread network of commercial channels facilitates the flow of food, textiles, machinery, chemicals, metals, and a multitude of other necessities all around the globe. The Founders would have heartily favored this flourishing development. However, they warned against the tendency to favor one nation over another or to mix political interdependence with commercial and economic interdependence. They steadfastly opposed alliances which involved political interdependence. Their motto seems to have been summed up in the phrase, "Coordination yes, but consolidation no."

In our day, when the nations of the world are being drawn closer together by transportation, communications, and commercial interdependence, the Founders' philosophy may seem a little old-fashioned, but Americans have learned during several recent wars that political and military interdependence is not the diplomatic prize its advocates had proclaimed it would be. In the end, the United States found itself trying to do a job which became impossible when its assumed allies flagrantly defaulted in their commitments and even their cooperation.

The formula drawn up by America's Founders now seems to have more merit than ever before, and modern Americans might do well to recapture the Founders' long-range dream and their carefully drawn plan to ultimately build a free, prosperous, and peaceful world.

On this theme George Washington had much to say, encouraging an approach that was fair to foreign nations, but still protected American interests.

Washington Describes the Founders' Plans

The universality of friendly foreign relations which Washington hoped to engender is reflected in the following statement from his famous Farewell Address:

> "Observe good faith and justice toward all nations. Cultivate peace and harmony with all. Religion and morality enjoin this conduct; and can it be that good policy does not equally enjoin it? It will be worthy of a free, enlightened, and, at no distant period, a great nation to give to mankind the magnanimous and too novel

> example of a people always guided by an exalted justice and benevolence."[2]

From experience, Washington was well aware of the natural tendency to classify nations as "friends" or "enemies." He felt that in the absence of actual hostility toward the United States, every effort should be made to cultivate friendship with all. He wrote:

> "In the execution of such a plan nothing is more essential than that permanent, inveterate antipathies against particular nations and passionate attachments for others should be excluded, and that in place of them just and amicable feelings toward all should be cultivated. The nation which indulges toward another an habitual hatred or an habitual fondness is in some degree a slave. It is a slave to its animosity or to its affection, either of which is sufficient to lead it astray from its duty and its interest."[3]

Washington pointed out that "antagonism by one nation against another disposes each more readily to offer insult and injury, to lay hold of slight causes of umbrage, and to be haughty and intractable when accidental or trifling occasions of dispute occur."[4]

The Problem with "Playing Favorites"

There is also a danger in having the United States become overly attached to some nations because of kinship or sentimental affection toward them. Washington warned:

> "So, likewise, a passionate attachment of one nation for another produces a variety of evils. Sympathy for the favorite nation, facilitating the illusion of an imaginary common interest in cases where no real common interest exists, and infusing into one the enmities of the other, betrays the former into a participation in the quarrels and wars of the latter without adequate inducement or justification. It leads also to concessions to the favorite nation of privileges denied to others, which is apt doubly to injure the nation making the concessions, by unnecessarily parting with what ought to have been retained, and by exciting jealousy, ill will, and disposition to retaliate in the parties from whom equal privileges are withheld."[5]

---

2. Fitzpatrick, The Writings of George Washington, op. cit., 35:231.
3. Ibid., 35:231.
4. Ibid.
5. Ibid., 35:232.

Concerning Most-favored Nations

Washington also warned against giving "most-favored" status to particular nations. It opens up the United States to strong foreign influences which could subvert the security or best interests of the United States. In fact, American officials seeking to accommodate friendly allies could inadvertently compromise American interests to a very dangerous extent. Washington said:

> "Against the insidious wiles of foreign influence, I conjure you to believe me, fellow citizens, the jealousy of a free people ought to be constantly awake, since history and experience prove that foreign influence is one of the most baneful foes of republican government. But that jealousy, to be useful, must be impartial, else it becomes the instrument of the very influence to be avoided instead of a defense against it. Excessive partiality for one foreign nation and excessive dislike of another cause those whom they actuate to see danger only on one side and serve to veil and even second the arts of influence on the others. Real patriots, who may resist the intrigues of the favorite, are liable to become suspected and odious, while its tools and dupes usurp the applause and confidence of the people to surrender their interests."[6]

What American Foreign Policy Should be

Washington then made his famous declaration of the Founders' policy of foreign relations:

> "The great rule of conduct for us, in regard to foreign nations, is in extending our commercial relations to have with them as little political connection as possible. So far as we have already formed engagements, let them be fulfilled with perfect good faith. Here let us stop."[7]

Washington had seen certain American politicians getting the United States embroiled in European quarrels. He saw these operating to the distinct disadvantage of the United States. Therefore, he warned:

> "Europe has a set of primary interests which to us have none, or a very remote relation. Hence she must be engaged in frequent controversies, the causes of which are essentially foreign to our concerns. Hence, therefore, it must be unwise in us to implicate

---

6. Ibid., 35:233.
7. Ibid.

> ourselves, by artificial ties, in the ordinary combinations and collusions of her friendships or enmities ... Why, by interweaving our destiny with that of any part of Europe, entangle our peace and prosperity in the toils of European ambition, rivalship, interests, humor, or caprice?" [8]

A World Policy

And what he had said concerning Europe he would say to the rest of the world:

> "It is our true policy to steer clear of permanent alliances with any portion of the foreign world. So far, I mean, as we are now at liberty to do it, for let me not be understood as capable of patronizing infidelity to existing engagements (I hold the maxim no less applicable to public than to private affairs that honesty is always the best policy). I repeat it, therefore: let those engagements be observed in their genuine sense. But, in my opinion, it is unnecessary and would be unwise to extend them." [9]

He said that "temporary alliances" may be justified for "extraordinary emergencies," but otherwise, "harmony, liberal intercourse with all nations are recommended by policy, humanity, and interest." [10]

Visualizing America as a World Peacemaker

It was the hope of the Founders that the strength of America would provide such a bulwark of defense for the free world that it would discourage warmongering nations from unleashing an attack on weaker neighbors. In our nuclear age this has become of paramount importance. There must be some means of neutralizing the effect of a surprise attack which could obliterate millions of people. The United States has taken the initiative in developing a defensive "peacemaker"—a defense mechanism that will destroy military *weapons* instead of *people*. On June 10, 1984, an intercontinental ballistic missile was experimentally fired from the coast of California, and when it was a hundred miles above the earth it was shot down by a new, non-nuclear defense weapon fired from an atoll far out in the Pacific.

This marked the beginning of a promising new era. If non-nuclear defense weapons can provide a protective network around the earth, no nation could

8. Ibid., 35:234.
9. Ibid.
10. Ibid., 35:235.

fire a nuclear warhead without having it destroyed soon after takeoff. Such a system could be made available to all nations, so that no nation could make war with nuclear missiles, regardless of their political ideology. This new American effort is appropriately called MAS—Mutually Assured Survival. The continued dispersal of nuclear weapons among nations hostile to the United States makes it imperative that the Strategic Defense Initiative should be perfected and deployed at the earliest possible date.

The Moral Willpower to Stand up for Peace

J. Reuben Clark, former Under Secretary of State and former U.S. Ambassador to Mexico, described the role of America as a great world peacemaker. He wrote:

> "America, multi-raced and multi-nationed, is by tradition, by geography, by citizenry, by natural sympathy, and by material interest, the great neutral nation of the earth. God so designed it. Drawn from all races, creeds, and nations, our sympathies run to every oppressed people. Our feelings, engaged on opposite sides of great differences, will in their natural course, if held in due and proper restraint, neutralize the one [with] the other. Directed in right channels, this great body of feeling for the one side or the other will ripen into sympathy and love for all misguided and misled fellowmen who suffer in any cause, and this sympathy and love will run out to all humanity in its woe ....
>
> "Having in mind our position as the great world neutral, ... we should announce our unalterable opposition to any plan to starve these innocent peoples ...—the women, the children, the sick, the aged, and the infirm—and declare that when actual and bona fide mass starvation shall come to any of them, no matter who they are, we shall do all that we properly may do to see that they are furnished with food ....
>
> "If we shall rebuild our lost moral power and influence by measures such as these which will demonstrate our love for humanity, our justice, our fair-mindedness, we ... shall then be where ... we can offer mediation between the two belligerents.
>
> "America, the great neutral, will thus become the Peacemaker of the world, which is her manifest destiny if she lives the law of peace."[11]

11. Skousen, The Five Thousand Year Leap, op. cit., pp. 276-278.

The Challenge for Today

America can be "the Peacemaker of the World." She *can* help other nations discover the formula for freedom and prosperity. But there is an important prerequisite: Americans must first rediscover that formula for themselves, as it is embodied in the principles found in the Constitution.

It is helpful to remember that the Constitution is not a stale, dead document. Rather, it is a vital, living blueprint for the success of the United States as a nation and its citizens as individuals.

A quick comparison between the constitutional principles and our practices today will show where we have gone astray. And the remedy is simple: return to the basic principles of the Founders' formula.

Of course, the first step to improvement and reform is *education*. The next step is *action*. The principles of the Constitution were not meant only to be studied, but to be restored and put into full operation. Much of this could be done now, but God will expect the rest to be done after the cleansing.

STATUTES

The Famous Statutes of God's Law

Alphabetical, By Topic

Abortion

The Law of the Covenant provided protection for both the mother and the unborn child:

"If men strive, and hurt a woman with child, so that her fruit depart from her, and yet no mischief follow: he shall be surely punished, according as the woman's husband will lay upon him: and he shall pay as the judges determine. And if any mischief follow, then thou shalt give life for life."[1]

However, the judges would probably rule that the mother's death was not intentional and therefore the death penalty would not be mandatory. This leaves a wide range of penalties which the judges might impose to fit the circumstances and allow the offender to save his life. For example,

"If there be laid on him a sum of money, then he shall give for the ransom of his life whatsoever is laid upon him."[2]

As indicated above, Jesus refers to the usual practice of enforcing the payment:

"And his lord was wroth, and delivered him to the tormentors [whip masters] till he should pay all that was due."[3]

However, even in the most extreme cases, whipping was limited to 40 stripes. The judge must witness the whipping to insure that the punishment is carried out as intended.[4]

Adultery

See also: *Fornication, Idolatry, Incest, and Rape.*

---

1. Exodus 21:22-23.
2. Exodus 21:30.
3. Matthew 18:34.
4. Deuteronomy 25:2-3.

Adultery is defined as an act of unlawful sexual intercourse between a married person and one of the opposite sex, whether married or single. Here are the commandments relating to this offense.

"Thou shalt not commit adultery." [5]

"He that committeth adultery with his neighbor's wife, the adulterer and the adulteress shall surely be put to death." [6]

However, as we have mentioned, death was not mandatory. The judge has a number of options to provide a semblance of justice between the parties.

Nevertheless, as we shall see later, the threat of death is included for adultery in case the offenders are so profligate that the judges feel they should be forcibly banished from the community. The parties are told that if they remain in the community after a certain date, it will be at "the risk of their lives."

In John 8:3-11 a woman was taken in adultery and brought to Jesus. Her accusers reminded Jesus that the penalty for adultery could be stoning, but the Romans did not allow a person to be put to death for this type of offense. The scripture says they were "tempting him," because if he said to stone her, the Romans would arrest him. If he said not to stone her the accusers would say he was against Moses. But Jesus did not answer. In the first place there was something wrong with this situation because the accusers brought only the woman. The law required that both offenders—the woman and the man—be brought before the judge.[7] But Jesus was not interested in technicalities. He had something more important to teach these "tempters."

He said, "He that is without sin … let him first cast a stone at her." Then he stooped down and made markings in the dust of the pavement. One by one her accusers crept away. Then Jesus asked the woman, "Woman … hath no man condemned thee? She said, "No man Lord, and Jesus said unto her, Neither do I condemn thee; go, and sin no more."

A modern translation adds a significant postscript that is not in the King James Version. It says: "And the woman glorified God from that hour, and believed on his name." [8] So that is the happy ending to this story.

5. Exodus 20:14.
6. Leviticus 20:10.
7. Ibid.
8. JST John 8:11.

Animals: Responsibility of Owner

In my early youth my family lived in a country community and I can vividly remember how frightening it was to have a mean bull escape onto the streets of thc town. We even had a neighbor that had a mean rooster that would often attack children. Then there were stray cows and horses that would ruin our gardens or get into grain fields. The fixing of responsibility for the control of domestic animals involves a whole series of situations. God's law guided the judges as follows:

> "If an ox gore a man or a woman, that they die: then the ox shall be surely stoned, and his flesh shall not be eaten; but the owner of the ox shall be quit."[9]

In other words, it was treated as an accidental death that was to be occasionally expected from this type of animal. People were expected to be cautious in protecting themselves and their children from these neutered bulls which were often ill-tempered. God's law continued:

> "But if the ox were wont to push with his horn in time past, and it hath been testified to his owner, and he hath not kept him in, but that he hath killed a man or a woman; the ox shall be stoned, and his owner also shall be put to death. If there be laid on him a sum of money [in lieu of death], then he shall give for the ransom of his life whatsoever is laid upon him."[10]

The same rules apply to the goring of a child by an ox.[11] If the ox attacked an employee or a servant, the law said:

> "If the ox shall push a manservant or a maidservant; he shall give unto their master thirty shekels of silver, and the ox shall be stoned."[12]

Then there is the situation where one ox attacks the ox of another. The law read:

> "And if one man's ox hurt another's, that he die; then they shall sell the live ox, and divide the money of it; and the dead ox also they shall divide. Or if it be known that the ox hath used to push in time past, and his owner hath not kept him in; he shall surely pay ox for ox; and the dead shall be his own."[13]

Another problem relates to stray animals or letting animals feed in another person's field:

---

9. Exodus 21:28.
10. Exodus 21:29-30.
11. Exodus 21:31.
12. Exodus 21:32.
13. Exodus 21:35-36.

"If a man shall cause a field or vineyard to be eaten, and shall put in his beast, and shall feed in another man's field; of the best of his own field, and of the best of his own vineyard, shall he make restitution." [14]

Of course, if this offense includes a deliberate trespass, by putting the animals in another's field, there was not only the payment of damages but an additional penalty of one-fifth to discourage the offender from repeating such depredations in the future.[15]

Animals: Purebred Strains to Be Maintained

Pure-bred cattle are those with distinctive characteristics which have been developed through generations of unmixed descent. The Israelites were to perpetuate the strains of purebred cattle in their possession:

"Ye shall keep my statutes. Thou shalt not let thy cattle gender with a diverse kind." [16]

No penalty is indicated, but since this is the law of the Lord, those who offended would no doubt be subject to an appropriate penalty which the judges would select from those we have already mentioned.

Appeals

Since Israel was organized in a hierarchy of tens, fifties, hundreds, thousands, etc., there was a direct line of appeal to insure the highest quality of justice possible. However there was also a provision to prevent the system from being abused or the final decision from being ignored or rejected. Here is what the law provided:

"If there arise a matter too hard for thee in judgment, between blood and blood, between plea and plea, and between stroke and stroke, being matters of controversy within thy gates: then shalt thou arise, and get thee up into the place which the Lord thy God shall choose;

"And thou shalt come unto the priests the Levites, and unto the judge that shall be in those days, and inquire; and they shall shew thee the sentence of judgment: And thou shalt do according to the sentence, which they of that place which the Lord shall choose shall shew thee; and thou shalt observe to do according to all that they inform thee:

"According to the sentence of the law which they shall teach thee, and according to the judgment which they shall tell thee, thou shalt do: thou shalt not

14. Exodus 22:5.
15. Numbers 5:7.
16. Leviticus 19:19.

decline from the sentence which they shall shew thee, to the right hand, nor to the left. And the man that will do presumptuously, and will not hearken unto the priest that standeth to minister there before the Lord thy God, or unto the judge, even that man shall die: and thou shalt put away the evil from Israel."[17]

This simply provides that a person can appeal clear up to the final authority if necessary, but once the final decree has been issued it has to be honored and carried out. It was a capital crime to stir up a mob against the final decree or refuse to carry it out. Notice that this mandate applied to the decisions of a lower court that had been overruled on appeal. The lower judges were duty-bound to accept the final decision or suffer the consequences.

Arrest: Authority for

Officers were authorized to arrest offenders and put them "in ward" (in a watched-over place) or in custody until the final disposition of a case.

"And they put him in ward, that the mind of the Lord might be shewed them."[18]

"And they put him in ward because it was not declared what should be done to him."[19]

It was also part of the law that any person or group of citizens who caught a person in the act of committing an offense could seize the person and bring him before the judges. This is called a "citizen's arrest." Two things were required for this type of arrest:

1. The person seizing the offender had to be an actual witness to the offense.

2. The person or group of persons who witnessed the crime had to be strong enough to immobilize the offender and take him into custody. Otherwise the regular officers had to be summoned.

Under the topic of Adultery we described a woman who was taken in the act of committing adultery and subjected to a citizens arrest so she could be brought to Jesus for judgment. The outcome of this incident is interesting. (See *Adultery* above).

Arson or Fire-setting

Arson is defined as deliberately setting fire to the property of another person or setting fire to one's own property to collect insurance.

In ancient Israel there was no insurance, but it was customary for the neighbors to help build a new house or barn if one burned down. Of course, if a man burned

17. Deuteronomy 17:8-12.
18. Leviticus 24:12.
19. Numbers 15:34.

down his barn or house just to get a new one, it would be arson and he would be punished instead of helped.

However, the more common problem was accidental fires:

"If fire break out, and catch in thorns, so that the stacks of corn, or the standing corn, or the field, be consumed therewith; he that kindled the fire shall surely make restitution." [20]

Any one of the more serious punishments would apply if the arsonist proved to be a pathological fire-bug or loss of life resulted from the fire. The motive of revenge would also give the fire a criminal element which the judges would have to take into consideration in selecting the appropriate punishment.

One of the most dangerous types of arsonists is the psychopath who sets fire incidental to his sexual activities. These are extremely difficult "fire-bugs" to detect and they can destroy millions of dollars worth of property. Then there are "serial arsonists" like the one in California who went down the coast setting fires as he went. The damages were estimated at two billion dollars. The psychopathic arsonist tends to boast to someone what he has done and this is the principal means by which they are caught.

Assassination

See also: *Murder*.

This offense generally refers to the murder of a ruler or high official in the government. It is often employed by those who want to overthrow the government or terminate the administration of a particular party. In ancient times this was the most prevalent device employed by the "secret combinations" to seize political power or, as with the modern *mafia*, punish those who did not obey the orders of the secret band of leaders.

One of the greatest accomplishments of modern popular governments has been the "peaceful transfer of power." Nevertheless, in the United States there have been four presidential assassinations: Lincoln in 1965, Garfield in 1881, McKinley in 1901, Kennedy in 1963, and an attempted assassination of President Reagan in 1981.

In contrast to this consider the Roman Empire. Of the first 47 emperors, 24 were assassinated.

Assault

See: *Battery*.

---

20. Exodus 22:6.

Asylum

There were six cities set aside where fugitives could flee for safety until the charges against them could be adjudicated.

Down through the ages it has been terribly destructive to any society if the people begin feuding among themselves. This is where the offended parties take the law into their own hands. Mobs of vigilantes may also roam across the land doing the same thing.

People are tempted to do this where they feel the judicial process is too slow or the offender will get away without being adequately punished.

To discourage feuding, the Lord set it up so that a person suspected of a crime could flee to a city of asylum and remain there in safety until "due process" could be arranged. This whole process is carefully set forth in Deuteronomy, chapter 19.

In modern times when the Nazis, Soviets and Communist Chinese waged genocidal warfare against minorities and dissidents in their own countries, millions were slaughtered. Any individual who could escape was offered political asylum in America, England, France, Switzerland, and certain other countries. Among the German-Jewish refugees were some of the foremost scientists who developed the atomic bomb that helped win World War II. Of those who did not escape, four to six million were sent to gas chambers or otherwise executed.

Banishment

See also: *Enforcement of the Law, Penalties*.

The object of law in a civilized country is to insure the peace and security of its inhabitants. Individual offenses are punished as they occur. However, when the pattern of the offenses become so frequent or so flagrant that the offender was considered a perpetual threat to the community it was not unusual to permanently banish (the Hebrew word is "root out") the offender from that region. Banishment was always accompanied by a declaration that if the person returned he would be killed.

Banishment was also frequently associated with the confiscation of property and the loss of the offender's inheritance.

Ezra mentions banishment as one of the remedies for the violations of God's law,[21] and it is believed that since nearly all of the offenses which would destroy a Zion society carry the ultimate punishment of death, we have concluded that the intent of the Lord was to employ the threat of death to enforce the decree of banishment. As we go through the statutes of the law it will be observed that some rather minor offenses carry the maximum penalty, but this would only be justified where these minor offenses (such a violating the sabbath) have become so flagrant

21. Ezra 7:26.

that the offender is spreading a spirit of rebellion and defiance which is inimical to the survival of a godly society. Under such circumstances a judgment of banishment under threat of death may then be the only viable remedy. In fact, it is likely in most cases where the judges make such a decisive pronouncement there will be electrifying motivation for some speedy repentance.

Battery

Battery is defined as the unlawful beating of another.

"And if men strive together, and one smite another with a stone, or with his fist, and he die not, but keepeth his bed: If he rise again, and walk abroad upon his staff, then shall he that smote him be quit: only he shall pay for the loss of his time, and shall cause him to be thoroughly healed."[22]

Of course, such an altercation could result in much more serious consequences, and even result in the death of the victim. After considering all the circumstances, the judges would have to determine whether it was an accidental death provoked by an unexpected quarrel, or whether it was a deliberate attempt by the assailant to commit murder from the beginning.

The Law of the Covenant made rather generous allowances for violence occurring during the heat of a quarrel, but if there was evidence of a premeditated taking of life, death would be mandatory.

Bestiality

Bestiality is defined as sexual relations between mankind and an animal. This was one of the characteristics of pagan practices in some countries and was sometimes associated with idolatry. For this reason it was looked upon as extremely offensive to God and a threat to the entire culture of Israel. The Lord said:

"Ye shall not walk in the manners of the nation, which I cast out before you: for they committed all these things, and therefore I abhorred them."[23]

There were many things God abhorred among the heathens but bestiality was among the worst. The Lord told Moses:

"Whosoever lieth with a beast shall surely be put to death."[24]

"Neither shalt thou lie with any beast to defile thyself therewith: neither shall any woman stand before a beast to lie down thereto: it is confusion."[25]

22. Exodus 21:18-19.
23. Leviticus 20:23.
24. Exodus 22:19.
25. Leviticus 18:23.

"And if a man lie with a beast, he shall surely be put to death: and ye shall slay the beast."[26] The beasts were slain because often they had been trained to perform obscene acts.[27]

"And if a woman approach unto any beast, and lie down thereto, thou shalt kill the woman, and the beast: [Concerning the slaying of the beast, see the citation above.] They shall surely be put to death; their blood shall be upon them."[28]

In certain situations the judges might allow some leniency where the offender was a young person or a first time offender and was bitterly remorseful for what had happened. In that case the judge had the option of allowing the offender to ransom his or her life as provided in Exodus 21:30.

In most cases, however, these offenses were considered to be such serious acts of debauchery that the death penalty was promptly administered, or, in fear of his life, the offender fled and became a permanent exile in some other region or country.

In modern times sexuality with animals has been associated with a number of scandals involving motion picture stars and habitual degenerates.

Blasphemy

Blasphemy is defined as any speech, act, portrayal, or device, which defames God.

"And he that blasphemeth the name of the Lord, he shall surely be put to death, and all the congregation shall certainly stone him."[29]

Idolatry (the worship of false gods) was considered a form of blasphemy and the penalty was death[30] although the person could ransom his or her life under Exodus 21:30.

Jesus was accused of blasphemy when he said he could forgive sin;[31] when he said he was the Son of God;[32] also when he said they would someday see him "sitting on the right hand of power, and coming in the clouds of heaven."[33]

Jesus was also accused of blasphemy when he said he could destroy "this temple" [meaning his body] and rebuild it in 3 days.[34] Stephen was accused of

26. Leviticus 20:15.
27. See Adam Clarke, Bible Commentary, New York: Eaten and Mains, 1:565, 569.
28. Leviticus 20:16.
29. Leviticus 24:16.
30. Exodus 22:20.
31. Matthew 9:2-3; Luke 5:21.
32. John 10:22-36; 19:7.
33. Matthew 26:64-65.
34. Matthew 26:59-61.

blasphemy and stoned because he said he beheld a vision in which he saw the Son of Man standing on the right hand of God.[35]

The apostles accused the people of Jerusalem of blasphemy for the way they treated Jesus and his disciples.[36]

Of course, the penalty of death was not mandatory even in cases of genuine blasphemy. Any of the lesser punishments could be invoked which we mentioned under "penalties." It was up to the judges to determine what was appropriate.

Bond Servant

See: *Servitude.*

Borrowing

See also: *Lending.*

Borrowing was not begging. It was requesting money or the use of some animal or thing with the promise that the same would be returned in as good a condition as when it was borrowed:

"And if a man borrow ought of his neighbor, and it be hurt, or die, the owner thereof being not with it, he shall surely make it good." [37]

However, if a man were hired to plow a field or perform some other service, and his animals were hurt or killed, the employer would not be held responsible since the risk of such injuries was included in the amount of the hire. The law stated:

"But if the owner thereof be with it, he shall not make it good: if it be an hired thing, it came for his hire." [38]

The Psalms pronounced a judgment on those who borrowed but did not repay:

"The wicked borroweth, and payeth not again." [39]

And the law provided stringent remedies to see that the delinquent borrower did pay:

"And his lord was wroth, and delivered him to the tormentors [whip masters] till he should pay all that was due." [40]

35. Acts 7:56-58.
36. Luke 22:63-65; Acts 13:45.
37. Exodus 22:14.
38. Exodus 22:15.
39. Psalms 37:21.
40. Matthew 18:34.

However, even in the most extreme cases, whipping was limited to 40 stripes. The judge must witness the whipping to insure that the punishment is carried out as intended.[41]

Another option was the confiscation of goods or property of the debtor.[42]

Breach of Trust

See: *Embezzlement.*

Bribery

Bribery is defined as giving money, goods, or promising some special advantage to induce a person to do something illegal or contrary to his will.

"And thou shalt take no gift: for the gift blindeth the wise, and perverteth the words of the righteous." [43]

The penalty for bribery was left to the discretion of the judges. If it involved a judge or some official of any kind it could mean immediate removal from office. There could also be heavy fines, whipping, or confiscation of property. In extreme cases there could be banishment to some foreign country.

Bribery constitutes the most prevalent cause of corruption in governments and commercial institutions today. However, it is usually excused as merely "doing favors" and winning "good will" with one another.

For example, a contractor gives a building inspector a case of whiskey and asks him to overlook certain deficiencies. Is this bribery? A politician promises certain special interest groups to pass laws giving this group subsidies or taxpayers' money or "entitlements" if they will vote for him. A President tells a congressman he needs his vote on a certain bill and will give him no help at the next election unless he votes in favor of the bill the congressman had intended to oppose.

Bribery comes in many forms and flavors.

Burglary

Burglary is defined as the act of breaking into any building at any time to commit a theft or other felony.

"Thou shalt not steal." [44]

41. Deuteronomy 25:2.
42. Ezra 7:26.
43. Exodus 23:8; Deuteronomy 16:19.
44. Exodus 20:15.

"If a thief be found breaking up [or breaking into a building], and be smitten [at nighttime] that he die, there shall no blood be shed for him."[45] (In other words, it is considered an excusable homicide.)

The next verse makes it clear that this is referring only to the killing of a burglar at night because it says:

"If the sun be risen upon him, there shall be blood shed for him; for he should make full restitution; if he have nothing, then he shall be sold for his theft."[46]

In other words, if the burglary occurs in the daytime the thief can be identified and a restitution made by him. At nighttime the burglar cannot be identified and the property owner has no remedy. Therefore, slaying the burglar at night was an excusable homicide whereas deliberately slaying a burglar in the daytime was an unlawful killing unless, of course, it was done in self defense.

As we have mentioned earlier, a householder who slew a burglar in broad daylight must make restitution to his family for the unnecessary slaying of the burglar. The point here is that human life is sacred, and if the burglar could be identified and arrested there was no need to kill him. Nevertheless, circumstances in each case would be evaluated by the judge and justice rendered according to the facts.

Police records show that modern burglars often pose more of a threat to a home than merely stealing money and goods. Often when burglars find a woman alone or even a couple alone, they will sexually assault the woman and often beat the man senseless. Security against burglaries in our day means much more than merely protecting property.

Business Ethics

The instinct to violate business ethics is primarily greed, and there is no greater remedy than a conversion and a commitment to the Golden Rule. But in the absence of that, the moment a party to a transaction treats the other party differently than he would like to be treated himself, the temptation of fraud arises.

The Lord was very specific in referring to fraud. He said:

"Thou shalt not defraud thy neighbor."[47] Then he went on to say:

"Ye shall do no unrighteousness in judgment, in meteyard, in weight, or in measure. Just balances, just weights, a just ephah, and a just hin, shall ye have."[48]

Later he emphasized the same point when he said:

45. Exodus 22:2.
46. Exodus 22:3.
47. Leviticus 19:13.
48. Leviticus 19:35-36.

"Thou shalt not have in thy bag divers weights, a great and a small. Thou shalt not have in thine house divers measures, a great and a small. But thou shalt have a perfect and just weight, a perfect and just measure shalt thou have ... For all that do such things [as using dishonest weights and measures], and all that do unrighteously, are an abomination unto the Lord thy God." [49]

It will be noted that the penalty is left to the discretion of the judges in all of these violations. The first rule will require complete reparation to the victim. The second rule will be an appropriate punishment to discourage the offender from repeating the offense. This could be in the form of fines, whipping, confiscation of property, or even banishment in extreme cases.

Castration

Legal definition: To emasculate or surgically remove the testicles of a male.

This mode of punishment is not mentioned in the Bible. However, all of the serious sex crimes under God's law carried the ultimate punishment of death. The Bible speaks of a person being able to "ransom" his life from a death penalty by satisfying the judges that this offense will never be committed again and that the offender is willing to undergo whatever sacrifice is necessary to escape the supreme penalty.[50]

It is entirely conceivable that in the case of a violent sex offender he might ask the judges to allow him to undergo voluntary emasculation to save his life. However, there is no provision in God's law for compulsory emasculation.

Children: Their Rights and Responsibilities

The rights of children and the responsibilities of parents toward children are emphasized all through the scriptures. This includes important responsibilities of adults toward children other than their own. The scriptures state:

"Thou shalt not avenge, nor bear any grudge against the children of thy people, but thou shalt love thy neighbour as thyself." [51]

The rights of children are unalienable just as the God-given rights of their parents are unalienable. Members of the community were forbidden to punish children to get even with their parents or vice versa:

"The fathers shall not be put to death for the children, neither shall the children be put to death for the fathers: every man shall be put to death for his own sin." [52]

49. Deuteronomy 25:13-16.
50. Exodus 21:30.
51. Leviticus 19:18.
52. Deuteronomy 24:16.

As children grew to maturity the Mosaic law required that they begin to assume responsibilities and conduct themselves according to the laws their parents had taught them. It is interesting that as soon as children reached "the age of accountability" (usually around eight) they were treated as adults where crimes were concerned. Judges might ameliorate the punishment because of youthfulness, but as far as the child was concerned, he or she knew that the full requirements of the law might be imposed upon them.

Special provisions were made for the criminal delinquent who became "stubborn and rebellious," and was a "glutton and a drunkard."[53] The penalty for such defiant profligacy was death,[54] providing, of course, the parents who were witnesses against him would cast the first stone.[55]

As might be expected, there is no single instance recorded where this extremity was ever used, nevertheless, every son of Israel knew that it was a most serious offense to rebel against parents because it was a capital crime.

Juveniles were forbidden by God to hold their parents in disdain as many do in modern times.

The Lord required parents to teach their children eternal truths throughout their lives:

"And thou shalt teach them diligently unto thy children, and shalt talk of them when thou sittest in thine house, and when thou walkest by the way, and when thou liest down, and when thou risest up."[56]

Parents were to teach their children religious history so they would understand the purposes of God in giving certain commandments to the people and also help them understand why certain rituals and procedures were to be followed:

"And when thy son asketh thee in time to come, saying, What mean the testimonies, and the statutes, and the judgments, which the Lord our God hath commanded you? Then thou shalt say unto thy son, We were Pharaoh's bondmen [slaves] in Egypt; and the Lord brought us out of Egypt with a mighty hand: and the Lord shewed signs and wonders, great and sore, upon Egypt ... and he brought us out from thence ....

"And the Lord commanded us to do all these statutes, to fear the Lord our God, for our good always, that he might preserve us alive ... And it will be our righteousness, if we observe to do all these commandments before the Lord our God, as he hath commanded us."[57]

53. Deuteronomy 21:18, 20.
54. Deuteronomy 21:20-21.
55. Deuteronomy 17:7.
56. Deuteronomy 6:7.
57. Deuteronomy 6:20-25.

Child Abuse

See also: *Incest, Idolatry, Homosexuality.*

Among pagan or apostate societies many children were subject to the most egregious cruelty, abuse and neglect. Historical records are replete with the gross mistreatment of children that are abhorrent to contemplate. When the Israelites apostatized, the prophets scorched them for their inhuman treatment of their children:

"Yea, they sacrificed their sons and their daughters unto devils, and shed innocent blood, even the blood of their sons and of their daughters, whom they sacrificed unto the idols of Canaan: and the land was polluted with blood." [58]

Apostate Israelites received the wrathful curse of God for having their children burned alive in the red hot arms of Molech, a pagan idol with a furnace in its belly and hollow arms in which a child could be roasted. The mandate of the Lord proclaimed his law:

"Thou shalt not let any of thy seed pass through the fire to Molech." [59]

The exploitation of children in torturous forced labor, putting their daughters out to harlotry, or emasculating their sons to bring a higher price as slaves,[60] were all part of the degradation of children during the days of Israel's apostasy.

But the deepest dungeons of hell were reserved for parents or other adults who sexually desecrated little children. God has given children into the custody of parents and the community of adults as a special gift from heaven. They are to be taught, trained and raised up to be righteous servants of the Most High. Any adults who violate that trust come under the same denunciation as that which Jeremiah pronounced when he said:

"Forgive not their iniquity, neither blot out their sin from thy sight, but let them be overthrown before thee; deal thus with them in the time of thine anger." [61]

Children: Their Age of Accountability

Through the ages there has been a tendency to excuse the criminal conduct on the part of children or youths because it was assumed their misconduct was the result of inexperience or poor judgment. Even today this is the view of the school of Behavioral Psychology. These scholars tend to blame crime and violence on "society" rather than individuals. Under this philosophy the people passed the Juvenile Delinquency Acts giving every state in the country a system of juvenile courts where the youth are assigned even if they have committed a violent adult

58. Psalms 106:37-38.
59. Leviticus 18:21.
60. Hastings' Dictionary of the Bible, under "eunuchs."
61. Jeremiah 18:23.

crime. Too often these courts brushed aside violent crimes by children and youths or punished them very lightly.

But it didn't work. This policy of leniency and tolerating robberies, arson, muggings, rapes, drive-by shootings and even murders has produced the highest crime rate in the world. Some have come to feel that our entire civilization has reached an advanced state of decay.

It is interesting that God's law concerning children takes an entirely different approach.

According to God's law a child may be mischievous or a trouble maker, but no "sin" is attributed to that child by the Lord until after he or she has reached the age of accountability. For the ordinary, normally developed child this has been designated by the Lord as age eight.[62] This means that a child is "officially" innocent of any misbehavior until age eight even though the parents may have been held responsible for the child's injuries or damages to others.

Nevertheless, by the age of eight every child should clearly understand that any misconduct or violations of God's commandments in the future will come under the direct scrutiny of the judges as well as the heavens. The scripture says:

"No one can be received … unless he has arrived unto the years of accountability before God, and is capable of repentance." [63]

And again:

"Their children shall be baptized for the remission of their sins when eight years old, and receive the laying on of hands. And they shall also teach their children to pray and to walk uprightly before the Lord." [64]

Making certain that children understand God's law becomes extremely important because under this system, all violations are adult violations. At least "a violation is a violation" and there are no "juvenile" crimes as such. Of course, when it comes to punishment or having the youthful offender provide "satisfaction" to the victim, the judge will take the age and experience of the offender into consideration.

Contracts

A contract is a compact or covenant between two or more people to do something which is enforceable under the law.

When an Israelite made a vow or contract, he was under a religious obligation as well as a legal duty to fulfill it:

---

62. JST Genesis 16:11; see Skousen, The First 2,000 Years, op. cit., p. 309.
63. JST Genesis 17:11; see Skousen, The First 2000 Years, op cite p. 254.
64. Ibid

"If a man vow a vow unto the Lord, or swear an oath to bind his soul with a bond; he shall not break his word, he shall do according to all that proceedeth out of his mouth."[65]

A vow by a minor could be disavowed by a father so that conniving people could not take advantage of a youth.[66]

If a wife made a vow or contract, it could be disavowed by her husband for the very practical reason that in all likelihood he would have to provide the money or otherwise help fulfill the vow.[67]

However, if the husband learns of the vow and keeps silent it is assumed that he has confirmed the vow made by his wife, and he will therefore be required to fulfill agreement if his wife does not.[68]

Cults: Religious and Fraternal

A cult usually refers to a group who have become obsessed in their attachment to a person, a principle, or an idea which is extreme or bizarre, perhaps even hostile to the community or the country.

Cults are known for their signs, fraternal signals and sometimes their dress and hair styles.

It was customary among some of the heathens to identify themselves with fellow-cultists by cutting their hair and beards in a round style. Herodotus makes special mention of those who worshipped Bacchus by shaving or cutting their hair "round."[69]

Concerning this the Lord says:

"Ye shall not round the corners of your heads, neither shalt thou mar the corners of thy beard."[70]

Another heathen custom which still prevails among many primitive peoples was cutting the flesh to show remorse for the death of a relative or friend. In Borneo the natives still cut off joints of fingers as funeral offerings. Often children are badly maimed before reaching adolescence because of this practice.

Another practice condemned by the Lord was tattooing or marking the body with elaborate religious symbols. The Lord declared:

---

65. Numbers 30:2.
66. Numbers 30:3-5.
67. Numbers 30:6-8.
68. Numbers 30:9-14.
69. Adam Clarke, Bible Commentary, 1:573.
70. Leviticus 19:27.

"Ye shall not make any cuttings in your flesh for the dead, nor print any marks upon you: I am the Lord." [71]

Debts

See: *Borrowing and Lending.*

The policy of God's law was to avoid the curse of perpetual debt or the loss of one's inheritance because of debt. In most societies the greatest burden of the people consists of taxes on the land and accumulated interest on debts.

God's law did not provide for any taxes on land. Therefore, the government could not confiscate or foreclose on land for failure to pay taxes.[72]

Debts could not extend beyond six years. The seventh year was called the "Lord's release." [73]

Loans made to the poor were to be without interest or usury.[74]

Mortgages or leases on land could not extend beyond 49 years. The fiftieth year was a time of Jubilee when debts were forgiven and the land had to be returned to the original owners. By this means each inheritance remained within each family on a perpetual basis.

Divorce

It is obvious that the Mosaic Law was designed to preserve the family and implement the marriage relationship. To maintain its integrity, adultery was considered to be almost as serious as murder.[75]

To get marriage off to a good start not even war was allowed to disrupt it:

"When a man hath taken a new wife, he shall not go out to war, neither shall he be charged with any business: but he shall be free at home one year, and shall cheer up his wife which he hath taken." [76]

Jesus made it plain that God had intended the marriage vow to be so sacred that it could not be broken except for extremely serious reasons. However, the Pharisees tempted him by pointing out that Moses had authorized husbands in ancient Israel to put away their wives[77] whenever they desired by simply giving them a bill or declaration of divorcement:

---

71. Leviticus 19:28.
72. Howard B. Rand, Digest of the Divine Law, Marrimac, Massachusetts: Destiny Publishing Company, 1959, p. 111.
73. Deuteronomy 15:1-2.
74. Leviticus 25:35-36.
75. Deuteronomy 22:22-24.
76. Deuteronomy 24:5.
77. Deuteronomy 24:1-4.

"And Jesus answered and said unto them, For the hardness of your heart he wrote you this precept. But from the beginning of the creation God made them male and female. For this cause shall a man leave his father and mother, and cleave to his wife; And they twain shall be one flesh: so then they are no more twain, but one flesh. What therefore God hath joined together, let not man put asunder." [78]

Up to this point, it almost appears that the Lord is holding the man primarily responsible for holding the marriage together. Later, however, the disciples of Jesus asked him further concerning this subject:

"And he saith unto them, Whosoever shall put away his wife, and marry another, committeth adultery against her. And if a woman shall put away her husband, and be married to another, she committeth adultery." [79]

Nevertheless, God gave to his ordained servants the power to both seal and unseal. Therefore, when his servants feel that a divorce is warranted they have the power to grant a divorce and have it recognized in heaven.[80]

Drunkenness

The vice of drunkenness is widely denounced throughout the scriptures. Its greatest element of evil is the suppression of reason and conscience so that a mild and inoffensive person can be turned into a raging maniac. Proverbs calls it "the wine of violence." [81] Paul says "drunkards" shall not inherit the kingdom of God.[82]

An habitual drunkard is suffering from an addiction and his most effective remedy is compulsory incarceration until he has "dried out." Ezra mentions imprisonment.[83] Whipping is also associated with public drunkenness. In listing all of the corrupt vices which Paul considered the most reprehensible, he includes the following:

"Now the works of the flesh are manifest, which are these; adultery, fornication, uncleanness, lasciviousness, idolatry, witchcraft, hatred, variance, emulations, wrath, strife, seditions, heresies, envyings, murders, *drunkenness*, revellings, and such like: of the which I tell you before, as I have also told you in time past, that they which do such things shall not inherit the kingdom of God." [84]

Emasculation

See: *Castration*.

78. Mark 10:5-9.
79. Mark 10:11-12.
80. Matthew 16:19; 18:18.
81. Proverbs 4:17.
82. 1 Corinthians 6:10.
83. Ezra 7:26.
84. Galatians 5:19-21.

Embezzlement by a Trustee

Legal definition: The fraudulent appropriation to one's own use or benefit, the property or money entrusted to him by another.

"If a man shall deliver unto his neighbour money or stuff to keep, and it be stolen out of the man's house; if the thief be found, let him pay double. If the thief be not found, then the master of the house shall be brought unto the judges, to see whether he have put his hand unto his neighbour's goods."[85]

If the investigation by the judges fails to implicate the custodian or trustee, then he shall take a sacred oath "in the name of God" that he is innocent and if he does so, he was to be considered absolved. Dr. Adam Clarke's comment on this principle is as follows:

"Whatever goods were thus left in the hands of another person, that person, according to Mosaic law, became responsible for them: if they were stolen, and the thief was found, he was to pay double; if he could not be found, the oath of the person who had them in keeping, made before the magistrates, that he knew nothing of them, was considered a full acquittance."[86]

If a trustee is careless and allows bailments to be stolen from him, "he shall make restitution unto the owner thereof."[87]

If an animal is given into his custody and it is accidentally "torn in pieces, then let him bring it for witness, and he shall not make good that which was torn."[88]

Elderly People Entitled to Respect

Under God's law there was a religious, family, and civilian responsibility toward the elderly and the infirm.

"Thou shalt rise up before the hoary head, and honor the face of the old man, and fear thy God."[89]

The means of enforcing this commandment was discretionary with the judges. However, public opinion and the reprimands of religious leaders were about the only enforcement devices employed.

Employer-Employee Relationships

If a man hires another to work for him and the employee uses his own animals to plow, haul, etc., the injury or death of any such animals is considered to be

85. Exodus 22:7-8.
86. Adam Clarke, Bible Commentary, 1:412.
87. Exodus 22:12.
88. Exodus 22:13.
89. Leviticus 19:32.

the responsibility of the hired employee since his wage included the risk of such injuries.[90]

Because an employer is in a superior position, the possibility of abuse called for a word of caution. The Lord holds employers responsible for the way they treat their employees:

"Ye shall not therefore oppress one another; but thou shalt fear thy God: for I am the Lord your God."[91] "Thou shalt not rule over him with rigour; but shalt fear thy God."[92]

"Thou shalt not oppress an hired servant that is poor and needy, whether he be of thy brethren, or of thy strangers that are in thy land within thy gates: at his day thou shalt give him his hire, neither shall the sun go down upon it; for he is poor, and setteth his heart upon it: lest he cry against thee unto the Lord, and it be sin unto thee."[93]

Enforcement of the Law

See also: *Penalties*.

One of the unique features of God's law is the fact that it was not administered by a body of "enforcement officers" but by the people themselves. Everybody had the responsibility to be on the alert for any violations of the law.

So this explains why ancient Israel did not appear to have any corps of semi-military officers constantly policing the people to see if there were any violators. Instead, the judges waited until the people brought a complaint. Then the judges had the sacred responsibility to "inquire diligently" to see if the charges were true.[94]

This implies an investigation as well as a hearing. As soon as the judges had all the facts at their disposal, they passed judgment.

But even the execution of the judgment depended to a large extent upon the people. This was particularly true in any case involving the death sentence.

As we have already pointed out, the only time the judges were duty-bound to invoke the death sentence was in the case of murder.[95] However, the death sentence could be invoked for a great variety of offenses where the offender was rebellious, unrepentant, and refused to leave the territory voluntarily or make any attempt to provide "satisfaction".

90. Exodus 22:14-15.
91. Leviticus 25:17.
92. Leviticus 25:43.
93. Deuteronomy 24:14-15.
94. Deuteronomy 17:2-5; 19:18.
95. Numbers 35:31.

But in any case, capital punishment required that the accusers as witnesses be the ones to cast the first stones. It is one thing to accuse a person of a capital crime and have the government do the investigating and then, if the offender was found guilty, do the executing. Obviously, it is quite a different thing where the private citizens who brought the original charges are required to support their accusation by casting the first stone. But this is what God's law required. The Lord said:

"The hands of the witnesses shall be first upon him to put him to death, and afterward the hands of all the people. So thou shalt put the evil away from among you."[96]

Note that no matter how inflamed a community might be against the accused, they could not execute the offender until after the citizens who brought the charges (and thereby inflamed the community's wrath) had cast the first stone. If these witnesses failed to act, then it was presumed that there was something wrong with their testimony. That is why the elders of a community were legally prohibited from carrying out the death sentence unless the accusing witnesses would strike the first blow.

A good example of the way the law was administered can be found in the provision dealing with a dissolute, disobedient and obstreperous son. Here, certainly, it would seem harsh to impose the death penalty. Yet every son of Israel knew that it was a most serious offense to rebel against one's parents because it was a capital offense.

At the same time, the law required that parents exhibit the utmost patience with a rebellious son and try to work with him to overcome his evil ways. This is clearly evident from the fact that before the parents could declare their son anathema the following was required of them:

"If a man have a stubborn and rebellious son, which will not obey the voice of his father, or the voice of his mother, and that, when they have chastened him, will not hearken unto them: Then shall his father and his mother lay hold on him, and bring him out unto the elders of his city, and unto the gate of his place; And they shall say unto the elders of his city, This our son is stubborn and rebellious, he will not obey our voice; he is a glutton, and a drunkard."[97]

At this point the parents had to pick up a stone and be the first to strike their son down.[98]

No wonder we have no record of this procedure ever being used! Parents, no matter how provoked, would be extremely unlikely to resort to such desperate measures. Nevertheless, the provision in the law had an important psychologi-

96. Deuteronomy 17:7.
97. Deuteronomy 21:18-20.
98. Deuteronomy 13:9; 17:7.

cal value. It impressed upon the youth of Israel that their parents did have legal authority over their very lives if they became violently rebellious.

In extreme cases where parents were compelled to take some kind of action, they had several options. One was having an offending son ransom his life. The scripture says:

"If there be laid on him a sum of money, then he shall give for the ransom of his life whatsoever is laid upon him." [99]

Jesus refers to the usual practice of enforcing such payments when he said that the offender was delivered "to the tormenters [whip masters] till he should pay all that was due." [100]

But, as we have pointed out before, whipping even in the most extreme cases was limited to 40 stripes. The judge was required to witness the whipping to insure that the punishment is carried out but not extended.[101]

Ezra also mentions other options available to the judges in lieu of death.[102] These include:

1. Confiscation of goods to enforce fines or assessed damages.
2. Imprisonment where necessary for public safety.
3. Banishment (under threat of death if he refuses or tries to return).

Exile

See: *Enforcement of the Law and Banishment.*

Eye for an Eye

Probably no aspect of the Law of the Covenant was more misunderstood than this provision. Here is what the scripture says:

"And thine eye shall not pity: but life shall go for life, eye for eye, tooth for tooth, hand for hand, foot for foot." [103]

The object of this provision was to threaten a comparable injury to the offender unless he made it up to his victim in compensation or some other form of "satisfaction." Another way of saying it would be, "He who hurts must be hurt or make full satisfaction to his victim." This policy is reflected in the passage which says:

99. Exodus 21:30.
100. Matthew 18:34.
101. Deuteronomy 25:2.
102. Ezra 7:26.
103. Deuteronomy 19:21.

"Moreover ye shall take no satisfaction for the life of a murderer, which is guilty of death: but he shall be surely put to death. And ye shall take no satisfaction for him that is fled to the city of his refuge, that he should come again to dwell in the land, until the death of the priest." [104]

In other words, there were only two situations where satisfaction could not be negotiated between the offender and the victim. This authorized the working out of "satisfaction" or compensation in all other cases.

When we come to the discussion of "penalties," the application of the principle of reparation or satisfaction will be discussed in more detail.

Familiar Spirits

See: *Spiritualism.*

Father

See: *Parents.*

Fire Hazard

See: *Arson.*

First Fruits

In an agrarian society the firstfruits of the fields and the flocks were gratefully acknowledged to be a manifestation of God's beneficent blessings. The Law of the Covenant took advantage of this feeling and accomplished several desirable purposes of the Lord. The scripture says:

"The first of the firstfruits of the land thou shalt bring into the house of the Lord thy God." [105] "As for the oblation of the firstfruits, ye shall offer them unto the Lord: but they shall not be burnt on the altar for a sweet savour." [106]

"And this shall be the priest's due from the people, from them that offer a sacrifice, whether it be ox or sheep; and they shall give unto the priest the shoulder, and the two cheeks, and the maw. The first-fruit also of thy corn, of thy wine, and of thine oil, and the first of the fleece of thy sheep, shalt thou give him." [107]

Fornication

See also: *Adultery, Bestiality, Idolatry, Incest, Sodomy.*

Fornication is defined as any unlawful sexual intercourse.

104. Numbers 35:31-32.
105. Exodus 23:19.
106. Leviticus 2:12.
107. Deuteronomy 18:3-4.

In all ages and dispensations, sexual purity has been required. As Paul wrote:

"For ye know what commandments we gave you by the Lord Jesus. For this is the will of God, even your sanctification, that ye should abstain from fornication: That every one of you should know how to possess his vessel in sanctification and honor; Not in the lust of concupiscence, even as the Gentiles which know not God." [108]

"Nevertheless, to avoid fornication, let every man have his own wife, and let every woman have her own husband." [109]

"And if a man entice a maid that is not betrothed, and lie with her, he shall surely endow her to be his wife. If her father utterly refuse to give her unto him, he shall pay money according to the dowry of virgins." [110]

Dr. Adam Clarke points out the practical wisdom of this provision. He says:

"This was an exceedingly wise and humane law, and must have operated powerfully against seduction and fornication, because the person who might feel inclined to take advantage of a young woman knew that he must marry her, and give her dowry, if her parents consented; and if they did not consent that their daughter should wed her seducer, in this case he was obliged to give her the full dowry which could have been demanded had she still been a virgin." [111]

Fraud

See: *Business Ethics.*

Gossiping

Gossip is defined as idle chatter made up of rumors or tales about the misfortunes of others. Because of the scandalous nature of gossip, it spreads through the community like wild fire before the wind, and no amount of explanatory truth seems capable of catching up with it. Therefore, the Lord says:

"Thou shalt not go up and down as a talebearer among thy people: neither shalt thou stand against the blood of thy neighbour: I am the Lord." [112] "Thou shalt not raise a false report: put not thine hand with the wicked to be an unrighteous witness." [113]

Modern law provides a heavy penalty in damages where the reputation of a person has been injured by libelous or slanderous gossip. In some cases damages have been allowed even where the slander was true. This is on the basis that the

108. 1 Thessalonians 4:2-5.
109. 1 Corinthians 7:2.
110. Exodus 22:16-17.
111. Adam Clarke, Bible Commentary, 1:413.
112. Leviticus 19:16.
113. Exodus 23:1.

offender deliberately spread the gossip for malicious purposes and with the intent of injuring the reputation of the victim.

Hate

Hate is defined as a passionate aversion or intense dislike which is aimed at some person or thing. Psychologically, hate feeds on itself and often festers into individual violence or collective mobocracy. This type of internalized passion for revenge or injury to another becomes particularly explosive when it involves close relatives or former friends. Therefore the Lord said:

"Thou shalt not hate thy brother in thine heart: [but] thou shalt … rebuke thy neighbor, and not suffer sin upon him." [114]

Note that it is not hate to point out to a person that he or she is following a path that is leading to their own destruction. The Lord says each individual has a duty to try and help others if possible.

However, some people cannot stand criticism no matter how kindly or constructive it might be. Like small children they resist criticism by equating it with "hate" and throw a frenzied tantrum of protest by exclaiming, "That man hates me!" The Lord makes it clear that helping someone see the error of his ways is not to be equated with hate. But in those cases where the offender becomes violent and rises up against his well-meaning neighbor, the Lord says:

"But if any man hate his neighbour, and lie in wait for him, and rise up against him, and smite him mortally that he die, and fleeth into one of these cities: Then the elders of his city shall send and fetch him thence, and deliver him into the hand of the avenger of blood, that he may die. Thine eye shall not pity him, but thou shalt put away the guilt of innocent blood from Israel, that it may go well with thee." [115]

During his ministry Jesus told his disciples how to solve the problem of hate. This is probably the most difficult commandment set forth in the entire Sermon on the Mount. He said:

"But I say unto you which hear, Love your enemies, do good to them which hate you, Bless them that curse you, and pray for them which despitefully use you." [116]

Handicapped Should Be Treated with Compassion and Kindness

The Lord has always required that his people who have been blessed with normal faculties and attributes, should show a very special kindness and consider-

114. Leviticus 19:17.
115. Deuteronomy 19:11-13.
116. Luke 6:27-28.

ation toward those less fortunate. He even indicates that those who take advantage of the handicapped are committing a sin against God. He said:

"Thou shalt not curse the deaf, nor put a stumbling block before the blind, but shall fear thy God: I am the Lord." [117]

Homosexuality

Homosexuality is defined as any unnatural sexual relations, but particularly with a person of the same sex. The Lord says:

"Thou shalt not lie with mankind, as with womankind: it is an abomination." [118]

"If a man also lie with mankind, as he lieth with a woman, both of them have committed an abomination: they shall surely be put to death; their blood shall be upon them." [119]

As we have already observed, the death penalty is mentioned in connection with a number of offenses but it was not mandatory except in the case of first degree murder. Nevertheless, it demonstrates the Lord's abhorrence toward this type of heinous offense when he says a sentence of death is permissible if the judges felt so inclined.

As in all cases, however, the object is reform, not revenge, and therefore both compassion and kindness would be employed to salvage as many offenders as possible.

Nevertheless, homosexuality has destroyed every civilization in which this form of depravity became established as an important part of the people's lifestyle. Paul wrote:

"And likewise also the men, leaving the natural use of the woman, burned in their lust one toward another; men with men working that which is unseemly, and receiving in themselves that recompense of their error which was meet." [120]

"Know ye not that the unrighteous shall not inherit the kingdom of God? Be not deceived: neither fornicators, nor idolaters, nor adulterers, nor effeminate, nor abusers of themselves with mankind." [121]

The same warning was given by Moses:

"Defile not ye yourselves in any of these things: for in all these the nations are defiled which I cast out before you." [122] "For whosoever shall commit any of these

117. Leviticus 19:14.
118. Leviticus 18:22.
119. Leviticus 20:13.
120. Romans 1:27.
121. 1 Corinthians 6:9.
122. Leviticus 18:24.

abominations, even the souls that commit them shall be cut off from among their people."[123]

This meant death or banishment.

Apparently "lesbianism" had also crept into the culture and therefore women who tried to play the role of men or men who wore the clothes of women were denounced because the Lord knew their clothes simply advertised their professional debauchery. The Lord said:

"The woman shall not wear that which pertaineth unto a man, neither shall a man put on a woman's garment: for all that do so are abomination unto the Lord thy God."[124]

Human Sacrifices

In the days of ancient Israel, human sacrifices, particularly of children, was a common practice among the pagan nations.

Although the penalty for human sacrifice was death under the Law of Moses, nevertheless, the Israelites indulged in these wretched practices during the days of their apostasy. Hear the charges of God against Israel. He said:

"Yea, they sacrificed their sons and their daughters unto devils, And shed innocent blood, even the blood of their sons and of their daughters, whom they sacrificed unto the idols of Canaan: and the land was polluted with blood."[125]

The Lord made capital punishment mandatory for this crime because it involved premeditated murder:

"Again, thou shalt say to the children of Israel, Whosoever be of the children of Israel, or of the strangers that sojourn in Israel, that giveth any of his seed unto Molech [as human sacrifices]; he shall surely be put to death: the people of the land shall stone him with stones. And I will set my face against that man, and will cut him off from among his people; because he hath given of his seed to Molech, to defile my sanctuary, and to profane my holy name."[126]

Idolatry

Idolatry is defined as an ardent devotion to or worship of something which is a substitute for the one true God.

Idolatry, by itself, was an insult to God by worshipping a stick, a stone, or some man-made image. However the degenerate aspects of pagan idolatry [which

---

123. Leviticus 18:29.
124. Deuteronomy 22:5.
125. Psalms 106:37-38.
126. Leviticus 20:2-3.

Israel gradually adopted] was depraved sexual orgies and human sacrifices. This is why the Lord denounced idolatry with such vehemence, and said:

"He that sacrificeth unto any god, save unto thc Lord only, he shall be utterly destroyed."[127]

"If there be found among you, within any of thy gates which the Lord thy God giveth thee, man or woman, that hath wrought wickedness in the sight of the Lord thy God, in transgressing his covenant, And hath gone and served other gods, and worshipped them, either the sun, or moon, or any of the host of heaven, which I have not commanded;

"And it be told thee, and thou hast heard of it, and inquired diligently, and, behold, it be true, and the thing certain, that such abomination is wrought in Israel: Then shalt thou bring forth that man or that woman, which have committed that wicked thing, unto thy gates, even that man or that woman, and shalt stone them with stones, till they die."[128]

Note the implication of the Lord in the following passage that idolatry, human sacrifices and obscene sexual practices were all part of the pagan idolatry. The Lord rebuked Israel, saying:

"And they shall no more offer sacrifices unto devils, after whom they have gone a whoring."[129]

As we have just mentioned, heathen idolatry almost invariably involved some form of fertility worship, implicating the worshippers in acts of degeneracy, bestiality, perversion, and promiscuous sexual indulgence.

Around 24,000 Israelites were destroyed by the Lord as a result of their involvement in the corrupting idol worship and immorality of Baal-Peor in Moab.[130]

Dr. Adam Clarke says: "It is well known that Baal-Peor and Ashtaroth were worshipped with unclean rites; and that public prostitution formed a grand part of the worship of many deities among the Egyptians, Moabites, Canaanites, Greeks, and Romans.[131]

Speaking of the abominable rites of heathen worship, the Lord refers to the sacrifice of children to Molech as well as the depraved immorality associated with pagan worship:

"And thou shalt not let any of thy seed pass through the fire to Molech, neither shalt thou profane the name of thy God: I am the Lord. Thou shalt not lie with mankind, as with womankind: it is abomination. Neither shalt thou lie with any

127. Exodus 22:20.
128. Deuteronomy 17:2-5.
129. Leviticus 17:7.
130. Numbers 25:1-9.
131. Clarke, Bible Commentary, 1:565, see also 1:569.

beast to defile thyself therewith: neither shall any woman stand before a beast to lie down thereto: it is confusion. Defile not ye yourselves in any of these things: for in all these the nations are defiled which I cast out before you ....

"Ye shall therefore keep my statutes and my judgments, and shall not commit any of these abominations; neither any of your own nation, nor any stranger that sojourneth among you: (For all these abominations have the men of the land done, which were before you, and the land is defiled;) That the land spue not you out also, when ye defile it, as it spued out the nations that were before you.

"For whosoever shall commit any of these abominations, even the souls that commit them shall be cut off from among their people. Therefore shall ye keep mine ordinance, that ye commit not any one of these abominable customs, which were committed before you." [132]

Incest

Incest is defined as "sexual cohabitation between near relatives."

Among primitive or degenerate heathen cultures it was customary to have the most promiscuous sexual relations within family groups or among close relatives. These often include elements of incest such as immoral relations between mothers and sons, fathers and daughters, brothers and sisters, etc. Sometimes, however, such unions were solemnized by actual marriage. This was particularly true of brothers and sisters, and became a regular practice in Egypt among the ruling Pharaohs. Concerning the problem of incest and relations within the boundaries of prohibited consanguinity, the Lord said:

"After the doings of the land of Egypt, wherein ye dwelt, shall ye not do: and after the doings of the land of Canaan, whither I bring you, shall ye not do: neither shall ye walk in their ordinances. Ye shall do my judgments, and keep mine ordinances, to walk therein: I am the Lord your God. Ye shall therefore keep my statutes, and my judgments: which if a man do, he shall live in them: I am the Lord. None of you shall approach to any that is near of kin to him, to uncover their nakedness: I am the Lord." [133]

Immorality between members of a family or close relatives carried the death penalty unless the judges allowed the offenders to ransom their lives with payments to the victim or to the high priest if the incest was by mutual consent.[134]

Jubilee

A jubilee is defined as a year-long celebration held every fifty years. It means a time of jubilation or rejoicing. The unique thing about the jubilee year is that it

132. Leviticus 18:21-30.
133. Leviticus 18:3-6; the laws of consanguinity are verses 7-10.
134. See Leviticus 20:11-12, 17, 19-21.

came right after a sabbath year. This means that there were two consecutive years of celebration and rest. This is made clear in the following scripture.

"And thou shalt number seven sabbaths of years unto thee, seven times seven years; and the space of the seven sabbaths of years shall be unto thee forty and nine years. Then shalt thou cause the trumpet of the jubilee to sound on the tenth day of the seventh month, in the day of atonement shall ye make the trumpet sound throughout all the land.

"And ye shall hallow the fiftieth year, and *proclaim liberty throughout all the land unto all the inhabitants thereof*; it shall be a jubilee unto you; and ye shall return every man unto his possession, and ye shall return every man unto his family." [135]

The italicized words in this last verse were adopted by the American Founding Fathers and inscribed on the Liberty Bell. The Lord concludes by saying:

"A jubilee shall that fiftieth year be unto you: ye shall not sow, neither reap that which groweth of itself in it, nor gather the grapes in it of thy vine undressed." [136]

One can well imagine the rejoicing which took place during the jubilee year. All debts were forgiven. All mortgages were marked "paid." All those who were working to pay off debts, fines, or penalties for past offenses, were forgiven and told to return home. In other words, the whole nation started over with no obligation to work for a year—a year's vacation—no debts, no mortgages, and no one in prison. Interestingly, they had just completed the 49th year which was a sabbath, so they really had two years of vacation to go along with all the other reasons for celebrating.

A person would have to live during a jubilee to learn how the details were all worked out, both socially and economically, but in general terms it must have been the most glorious time in the history of each generation.

Judges

As we have indicated earlier, a "judge" in Israel was more than a judicial officer. He was a "ruler" [137] who had responsibilities in a wide variety of administrative capacities. However, deciding disputes between contending parties was no small part of these responsibilities and therefore the title of "judge" was appropriate.

Judges and public officers were supposed to be of the highest caliber:

"Moreover thou shalt provide out of all the people able men, such as fear God, men of truth, hating covetousness; and place such over them, to be rulers of

135. Leviticus 25:8-10.
136. Leviticus 25:11.
137. Deuteronomy 1:13.

thousands, and rulers of hundreds, rulers of fifties, and rulers of tens: And let them judge the people at all seasons: and it shall be, that every great matter they shall bring unto thee, but every small matter they shall judge: so shall it be easier for thyself, and they shall bear the burden with thee." [138]

Judges were to be "wise men, and understanding, and known among your tribes, and I will make them rulers over you," so that they would have the confidence of the people.[139]

They were to accept no gifts for "a gift doth blind the eyes of the wise, and pervert the words of the righteous." [140]

Judges were to make decisions only after a thorough investigation. They were to "make diligent inquisition" concerning the facts in each case.[141]

Judges were not to find a person guilty of a capital crime unless there were at least "two or three witnesses" who could prove his guilt. One witness was never sufficient.[142] This did not mean that the guilty person got away with his or her crime. It simply meant that the case would be left to the judgment of God in the next world. It is too dangerous for a society to execute people on the word of a single witness who might be vindictive or otherwise motivated to make the allegation.

When a matter had been appealed to the chief judge or High Priest and the case had been settled, it was a capital offense to stir up insurrection against the decision.[143] This applied to the parties in the case and also the judges of original jurisdiction who might be offended by a reversal.

Moses said to the judges:

"Hear the causes between your brethren, and judge righteously between every man and his brother, and the stranger that is with him. Ye shall not respect [discriminate against] persons in judgment; but ye shall hear the small as well as the great; ye shall not be afraid of the face of man; for the judgment is God's: and the cause that is too hard for you, bring it unto me, and I will hear it." [144]

"Ye shall do no unrighteousness in judgment: thou shalt not respect [discriminate against] the person of the poor, nor honor the person of the mighty: but in righteousness shalt thou judge thy neighbor." [145]

---

138. Exodus 18:21-22.
139. Deuteronomy 1:13.
140. Deuteronomy 16:19.
141. Deuteronomy 19:18.
142. Numbers 35:30; Deuteronomy 17:6.
143. Deuteronomy 17:12.
144. Deuteronomy 1:16-17.
145. Leviticus 19:15.

Juvenile Delinquency

See: *Children.*

Kidnaping

Kidnaping is defined as stealing a human being and holding that child or adult by force against his will, usually for ransom. However, during both ancient and modern times, women and children were often captured or kidnaped to be sold or forced into slavery.

The Lord made it clear how he felt about this cruel and inhuman practice:

"And he that stealeth a man, and selleth him, or if he be found in his hand, he shall surely be put to death." [146] "If a man be found stealing any of his brethren of the children of Israel, and maketh merchandise of him, or selleth him; then that thief shall die; and thou shalt put evil away from among you." [147]

Kidnaping was a heinous crime, but it would not automatically require the offender to be executed unless the victim was killed. In the absence of murder, the lesser penalties could be applied. However, the law allowed the judges to sentence the kidnaper to death if the circumstances warranted it. Kidnaping as such did not make the death penalty mandatory.[148]

Kings—Their Calling and Responsibilities

The Lord anticipated that after the Israelites entered the Promised Land, they would want a king:

"When thou art come into the land which the Lord thy God giveth thee, and shalt possess it, and shall dwell therein, and shalt say, I will set a king over me, like as all the nations that are about me." [149]

Furthermore, the Lord knew that no matter how well meaning the Israelites might be in thinking a king would serve them better than their elected judges, experience would soon demonstrate that they would actually be abandoning the open and prosperous society of a government under elected judges, and subjecting themselves to the whims and high taxes of an autocratic sovereign.

The main difference between a king (even one approved by the people) and elected judges, is the fundamental fact that judges do not make laws. They have no legislative power. Kings, on the other hand, have always assumed the authority to issue personal edicts as laws. Kings somehow develop the idea that they are "sovereign." They rapidly acquire powers by asserting broad authority over the

---

146. Exodus 21:16.
147. Deuteronomy 24:7.
148. Numbers 35:31-32.
149. Deuteronomy 17:14.

people and are backed up by the army. Those elements of power and aggrandizement soon corrupt both the king and the people. In one generation the people find themselves losing their freedom and drifting into tyranny.

However, the Lord said that a righteous king could avoid these pitfalls if he would accept the Lord's guidance. He therefore outlined certain principles which would tend to give the people a righteous king if he followed the restrictions laid down by the Lord. Here are the Lord's suggestions:

1. He must be a citizen of Israel and not a stranger.[150]

2. He should be a person "whom the Lord thy God shall choose."[151]

3. He should not try to "multiply horses" which was a common characteristic of pagan kings, especially the extravagant and war-making kings of Egypt.[152]

4. The king was not to multiply wives. This was a common practice to bind other nations to the king. Some kings had several hundred wives taken from the principal families of surrounding territories.[153]

5. The king was not to "multiply to himself silver and gold," which would have to be extracted from the people.[154]

6. The task of the king was to be a great scholar, judge, general, and righteous policy maker. To do this, he was to have his own personal copy of the law and he was to "read therein all the days of his life; that he may learn to fear the Lord his God, to keep all the words of the law and these statutes, to do them."[155]

LAND

No person was to look upon land as "his" but rather he was to consider it a stewardship from the Lord. As the Lord said:

"The land shall not be sold for ever; for the land is mine; for ye are strangers and sojourners with me."[156]

In other words, once a man and his family had received a stewardship inheritance in the promised land, they could not quit-claim the land lest it disinherit their children after them.

The most they could do was to lease the land for 49 years. Every fiftieth year (at the time of the Jubilee) the land went back to the family who originally received

150. Deuteronomy 17:15.
151. Ibid.
152. Deuteronomy 17:16.
153. Deuteronomy 17:17.
154. Ibid.
155. Deuteronomy 17:19.
156. Leviticus 25:23.

it as a stewardship.[157] As a result, the cost of leasing land depended upon the length of time remaining until the next Jubilee.[158]

If a poor Israelite had been forced to lease his land through economic necessity, he was able to redeem it and get it back at any time by paying the pro-rated amount for the remainder of the lease.[159] All leases and mortgages terminated at the time of the Jubilee which came around every fifty years.[160]

In all of these transactions the Lord required the utmost honesty on the part of both the buyer and the seller:

"Ye shall not therefore oppress one another; but thou shalt fear thy God." [161]

The above rules applied not only to land but also to any house or real estate located in the villages and unwalled cities.[162]

However, a different rule applied to a house located in a fortress city—a walled city. There the owner of a house could sell it and have one year to buy it back. If he did not do so within the prescribed time the property went to the new owner in *fee simple* or as a permanent stewardship and was not affected by the Jubilee.[163]

A special rule applied to the Levites. These people had no inheritance except certain cities which were given to them. It was therefore impossible for a Levite to dispose of his land in the suburbs of his city even under lease.[164]

Nevertheless, a Levite could lease his house but at the time of the Jubilee it had to be returned to him. Even in a walled city a Levite could not permanently dispose of a house.[165]

Each Israelite was to try to increase the ownership of land among those who lived under God's laws. Therefore, if a poor Israelite came into the community who had no inheritance, the other Israelites were expected to help him get started so he could buy an inheritance:

"And if thy brother be waxen poor, and fallen in decay with thee: then thou shalt relieve him: yea, though he be a stranger, or a sojourner; that he may live with thee." [166]

---

157. Leviticus 25:13.
158. Leviticus 25:16.
159. Leviticus 25:24-28.
160. Leviticus 25:8-11.
161. Leviticus 25:17.
162. Leviticus 25:31.
163. Leviticus 25:29-30.
164. Leviticus 25:33-34.
165. Leviticus 25:32.
166. Leviticus 25:35.

If money were loaned to a fellow Israelite on this basis, it was to be without interest or usury:

"Take thou no usury of him, or increase: but fear thy God; that thy brother may live with thee [in harmony, not in the same domicile]. Thou shalt not give him thy money upon usury, nor lend him thy victuals for increase." [167]

The Lord's program of expanding the ownership or inheritance of the Israelites until they occupied practically the entire territory, may have been considered unfair by the non-Israelites. However, these purchases were done on the open market like any other business transaction, and did not involve any extortion or compulsion against the seller. The object was to fill up the land with people who were willing to live under God's law.

If a gentile or pagan became converted and covenanted to live according to the revealed principles of righteousness, he automatically became an Israelite and was counted the "seed of Abraham" by adoption.[168] He was therefore entitled to all of the privileges of an Israelite.

This is undoubtedly one of the reasons the Lord urged the Israelites to buy bond servants from among the non-Israelites[169] so that by living with the Israelites they could see the advantages of their lifestyle and become converted. If they did so they would be looked upon as a "brother" and would be released at the next Jubilee along with their families. (See Leviticus 25:39-40 for the treatment of any "brother" serving as a bond servant.) Thereafter they would obtain an inheritance like any other Israelite.

The scripture is clear, however, that if a gentile bond servant did not respond to the message, he would be considered chattel property just as all the other nations considered bond servants at that time.[170] Nevertheless an Israelite was under obligation to treat bond servants with kind and human consideration. (See: *Servitude*)

The land, like the people, had its sabbath:

"Six years thou shalt sow thy field, and six years thou shalt prune thy vineyard, and gather in the fruit thereof; But in the seventh year shall be a sabbath of rest unto the land, a sabbath for the Lord: thou shalt neither sow thy field, nor prune thy vineyard.That which groweth of its own accord of thy harvest thou shalt not reap, neither gather the grapes of thy vine undressed: for it is a year of rest unto the land." [171]

"And six years thou shalt sow thy land, and shalt gather in the fruits thereof: But the seventh year thou shalt let it rest and lie still; that the poor of thy people

167. Leviticus 25:36-37.
168. Romans 8:14-24; Galatians 3:7-9, 29; 4:5; Ephesians 1:5.
169. Leviticus 25:45.
170. Leviticus 25:45-46.
171. Leviticus 25:3-5.

may eat: and what they leave the beasts of the field shall eat. In like manner thou shalt deal with thy vineyard, and with thy oliveyard." [172]

The question automatically arises, what did the people eat during the seventh year and on up to the beginning of the ninth year when the new harvest was available? Concerning this, the Lord said:

"And if ye shall say, What shall we eat the seventh year? behold, we shall not sow, nor gather in our increase: Then I will command my blessing upon you in the sixth year, and it shall bring forth fruit for three years. And ye shall sow the eighth year, and eat yet of old fruit until the ninth year; until her fruits come in ye shall eat of the old store." [173]

As noted in Leviticus 25:3-5, only the poor and the stranger could go into the field or the vineyard to gather that which "groweth of its own accord." Technically, even the owner could do this if he were "poor" and did not have enough to carry him over until the beginning of the ninth year.

Concerning the Israelites who were "poor," the Lord said:

"When thou comest into thy neighbor's vineyard, then thou mayest eat grapes thy fill at thine own pleasure; but thou shalt not put any in thy vessel. When thou comest into the standing corn of thy neighbor, then thou mayest pluck the ears with thine hand; but thou shalt not move a sickle unto thy neighbor's standing corn." [174]

Law of the Covenant

The scripture says, "the Law of the Lord is *perfect*." [175] In this scripture it says it reflects the goodness of God even to "converting the soul." Furthermore, by learning this law, it makes even the "simple" seem wise.

The Lord knew that on the basis of the laws and principles in this book, every Israelite could be judged in a fair and just manner. So he said:

"Take this book of the law, and put it in the side of the ark of the covenant of the Lord your God, that it may be there for a witness against thee." [176]

Of course, if they had obeyed the law, it would be a witness for them. Therefore he wanted these laws taught to every generation of the Israelites. The Lord said:

"And these words, which I command thee this day, shall be in thine heart: And thou shalt teach them diligently unto thy children, and shalt talk of them when thou sittest in thine house, and when thou walkest by the way, and when thou liest down, and thou risest up, And thou shalt bind them for a sign upon thine hand, and they

172. Exodus 23:10-11.
173. Leviticus 25:20-22.
174. Deuteronomy 23:24-25.
175. Psalms 19:7.
176. Deuteronomy 31:26.

shall be as frontlets between thine eyes. And thou shalt write them upon the posts of thy house, and on thy gates." [177]

The Israelites took these last two verses literally. They wrote several scriptures on vellum, divided them between two boxes, and then wore one on the forehead and the other inside the upper arm. These became known as "prayer ornaments," or "phylacteries," which means a charm, a fortress, or a protection against evil.

But the important verse is number 6 where the Lord said he wanted these laws engraved on their *hearts*, not pieces of vellum.

The Lord also wanted it thoroughly understood that his laws were to apply to everyone throughout the land—both strangers and Israelites. He said:

"Ye shall have one manner of law, as well for the stranger, as for one of your own country: for I am the Lord your God." [178]

Just so every Israelite and stranger would know the law, the Lord had it read to the whole nation on a special occasion. He told Moses how it should be done and we therefore read:

"Moses wrote this law, and delivered it unto the priests the sons of Levi … And Moses commanded them, saying, At the end of every seven years, in the solemnity of the year of release, in the feast of tabernacles, … thou shalt read this law before all Israel in their hearing. Gather the people together, men, and women, and children, and the stranger that is within thy gates, that they may hear, and that they may learn, and fear the Lord your God, and observe to do all the words of this law: And that their children which have not known any thing, may hear, and learn to fear the Lord your God." [179]

Lending

The Lord makes a distinction between lending for commercial purposes (for interest) and lending to a person in desperate need. He said:

"If thou lend money to any of my people that is poor by thee, thou shalt not be to him as an usurer, neither shalt thou lay upon him usury. If thou at all take thy neighbor's raiment to pledge, thou shalt deliver it unto him by that the sun goeth down: For that is his covering only, it is his raiment for his skin: wherein shall he sleep? and it shall come to pass when he crieth unto me, that I will hear: for I am gracious." [180]

"And if thy brother be waxen poor, and fallen in decay with thee; then thou shalt relieve him: yea, though he be a stranger, or a sojourner; that he may live with

177. Deuteronomy 6:6-9; 11:18-20.
178. Leviticus 24:22.
179. Deuteronomy 31:9-13.
180. Exodus 22:25-27.

thee. Take thou no usury of him, or increase: but fear thy God; that thy brother may live with thee. Thou shalt not give him thy money upon usury, nor lend him thy victuals for increase."[181]

It will be recalled that during the Jubilee, there was a forgiving of debts and a "time of release." But this occurred every *seven* years as well. The Lord said:

"At the end of every seven years thou shalt make a release. And this is the manner of the release: Every creditor that lendeth ought unto his neighbor shall release it; he shall not exact it of his neighbor, or of his brother; because it is called the Lord's release. Of a foreigner thou mayest exact it again: but that which is thine with thy brother thine hand shall release; *Save when there shall be no poor among you.*"[182]

Note that this rule is to help Israelites who are poor. The Lord said this would no longer be necessary "when there shall be no more poor among you." The goal was to build a society like Enoch of old. Under the Law of the Covenant it has been demonstrated that both poverty and crime can be eliminated within a very short period of time.

Throughout this discussion the Lord continues to distinguish between commercial lending and lending to the poor. Concerning the poor, the Lord commends generosity and warns against stinginess just because the "year of release" is near when all debts will be forgiven.

"If there be among you a poor man of one of thy brethren within any of thy gates in thy land which the Lord thy God giveth thee, thou shalt not harden thine heart, nor shut thine hand from thy poor brother: But thou shalt open thine hand wide unto him, and shalt surely lend him sufficient for his need, in that which he wanteth.

"Beware that there be not a thought in thy wicked heart, saying, The seventh year, the year of release, is at hand; and thine eye be evil against thy poor brother, and thou givest him nought; and he cry unto the Lord against thee, and it be sin unto thee. Thou shalt surely give him, and thine heart shall not be grieved when thou givest unto him: because that for this thing the Lord thy God shall bless thee in all thy works, and in all that thou puttest thine hand unto.

"For the poor shall never cease out of the land: [because, as Moses would later learn, they would never equal the accomplishments of Enoch[183]] therefore I command thee, saying, Thou shalt open thine hand wide unto thy brother, to thy poor, and to thy needy, in thy land."[184]

181. Leviticus 25:35-37.
182. Deuteronomy 15:1-4.
183. Deuteronomy 31:27-29.
184. Moses 7:18; see Skousen, The First 2,000 Years, op. cit., p. 174.

Levites

The Levites were the civil servants, the teachers of Biblical law, the functionaries at the tabernacle, and the religious leaders or priests for all of the tribes of Israel.

These specialized assignments came after the "golden calf" incident at the foot of Mount Sinai. When Moses came down from the Mount and saw what was happening, he called out, "Who is on the Lord's side?" [185] Only the Levites stepped forward and joined Moses. The rest were ashamed that they had allowed this wicked ritual to take place. The Levites were then ordered into the pit where the drunken, naked fertility worshipers were gathered, and 3,000 were slain that day.[186]

These lewd fertility worshipers had so outraged the Lord, that they had put the whole camp in jeopardy. Even before Moses came down off the Mount, the Lord had told Moses that he intended to have everyone over 20 years of age brought back to the spirit world. Moses pleaded with the Lord to let him see if he could reform them. (For details see Skousen, *The Third Thousand Years*, pp. 315-320.)

Sometime later, the Lord said:

"I have taken the Levites for all the firstborn of the children of Israel. And I have given the Levites as a gift to Aaron and to his sons from among the children of Israel, to do the service … in the tabernacle of the congregation." [187]

"The Levites: from twenty and five years old and upward they shall go in to wait upon the service of the tabernacle of the congregation. And from the age of fifty years they shall cease waiting upon the service thereof, and shall serve no more." [188]

So the Levites began their careers of specialized service. When they arrived in the Promised Land, the Levites were not given an inheritance like the other tribes, but they were given 48 cities scattered throughout the nation where they could serve as priests, tax collectors, and teachers.

For their sustenance they received a tenth of the tithes[189] along with the poll tax or redemption tax for the firstborn and the poll tax at the time of census. They also received the firstborn of the calves, sheep, and goats. In addition they received the heave offerings of animals brought to be sacrificed.

185. Exodus 32:26.
186. Exodus 32:28.
187. Numbers 8:18-19.
188. Numbers 8:24-25.
189. Numbers 18:26.

Lying

Falsehood, misrepresentation, deceit, cheating, deception, are all treated here under the general topic of "lying." The Lord said:

"Thou shalt not bear false witness against thy neighbor." [190]

"Ye shall not steal, either deal falsely, neither lie one to another." [191]

Notice that no specific penalty is mentioned for deceit or lying. This was left to the discretion of the judges.

Mayhem

Mayhem is defined as deliberately mutilating a person's body or injuring him so that he can no longer function with all his faculties. The Lord said:

"And if men strive together, and one smite another with a stone, or with his fist and he die not, but keepeth his bed: If he rise again, and walk abroad upon his staff, then shall he that smote him be quit: only he shall pay for the loss of his time, and shall cause him to be thoroughly healed." [192]

Military Service

Moses was asked to set up the military service of Israel in such a way that it would be counted a great honor to serve in its ranks. Battalions were formed from each tribe.[193]

This would tend to make each contingent anxious to uphold the standard of its tribe.

Then Moses was told to eliminate from the ranks of the armies of Israel any who would tend to be distracted by affairs at home:

"And the officers shall speak unto the people, saying, What man is there that hath built a new house, and hath not dedicated it? let him go and return to his house, lest he die in the battle, and another man dedicate it. And what man is he that hath planted a vineyard, and hath not yet eaten of it? let him also go and return unto his house, lest he die in the battle, and another man eat of it. And what man is there that hath betrothed a wife, and hath not taken her? let him go and return unto his house, lest he die in the battle, and another man take her." [194]

Moses was also told to eliminate any who were fearful or faint hearted:

---

190. Exodus 20:16.
191. Leviticus 19:11.
192. Exodus 21:18-19.
193. Numbers 31:3-5.
194. Deuteronomy 20:5-7.

"And the officers shall speak further unto the people, and they shall say, What man is there that is fearful and faint-hearted? let him go and return unto his house, lest his brethren's heart faint as well as his heart." [195]

A dramatic illustration of how these principles worked in actual practice is found in Gideon's campaign against the Midianites. When Gideon had assembled 32,000 troops who were all duty-bound to fight, the Lord told Gideon to subject the army to a self-purging process as previously outlined by Moses. When this was done Gideon had only 10,000 men left.[196] The others went home but participated later in the mopping up process. As for Gideon, he ended up with only 300 to put the Midianites to flight.

Modern armies tend to build elite corps out of their best fighting components and these make the first contact with the enemy. The reserve units, as well as the crews who build installations and set up occupation camps, follow along later. It is considered a great honor to be chosen for the elite corps or crack assault units. It was the same policy advocated by the Lord for the armies of ancient Israel as they went through the screening or selection process we have just described.

When the tribal battalions were assembled they were to select "captains of the armies to lead the people." [197]

Apparently this selection was by a democratic procedure.

Military Attack—Three Modes

It is interesting that the purpose of the armies of Israel was to restore peace and at the same time compel the pagan cities or nations to give up their human sacrifices and other abominations which plagued the land. For this reason, the Lord gave them three different formulas with instructions to apply the one which fit the circumstances. Here is what he said:

"When thou comest nigh unto a city to fight against it, *then proclaim peace unto it*. And it shall be, if it makes the answer of peace, and open unto thee, then it shall be, that all the people that is found therein shall be tributaries unto thee, and they shall serve thee." [198]

In this case there would be no war and the people would come under the supervision of the Israelites who would eliminate their practices which were so reprehensible to the Lord.

But what if they would not make peace?

195. Deuteronomy 20:8.
196. Judges 7:3.
197. Deuteronomy 20:9.
198. Deuteronomy 20:10-11.

"And if it will make no peace with thee, but will make war against thee, then thou shalt besiege it: And when the Lord thy God hath delivered it into thine hands, thou shalt smite every male thereof with the edge of the sword: But the women, and the little ones, and the cattle, and all that is in the city, even all the spoil thereof, shalt thou take unto thyself; and thou shalt eat the spoil of thine enemies, which the Lord thy God hath given thee ...." [199]

Now we come to those cities which God had declared anathema. These are the people who had slaughtered their children by burning and other forms of human sacrifice. Five centuries before God had told Abraham how he abhorred the wickedness of these Amorite nations in Canaan. But he told Abraham that his descendants would not immediately inherit the land because "the wickedness of the Amorites is not yet full." By the time of Joshua who succeeded Moses, their day of doom had come.

The Psalms describe how they lived:

"They sacrificed their sons and their daughters unto devils, and shed innocent blood, even the blood of their sons and of their daughters, whom they sacrificed unto the idols of Canaan: and the land was polluted with blood." [200]

Therefore the Lord described to Moses how he wanted these Amorite cities annihilated:

"But of the cities of these people ... thou shalt save alive nothing that breatheth: But thou shalt utterly destroy them; namely, the Hittites, and the Amorites, the Canaanites, and the Perizzites, the Hivites, and the Jebusites; as their Lord thy God hath commanded thee." [201]

Mobocracy

Mobs, even for a "good cause," represent society at its lowest ebb. A mob usually ends up in the hands of the criminally minded who whip the crowd into a rash of violence, looting, and burning. The Lord had this in mind when he said:

"Thou shalt not follow a multitude to do evil; neither shalt thou speak in a cause to decline after many to wrest judgment." [202]

This last phrase has reference to those who decline to accept a judgment of the court and who gather in a mob to "wrest judgment" or take the law into their own hands.

199. Deuteronomy 20:12-14.
200. Psalms 106:37-38.
201. Deuteronomy 20:16-17.
202. Exodus 23:2.

Mother

See: *Parents*.

Murders and Accidental Homicides

The law of the Covenant clearly distinguished between premeditated killing and accidental homicide. There were four types of homicide problems which the Law of the Covenant described.

1. *First Degree Murder*. This is the deliberate, premeditated killing of another human being. The mandatory penalty was death.[203]

No amount of "satisfaction" could ameliorate the crime of murder. The scripture says: "He shall surely be put to death."[204]

The conviction of a murderer had to be based on the testimony of two or more witnesses, otherwise the matter must wait on God's judgment.

The victim's nearest kinsman had the responsibility of bringing the murderer to trial and avenging his death.[205]

2. *Accidental homicide.* The accidental killing of another was not punishable.[206]

If the victim's kinsman accused the accidental killer of murder, then the latter could flee to the altar of the temple[207] or to one of the cities of refuge after they were built. There he had to remain until he could have a fair trial. However, he had to be returned to the city where the killing occurred for his trial.

If he were found innocent of deliberate homicide (murder), but the kinsman would not believe the findings of the judge, then the accused was to be sent back to the city of refuge and remain there until the High Priest died.[208]

Once the alleged offender was assigned to a city of refuge, he was not allowed to give "satisfaction" to the avenger of blood in order to return home before the High Priest died. It was felt he might be tricked.[209]

However, if he wandered from the city of refuge before the appointed time and was slain, the kinsman would not be punished because the accused had violated the limits of his sanctuary.[210]

---

203. Numbers 35:16-18, 20-21, 30; Deuteronomy 19:11-13.
204. Numbers 35:31.
205. Number 35:19.
206. Leviticus 21:13; Numbers 35:22-23,32; Deuteronomy 19:4-5.
207. Exodus 21:14.
208. Numbers 35:24-25.
209. Numbers 35:32.
210. Numbers 35:26-28.

After the High Priest died, the accused could return to his own city and the avenger of blood or kinsman had to leave him unmolested.[211]

The application of this law applied to "strangers" as much as it did to Israelites.[212]

3. *Excusable homicides*:

"If a thief be found breaking up [breaking into a building], and be smitten [at nighttime] that he die, there shall no blood be shed for him."[213] In other words, it would be considered excusable.

"If the sun be risen upon him, there shall be blood shed for him."[214] To kill a person in broad day light was not excusable because the thief could be identified and apprehended with greater facility than at night. Therefore, it was not excusable.

4. *Unsolved murders*. In order to preserve the sanctity of human life, the Lord required that every murder be treated as a major issue whether the perpetrator was found or not. In those cases where "it be not known who hath slain him," the elders of the city nearest to the place where the body was found were required to take a heifer into "a rough valley, which is neither eared nor sown [still a wilderness], and shall strike off the heifer's neck ...."[215]

They would then wash their hands over the heifer and say, "Our hands have not shed this blood, neither have our eyes seen it. Be merciful, O Lord, unto thy people Israel, whom thou hast redeemed, and lay not innocent blood unto thy people of Israel's charge." 32 The Lord said that in this manner "shalt thou put away the guilt of innocent blood from among you ...."[216]

Neighbors—Duties Toward

The most valuable asset of a home is the environment of the neighborhood in which it is located. The purpose of God's law was to make every neighborhood a haven of security and peace. So the Lord declared:

"Thou shalt not avenge, nor bear any grudge against the children of thy people, but *thou shalt love thy neighbor as thyself*."[217]

This is the passage quoted by Jesus and identified as the second greatest commandment.[218]

---

211. Number 35:28.
212. Numbers 35:15; also 15:16.
213. Exodus 22:2.
214. Exodus 22:3.
215. Deuteronomy 21:4.
216. Deuteronomy 21:9.
217. Leviticus 19:18.
218. Matthew 22:39.

"If thou meet thine enemy's ox or his ass going astray, thou shalt surely bring it back to him again."[219]

"Thou shalt not see thy brother's ox or his sheep go astray, and hide thyself from them: thou shalt in any case bring them again unto thy brother. And if thy brother be not nigh unto thee, or if thou know him not, then thou shalt bring it unto thine own house, and it shall be with thee until thy brother seek after it, and thou shalt restore it to him again. In like manner shalt thou do with his ass; and so shalt thou do with his raiment; and with all lost things of thy brother's, which he hath lost, and thou hast found, shalt thou do likewise: thou mayest no hide thyself. Thou shalt not see thy brother's ass or his ox fall down by the way, and hide thyself from them: thou shalt surely help him to lift them up again."[220]

"Thou shalt not defraud thy neighbor, neither rob him."[221]

"Thou shalt not hate thy brother in thine heart: thou shalt in any wise [nevertheless] rebuke thy neighbor, and not suffer sin upon him."[222]

The Lord imposed heavy duties on an Israelite concerning any of his neighbors who were poor. The poor were to be given generous assistance without usury.[223]

If a poor neighbor could not pay his debts by the end of the Sabbath Year, the debt was to be written off and forgotten.[224]

An Israelite was not to be reluctant to lend to a poor neighbor just because the Sabbath Year was near when the debt would be automatically cancelled.[225]

Oaths

See also: *Contracts*

The oath was originally designed as the most solemn procedure for covenant-making. It involved not only a covenant with another person or society but also a covenant with God that the oath-taker would fulfill his promise. This is why the oath was always to be taken in the name of God and not in the name of anything else:

"Thou shalt fear the Lord thy God, and serve him, and *shalt swear by his name*."[226]

219. Exodus 23:4.
220. Deuteronomy 22:1-4.
221. Leviticus 19:13.
222. Leviticus 19:17.
223. Exodus 22:25-27; Leviticus 25:35-37.
224. Deuteronomy 15:1-2.
225. Deuteronomy 15:7-11.
226. Deuteronomy 6:13.

Once the oath was taken, it was to be given the highest priority in the life of the covenant-maker so that he made certain it was carefully fulfilled. This is the meaning of the third commandment:

"Thou shalt not take the name of the Lord thy God in vain: for the Lord will not hold him guiltless that taketh his name in vain." [227]

Oaths have been primarily reserved for the temple, for the giving of testimony, the coronation of kings and queens, the initiation into an important office, initiation into the military, and the confirming of some important official act.

The oath was never intended to be a daily vehicle for confirming a questioned statement or some superfluous triviality. Nevertheless, with the passing of time, the Israelites followed the pagan practice of "swearing" by the heavens, the earth, the head, etc. that such and such was true or that such and such would be done. This type of "swearing" was actually a form of profanity—an unauthorized type of oath which profaned the oath-taking procedure, and therefore the name of God.

This is why Jesus denounced this type of "market-place swearing" which was so common in his day. He said:

"Swear not at all: neither by heaven; for it is God's throne: nor by the earth; for it is his footstool: neither by Jerusalem; for it is the city of the great King. Neither shalt thou swear by thy head; because thou canst not make one hair white or black. But let your communication be, Yea, yea; Nay, nay: for whatsoever is more than these cometh of evil." [228]

Some interpreted this to mean that Jesus had outlawed sacred oaths. However, they missed the point. Jesus was talking about daily "communications" or conversation. It was the continuous "swearing" by the head, by the heavens, by the City of Jerusalem, etc., to which he objected. The sacred oath was an entirely different subject.

The use of the oath in judicial matters was an important part of the Law of the Covenant. For example:

"If a man deliver unto his neighbor an ass, or an ox, or a sheep, or any beast, to keep; and it die, or be hurt, or driven away, no man seeing it: then shall an oath of the Lord be between them both, that he hath not put his hand unto his neighbor's goods; and the owner of it shall accept thereof, and he shall not [be required] to make it good." [229]

Another example of this type of procedure, based on an oath, will be found in Deuteronomy 21:4-9.

---

227. Exodus 20:7.
228. Matthew 5:34-37.
229. Exodus 22:10-11.

Parents

Under God's law parents had prime responsibilities, and they were entitled to a high degree of respect and appreciation.

Therefore the Lord said:

"Honor thy father and thy mother: that thy days may be long upon the land which the Lord thy God giveth thee."[230]

"And he that curseth his father, or his mother, shall surely be put to death."[231]

"And he that smiteth his father, or his mother, shall surely be put to death."[232]

The only problem with these severe penalties was the fact that the parents had to cast the first stone.[233] Furthermore, there was a ritual required of the law before the rebellious son could be declared *anathema*. The law read:

"If a man have a stubborn and rebellious son, which will not obey the voice of his father, or the voice of his mother, and that, when they have chastened him, will not hearken unto them: Then shall his father and his mother lay hold on him, and bring him out unto the elders of his city, and unto the gate of his place; And they shall say unto the elders of his city, This our son is stubborn and rebellious, he will not obey our voice; he is a glutton, and a drunkard."[234]

At this point the parents had to pick up a stone and be the first to strike their son down. We have no record of any instance where this ever took place. Instead, the parents would resort to some of the other options in lieu of death. For example:

"If there be laid on him a sum of money, then he shall give for the ransom of his life whatsoever is laid upon him."[235]

Jesus refers to the usual practice of enforcing the payment:

"And his lord was wroth, and delivered him to the tormentors [whip masters] till he should pay all that was due."[236]

However, even in the most extreme cases, whipping was limited to 40 stripes. The judge must witness the whipping to insure that the punishment is carried out as intended.[237]

---

230. Exodus 20:12.
231. Exodus 21:17.
232. Exodus 21:15.
233. Deuteronomy 13:9; 17:7.
234. Deuteronomy 21:18-20.
235. Exodus 21:30.
236. Matthew 18:34.
237. Deuteronomy 25:2.

We have already mentioned Ezra who speaks of other options in lieu of death.[238]

1. Confiscation of goods to enforce fines or assessed damages.
2. Imprisonment where necessary for public safety.
3. Banishment (self-exile under threat of death if he refuses).

Penalties

See also: *Enforcement of the Law*.

Some have thought the penalties under the Law of the Covenant were particularly harsh. It has been called a system of *lex talionis* or a law of revenge. This is because the phrase, "an eye for an eye" was interpreted to mean a literal destruction of the offender's eye when it was actually the *threat* of losing his eye that provided the motivation so the offender would give his victim "satisfaction" or compensation for damages.

In other words, the Law of the Covenant was specifically designed to give the victims of a tort or a crime the degree of compensation which the offense warranted.

It even provided a punitive element to teach the offender not to repeat his offense. Here are some examples of reparation plus punitive damages:

"If the theft be certainly found in his hand alive, whether it be ox, or ass, or sheep; he shall restore *double*."[239]

"If a man shall steal an ox, or a sheep, and *kill* it, or *sell* it; he shall restore *five* oxen for an ox, and *four* sheep for a sheep."[240]

Notice that if the stolen animal was still alive it could be returned to the owner with an additional animal of the same kind as punitive damages. However, if he had killed the animal it obviously could not be returned alive to the owner so it would make the offender subject to a much more severe penalty.

Furthermore, if he had sold the stolen animal or animals, it would be prima facie evidence to the judge that he was a cattle rustler and therefore the judge would require the offender to restore five oxen for every stolen ox, or four sheep for every stolen sheep. It is interesting to note the extremely severe penalty imposed on a person who was involved in commercial criminality. This law was intended to send the message throughout Israel that under the Law of the Covenant crime does not pay.

Here was the penalty for trespass:

---

238. Ezra 7:26.
239. Exodus 22:4.
240. Exodus 22:1.

"Then they shall confess their sin which they have done: and he shall recompense his trespass with the principal thereof, and add unto it the *fifth* part thereof, and give it unto him against whom he hath trespassed." [241]

In case the authorities could not discover who owned the property that had been trespassed upon, here was the rule:

"But if the man have no kinsman to recompense the trespass unto, let the trespass be recompensed unto the Lord, even to the priest; beside the ram of the atonement, whereby an atonement shall be made for him." [242]

The same principle applied where a person was injured or whose property had been damaged. The offender had to make "satisfaction" to the injured person or have the same injury imposed on him. This is the meaning of the following scripture:

"And he that killeth a beast shall make it good; beast for beast. And if a man cause a blemish in his neighbor; as he hath done, so shall it be done to him; Breach for breach, eye for eye, tooth for tooth: as he hath caused a blemish in a man, so shall it be done to him again." [243]

In all of these cases the offender could avoid being subjected to a similar injury to himself or property by providing "satisfaction." This was usually in the form of money damages.

If he did not have the money, he was required to sell his services under a bond, but it could not exceed six years.[244]

There were only two instances where "satisfaction" was not allowed:

"Moreover ye shall take no satisfaction for the life of a murderer, which is guilty of death: but he shall be surely put to death. And ye shall take no satisfaction for him that is fled to the city of his refuge, that he should come again to dwell in the land, until the death of the priest." [245]

We observed earlier that the penalty for offenses which would corrupt the culture of Israel was often "death," but in all cases other than the two exceptions just cited, the offender was usually assessed money damages:

"If there be laid on him a sum of money, then he shall give for the ransom of his life whatsoever is laid upon him." [246]

241. Numbers 5:7.
242. Numbers 5:8.
243. Leviticus 24:18-20.
244. Deuteronomy 15:12.
245. Numbers 35:31-32.
246. Exodus 21:30.

Other options cited by Ezra include banishment, confiscation of property, or imprisonment.[247]

As was mentioned above, Moses said the offender: "shall make full restitution [but] if he have nothing, then he shall be sold for his theft [or for any injury he had caused]."[248]

In other words, he would be sold as a bond servant. However, it says a bond servant could only be sold for six years:

"Six years he shall serve: and in the seventh he shall go out free for nothing."[249]

As we indicated, the death penalty was indicated for practically all offenses which would destroy the culture of the people, but as we have also noted, "repentance" plus providing "satisfaction" in terms of damages or some other penalty would allow the individual to "ransom" his life except in the two instances mentioned in Numbers 35:31-32.

Among the several options available to the judges when the offender either refused to repent or was unwilling to provide "satisfaction" to his victim, there was the option of voluntary exile or banishment. The scripture speaks of this penalty as being "cut off from among his people." Notice that he was not cut off from all people but just his people.

The judges, in effect, would simply say to a recalcitrant offender that since he would not repent and provide "satisfaction" to his victim, they will declare him an outlaw.

This means that if he is still in Israel after a certain date he will be there at the risk of his life. This action would be taken to motivate an uncooperative offender to leave Israel so he would no longer be able to corrupt the cultural society of God's people. If he did not, he would very likely be slain. Being an outlaw, he could claim no protection if he stayed among his people.

Of course, going into exile carried with it some definite hardships. Not only would the offender be compelled to start a new life, but he would lose his entire inheritance in Israel. He would also lose his association with loved ones and friends. There are numerous references to the use of exile as an alternative punishment for those who would not repent or make satisfaction.[250]

There were certain types of offenses which were against the community such as public drunkenness, prostitution, rioting, etc.

In these cases satisfaction could not be made to any individual, and therefore the punishment was by whipping the offender. However, this was not to be a brutal

247. Ezra 7:26.
248. Exodus 22:3.
249. Exodus 21:2.
250. See Exodus 30:33; 30:38; Leviticus 7:20-21, 25; 17:4; 19:8; 20:6.

flogging, and in no case could the number of "stripes" be more than 40. Here is what the scripture says about whipping:

"And it shall be, if the wicked man be worthy to be beaten, that the judge shall cause him to lie down, and to be beaten before his face, according to his fault, by a certain number. Forty stripes he may give him, and not exceed: lest, if he should exceed, and beat him above these with many stripes, then thy brother should seem vile unto thee."[251]

Jesus also referred to the practice of whipping where a person would not pay the damages to his victim. He said the offender was delivered "to the tormentors [whip masters], till he should pay all that was due."[252]

When the death penalty was invoked it was usually by stoning or hanging:

"And if a man have committed a sin worthy of death and he be … put to death, and thou hang him on a tree: His body shall not remain all night upon the tree, but thou shalt in any wise bury him that day; (for he that is hanged is accursed of God;) that thy land be not defiled, which the Lord thy God giveth thee for an inheritance."[253]

Phylacteries

See: *Law of the Covenant.*

Poll Tax

A poll tax is levied against each person "by the head," which is what "poll" means. Regardless of circumstances, each person is taxed the same. Israel had such a tax:

"When thou takest the sum [census] of the children of Israel after their number, then shall they give every man a ransom for his soul unto the Lord … Every one that passeth among them that are numbered from twenty years old and above, shall give an offering unto the Lord. The rich shall not give more, and the poor shall not give less than half a shekel when they give an offering unto the Lord, to make an atonement for your souls. And thou shalt take the atonement money of the children of Israel, and shalt appoint it for the service of the tabernacle of the congregation; that it may be a memorial unto the children of Israel before the Lord, to make an atonement for your souls."[254]

251. Deuteronomy 25:2-3.
252. Matthew 18:34.
253. Deuteronomy 21:22-23.
254. Exodus 30:12-16.

There was also a poll tax (so much per head) for the firstborn of the Israelites and also of their animals except for the firstborn of a cow, sheep, or goat, which were sacrificed and eaten.[255]

All the rest of the firstborn had to be redeemed at so much per head:

"Every thing that openeth the matrix in all flesh, which they bring unto the Lord, whether it be of men or beasts, shall be thine: nevertheless the firstborn of man shalt thou surely redeem, and the firstling of unclean beasts shalt thou redeem. And those that are to be redeemed from a month old shalt thou redeem, according to thine estimation, for the money of five shekels, after the shekel of the sanctuary ... But the firstling of a cow, or the firstling of a sheep, or the firstling of a goat, thou shalt not redeem; they are holy."[256] (Then it goes on to say how they shall be sacrificed.)

The poll taxes, including the redemption tax, were turned over to the Levites for their sustenance, along with a tenth of the tithe.[257]

The Poor

See also: *Lending and Debts.*

As we have already seen, the Law of the Covenant required more than mere compassion for the poor. It required constructive generosity. Although mankind are all created equal before the law, they are never equal in their circumstances. The purpose of God's law was to improve the equality of opportunity to obtain the necessities of life. There was a further mandate under God's law to encourage those who had been favored by circumstances to share with those less fortunate.

In fact, the law which was given directly from heaven to Moses imposes many responsibilities on the whole people which favored the poor. These, of course, were adapted to the circumstances of those days. The important element was simply that just because a person might be poor, it was no reason for treating him in a demeaning manner.

"When thou dost lend thy brother any thing, thou shalt not go into his house to fetch his pledge. Thou shalt stand abroad, and the man to whom thou dost lend shall bring out the pledge abroad unto thee. And if the man be poor, thou shalt not sleep with his pledge: In any case thou shalt deliver him the pledge again when the sun goeth down, that he may sleep in his own raiment, and bless thee: and it shall be righteousness unto thee before the Lord thy God.

"Thou shalt not oppress an hired servant that is poor and needy, whether he be of thy brethren, or of thy strangers that are in thy land within thy gates: At his day thou shalt give him his hire, neither shall the sun go down upon it; for he is poor,

255. Deuteronomy 15:19-20.
256. Numbers 18:15-17.
257. Numbers 18:1, 21, 26.

and setteth his heart upon it: lest he cry against thee unto the Lord, and it be sin unto thee ....

"When thou cuttest down thine harvest in thy field, and hast forgot a sheaf in the field, thou shalt not go again to fetch it: it shall be for the stranger, for the fatherless, and for the widow: that the Lord thy God may bless thee in all the work of thine hands.

"When thou beatest thine olive tree, thou shalt not go over the boughs again: it shall be for the stranger, for the fatherless, and for the widow. When thou gatherest the grapes of thy vineyard, thou shalt not glean it afterward: it shall be for the stranger, for the fatherless, and for the widow."[258]

"And when ye reap the harvest of your land, thou shalt not wholly reap the corners of thy field, neither shalt thou gather the gleanings of thy harvest. And thou shalt not glean thy vineyard, neither shalt thou gather every grape of thy vineyard; thou shalt leave them for the poor and stranger: I am the Lord your God."[259]

One of the greatest benefits to the poor was a provision to prevent anyone from getting into perpetual debt. Every seven years debts were automatically canceled! The Lord said:

"At the end of every seven years thou shalt make a release. And this is the manner of the release: Every creditor that lendeth ought unto his neighbor shall release it; he shall not exact it of his neighbor, or of his brother; because it is called the Lord's release."[260]

The long-range goal of the Law of the Covenant was to train the people to become directly involved in the economic system and help young people and the poor to be self-sustaining. The Lord even looked forward to the time when "there shall be no poor among you."[261]

Israel was not expected to do this for the whole world, but to demonstrate to the world that by living the Law of the Covenant poverty could be eliminated. Even "strangers" could participate in the system by coming under the Lord's law, but otherwise, they were considered outsiders. Concerning loans to the poor, the Lord said:

"Of a foreigner thou mayest exact it again: but that which is thine with thy brother thine hand shall release."[262]

People of means were specifically instructed by the Lord to be generous with the poor even though the Sabbath was near when debts would be canceled:

---

258. Deuteronomy 24:10-15, 19-21.
259. Leviticus 19:9-10.
260. Deuteronomy 15:1-2.
261. Deuteronomy 15:4.
262. Deuteronomy 15:3.

"If there be among you a poor man of one of thy brethren within any of thy gates in thy land which the Lord thy God giveth thee, thou shalt not harden thine heart, nor shut thine hand from thy poor brother: But thou shalt open thine hand wide unto him, and shalt surely lend him sufficient for his need, in that which he wanteth.

"Beware that there be not a thought in thy wicked heart, saying, The seventh year, the *year of release*, is at hand; and thine eye be evil against thy poor brother, and thou givest him nought; and he cry unto the Lord against thee, and it be sin unto thee.

"Thou shalt surely give him, and thine heart shall not be grieved when thou givest unto him: because that for this thing the Lord thy God shall bless thee in all thy works, and in all that thou puttest thine hand unto."[263]

Private Property

Under the Law of the Covenant, the base for the building of an inheritance was the inalienable rights associated with private property. Various passages refer to the protection of property.

"When thou dost lend thy brother any thing, thou shalt not go into his house to fetch the pledge. Thou shalt stand abroad, and the man to whom thou doest lend shall bring out the pledge abroad unto thee."[264]

"Thou shalt not remove thy neighbor's landmark, which they of old time had set in thine inheritance, which thou shalt inherit in the land that the Lord thy God giveth thee to possess it."[265]

"Then they shall confess their sin which they have done: and he shall recompense his trespass with the principal thereof, and add unto it the fifth part thereof, and give it unto him against whom he hath trespassed."[266]

Under *Penalties* we have already seen how the theft of private property was rigorously prosecuted. The thief was required to compensate his victim two to five times what he had taken.

But in spite of all this, there was a time when the Lord allowed a little leniency. It was when the fruit was ripe in the orchards and the grain was ripe in the field:

"When thou comest into thy neighbor's vineyard, then thou mayest eat grapes thy fill at thine own pleasure; but thou shalt *not put any in thy vesse*l. When thou

263. Deuteronomy 15:7-10.
264. Deuteronomy 24:10-11.
265. Deuteronomy 19:14.
266. Numbers 5:7.

comest into the standing corn of thy neighbor, then thou mayest pluck the ears with thine hand; but thou *shalt not move a sickle unto thy neighbor's standing corn.*"[267]

Prophets—True or False?

The prophetic calling is based on a scientific principal rather than mystical imagination. A prophet speaks that which he has been told and describes that which he has seen. Unless he has received instructions from the Lord or has been shown a vision he has no more knowledge on the subject than other men and women and must not pretend otherwise.

Sometimes, however, those who aspire to the prophetic calling presume to speak in the name of the Lord when the Lord has not spoken to them. There have been such people in all ages and it has therefore resulted in confusion among the Lord's people as well as others who are seeking the will of the Lord. Accordingly, Moses gave the following test concerning any person who came speaking in the name of the Lord:

"And if thou say in thine heart, How shall we know the word which the Lord hath not spoken? When a prophet speaketh in the name of the Lord, if the thing follow not, nor come to pass, that is the thing which the Lord hath not spoken, but the prophet hath spoken it presumptuously: thou shalt not be afraid of him."[268]

Not only were the people free to ignore men who thus violated their calling or presumed to speak without authority, but the Lord reflected his indignation against those who did so:

"But the prophet, which shall presume to speak a word in my name, which I have not commanded him to speak, or that shall speak in the name of other gods, even that prophet shall die."[269]

Of course, death was not mandatory unless the false prophet was involved in human sacrifices, putting children through the fire of Molech, and so forth. Otherwise, his punishment could be any of the penalties we have already mentioned such as fines, imprisonment, or banishment.[270]

Prostitution

A prostitute is defined as a person who engages in promiscuous sexual relations for pay.

Among the heathen nations, prostitution was a respectable institution. The pagan temples had professional prostitutes who were referred to as "temple virgins!"

267. Deuteronomy 23:24-25.
268. Deuteronomy 18:21-22.
269. Deuteronomy 18:20.
270. Ezra 7:26.

Among the Israelites, during their apostasy, parents sometimes sold their daughters into prostitution.

"Do not prostitute thy daughter, to cause her to be a whore; lest the land fall to whoredom, and the land become full of wickedness."[271]

Public Nuisances

In every community there seem to be a few careless and indifferent souls who conduct their affairs without any concern for others. Where they create a public nuisance or a situation which would be dangerous for children, animals, or even adults, the Lord had this to say:

"And if a man shall open a pit, or if a man shall dig a pit, and not cover it, and an ox or an ass fall therein; The owner of the pit shall make it good, and give money unto the owner of them; and the dead beast shall be his."[272]

Punishments

See: *Penalties*.

Ransom—an Offender May Ransom His Life

"If there be laid on him a sum of money, then he shall give for the ransom of his life whatsoever is laid upon him."[273]

Rape

Rape is defined as forcible sexual intercourse against the will of the victim or sexual intercourse with a victim who is too young to give legal consent.

The Law of the Covenant stated:

"But if a man find a betrothed damsel in the field, and the man force her, and lie with her: then the man only that lay with her shall die: But unto the damsel thou shalt do nothing; there is in the damsel no sin worthy of death: for as when a man riseth against his neighbor, and slayeth him, even so is this matter."[274]

"If a damsel that is a virgin be betrothed unto an husband, and a man find her in the city, and lie with her; Then ye shall bring them both out unto the gate of that city, and ye shall stone them with stones that they die; the damsel, because she cried not, being in the city; and the man, because he hath humbled his neighbor's wife: so thou shalt put away evil from among you."[275]

---

271. Leviticus 19:29.
272. Exodus 21:33-34.
273. Exodus 21:30.
274. Deuteronomy 22:25-26.
275. Deuteronomy 22:23-24.

Of course, if she could prove that she was intimidated and dared not cry out, the judges would treat her case accordingly.

If the problem was one of seduction of a maiden rather than forced rape, the rule was as follows:

"If a man find a damsel that is a virgin, which is not betrothed, and lay hold on her, and lie with her, and they be found; Then the man that lay with her shall give unto the damsel's father fifty shekels of silver, and she shall be his wife; because he hath humbled her, he may not put her away all his days."[276]

Sabbath Day

All through the scripture the sanctity of the sabbath day is emphasized:

"Remember the Sabbath day, to keep it holy. Six days shalt thou labour, and do all thy work: but the seventh day is the Sabbath of the Lord thy God: in it thou shalt not do any work, thou, nor thy son, nor thy daughter, thy man-servant, nor thy maid-servant, nor thy cattle, nor thy stranger that is within thy gates."[277]

"Speak thou also unto the children of Israel, saying, Verily my sabbaths ye shall keep: *for it is a sign between me and you* throughout your generations; that ye may know that I am the Lord that doth sanctify you. Ye shall keep the sabbath therefore; for it is holy unto you: every one that defileth it shall surely be put to death: for whosoever doeth any work therein, that soul shall be cut off from among his people."[278]

Servitude

No adult Israelite could be forced into servitude unless he was guilty of a theft and had been compelled to take up servitude in order to make retribution:

"If the sun be risen upon him, there shall be blood shed for him; for he should make full restitution; if he have nothing, then he shall be sold for his theft."[279]

But whether an Israelite had become a servant voluntarily or under the above circumstances, he could not be compelled to serve longer than six years:

"If thou buy an Hebrew servant, six years he shall serve: and in the seventh he shall go out free for nothing."[280]

Occasionally, however, a person would become almost like a member of his master's household and wish to remain. In this situation he would go with his

276. Deuteronomy 22:28-29.
277. Exodus 20:8-10.
278. Exodus 31:13-14.
279. Exodus 22:3.
280. Exodus 21:2.

master to the "judges" of the community so they could be certain the servant was not making his request under duress:

"And if thy servant shall plainly say, I love my master, my wife, and my children; I will not go out free: Then his master shall bring him unto the judges; he shall also bring him to the door, or unto the door post; and his master shall bore his ear through with an awl; and he shall serve him for ever." [281]

There was a difference between a person who was compelled to become a bond servant to pay for damages and one who felt compelled to work as a house servant because of poverty:

"And if thy brother that dwelleth by thee be waxen poor, and be sold unto thee; thou shalt not compel him to serve as a bond servant: But as an hired servant, and as a sojourner, he shall be with thee, and shall serve thee unto the year of jubilee." [282]

The Lord made it clear that cruel masters who abused their servants would be accountable to him:

"Thou shalt not rule over him with rigor; but shalt fear thy God." [283]

"And if a man smite his servant, or his maid, with a rod, and he die under his hand; he shall be surely punished." [284]

However, if the servant is injured but does not die, the master was not punished.

"Not withstanding, if he continue a day or two, he shall not be punished: for he is his money." [285]

"And if a man smite the eye of his servant, or the eye of his maid, that it perish; he shall let him go free for his eye's sake. And if he smite out his manservant's tooth, or his maidservant's tooth; he shall let him go free for his tooth's sake." [286]

Seventy Elders—A Permanent Senate

When Moses felt overwhelmed by the burden of managing somewhere around three million Israelites, he cried out:

"I am not able to bear all this people alone, because it is too heavy for me. And if thou deal thus with me, kill me, I pray thee, out of hand ....

"And the Lord said unto Moses, Gather unto me seventy men of the elders of Israel, whom thou knowest to be the elders of the people, and officers over them;

281. Exodus 21:5-6.
282. Leviticus 25:39-40.
283. Leviticus 25:43.
284. Exodus 21:20.
285. Exodus 21:21.
286. Exodus 21:26-27.

and bring them unto the tabernacle of the congregation, that they may stand there with thee.

"And I will come down and talk with thee there: and I will take of the spirit which is upon thee and will put it upon them; and they shall bear the burden of the people with thee, that thou bear it not thyself alone."[287]

It would appear that it was this same group that had been allowed to come part way up Mount Sinai and see the glory of the Lord.

"And he said unto Moses, Come up unto the Lord, thou, and Aaron, Nadab, and Abihu, and seventy of the elders of Israel; and worship ye afar off....

"Then went up Moses, and Aaron, Nadab, and Abihu, and seventy of the elders of Israel. And they saw the God of Israel: and there was under his feet as it were a paved work of a sapphire stone, and as it were the body of heaven in his clearness. And upon the nobles of the children of Israel he laid not his hand: also they saw God, and did eat and drink."[288]

This governing body of Seventy Elders gave "advice and consent" to important decisions proposed by Moses or the Council of Elders representing the various tribes of Israel. It served as an advisory body in selecting principal administrators and in making decisions concerning peace and war or relations with surrounding nations. It also served as a judicial body and this became its principal function when it became known as the Sanhedrin of the Jews.

The United States Constitution made the Senate the body which would give advice and consent in all major appointments by the president. It gives its advice and consent to all declarations of war, to all treaties, including peace treaties. It must give its advice and consent to all proposals passed by the House of Representatives. It serves as a judicial body to try all cases of impeachment.

It is obvious why the Council of Seventy Elders in ancient Israel is often referred to as the prototype for the United States Senate.

Sodomy

See: *Homosexuality, Bestiality.*

Sodomy is defined as any of the unnatural acts of sexual perversion attributed to the ancient city of Sodom near the Dead Sea which God destroyed by fire.[289] It usually refers to anal sexuality or human sexual relations with animals.

These degenerate and perverted practices were popularized among pagan nations and had such a denigrating effect on the cultural and moral life of the

287. Numbers 11:14-17.
288. Exodus 24:1, 9-11.
289. Genesis 19:24-25.

people that they are often cited as the primary factor in the fall of major civilizations of the past.

Sodomy and similar practices were often associated with fertility worship and rituals identified with various forms of idolatry.

Spiritualism

Spiritualism is the belief in the occult—that mankind on earth can communicate with the spirits of the dead through a seance or some mystical ritual.

"And the soul that turneth after such as have familiar spirits, and after wizards, to go a whoring after them, I will even set my face against that soul, and will cut him off from among his people." [290]

"When thou art come into the land which the Lord thy God giveth thee, thou shalt not learn to do after the abominations of those nations. There shall not be found among you any one that maketh his son or his daughter to pass through the fire, or that useth divination, or an observer of times, or an enchanter, or a witch,

"Or a charmer, or a consulter with familiar spirits, or a wizard, or a necromancer [one who pretends to tell the future by messages from the dead]. For all that do these things are an abomination unto the Lord: and because of these abominations the Lord thy God doth drive them out from before thee." [291]

Among the wicked there has always been a concerted attempt to communicate with "familiar spirits" or occult powers to replace the principle of direct revelation from God. It will be recalled that when Saul could not get a message from the Lord by the Urim and Thummim he resorted to the services of a witch who had survived Saul's earlier order to have all of them killed.[292] Of course, the woman falsely pretended to bring up Samuel which is typical of those dealing with familiar spirits. God's prophets do not communicate their messages through witches or spiritual seances.

Stealing

Stealing or theft is defined as taking or appropriating another's property without the consent of the owner.

"Thou shalt not steal." [293]

"If a man shall steal an ox, or a sheep, and kill it, or sell it; he shall restore *five* oxen for an ox, and *four* sheep for a sheep." [294]

290. Leviticus 20:6.
291. Deuteronomy 18:9-12.
292. 1 Samuel 28:3-20.
293. Exodus 20:15.
294. Exodus 22:1.

"If the theft be certainly found in his hand alive, whether it be ox, or ass, or sheep; he shall restore *double*."[295]

"If the sun be risen upon him, there shall be blood shed for him; for he should make full restitution; if he have nothing, then he shall be sold for his theft."[296]

Notice how God's law handled commercial cattle stealing. In the old west the punishment was hanging, but God's law took the profit out of this type of crime by having the offender pay two, four or five times the value of each animal stolen, depending on the kind. Obviously this was to send forth the message that in Israel "crime does not pay."

Strangers, Treatment of

God has always required that his chosen servants extend the greatest courtesy and consideration to the stranger "within your gates."

Moses emphasized this doctrine repeatedly as it was given to him by the Lord:

"For the Lord your God is God of gods, and Lord of lords, a great God, a mighty, and a terrible, which regardeth not persons, nor taketh reward: He doth execute the judgment of the fatherless and widow, and loveth the stranger, in giving him food and raiment. Love ye therefore the stranger: for ye were strangers in the land of Egypt."[297]

"Thou shalt neither vex a stranger, nor oppress him: for ye were strangers in the land of Egypt."[298]

"But the stranger that dwelleth with you shall be unto you as one born among you, and thou shalt love him as thyself; for ye were strangers in the land of Egypt: I am the Lord your God."[299]

"One law and one manner shall be for you, and for the stranger that sojourneth with you."[300]

Now we come to a glaring contradiction to the above passages:

"Ye shall not eat of any thing that dieth of itself: thou shalt give it unto the stranger that is in thy gates, that he may eat it; or thou mayest sell it unto an alien: for thou art an holy people unto the Lord thy God."[301]

---

295. Exodus 22:4.
296. Exodus 22:3.
297. Deuteronomy 10:17-19.
298. Exodus 22:21.
299. Leviticus 19:34.
300. Numbers 15:16.
301. Deuteronomy 14:21.

Modern texts demonstrate that this verse has been improperly rendered. Originally, it said: "Thou shalt not give it unto the stranger … thou mayest not sell it unto an alien."[302]

The scripture consistently emphasized that "strangers" were to be treated with kindness and generosity. Strangers who were poor were to have the same privileges as Israelites who were poor.

"And when ye reap the harvest of your land, thou shalt not wholly reap the corners of thy field, neither shalt thou gather the gleanings of thy harvest. And thou shalt not glean thy vineyard, neither shalt thou gather every grape of thy vineyard; thou shalt leave them for the poor and *stranger*: I am the Lord your God."[303]

Tattooing

Among pagan nations, as we point out under "cults," it was customary to mark, scar or mutilate the body as an identification, a decoration, or a symbol of some heroic act. It was also a custom to cut off fingers or toes as funerary offerings when someone died. This was frequently done by cutting off the fingers or toes of children. In fact the natives in Borneo do it today. All of these mutilating devices were abhorrent to the Lord:

"Ye shall not make any cuttings in your flesh for the dead, nor print any marks upon you: I am the Lord."[304]

Theft

See: *Stealing*.

Tithes

Tithes are defined as one-tenth of one's increase.

"And all the tithe of the land, whether of the seed of the land, or of the fruit of the tree, is the Lord's: it is holy unto the Lord. And if a man will at all redeem ought of his tithes, he shall add thereto the fifth part thereof.

"And concerning the tithe of the herd, or of the flock, even of whatsoever passeth under the rod, the tenth shall be holy unto the Lord. He shall not search whether it be good or bad, neither shall he change it: and if he change it at all, then both it and the change thereof shall be holy; it shall not be redeemed."[305]

"And, behold, I have given the children of Levi all the tenth in Israel for an inheritance, for their service which they serve, even the service of the tabernacle

302. JST Deuteronomy 14:21; see Skousen, The Third Thousand Years, op. cit., p. 679-680.
303. Leviticus 19:9-10.
304. Leviticus 19:28.
305. Leviticus 27:30-33.

of the congregation. Neither must the children of Israel henceforth come nigh the tabernacle of the congregation, lest they bear sin, and die.

"But the Levites shall do the service of the tabernacle of the congregation, and they shall bear their iniquity: it shall be a statute for ever throughout your generations, that among the children of Israel they have no inheritance.

"But the tithes of the children of Israel, which they offer as an heave offering unto the Lord, I have given to the Levites to inherit: therefore I have said unto them, Among the children of Israel they shall have no inheritance.

"And the Lord spake unto Moses, saying, Thus speak unto the Levites, and say unto them, When ye take of the children of Israel the tithes which I have given you from them for your inheritance, then ye shall offer up an heave offering of it for the Lord, even a tenth part of the tithe.

"And this your heave offering shall be reckoned unto you, as though it were the corn of the threshing floor, and as the fullness of the winepress. Thus ye also shall offer an heave offering unto the Lord of all your tithes, which ye receive of the children of Israel; and ye shall give thereof the Lord's heave offering to Aaron the priest." [306]

The Israelites also had a second tithe which was laid up in store so they could afford to attend the three feasts each year and also take provisions to the Levite Priests who worked without compensation throughout the year to prepare these feasts.

"Thou shalt truly tithe all the increase of thy seed, that the field bringeth forth year by year. And thou shalt eat before the Lord thy God, in the place which he shall choose to place his name there, the tithe of thy corn, of thy wine, and of thine oil, and the firstlings of thy herds and of thy flocks; that thou mayest learn to fear the Lord thy God always.

"And if the way be too long for thee, so that thou art not able to carry it; or if the place be too far from thee, which the Lord thy God shall choose to set his name there, when the Lord thy God hath blessed thee: Then shalt thou turn it into money, and bind up the money in thine hand, and shalt go unto the place which the Lord thy God shall choose:

"And thou shalt bestow that money for whatsoever thy soul lusteth after, for oxen, or for sheep, or for wine, or for strong drink, or for whatsoever thy soul desireth: and thou shalt eat there before the Lord thy God, and thou shalt rejoice, thou, and thine household,

"And the Levite that is within thy gates; thou shalt not forsake him; for he hath no part nor inheritance with thee.

306. Numbers 18:21-28.

"At the end of three years thou shalt bring forth all the tithe of thine increase the same year, and shalt lay it up within thy gates:

"And the Levite, (because he hath no part nor inheritance with thee,) and the stranger, and the fatherless, and the widow, which are within thy gates, shall come, and shall eat and be satisfied; that the Lord thy God may bless thee in all the work of thine hand which thou doest." [307]

It should be observed that the first scripture under "Tithes" states that if a person wanted to purchase back something he had given as a tithe, he could do so by adding a fifth of its value. Let us quote that passage again:

"And if a man will at all redeem ought of his tithes, he shall add thereto the fifth part thereof." [308]

The honest payment of tithes was considered an extremely sacred obligation to the Lord. The prophet Malachi emphasized this principle in the last book of the Old Testament:

"Will a man rob God? Yet ye have robbed me. But ye say, Wherein have we robbed thee? *In tithes and offerings*. Ye are cursed with a curse: for ye have robbed me, even this whole nation. Bring ye all the tithes into the storehouse, that there may be meat in mine house, and prove me now herewith, saith the Lord of hosts, if I will not open you the windows of heaven, and pour you out a blessing, that there shall not be room enough to receive it." [309]

Transvestites

These are defined as those who adopt the dress and often the behavior of the opposite sex. This was often done by homosexuals and lesbians to advertise their sexual preferences. Therefore it was an abomination to the Lord.

"The woman shall not wear that which pertaineth unto a man, neither shall a man put on a woman's garment: for all that do so are abomination unto the Lord God." [310]

Trees—In Wartime Spare the Fruit Trees

Trees were used by invading armies to build scaffolds and other devices connected with a siege—or even to provide kindling for their armies. This resulted in the gradual denuding of the land. The Lord realized that an invading army would use some trees in spite of any command to the contrary, and therefore he restricted his mandate to the fruit trees—at least, spare the fruit trees!

307. Deuteronomy 14:22-29.
308. Leviticus 27:31.
309. Malachi 3:8-10.
310. Deuteronomy 22:5.

"When thou shalt besiege a city a long time, in making war against it to take it, thou shalt not destroy the trees thereof by forcing an axe against them ... Only the trees which thou knowest that they be not trees for meat, thou shalt destroy and cut them down; and thou shalt build bulwarks against the city that maketh war with thee, until it be subdued."[311]

Trespassing

This is defined as any trespass against the law of the Lord or the rights of another. This was usually an offense of the lesser variety and therefore the penalty, in addition to damages, was only one-fifth. The law stated:

"Then they shall confess their sin which they have done: and he shall recompense his trespass with the principal thereof, and add unto it the *fifth* part thereof, and give it unto him against whom he hath trespassed. But if the man have no kinsman to recompense the trespass unto, let the trespass be recompensed unto the Lord, even to the priest."[312]

Usury

See: *Lending.*

Weights and Measures

Confidence in the market economy of Israel depended upon honest weights and measures. Therefore the Lord said:

"Ye shall do no unrighteousness in judgment, in meteyard, in weight, or in measure. Just balances, just weights, a just ephah, and a just hin, shall ye have: I am the Lord your God, which brought you out of the land of Egypt."[313]

The penalty for dishonest weights and measures was left to the discretion of the judges. However, as Ezra pointed out, the options included not only whipping but confiscation of goods, imprisonment, or banishment.[314]

Whipping

See: *Penalties and Enforcing the Law.*

Widows and Orphans

The law of the covenant is filled with provisions to protect the weak, the elderly, the infirm and the handicapped. In this same spirit it provided a strong warning against those who neglected, persecuted, or took advantage of widows and orphans:

311. Deuteronomy 20:19-20.
312. Numbers 5:7-8.
313. Leviticus 19:35-36.
314. Ezra 7:26.

"If thou afflict them in any wise, and they cry at all unto me, I will surely hear their cry; And my wrath shall wax hot, and I will kill you with the sword; and your wives shall be widows, and your children fatherless." [315]

"Thou shalt not pervert the judgment of the stranger, nor of the fatherless; nor take a widow's raiment to pledge." [316]

"When thou cuttest down thine harvest in thy field, and hast forgot a sheaf in the field, thou shalt not go again to fetch it: it shall be for the stranger, for the fatherless, and for the widow: that the Lord thy God may bless thee in all the work of thine hands.

"When thou beatest thine olive tree, thou shalt not go over the boughs again: it shall be for the stranger, for the fatherless, and for the widow. When thou gatherest the grapes of thy vineyard, thou shalt not glean it afterward: it shall be for the stranger, for the fatherless, and for the widow." [317]

"And when ye reap the harvest of your land, thou shalt not wholly reap the corners of thy field, neither shalt thou gather the gleanings of thy harvest. And thou shalt not glean thy vineyard, neither shalt thou gather every grape of thy vineyard; thou shalt leave them for the poor and stranger: I am the Lord your God." [318]

Witchcraft

See also: *Spiritualism*.

"Thou shalt not suffer a witch to live." [319]

Although this is the passage usually quoted to justify the killing of suspected witches, a modern translation says, "Thou shalt not suffer a murderer to live." [320]

Another passage often quoted to justify the complete suppression of witchcraft is the following:

"There shall not be found among you any one that maketh his son or his daughter to pass through the fire, or that useth divination, or an observer of times [astrologers], or an enchanter, or a witch." [321]

Notice that witchcraft is rated along with idolatry and other offenses that were subversive to the entire culture of Israel. The death penalty was not mandatory but it was invoked in the days of Saul and on other occasions. Banishment under threat of death would have been an option but that was seldom used. Witchcraft

---

315. Exodus 22:23-24.
316. Deuteronomy 24:17.
317. Deuteronomy 24:19-21.
318. Leviticus 19:9-10.
319. Exodus 22:18.
320. JST Exodus 22:18.
321. Deuteronomy 18:10.

was punished by death even more consistently than the punishment of idolatry by death.

The Law of Witnesses

The role of witnesses was extremely important in the culture of the Law of the Covenant. It was equally important to root out professional false witnesses who would say anything for a price.

"At the mouth of two witnesses, or three witnesses, shall he that is worthy of death be put to death; but at the mouth of one witness he shall not be put to death. The hands of the witnesses shall be first upon him to put him to death, and afterward the hands of all the people. So thou shalt put the evil away from among you." [322]

"One witness shall not rise up against a man for any iniquity, or for any sin, in any sin that he sinneth: at the mouth of two witnesses, or at the mouth of three witnesses, shall the matter be established." [323]

"Thou shalt not bear false witness against thy neighbor." [324]

"Thou shalt not raise a false report: put not thine hand with the wicked to be an unrighteous witness." [325]

"If a false witness rise up against any man to testify against him that which is wrong; then both the men, between whom the controversy is, shall stand before the Lord, before the priests and the judges, which shall be in those days; and the judges shall make diligent inquisition: and, behold, if the witness be a false witness, and hath testified falsely against his brother; then shall ye *do unto him*, as he had thought to have done unto his brother: so shalt thou put the evil away from among you." [326]

One of the unique aspects of the law given to Israel was that if a convicted criminal was to be executed by stoning, the witnesses against him had to cast the first stone:

"If thy brother … entice thee secretly, saying, Let us go and serve other gods … thou shalt surely kill him; thine hand shall be first upon him to put him to death, and afterwards the hand of all the people." [327]

Obviously, if a witness would not participate in the execution there was a presumption that there might be something wrong with his accusation.

---

322. Deuteronomy 17:6-7.
323. Deuteronomy 19:15.
324. Exodus 20:16.
325. Exodus 23:1.
326. Deuteronomy 19:16-19.
327. Deuteronomy 13:6, 9.

BIBLIOGRAPHY

1996 World Almanac, Mahwah, New Jersey: Funk and Wagnalls Corp, 1996.

Adams, Charles Francis, ed., The Works of John Adams, Boston: Little, Brown and Co., 1850-56.

Allison, Andrew, The Real Benjamin Franklin, Washington D.C.: National Center for Constitutional Studies, 1987.

Allison, Andrew, The Real Thomas Jefferson, Washington, D.C.: The National Center for Constitutional Studies, 1983.

Andrus, Hyrum, Doctrines of the Kingdom, Salt Lake City: Bookcraft Publishers, 1973.

Aristotle, Great Books of the Western World, Chicago: Encyclopedia Britannica, 1952.

Atwood, Harry, Our Republic, Merrimac, Massachusetts: Destiny Publishers, 1974.

Barker, James L., Apostasy from the Divine Church, published by Kate Montgomery Barker, Salt Lake City, 1960.

Bartlett, John, Familiar Quotations, Boston: Little, Brown, and Co., 14th edition, 1968.

Bergh, Albert Ellery, The Writings of Thomas Jefferson, Washington, D.C.: The Thomas Jefferson Memorial Association, 1907.

Birmingham, Stephen, The Grandees, New York: Harper and Roe, 1971.

Black, Henry Campbell, Black's Law Dictionary, 4th ed., St. Paul: West Publishing Company, 1968.

Blackstone, William, Commentaries on the Laws of England, William Carey Jones, ed., San Francisco: Bancroft-Whitney Company, 1916.

Bowen, Catherine Drinker, Miracle at Philadelphia, London: Hamish Hamilton, 1967.

Boyd, Julian P., ed., The Papers of Thomas Jefferson, Princeton, N.J.: Princeton University Press, 1950.

Boyle, Donzella Cross, Quest of a Hemisphere, Boston: Western Islands, 1970.

Bradford, William, History of Plymouth, 1606-1642, Collections of Massachusetts Historical Society, Fourth Series, 1856.

Brant, Irving, James Madison, Indianapolis: The Bobbs-Merrill Company, 1941.

Burnaby, Andrew, Travels in the Middle Settlements in North America in the Year 1759 and 1760, 2nd ed. in John Pinkerton, ed., A General Collection of the Best and Most Interesting Voyager and Travels, London, 1812.

Cherry, Conrad, God's New Israel, Englewood, N.J.: Prentice-Hall, Inc., 1971.

Chinard, Charles, Thomas Jefferson, The Apostle of Americanism, Ann Arbor, Mich.: University of Michigan Press, 1964.

Clark, J. Reuben, Stand Fast By Our Constitution, Salt Lake City: Deseret Book Company, 1973.

Clarke, Adam, Bible Commentary, New York: Eaten and Mains.

Constitution of the United States, Skousen, The Making of America, pp. 785-798.

Corwin, Constitution of the United States, Washington, D.C.: U.S. Government Printing Office, 1964.

Cousins, Norman, In God We Trust, New York: Harper Brothers, 1958.

Dawson, R. MacGregor, The Government of Canada, Toronto: The University of Toronto Press, 1970.

Dummelow's Bible Dictionary, New York: The Macmillan Company, 1961.

Durant, Will, The Reformation, New York: Simon and Schuster, 1957.

Durant, Will, The Story of Civilization, New York: Simon and Schuster, 1939.

Ebenstein, William, Great Political Thinkers, New York: Holt, Rinehart and Winston, 1963.

Eidsmoe, John, Christianity and the Constitution, Grand Rapids: Baker Book House, 1987.

Elliot, Jonathan, ed., The Debates in the Several State Conventions, Philadelphia: B. Lippincott Co., 1901.

Emery, Noemie, Alexander Hamilton, An Intimate Portrait, New York: G. P. Putnam's Sons, 1982.

Encyclopedia Britannica, Cambridge: Cambridge University Press, scholars ed. (11th), 1910.

Encyclopedia Britannica, Micropedia Ready Reference, Chicago, 1974.

Essays on Liberty, 12 vols., The Foundation for Economic Education, Inc., 1952-1965.

Farrand, Max, Records of the Federal Convention of 1787, New Haven: Yale University Press, 1974.

"Fate Joins the Flu Fighters," American Medical Association, Hygeia, Mar., 1941.

Ferguson, Ida M., Heraldry and the United States of America, Vancouver, B.C., Canada: The Covenant People.

Fiske, John, The Beginning of New England, Boston: Houghton Mifflin Co., 1902.

Fiske, John, Historical Writings, Boston: Houghton Mifflin Co., 1902.

Fitzpatrick, John C., The Writings of George Washington, 39 vols., Washington, D.C.: U.S. Government Printing Office.

Flexner, James Thomas, Washington, The Indispensable Man, Boston: Little, Brown and Company, 1974.

Ford, Paul Leicester, The Writings of Thomas Jefferson, New York: G. P. Putnam's Sons, 1892.

Frothingham, Richard, The Rise of the Republic of the United States, Boston: Little, Brown and Company, 1873.

Graebner, Norman A., et al., A History of the American People, New York: McGraw-Hill Book Company, 1970.

Green, John Richard, A Short History of the English People, New York: A. L. Burt Company, 1900.

Hastings' Dictionary of the Bible, Edinburgh: T. and T. Clark, 1942 ed.

House, H. Wayne, ed., Restoration of the Constitution, Dallas: Probe Books, 1987.

Howe, Daniel Waite, The Puritan Republic, Indianapolis: The Bowen-Merrill Company, 1899.

Howe, John R., The Changing Political Thought of John Adams, Princeton, N.J.: Princeton University Press, 1966.

Huszar, George B. de, ed., Basic American Documents, Ames, Iowa: Littlefield, Adams and Company, 1953.

International Dictionary, Boston: Houghton Mifflin Company, 1979.

James, Marquis, The Life of Andrew Jackson, New York: Garden City Publishing Co., Inc., 1940.

Jefferson, Thomas, Letters, New York: The Library of America, 1984.

Jefferson, Thomas, The Autobiography of Thomas Jefferson, New York: The Library of America, 1984.

Josephus, Antiquities of the Jews, Grand Rapids, Michigan: Kregel Publications, 1966.

Journal of Discourses, 26 vols.

Koch, Adrienne, ed., The American Enlightenment, New York: George Braziller, 1965.

Locke, John, Second Essay on Civil Government, Great Books of the Western World, Chicago: Encyclopedia Britannica, 1952.

Lodge, Henry Cabot, ed., The Works of Alexander Hamilton, New York: G. P. Putnam's Sons, 1904.

Long, Hamilton Albert, Your American Yardstick, Philadelphia: Your Heritage Books, Inc., 1963.

Lutz, Donald S., The Relative Influence of European Writers on Late Eighteenth Century American Political Thought, 78 American Political Science Review.

Madison, James and Hamilton, Alexander, Federalist Papers, New York: New American Library, Mentor's Book editon.

Marlow, H. Carlton and Davis, Harrison M., The American Search for Women, Santa Barbara, California: Clio Books, 1976.

McDonald, Forest, Alexander Hamilton, NY: W. C. Norton & Company, 1979.

McDonald, Forest, A Constitutional History of the United States, New York: Franklin Watts, 1982.

Mosheim, John Laurence von, Institutes of Ecclesiastical History, London: Longman, Brown, Green and Longman, 1850.

Montesquieu, Charles de, The Spirit of the Laws, Great Books of the Western World, Chicago: Encyclopedia Britannica, Inc., 1953.

Morison, Samuel Eliot, The Oxford History of the American People, New York: Oxford University Press, 1965.

New York Times, December 26, 1964 and November 9, 1995.

Nibley, Hugh, Old Testament and Related Studies, Salt Lake City: Deseret Book, 1986.

Nicolay and Jay, Complete Works of Abraham Lincoln, New York: Francis D. Tandy Co., 1894.

Norton, Thomas James, Undermining the Constitution—A History of Lawless Government, New York: Devin-Adair Co., 1950.

Padover, Saul K., ed., The Washington Papers, NY: Harper & Brothers, 1955.

Padover, Saul K., ed., The Complete Jefferson, New York: Tudor Publishing Company, 1943.

Parry, Jay A. and Allison, Andrew M., The Real George Washington, Washington, D.C.: The National Center for Constitutional Studies, 1991.

Patterson, Richard S. and Dougall, Richardson, The Eagle and the Shield—A History of the Great Seal of the United States, Washington, D.C.: U.S. Department of State, 1976.

Plato, The Republic, Great Books of the Western World, Chicago: Encyclopedia Britannica, 1952.

Plato, Timaeus, Great Books of the Western World, Chicago: Encyclopedia Britannica, 1952.

Rand, Howard B., Digest of the Divine Law, Marrimac, Massachusetts: Destiny Publishing Company, 1959.

Rivers and Fendall, eds., Letters and Other Writings of James Madison, Philadelphia: J. P. Lippincott, 1865.

Rutland, Robert A., The Papers of James Madison, Chicago: University of Chicago Press, 1962.

Salt Lake Tribune, October 26, 1985.

Shannon, Fred Albert, Economic History of the People of the United States, New York: The Macmillan Company, 1934.

Shelley, Bruce L., Church History in Plain Language, Waco, Texas: Word Books, 1982.

Skousen, Mark, Forecasts & Strategies, Phillips Publishing, Inc., Sept., 1995.

Skousen, W. Cleon, Days of the Living Christ, Salt Lake City: Ensign Pub., 1992.

Skousen, W. Cleon, "God's Covenant People," a speech given on Dec. 18, 1991.

Skousen, W. Cleon, Prophecy and Modern Times, sixth edition, Salt Lake City: Ensign Publishing, 1996.

Skousen, W. Cleon, The First 2,000 Years, Salt Lake City: Bookcraft, 1953.

Skousen, W. Cleon, The Third Thousand Years, SLC: Bookcraft Inc., 1964.

Skousen, W. Cleon, The Fourth Thousand Years, Salt Lake City: Bookcraft, 1966.

Skousen, W. Cleon, The Five Thousand Year Leap, Washington, D.C.: National Center for Constitutional Studies, 1981.

Skousen, W. Cleon, The Making of America, Washington, D.C.: National Center for Constitutional Studies, 1987.

Skousen, W. Cleon, The Miracle of America, SSLC: Freemen Institute, 1981.

Skousen, W. Cleon, The Urgent Need for a Comprehensive Monetary Reform, Salt Lake City: Freemen Institute. 1982.

Smith, Adam, The Wealth of Nations, Garden City, New York: Doubleday & Company, 1962.

Smyth, Albert Henry, ed., The Writings of Benjamin Franklin, New York: The Macmillan Company, 1905-1907.

Tansill, Charles Callan, The Making of the American Republic, New Rochelle, N.Y.: Arlington House, 1987.

The Annals of America, 1796, Chicago: Encyclopedia Britannica, 1968.

The Apocrypha According to the Authorized Version, Merrimac, Massachusetts: Destiny Publishers, 1946.

The Constitution magazine, Washington, D.C.: National Center for Constitutional Studies, July, 1987.

The Improvement Era magazine, June, 1957.

"The Inspired Constitution and J. Reuben Clark, Jr.," The Freemen Digest, March, 1978.

The Nicene and Post-Nicene Fathers of the Christian Church, Grand Rapids, Michigan: William B. Eerdmans Publishing Company, 1952.

The U.S. Government Manual, National Archives and Records Administration.

"The Worst Pestilence in Modern Times," Scribner's, January 1938.

Tocqueville, Alexis de, Democracy in America, Rochelle, New York: Arlington House, 1840 Heirloom Edition.

Toffler, Alvin, The Third Wave, New York: Bantam Books, 1981.

Turner, Sharon, The History of the Anglo Saxons, London: Longman Reese, et al., 1936.

Tuveson, Ernest Lee, Redeemer Nation, Chicago: Univ. of Chicago Press, 1968.

Van Doren, Carl, The Great Rehearsal, New York: The Viking Press, 1948.

Wallace, Irving, et al., "Hebrew: National Language of the U.S.", Parade Magazine, New York: Parade Publications, May 30, 1982.

Wallechinsky, David and Wallace, Irving, Peoples Almanac, New York: William Morrow and Company, 1978.

Weinberg, Albert, Manifest Destiny, Gloucester, Massachusetts: Peter Smith Publishers, 1958.

Wells, William V., The Life and Public Services of Samuel Adams, Boston: Little, Brown and Company, 1965.

Willison, George F., Saints and Strangers, New York: Reynal and Hitchcock, 1945.

Wood, Gordon S., The Creation of the American Republic, Chapel Hill, N.C.: The University of North Carolina Press, 1969.

Yonge, Charlotte M., Germany, Boston: D. Lothrop Company, 1878.

INDEX

A

B

D

H

I

J

N

O

P

R

After victory at Yorktown, 318
Washington's dilemma, 319
He avoided the mistake of Cromwell, 319
Rhode Island
Flight of Roger Williams from Massachusetts, 290
Supported by Baptists, 291
Ann Hutchinson, 291
Indian massacre, 292
Rolfe, John
Married Pocahontas, 274
Takes her to England, 274
Son, Thomas, born in England, 274
Pocahontas dies in England, 275
Returns to Virginia, 275
Killed by Indians, 275
Rolfe, Thomas
Born to Pocahontas in England, 274
Mother dies in England, 275
Raised by Sir Lewis Stuckeley in England, 275
In maturity, moved to Virginia, 275
Married and raised a large posterity, 275
Rome
A mighty empire, 13
Split in two in 395 A.D., 13
Disintegrated into numerous nations, 13
The Roman Senate, 169
From "Wards" to "Hundreds" 170
Two Consuls or executive, 171
The Censors and Tribunes, 172
Assembly of the Tribes, 173
Roman military organization, 173
Rome unites church and state, 174
Founders' view of the Roman system, 175
Roman Law, 176
Cicero's attempt to save Rome, 179
Rossiter, Clinton
America's sense of mission, 19
Rutgers University
Funded by Dutch Reformed churches, 2

S

Sabbath day, 55
Seventh day a sabbath, 618
Changed to first day of week, 105
Salamon, Haym
Background, 26
Knew six languages, 26
Allowed to get university education, 26
Raised $400,000 for war effort, 27
Personal loans to many Founders, 27
Including Washington and Madison, 27
Charged no interest on personal loans, 27
Charged only 1/4 of one percent, 27
Best war-bond salesman in America, 26
Sand, house of, and house of rock, 128
Schoolmaster law
Carnal law not part of God's law, 36
Seal of the United States
History of first seal, 355
One side portrayed ancient Israel, 356
Other side, Anglo Saxons, 356
Present seal a substitute, 357
Senate
In Israel, 70 "wise men" 59
Some aspects copied by United States, 60
Separation of Powers
Not needed by ancient Israel, 58
Servitude, 55, 618
Seventy Elders -- Israel's senate, 55, 619
Slavery issue, 415
Jefferson had best solution, 414
Northwest Ordinance outlaws slavery, 416
Decision at Constitutional Convention, 416
In 1808 Congress makes huge mistake, 417
Resulted in Civil War, 418
Smith, Adam
The Nature and Causes of the Wealth of Nations, 412
Published in 1776, 412
The four great economic freedoms, 413, 542
Four times when government intervention required, 413, 542
Isn't 'profit' a form of robbery? 542
Free Enterprise makes things abundant, 543
Free enterprise makes things cheap, 543
Why competition is not wasteful, 544
Why price controls always fail, 544
Why they produce black markets, 545
Smith, John (1580-1631)
Early craving for adventure, 266
Fought in Europe 3 years, 266
Joins crusade against infidels, 266
Smith becomes a captain, 267
Beheads three of the enemy, 267
Taken prisoner and made a slave, 268

T

U

V

Z